D0515155

Marketing Strategy

Planning and Implementation

The Irwin Series in Marketing
Consulting Editor
Gilbert A. Churchill, Jr.
University of Wisconsin, Madison

Marketing Strategy

Planning and Implementation

Orville C. Walker, Jr.
James D. Watkins Professor of Marketing
University of Minnesota

Harper W. Boyd, Jr.
Donaghey Distinguished Professor of Marketing
University of Arkansas—Little Rock

Jean-Claude Larréché
Professor of Marketing
European Institute of Business Administration
INSEAD

IRWIN

Homewood, IL 60430
Boston, MA 02116

This symbol indicates that the paper in this book is made from recycled paper. Its fiber content exceeds the recommended minimum of 50% waste paper fibers as specified by the EPA.

© RICHARD D. IRWIN, INC., 1992

All rights reserved. No part of this publication may be reproduced, stored in a retrieval system, or transmitted, in any form or by any means, electronic, mechanical, photocopying, recording, or otherwise, without the prior written permission of the publisher.

Sponsoring editor: Steve Patterson
Developmental editor: Eleanore Snow
Project editor: Paula M. Buschman
Production manager: Carma W. Fazio
Designer: Becky Lemna
Compositor: Weimer Typesetting Co., Inc.
Typeface: 10/12 Bembo
Printer: R. R. Donnelley & Sons Company

Library of Congress Cataloging-in-Publication Data

Walker, Orville C.
   Marketing strategy : planning and implementation / Orville C.
Walker, Jr., Harper Boyd, Jr., Jean-Claude Larréché.
      p.   cm.
   ISBN 0-256-09005-X   ISBN 0-256-11271-1 (Int'l ed.)
   1. Marketing—Management.   I. Boyd, Harper W.   II. Larréché, Jean
-Claude.   III. Title.
HF5415.13.W249   1992
658.8′02—dc20   91–27772

Printed in the United States of America
1 2 3 4 5 6 7 8 9 0 DOC 8 7 6 5 4 3 2 1

Preface

At the top of many executives' "things-to-do" lists for the 1990s is the objective of making their organizations more market-oriented, more tuned-in to customer needs and competitive threats, and quicker to respond to changing market conditions. The question is, How can that goal be achieved? Recent studies have concluded that the activities essential for achieving a market orientation are too important and pervasive to be left solely to marketers. Employees in every functional area must be trained and motivated to pay attention to and direct their efforts toward satisfying customer needs and desires.[1] A director of the Marketing Science Institute recently reinforced this broad view of the importance and scope of marketing activities by predicting that marketing as a stand-alone function will become extremely rare in the typical organization of the future. Instead, marketing—in the sense of doing what is necessary to serve and satisfy customers—will become everybody's business, at least within those organizations that survive and prosper in an increasingly competitive climate.[2]

Of course, even when the day-to-day responsibility for marketing activities is diffused across employees in every part of the organization, someone still has to plan, coordinate, and control those activities for each product or service the firm offers the market. Someone must devise a marketing strategy aimed at providing value to customers and gaining an advantage over competitors, and someone must ensure that the various functional activities necessary to implement that strategy are effectively carried out. That "someone" might be a traditional product or marketing manager, a vice president of marketing, a general manager of a business unit, or even a team of managers

---

[1] For example, see Ajay K. Kohli and Bernard J. Jaworski, "Market Orientation: The Construct, Research Propositions, and Managerial Implications," *Journal of Marketing,* April 1990, pp. 1–14.

[2] Frederick E. Webster, Jr., "It's 1990—Do You Know Where Your Marketing Is?" MSI White Paper (Cambridge, Mass.: Marketing Science Institute, April 14, 1989).

drawn from a variety of functional areas. Regardless of who bears the responsibility, that process of formulating and managing the marketing strategy for a given market entry is the central focus of this book.

It is also important to recognize, however, that marketing strategies are not formulated or implemented in a vacuum. Most organizations have corporate and business-level strategies that establish guidelines concerning objectives to be attained, directions for future growth, and how the organization will compete and seek to gain a sustainable advantage in the marketplace. These guidelines impose constraints on the range of marketing strategies a marketing manager can pursue within the larger strategic context of his or her organization. But, on the other hand, marketing managers are also uniquely positioned to provide information and insights for the development of corporate and business strategies because they straddle the boundary between the external environment and the inner-workings of the firm. Thus, as organizations strive to become more customer-oriented and face ever more hostile and rapidly changing competitive environments, the marketer's role in strategy formulation is likely to increase.

Similarly, while marketing managers play a crucial role in translating the firm's broad objectives into strategic marketing programs designed to win customer acceptance and competitive advantage in specific markets, they do not implement those programs by themselves. Effective execution requires cooperative and coordinated efforts across many functional areas. Thus, the range of viable marketing strategies available to a manager is constrained by the resources and functional competencies available within his or her organization. And the successful implementation of a chosen strategy depends on the marketer's ability to win the cooperation and support of people in other functional areas.

WHY WE WROTE THIS BOOK

As the above discussion suggests, the process of formulating and implementing marketing strategy is intimately linked with strategic decisions made at higher organizational levels and with the operational decisions and actions taken in a variety of functional departments. It is these internal linkages—together with their direct links to the external market and competitive environment—that make the management of strategic marketing programs such a challenging and interesting endeavor.

Unfortunately, most of the existing marketing management and strategy textbooks do not provide a very complete picture of the complexities involved in managing marketing strategies. Some examine strategic decisions that are made at the corporate or business level but devote relatively little attention to how those decisions might best be translated into strategic marketing programs for individual products or services. Others tend to treat marketing management as a stand-alone business function. While they do a good job of describing the concepts, analytical tools, and planning techniques that are useful for formulating marketing strategies, they pay only scant attention to the web of internal strategic and operational relationships that surround that formulation process. Consequently, our major motivation for writing this book was a desire to provide a broader, more complete and realistic view of marketing's strategic and operational roles and relationships within today's organizations.

A focus on the strategic planning process

As a basis for understanding the strategic role of marketing, one must first understand *how* strategies are formulated: the planning processes and the analytical tools and techniques managers might use when developing strategies. Thus, this book is structured around the analytical and decision-making processes involved in formulating, implementing, and controlling a strategic marketing program for a given product-market entry. It includes discussions of customer, competitor, and environmental analysis; market segmentation and targeting; competitive positioning; implementation; and control. Because we assume that the reader is already familiar with many of the concepts and analytical tools relevant to these topics, however, we go beyond a simple review of definitions and procedures to examine strategic implications. In our discussion of positioning decisions in Chapter 7, for instance, we not only review the techniques a manager might use to analyze a product's competitive position in the marketplace, we also discuss various positioning strategies and the conditions under which each is likely to be most appropriate.

A unique focus on strategic and interfunctional relationships

This book differs from other marketing management and strategy texts in that it examines in detail how marketing interacts with other levels of strategy and with other functional departments within an organization. Specifically, it includes an examination of three sets of relationships that are given little or no attention in other texts.

1. *The relationships between corporate, business-level, and marketing strategies.* As mentioned, managers responsible for developing and implementing marketing strategies for specific products and target markets are also uniquely qualified to provide insights and information needed to formulate competitive strategies at the business and corporate levels of the organization. And as organizations strive to become more customer-oriented, the marketing manager's role in strategic planning is likely to increase. At the same time, those higher-level strategic decisions often impose guidelines and constraints on the marketing manager's freedom of action when designing marketing strategies and programs for individual products or services.

   This book examines this complex set of relationships between the different levels of strategy in several ways. First, Chapter 1 presents a general discussion of the hierarchy of strategies found in most multiproduct organizations, their interrelationships, and the marketer's role in helping to formulate strategies at different organizational levels. Chapter 3 provides a more specific, and unique, discussion of business-level competitive strategies and their implications for marketing strategies and actions appropriate for individual products or services within the business unit. Finally, each of the chapters discussing alternative strategic marketing programs appropriate for specific market conditions (Chapter 8–11) examines how those programs should fit the firm's higher-level strategies.

2. *Relationships between the content of marketing strategies and the strategic environment.* Most texts talk in general terms about how the marketing strategy for a given product or service should fit the characteristics of the market and competitive environment. But they usually do not provide much detail concerning the specific kinds of strategic marketing programs that are best suited to different environmental contexts. Nor do they discuss the specific tactical decisions and actions necessary to effectively carry out each strategy.

    In contrast, this book provides an entire section of four chapters that discuss the marketing strategies and tactics best suited to specific environmental situations. Those situations are defined both in terms of market characteristics as defined by the stage in the product life cycle and by the product's relative competitive position. Thus, Chapter 8 discusses marketing strategies for new-market entries. Chapter 9 examines strategies for growth markets, both share-maintenance strategies for market leaders and growth strategies for low-share followers. Strategies for mature and declining markets are described in Chapter 10. Finally, global marketing strategies are detailed in Chapter 11.

3. *Relationships between marketing and other functional areas.* A marketing manager's ability to effectively implement a strategic marketing program depends in large measure on the cooperation and competence of other functional areas within the organization. Consequently, we devote substantial attention to the interfunctional implications of specific marketing strategies. Each of the marketing strategies appropriate for the particular circumstances described in Chapters 8 through 11 are also examined in terms of the requirements they impose on other functional departments such as product and process R&D, production, quality control, logistics, and finance. In addition, Chapter 12 provides an overview of the functional competencies required to effectively implement different competitive and marketing strategies. It also discusses organizational mechanisms appropriate for coordinating efforts and resolving conflicts across functional areas.

THE TARGET AUDIENCE FOR THIS BOOK

Most MBA programs offer at least one course on marketing strategy. While they carry many different names—such as "Marketing Policy," "Strategic Marketing," or "Advanced Marketing Management"—they are usually positioned as capstone courses whose primary purpose is to help students integrate what they have learned about the analytical tools and the 4 Ps of marketing within a broader framework of competitive strategy. Thus, such courses are often required of all marketing majors toward the end of their academic programs. And similar capstone courses are usually either required or offered as electives in many of the better undergraduate marketing programs as well. We designed this book primarily to serve the needs of students in these kinds of courses.

FEATURES APPROPRIATE FOR A CAPSTONE MARKETING STRATEGY COURSE

We think this book's organization structure and its unique content makes it particularly well suited for use in integrative, capstone courses at either the graduate or advanced undergraduate level. Some particularly relevant features include the following.

- Because the book is organized around the analytical and decision-making processes involved in formulating and implementing marketing strategies, it provides the opportunity for students to review and integrate many of the concepts and techniques they encountered in earlier courses. But rather than simply rehash basic definitions and descriptions, this text emphasizes the strategic implications of such topics as market segmentation, competitor analysis, target market selection, and positioning.

- On the other hand, this text gives substantial coverage to a few technical topics that are often not covered in much detail in other marketing courses, such as secondary sources of competitive and market intelligence, the techniques of value-based planning, and the contents of an annual strategic marketing plan. However, to preserve the text's readability and provide instructors with greater flexibility in adapting the book to their individual course outlines, these topics are dealt with in separate appendices at the end of the relevant text chapters.

- The book also provides a sound review of the tactical elements—the 4 Ps—of marketing. But rather than forcing students to wade through yet another set of chapters on product, pricing, promotion, and distribution decisions, each of these program elements is discussed within the context of a variety of alternative marketing strategies, the objectives they are designed to accomplish, and the situations where their use is most appropriate.

- This book pays a great deal of attention to the role of marketing managers in the formulation and implementation of higher-level strategies within the firm and to the influences and constraints those higher-level strategies subsequently impose on the range of marketing actions appropriate for individual products or services. This helps students more fully understand and appreciate the linkages and interactions among an organization's corporate, business, and marketing strategies.

- We also provide unusually extensive discussions of the various functional competencies and resources required by different types of marketing strategies and the kinds of interfunctional coordination necessary to implement those strategies effectively. Thus, this book provides a good framework for reviewing and integrating the material that students have been exposed to in courses in other functional areas as well as in previous marketing courses.

- The ultimate objective of any capstone course is to prepare students to make a smooth transition from their academic program into the business world. All of the above features should help prepare students to better understand and deal with the kinds of activities and decisions they will soon face on the job. But in addition, we have attempted to write the book in a way that reflects both the excitement and the practical realities of marketing management as it happens in a variety of real world settings. The book incorporates hundreds of up-to-date examples that demonstrate marketing strategies and practices as they are applied to industrial as well as consumer products, services as well as goods, not-for-profit organizations as well as business firms, and foreign as well as domestic markets. And to further enhance student interest and understanding, every chapter begins with a mini-case example that serves to introduce and illustrate the major concepts or strategies discussed in that chapter. These introductory examples are referred to at appropriate places throughout each chapter to further help the student see the relationships among concepts and their relevance to real problems.

FEATURES APPROPRIATE FOR DIFFERENT TEACHING APPROACHES

Capstone courses dealing with marketing strategy not only parade under a variety of different titles, they are also taught in a variety of different ways. Consequently, this book and its package of supporting materials were designed to fit a variety of teaching approaches. While we have tried to avoid excessive repetition and thereby keep the book relatively short and succinct, instructors who prefer a lecture-discussion approach will find ample material for either a quarter or semester course. For those who prefer case-oriented instruction, the book provides a solid foundation of concepts, techniques, and examples to prepare students for more effective case analysis and discussion. Many other features of the book and its supporting materials are designed to stimulate student interest and involvement and to facilitate the instructor's teaching performance, regardless of the chosen pedagogical approach. These features include:

- A computerized simulation case (the SAMAR case) has been developed to integrate a number of strategic issues involved in deciding how to allocate marketing resources among a portfolio of both existing and potential new products within a business. It provides an appropriate way to expose students to the dynamics of resource allocation problems in a simulation context in which they can manage a firm over a period of time, analyze situations, make decisions, receive rapid feedback, and adjust their strategies. It also gives the instructor the opportunity to expose students to an integrative simulation without devoting as large a proportion of the total course to the exercise as many more extensive simulation games require. SAMAR can be used as a team project outside the class or as a part of the course requiring only one to three class sessions. The teaching note in the Instructor's Manual suggests a variety of ways SAMAR can be integrated with material in various parts of the text and with different course outlines, including those for executive courses.

- For those who prefer to incorporate a more extensive simulation game—either in addition to or instead of the SAMAR case—within their course, the Instructor's Manual includes suggestions from Jean-Claude Larréché, a coauthor of both MARKSTRAT and INDUSTRAT, concerning how those simulations can best be integrated with material in the text.

- While no cases other than SAMAR are included in the text, the Instructor's Manual includes a detailed annotated bibliography of more than 280 domestic and global marketing cases from a variety of published sources. Each case summary is keyed to appropriate topics and chapters within the text.

- The Instructor's Manual also includes a set of discussion questions geared to the material covered in each chapter. These questions are designed to provide a vehicle for meaningful student exercises or class discussions. Rather than being simple review questions that ask students to regurgitate answers found in the chapter, these questions are more application-oriented and often take the form of mini-cases that reflect actual company problems.

- The Instructor's Manual also includes a list of additional readings from a variety of up-to-date sources that illustrate or expand upon major topics in each chapter of the text.

- Finally, a set of overhead transparencies that reproduce, and in some cases expand upon, important exhibits found in the text is available to adopters.

ACKNOWLEDGMENTS

A book like this is never solely the work of the authors whose names appear on the cover. Instead, many people aided and abetted this enterprise, and we gratefully acknowledge their contributions.

First, we thank our faculty colleagues in our respective schools for their wise counsel and advice. We are also grateful to our friends in industry. Our conversations with them over the years, both informally and within various executive programs, have contributed much to our understanding of how.

marketing strategy works in the real world and have produced many of the most interesting examples in this book.

In a concerted effort to practice what we marketing academicians constantly preach, we have tried to be customer-oriented and to write a book that is responsive to the needs of both instructors and students. Consequently, we offer special thanks to our many undergraduate, graduate, and executive program students for their patience in serving as guinea pigs during the classroom testing of parts of this book at various stages of its development. Their constructive criticism and useful suggestions helped make this a better book. Similarly we greatly appreciate the work of the following colleagues who provided detailed and constructive reviews of this manuscript.

Roger J. Calantone
Michigan State University

Alan G. Sawyer
University of Florida

Sang T. Choe
University of Southern Indiana

Robert W. Schaffer
California State Polytechnic University

Michael D. Hutt
Arizona State University

Robert B. Woodruff
University of Tennessee

Wayne Norvell
Kansas State University

Murry Young
University of Denver

Their insightful comments and suggestions greatly aided our efforts to make this book a useful tool for teaching and learning.

We owe a large debt of gratitude to Professor Gil Churchill of the University of Wisconsin-Madison—the Consulting Editor for Irwin's marketing series—for helping to identify a market opportunity for a book such as this and for his wise counsel throughout its development. We also appreciate the efforts of Margaret Morrison, Coordinator of Public Services of the Torreyson Library at the University of Central Arkansas, for her valuable assistance in preparing the appendix on sources of competitive and market intelligence. And we salute Roberta Moore for her unfailing good grace and her competence in helping prepare the manuscript.

We also thank the staff at Richard D. Irwin, Inc. for their unmatched skill at turning a rough manuscript into an attractive and readable book. In particular, Eleanore Snow, our Developmental Editor, has once again earned our heartfelt appreciation. In our view, Eleanore's name should appear above the title ("Eleanore Snow Presents . . .") much as the names of Cecil B. DeMille, Howard Hawks, and other great Hollywood producer-directors appeared in their films. Like them, Eleanore played a crucial and pervasive role in shaping the final product. Her insightful suggestions contributed greatly to both the form and substance of the book, her administrative skills were crucial for maintaining some degree of coordination among three rather willful and geographically dispersed authors, and her consummate skill at wielding an iron fist cloaked in a soft velvet glove was solely responsible for bringing the project to a timely conclusion.

Finally, because each of our lives has been touched and enriched by different people, we each dedicate this book to individuals who hold special places in our separate hearts. Orville Walker thanks Linda Keefe for bringing the gravy. Harper Boyd thanks Cindy and Sarah Victoria for making him a very proud father. And Jean-Claude Larréché thanks Denyse for each of the last 20 years. This book is dedicated, with love, to them.

Orville C. Walker, Jr.
Harper W. Boyd, Jr.
Jean-Claude Larréché

Contents in Brief

S E C T I O N   F I V E
THE SAMAR CASE

Contents

INTRODUCTION TO STRATEGY

The Strategic Role of Marketing

AMERICAN EXPRESS: SERVICE THAT SELLS[1]

Do you really know American Express? Most people think of the firm as a credit-card company. Many also know that it was among America's most successful and admired corporations in the 1980s. During that period it more than tripled its revenues, earned an average return on shareholders' equity of better than 15 percent a year, and was cited as the most admired financial services firm in *Fortune*'s surveys of top executives every year after 1986. But where did that revenue and earnings growth come from? What strategies guided the success of American Express?

Corporate strategy—two avenues toward growth

American Express Corporation has traditionally focused on two main businesses, financial services and travel. During the first half of the 80s, much of the firm's growth resulted from a strategy aimed at broadening its product line and market coverage in the financial services business through a series of acquisitions, such as the investment firm Shearson Loeb Rhoades and Investors Diversified Services (IDS).

The purchase of IDS in 1984 was a particularly important strategic move for two reasons. First, it added some rapidly growing products to the firm's line. As James D. Robinson III, the CEO of American Express, points out, "it helped open up the savings and investment side of the equation." Whether consumers spent with the card or saved with IDS, American Express benefited. The acquisition also helped American Express appeal to a new

---

[1]This example is based on material found in John P. Newport, Jr., "American Express: Service That Sells," *Fortune*, November 20, 1989, pp. 80–94; and Sarah Smith, "America's Most Admired Corporations," *Fortune*, January 29, 1990, pp. 59–92.

EXHIBIT 1-1
Revenue and Net Income for Each Division of the American Express Co.

Business	1988 Revenue (in millions)	1988 Net Income (in millions)
Travel Related Services	$6,853.5	$709.7
American Express Bank	$1,738.5	$149.0
IDS Financial Services	$1,556.5	$147.6
Information Services Company	$446.9	$63.0
Shearson Lehman Hutton	$10,528.5*	$50.0*

*Reflects consolidation of 60 percent of Shearson.

Source: The American Express Company, as reported in John Paul Newport, Jr., "American Express: Service That Sells," *Fortune,* November 20, 1989, p. 80. *Fortune,*© 1989 The Time Inc. Magazine Company. All rights reserved.

segment of the financial services market. While the firm's credit cards and other services were targeted primarily at upper-income groups, IDS sold annuities, life insurance, and mutual funds to middle-income households through a salesforce of 6,000 financial planners. IDS proved a successful addition to American Express, as Exhibit 1–1 shows, contributing nearly $148 million to the corporation's bottom line in 1988, about 13 percent of the total.

Much of the company's growth in revenue and profit during the last half of the 1980s, however, was generated by internal expansion into new, though related, businesses and market segments. Indeed, adaptability and an entrepreneurial spirit have become the keystone of corporate strategy at American Express. As Robinson argues, "change is going to happen, and we should be excited by that. We should be out there helping change to happen so that we can be the first to take advantage of it."

Business-level competitive strategy

The engine that provides both the resources and the strategic foundation to support the firm's internal expansion is the Travel Related Services (TRS) division, particularly its American Express credit cards. In the 1970s and early 1980s, the company expanded the number of its cardholders by heavily promoting the prestige and security associated with carrying the little piece of green plastic. But by the mid-80s, the company's "Do you know me?" advertising campaign began to lose its impact. And bankcards—such as MasterCard and Visa—proliferated by offering cheaper annual fees and enticing lines of credit. But throughout the decade, American Express managed to increase its share of cards outstanding in the United States from about 7 percent in 1979 to 10 percent in 1988, or 22 million cards, and its share of domestic charge volume grew from 20 percent to 27 percent, or $69 billion.

How did American Express improve its performance in the face of increasing competition? By finding ways to differentiate its card from all others on the basis of superior service.

In the mid-70s, when James Robinson was head of the TRS division, he developed a system for measuring service quality that is still used. Managers review how long it takes operators in service centers to answer the phone (the standard is seven seconds) and how long it takes to replace lost cards (48 hours is the goal). The company also has a group of managers who develop new ways to improve and measure service quality, and it convenes periodic quality conferences to help devise methods for sharpening the firm's competitive advantage. It even maintains a "Quality University" that provides regular training for line employees and their managers to ensure that new ideas for improving customer service are put into practice.

Marketing strategy

Of course, efforts to improve service quality do little to give the firm a competitive advantage unless customers perceive that those efforts really do result in superior service. One way to improve perceptions about the company's superior service is through advertising and promotion. Thus, American Express spends as much as $250 million a year—twice as much as MasterCard and Visa combined—reminding peo-ple that "Membership has its privileges" and convincing them that the American Express card offers more services and prestige than any of its competitors.

More important, though, American Express works diligently to keep abreast of customer wants and to find ways to satisfy them. The firm surveys customers and potential customers relentlessly, and its marketing managers are constantly refining and test-marketing new ideas. The company also maintains and updates weekly a profile of 450 attributes— such as age, sex, and purchasing patterns—on every cardholder. This information is used to segment the market based on income and life-style characteristics and to determine what service attributes appeal most to each segment.

American Express's marketing managers have used the information gained through their ongoing market analysis to design card enhancements targeted at specific customer segments, such as limousine pickup at airports for platinum card members, extra travel insurance for security-conscious senior citizens, and a special magazine for students. They also developed a "flanker" product designed to compete head-to-head with bankcards without cannibalizing or injuring the prestige of their premier brand. Thus, the Optima card was introduced in 1987, but it was only offered to existing cardholders as an add-on. Members can use Optima to charge items they don't want to put on their green card and pay for promptly without having to resort to one of the other bankcards.

Optima exceeded expectations and had captured an estimated 2 percent of the bankcard market by 1989.

American Express's knowledge of its customers has also enabled it to expand into new businesses. For example, once the company gets a good customer into the data base, it prods with bill stuffers and catalogs to see what else he or she might buy. The firm sells a wide variety of merchandise (jewelry and stereo equipment) and financial services (insurance and mutual funds) through the mail. The cardholder data base also provides the primary hunting ground for subscribers to the magazines produced by the company's publishing operation, such as *Travel and Leisure* and *Food and Wine*. Such direct-marketing operations generated revenues of about $600 million in 1989 and were the firm's fastest growing businesses.

Finally, American Express is also pursuing growth by attempting to improve the penetration of its credit cards and financial services into global markets where demand is growing faster than it is domestically. Consequently, the company is actively trying to improve its international competitive environment by engaging in lobbying activities aimed at changing governments' trade and economic policies. For example, the firm is currently trying to persuade governments to include its services in future tariff agreements and to find ways to solve the Third World debt crisis.

Implementation

It is easy to formulate corporate, competitive, and marketing strategies based on catch phrases like "understanding the customer," "offering superior service," and "embracing change." But it is not always so easy to convince employees to take such concepts to heart or to take the actions necessary to make the strategies work. Among the keys to American Express's success, then, is that top management has clearly demonstrated its commitment to the firm's strategic principles, and that the organization's structure, policies, and processes are designed to enable and encourage employees to perform in ways that are consistent with those principles.

CEO Robinson communicates top management's commitment to the company's strategic themes by hammering on the importance of customer service and openness to change every chance he gets. For example, in one 25-minute tour of an Amexco travel agency in Manhattan he uttered the word "quality" 10 times. He constantly promotes his vision of American Express as one of the world's premier service providers by preaching homilies like "Quality is the only patent protection we've got" to nearly every gathering of employees.

More substantively, the organization and its internal processes are designed to facilitate and reward behavior that is consistent with the company's strategic thrust. To encourage innovation and entrepreneurial actions by business and marketing managers, for instance, decision-making authority is relatively decentralized. The firm tries to hire strong, ambitious managers and then give them substantial freedom to manage their own businesses and to react quickly to new opportunities in the environment. The company also constantly monitors its employees' performance, and it ties financial rewards and promotions to that performance. As a result, American Express's strategies are more than just plans on paper, as its record of continuing growth and profitability reflects.

MULTIPLE LEVELS OF STRATEGY: DIFFERENT ISSUES AT DIFFERENT LEVELS

The recent history of American Express illustrates some important points about strategy that will be recurring themes throughout this book. First, most firms—particularly those with multiple business units—pursue a hierarchy of interdependent strategies. Each strategy is formulated at different levels in the organization and deals with different issues. For example, American Express's decision to seek future growth primarily through the internal development of new businesses that take advantage of the firm's customer knowledge and its reputation for high-quality service reflects its new corporate strategy. This level of strategy provides direction on the company's mission, the kinds of businesses it should be in, and its growth policies. On the other hand, attempts to differentiate the American Express card from competing bankcards by providing and promoting superior service reflects the business-level strategy of the firm's Travel Related Services (TRS) division. This level of strategy primarily addresses the way a business competes within its industry. Finally, interrelated functional decisions about how to divide the market into customer segments, which segments to target, what products and service enhancements to offer each segment, what promotional appeals and media to employ, and what fees to charge all reflect the **marketing strategies** for each of American Express's various product-market entries. Each marketing strategy provides a plan for pursuing the company's objectives within a specific market segment.

Because the different levels of strategy are interrelated, individual marketing strategies and programs are not created in a vacuum. Instead, the marketing objectives and strategy for a particular product-market entry should be consistent with the direction and resources provided by the firm's corporate and business-level strategies. Thus, a marketing manager's freedom of action is constrained by strategic decisions made at higher levels within the firm. For instance, it is unlikely that the manager responsible for introducing the new Optima card would have been allowed to position it as a low-cost, stand-alone card targeted at the moderate-income masses because such a marketing strategy would be inconsistent with the TRS division's competitive strategy of offering superior service and with its prestigious image.

On the other hand, a major part of the marketing manager's job is to monitor and analyze the needs and wants of customers and potential customers and identify emerging opportunities and threats posed by competitors and trends in the external environment. Marketers thus often play a major role in providing inputs to and influencing the development of corporate and business-level strategies. For instance, the shift in American Express's corporate-growth strategy from one of acquisition to one of internal development of new businesses was triggered by the large base of customer knowledge accumulated by marketers in the TRS division and by their success at identifying new products and services to satisfy those customers.

Regardless of who is involved in formulating the various levels of strategy or how appropriate those strategies are, they will not lead to successful outcomes unless implemented effectively. As American Express exemplifies, sound implementation requires a clear vision and solid support from top management. And the organization's structure, policies, and processes must be designed to enable and encourage employees at all levels to take the actions necessary to make the strategy work.

The next section takes a closer look at the nature of and the interrelationships among corporate, business, and marketing strategies. We then examine some of the alternative processes that different firms use to formulate such strategies and the important role that marketing managers often play in those processes. The various processes and decisions involved in formulating and implementing marketing strategies for a particular product over the course of its competitive life provide a framework for organizing the remaining chapters in this book.

Strategy: a definition

Although strategy first became a popular business buzzword during the 1960s, it continues to have widely differing definitions and interpretations. The following definition, however, captures the essence of the term as it is most commonly used.

> A **strategy** *is a fundamental pattern of present and planned objectives, resource deployments, and interactions of an organization with markets, competitors, and other environmental factors.*[2]

As this definition suggests, a good strategy should specify (1) what is to be accomplished; (2) where, that is, on which industries or product-markets it will focus; and (3) how, or which resources and activities will be allocated to each product-market to meet environmental opportunities and threats and to gain a competitive advantage.

---

[2]For a summary of the definitions offered by a number of other authors, see Roger A. Kerin, Vijay Mahajan, and P. Rajan Varadarajan, *Contemporary Perspectives on Strategic Market Planning* (Boston: Allyn and Bacon, 1990), pp. 8–9. Our definition differs from some others, however, in that we view the setting of objectives as an integral part of strategy formulation whereas they see it as a separate process. Because a firm's objectives are influenced and constrained by many of the same environmental and competitive factors as the other elements of strategy, it seems logical to treat both the setting of objectives and the allocation of resources aimed at reaching those objectives as two parts of the same strategic planning process.

The components of strategy

There are five components, or sets of issues, within a well-developed strategy.

1. *Scope.* The scope of an organization refers to the breadth of its strategic domain, that is, the number and types of industries, product lines, and market segments it competes in or plans to enter. Decisions about an organization's strategic scope should reflect management's view of the firm's *mission* or *strategic intent.* This common thread among its various activities and product-markets defines the essential nature of what its business is and what is should be in the future.

2. *Goals and objectives.* Strategies should also specify desired levels of accomplishment on one or more dimensions of performance—such as volume growth, profit contribution, or return on investment—over specified periods for each of the firm's businesses and product-markets and for the organization as a whole.

3. *Resource deployments.* Every organization has limited financial and human resources. Thus, a strategy should specify how such resources are to be obtained and allocated across businesses, product-markets, functional departments, and activities within each business or product-market.

4. *Identification of a sustainable competitive advantage.* Perhaps the most important part of any strategy is a specification of how the organization will compete in each business and product-market within its domain. How can it position itself to develop and sustain a differential advantage over current and potential competitors? To answer such questions, managers must examine the market opportunities in each business and product-market (i.e., what customer needs are not being satisfied as well as they might be?) and the company's distinctive competencies or strengths relative to its competitors.

5. *Synergy.* Synergy exists when the firm's businesses, product-markets, resource deployments, and competencies complement and reinforce one another. Synergy enables the total performance of the related businesses to be greater than it would be otherwise: the whole becomes greater than the sum of its parts. Consequently, strategies should be designed to exploit potential sources of synergy across the firm's businesses and product-markets as a means of improving the organization's overall efficiency and effectiveness.

The hierarchy of strategies

Explicitly or implicitly, these five basic dimensions are part of all strategies. However, rather than a single comprehensive strategy, most organizations pursue a hierarchy of interrelated strategies, each formulated at a different level of the firm.[3] The three major levels of strategy in most large, multiproduct organizations are (1) **corporate strategy,** (2) **business-level strategy,** and (3) **functional strategies** focused on a particular product-market entry.[4] These three types are diagrammed in Exhibit 1–2.

Although our primary focus is on the development of marketing strategies and programs for individual product-market entries, Exhibit 1–2 shows that other functional departments, such as R&D and production, also have strategies and plans. Thus, the organization's success in a given product-market depends on the effective coordination of strategies and activities across functional departments. Throughout this book, then, we will pay attention to the interfunctional implications of various marketing strategies, the potential conflicts across functional areas, and the mechanisms that firms use to resolve those conflicts.

Strategies at all three levels contain the five components outlined above, but because each strategy serves a different purpose within the organization, each emphasizes different sets of issues. Exhibit 1–3 summarizes the focus and the specific issues dealt with at each level of strategy, which are discussed below.

Corporate strategy

At the corporate level, managers of today's complex organizations must coordinate the activities of multiple business units and, in the case of conglomerates, even separate legal business entities. Consequently, decisions about the organization's scope and appropriate resource deployments across its various divisions or businesses are the primary focus of corporate strategy. The essential questions to be answered at this level are: What business(es) are we in?, What businesses should we be in?, and What portion of our total resources should be devoted to each business to achieve the organization's overall goals and objectives? Thus, American Express's investment of substantial resources to develop new magazine publishing and direct-mail merchandising businesses reflects corporate strategy decisions made at the highest management level in the company.

Attempts to develop and maintain distinctive competencies at the corporate level tend to be broadly focused, concentrating on such things as gener-

---

[3]The recognition of a hierarchy of strategies within a single firm is a relatively recent but increasingly common concept in both the strategic management and marketing literatures. For example, see George S. Day, *Strategic Market Planning: The Pursuit of Competitive Advantage* (St. Paul, Minn.: West Publishing Co., 1984), p. 44, and Kerin, Mahajan, and Varadarajan, *Contemporary Perspectives,* pp. 11–26.

[4]Of course, it is possible to identify more than three levels of strategy. For instance, marketing management texts often discuss "subfunctional strategies," that is, strategies for specific activities within the marketing mix, such as advertising, pricing, and distribution. However, many managers refer to such activity plans as tactics rather than strategies. At the opposite end of the spectrum, some authors discuss the need for a macrolevel "enterprise strategy" addressing the question of how an organization can best maintain its political legitimacy and improve its relations with other organizations and stakeholders in the face of changes in its environment. For example, see H. I. Ansoff, "Strategic Issue Management," *Strategic Management Journal,* April–June 1980, pp. 131–48.

EXHIBIT 1-2
The Hierarchy of Strategies

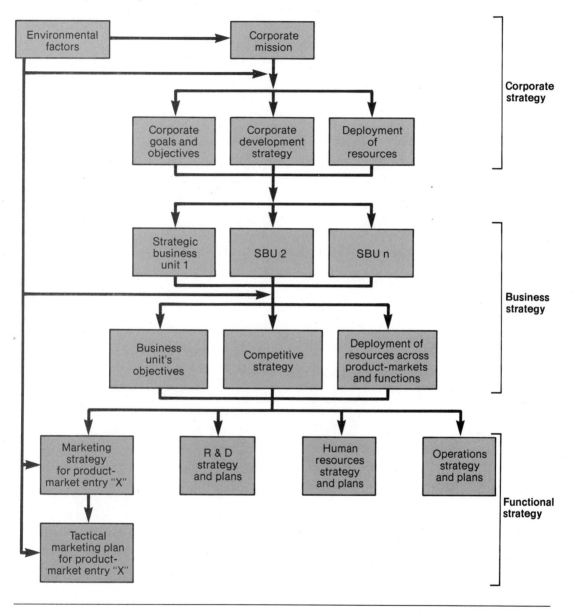

ating superior financial, capital, and human resources; designing effective organizational structures and processes; and seeking synergy among the firm's various businesses. Synergy can become a major competitive advantage in firms where related businesses reinforce one another by sharing corporate staff, R&D, financial resources, production technologies, distribution

EXHIBIT 1-3

Key Components of Corporate, Business, and Marketing Strategies

Strategy components	Corporate strategy	Business strategy	Marketing strategy

Scope	• Corporate domain— "Which businesses should we be in?"
	
	• Corporate development strategy
	    Conglomerate diversification (expansion into unrelated businesses)
	    Vertical integration
	    Acquisition and divestiture policies
		• Business domain— "Which product-markets should we be in within this business or industry?"
		• Business development strategy
		    Concentric diversification (new products for existing customers or new customers for existing products)
			• Target market definition
			• Product-line depth and breadth
			• Branding policies
			• Product-market development plan
			• Line extension and product elimination plans

Goals and objectives	• Overall corporate objectives aggregated across businesses
	    Revenue growth
	    Profitability
	    ROI (return on investment)
	    Earnings per share
	    Contributions to other stakeholders
		• Constrained by corporate goals
		
		• Objectives aggregated across product-market entries in the business unit
		    Sales growth
		    New product or market growth
		    Profitability
		    ROI
		    Cash flow
		    Strengthening bases of competitive advantage
			• Constrained by corporate and business goals
			• Objectives for a specific product-market entry
			    Sales
			    Market share
			    Contribution margin
			    Customer satisfaction

Allocation of resources	• Allocation among businesses in the corporate portfolio • Allocation across functions shared by multiple businesses (corporate R&D, MIS)	• Allocation among product-market entries in the business unit • Allocation across functional departments within the business unit	• Allocation across components of the marketing plan (elements of the marketing mix) for a specific product-market entry
Sources of competitive advantage	• Primarily through superior corporate financial or human resources; more corporate R&D; better organizational processes or synergies relative to competitors across all industries in which the firm operates	• Primarily through competitive strategy; business unit's competencies relative to competitors in its industry	• Primarily through effective product positioning; superiority on one or more components of the marketing mix relative to competitors within a specific product-market
Sources of synergy	• Shared resources, technologies, or functional competencies across businesses within the firm	• Shared resources (including favorable customer image) or functional competencies across product-markets within an industry	• Shared marketing resources, competencies, or activities across product-market entries

SOURCE: Harper W. Boyd, Jr. and Orville C. Walker, Jr., *Marketing Management: A Strategic Approach* (Homewood, Ill.: Richard D. Irwin, Inc., 1990), pp. 46–47.

channels, or marketing programs. American Express sought such synergy when it developed new businesses to take advantage of the mailing lists and the detailed customer information collected by the TRS division from its credit-card customers.

Business-level strategy

How a business unit will compete within its industry is the critical focus of business-level strategy.[5] Thus, a major issue addressed in a business strategy is how to achieve and sustain a competitive advantage. What distinctive competencies can give the business unit a competitive advantage? And which of those competencies best match the needs and wants of the customers in the business's target segment(s)? For example, a business with low-cost sources of supply and efficient, modern plants might adopt a low-cost competitive strategy, while one with a strong marketing department and a competent salesforce might compete by offering superior customer service.

Since different customer segments may want different benefits from the same category of products, a business unit may not have the competencies needed to compete effectively in all market segments. Therefore, another important issue a business-level strategy must deal with is appropriate scope: How many and which market segments to compete in, and what product offerings and marketing programs are needed to appeal to these segments.

Finally, synergy should be sought across product-markets and across functional departments within the business. Thus, American Express's TRS division sometimes stuffs promotional materials for products offered by its publishing and merchandising operations in the bills mailed to its credit-card customers.

Marketing strategy

The primary purpose of a marketing strategy is to effectively allocate and coordinate marketing resources and activities to accomplish the firm's objectives within a specific product-market. Therefore, decisions about the scope of a marketing strategy involve specifying the target-market segment(s) to be pursued and the product line to be offered. Then, firms seek a competitive advantage and synergy, planning a well-integrated program of marketing-mix elements (primarily the 4 Ps of product, price, promotion, and place of distribution) tailored to the needs and wants of customers in the target segments. For example, a broad line of customer services and heavy advertising focused on upper-income professionals and stressing service and prestige are elements of the marketing strategy for the American Express card.

---

[5]Donald C. Hambrick, "Operationalizing the Concept of Business-Level Strategy," *Academy of Management Review* 5 (1980), pp. 567–75.

STRATEGIC PLANNING SYSTEMS

American Express is an example of a company with well-developed, integrated strategies at all three levels. However, such is not the case with all companies. There are wide variations across firms in the extensiveness of strategic planning and the procedures followed in formulating strategies.

The value of formal planning systems

At one extreme, some companies—particularly smaller, entrepreneurial firms—employ few, if any, formal strategic planning procedures. Of course, this does not necessarily mean that they have no strategy. The owner or top executive may have had a clear strategic vision in the beginning. And he or she may give some sporadic thought to strategic issues as the firm and its industry evolve over time. Nevertheless, evidence suggests that such piecemeal, informal approaches to strategic planning are less effective than more formal systems for formulating strategy. For example, a review of 15 studies comparing firms with formal planning systems to firms without such systems found that the formal planners outperformed the informal planners in 10 cases, the two types of firms performed about equally in 3 studies, and the informal planners achieved superior performance in only 2 cases.[6]

The fact that firms with formal planning systems typically outperform those without such systems may seem a bit surprising, given the rapidly changing market and competitive conditions many firms face in today's environment. Indeed, some managers argue that extensive planning is a waste of time because changing circumstances often force management to revise its plan or scrap it entirely in favor of a new one. But even though plans may need to be revised or adapted, most organizations still benefit from the process of developing them.

For one thing, a formal planning process forces managers to take time from daily activities to consider strategic issues that might otherwise be overlooked. It also helps structure and operationalize the otherwise daunting task of responding to a dynamic environment and strategically managing a complex organization with limited resources. Thus, research suggests that formal planning is even more useful under conditions of major change in the firm or its environment, when uncertainty is high, and when complex decisions must be reached.[7]

Finally, a formal plan can help prevent firms from making too many erratic changes in response to short-lived environmental disruptions, which only confuses both employees and customers. As one author suggests, a for-

---

[6]J. Scott Armstrong, "The Value of Formal Planning for Strategic Decisions: Review of Empirical Research," *Strategic Management Journal* 3 (1982), pp. 197–212.
[7]Ibid.

mal plan is like the rudder on a ship. The plan may be disrupted by changing conditions, just as a ship's rudder may not be very useful during heavy seas. Yet a plan, like a rudder, is essential for providing direction and holding the firm on course when the storm is over.

Evolution of planning systems

Even among firms that do employ formal planning systems, there are great differences in who participates, the procedures followed, and the content of the strategic plans ultimately produced. In spite of this diversity, some attempts have been made to categorize broad types of planning systems. In one of the best-known studies, Gluck, Kaufman, and Walleck of the McKinsey consulting firm examined the planning procedures followed by 120 firms in seven different countries.[8] They identified four types of planning systems: financial planning, long-range planning, strategic planning, and strategic management.

Gluck and his colleagues argue that these four systems reflect an evolutionary process; each type appeared at a different time during the 20th century and each subsequent system added to, rather than replaced, earlier systems. They also found that planning systems within individual companies tend to develop along a similar evolutionary path, with new start-ups concentrating on financial planning but then moving toward strategic management as they grow and the strategic issues they face become more complex. As we shall see, though, many firms have not yet developed the most sophisticated types of planning systems. Major characteristics of each type are summarized in Exhibit 1–4 and are discussed below.

Financial planning systems

This type of system planning consists mainly of an annual budgeting process which focuses on forecasting revenue, costs, and capital requirements. Annual budgets are then set for the firm's various businesses and departments, and careful attention is paid to deviations from those budgets to find explanations and determine whether remedial actions are required.

The assumption underlying financial planning systems is that the past will repeat itself, that the market and competitive environment a business will face next year will be largely the same as this year. Thus, detailed strategies are seldom formalized, although implicit strategies often are reflected in the resource allocation decisions made by top management when they approve or adjust budgets for their various businesses. As a result, the planning process, such as it is, under this kind of system is highly centralized at the top levels of corporate management.

---

[8]Frederick W. Gluck, Stephen P. Kaufman, and A. Steven Walleck, "The Four Phases of Strategic Management," *Journal of Business Strategy* 3 (1982), pp. 9–21.

EXHIBIT 1–4

Characteristics of Alternative Planning Systems

Characteristic	Type of planning system			
	Financial planning	**Long-range planning**	**Strategic planning**	**Strategic management**
Management emphasis	Control budget deviations	Anticipate growth and manage complexity	Creative response to changing environment by changing strategic thrust and capabilities	Cope with strategic surprises and fast-developing opportunities or threats
Major assumptions	The past repeats	Past trends will continue	New trends and discontinuities are predictable	Planning cycles are inadequate to deal with rapid changes
Direction of strategic decision making	Top-down	Bottom-up	Mixed (leaning toward top-down)	Mixed (leaning toward bottom-up)
Planning time frame	Periodic	Periodic	Periodic	Real time
Underlying value system	Meet the budget	Predict the future	Think strategically	Create the future
Time period when first developed	Early 1900s	1950s	1960s	mid-1970s

SOURCE: Adapted from material found in F. Gluck, S. Kaufman, and A. Walleck. "The Four Phases of Strategic Management," *Journal of Business Strategy,* Winter 1982, pp. 9–21; D. Aaker, *Strategic Market Management,* 2nd ed. (New York: John Wiley & Sons, 1988), p. 10; and R. Kerin, V. Mahajan, and P. Varadarajan, *Contemporary Perspectives on Strategic Market Planning* (Boston: Allyn and Bacon, 1990), p. 18.

Financial planning systems were first widely adopted by firms during the first half of the 20th century. Yet over half the businesses Gluck and colleagues surveyed in the early 1980s, including some very successful firms, still followed this kind of "meeting-the-numbers" approach.

Long-range planning systems

Relative to financial planning and its emphasis on annual budgets, long-range planning systems cover longer time frames (5 or 10 years) and are more future-oriented. Focusing on anticipating growth and managing increasing complexity, they attempt to project future sales, costs, technological changes, and the like. Any gaps between projected sales and profits and the organization's goals are analyzed to determine what operational changes—such as a new plant or a larger salesforce—might be necessary to achieve long-term objectives.

A major assumption underlying long-range planning systems is that past trends can be extrapolated into the future. Unfortunately, this means that little consideration is given to anticipating new opportunities or initiating new directions. Resources tend to be allocated across businesses and product-markets already in the firm's portfolio.

Because many of the projections and forecasts that serve as the foundation for long-range planning are produced by the managers of individual businesses within the firm, such systems tend to be relatively decentralized. While top management makes major resource allocation decisions and monitors the short-term performance of each business, objectives are often set from the bottom up, with each business bearing the responsibility for determining its own goals and strategies.

In spite of their shortcomings, long-range planning systems continue to be widely used. Indeed, Gluck and his colleagues report that most planning systems in use in the 1980s did not go much beyond this kind of "planning by extrapolation."

Strategic planning systems

Increasingly rapid and disruptive changes in the market environment—such as the energy crisis, high inflation, and increased foreign competition—helped precipitate the development of strategic planning during the 1960s and early 1970s. Because such changes caused discontinuities and shifts in past trends, simply extrapolating such trends into the future was no longer an adequate basis for planning in many industries.

Consequently, strategic planning systems attempt to achieve a more in-depth understanding of the firm's market environment, particularly its customers and competitors. The objective is to anticipate changes and shifts that might have strategic implications. Thus, strategic planning is more dynamic than earlier systems. It focuses on identifying possible opportunities or threats in the environment, evaluating alternative responses, and, when necessary, changing the strategic direction and capabilities of the firm. Current business units and their strengths and weaknesses are not assumed as given; they can change according to market conditions. Thus, a firm's various businesses are not all expected to perform in the same way, and each may pursue its own competitive strategy and objectives.

Like earlier systems, though, strategic planning is a periodic, usually annual, process. Most organizations employing such systems update their strategic plans in the spring or summer. Then, during the fall, those plans provide a foundation for developing annual operating plans and budgets for the individual businesses and products within the firm. For example, General Electric's strategic planning cycle is diagrammed in Exhibit 1–5.

While marketing and business-unit managers often have some input into the annual strategic planning process, top corporate executives usually make final decisions concerning strategic directions and the allocation of resources. As Exhibit 1–5 indicates, for instance, corporate management hands down strategy and budget guidelines to the business units; it also reviews and approves business plans and budgets. Thus, while most strategic planning systems involve elements of both bottom-up and top-down planning, top corporate management tends to play a dominant role.

One advantage of annual strategic planning is that it forces managers to address strategic issues at scheduled times. Without such a formal process,

EXHIBIT 1-5

General Electric's Corporate Strategic Planning Cycle

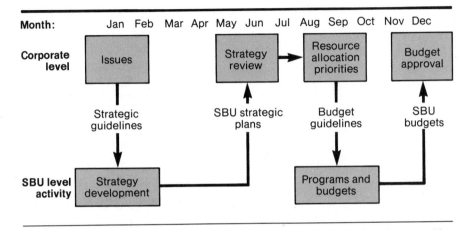

SOURCE: Dale J. Hedhuis, "Commentary," in Dan E. Schendel and Charles W. Hofer, eds. *Strategic Management* (Boston: Little, Brown, Inc., 1979), p. 243.

managers might become absorbed in day-to-day problems and lose sight of the bigger strategic picture. On the other hand, environmental threats and market opportunities can arise so quickly that being tied to an annual planning process can be disastrous. A study of how 10 companies made major changes in strategy found that most such changes were precipitated by critical events, such as an energy crisis or the development of a breakthrough technology, that were difficult to foresee and over which management had no control.[9] Typically, the organizations reacted to such events by making a series of small, incremental decisions that ultimately added up to a major shift in strategy. And most of these incremental decisions were made on an ad hoc, spur-of-the-moment basis rather than as part of an annual formal strategic planning process.[10]

Strategic management systems

By the mid-70s some firms—particularly diversified manufacturing companies in dynamic industries such as electronics—perceived that an annual formal strategic planning cycle was inadequate to respond to the rapid changes occurring in their global market and competitive environments. Conse-

---

[9]James Brian Quinn, "Strategic Change: 'Logical Incrementalism'," *Sloan Management Review,* Fall 1978, pp. 7–23.

[10]The new strategies that sometimes develop as the result of a series of ad hoc, incremental decisions are referred to as *emergent* strategies. For a discussion of such strategies and the processes involved in their development, see Michael D. Hutt, Peter H. Reingen, and John R. Ronchetto, Jr., "Tracing Emergent Processes in Marketing Strategy Formation," *Journal of Marketing,* January 1988, pp. 4–19.

quently, they developed strategic management systems that supplement the formal planning process with procedures and structures designed to enable the organization to be more responsive to fast-developing opportunities and threats.[11]

Firms pursuing strategic management have adopted a variety of new procedures and structures to improve the responsiveness of their decision making, including: more detailed environmental scanning; continuous, real-time information systems; decentralization of strategic decisions; encouragement of entrepreneurial thinking among lower-level managers; and the use of interfunctional management teams to analyze issues and initiate strategic actions outside the formal planning process. At American Express, for instance, the extensive data base of customer demographic and lifestyle variables is updated weekly to keep abreast of emerging trends and opportunities. The corporate culture encourages and rewards entrepreneurial thinking at all management levels. And interfunctional teams of managers are assigned to deal with ongoing strategic issues such as finding new ways to improve customer service.

Because strategic management systems emphasize staying in close and constant touch with the environment and decentralized decision processes, lower-level managers tend to play a more crucial role in formulating strategy. Of course, top management is still responsible for defining the organization's basic strategic thrust and has the final authority to approve or reject new strategic initiatives emanating from the lower ranks. Thus, strategic management systems also involve elements of both bottom-up and top-down planning. However, lower-level mangers tend to be more active and influential participants in such systems than in firms that rely on more formal, periodic strategic planning.

Characteristics of effective planning systems

As planning systems have evolved over the years, each new type has added features to, rather than replaced, earlier systems. But the fact that the newer systems represent attempts to improve upon and overcome the weaknesses of earlier ones should not be interpreted as meaning that the newest planning approach—strategic management—is the most appropriate and effective for all organizations. Research suggests that any type of planning system can be effective if tailored to the firm's environment, the nature of its businesses, and the organizational context.[12] Thus, for a firm engaged in commodity businesses that competes primarily on price in relatively predictable market and competitive environments, a financial or long-range planning system might be adequate. For example, Cargill—one of the nation's largest dealers

---

[11]Some authors refer to the kind of responsive, real-time strategic decision making envisioned by strategic management systems as *adaptive planning*. For a more detailed discussion of the rationale for and procedures involved in such systems see, George S. Day, *Market-Driven Strategy: Processes for Creating Value* (New York: The Free Press, 1990), chaps. 3 and 4.

[12]Balaji Chakravarthy, "On Tailoring a Strategic Planning System to Its Context: Some Empirical Evidence," *Strategic Management Journal,* November–December 1987, pp. 517–34.

in agricultural grains like wheat and soybeans—reaches many of its strategic decisions through long-range planning based on projections of future grain production and global demand.

Regardless of the type of system used, firms effective at strategic planning have three things in common.[13] First, there is little resistance to the planning process within the firm. Managers strongly believe that planning is essential for the organization's continued success. Consequently, they are active, willing participants in the planning process; and they are committed to successfully implementing the strategies that are developed.

A second, and closely related, characteristic is strong support from top management. Clearly, other employees are more likely to take planning seriously when top executives are strongly committed to the planning process and its outcomes. However, that commitment must be backed with resources for environmental scanning, market analysis, and other systems needed to provide adequate information inputs to planning and sufficient human resources to enable managers to spend some time planning.

Finally, effective planning systems strike a balance between creativity and control. That is, they encompass elements of both top-down and bottom-up planning. Top management must formulate a clear strategic vision for the firm, guard against the various business and product-market strategies straying too far from that vision, and make sure that strategies at different levels are coordinated with one another. At the same time, lower-level managers must be encouraged to stay in close touch with the market environment, identify emerging threats and opportunities, and initiate strategic responses when necessary.

While all four types of planning systems are in use today, many analysts argue that most companies will need to move toward the more adaptive strategic management-type systems to remain competitive. Increasingly dramatic and rapid environmental changes, brought about by advancing technology, fragmenting markets, global competition, and the like, will require firms to become more market-oriented and more strategically responsive.[14] But the changing business environment not only necessitates changes in how companies formulate and implement their strategies, it is also likely to affect the role that marketing and marketing managers play in those processes.

THE ROLE OF MARKETING IN FORMULATING AND IMPLEMENTING STRATEGIES

Marketing managers bear the primary responsibility for formulating and implementing strategic marketing plans for individual product-market entries. As mentioned earlier, though, their freedom of action in designing such plans

---

[13]V. Ramanujam, N. Venkatraman, and John C. Camillus, "Multi-Objective Assessment of Effectiveness of Strategic Planning: A Discriminant Analysis Approach," *Academy of Management Journal,* June 1986, pp. 347–72.

[14]For a more detailed discussion of this argument, see George S. Day, *Market-Driven Strategy: Processes for Creating Value* (New York: The Free Press, 1990), chap. 1.

is often constrained by their firm's corporate and business-level strategies. The marketing manager for Heinz ketchup, for instance, probably could not gain approval for an aggressive promotional campaign aimed at increasing Heinz's already commanding share of its market. Such a marketing strategy would be inconsistent with a corporate growth strategy that allocates the bulk of the firm's marketing resources to newer, more rapidly growing product categories—such as the Weight Watchers' line of entrees—and with a business strategy dedicated to competing in basic food categories by maintaining the lowest-cost position in the industry.[15]

On the other hand, the essence of strategic planning at all levels is identifying threats to avoid and opportunities to pursue. The primary strategic responsibility of any manager is to look outward continuously to keep the firm or business in step with changes in the environment. Because they occupy positions at the boundary between the firm and its customers, distributors, and competitors, marketing managers are usually most familiar with conditions and trends in the market environment. Consequently, they are responsible not only for developing strategic plans for their own product-market entries, but also are often primary participants and contributors to the planning process at the business and corporate level as well. As an example, see the wide-ranging influence of marketing managers on strategic planning within SBUs at General Electric, as outlined in Exhibit 1–6. GE's marketing managers have primary responsibility for, or are among the key participants in, formulating nearly all aspects of an SBU's business strategy, as well as planning and implementing many functional program elements within the business unit.

Factors that mediate marketing's role in strategic planning

Unfortunately, marketing managers do not play so extensive a strategic role in all organizations as they do at General Electric. This is because GE is more market-oriented than many firms. Not surprisingly, marketers tend to have the greatest influence on strategy at all levels in corporations that embrace a market-oriented business approach.

Market-oriented management

While there are many views about what it means for a firm to be market-oriented, most agree that market-oriented companies firmly embrace the business philosophy known as the marketing concept.[16] As originally stated

---

[15]Bill Saporito, "Heinz Pushes to Be the Low-Cost Producer," *Fortune*, June 24, 1985, pp. 44–54.

[16]For a discussion of how being "market-oriented" differs from "getting close to the customer," see Benjamin P. Shapiro, " What the Hell Is Market-Oriented?" *Harvard Business Review*, November–December 1988, p. 119; and Ajay Kohli and Bernard J. Jaworski, "Market Orientation: The Construct, Research Propositions, and Managerial Implications," *Journal of Marketing*, April 1990, pp. 1–18. For an instrument used to measure the relative degree of market orientation across firms and business units, see John C. Narver and Stanley F. Slater, "The Effect of Market Orientation on Business Profitability," *Journal of Marketing*, October 1990, pp. 20–35.

EXHIBIT   1–6

Participation in Strategic Planning by Marketing Managers at General Electric

Strategic planning activity	Marketing's role
Determination of SBU's objectives and scope	Key participant along with SBU's general manager
Environmental assessment (customers; economic, political, regulatory trends)	Primary contributor and a major beneficiary of the results
Competitive assessment (actual and potential competitors	Primary contributor, working with other functional managers and staff planners
Situation assessment (inputs to portfolio analysis; industry and market attractiveness; firm and product position)	Primary contributor, working with staff planners and general manager
Objectives and goals	Key participant with other functional managers, including responsibility for measuring several performance indicators
Strategies	Major contributor to determination of SBU's competitive strategy; responsible for marketing strategy and for coordinating plans with other functional strategies

Key program elements	Marketing's role
Product-market development	Leadership role
Product quality	Leading responsibility for quality
Distribution	Primary responsibility
Technology	Varies according to the importance of technology to the product or service
Human resources	Responsible for functional area
Business development*	Key supporting role with strategic planning and manufacturing responsible for implementation
Manufacturing facilities	Typically, only limited involvement

*Decisions to expand, improve, or contract the business.

SOURCE: Adapted from a speech presented by Stephen G. Harrell (then of the General Electric Company) at the American Marketing Association Educators' Conference, Chicago, August 5, 1980. Mr. Harrell is currently a partner in Megamark Partners, a consulting firm specializing in marketing and new-product development.

by General Electric four decades ago, the **marketing concept** holds that the planning and coordination of all company activities around the primary goal of satisfying customer needs is the most effective means to attain and sustain a competitive advantage and achieve company objectives over time.

Thus, market-oriented firms are characterized by a consistent focus by personnel in all departments and at all levels on customers' needs and competitive circumstances in the market environment. They are also willing and able to quickly adapt products and functional programs to fit changes in that environment. Such firms pay a great deal of attention to customer research *before* products are designed and produced. They embrace the concept of market segmentation by adapting product offerings and marketing programs to the special needs of different target markets. Finally, their organizational structures and procedures reflect a market orientation. Marketing managers or product teams play an active role in planning strategies, developing products, and coordinating activities across functional departments to ensure that they are all consistent with the desires of target customers. Thus, the market-oriented firm keeps its businesses focused on well-defined market segments and continually seeks to enhance its competitive advantages.

Rubbermaid, Inc.—a firm that generates well over $1 billion in sales from a line of "homely" plastic housewares, such as ice cube trays and dish drainers—illustrates the link between market orientation and strategic success. A major part of the firm's growth strategy is a focus on new-product and new-market development. It launches nearly 200 new products annually. Most are targeted at specific segments, such as singles living in relatively small apartments and town homes. Rubbermaid reports an unusually high success rate (90 percent) for its new-product introductions, attributed in large measure to the firm's market orientation. Rubbermaid managers continually monitor and adapt to changing consumer preferences and lifestyles, competitive actions, and the concerns of retailers. As Stanley Gault, the firm's CEO, declares: "Our formula for success is very open. We absolutely watch the market, and we [all] work at it 24 hours a day."[17]

Unfortunately, not all companies are so market-oriented as Rubbermaid or General Electric. For a variety of reasons, many American companies are inner-directed and give unbalanced emphasis to internal aspirations, technological developments, and short-run efficiency considerations. Among the reasons why firms are not always in close touch with the market environment are:

- Competitive conditions may enable a firm to be successful in the short run without being particularly sensitive to customer desires.
- The firm may suffer from strategic inertia—the automatic continuation of strategies successful in the past, even though current market conditions are changing.
- Resource constraints and short-run financial pressures can divert management's attention from the actions needed to adapt to changing market and competitive conditions.

Competitive factors affecting a firm's market orientation

One reason some firms are not particularly market-oriented is that the market and competitive conditions they face enable them to be successful in the short term without paying much attention to their customers. Early entrants into

---

[17]Alex Taylor III, "Why the Bounce at Rubbermaid?" *Fortune*, April 13, 1987, pp. 77–78.

newly emerging industries—particularly industries based on new technologies—are especially likely to be internally focused and not very market-oriented. This is because there are likely to be relatively few strong competitors during the formative years of a new industry, customer demand for the new product is likely to grow rapidly and outstrip available supply, and production problems and resource constraints tend to represent more immediate threats to the survival of such new businesses.

Businesses facing such market and competitive conditions are often **product- or production-oriented.** They focus most of their attention and resources on such functions as product and process engineering, production, and finance in order to acquire and manage the resources necessary to keep pace with growing demand. The business is primarily concerned with producing more of what it wants to make, and marketing generally plays a secondary role in formulating and implementing strategy. Indeed, such firms commonly rely on financial or long-range planning systems and base their strategies on extrapolations of the current situation. Some other functional differences between production-oriented and market-oriented firms are summarized in Exhibit 1–7.

As industries grow, they become more competitive. New entrants are attracted and existing producers attempt to differentiate themselves through improved products and more efficient production processes. As a result, industry capacity often grows faster than demand and the environment shifts from a seller's market to a buyer's market. Firms often respond to such changes with aggressive promotional activities—such as hiring more salespeople, increasing their advertising budgets, or offering frequent price promotions—to maintain market share and hold down unit costs.

Unfortunately, this kind of **sales-oriented** response to increasing competition still focuses on selling what the firm wants to make rather than customer needs. Worse, competitors can easily match such aggressive sales tactics. In other words, simply spending more on selling efforts usually does not create a sustainable competitive advantage.

As industries mature, sales volume levels off and technological differences among brands tend to disappear as manufacturers copy the best features of each other's products. Consequently, a firm must seek new market segments or steal share from competitors by offering lower prices, superior services, or intangible benefits other firms cannot match.[18] At this stage, managers can most readily appreciate the benefits of a market orientation, and marketers are often given a bigger role in developing competitive strategies. It is not surprising, then, that many of America's most market-oriented firms—and those working hardest to become market-oriented—are well-established competitors in relatively mature industries.

---

[18]James B. Quinn, Thomas L. Doorley, and Penny C. Paquette, "Beyond Products: Service-Based Strategy," *Harvard Business Review,* March–April 1990, pp. 58–67.

EXHIBIT 1–7

Differences between Production-Oriented and Market-Oriented Firms

Business activity or function	Production orientation	Market orientation
Product offering	Company sells what it wants to make; primary focus on technology, functional performance, and cost.	Company makes what it can sell; primary focus on customer needs and market opportunities.
Product line	Narrow; primary concern is to design standardized products so production runs will be long and unit costs minimized.	Broad; primary concern is to customize offerings to meet the unique needs of various target segments.
Pricing	Based on production and distribution costs.	Based on perceived benefits provided.
Research	Technical research; focus on product improvement and cost cutting in the production process.	Market research; focus on identifying new opportunities and applying new technology to satisfy customer needs.
Packaging	Protection for the product; designed to minimize costs.	Designed for customer convenience; a promotional tool.
Credit	A necessary evil; minimize bad debt losses.	A customer service; a tool to facilitate customer purchases.
Promotion	Emphasis on product features, quality, and price.	Emphasis on product benefits and ability to satisfy customers' needs or solve problems.
Strategic planning	Financial and/or long-range planning systems; top-down planning.	Strategic planning or strategic market management systems; more participation from lower levels of management.

Strategic inertia

In some cases, a firm that achieved success by being in tune with its environment loses touch with its market because managers become reluctant to tamper with strategies and marketing programs that worked in the past. They begin to believe there is "one best way" to satisfy their customers. Such strategic inertia is dangerous for the simple reason that customers' needs and competitive offerings change over time. Staying successful requires constant analysis of and adjustments to changes in what customers want and competitors offer. Thus, in environments where such changes happen frequently, the strategic planning process needs to be ongoing and adaptive, and marketers need to provide detailed information about what is happening with their customers and competitors.[19]

---

[19]Thomas V. Bonoma, "Marketing Success Can Breed 'Marketing Inertia'," *Harvard Business Review,* September–October 1981, pp. 115–21.

Short-run financial pressures

Ironically, another reason that some firms' commitment to a market orientation waned during the 1970s and 1980s was the growing popularity of strategic planning. As we have seen, strategic planning systems are often dominated by a top-down planning process, where top executives hand down decisions about strategic directions for, and the resources to be allocated to, a firm's business units and products. While such decisions should take into account information from lower-level managers about future threats and opportunities in the market environment, top managements' short-term financial imperatives can outweigh such information.

This bias toward short-run financial concerns was exacerbated during the late 1970s and early 1980s by the popularity of portfolio planning models and other techniques focused on managing market share and cash flows to conserve scarce financial resources and by the growing threat of hostile takeovers of firms whose stock appeared to be undervalued. As a consequence, even some historically market-driven firms lost their customer focus during this period and relegated marketing decisions to short-run tactical concerns.[20] In many cases, such lapses were adroitly exploited by foreign competitors who invested heavily to bring new products and processes to customer segments underserved by domestic competitors.

The growing importance of a market orientation for future success

Both financial and long-range planning systems are based on the assumption that past trends can be extrapolated into the future. And periodic strategic planning assumes that discontinuities can be predicted and that the organization can react and adjust its programs faster than changes occur in its environment. These assumptions may still be valid in some industries where markets are stable or slowly evolving in predictable ways and where all competitors play by well-established rules. Unfortunately, such assumptions are becoming increasingly dangerous in a growing number of industries because of increasing rates and magnitudes of change resulting from such things as:

- Mature markets fragmenting into smaller segments with unique needs and preferences.
- Previously self-contained national markets being transformed into linked global markets.
- Technological, demographic, and lifestyle changes creating new market opportunities.
- Competitive advantages becoming harder to sustain as product life cycles shorten and global competitors contest more markets.

---

[20]For a more detailed elaboration of these arguments, see Frederick E. Webster, Jr., "Rediscovering the Marketing Concept," *Business Horizons,* May–June 1988, pp. 29–39.

- Overcapacity intensifying competitive pressures by giving customers greater bargaining power.
- New information technologies enabling closer links between customers and their suppliers and improving customers' ability to evaluate the performance of alternative suppliers.

In light of such changes, many experts argue that firms in most, if not all, industries will have to focus on customer needs and utilize ongoing, adaptive planning processes to succeed and prosper in the future.[21] This, in turn, suggests that marketing managers are likely to play even larger roles in formulating strategies at all organizational levels in the years to come.

THE PROCESS OF FORMULATING AND IMPLEMENTING MARKETING STRATEGY

This book's primary focus is on the development and implementation of marketing strategies for individual product-market entries. Exhibit 1–8 briefly diagrams the activities involved in this process, and it also serves as the organizational framework for the rest of this book.

Interrelationships among different levels of strategy

Before we can discuss the development of a marketing strategy for a specific product, however, we must first examine corporate and business-level strategies in more detail. As we have seen, marketers often play a major role in formulating such strategies, and that role is likely to expand in the future. At the same time, strategic decisions at the corporate and SBU level often influence or constrain the range of options a marketing manager can realistically consider when designing a marketing strategy for his or her product. After all, the marketing program for an individual product must be consistent with the strategic direction, competitive thrust, and resource allocations decided on at higher management levels. Therefore, Chapters 2 and 3 examine the components of corporate and business-level strategies and their implications for the design and implementation of marketing strategies at the product-market level.

Market opportunity analysis

A major factor in the success or failure of a strategy at any level is whether it fits the realities of the firm's external environment. Thus, in developing a marketing strategy for a product, the marketing manager must first monitor

---

[21]George S. Day, *Market-Driven Strategy: Processes for Creating Value* (New York: The Free Press, 1990), chap 1.

E X H I B I T   1 – 8
The Process of Formulating and Implementing Marketing Strategy

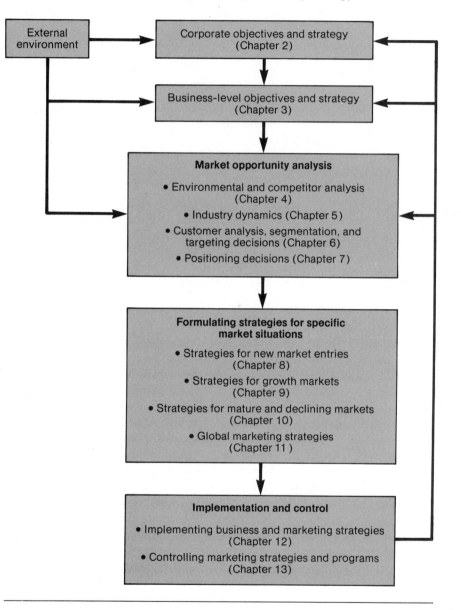

and analyze the opportunities and threats posed by factors outside the organization.

Environmental, industry, and competitor analysis

To understand potential opportunities and threats over the long term, marketers must first attempt to identify and predict the impact of broad trends in the economic and social environment. In some situations, a firm might even try to influence the direction of such trends. For example, American Express engaged in lobbying activities in a number of European and Asian countries aimed at persuading their governments to adopt more favorable trade and economic policies. Chapter 4 discusses a number of macroenvironmental factors that marketing managers should pay attention to, along with some methods for monitoring, analyzing, and perhaps influencing the impact of those factors on the future performance of their product-market entries.

One of the most critical aspects of the external environment for marketers to keep tabs on is the competition. What are the strengths and weaknesses of existing and potential competitors relative to those of the firm? How might the firm gain a sustainable competitive advantage in a given product-market? How might those competitors react to changes in the environment and to the firm's marketing actions in the future? Chapter 4 presents some methods for attempting to answer such questions.

Of course, the competitive environment of an industry is not static but can change dramatically over time. For example, the growth of major competitors such as MasterCard and Visa during the 1980s forced American Express to increase its promotional budget and work even harder to improve customer service to maintain its share of the credit-card market. Chapter 5 explores the competitive dynamics of an industry, particularly emphasizing how competition and customers' buying patterns are likely to change as the industry or product-market moves through various life-cycle stages.

Customer analysis: segmentation, targeting, and positioning

The primary purpose of any marketing strategy is to facilitate and encourage exchange transactions with potential customers. One of a marketing manager's major responsibilities, then, is to analyze the motivations and behaviors of present and potential customers. Of course, it is unlikely that every potential customer will have the same needs, seek the same product benefits, or be influenced in the same way by the same marketing program. Thus, marketing managers must also determine whether there are multiple market segments that will respond differently to their products and marketing programs and how to best define, identify, and appeal to those segments. Chapter 6, therefore, examines dimensions and techniques that can be used to analyze customers and to define and identify market segments in both consumer and organizational markets.

But not every segment of a market is likely to be equally attractive to a firm. Some may be too small to be profitable, and others may desire benefits the firm cannot provide so efficiently or effectively as some competitors. Given its prestigious image and its strategy of providing superior service at premium prices, for instance, American Express does not try to attract the lower-income segments of the charge-card market. Therefore, after examining customer needs and competitive strengths and weaknesses, a marketing manager must decide which market segment or segments to target and how to position the product in the target segment relative to competitive offerings. Chapter 6 examines some considerations in selecting target segments, and Chapter 7 discusses various methods for choosing a competitive position for the product within those markets.

Formulating strategies for specific market situations

The strategic marketing program for a particular product-market entry should reflect market demand and the competitive situation within the target market. As demand and competitive conditions change over time, the marketing strategy should also be adjusted. During the 1970s, for instance, American Express's successful "Do you know me?" promotional campaign was aimed at building primary demand by emphasizing the convenience and prestige of carrying a credit card. But as competing bankcards proliferated, American Express switched to a "Membership has its privileges" campaign designed to differentiate the green card from its competitors by promoting superior customer service.

Because demand and competitive conditions change as product-markets grow and mature, the third section of this book discusses a variety of different marketing strategies appropriate for different stages in a market's life cycle. Chapter 8 examines some marketing strategies for introducing new products or services to the market. Chapter 9 discusses strategies appropriate for building or maintaining a product's share of a growing market in the face of increasing competition. And Chapter 10 considers the strategies a marketing manager might adopt in mature or declining product-markets. Finally, many companies try to grow by pursuing target markets in other countries. However, cultural and political differences across nations often require different strategic approaches for marketing success. Chapter 11, therefore, discusses global marketing strategies.

Implementation and control

A final critical determinant of a strategy's success is the firm's ability to implement it effectively. And this, in turn, depends on whether the strategy is consistent with the firm's resources, organizational structure, coordination and control systems, and the skills and experience of company personnel. In other words, managers must design a strategy that fits existing company resources, competencies, and procedures—or try to construct new structures and systems to fit the chosen strategy.[22] American Express's strategy of offering superior service and pursuing growth through internal new-product development, for example, would not have been so successful without its extensive data base of customer information and its various systems and procedures for measuring and improving service quality. Therefore, Chapter 12 discusses the structural variables, planning and coordination processes, and personnel and corporate culture characteristics related to the successful implementation of different marketing strategies.

Finally, the marketing manager must determine whether the marketing program is achieving its objectives and adjust the strategy when performance is disappointing. This evaluation and control process provides feedback to managers and serves as the basis for a subsequent market opportunity analysis. Chapter 13 examines ways to evaluate marketing performance and develop contingency plans for when things go wrong.

SUMMARY

This chapter argues that a strategy should specify *what* is to be accomplished, *where* it is to be accomplished (which industries and product-markets to focus on), and *how* (the resources and activities to be allocated to each product-market to meet environmental opportunities and threats and gain a competitive advantage). Consequently, there are five components within a well-developed strategy: (1) scope, or the desired breadth of the organization's strategic domain, (2) goals and objectives, (3) resource deployments, indicating how financial and human resources are to be distributed across businesses, product-markets, and/or functional departments and activities, (4) identification of a source of sustainable competitive advantage, and (5) specification of potential sources of synergy across businesses and/or functional departments.

Most firms—especially those with multiple businesses or divisions—do not have a single comprehensive strategy but a hierarchy of corporate strategy, business-level strategies, and functional strategies focused on individual product-market entries. A marketing manager's strategy for a specific product-market entry is constrained by the strategic decisions made at the corporate and business-unit levels. On the other hand, marketing managers often play a crucial role in providing necessary information and analyses to the strategic planning process at higher levels of the organization.

The extent of the marketer's role in strategic planning is mediated by the type of planning system the firm uses. As firms grow and mature, their planning systems tend to evolve from the simplest kind of financial planning to long-range and strategic planning. And in some cases, firms ultimately

---

[22]N. Venkatraman and John C. Camillus, "Exploring the Concept of 'Fit' in Strategic Management," *Academy of Management Review* 9 (1984), pp. 513–25.

embrace the most adaptive, ongoing type of strategic market management planning system. As this evolution occurs, the role of marketing managers in the strategic planning process tends to increase in importance.

The marketer's role in formulating and implementing strategy is also influenced by the market orientation of the firm and its top managers. Some firms are not very market-oriented because competitive conditions may enable the firm to be successful without being particularly sensitive to customer desires, the firm may be committed to past policies that are no longer appropriate in view of changing conditions in the market, or market and competitive concerns may be outweighed by short-term financial imperatives. However, a clearer focus on customer needs and competitive responses is likely to become more crucial for the future strategic success of most firms because of the increasing rate and magnitude of changes occurring in the domestic and global market environments. And this suggests that marketers will play an even more important strategic role in the years to come.

Corporate Strategy Decisions

BORDEN, INC.: REMAKING ELSIE[1]

Ever since Gail Borden patented a process for condensing milk in 1856, Borden has meant milk to most Americans. And ever since her debut in a 1935 radio ad, Elsie the Cow has been the cheery goodwill ambassador for Borden's dairy products. But in 1989, Borden began a partial retreat from the dairy business by announcing it would sell or close 20 dairy processing facilities. This withdrawal from what had long been the firm's core business not only took the company out of major dairy markets in the Southeast and Midwest, it also accounted for 40 percent of a $570 million (pretax) one-time restructuring charge the firm wrote off in 1989.

Why such a drastic move? Borden executives blamed intense competition and high raw milk prices for making the dairy business less profitable and attractive—at least in some regions of the country—than many other food product categories. However, some observers speculate that lawsuits filed against Borden and some of its competitors for bid-rigging on school milk contracts in several southeastern and midwestern states may have also influenced the decision. In Florida, for example, Borden did not admit any wrong-doing, but it paid over $10 million to settle the case and subsequently closed four of its dairy plants in the state.

Borden's broader scope and new corporate mission

Regardless of the company's reasons for pulling out of bulk milk markets in the Southeast and Midwest, the firm still hopes to retain its number-one share of the national dairy products market by focusing on less

---

[1]This example is based on material found in Norm Alster, "Remaking Elsie," *Forbes,* December 25, 1989, pp. 106–10; and *Borden 1989 Annual Report* (New York: Borden, Inc., 1990).

competitive markets in the South and West. Nevertheless, Borden will depend less and less on its dairy business as a source of sales and profits in coming years. Instead, the firm has broadened the scope of its operations and adopted a mission of becoming a leading player in six packaged food, consumer, and industrial goods categories. As stated in its 1989 annual report, Borden's purpose since 1986 has been to engage in "purchasing, manufacturing, processing, and distributing a broad range of pasta, snacks, niche grocery products, dairy products, nonfood consumer products, and films and adhesives both domestically and in foreign countries."

Growth through acquisition

Borden's new mission was to focus on more attractive market opportunities where its competencies and resources could give it a sustainable competitive advantage and generate profitable revenue growth. The firm already had a presence (though in some cases only a small one) in a number of high-margin, nondairy product categories by the mid-80s. For example, it produced Creamettes pasta, Cheez Doodles snacks, specialty grocery items such as ReaLemon lemon juice, and a number of nonfood products like Elmer's Glue. To strengthen its position in these categories and successfully pursue its new corporate mission, however, the firm launched an aggressive strategy of growth through acquisition in 1986. Within three years it spent more than $3 billion to purchase 78 businesses, each carefully chosen to fit into one

of the six growth areas specified in the firm's mission statement. During the same period, Borden divested 22 businesses with annual sales of over $1 billion that no longer fit the firm's focus, including such things as a large commodity chemicals operation.

Borden's development of its pasta business illustrates its growth strategy. The Creamette Company, like most other pasta makers, was a regional manufacturer when Borden acquired it in 1979. Borden had hoped to use its size and marketing muscle to build Creamettes into the first national pasta brand. But each time it tried to break into new markets, Creamette met fierce defensive promotion and advertising by an entrenched local brand. Borden's solution was simply to buy the local brand, thereby gaining local distribution and eliminating a competitor. "We saw that the only way to ever get national in pasta was to acquire, so we acquired 17 regional brands," says Romeo Ventres, Borden's CEO. Now the firm can sell Creamettes alongside an acquired local brand in each region and use its superior resources and promotion skills to build national identity without local price wars. National distribution enabled Creamette to double its market share in three years, to over 12 percent in 1989.

Corporate organization and performance

Borden is organized into four operating divisions. Its Grocery and Specialty Products Division incorporates the firm's pasta brands and most of its specialty or niche

EXHIBIT   2 – 1

Sales and Operating Income of Borden's Four Divisions, 1987–89

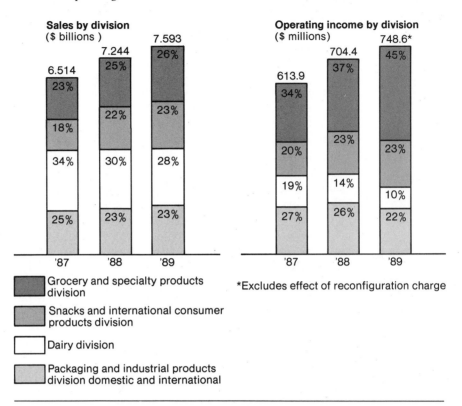

SOURCE: *Borden 1989 Annual Report* (New York: Borden, Inc., 1990), p. 29.

food products, such as Eagle Brand condensed milk, Cracker Jack, Wyler's bouillon, and Classico pasta sauce. As Exhibit 2–1 indicates, this division has grown substantially in recent years, and it produced nearly half the firm's profits in 1989.

Borden has pursued growth in the salty-snack category in the same way as in pasta: by acquiring and extending a number of strong regional brands. Total sales of brands like Wise, Jays, New York Deli, Bravos, and Krunchers! make the company number two in market share in the domestic salty-snack

market, right behind Frito-Lay. Borden is also the leading producer of sweet baked snacks in West Germany, and a major competitor in salty snacks in the United Kingdom, Spain, and other countries. These businesses are all housed within the firm's Snacks and International Consumer Products Division.

Borden's remaining bulk milk operations, together with its ice cream and yogurt brands, constitute the firm's Dairy Division. Finally, nonfood consumer products, such as Wall-Tex wallcoverings, and industrial films and adhesives are organized within the Packaging and Industrial Products Division.

Allocating resources to achieve future objectives

By the end of 1989, Borden had largely accomplished its objective of achieving "critical mass" in the six growth areas targeted in its mission statement through acquisition of smaller regional firms. The firm then shifted to a more internally focused growth strategy to improve the sales volumes and competitive positions of its various national and regional brands. The company's ultimate goal is to achieve a number-one market share position, nationally or regionally, for each of its consumer products. To accomplish this, the firm began shifting more resources (some $75 to $100 million) into marketing programs for brands thought to have future growth potential, such as Creamettes pasta, Classico pasta sauce, Krunchers! potato chips, and Borden Lite-Line cheese.

However, even if the firm achieves its volume growth objectives, management worries that its profits may not keep pace. Increasingly, profit margins on many Borden brands, particularly its snack products, are being squeezed. On one side, more intense competition from large national manufacturers

like Frito-Lay and Anheuser-Busch is forcing Borden to spend more on advertising and promotion and to lower prices to achieve its volume and share goals. On the other side, powerful grocery chains are demanding more trade promotion dollars and higher slotting fees in return for shelf space in their stores.

In an attempt to improve profit margins in the face of these trends, Borden adopted a second corporate objective. Its goal is to become the low-cost producer in each of its major product categories by 1992. The firm planned to spend $650 million on capital improvements in 1990 and 1991. The funds would be used to build 11 new large-scale, low-cost plants and to consolidate production within its most modern facilities. The company also initiated a program to reward employees for ideas on quality and productivity improvement at each plant by sharing with them the dollar savings from performance improvements.

Thus, while Elsie may be partially put out to pasture, Borden's well-defined, carefully implemented corporate strategy seems to be turning the company into a much more aggressive kind of animal. And it has put the firm in a position to milk substantial future sales and earnings growth from its revitalized consumer packaged goods businesses.

STRATEGIC DECISIONS AT THE CORPORATE LEVEL

Borden's corporate strategy provides a clear sense of direction and useful guidance for the company's managers because it speaks to all five dimensions of strategy discussed in Chapter 1. First, it defines the overall **scope, mission,** and **intent** of the company by targeting six specific product categories as areas for future growth and development. It also sets challenging, but specific and measurable, **objectives** for the company and its various businesses, such as the goal of becoming the low-cost producer in each product category by 1992.

One aspect of Borden's corporate strategy that has changed recently is the planned **direction for future growth and development**—the means by which the firm aims to achieve and sustain an overall competitive advantage. From 1986 through 1989, the firm focused on growth through acquisition of regional pasta and snack manufacturers to achieve a critical mass in those categories. Once it accomplished this goal, the firm shifted its strategy to focus on internal growth by building the volume, market shares, and profitability of its established brands through more aggressive marketing programs and more efficient production. This change in competitive direction also necessitated changes in the **allocation of resources** across different businesses and functional activities within the firm. The firm closed 20 milk processing plants and focused more funds on capital improvements and marketing programs in its grocery and snack businesses. Finally, Borden sought to take advantage of possible **synergies** by grouping related businesses into four separate divisions where they could benefit from sharing large-scale production facilities and marketing efforts.

The Borden example also demonstrates that a clearly defined corporate strategy can influence and constrain the decisions a firm's marketing managers make when designing marketing strategies and programs for individual products. The marketing plan for Creamettes pasta, for instance, must reflect the corporate goals of making it the first national pasta brand and of achieving a leading share position in its category.

In view of the influence of corporate-level decisions on the development and implementation of strategic programs for individual product-market entries, the remaining sections of this chapter discuss the five dimensions of a well-defined corporate strategy in more detail. As a guide, Exhibit 2–2 summarizes some of the crucial questions about each of these strategy components.

CORPORATE SCOPE: DEFINING THE FIRM'S MISSION AND INTENT

A well-thought-out mission statement guides an organization's managers as to which market opportunities to pursue and which fall outside the firm's strategic domain. A clearly stated mission can help instill a shared sense of direction, relevance, and achievement among employees, and a positive image of the firm among customers, investors, and other stakeholders.

To provide a useful sense of direction, a corporate mission statement must clearly define the organization's strategic scope. It should answer such fundamental questions as: What is our business? Who are our customers? What kinds of value can we provide to these customers? and What should our

EXHIBIT 2-2

Corporate Strategy Components and Issues

Strategy Component	Key Issues
Scope, mission, and intent	• What business(es) should the firm be in?
	• What customer needs, market segments, and/or technologies should be focused on?
	• What is the firm's enduring strategic purpose or intent?
Objectives	• What performance dimensions should the firm's business units and employees focus on?
	• What is the target level of performance to be achieved on each dimension?
	• What is the time frame in which each target should be attained?
Development strategy	• How can the firm achieve a desired level of growth over time?
	• Can the desired growth be attained by expanding the firm's current businesses?
	• Will the company have to diversify into new businesses or product-markets to achieve its future growth objectives?
Resource allocation	• How should the firm's limited financial resources be allocated across its businesses to produce the highest returns?
	• Of the alternative strategies that each business might pursue, which will produce the greatest returns for the dollars invested?
Sources of synergy	• What competencies, knowledge, and customer-based intangibles (e.g., brand recognition, reputation) might be developed and shared across the firm's businesses?
	• What operational resources, facilities, or functions (e.g., plants, R&D, salesforce, etc.) might the firm's businesses share to increase their efficiency?

business be in the future?[2] For example, a few years ago PepsiCo, the manufacturer of Pepsi-Cola, broadened its mission to focus on "marketing superior quality food and beverage products for households and consumers dining out." That clearly defined mission guided the firm's managers toward the acquisition of several related companies, such as Frito-Lay, Pizza Hut, and Taco Bell, and the divestiture of operations that no longer fit the firm's primary thrust.[3]

---

[2]Some organizations develop mission statements that go beyond a definition of the firm's strategic domain and include specific ethical principles or social values top management desires the organization to follow. Borden's 1989 *Annual Report,* for example, includes a section on "Social Responsibility" that outlines a set of guiding principles about how the company will treat its employees and policies concerning charitable contributions and environmental protection efforts (pp. 22–23). For the purpose of understanding a corporation's competitive strategy, however, we focus primarily on those aspects of mission statements that address the scope of a firm's product and market domain.

[3]"Pepsi's Marketing Magic: Nobody Does It Better," *Business Week,* February 10, 1986, pp. 52–57. Also see Patricia Sellers, " Pepsi Keeps on Going After No. 1," *Fortune,* March 11, 1991, pp. 62–70.

While managers often have a clear understanding of the firm's mission when a new organization is first formed, growth and expansion into new product-markets, employee turnover, and changing environmental conditions can all cloud or make inappropriate a firm's mission over time. Consequently, a review and, if necessary, a restatement of the organization's mission should be a periodic part of the corporate strategic planning process.

Factors that influence the corporate mission

Like any other component of strategy, an organization's mission should fit its internal characteristics, resources, and competencies and its external opportunities and threats. Thus, while defining the firm's mission is usually a first step in developing corporate strategy, it should be intertwined with analyses of the organization's strengths and weaknesses and of its environment.

A firm's mission statement should reflect internal characteristics such as the historical accomplishments, top management preferences, and shared values, myths, and symbols that, taken together, make up the company's culture.[4] The mission should also be compatible with the firm's more tangible internal characteristics: its resources, distinctive competencies, and possible synergies across its various businesses. Thus, after PepsiCo redefined its mission it divested its Wilson Sporting Goods and North American Van Lines divisions in part because the firm's marketing and product development skills were not much of an advantage in the moving or sporting goods businesses.

Finally, a firm's mission statement should take into account the opportunities and threats in its external environment. It should guide the organization toward product-markets where customer needs and competitive conditions offer attractive growth possibilities; at the same time, it should help steer the organization away from industries where stagnant demand, strong competitors, or emerging new technologies might make it difficult to establish a competitive advantage and achieve corporate objectives. In this sense, a mission statement represents both a response to environmental conditions and an attempt to control them by spelling out which markets and competitors a firm should avoid confronting in the future.[5] Thus, Borden's revised mission statement steered the firm away from bulk milk markets where commodity pricing, intense competition, and possibly legal difficulties reduced the chances for growth and profitability. Instead, it focused the company's attention on high-value-added packaged goods categories where competition is less intense and opportunities for future sales and profit growth are greater.

[4]Terrence E. Deal and Allan A. Kennedy, *Corporate Cultures* (Reading, Mass.: Addison-Wesley, 1982).

[5]John Child, "Organization Structure, Environment and Performance: The Role of Strategic Choice," *Sociology,* 1972, pp. 1–22.

Dimensions for defining the corporate mission

A number of dimensions can be used to define an organization's strategic scope or mission.[6] Some firms specify their domain in physical terms, focusing on products or services the company will produce or technologies it will use. Such mission statements, however, can lead to confusion and slow reaction times if technologies or customer demands change. For example, in a classic article Leavitt argues that Penn Central Railroad's view of its mission as being "the railroad business" helped cause the firm's failure. Penn Central did not respond to major changes in transportation technology, such as the rapid growth of air travel and the increased efficiency of long-haul trucking. Nor did it react to changes in customer preferences, such as a growing willingness to pay higher prices for the speed and convenience of air travel. Leavitt argues that it is better to define a firm's mission in terms of what customer needs are to be satisfied and the functions that must be performed to do so.[7] Products and technologies change over time, but basic customer needs tend to endure. Thus, if Penn Central had defined its mission as satisfying its customers' transportation needs rather than simply being a railroad, it might have been more willing to expand its domain to incorporate newer technologies.

One problem with Leavitt's advice, though, is that a mission statement focusing only on basic customer needs can be too broad to provide clear guidance and can fail to take into account the firm's specific competencies. If Penn Central had defined itself as a transportation company, should it have diversified into the trucking business? Started an airline? Considered manufacturing cars? As the upper-right quadrant of Exhibit 2–3 suggests, the most useful mission statements focus on both the customer need to be satisfied and how the firm will attempt to satisfy that need. They are specific as to the customer groups and the kinds of products or technologies on which the firm will concentrate its efforts.[8] Thus, instead of thinking of itself as being in the railroad business or as satisfying the transportation needs of all potential customers, Burlington Northern's mission is to provide long-distance transportation for large-volume producers of low-value, low-density products, such as coal and grain.

Strategic intent or vision: a motivational view of corporate mission

Recently, some writers have argued that mission statements stated in terms of specific customer needs, target markets, technologies, and/or products (such as Burlington Northern's) may also have some shortcomings as a foun-

---

[6]For a more detailed discussion of the various dimensions and variables an organization might use in defining its mission, see David A. Aaker, *Strategic Market Management,* 2nd ed. (New York: John Wiley and Sons, 1988), chap. 3.

[7]Theodore Leavitt, "Marketing Myopia," *Harvard Business Review,* July–August, 1960, pp. 45–56.

[8]Derek Abell, *Defining the Business: The Starting Point of Strategic Planning* (Englewood Cliffs, N.J.: Prentice Hall, 1980), chap. 3.

EXHIBIT 2-3
Characteristics of Effective Corporate Mission Statements

	Broad	**Specific**
Functional Based on customer needs	Transporation business	Long-distance transportation for large-volume producers of low-value, low-density products
Physical Based on existing products or technology	Railroad business	Long-haul, coal-carrying railroad

SOURCE: Reprinted by permission from p. 43 of *Strategy Formulation: Analytical Concepts* by C. W. Hofer and D. Schendel. Copyright © 1978 by West Publishing Company. All rights reserved.

dation for a corporate strategy.[9] For one thing, it can be hard to get company employees fired up over something as mundane as "providing long-distance transportation," no matter how necessary or desirable the task. Also, while such specific mission statements may accurately reflect the market situation and the firm's strengths and weaknesses at the present time, they may prove too rigid as things change. Employees may overlook some new market opportunities, or new ways of building on the company's strengths or overcoming its weaknesses, because the firm's stated mission doesn't explicitly recognize those approaches.

Those authors suggest that a firm's basic scope and focus might be more effectively defined by a more general but personally motivating statement of **strategic intent** or **vision.** Consider, for instance, the difference between Burlington Northern's mission statement and the rallying cry that expresses the strategic intent of one Japanese auto manufacturer: "Beat Benz!" The first accurately describes the scope of BN's business, but it fails to inspire. "Beat Benz," on the other hand, not only expresses the firm's ultimate goal of taking over world leadership in the manufacture of luxury cars, it appeals to every employee's competitive instinct and desire for accomplishment. This is the essence of a good statement of strategic intent or vision. It provides a motivational perspective on the corporate purpose by setting an enduring goal worthy of employee commitment, usually couched in terms of unseating the best, or remaining the best, worldwide.

While an effective statement of strategic intent is clear about the organization's long-term ends, it should be flexible as to means. It must leave room for employee improvisation. Indeed, strategic intent usually implies a sizable

[9]For a more detailed discussion of strategic intent and its implications for formulating corporate strategy, see Gary Hamel and C. K. Prahalad, "Strategic Intent," *Harvard Business Review,* May–June 1989, pp. 63–76; and James C. Collins and James I. Porras, " Making Impossible Dreams Come True," *Stanford Business School Magazine,* July 1989, pp. 14–19.

stretch for an organization. Whereas the traditional approach to strategic planning seeks a good fit between existing resources and current opportunities, strategic intent creates an extreme misfit between the firm's resources and future ambitions. Current capabilities and resources will not suffice. Instead, top management challenges the organization's employees to make the most of limited resources, to be more inventive, and to develop new capabilities. To increase the probability that such challenges will be met, the firm must first provide its employees with the necessary skills (usually via increased training) and then give them substantial freedom to initiate new procedures or programs aimed at moving the organization toward its goal. Such decentralization of decision making can increase both the amount of worker participation and the creativity brought to the process of defining the corporation's strategy.

The risk inherent in this approach, however, is similar to that which arises when a firm defines its mission in terms of satisfying a generic customer need. Although the ultimate objective is clear, there may be many ways to pursue it. And some of those ways may be inconsistent or compete with one another. Even a clear strategic vision, in other words, may not provide a sufficiently specific direction to focus employee efforts.

One possible solution to this dilemma is for management to combine a statement of strategic intent with a more traditional mission statement; one to stimulate employee commitment and the other to focus their efforts on a more clearly defined domain of product-markets. While PepsiCo employees are urged to "beat Coke," for instance, they also understand that their competitive efforts should be focused on "marketing superior quality food and beverage products for households and consumers dining out." Thus, when Coke entered the entertainment business a number of years ago via the acquisition of Columbia Pictures and other investments, PepsiCo did not follow because entertainment did not fit the firm's mission.

Management can also convert a broad statement of strategic intent into a more specific mechanism for focusing the organization's efforts by breaking it down into a sequential series of shorter-term objectives or challenges that must be accomplished for the intent to be realized. In attempting to move Borden toward becoming a major competitor in the packaged food industry, for instance, CEO Ventres first challenged his divisional managers to identify and acquire strong regional competitors in fragmented product categories like pasta and salty snacks to achieve national market coverage and a leading share position in those categories by 1989. Once that objective was accomplished, he issued a new challenge for the firm to become the low-cost producer in each of its major product categories by 1992.

A firm's strategic intent should remain constant over time. However, its shorter-term objectives often change in response to changing market and competitive circumstances and the firm's own changing competencies and resources as it moves toward its ultimate goal. Also, like strategic intent, shorter-term objectives should be both challenging and specific about the ends to be accomplished but flexible as to the means employees might use to achieve them. Finally, note that Borden wanted to accomplish its strategic objectives within specific time frames. As we will see in the next section, the above points are common characteristics of useful corporate objectives.

CORPORATE OBJECTIVES

Confucius said that "For one who has no objective, nothing is relevant." Formal objectives provide decision criteria that guide an organization's business units and employees toward specific dimensions and levels of performance. Those same objectives provide the benchmarks for evaluating actual performance. One factor that shaped Borden's decision to deemphasize its bulk milk operations, for instance, was the difficulty of achieving the firm's ambitious profit and return on equity objectives in such a commodity-like business. Since focusing more attention on its higher-value-added packaged foods businesses, Borden's overall return on equity increased from 14.3 percent in 1985 to 17.8 percent in 1988.

To be useful as decision criteria and evaluative benchmarks, corporate objectives must be both specific and measurable. Therefore, each objective should contain four components:

- A *performance dimension* or attribute sought.
- A *measure* or *index* for evaluating progress.
- A *target* or *hurdle level* to be achieved.
- A *time frame* within which the target is to be accomplished.

Enhancing shareholder value: the ultimate objective

In recent years, a growing number of executives of publicly held corporations have concluded that the organization's ultimate objective should be to increase its shareholders' economic returns, as measured by dividends plus appreciation in the company's stock price.[10] Management balances the interests of various corporate constituencies, including employees, customers, suppliers, debtholders, and stockholders. The firm's continued existence depends on a financial relationship with each of these parties. Employees want competitive wages. Customers want high quality at a competitive price. Suppliers and debtholders have financial claims that must be satisfied with cash when they fall due. And shareholders, as residual claimants, look for cash dividends and the prospect of future dividends reflected in the stock's market price.

If a company does not satisfy its constituents' financial claims, it ceases to be viable. Thus, a going concern must strive to enhance its ability to generate cash from the operation of its businesses and to obtain any additional funds needed from debt or equity financing.

---

[10]Jack L. Treynor, "The Financial Objective in the Widely Held Corporation," *Financial Analysts Journal,* March–April 1981, pp. 68–72; and Alfred Rappaport, *Creating Shareholder Value: The New Standard for Business Performance* (New York: The Free Press, 1986), chap. 1.

The firm's ability to attain debt financing (its ability to borrow) depends in turn on projections of how much cash it can generate in the future. Similarly, the market value of its shares, and therefore its ability to attain equity financing, depends on investors' expectations of the firm's future cash-generating abilities. People willingly invest in a firm only when they expect a better return on their funds than they could get from other sources without exposing themselves to any greater risks. Thus, management's primary objective should be to pursue capital investments, acquisitions, and business strategies that will produce future cash flows sufficient to return positive value to shareholders. Failure to do so will not only depress the firm's stock price and inhibit the firm's ability to finance future operations and growth, it may also make the organization more vulnerable to a takeover by outsiders who promise to increase its value to shareholders.

Given this rationale, many firms set explicit objectives targeted at increasing shareholders' value. These are usually stated in terms of a target return on shareholder equity, increase in the stock price, or earnings per share. When a previous CEO took over Borden in 1979, for instance, his primary objective was to boost the firm's return on shareholder equity from 11.9 percent to 15 percent before he retired in 1986, an objective the firm met handily. His commitment to that objective also may have been influenced by an incentive plan established by Borden's board of directors that awarded him a bonus each year earnings per share increased by 7 percent or more.[11]

Unfortunately, such broad shareholder-value objectives do not always provide adequate guidance for a firm's lower-level managers or benchmarks for evaluating performance. For one thing, standard accounting measures, such as earnings per share or return on investment, are not always reliably linked to the true value of a company's stock.[12] And as we shall see later in this chapter, tools are available to evaluate the future impact of alternative strategic actions on shareholder value; but those valuation methods have inherent pitfalls and can be difficult to apply at lower levels of strategy—as when trying to choose the best marketing strategy for a particular product-market entry.[13]

Finally, there is a danger that a narrow focus on short-term financial, shareholder-value objectives may lead managers to pay too little attention to actions necessary to provide value to the firm's customers and sustain a competitive advantage. In the long term, customer value and shareholder value converge; a firm can continue to provide attractive returns to shareholders only so long as it satisfies and retains its customers. But some managers may

---

[11]Alison Leigh Cowan, "Borden's No. 1 Product: Contented Shareholders," *Business Week,* July 28, 1986, pp. 78–80.

[12]Bradley T. Gale and Donald J. Swire, "The Tricky Business of Measuring Wealth," *Planning Review,* March–April 1988, pp. 14–17, & 47.

[13]Patrick Barwise, Paul R. Marsh, and Robin Wensley, "Must Finance and Strategy Clash?" *Harvard Business Review,* September–October 1989, pp. 85–90; and George S. Day and Liam Fahey, "Putting Strategy into Shareholder Value Analysis," *Harvard Business Review,* March–April 1990, pp. 156–62.

EXHIBIT 2-4

Schlitz: An Example of Increasing Stock Price at the
Expense of Competitive Position

In the early 1970s, Schlitz Brewing made the mistake of boosting its share price at the
expense of its competitive position. The firm shortened its brewing process by 50 percent, reduced labor costs, and switched to less costly ingredients. As a result, it became
the lowest-cost producer in the industry, its profits soared, and its stock price rose to a
high of $69 by 1974. Unfortunately, however, Schlitz's aggressive cost-cutting campaign
also degraded the quality of its beer. By 1976, the firm was receiving constant customer
and dealer complaints and its market share was slipping badly. In 1978, a new management team attempted to get product quality back on track, but by then consumers had
such a low opinion of Schlitz beer that the company could not recover. By 1981, Schlitz's
market share position had slipped from number two all the way to number seven, and its
share price had dropped to a mere $5.

SOURCE: George S. Day and Liam Fahey, "Putting Strategy into Shareholder Value Analysis," *Harvard
Business Review,* March–April 1990, pp. 156–62.

overlook this in the face of pressures to achieve aggressive short-term financial objectives, as illustrated by the experience of Schlitz Brewing discussed
in Exhibit 2–4.[14]

Most organizations pursue multiple objectives

Given the limitations of a single objective focused on enhancing shareholder
value, most companies establish multiple objectives to guide and evaluate
their managers' performance. Some of those objectives—such as increasing
market share, improving product quality, or reducing operating expenses—
relate to specific actions that directly influence the firm's ability to generate
future cash flows and greater shareholder value.[15] Others may aim at making
specific contributions to the firm's various constituencies, such as improving
the skill levels of the workforce or contributing to community charities. Exhibit 2–5 lists some common performance dimensions and measures used in
specifying such corporate, as well as business-unit and marketing, objectives.

Many firms have more than one objective, as the results of a study of the
stated objectives of 82 large corporations clearly demonstrate. While the largest percentage of respondents (89 percent) had explicit profitability objectives,
82 percent reported growth objectives, 66 percent had specific market share
goals, more than 60 percent mentioned social responsibility, employee welfare, and customer service objectives, and 54 percent of the companies had

---

[14]Day and Fahey, "Putting Strategy . . . ," p. 157.

[15]Alfred Rappaport, "Linking Competitive Strategy and Shareholder Value Analysis," *Journal
of Business Strategy,* Spring 1987, pp. 58–67.

EXHIBIT 2-5

Common Performance Criteria and Measures that Specify Corporate,
Business-Unit, and Marketing Objectives

Performance criteria	Possible measures or indexes
• Growth	$ sales Unit sales Percent change in sales
• Competitive strength	Market share Brand awareness Brand preference
• Innovativeness	$ sales from new products Percent of sales from product-market entries introduced within past five years Percent cost savings from new processes
• Profitability	$ profits Profit as percent of sales Contribution margin* Return on investment (ROI) Return on net assets (RONA) Return on equity (ROE)
• Utilization of resources	Percent capacity utilization Fixed assets as percent of sales
• Contribution to owners	Value to shareholders —dividends —stock price Earnings per share Price/earnings ratio
• Contribution to customers	Price relative to competitors Product quality Customer satisfaction
• Contribution to employees	Wage rates, benefits Personnel development, promotions Employment stability, turnover
• Contribution to society	$ contributions to charities or community institutions Growth in employment

*Business-unit managers and marketing managers responsible for a product-market entry often have little control over costs associated with corporate overhead, such as the costs of corporate staff or R&D. It can be difficult to allocate those costs to specific strategic business units (SBUs) or products. Consequently, profit objectives at the SBU and product-market level are often stated as a desired *contribution margin* (the gross profit prior to allocating such overhead costs).

R&D/new-product development goals.[16] These percentages add up to much more than 100 percent, showing that most firms had several objectives.

In addition, while the most commonly reported corporate objective involved some aspect of profitability or return on investment, more than three-

[16] Y. K. Shetty, "New Look at Corporate Goals," *California Management Review,* Winter 1979, pp. 71–79.

quarters of the respondents also had a growth or market share objective. Many firms thus face potential conflicts in trying to fulfill their objectives: the level of investment and expenditure required to aggressively pursue long-term growth may reduce short-term profitability.[17] Similar trade-offs can occur between social responsibility or employee welfare goals and short-term profit objectives. One way to reconcile such potentially conflicting goals is to rank them in a hierarchy, establishing priorities for action. Another approach is to state one of the conflicting goals as a constraint or hurdle. Thus, a firm might attempt to maximize growth subject to the constraint that ROI remain above a specified minimum level each year.

Business-unit and product-market objectives

Once broad corporate objectives have been set, they must be broken down into a consistent set of subobjectives for each of the businesses and product-markets in which the firm competes. In some cases, every business unit is expected to match the corporate objective. The 3M Company, for instance, expects each business division to meet the corporate goal of producing 25 percent of its sales volume from products introduced within the past five years as a means of stimulating innovation and growth. More commonly, however, the businesses and product-markets are assigned objectives that reflect differences in their competitive positions or the maturity of their markets. A business unit with large market shares in a number of mature product-markets, for example, might be given a lower sales growth objective but a higher profit goal than a unit with a weaker competitive position or more rapidly growing markets.

CORPORATE DEVELOPMENT STRATEGY

Often, the projected combined future sales and profits of a corporation's business units and product-markets fall short of the firm's long-run growth and profitability objectives. There is a gap between what the firm expects to become if it continues on its present course and what it would like to become. This is not surprising, since some high-growth markets are likely to mature over time, and some high-profit, mature businesses may decline to insignificance as they get older. Thus, to answer the critical question—Where is future growth coming from?—management must choose a specific strategy to guide future corporate development.

Essentially, a firm can go in two major directions in seeking future growth: **expansion** of its current businesses and activities, or **diversification** into new businesses, either through internal business development or acquisition. Exhibit 2–6 outlines some specific options a firm might pursue in seeking growth via each of these directions.

---

[17]Gordon Donaldson, *Managing Corporate Wealth* (New York: Praeger, 1984).

EXHIBIT 2-6

Alternative Corporate Growth Strategies

	Current products	**New products**

Current markets	**Market penetration strategies**
	• Increase market share
	• Increase product usage
	  Increase frequency of use
	  Increase quantity used
	  New applications
		Product development strategies
		• Product improvements
		• Product-line extensions
		• New products for same market

New markets	**Market development strategies**
	• Expand markets for existing
	  products
	  Geographic expansion
	  Target new segments
		Diversification strategies
		• Vertical integration
		  Forward integration
		  Backward integration
		• Diversification into related
		  businesses (concentric
		  diversification)
		• Diversification into unrelated
		  businesses (conglomerate
		  diversification)

Expansion

One way to expand current businesses is by increasing their share of existing markets, particularly if those markets are growing. This typically involves making product improvements, cutting prices, or outspending competitors on promotion. For example, in an effort to gain share in the full-size pickup truck market at the expense of industry-leading Ford, Chevrolet made product-design changes. To dramatize these improvements, it committed substantial funds to an aggressive new advertising campaign. Such actions often invite competitive retaliation, however, and Ford responded with its own product upgrading and strong advertising program.[18]

A second approach encourages current customers to use more of the product, use it more often, or use it in new ways. Packages of Kellogg's Cracklin' Oat Bran cereal, for example, include recipes for things like bran muffins that use the cereal as an ingredient and a coupon good for 50 cents off the purchase of another box.

---

[18]Joseph B. White, "Chevy Turns to Negative Ads in an Effort to Topple Ford as Pickup Truck Leader," *The Wall Street Journal,* December 13, 1988, p. 81.

A third way to expand existing businesses is to develop product-line extensions or new-product offerings for existing customers. For example, Arm & Hammer successfully introduced a laundry detergent, an oven cleaner, and a liquid detergent. Each capitalized on baking soda's image as an effective deodorizer and on the fact that 97 percent of consumers recognized the Arm & Hammer brand name.[19]

Finally, a firm might expand the markets for its current products, as when a domestic producer attempts to move into foreign markets. For example, Morgan Stanley, a large New York–based investment bank, opened a Tokyo branch concerned primarily with equity trading.[20]

Diversification

Firms also seek growth by diversifying their operations. This is typically riskier than the various expansion strategies because it involves new operations and customer groups. Nevertheless, about two-thirds of all Fortune 500 companies are diversified to one degree or another.[21]

Vertical integration is one way for corporations to diversify their operations. **Forward integration** occurs when a firm moves "downstream" in terms of the product flow—as when a manufacturer integrates by acquiring a wholesaler or retail outlet. **Backward integration** occurs when a firm moves "upstream" by acquiring a supplier. For example, The Limited, Inc., a firm that owns about 2,500 women's apparel stores, was one of the first clothing retailers to engage in backward integration. Its Mast Industries division consists of a worldwide network of manufacturers, which produces most of the merchandise sold through The Limited's stores.

Integration gives a firm access to scarce or volatile sources of supply or tighter control over the marketing, distribution, and servicing of its products. But it increases the risks inherent in committing substantial resources to a single industry. Also, the investment required to vertically integrate often offsets the additional profitability generated by those integrated operations, resulting in little improvement in return on investment.[22]

Related (or concentric) diversification occurs when a firm internally develops or acquires another business that does not have products or customers in common with its current businesses but that might contribute to internal synergy through the sharing of production facilities, brand names, R&D know-how, or marketing and distribution skills. Thus, Procter & Gamble decided to enter the packaged cookie business a few years ago to take

---

[19]J. J. Honomichl, "The Ongoing Saga of 'Mother Baking Soda,'" *Advertising Age,* September 20, 1982, pp. M2–M3.

[20]"How to Beat the Japanese," *U.S. News & World Report,* August 24, 1987, pp. 38–44.

[21]Richard P. Rumelt, *Strategy, Structure, and Economic Performance* (Boston: Harvard Business School, Division of Research, 1976).

[22]Robert D. Buzzell, "Is Vertical Integration Profitable?" *Harvard Business Review,* January–February 1983, pp. 92–102.

advantage of the popularity of its Duncan Hines brand and its massive promotional resources.

The motivations for **unrelated (or conglomerate) diversification** are primarily financial rather than operational. By definition, an unrelated diversification involves two businesses that have no commonalties in products, customers, production facilities, or functional areas of expertise. Such diversification most likely occurs when a disproportionate number of the firm's current businesses face decline due to decreasing demand, increased competition, or product obsolescence. The firm must seek new avenues to provide future growth. Other more fortunate firms may move into unrelated businesses because they have more cash than they need to expand their current businesses, or they wish to discourage takeover attempts.

Unrelated diversification is the riskiest growth strategy. Consequently, one might expect conglomerate firms to have inferior financial performance compared to less diversified organizations. Indeed, one study found that firms engaging in unrelated diversification produced an 18 percent lower average return on equity than that produced by all Fortune 500 firms during 1967–78.[23] However, a more recent study suggests that the financial performance of diversified firms is moderated by the industries they diversify into. This suggests that a firm's future success is determined as much by the accuracy of management's analysis of the attractiveness of potential product-markets, and of the firm's competitive advantages in those markets, as it is by the specific growth strategy it adopts.[24]

ALLOCATING CORPORATE RESOURCES

Diversified organizations have several potential advantages over more narrowly focused firms. They have a broader range of areas in which they can knowledgeably invest, and their growth and profitability rates may be more stable because they can offset declines in one business with gains in another. To exploit the advantages of diversification, though, corporate managers must make intelligent decisions about how to allocate financial and human resources across the firm's various businesses and product-markets. Two sets of analytical tools have proven especially useful in making such decisions: **portfolio models** and **value–based planning.**

Portfolio models

One of the most significant developments in strategic management during the 1970s and 1980s was the development and widespread adoption of portfolio models to help managers allocate corporate resources across multiple

[23]Malcolm S. Salter and Wolf A. Weinhold, *Diversification Through Acquisition* (New York: The Free Press, 1979).

[24]Richard A. Bettis and William K. Hall, "Diversification Strategy, Accounting Determined Risk, and Accounting Determined Return," *Academy of Management Journal* 25 (June 1982), pp. 254–64.

EXHIBIT 2-7

BCG's Market Growth/Relative Share Matrix

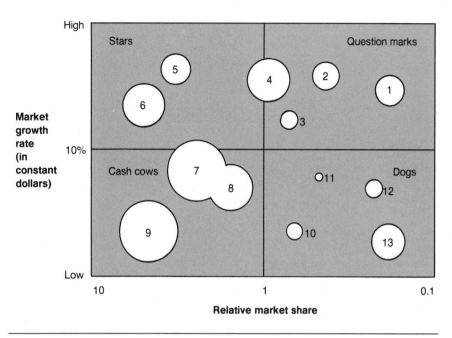

SOURCE: Reprinted with permission from *Long Range Planning* 10, Barry Hedley, "Strategy and the Business Portfolio." Copyright © 1977 Pergamon Press, Inc.

businesses. These models enable managers to classify and review their current and prospective SBUs by viewing them as a portfolio of investment opportunities and then evaluating each business's competitive strength and the attractiveness of the markets it serves.

The Boston Consulting Group's (BCG) growth-share matrix

One of the first, and best known, portfolio models is the growth-share matrix developed by the Boston Consulting Group (BCG). It analyzes the impact of investing resources in different business units on the corporation's future earnings and cash flows. Each business is positioned within a matrix, as shown in Exhibit 2–7. The vertical axis indicates the industry's growth rate, and the horizontal axis shows the business unit's market share relative to its largest competitor.

The growth-share matrix assumes that a firm must generate sufficient cash from businesses with strong competitive positions in mature markets to fund the investments necessary to build the market shares of other businesses in more rapidly growing industries that represent attractive future opportunities. Thus, the **market growth rate** shown on the vertical axis is a proxy measure for the maturity and attractiveness of an industry. This model views

EXHIBIT 2-8

Cash Flows across Businesses in the BCG Portfolio Model

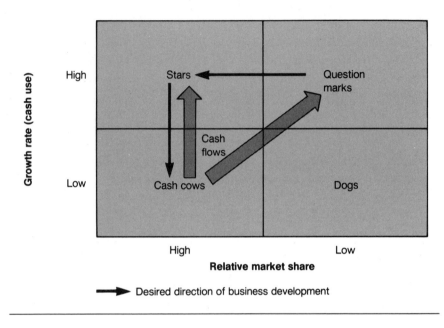

Desired direction of business development

businesses in relatively rapidly growing industries as more attractive investment opportunities for future growth and profitability. In Exhibit 2–7, an
annual market growth rate of 10 percent is the cutoff level between fast- and
slow-growing industries. This dividing line can vary, however, depending on
a corporation's objectives and available opportunities.

Similarly, a business's **relative market share** is a proxy for its competitive
strength within its industry. It is computed by dividing the business's absolute market share in dollars or units by that of the leading competitor in
the industry. Thus, in Exhibit 2–7 a business unit is in a strong competitive
position if its share is equal to, or larger than, that of the next leading competitor (i.e., a relative share of 1.0 or larger). But it is competitively weak
if the leading competitor holds a larger share of the market. Finally, in the
exhibit, the size of the circle representing each business unit is propor-
tional to that unit's sales volume. Thus, businesses 7 and 9 are the largest
volume businesses in this hypothetical company, while business 11 is the
smallest.

Resource allocation and strategy implications

Each of the four cells in the growth-share matrix represents a different
type of business with different strategy and resource requirements. The
implications of each are discussed below and summarized graphically in
Exhibit 2–8.

- *Question marks*. Businesses in high-growth industries with low relative market shares (those in the upper-right quadrant of Exhibit 2–8) are called *question marks* or *problem children*. Such businesses require large amounts of cash, not only for expansion to keep up with the rapidly growing market, but also for marketing activities (or reduced margins) to build market share and catch the industry leader. If management can successfully increase the share of a question mark business, it becomes a star. But if they fail, it eventually turns into a dog as the industry matures and the market growth rate slows. When this happens it can be difficult for the firm to recoup its past investments in the business. The strategic implication, then, is that management must be careful in selecting which question marks to invest in for future growth. Without sufficient resources and a competitive advantage it can exploit to successfully overtake the market leader, the firm is best advised to divest or harvest the business before its resources are drained.

- *Stars*. A star is the market leader in a high-growth industry. Stars are critical to the continued future success of the firm. As their industries mature, they move into the bottom-left quadrant and become cash cows. Paradoxically, while stars are critically important, they often are net users rather than suppliers of cash in the short run (as indicated by the possibility of a negative cash flow shown in Exhibit 2–8). This is because the firm must continue to invest in such businesses to keep up with rapid market growth and to support the R&D and marketing activities necessary to stave off competitors' attacks and maintain a leading market share. Indeed, share maintenance is crucial for star businesses to become cash cows rather than dogs as their industries mature.

- *Cash cows*. Businesses with a high relative share of low-growth markets are called *cash cows* because they are the primary generators of profits and cash in a corporation. Such businesses do not require much additional capital investment. Their markets are stable, and their share leadership position usually means they enjoy economies of scale and relatively high profit margins. Consequently, the corporation can use the cash from these businesses to support its question marks and stars (as shown in Exhibit 2–8). However, this does not mean the firm should necessarily maximize the business's short-term cash flow by cutting R&D and marketing expenditures to the bone—particularly not in industries where the business might continue to generate substantial future sales. When firms attempt to harvest too much cash from such businesses they risk suffering a premature decline from cash cow to dog status, thus losing profits in the long term.

- *Dogs*. Low-share businesses in low-growth markets are called *dogs* because although they may throw off some cash, they typically generate low profits, or losses. Divestiture is one option for such businesses, although it can be difficult to find an interested buyer. Another common strategy is to harvest dog businesses. This involves maximizing short-term cash flow by paring investments and expenditures until the business is gradually phased out. In some cases, though, an argument can be made for continuing to invest in a dog. Such a strategy may make sense, for instance, if the business can be focused on one or a few product-markets where it has some competitive strengths and additional profitable growth can be found.

Limitations of the growth-share matrix

Because the growth-share matrix uses only two variables as a basis for categorizing and analyzing a firm's businesses, it is relatively easy to understand. But while this simplicity helps explain its popularity, it also means that the model has limitations:

- *Market growth rate is an inadequate descriptor of overall industry attractiveness.* For one thing, market growth is not always directly related to profitability or cash flow. Some high-growth industries have never been very profitable, because low entry barriers and capital intensity has enabled supply to grow even faster, resulting in intense price competition. Also, rapid growth in one year is no guarantee that growth will continue in the following year.

- *Relative market share is inadequate as a description of overall competitive strength.* It is based on the assumption that an experience curve resulting from a combination of scale economies and other efficiencies gained through learning and technological improvements over time leads to continuing reductions in unit costs as a business's relative market share increases. But a large market share within an industry does not always give a business a significant cost advantage—especially when the product is a low-value-added item, when different products within the business require different production or marketing activities, where different competitors have different capacity and utilization rates, or where some competitors are more vertically integrated or have lower-cost suppliers than others.[25]

  Also, market share is more properly viewed as an outcome of past efforts to formulate and implement effective business-level and marketing strategies rather than as an indicator of enduring competitive strength.[26] If the external environment changes, or the SBU's managers change their strategy, the business's relative market share can shift dramatically.

- *The outcomes of a growth-share analysis are highly sensitive to variations in how "growth" and "share" are measured.* Using information from 15 business units within a single firm, one study explored how their positions within

[25]David B. Montgomery and George S. Day, "Experience Curves: Evidence, Empirical Issues, and Applications," in *Strategic Marketing and Strategic Management,* eds. David Gardner and Howard Thomas (New York: John Wiley & Sons, 1984), pp. 213–38.

[26]Robert Jacobson argues that market share and profitability are joint outcomes from successful strategies and, further, that management skills likely have the greatest impact on profitability. See "Distinguishing Among Competing Theories of the Market Share Effect," *Journal of Marketing,* October 1988, pp. 68–80.

a growth-share matrix would vary when different measures of growth and market were used. The study used four measures of share and four of growth (both past and forecasted future growth). Only 3 of the 15 businesses ended up in the same quadrant of the matrix no matter what measures were used.[27]

Another measurement problem has to do with how the industry and the SBU's "served market" (i.e., the target-market segments being pursued) should be defined. For example, Coke Classic holds about a 19 percent share of the U.S. soft-drink market but less than 8 percent of the market for all liquid beverages. Given that consumers substitute other beverages, such as coffee, bottled water, and fruit juice, for soft drinks to varying degrees, which is the most appropriate market definition to use?

- *While the matrix specifies appropriate investment strategies for each business, it provides little guidance to how best implement those strategies.* While the model suggests that a firm should invest cash in its question mark businesses, for instance, it does not consider whether there are any potential sources of competitive advantage that the business can exploit to successfully increase its share. Simply providing a business with more money does not guarantee that it will be able to improve its position within the matrix.

- *The model implicitly assumes that all business units are independent of one another except for the flow of cash.* If this assumption is not accurate, the model can suggest some inappropriate resource allocation decisions. For instance, if other SBUs depend on a dog business as a source of supply— or if they share functional activities, such as a common plant or salesforce, with that business—harvesting the dog might increase the costs or reduce the effectiveness of the other SBUs.

Alternative portfolio models

In view of the above limitations, a number of firms have attempted to improve the basic portfolio model. As indicated in Exhibit 2–9, such improvements have focused primarily on developing more detailed, multifactor measures of industry attractiveness and a business's competitive strength and on making the analysis more future-oriented.

Multifactor portfolio models, typically referred to as *industry attractiveness–business position matrices* or *directional policy matrices,* rely on factors other than just market growth to judge the future attractiveness of different industries. Similarly, they use multiple variables in addition to relative market share to judge the competitive strength and position of each of their businesses.

Exhibit 2–10 shows some of the factors that managers might use to evaluate industry attractiveness and a business's competitive position. Corporate managers must first select factors most appropriate for their firm and weight

---

[27]Yoram Wind, Vijay Mahajan, and Donald J. Swire, "An Empirical Comparison of Standardized Portfolio Models," *Journal of Marketing,* Spring 1983, pp. 89–99.

EXHIBIT 2-9

Developments in Portfolio Analysis

From analysis based on		To analysis based on
• One or two specified dimensions	→	• Dimensions selected by management
• Single-item measures	→	• Multifactor measures
• Unweighted measures	→	• Weighted measures
• Objective data	→	• Objective and perceptual data
• Single respondent	→	• Multiple respondents
• Historical data	→	• Projected data

SOURCE: Adapted from Roger A. Kerin, Vijay Mahajan, and P. Rajan Varadarajan, *Contemporary Perspectives on Strategic Market Planning* (Boston: Allyn and Bacon, 1990), p. 86.

them according to their relative importance. They then rate each business and its industry on the two sets of factors. Next they combine the weighted evaluations into summary measures used to place each business within one of the nine boxes in the matrix shown in Exhibit 2–10. Businesses falling into boxes numbered 1 (where both industry attractiveness and the business's ability to compete are relatively high) are good candidates for further investment for future growth. Businesses in the 2 boxes should receive only selective investment with an objective of maintaining current position. Finally, businesses in the 3 boxes are candidates for harvesting or divestiture.

These multifactor models are richer and more detailed than the simple growth-share model and consequently they provide more strategic guidance concerning the appropriate allocation of resources across businesses. They are also more useful for evaluating potential new product-markets. However, the multifactor measures in these models can be subjective and ambiguous, especially when managers must evaluate different industries on the same set of factors. Also, the conclusions drawn from these models still depend on the way industries and product-markets are defined.[28]

Recently, firms have also used portfolio analysis to evaluate how they should allocate resources across the different **technologies** (as opposed to particular businesses or products) in their asset base. A technology portfolio matrix typically categorizes different technologies according to whether the firm is, or will be, an industry leader or follower in the development of the technology, the amount of development needed to commercialize the technology, and the likely market potential for products based on the technology.[29] This form of portfolio analysis is particularly useful for high-tech

---

[28]For a more detailed discussion of the uses and limitations of multifactor portfolio models, see Roger A. Kerin, Vijay Mahajan, and P. Rajan Varadarajan, *Contemporary Perspectives on Strategic Market Planning* (Boston: Allyn and Bacon, 1990), chap. 3.

[29]Noel Capon and Rashi Glazer, "Marketing and Technology: A Strategic Coalignment," *Journal of Marketing,* July 1987, pp. 1–14.

EXHIBIT 2-10

The Industry Attractiveness–Business Position Matrix

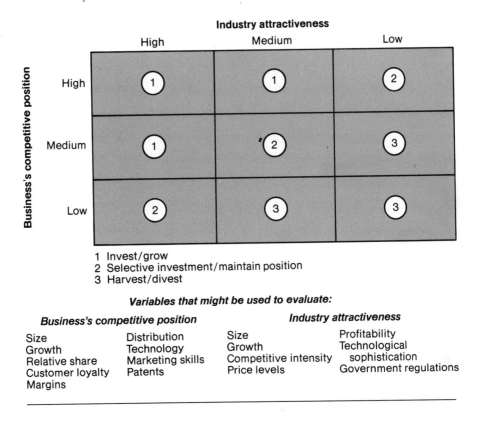

1 Invest/grow
2 Selective investment/maintain position
3 Harvest/divest

Variables that might be used to evaluate:

Business's competitive position		Industry attractiveness	
Size	Distribution	Size	Profitability
Growth	Technology	Growth	Technological
Relative share	Marketing skills	Competitive intensity	sophistication
Customer loyalty	Patents	Price levels	Government regulations
Margins			

firms or business units that have more potential new technologies and/or applications in the early stages of development than they have the resources to fully commercialize.

Value-based planning

As mentioned, one limitation of portfolio analysis is that it specifies how firms should allocate financial resources across their businesses without considering the competitive strategies those businesses are, or should be, pursuing. Portfolio analysis provides little guidance, for instance, in deciding which of two question mark businesses—each in attractive markets but following different strategies—is worthy of the greatest investment or in choosing which of several alternative competitive strategies a particular business unit should pursue.

Value-based planning is a resource allocation tool that attempts to address such questions by assessing the shareholder value a given strategy is likely to create. Thus, value-based planning provides a basis for comparing the economic returns to be gained from investing in different businesses pursuing different strategies or from alternative strategies that might be adopted by a given business unit.

A number of value-based planning methods[30] are currently in use across a variety of corporations, including Borden, NCR, TRW, and Sears. But all of these methods share three basic features. First, they assess the economic value a strategy is likely to produce by examining the cash flows it will generate rather than relying on distorted accounting measures, such as return on investment or earnings per share.[31] Second, they estimate the shareholder value that a strategy will produce by discounting its forecasted cash flows by the business's risk-adjusted cost of capital. Finally, they evaluate strategies based on the likelihood that the investments required by the strategy will deliver returns greater than the cost of capital.

This approach to evaluating alternative strategies is particularly appropriate for use in allocating investments across business units because the business level is where it becomes most obvious that a unit's net earnings are not always the same as the cash it produces. Suppose, for instance, that a firm experiences rapid sales growth and as a result must make ever-larger investments in noncash assets, such as inventory and accounts receivable. The company may show a handsome profit in an accounting sense, but its noncash assets may absorb much of its cash, leaving it with too little cash to meet its short-term expenses and obligations. This is exactly what happened to Endo-Lase, a distributor of medical lasers. Company sales tripled in 1984, and the firm reported substantial earnings. But accounts receivable increased at an even faster rate, leaving the firm strapped for working capital. Endo-Lase soon found it necessary to write down its receivables, and write off over 90 percent of its earnings. The company filed for bankruptcy in 1986.[32] This was a dramatic evaporation of shareholder value; but any company or business unit that persistently needs more cash than it generates is eating into shareholder value.

Discounted cash flow model

Perhaps the best known and most widely used approach to value-based planning is the discounted cash flow model proposed by Alfred Rappaport and the Alcar Group, Inc. In this model, as Exhibit 2–11 indicates, shareholder value created by a strategy is determined by the cash flow it generates, the

---

[30]Two of the most commonly used approaches to value-based planning are the market-to-book ratio model and the discounted cash flow model. The market-to-book ratio model is described in William W. Alberts and James M. McTaggart, "Value-Based Strategic Investment Planning," *Interfaces* 14 (January–February 1984), pp. 138–51. The discounted cash flow model, which is the approach focused on in this chapter, is detailed in Alfred Rappaport, *Creating Shareholder Value: A New Standard for Business Performance* (New York: The Free Press, 1986).

[31]For a detailed discussion of the shortcomings of accounting data for evaluating the value created by a strategy, see Rappaport, *Creating Shareholder Value*, chap. 2.

[32]"Now You See It . . . ," *Forbes*, February 9, 1987, p. 70.

EXHIBIT 2-11

Factors Affecting the Creation of Shareholder Value

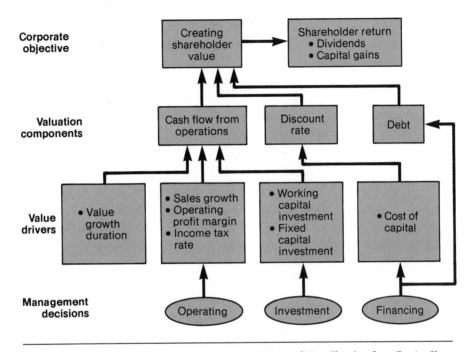

SOURCE: Reprinted with permission of The Free Press, a Division of Macmillan, Inc. from *Creating Share-holder Value* by Alfred Rappaport. Copyright © 1986 by Alfred Rappaport.

business's cost of capital (which is used to discount future cash flows back to their present value), and the market value of the debt assigned to the business. The future cash flows generated by the strategy are, in turn, affected by six factors or "value drivers." They are: the rate of sales growth the strategy will produce, the operating profit margin, the income tax rate, investment in working capital, fixed capital investment required by the strategy, and the duration of value growth.

The first five value drivers are self-explanatory, but the sixth requires some elaboration. The duration of value growth represents management's estimate of the number of years over which the strategy can be expected to produce rates of return that exceed the cost of capital. This estimate, in turn, is tied to two other management judgments. First, the manager must decide on the length of the planning period (typically three to five years); he or she must then estimate the residual value the strategy will continue to produce after the planning period is over. Such decisions are tricky, for they involve predictions of what will happen in the relatively distant future. Unfortunately, managers must wrestle with several such thorny estimation problems when implementing value-based planning. A detailed discussion of the procedure involved and the kinds of forecasts and predictions a manager must make in using discounted cash flow analysis to evaluate a business strategy appears in this chapter's appendix.

Some limitations of value-based planning[33]

Value-based planning is not a substitute for strategic planning; it is only one tool for evaluating strategy alternatives identified and developed through managers' judgments. It does so by relying on forecasts of many kinds to put a financial value on the hopes, fears, and expectations managers associate with each alternative. Projections of cash inflows rest on forecasts of sales volume, product mix, unit prices, and competitors' actions. Expected cash outflows depend on projections of various cost elements, working capital, and investment requirements.

While good forecasts are notoriously difficult to make, they are critical to the validity of value-based planning. Once someone attaches numbers to judgments about what is likely to happen, people tend to endow those numbers with the concreteness of hard facts. Consequently, the numbers derived from value-based planning can sometimes take on a life of their own, and managers can lose sight of the assumptions underlying them.

Consequently, inaccurate forecasts can create problems in implementing value-based planning. For one thing, there are natural human tendencies to overvalue the financial projections associated with some strategy alternatives and to undervalue others. For instance, managers are likely to overestimate the future returns from a currently successful strategy. Evidence of past success tends to carry more weight than qualitative assessments of future threats. Managers may pay too little attention to how competitive behavior, prices, and returns might change if, for example, the industry were suddenly beset by a slowdown in market growth and the appearance of excess capacity.

On the other hand, some kinds of strategy alternatives are consistently undervalued. Particularly worrisome from a marketing viewpoint is the tendency to underestimate the value of keeping current customers. Putting a figure on the damage to a firm's competitive advantage from *not* making a strategic investment necessary to maintain the status quo is harder than documenting potential cost savings or profit improvements that an investment might generate. For example, a few years ago Cone Drive Operations, a small manufacturer of heavy-duty gears, faced a number of related problems. Profits were declining, inventory costs were climbing, and customers were unhappy because deliveries were often late. Cone's management thought that a $2 million computer-integrated manufacturing system might help solve these problems; but a discounted cash flow analysis indicated the system would be an unwise investment. Because the company had only $26 million in sales, it was hard to justify the $2 million investment in terms of cost

---

[33]This section summarizes points made in more detail in George S. Day and Liam Fahey, "Putting Strategy into Shareholder Value Analysis," *Harvard Business Review,* March–April 1990, pp. 156–62.

savings. However, the financial analysis underestimated intangibles like improved product quality, faster order processing, and improved customer satisfaction. Management decided to install the new system anyway, and new business and nonlabor savings paid back the investment in just one year. More important, Cone retained nearly all of its old customers, many of whom had been seriously considering switching to other suppliers.

Finally, another kind of problem involved in implementing value-based planning occurs when management fails to consider all the appropriate strategy alternatives. Since it is only an analytical tool, value-based planning can evaluate alternatives, but it cannot create them. The best strategy will never emerge from the evaluation process if management fails to identify it.

To realize its full benefits, management must link value-based planning to sound strategic analysis—analysis rigorous enough to avoid the problems associated with undervaluing certain strategies, overvaluing others, and failing to consider all the options. As Day and Fahey argue:

> Managers must fully consider the competitive context of cash flows and ensure that cash flow projections are directly tied to competitive analysis projections. They must question whether the cash outflows contribute to competitive advantage and to what extent cash inflows are dependent on those advantages. Specifically, they should broaden the range of strategy alternatives, challenge the inherent soundness of each alternative, and test the sensitivity of each alternative to changes in cash inflows and outflows.[34]

In spite of its limitations, when value-based planning is used correctly as an integral part of the broader strategic planning process it can be a useful tool for evaluating, and deciding how to allocate resources among, alternative strategies. An example of a successful application of value-based planning at the Coca-Cola Company is discussed in Exhibit 2–12.

SOURCES OF SYNERGY

A final strategic concern at the corporate level is to increase synergy across the firm's various businesses and product-markets. As mentioned, synergy exists when two or more businesses or product-markets, and their resources and competencies, complement and reinforce one another so that the total performance of the related businesses is greater than it would be otherwise.

Some potential synergies at the corporate level are knowledge-based. The performance of one business can be enhanced by the transfer of competencies, knowledge, or customer-related intangibles—such as brand-name recognition and reputation—from other units within the firm. For instance, the technical knowledge concerning image processing and the quality reputation that Canon developed in the camera business helped ease the firm's entry into the officer copier business.

---

[34]George S. Day and Liam Fahey, "Putting Strategy . . . ," pp. 160–61.

EXHIBIT   2-12

A Strategic Application of Value-Based Planning at the Coca-Cola Company

> The Coca-Cola Company uses value-based planning to help make decisions both about what businesses to acquire or divest and about the relative attractiveness of alternative strategies within each of its businesses. An example of the usefulness of the approach is provided by Coke's recent experience within its soda fountain business. The firm had long considered this business to be very profitable since there were no bottles or cans to fill, transport, or store. But a discounted cash flow analysis revealed that the business was actually destroying shareholder value. Over time, the business had become quite capital intensive. As a result, the business's return on capital was only 12.6 percent, while its cost of capital was estimated to be 16 percent.
>
> The main culprit turned out to be the expensive, five-gallon, stainless steel containers used to transport the Coke syrup to retail outlets. Therefore, the business changed its distribution and packaging policies. It adopted cheaper, disposable bag-in-a-box containers and sent larger 50-gallon drums to its bigger customers. By thus reducing its investment in containers, the business's return on capital rose to 17 percent. At the same time, by increasing its financial leverage, Coke reduced its cost of capital to 14 percent. Thus, the soda fountain business was turned into a strong contributor to shareholder value.

SOURCE: Bernard C. Reimann, "Managing for the Shareholders: An Overview of Value-Based Planning," *Planning Review,* January–February 1988, pp. 10–22.

In part, such knowledge-based synergies are a function of the corporation's scope and mission—or how its managers answer the question, What businesses should we be in? When a firm's portfolio of businesses and product-markets reflects a common mission based on well-defined customer needs, market segments, or technologies, the company is more likely to develop core competencies, customer knowledge, and strong brand franchises that can be shared across businesses. However, the firm's organization structure and allocation of resources may also enhance knowledge-based synergy. A centralized corporate R&D department, for example, is often more efficient and effective at discovering new technologies with potential applications across multiple businesses than if each business unit bore the burden of funding its own R&D efforts. Similarly, some experts argue that strong corporate-level coordination and support is necessary to maximize the strength of a firm's brand franchise, and to glean full benefit from accumulated market knowledge, when competing in global markets.[35]

A second potential source of corporate synergy is inherent in sharing operational resources, facilities, and functions across business units. For instance, two or more businesses might produce products in a common plant or use a single salesforce to contact common customers. When such sharing helps increase economies of scale or experience-curve effects, it can improve the efficiency of each of the businesses involved. However, the sharing of operational facilities and functions may not produce positive synergies for all

---

[35]Gary Hamel and C. K. Prahalad, "Strategic Intent," *Harvard Business Review,* May–June 1989, p. 74.

business units. Such sharing can limit a business's flexibility and reduce its ability to adapt quickly to changing market conditions and opportunities. Thus, a business whose competitive strategy is focused on new-product development and the pursuit of rapidly changing markets may be hindered more than helped when it is forced to share operating resources with other units.[36] For instance, when Frito-Lay attempted to enter the packaged cookie market with its Grandma's line of soft cookies, the company relied on its 10,000 salty-snack route salespeople to distribute the new line to grocery stores. The firm thought its huge and well-established snack salesforce would give its cookies a competitive advantage in gaining shelf space and retailer support. But because those salespeople were paid a commission on their total sales revenue, they were reluctant to take time from their salty-snack products to push the new cookies. The resulting lack of a strong sales effort contributed to Grandma's failure to achieve a sustainable market share.

As we shall see in the next chapter, the type of competitive strategy a business unit chooses to pursue can have a number of implications for corporate-level decisions concerning organizational structure and resource allocation as well as for the marketing strategies and programs employed within the business.

SUMMARY

Decisions about the organization's scope or mission, its overall goals and objectives, avenues for future growth, resource deployments, and potential sources of synergy across business units are the primary components of corporate strategy.

A mission statement provides guidance to an organization's managers about which market opportunities to pursue and which fall outside the firm's strategic domain. Similarly, a statement of strategic intent establishes a long-term direction for the firm and motivates employee effort; but it is flexible in giving employees substantial freedom to decide what means are best for achieving the firm's purpose.

Formal objectives guide a firm's businesses and employees toward specific dimensions and levels of performance by establishing benchmarks against which performance can be compared and evaluated. Increasing shareholder value is the ultimate objective for publicly held companies. But difficulties in determining whether specific actions will create such value lead most firms to set specific objectives for performance outcomes such as sales volume, market share, and return on investment.

The corporate development strategy addresses the question of where the firm's future growth will come from. A company might seek growth either

---

[36]Robert W. Ruekert and Orville C. Walker, Jr., "Shared Marketing Programs and the Performance of Different Business Strategies," Report # 91-100 (Cambridge, Mass.: The Marketing Science Institute, 1991).

through the expansion of its current businesses or by diversifying into new business.

A firm should allocate its resources across its various businesses to reflect both the relative competitive strength of each business and variations in the attractiveness and growth potential of the markets they serve. Portfolio models help managers make these allocation decisions. Value-based planning is another useful resource allocation tool. It attempts to evaluate potential investments in a firm's businesses, and in the alternative strategies each business might pursue, on the basis of how much value those investments will produce for the firm's shareholders over time.

Finally, corporate synergy can be gained by developing competencies, knowledge, and customer-based intangibles, such as brand-name recognition and reputation, that can be shared across multiple businesses within the company. Similarly, synergy might be sought through the sharing of operational resources and functions, such as a common plant or salesforce, across businesses. Caution is necessary, however, because sharing operational facilities and activities can reduce a business's flexibility and hinder its ability to respond quickly to changing market conditions.

APPENDIX: VALUE-BASED PLANNING PROCEDURES

This Appendix briefly details the procedure involved in using a discounted cash flow analysis to evaluate a particular business strategy. The steps in this procedure are outlined in Exhibit A–1. Those interested in a more detailed discussion of the procedure and its rationale may wish to consult one of the recent books on the subject.[37]

The process begins with a forecast of the annual operating cash flows the strategy will produce over the course of the planning period. These consist of cash inflows [(sales) × (operating profit margin) × (1 − income tax rate)], plus depreciation, minus cash outflows [(incremental fixed capital investment) + (incremental working capital)]. Next, the analyst must calculate a risk-adjusted cost of capital for the business, weighted to reflect the proportion of debt and equity capital. In step 3, the forecasted annual cash flows are discounted back to the initial time period and summed to arrive at their present value. Step 4 requires the analyst to estimate the residual value of the strategy at the end of the planning period, which is then discounted back to its present value. Next, the total present value of the strategy is calculated by adding the present values of future cash flows and the residual value and subtracting the market value of debt assigned to the business, if any. The sixth step involves estimation of the business's initial or prestrategy shareholder value, which is the current value of the business assuming no additional value will be created by any prospective investments or strategy changes. Finally,

---

[37]For example, see Alfred Rappaport, *Creating Shareholder Value: A New Standard for Business Performance* (New York: The Free Press, 1986).

EXHIBIT A-1

Procedure for Conducting a Discounted Cash Flow
Analysis of a Proposed Business Strategy

	Step	Elaboration
Step 1:	Forecast annual operating cash flows for the strategy during the planning period.	A_i = net after-tax cash flow in year i = cash inflow [(sales) × (operating profit margin) × (1 − income tax rate)] − depreciation + cash outflow [(incremental fixed capital investment) + (incremental working capital investment)]
Step 2:	Calculate a risk-adjusted cost of capital for the business.	Cost of capital should be weighted to reflect the proportion of debt and equity capital.
Step 3:	Discount the forecasted cash flows back to their present value (PV_a).	$$PV_a = \sum_{i=1}^{t} \frac{Ai}{(1 + R)^i}$$ where t = planning period in years Ai = net after-tax cash flow in year i R = risk-adjusted cost of capital
Step 4:	Estimate the residual value at the end of the planning period and discount it back to the present (PV_b).	$$\text{Residual Value } (PV_b) = \frac{\text{Perpetuity cash flow}}{\text{Cost of capital}}$$
Step 5:	Compute the total present value of the strategy by summing the present values of future cash flows and the residual value.	Total present value = $PV_a + PV_b$
Step 6:	Calculate the prestrategy shareholder value of the business.	Prestrategy value = $$\frac{\text{Current cash flow before new investment}}{\text{Cost of capital}}$$ − Market value of assignable debt
Step 7:	Compute the strategy's value creation potential.	Strategy's value creation potential = Total present value − Prestrategy value

the shareholder value creation potential of the strategy can be calculated by subtracting the prestrategy value of the business estimated in step 6 from the total present value determined in step 5.

A simple illustration of discounted cash flow analysis applied to the evaluation of a business strategy is shown in Exhibit A–2. In this example, provided by Bernard Reimann,[38] the following assumptions are made:

[38]Bernard C. Reimann, "Stock Price and Business Success: What Is the Relationship?" *Journal of Business Strategy*, Spring 1987, pp. 38–49.

EXHIBIT A-2

An Example of the Use of Discounted Cash Flow Analysis to Evaluate a Business-Unit Strategy

	Current Values 1985	Income Statement Projections					Residual Value 1990+
		1986	1987	1988	1989	1990	
Sales*	$100.00	110.00	121.00	133.10	146.41	161.05	161.05
Gross margin (= 25%)	25.00	27.50	30.25	33.28	36.60	40.26	40.26
S. & G. A. (= 10%)	10.00	11.00	12.10	13.31	14.64	16.11	15.11
Profit before tax	$ 15.00	16.50	18.15	19.97	21.96	24.16	24.16
Income tax	7.50	8.25	9.08	9.98	10.98	12.08	12.08
Net profit	$ 7.50	8.25	9.08	9.98	10.98	12.08	12.08
	Statement of Financial Position (Year-End)						
Net working capital	10.00	11.00	12.10	13.31	14.64	16.11	16.11
Depreciable assets	30.00	33.00	36.30	39.93	43.92	48.32	48.32
Assets employed	$ 40.00	44.00	48.40	53.24	58.56	64.42	64.42
Return on assets	18.8%	18.8%	18.8%	18.8%	18.8%	18.8%	18.8%
	Cash Flow Statement						
Net earnings	7.50	8.25	9.08	9.98	10.98	12.08	12.08
Depreciation	7.00	3.00	3.30	3.63	3.99	4.39	4.39
Capital expenditures		6.00	6.60	7.26	7.99	8.78	4.39
Increase in working capital		1.00	1.10	1.21	1.33	1.46	0.00
Cash flow		$ 4.25	4.68	5.14	5.66	6.22	12.08
PV factor (at 15% discount)		0.87	0.76	0.66	0.57	0.50	3.31†
Present value of cash flow		3.70	3.53	3.38	3.23	3.09	40.04
Total present value	$56.98	(Annual cash flows + residual value)					
Current (preplan) value	50.00	(Year 0 net operating earnings/discount rate)					
Net present value	$ 6.98	= Shareholder value contribution					

*Sales growth: 10%

†"Perpetuity" assumption: PV factor/discount rate = 50/.15

SOURCE: Bernard C. Reimann, "Stock Price and Business Success: What Is the Relationship?" *Journal of Business Strategy*, Summer 1987, p. 44.

- Sales growth remains constant at 10 percent per year.
- Gross margins and selling, general, and administrative expenses remain constant at 25 percent and 10 percent, respectively.
- Asset turnover remains constant.
- The risk-adjusted cost of capital (discount rate) is 15 percent.
- Aftertax earnings in the initial period are equivalent to cash flow, since no incremental investment exists.
- The business unit has no assignable debt.

Note that the strategy examined in Exhibit A–2 is estimated to have a total present value (i.e., the present value of annual cash flows during the five-year planning period plus its residual value) of $56.98 million. Its prestrategy value—assumed to be the cash flow in the current year divided by the discount rate—is $50 million. Thus, the strategy has the potential for creating an additional $6.98 million in shareholder value if adopted. The strategy is therefore worth the investment from a shareholder value point of view, assuming other strategy alternatives available to the business unit wouldn't create even more value.

Estimation problems

This rather bland examination of the steps involved in a discounted cash flow analysis downplays some difficult judgment calls and produces hard numbers that may carry an unwarranted aura of precision. Three variables are especially difficult for managers to estimate and may be subject to dubious assumptions: the cost of capital, the residual value of the strategy, and the prestrategy or initial value of the business.[39]

The cost of capital

The rate used for discounting the cash flow stream of a strategy should be the weighted average costs of debt and equity capital. This rate may differ considerably across businesses within the same corporation because of differences in their risk exposure and amount of debt needed to finance their assets.

The cost of debt capital is relatively easy to estimate. It is the rate the parent company would have to pay for new debt given its capital structure. To determine the cost of equity capital, however, the analyst must estimate three components that reflect the minimum return expected by shareholders: (1) a "real" interest rate, or their compensation for making a risk-free investment, (2) further compensation for expected inflation, and (3) a risk premium to offset the possibility that actual results will fall short of expectations. The risk premium is the most difficult to estimate. In theory, it should be correlated with stock price movements. But this is not practical with business units, since they have no publicly traded stock. Therefore, analysts have to resort to indirect estimation methods, such as examining the stock price movements of surrogate publicly traded firms. Because good surrogates are hard to find, risk is often gauged judgmentally by looking at the variability of the business's past earnings, the size of differences between its projected and actual earnings, and the susceptibility of its future earnings to environmental changes.

---

[39]The following discussion summarizes material found in George S. Day, *Market-Driven Strategy: Processes for Creating Value* (New York: The Free Press, 1990), chap. 13.

Residual value

The question of how much residual value will be created after the planning period is crucial, since the residual is often the largest portion of the total present value of a strategy. For instance, a study of 620 businesses found that more than 30 percent were net cash users during an entire five-year planning period. On the other hand, the study also confirmed the propensity of American managers for near-term results, as more than half the businesses had positive cash flows during the planning period at the expense of a reduction in total shareholder value.[40]

The amount of residual value depends on the length of the planning period the analyst chose, the strategy being considered, and assumptions about the competitive situation that will exist at the end of the planning period. The planning period should be long enough to enable the strategy to be implemented and to observe its results in the market. But if the strategy involves building a business's position by increasing its investment in R&D and launching new products, for instance, even a relatively long planning period may encompass nothing but negative or negligible cash flows. Virtually all the value generated by such a strategy is likely to come from exploiting the business's enhanced market share position after the planning period ends. On the other hand, a harvest strategy might generate significant cash flows over a short planning period at the expense of an eroded residual value at the end of the period.

No matter the length of a planning period, most managers agree that beyond the end of it the future is too murky to forecast. So how can they generate an estimate of a strategy's residual value? Perhaps the most popular method—and the one employed in the example in Exhibit A–2—is the **perpetuity approach.** Its rationale is the assumption that any business able to generate returns greater than the cost of capital will attract competition. Eventually, the entry of competitors will drive profits down to the minimum acceptable level—a level equal to the cost of capital. Thus, by the end of the planning period, the business will be earning only the cost of capital on an average new investment. Once the rate of return has fallen to this level, period-to-period differences in cash flows do not alter the value of the business. Thus, these future cash flows can be treated as though they were a perpetuity, or an infinite stream of identical cash flows. Because the present value of any financial perpetuity is the annual cash flow divided by the cost of capital, it follows that:

$$\text{Residual value} = \frac{\text{Perpetuity cash flow}}{\text{Cost of capital}}$$

One reason for the popularity of the perpetuity method is its simplifying assumption that any cash flows from investments made after the planning

---

[40]Robert D. Buzzell and Bradley T. Gale, *The PIMS Principles: Linking Strategy to Performance* (New York: The Free Press, 1987).

period can be ignored because they will not change the value of the business. However, the method also assumes that the annual cash flows will be maintained at the same level they reached at the end of the planning period. This assumption is worrisome, since it ignores differences across businesses in the sustainability of size or access advantages that are the basis for superior performance.

Prestrategy value

A business's prestrategy value is the benchmark for determining whether proposed strategies will further enhance shareholder value over what would otherwise be produced. Once again, the perpetuity approach is a popular method for estimating a business's prestrategy value. It assumes that, if the business were to stay with its current strategy, no additional value would be created through prospective new investments. This assumption allows the annual cash flows of the current strategy to be treated as a financial perpetuity, in which case the prestrategy value of the business is the cash flow from the most recent period divided by the cost of capital.

While the perpetuity assumption is convenient and makes estimation of prestrategy value more tractable, it does not fit well with reality. Even if a business does not change its current strategy, it is still likely to adjust to changes in the market and competitive situation by making investments necessary to maintain its position as the market evolves. Some of these investments, such as adding plant capacity to keep up with growing demand, may further increase shareholder value. Consequently, a more realistic alternative to the perpetuity approach for estimating prestrategy value might be to forecast the financial outcomes of the current strategy after taking into account likely adjustments for anticipated trends in market demand and competitive actions. Unfortunately, introducing strategic and environmental considerations into the baseline forecast of value creation opens up even more possibilities for subjectivity and bias.

Business Strategies and Their Marketing Implications

BUSINESS STRATEGIES AND MARKETING PROGRAMS AT 3M

The Minnesota Mining and Manufacturing Company, better known as 3M, began manufacturing sandpaper about nine decades ago.[1] Today it is a leader in more than 100 technical areas from fluorochemistry to optical recording, and its 50,000 different products produced $13 billion in sales and better than a 24 percent return on investment in 1990. Recent trends in the firm's sales, earnings, and R&D expenditures are shown in Exhibit 3–1.

As you might expect of a firm with so many products, 3M is organized into a large number of strategic business units (SBUs). The company contains 44 such units organized into four sectors or groups: the Industrial and Electronic Sector, making such things as pressure-sensitive tapes, abrasives,

adhesives, and electronic connectors; the Life Sciences Sector, consisting of such diverse businesses as pharmaceuticals and reflective materials, all designed to enhance health and safety; the Information and Imaging Technologies Sector, concerned with the areas of commercial graphics, audio visuals, magnetic media, and imaging systems; and the Commercial and Consumer Sector, responsible for Post-it brand respositionable notes and Scotch brand Magic Transparent Tape.

3M has acquired a number of smaller firms over the years to fill out a product line or gain some particular technical expertise. But the company's growth strategy has always focused primarily on internal new-product development, emphasizing both improved products for

---

[1]Material for this example was drawn from *The 3M Company, 1990 Annual Report* (St. Paul, Minn.: The 3M Company, 1991); and A. Johnson, "The 3M Company: Organized to Innovate," *Management Review,* July 1986, pp. 38–39.

EXHIBIT 3-1

Recent Trends in 3M's Sales, Earnings, and R&D Expenditures

	Net Sales ($)			Net Income ($)			R&D ($)	
	Total	U.S.	Int'l	Total	Dividends	Retained Earnings	Total	Percent of Sales
1990	$13,021	51%	49%	$1,308	49%	51%	$865	6.6%
1989	$11,990	54%	46%	$1,244	46%	54%	$784	6.5%
1988	$11,323	55%	45%	$1,154	42%	58%	$721	6.4%
1987	$10,004	57%	43%	$ 918	46%	54%	$650	6.5%
1986	$ 9,056	58%	42%	$ 779	53%	47%	$586	6.5%

Note: all dollars are in millions.

existing customers and new products for new markets. Indeed, one of the formal objectives assigned to every business unit is to obtain at least 25 percent of annual sales from products introduced within the last five years. The company supports this objective with an R&D budget of over $865 million, more than 6.6 percent of total revenues.

3M also pursues growth through the aggressive development of foreign markets for its many products, especially in Europe, Asia, and South America. As Exhibit 3–1 indicates, the percentage of sales attained from international markets has increased steadily in recent years and now accounts for nearly half the firm's total revenue.

Differences in customer needs, product life-cycle stage, and the maturity of technologies across industries, however, lead the various business units to pursue their growth objectives in different ways. The Industrial Tape business unit, for example, operates in an industry where both the basic technologies and the customer segments are mature and relatively stable. Growth in

this SBU results from extending the scope of adhesive technology (e.g., attaching weather-stripping to auto doors), product improvements and line extensions targeted at existing customers, and expansion into global markets.

In contrast, the firm's Medical Products unit develops new medical applications and markets for emerging technologies. It sells a broad range of innovative medical devices (such as a powered bone stapler), pharmaceuticals (a drug to control irregular heartbeat), and dental products (tooth-colored fillings). Most of the unit's growth, therefore, comes from developing totally new products directed at new markets.

The competitive strategies of 3M's various business units also differ. For instance, the company's tapes hold a commanding share of most market segments, even though it charges higher prices and earns bigger margins than its competitors. As a result, the Industrial Tape business unit is primarily concerned with maintaining its share position in existing markets while preserving or even improving its profitability. Its competitive strategy is to differentiate itself from competitors on the basis of high product quality and excellent customer service.

On the other hand, the Medical Products unit's strategy is to avoid head-to-head competitive battles by being the technological leader in the industry and introducing a constant stream of unique products. This focus means, however, that to build viable markets for its new products it must devote substantial resources both to R&D and to the stimulation of primary demand. Thus, its main objective is volume growth; and it must sometimes sacrifice short-run profitability to fund the product development and marketing efforts needed to accomplish that goal.

These differences in competitive strategies also influence the strategic marketing programs of the various business units. For instance, because most of 3M's tapes are mature products in established markets, the firm spends few resources on advertising or sales promotion for tape products. However, the business unit does maintain a large, well-trained technical salesforce that provides valuable assistance to customers and feedback to the firm's R&D personnel about potential new applications and product improvements. The unit also maintains substantial inventories of tapes in company distribution centers to ensure rapid delivery—another critical aspect of good service in the tape industry.

In contrast, the pioneering nature of many of the Medical Products unit's products and services calls for more extensive promotion programs to develop customer awareness and stimulate primary demand. Consequently, the unit devotes a relatively large proportion of its revenues to advertising in technical journals aimed at physicians, hospital administrators, and medical technicians. It also supports a large technical salesforce; but those salespeople spend much of their time demonstrating new products and prospecting for new accounts in addition to servicing existing customers. Finally, the unit uses marketing research extensively to test new-product concepts and forecast their demand potential.

THE CONCEPT OF STRATEGIC FIT

The situation at 3M again illustrates that firms with multiple businesses usually have a hierarchy of strategies extending from the corporate level down to the individual product-market entry. As we saw in the last chapter, corporate strategy addresses such issues as the firm's mission and scope and the directions it will pursue for future growth. Thus, 3M's corporate growth strategy focuses primarily on developing new products and new applications for emerging technologies.

The major strategic question addressed at the business-unit level is How should we compete in this business? For instance, 3M's Industrial Tape unit attempts to maintain its commanding market share and high profitability by differentiating itself on the basis of high quality and good customer service. On the other hand, the Medical Products unit seeks high growth via aggressive new-product and market development.

Finally, the strategic marketing program for each product-market entry within a business unit attempts to allocate marketing resources and activities in a manner appropriate for accomplishing the business unit's objectives. Thus, most of the strategic marketing programs within 3M's Medical Products SBU involve relatively large expenditures for marketing research and introductory advertising and promotion campaigns aimed at achieving sales growth.

One key reason for 3M's continuing success is that all three levels of strategy within the company have usually been characterized by good internal and external consistency, or **strategic fit.** 3M's managers have done a good job of monitoring and adapting their strategies to the market opportunities, technological advances, and competitive threats in the company's external environment. The firm's marketing and sales managers play critical roles both in developing market-oriented strategies for individual products and in influencing and helping to formulate corporate and business-level strategies that are responsive to environmental conditions. At the same time, those strategies are usually internally compatible. Each strategy fits with those at other levels as well as with the unique competitive strengths and competencies of the relevant business unit and the company as a whole.[2]

Fit with the external environment

Because marketing managers occupy positions at the boundary between the firm and its customers, distributors, and competitors, they are usually most familiar with conditions and trends in the market environment. Thus, they often bear the primary responsibility for monitoring and interpreting environmental threats and opportunities. Their knowledge and expertise often enable them to be influential in strategic planning at the corporate and business-unit levels as well as for their own product-market entries. This is particularly true in consumer goods organizations; but it is also true in market-oriented industrial goods and services firms.[3]

These firms often use bottom-up planning processes—such as the strategic management systems discussed in Chapter 1—that begin with an analysis of potential opportunities and threats at the individual product-market level. They formulate marketing strategies for each product-market entry and then aggregate them to serve as a starting point for the resource allocation decisions that must be made at the business-unit level. Business-unit plans, in

---

[2]For a more detailed discussion of the concept of strategic fit and the role of various external and internal variables in influencing the effectiveness of a firm's strategies, see N. Venkatraman and James Camillus, "The Concept of 'Fit' in Strategic Management," *Academy of Management Review* 9 (1984), pp. 513–25.

[3]George S. Yip, "The Role of Strategic Planning in Consumer-Marketing Businesses," Working Paper #84-103 (Cambridge, Mass.: Marketing Science Institute, 1984).

turn, serve as a springboard for the formulation of corporate strategies. Thus, a firm may periodically adjust its corporate and business-unit domains, objectives, and resource allocation decisions to fit new environmental opportunities and threats identified by marketing managers operating at the product-market level.

Fit with internal capabilities

No matter how well a strategy fits the firm's market and competitive environment, though, it will not be successful unless the company can carry it out effectively. Indeed, there is evidence that differences in the way a strategy is implemented can account for more variance in performance across businesses in a given environment than the kinds of strategies they choose.[4] Thus, a strategy should fit the company's internal capabilities, resources, organizational structure, policies, and operating procedures. 3M is able to successfully pursue a strategy of internal growth through the development of high-tech products and applications partly because it has substantial financial resources, a large staff of competent scientists and engineers, excellent technical sales and marketing capabilities, and corporate procedures and reward systems that encourage product innovation. Firms that lack one or more of these essential capabilities are likely to be less successful at implementing strategies focused on innovation and new-product development. Such companies would be better off pursuing strategies more consistent with their own internal capabilities, such as growth through acquisition.

Another requirement for successful implementation of a strategy is that it be consistent and coordinated with the strategies formulated at other levels within the firm. Each business unit's strategy should fit with corporate-level decisions concerning the firm's mission and scope, overall objectives, avenues for future growth, and allocation of resources across businesses. Similarly, the strategic marketing program for each product-market entry within a business should fit with the unit's objectives, competitive strategy, and resource allocation decisions.

This need for compatibility across levels of strategy imposes both imperatives and constraints on managers formulating strategic marketing programs for individual products. The marketer may be influential in formulating corporate and business-unit strategies, but once in place, those strategies limit the objectives and actions he or she chooses for the product's marketing plan. It would be difficult, for instance, for a marketing manager responsible for masking tape within 3M's Industrial Tape unit to win acceptance for heavy advertising expenditures and price promotions aimed at expanding sales volume and market share at the expense of short-term profitability. Such a pro-

---

[4]For example, see Charles C. Snow and Lawrence G. Hrebiniak, "Strategy, Distinctive Competence and Organizational Performance," *Administrative Science Quarterly* 25 (1980), pp. 317–35; and Donald C. Hambrick, "High Profit Strategies in Mature Capital Goods Industries: A Contingency Approach," *Academy of Management Journal* 26 (1983), pp. 687–707.

gram would be inconsistent with the business unit's established objectives and competitive strategy.

These interdependencies among strategies—particularly those at the business and product-market levels—are the major focus of the rest of this chapter. First, we briefly examine the strategic decisions that must be made at the business level, paying particular attention to a number of generic competitive strategies a business unit might choose to pursue and the environmental circumstances in which each type is most appropriate. We then examine the implications those strategies have for the marketing activities and programs that are most appropriate for businesses pursuing each type.

STRATEGIC DECISIONS AT THE BUSINESS-UNIT LEVEL

When a firm is involved in multiple businesses, it is typically organized in separate components responsible for each business. While these organizational components go by many different names, they are most commonly called **strategic business units** or **SBUs.** Managers of each unit must decide what objectives and strategies to pursue within their specific business, subject to the approval of corporate management.

The first step in developing business-level strategies, then, is for the firm to decide how to divide itself into SBUs. The managers of each business unit then must make recommendations about the SBU's objectives and scope, how resources should be allocated across its product-market entries and functional departments, and which competitive strategy to pursue to build a sustainable advantage in its product-markets.

Defining strategic business units

Ideally, a strategic business unit should be designed to incorporate a unique set of products aimed at a homogeneous set of markets. It should also have responsibility for its own performance and control over the resources that affect that performance.

As Exhibit 3–2 indicates, there is a rationale for each of these desired business-unit characteristics. But as might be expected, firms do not always meet all of these ideals when designing their SBUs. There are usually trade-offs between having many small homogeneous business units versus fewer, but larger and more diverse, SBUs that top management can more easily supervise.

The crucial question, then, is What criteria should be used when deciding which product-markets to cluster into a business unit? The three dimensions suggested earlier as criteria for defining the scope and mission of the entire corporation can also serve as the basis for defining individual SBUs:

- *Technical compatibility,* particularly with respect to product technologies and operational requirements, such as the use of similar production facilities and engineering skills.

EXHIBIT 3-2

Characteristics of the Ideal Strategic Business Unit

Characteristic	Rationale
• Serves a homogeneous set of markets with a limited number of related technologies	Minimizing the diversity of a business unit's product-market entries enables the unit's manager to do a better job of formulating and implementing a coherent and internally consistent business strategy.
• Serves a unique set of product-markets	No other SBU within the firm should compete for the same set of customers with similar products. This enables the firm to avoid duplication of effort and helps maximize economies of scale within its SBUs.
• Has control over the factors necessary for successful performance, such as R&D, production, marketing, and distribution	This is not to say that an SBU should never share resources, such as a manufacturing plant or a salesforce, with one or more business units; but the SBU should have authority to determine how its share of the joint resource will be used to effectively carry out its strategy.
• Has responsibility for its own profitability	Because top management cannot keep an eye on every decision and action taken by all its SBUs, the success of an SBU and its managers must be judged by monitoring its performance over time. Thus, the SBU's managers should have control over the factors that affect performance, and then be held accountable for the outcomes.

- Similarity in the *customer needs* to be satisfied or the product benefits sought by customers in the target markets.
- Similarity in the *personal characteristics* or behavior patterns of customers in the target markets.

In practice, it is often not possible to meet all three criteria. Instead, the choice is often between technical/operational compatibility and customer homogeneity. Management commonly defines SBUs on the basis of technical and operational interdependence, clustering product-market entries that require similar technologies, production facilities, and employee skills to minimize the coordination problems involved in administering the unit. In some firms, however, the marketing synergies gained from coordinating technically different products aimed at the same customer need or market segment outweigh operational considerations. In these firms, managers group product-market entries into SBUs based on similarities across customer or distribution systems. For instance, 3M's Medical Products unit includes a wide range of products involving very different technologies and production processes. They are grouped within the same business unit, though, because they all address health needs, they are marketed to physicians and other health professionals, and they can be sold through a common salesforce and distribution system.

Business-unit objectives

Companies break down corporate objectives into subobjectives for each SBU. In most cases, those subobjectives vary across SBUs according to the attractiveness of their industries, the strength of their competitive positions within those industries, and resource allocation decisions by corporate management. For example, corporate managers may assign an SBU in a rapidly growing industry higher volume and share-growth objectives but lower ROI objectives than an SBU with a large share in a mature industry.

A similar process of breaking down overall SBU objectives into a set of subobjectives should occur for each product-market entry within the unit. Those subobjectives obviously must help the SBU's overall objectives; but once again they may vary across product-market entries according to the attractiveness and growth potential of individual market segments and the competitive strengths of the company's product in each market. For example, when Nabisco first introduced its new Almost Home line of cookies in the mid-80s its objective was to capture a large share of the emerging soft-and-chewy cookie segment and fend off the competitive threat of Procter & Gamble's Duncan Hines brand. Nabisco wanted to maximize Almost Home's volume growth and market share even if the line did not break even for several years. At the same time, though, the company maintained high profit goals for its other established cookie brands to provide the cash required for Almost Home's introduction and to preserve the profit level of its cookie SBU.

Allocating resources within the business unit

Once an SBU's objectives and budget have been approved at the corporate level, its managers must decide how the available resources should be allocated across the unit's various product-market entries. Because this allocation process is quite similar to allocating corporate resources across SBUs, many firms use the same portfolio analysis tools for both.[5] Of course, at the SBU level, managers must determine the attractiveness of individual target markets and the competitive position of their products within those markets rather than analyzing industry attractiveness and the overall competitive strengths of the firm.

Unfortunately, value-based planning is not as useful a tool for evaluating alternative resource allocations across product-market entries as it is for evaluating allocations across SBUs. This is because the product-market entries within a business unit often share the benefits of common investments and

---

[5]Phillipe Haspeslagh, "Portfolio Planning: Uses and Limits," *Harvard Business Review,* January–February 1982, pp. 59–73.

the costs of functional activities, as when multiple products are produced in the same plant or sold by the same salesforce. The difficulty of deciding what portion of such common investments and shared costs should be assigned to specific products increases the difficulty of applying a discounted cash flow analysis at the product-market level.

The business unit's competitive strategy

The essential question to be answered in formulating a business strategy is, How will the business unit compete to gain a sustainable competitive advantage within its industry? Achieving a competitive advantage requires a business unit to make two choices:

- What is the SBU's *competitive domain or scope?* What market segments should it target, and what customer needs will the unit attempt to satisfy? This decision provides guidelines for the desired breadth and complexity of the unit's product line and a foundation for the formulation of marketing strategies for each product-market entry.
- How will the business unit *distinguish itself from competitors* in its target market(s)? What distinctive competencies can it rely on to achieve a unique position relative to its competitors?

Even though a business unit may contain a number of different product-market entries, most analysts argue that the unit should pursue the same overall source of competitive advantage in all of them. In this way the SBU can take full advantage of its particular strengths and downplay its weaknesses. As Porter argues in his book on competitive advantage,

> If a [business] is to attain a competitive advantage, it must make a choice about the type of competitive advantage it seeks to attain and the scope within which it will attain it. Being "all things to all people" is a recipe for strategic mediocrity and below-average performance, because it often means that a [business] has no competitive advantage at all.[6]

Porter argues that a business might seek a competitive advantage on two broad dimensions: it can try to be the low-cost producer within its target markets, or it can differentiate itself from the competition through its product offerings or marketing programs. It might achieve differentiation, for example, by offering a higher-quality or more technically advanced product, more extensive promotion, broader distribution, or better customer service.[7] Indeed, some businesses attempt to differentiate their various product offerings on multiple dimensions by developing an entire set of competencies. IBM, for instance, differentiates its AS/400 computer system by offering superior system design and postsale services as well as outstanding technical features and product performance. This multidimensional approach to developing a

---

[6]Michael E. Porter, *Competitive Advantage: Creating and Sustaining Superior Performance* (New York: The Free Press, 1985), p. 12.

[7]Also see, Michael E. Porter, *Competitive Strategy* (New York: The Free Press, 1980).

EXHIBIT 3-3

Porter's Four Business Strategies

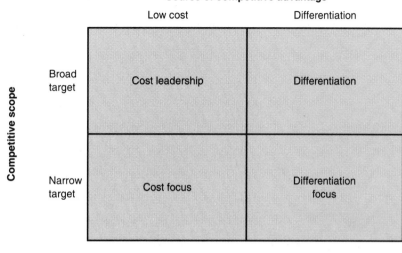

SOURCE: Adapted with permission of The Free Press, a Division of Macmillan, Inc. from *Competitive Advantage: Creating and Sustaining Superior Performance* by Michael E. Porter. Copyright © 1985 by Michael E. Porter.

differentiated competitive strategy is often referred to as **total quality management.**[8]

Also, a business unit's strategic scope might be defined either broadly or narrowly. That is, it might pursue a wide range of market segments within its industry or focus on only one or a few target segments. As Exhibit 3–3 indicates, then, Porter suggests that there are four basic or "generic" competitive strategies that a business unit might adopt: (1) **cost leadership** across a broad range of product/market entries, (3) cost leadership focusing on a narrow group of target segments, (3) **differentiation** across a wide variety of segments, or (4) more narrowly focused differentiation.

Of course, there are other dimensions besides low cost, high quality, or superior service on which a business unit may try to gain a competitive advantage. For example, Miles and Snow have identified another set of business strategies based on a business's intended rate of product-market development (i.e., new product development, penetration of new markets, etc.).[9] They classify business units into four strategic types: **prospectors, analyzers, defenders,** and **reactors.** Exhibit 3–4 describes each of these business

---

[8]Frank Rose, "Now Quality Means Service Too," *Fortune,* April 22, 1991, pp. 97–111.

[9]Robert E. Miles and Charles C. Snow, *Organizational Strategy, Structure and Process* (New York: McGraw-Hill, 1978).

EXHIBIT 3–4

Summary Definitions of Miles and Snow's Four Business Strategies

Prospector
- Operates within a broad product-market domain that undergoes periodic redefinition.
- Values being a "first mover" in new-product and market areas, even if not all of these efforts prove to be highly profitable.
- Responds rapidly to early signals concerning areas of opportunity; and these responses often lead to new rounds of competitive actions.
- Competes primarily by stimulating and meeting new market opportunities, but may not maintain strength over time in all markets it enters.

Defender
- Attempts to locate and maintain a secure position in relatively stable product or service areas.
- Offers relatively limited range of products or services compared to competitors.
- Tries to protect its domain by offering lower prices, higher quality, or better service than competitors.
- Usually not at the forefront of technological/new-product development in its industry; tends to ignore industry changes not directly related to its area of operation.

Analyzer
- An intermediate type; makes fewer and slower product-market changes than prospectors, but is less committed to stability and efficiency than defenders.
- Attempts to maintain a stable, limited line of products or services, but carefully follows a selected set of promising new developments in its industry.
- Seldom a "first mover," but often a second or third entrant in product-markets related to its existing market base—often with a lower cost or higher quality product or service offering.

Reactor
- Lacks any well-defined competitive strategy.
- Does not have as consistent a product-market orientation as its competitors.
- Not as willing to assume the risks of new-product or market development as its competitors.
- Not as aggressive in marketing established products as some competitors.
- Responds primarily when it is forced to by environmental pressures.

SOURCE: Adapted from R. E. Miles and C. C. Snow, *Organizational Strategy, Structure and Process*, © 1978 McGraw-Hill, Inc. Reprinted by permission of the publisher.

strategies briefly. As indicated, businesses pursuing a prospector strategy focus on growth through the development of new products and markets. 3M's Medical Products business unit provides a good example of this. Defender businesses concentrate on maintaining their positions in established product-markets while paying less attention to new-product development, as is the case with 3M's Industrial Tape business unit. The analyzer strategy falls in between these two. An analyzer business attempts to maintain a strong position in its core product-market(s) but also seeks to expand into new, but usually closely related, product-markets. Finally, reactors are businesses with no clearly defined strategy.

Even though both the Porter and the Miles and Snow typologies have received popular acceptance and research support, neither is complete by it-

EXHIBIT 3–5

Combined Typology of Business-Unit Competitive Strategies

Emphasis on new product-market growth

Heavy emphasis ←——————————————→ No emphasis

	Prospector	Analyzer	Defender	Reactor
Differentiation	Units primarily concerned wtih attaining growth through aggressive pursuit of new product-market opportunities	Units with strong core business; actively seeking to expand into related product-markets with differentiated offerings	Units primarily concerned with maintaining a **differentiated** position in mature markets	Units with no clearly defined product-market development or competitive strategy
Cost leadership		Units with strong core business; actively seeking to expand into related product-markets with low-cost offerings	Units primarily concerned with maintaining a **low-cost** position in mature markets	

(Left axis label: **Competitive strategy**)

self. For example, a defender business unit might pursue either of Porter's sources of competitive advantage—a low-cost position or differentiation—to protect its market position. Thus, we have combined the two typologies in Exhibit 3–5 to provide a more comprehensive overview of possible business strategies. The exhibit classifies business strategies on two primary dimensions: the unit's desired rate of product-market development and the unit's intended method of competing in its established product-markets.[10]

Of course, each strategy in Exhibit 3–5 could be further subdivided according to whether a business applies the strategy across a broadly defined product-market domain or concentrates on a narrowly defined segment where it hopes to avoid direct confrontation with major competitors (i.e., the focus strategy of Porter). While this is a useful distinction to make, it is more relevant to a discussion of the business's choice of a target-market strategy (as examined in Chapter 6) than to its competitive strategy. Most businesses compete in a consistent way (at least in terms of basic dimensions) across all of their product-markets, whether their domain is broad or narrow.

---

[10]For a more detailed discussion of this "hybrid" taxonomy of generic business strategies, see Orville C. Walker, Jr. and Robert W. Ruekert, "Marketing's Role in the Implementation of Business Strategies: A Critical Review and Conceptual Framework," *Journal of Marketing*, July 1987, pp. 15–33.

Note too that Exhibit 3–5 describes only six different business strategies rather than the eight that one might expect. One reason for this is that we view reactor and prospector businesses as two homogeneous categories.

Evidence suggests that a substantial number of businesses fall into the reactor category. One study, for instance, found that 50 out of 232 businesses examined could be classified as reactors.[11] However, these businesses do not have well-defined or consistent approaches to either new-product or market development or to ways of competing in their existing product-markets. As a manager of Sheldahl, Inc.—a firm that designs and manufactures flexible circuit boards and other components for the electronics and defense industries—complained in a discussion with one of the authors,

> Our division is a reactor in the sense that we are constantly changing directions and getting into new areas in response to actions taken by our competitors or special requests from large customers. We are like a job-shop; we take on new projects without ever asking whether there will be a viable future market for what we are doing. Consequently, neither our volume growth nor our profitability has been as good as it should have been in recent years.

The first action managers should take to improve the performance of reactors is to develop and implement a clearly defined and coherent competitive strategy—one that corresponds to one of the other generic strategies outlined in Exhibit 3–5. But because most reactors have no consistent competitive strategy, we largely ignore them in the remainder of this discussion.

Prospectors are also discussed as a single strategic category because the desire for rapid new-product or market development is the overriding aspect of their strategy. There is little need for a prospector to consider how it will compete in the various new product-markets it develops. It usually faces little or no competition in those markets—at least not until those markets become established and other firms begin to enter. In 3M's Medical Products SBU, for example, most marketing programs are aimed at generating awareness and stimulating primary demand instead of offering low prices or finding ways to differentiate products because they are unchallenged by any competitors.

THE UNDERLYING DIMENSIONS OF ALTERNATIVE BUSINESS STRATEGIES

In Chapter 2 we said that all strategies consist of five components or underlying dimensions: scope (or the breadth of the strategic domain); goals and objectives; resource deployments; a basis for achieving a sustainable competitive advantage; and synergy. The generic business strategies outlined in Exhibit 3–5 are defined largely on the basis of their differences on only one of

---

[11]Charles C. Snow and Lawrence G. Hrebiniak, "Strategy, Distinctive Competence and Organizational Performance," *Administrative Science Quarterly* 25 (1980), pp. 317–35.

these dimensions: the nature of the competitive advantage sought. However, each strategy also involves some important differences on the other four dimensions. Those underlying differences provide some useful insights about the conditions under which each strategy is most appropriate and about the relative importance of different functional activities, particularly marketing actions, in implementing them effectively.

Differences in scope

Both the breadth and the stability of a business's domain are likely to vary with different strategies. This, in turn, can affect the variables the corporation uses to define its various businesses. At one extreme, defender businesses, whether low cost or differentiated, tend to operate in relatively well-defined, narrow, and stable domains where both the product technology and the customer segments are mature. A company can define and group related product-market entries into such business units on the basis of the three criteria discussed earlier: technical compatibility, the customer need to be satisfied, and similarity of customer characteristics and behavior patterns. For example, Pillsbury's Prepared Dough Products business unit is a differentiated defender consisting of several product-market entries, such as Hungry Jack Biscuits and Crescent Rolls. All the products in the SBU hold a commanding share of their product category, appeal to traditional households who want fresh-baked breadstuffs, and are based on the same dough-in-a-can technology. Consequently, the SBU is largely self-contained with respect to production facilities, marketing, and distribution.

At the other extreme, prospector businesses usually operate in broad and rapidly changing domains where neither the technology nor customer segments are well established. The scope of such businesses often undergo periodic redefinition. Also, it is usually impossible to organize such units according to all three of the preceding criteria. Thus, prospector businesses are typically organized around either a core technology that might lead to the development of products aimed at a broad range of customer segments or a basic customer need that might be met with products based on different technologies. The latter is the approach taken by 3M's Medical Products SBU. Its mission is to satisfy the health needs of a broad range of patients with new products and services developed from technologies drawn from other business units within the firm. For example, it has developed a variety of innovative drug delivery systems using aerosols, adhesives, and other 3M technologies.

Analyzer businesses, whether low cost or differentiated, fall somewhere in between the two extremes. They usually have a well-established core business to defend, and often their domain is primarily focused on that business. However, businesses pursuing this intermediate strategy are often in industries that are still growing or experiencing technological changes. Consequently, they must pay attention to the emergence of new customer segments and/or new product types. As a result, managers must review and adjust the domain of such businesses from time to time.

Differences in goals and objectives

Another important difference across generic business-level strategies with particular relevance for the design and implementation of appropriate marketing programs is that different strategies often focus on different objectives. SBU and product-market objectives might be specified on a variety of criteria; but to keep things simple, we focus on only three performance dimensions of major importance to both business-unit and marketing managers:

1. *Effectiveness.*   The success of a business's products and programs relative to those of its competitors in the market. Effectiveness is commonly measured by such items as *sales growth* relative to competitors or *changes in market share.*

2. *Efficiency.*   The outcomes of a business's programs relative to the resources used in implementing them. Common measures of efficiency are *profitability* as a percent of sales, and *return on investment.*

3. *Adaptability.*   The business's success in responding over time to changing conditions and opportunities in the environment. Adaptability can be measured in a variety of ways, but the most common ones are the *number of successful new products* introduced relative to competitors, or the *percent of sales accounted for by products introduced within the last five years.*

However, it is very difficult for any SBU, regardless of its competitive strategy, to simultaneously achieve outstanding performance on even this limited number of dimensions, because they involve substantial trade-offs. Good performance on one dimension often means sacrificing performance on another.[12] For example, developing successful new products or attaining share growth often involves large marketing budgets, substantial up-front investment, high operating costs, and a shaving of profit margins—all of which reduce ROI. This suggests that managers should choose a competitive strategy with a view toward maximizing performance on one or two dimensions while expecting to sacrifice some level of performance on the others, at least in the short term. Over the longer term, of course, the chosen strategy should promise discounted cash flows that exceed the business's cost of capital and thereby increase shareholder value.

As Exhibit 3–6 indicates, prospector businesses are expected to outperform defenders on both new-product development and market share growth. For instance, the Life Sciences sector of 3M, which includes a large proportion of prospector businesses, produced revenue growth of more than 40 percent from 1987 through 1990, and more than a third of the sector's sales were generated by new products. In comparison, 3M's total revenues grew only about 30 percent during the same period.

On the other hand, both defender strategies should lead to better returns on investment. Differentiated defenders likely produce higher returns than low-cost defenders, assuming that the greater expenses involved in maintain-

---

[12]Gordon Donaldson, *Managing Corporate Wealth* (New York: Praeger, Inc., 1984).

EXHIBIT 3–6

Differences in Scope, Goals and Objectives, Resource Deployments, and Synergy across Different Business Strategies

Dimensions	Prospector	Analyzer	Differentiated defender	Low-cost defender
• Scope	Broad/dynamic domains: technology and customer segments not well established	Mixture of defender and prospector strategies	Mature/stable/well-defined domain; mature technology and customer segments	Mature/stable/well-defined domain; mature technology and customer segments
• Goals and objectives Adaptability (new-product success)	Extensive	Mixture of defender and prospector strategies	Little	Very little
Effectiveness (increase in market share)	Large	Mixture of defender and prospector strategies	Little	Little
Efficiency (ROI)	Low	Mixture of defender and prospector strategies	High	High
• Resource deployment	Need cash for product development (question marks or stars)	Need cash for product development but less so than prospectors	Generate excess cash (cash cows)	Generate excess cash (cash cows)
• Synergy	Danger in sharing operating facilities and programs—better to share technology/marketing skills	Danger in sharing operating facilities and programs—better to share technology/marketing skills	Need to seek operating synergies to achieve efficiencies	Need to seek operating synergies to achieve efficiencies

ing their differentiated positions can be more than offset by the higher margins gained by avoiding the intense price competition low-cost competitors often face. Once again, both low-cost and differentiated analyzer strategies likely fall between the two extremes.

The validity of the expected performance differences outlined in Exhibit 3–6 is supported by some empirical evidence. One study found that businesses pursuing defender strategies significantly outperformed prospector businesses on return on investment and cash flow on investment regardless of the type of environment they faced, while prospectors generated significantly greater rates of market share growth—particularly in innovative or rapidly growing markets.[13] Similarly, a more recent study found that both prospectors and analyzers outperformed defenders on market share growth and

---

[13]Donald C. Hambrick, "Some Tests of the Effectiveness and Functional Attributes of Miles and Snow's Strategic Types," *Academy of Management Journal* 26 (1983), pp. 5–26.

return on equity in markets experiencing steady growth. Surprisingly, though, the same study found that defenders outperformed all other strategies on both efficiency and effectiveness dimensions in highly volatile markets.[14] This unexpected finding might be attributable to the episodic periods of both growth and contraction that volatile markets experience. Thus, while aggressive prospector and analyzer businesses may outperform the more conservative defenders during growth periods, they may also suffer greater volume and financial losses during periods of market decline.

Differences in resource deployments

Businesses following different strategies also tend to allocate their financial resources differently across product-markets, functional departments, and activities within each functional area. Prospector—and to a lesser degree, analyzer—businesses devote a relatively large proportion of resources to the development of new product-markets. Because such product-markets usually require more cash to develop than they produce short term, businesses pursuing these strategies often need infusions of financial resources from other parts of the corporation. In portfolio terms, they are "question marks" or "stars."

Defenders, on the other hand, focus the bulk of their resources on preserving existing positions in established product-markets. These product-markets are usually profitable; therefore, defender businesses typically generate excess cash to support product and market development efforts in other business units within the firm. They are the "cash cows." Pillsbury's Prepared Dough Products business unit, for example, generated about half of all the profits produced by the corporation's packaged food operations in the late 1980s. Much of those profits were subsequently reallocated to market and product development efforts (such as the introduction of microwave cake mix) carried out within other SBUs.

Resource allocations among functional departments and activities within the SBU also vary across businesses pursuing different strategies. For instance, marketing budgets tend to be the largest as a percentage of an SBU's revenues when the business is pursuing a prospector strategy; they tend to be the smallest as a percentage of sales under a low-cost defender strategy. We discuss this in more detail later in this chapter.

Differences in sources of synergy

Because different strategies emphasize different methods of competition and different functional activities, a given source of synergy may be more appropriate for some strategies than for others.

---

[14]Daryl O. McKee, P. Rajan Varadarajan, and William M. Pride, "Strategic Adaptability and Firm Performance: A Market-Contingent Perspective," *Journal of Marketing*, July 1989, pp. 21–35.

At one extreme, the sharing of operating facilities and programs may be an inappropriate approach to gaining synergy for businesses following a prospector strategy. And to a lesser extent, this may also be true for both types of analyzer strategies. Such sharing can reduce an SBU's ability to adapt quickly to changing market demands or competitive threats. Commitments to internally negotiated price structures and materials, as well as the use of joint resources, facilities, and programs, increase interdependence among SBUs and limit their flexibility. Because prospector and analyzer businesses seek growth through new-product and market development, a lack of flexibility makes it difficult for them to successfully implement their chosen strategy. It is more appropriate for such businesses to seek synergy through the sharing of a technology, engineering skills, or market knowledge—expertise that can help improve the success rate of their product development efforts. Thus, 3M's Medical Products SBU attempts to find medical applications for new technologies developed in many of the firm's other business units.

At the other extreme, however, low-cost defenders should seek operating synergies that will make them more efficient. Synergies that enable such businesses to increase economies of scale and experience curve effects are particularly desirable. They help reduce unit costs and strengthen the strategy's basis of competitive advantage. The primary means of gaining such operating synergies is through the sharing of resources, facilities, and functional activities across product-market entries within the business unit or across related business units. Emerson Electric, for instance, has formed an "operating group" of several otherwise autonomous business units that make different types of electrical tools. By sharing production facilities, marketing activities, and a common salesforce, the group has been able to reduce per-unit production and marketing costs.[15]

THE FIT BETWEEN BUSINESS STRATEGIES AND THE EXTERNAL ENVIRONMENT

Because different strategies pursue different objectives in different domains with different competitive approaches, they do not all work equally well under the same environmental circumstances. The question is, Which environmental situations are most amenable to the successful pursuit of each type of strategy? Exhibit 3–7 briefly outlines some of the major market, technological, and competitive conditions—plus a business unit's strengths relative to its competitors—that are most favorable for the successful implementation of each generic business strategy. We next discuss the reasons why each strategy fits best with a particular set of environmental conditions.

---

[15]"Emerson Electric: High Profits From Low Tech," *Business Week,* April 4, 1983, p. 62.

EXHIBIT 3-7
External Factors Favorable to the Adoption of Individual Business Strategies

External factors	Prospector	Analyzer	Differentiated defender	Low-cost defender
Market characteristics	Industry in introductory or early growth stage of life cycle; many potential customer segments as yet unidentified and/or undeveloped.	Industry in late growth or early maturity stage of life cycle; one or more product offerings currently targeted at major customer segments, but some potential segments may still be undeveloped.	Industry in maturity or decline stage of life cycle; current offerings targeted at all major segments; sales primarily due to repeat purchases/ replacement demand.	Industry in maturity or decline stage of life cycle; current offerings targeted at all major segments; sales primarily due to repeat purchases/ replacement demand.
Technology	Newly emerging technology; many applications as yet undeveloped.	Basic technology well-developed but still evolving; product modifications and improvements—as well as emergence of new competing technologies—still likely.	Basic technology fully developed and stable; few major modifications or improvements likely.	Basic technology fully developed and stable; few major modifications or improvements likely.
Competition	Few established competitors; industry structure still emerging; single competitor holds commanding share of major market segments.	Large number of competitors, but future shakeout likely; industry structure still evolving; one or more competitors hold large shares in major segments, but continuing growth may allow rapid changes in relative shares.	Small to moderate number of well-established competitors; industry structure's stable, though acquisitions and consolidation possible; maturity of markets means relative shares of competitors tend to be reasonably stable over time.	Small to moderate number of well-established competitors; industry structure's stable, though acquisitions and consolidation possible; maturity of markets means relative shares of competitors tend to be reasonably stable over time.
Business's relative strengths	SBU (or parent) has strong R&D, product engineering, and marketing research and marketing capabilities.	SBU (or parent) has good R&D, product engineering, and marketing research capabilities, but not as strong as some competitors; has either low-cost position or strong sales, marketing, distribution, or service capabilities in one or more segments.	SBU has no outstanding strengths in R&D or product engineering; costs are higher than at least some competitors; SBU's outstanding strengths are in process engineering and quality control and/or in marketing, sales, distribution, or customer services.	SBU (or parent) has superior sources of supply and/or process engineering and production capabilities that enable it to be low-cost producer; R&D, product engineering, marketing, sales, or service capabilities may not be as strong as some competitors'.

Appropriate conditions for a prospector strategy

A prospector strategy is particularly well suited to unstable, rapidly changing environments resulting from new technology, shifting customer needs, or both. In either case, such industries tend to be at an early stage in their life cycles and offer many opportunities for new product-market entries. Industry structure is often unstable because few competitors are present and their relative market shares can shift rapidly as new products are introduced and new markets develop. Prospector strategies are common in industries where new applications and customer acceptance of existing technologies are still developing (such as the personal computer, computer software, and information technologies industries), and industries with rapid technological change (such as biotechnology, medical care, and aerospace).

Because they emphasize the development of new products and/or new markets, the most successful prospectors are usually strong in and devote substantial resources to two broad areas of competence. First, R&D, product engineering, and other functional areas that identify new technology and convert it into innovative products. Second, marketing research, marketing, and sales: functions necessary for the identification and development of new market opportunities.

In addition, successful prospector SBUs usually have a high degree of decision making and operational autonomy. Such businesses can react quickly to new technological developments and market needs. Illinois Tool Works (ITW)—an 80-year-old manufacturer that earned $164 million on sales of $2.2 billion worth of a variety of tools and components in 1989—is a good example of a firm that gives substantial autonomy to its prospector business units.[16] For a description of how ITW's organizatinoal structure and policies facilitate the success of those units, see Exhibit 3–8.

In some cases, however, even though a prospector business has strong product development and marketing skills, it may lack the resources to maintain its early lead as product-markets grow and attract new competitors. For example, Minnetonka was the pioneer in several health and beauty-aid product categories with brands like Softsoap liquid soap and Check-Up plaque-fighting toothpaste. However, after hitting a sales peak of $151 million in 1987, the firm was unable to maintain its leading share position in these markets because competitors like Procter & Gamble and Colgate-Palmolive introduced competing brands with advertising and promotion budgets much larger than Minnetonka could match. The firm was eventually forced to change its strategy and concentrate on manufacturing products under licenses from larger firms, such as the Obsession line of fragrances licensed from Calvin Klein.

---

[16]Ronald Henkoff, "The Ultimate Nuts & Bolts Co.," *Fortune*, July 16, 1990, pp. 70–73.

E X H I B I T   3 - 8

Illinois Tool Works—Organizational Structure and Policies Favorable
to the Performance of Prospector Businesses

Unglamorous and low-profile, ITW manufactures a diverse array of items that are typically attached to, embedded in, or swathed around somebody else's goods. It makes nails, screws, bolts, strapping, wrapping, valves, capacitors, filters, and adhesives—as well as the tools and machines to apply them.

ITW is not a firm where senior managers hog power, build empires, or bark orders. The company has 90 SBUs or divisions loosely organized into nine groups. The largest, the $420-million-a-year construction products group, has only three central administrators—a president, a controller, and a shared secretary.

While many of ITW's SBUs are defender businesses with well-established products in mature markets, a surprising number are newly developed prospector businesses. Part of the reason for this is that when engineers and marketers in an existing division develop and commercialize a highly successful new product, it is often split off to form a new business unit. This is how a unit known as Nexus came into being. A researcher in an established division invented a durable, safety-rated plastic buckle for a customer who makes life jackets. Six years later, Nexus—along with its licensees—sold $45 million of the buckles for backpacks, bicycle helmets, and pet collars.

ITW's prospector divisions are typically small, with less than $30 million in annual revenues. Most seek out, and often dominate, market niches where there are no established competitors. And to ensure their continued autonomy and flexibility, each division's chief is given control over the unit's R&D, manufacturing, and marketing operations.

SOURCE: Based on material found in Ronald Henkoff, "The Ultimate Nuts & Bolts Co.," *Fortune*, July 16, 1990, pp. 70–73. *Fortune*, © 1989 The Time Inc. Magazine Company. All rights reserved.

Appropriate conditions for an analyzer strategy

The analyzer strategy is a hybrid. On one hand, analyzers are concerned with defending—via low costs or differentiation in quality or service—a strong share position in one or more established product-markets. At the same time, the business must pay attention to new-product development in order to avoid being leapfrogged by competitors with more technologically advanced products or being left behind in newly developing application segments within the market. This dual focus makes the analyzer strategy appropriate for well-developed industries that are still experiencing some amount of growth and change due to evolving customer needs and desires or continuing technological improvements.

Commercial aircraft manufacturing is an example of such an industry. Both competitors and potential customers are few and well established. But technology continues to improve; the increased competition among airlines since deregulation has changed the attributes those firms look for when buying new planes; and mergers have increased the buying power of some customers. Thus, Boeing's commercial aircraft division has had to work harder to maintain its 50 percent share of worldwide commercial plane sales. Although the firm continues to enjoy a reputation for producing high-quality and reliable planes, it had to make price concessions and increase customer services during the late 1980s to stave off threats from competitors like the European Airbus consortium. For example, in one deal with American Airlines, Boeing agreed to lease rather than sell more than $2 billion worth of planes and to allow American to cancel the leases with as little as 30 days' notice. At the same time, the firm's commercial aircraft division was also engaged in a product development effort with more than a $2 billion budget aimed at producing a new generation of airplanes to recapture the technological lead enjoyed by Airbus's new A-320 jet.[17]

One problem with an analyzer strategy is that few businesses—even very large ones like Boeing's commercial aircraft division—have the resources and competencies needed to successfully defend an established core business while also generating new products. Success on both dimensions requires strengths across virtually every functional area. Few businesses or their parent companies have such universal strengths relative to competition; therefore, analyzers are often not as innovative in new product development as prospectors. And they may not be as profitable in defending their core businesses as defenders. Thus, in addition to seeing its technological lead in the industry eroded, Boeing's commercial aircraft division also saw its market share fall from 70 percent in 1981 to 50 percent in 1987 and its earnings as a percent of revenues slump dramatically. Revenues have since improved, but largely because of a strong increase in demand for commercial airliners.

Appropriate conditions for a defender strategy

A defender strategy makes sense only when a business has something worth defending. It is most appropriate for units with a profitable share of one or more major segments in a relatively mature, stable industry. A defender may initiate some product improvements or line extensions to protect and strengthen its position in existing segments; but it devotes relatively few resources to basic R&D or the development of innovative new products. Thus, a defender strategy works best in industries where the basic technology is not very complex or where it is well developed and unlikely to change dramatically over the short run. Pillsbury's Prepared Dough Products SBU, for instance, has introduced a number of line extensions over the years; but as noted earlier, most have been reconfigurations of the same basic dough-in-a-can technology, such as Soft Breadsticks.

Differentiated defenders

To effectively defend its position by differentiation, a business must be strong in those functional areas critical for maintaining its particular competitive advantage over time. If a business's differentiation is based on superior product quality, those key functional areas include production, process engineering, quality control, and perhaps product engineering to develop product improvements. Interestingly, successful differentiation of its offerings on the

[17]Kenneth Labich, "Boeing Battles to Stay on Top," *Fortune,* September 28, 1987, pp. 64–72.

EXHIBIT 3–9

The Relationship between Product Quality and Pretax ROI by Business Type

		Quality level			
	Lowest	Below average	Average	Above average	Highest
Consumer durables	16%	18%	18%	26%	32%
Consumer nondurables	15	21	17	23	32
Capital goods	10	8	13	20	21
Raw materials	13	21	21	21	35
Components	12	20	20	22	36
Supplies	16	13	19	25	36

NOTE: Numbers refer to percent average ROI.
SOURCE: Robert D. Buzzell, "Product Quality," *Pimsletter* no. 4 (Cambridge, Mass.: The Strategic Planning Institute, 1981), p. 5.

quality dimension has a strong impact on a business's return on investment—a critical performance objective for defenders. The positive correlation between quality and ROI holds true even after allowing for the effects of market share and investment intensity. As Exhibit 3–9 shows, the pretax return on investment is higher in all businesses for firms selling above-average and highest-quality products than for firms selling average or below-average quality offerings.

Regardless of the basis for differentiation, marketing is also important for the effective implementation of a differentiated defender strategy. Marketing activities that track changing customer needs and competitive actions and communicate the product offering's unique advantages through promotional and sales efforts to maintain customer awareness and loyalty are particularly important.

Low-cost defenders

Successful implementation of a low-cost defender strategy requires the business to be more efficient than its competitors.[18] Thus, the business must establish the groundwork for such a strategy early in the growth stage of the industry. Achieving and maintaining the lowest per-unit cost usually means that the business has to seek large volume from the beginning—through some combination of low prices and promotional efforts—to gain economies

---

[18]Efficiency and competition based on low price are primary elements of low-cost defenders' business strategies. However, businesses pursuing other competitive strategies should also hold down their costs as much as possible given the functional activities and programs necessary to implement those strategies effectively. Indeed, some of the most successful businesses are those that work aggressively to simultaneously lower costs and improve quality and service. For example, see Ronald Henkoff, "Cost Cutting: How to Do It Right," *Fortune*, April 9, 1990, pp. 40–49.

of scale and experience. At the same time, such businesses must also invest in more plant capacity in anticipation of future growth and in state-of-the-art equipment to minimize production costs. This combination of low margins and heavy investment can be prohibitive unless the parent corporation can commit substantial resources to the business or extensive sharing of facilities, technologies, and programs with other business units is possible.

The low-cost defender's need for efficiency also forces the standardization of product offerings and marketing programs across customer segments to achieve scale effects. Thus, such a strategy is usually not so effective in fragmented markets desiring customized offerings as it is in commodity industries such as basic chemicals, steel, or flour, or in industries producing low-technology components such as electric motors or valves.

Changing strategies at different stages in the industry life cycle

A business may have to change its objectives and competitive strategy as the industry and the business's competitive position within it mature and stabilize. Thus, a prospector strategy is most appropriate during the early stages of a product category's life cycle as a business attempts to build a successful product line and increase its market share. As the industry matures and the competitive environment stabilizes, analyzer, and ultimately defender, strategies become more appropriate as the business turns its attention to maintaining and reaping the higher ROI and cash flows of its hard-won market position.

The problem is that the effective implementation of different business strategies not only requires different functional competencies and resources, but also different organizational structures, decision-making and coordination processes, reward systems, and even personnel. Because such internal structures and processes are hard to change quickly, it can be very difficult for an entire SBU to make a successful transition from one basic strategy to another.[19] For example, many of Emerson Electric's SBUs historically were successful low-cost defenders; but accelerating technological change in their industries caused the corporation to try to convert them to low-cost analyzers who would focus more attention on new-product and market development. Initially, however, this attempted shift in strategy resulted in some culture shock, conflict, and mixed performance outcomes from within those units.[20]

In view of the implementation problems involved, some firms do not try to make major changes in the basic competitive strategies of their existing

---

[19]Although there is disagreement about how they occur, most people who have studied the transitions from one strategy to another within companies agree that it takes at least several years for them to be implemented successfully. See, for example, James B. Quinn, *Strategies for Change: Logical Incrementalism* (Homewood, Ill.: Richard D. Irwin, 1980); and Danny Miller and Peter H. Friesen, *Organizations: A Quantum View* (Englewood Cliffs, N.J.: Prentice Hall, 1984).

[20]"Emerson Electric: High Profits From Low Tech," *Business Week,* April 4, 1983, p. 2.

business units. Instead, they might form entirely new prospector SBUs to pursue emerging new technologies and industries rather than expecting established units to handle extensive new-product development efforts. As individual product-market entries gain successful positions in well-established markets, some firms move them from the prospector unit that developed them to an analyzer or defender unit that is better suited to reaping profits from them as their markets mature. Finally, some firms that are technological leaders in their industries may divest or license individual product-market entries as they mature rather than defend them in the face of increasing competition and eroding margins. This is an approach commonly taken by such companies as 3M and DuPont.

MARKETING IMPLICATIONS OF DIFFERENT BUSINESS STRATEGIES

Business units typically incorporate a number of distinct product-markets. A given entry's marketing manager monitors and evaluates the product's environmental situation and develops a marketing program suited to it. However, the manager's freedom to design such a program is constrained by the business unit's competitive strategy. This is because different strategies focus on different objectives and seek to gain and maintain a competitive advantage in different ways. As a result, different functions within the SBU—and different activities within a given functional area, such as marketing—are critical for the success of different strategies.

There are, therefore, different functional key factors for success inherent in the various generic business strategies.[21] This constrains the individual marketing manager's freedom of action in two basic ways. First, because different functions within the business unit are more important under different strategies, they receive different proportions of the SBU's total resources. Thus, the SBU's strategy influences *the amount of resources committed to marketing* and ultimately the budget available to an individual marketing manager within the business unit. Second, the SBU's choice of strategy influences both the kind of *market and competitive situation* that individual product-market entries are likely to face and the *objectives* they are asked to attain. Both constraints have implications for the design of marketing programs for individual products within an SBU.

Of course, it is somewhat risky to draw broad generalizations about how specific marketing policies and program elements might fit within different business strategies. While a business strategy is a general statement about how an SBU chooses to compete in an industry, that unit may comprise a number of different product-market entries facing different competitive situ-

---

[21]For more detailed discussions of the "key factors for success" in implementing different strategies—particularly those involving the functional competencies of the business—see Kenichi Ohmae, *The Mind of the Strategist* (New York: McGraw-Hill Book Company, 1982), chap. 3; and James B. Quinn, Thomas L. Doorley, and Penny C. Paquette, "Beyond Products: Services-Based Strategy," *Harvard Business Review,* March–April 1990, pp. 58–67.

EXHIBIT 3-10

Differences in Marketing Policies and Program Components
across Businesses Pursuing Different Strategies

Marketing policies and program components	Strategy		
	Prospector	Differentiated defender	Low-cost defender
Product policies			
• Product line breadth relative to competitors	+	+	−
• Technical sophistication of products relative to competitors	+	+	−
• Product quality relative to competitors	?	+	−
• Service quality relative to competitors	?	+	−
Price policies			
• Price levels relative to competitors	+	+	−
Distribution policies			
• Degree of forward vertical integration relative to competitors	−	+	?
• Trade promotion expenses as percent of sales relative to competitors	+	−	−
Promotion policies			
• Advertising expenses as percent of sales relative to competitors	+	?	−
• Sales promotion expenses as percent of sales relative to competitors	+	?	−
• Salesforce expenses as percent of sales relative to competitors	?	+	−

Key: + Greater than the average competitor
   − Smaller than the average competitor
   ? Uncertain relationship between strategy and marketing policy or program component

ations in different markets. Thus, there is likely to be a good deal of variation
in marketing programs, and in the freedom individual marketing managers
have in designing them, across products within a given SBU. Still, a business's strategy does set a general direction for the types of target markets it
will pursue and how the unit will compete in those markets. And it does
have some influence on marketing policies that cut across product-markets.
Exhibit 3–10 outlines some differences in marketing policies and program
elements that occur across businesses pursuing different strategies, and those
differences are discussed below.

Product policies

One set of marketing policies defines the nature of the products the business
will concentrate on offering to its target markets. These policies concern the
breadth or diversity of product lines, their *level of technical sophistication,* and the
target *level of product quality* relative to competitors.

Because prospector businesses rely heavily on the continuing development of unique new products and the penetration of new markets as their primary competitive strategy, policies encouraging broader and more technically advanced product lines than those of competitors should be positively related to performance on the critical dimension of share growth. The diverse and technically advanced product offerings of 3M's Medical Products SBU are a good example of this.

Whether a prospector's products should be of higher quality than competitors' products is open to question. Quality is hard to define—it can mean different things to different customers. Even so, it is an important determinant of business profitability.[22] Thus, Hambrick suggests that in product-markets where technical features or up-to-the-minute styling are key attributes in customers' definitions of quality, high-quality products may play a positive role in determining the success of a prospector strategy. On the other hand, in markets where the critical determinants of quality are reliability or brand familiarity, the maintenance of relatively high product quality is likely to be more strongly related to the successful performance of defender businesses, particularly differentiated defenders.[23]

Differentiated defenders compete by offering more or "better" choices to customers than their competitors. For example, 3M's commercial graphics business, a major supplier of sign material for truck fleets, has strengthened its competitive position in that market by developing products appropriate for custom-designed signs. Until recently, the use of film for individual signs was not economical. But the use of computer-controlled knives and a new Scotch-brand marking film produce signs of higher quality and at lower cost than those that are hand-painted. This kind of success in developing relatively broad and technically sophisticated product lines should be positively related to the long-term ROI performance of most differentiated defender businesses. However, such policies are inconsistent with the efficiency requirements of the low-cost defender strategy. Broad and complex product lines lead to short production runs and large inventories. Maintaining technical sophistication in a business's products requires continuing investments in product and process R&D. Consequently, the adoption of such policies is apt to be less common in low-cost defender businesses.

Instead of, or in addition to, competing on the basis of product characteristics, businesses can distinguish themselves relative to competitors on the *quality of service* they offer. Such service might take many forms, including engineering and design services, alterations, installation, training of customer personnel, or maintenance and repair services. A policy of high service quality is particularly appropriate for differentiated defenders because it offers a way to maintain a competitive advantage in well-established markets.

The appropriateness of an extensive service policy for low-cost defenders, though, is more questionable if higher operating and administrative costs off-

---

[22]Robert Buzzell, "Product Quality," *Pimsletter No. 4* (Cambridge, Mass.: The Strategic Planning Institute, 1986).

[23]Hambrick, "Some Tests of the Effectiveness and Functional Attributes."

set customer satisfaction benefits. Those higher costs may detract from the business's ability to maintain the low prices critical to its strategy, as well as lowering ROI—at least in the short term. On the other hand, even low-cost defenders may have difficulty holding their position over the long term without maintaining at least competitive parity with respect to critical service attributes.[24]

Pricing policies

Success in offering low prices relative to competitors should be positively related to the performance of low-cost defender businesses—for low price is the primary competitive weapon of such a strategy. However, such a policy is inconsistent with both differentiated defender and prospector strategies. The higher costs involved in differentiating a business's products on either a quality or service basis require higher prices to maintain profitability. Differentiation also provides customers with additional value for which higher prices can be charged. Similarly, the costs and benefits of new-product and market development by prospector businesses require and justify relatively high prices. Thus, differentiated defenders and prospectors seldom adhere to a policy of low competitive prices.

Distribution policies

Some observers argue that prospector businesses should show a greater degree of *forward vertical integration* than defender businesses.[25] The rationale for this view is that the prospector's focus on new-product and market development requires superior market intelligence and frequent reeducation and motivation of distribution channel members. This can best be accomplished through tight control of company-owned channels. However, these arguments seem inconsistent with the prospector's need for flexibility in constructing new channels to distribute new products and reach new markets.

Attempting to maintain tight control over the behavior of channel members is a more appropriate policy for defenders who are trying to maintain strong positions in established markets. This is particularly true for defenders who rely on good customer service to differentiate themselves from competitors. Thus, it seems more likely that a relatively high degree of forward vertical integration is found among defender businesses, particularly differentiated defenders, while prospectors rely more heavily on independent channel members—such as manufacturer's representatives or wholesale distributors—to distribute their products.[26]

---

[24]For additional arguments in the debate about the relative costs and competitive benefits of superior customer service, see Frank Rose, "Now Quality Means Service Too."

[25]Miles and Snow, *Organizational Strategy, Structure, and Process;* and Hambrick, "Some Tests of the Effectiveness and Functional Attributes."

[26]Although Hambrick argued for the reverse relationship, data from his study of 850 SBUs actually support our contention that defenders have more vertically integrated channels than prospectors. See Hambrick, ibid.

Because prospectors focus on new products where success is uncertain and sales volumes are small in the short run, they are likely to devote a larger percentage of sales to *trade promotions* than defender businesses. Prospectors rely on trade promotion tools such as quantity discounts, liberal credit terms, and other incentives to induce cooperation and support from their independent channel members.

Promotion policies

Extensive marketing communications also play an important role in the successful implementation of both prospector and differentiated defender strategies. The form of that communication, however, may differ under the two strategies. Because prospectors must constantly work to generate awareness, stimulate trial, and build primary demand for new and unfamiliar products, high advertising and sales promotion expenditures are likely to bear a positive relationship to the new-product and share-growth success of such businesses. 3M's Medical Products SBU, for instance, devotes substantial resources to advertising in professional journals and distributing samples of new products, as well as to maintaining an extensive salesforce.

Differentiated defenders, on the other hand, are primarily concerned with maintaining the loyalty of established customers by adapting to their needs and providing good service. These tasks can best be accomplished—particularly in industrial goods and services industries—by an extensive, well-trained, well-supported, salesforce. Therefore, differentiated defenders are likely to have higher salesforce expenditures than competitors.

Finally, low-cost defenders appeal to their customers primarily on price. Thus, high expenditures on advertising, sales promotion, or the salesforce would detract from their basic strategy and may have a negative impact on their ROI performance. Consequently, such businesses are likely to make relatively low expenditures as a percentage of sales on those promotional activities.

SERVICE BUSINESSES: DO THEY REQUIRE DIFFERENT STRATEGIES?

The service component of the U.S. economy accounts for over 70 percent of all nonfarm jobs and about 67 percent of all economic activity, compared to 21 percent for manufacturing. Since 1970, services have added some 30 million jobs, while manufacturing employment has stayed relatively constant at 19 million for the past 20 years. Services outpace manufacturing in capital spending by nearly $50 billion, corporate profits by over $25 billion, and international trade, where they generate a small profit compared to a huge merchandise deficit.[27]

---

[27]John S. McClenahen and Perry Pascarella, "America's New Economy," *Industry Week,* January 26, 1987, pp. 26–32.

As the number of two-wage-earner families and single-person households continue to grow, time becomes increasingly valuable for more and more people. This, coupled with increasing household incomes and other factors, suggests that growth in the demand for services is likely to outstrip growth in the manufacturing sector of our economy well into the future.

But what is a service? Basically, services can be thought of as **intangibles** and goods as **tangibles.** The former can rarely be experienced in advance of the sale, while tangible products can be experienced, even tested, before purchase.[28] Using this distinction, a **service** can be defined as "any activity or benefit that one party can offer to another that is essentially intangible and that does not result in the ownership of anything. Its production may or may not be tied to a physical product."[29]

We typically associate services with nonmanufacturing businesses, even though service is often an indispensable part of a goods producer's offering. Services like applications engineering, system design, delivery, installation, training, and maintenance can be crucial for building long-term relationships between manufacturers and their customers, particularly in consumer durable and industrial products businesses. Thus, almost all businesses are engaged in service to a greater or lesser extent.

On the other hand, many organizations are concerned with producing and marketing a service as their primary offering rather than as an adjunct to a physical product. These organizations include firms providing personal services, such as health care, communications, retailing, and finance companies; commercial service organizations, such as accounting, legal, and consulting firms; public sector services like the military, police and fire departments, and schools; and not-for-profit service organizations, such as churches, hospitals, universities, and arts organizations. The crucial question is whether such organizations must employ different strategies and functional programs than goods manufacturers to be successful.

There are substantial similarities in the strategic issues both goods and service producers face, especially when deciding how to compete at the business level. However, the intangibility, as well as some other special characteristics, of services can cause unique marketing and operational problems for service organizations, as discussed below.

Business-level competitive strategies

The framework we used to classify the business-level competitive strategies pursued by goods producers is equally valid for service businesses. Some service firms—such as Super 8 or Days Inn in the lodging industry—attempt to minimize costs and compete largely with low prices. Other firms, like Marriott, differentiate their offerings on the basis of high service quality or unique benefits. Similarly, some service businesses adopt prospector strategies and aggressively pursue the development of new offerings or markets. As

---

[28]Theodore Leavitt, *The Marketing Imagination* (New York: The Free Press, 1986), pp. 94–95.

[29]Philip Kotler and Gary Armstrong, *Principles of Marketing* (Englewood Cliffs, N.J.: Prentice Hall, 1989), p. 575.

we saw in the first chapter, for instance, American Express's Travel Related Services division has developed a variety of new services tailored to specific segments of the firm's credit-card holders. Other service businesses focus narrowly on defending established positions in current markets. Still others can best be described as analyzers pursuing both established and new markets or as reactors who lack any consistent strategy.

A recent study of the banking industry provides some empirical evidence that service businesses actually do pursue the same types of competitive strategies as goods producers. The 329 bank CEOs who responded to the survey had little trouble categorizing their institutions' competitive strategies into one of Miles and Snow's four types. Fifty-four of the executives reported that their banks were prospectors, 87 identified their firms as analyzers, 157 as defenders, and 31 as reactors.[30]

The impact of service characteristics on marketing[31]

The business-level competitive strategy pursued by a service business has the same implications for marketing policies and program elements as those discussed earlier for goods producers. For example, a bank pursuing a prospector strategy likely offers a broader range of services, promotes them more extensively, has broader distribution (i.e., more branch offices), and charges more for its services than one following a defender strategy. However, services have some characteristics that often give rise to special marketing problems and therefore demand special marketing policies and actions. These characteristics are that services are intangible and perishable, they often require substantial customer contact, and their quality can vary from one transaction to the next.

Intangibility

The intangibility of services can make it more difficult to win and hold on to customers. Because prospective customers have difficulty experiencing (seeing, touching, smelling, feeling) the service offering in advance, they are forced to buy promises. But promises are also intangible; hence, metaphors and similes become surrogates for the tangibility that is lacking. This helps explain the solid, reassuring decor of most banks and law offices; the neat, cheerful uniforms worn by employees at McDonald's or Burger King; and

---

[30]Daryl O. McKee, P. Varadarajan, and William Pride, "Strategic Adaptability and Firm Performance: A Market-Contingent Perspective," *Journal of Marketing,* July 1989, pp. 21–35.

[31]For a more detailed discussion of the unique marketing problems faced by service businesses, see Valarie A. Zeithaml, A. Parasuraman, and Leonard L. Berry, "Problems and Strategies in Services Marketing," *Journal of Marketing,* Spring 1985, pp. 33–46; and Valarie A. Zeithaml, A. Parasuraman, and Leonard L. Berry, *Delivering Quality Service: Balancing Customer Perceptions and Expectations* (New York: The Free Press, 1990). Also, for an examination of some of the special problems involved in marketing professional services—such as those provided by lawyers, physicians, and business consultants—see, Paul N. Bloom, "Effective Marketing for Professional Services," *Harvard Business Review,* September–October 1984, pp. 102–10.

the elegant decor and atmosphere of upscale shops and hotels. These things become the tangible symbols of the intangible services being offered.

A further difficulty with intangibility is that customers often don't know what criteria to use in evaluating a service. How do you rate a stockbroker's advice *before* you follow it? Or a doctor's? Typically, customers approach the purchase of services with optimistic expectations. Disappointment is all too easy to come by under these conditions.

One special marketing challenge facing most service businesses, then, is to find ways to make their offerings more tangible to potential customers. Some methods for accomplishing this include:

- *Designing facilities and products and training personnel to serve as symbols of service quality.* As mentioned above, the firm should attempt to design all aspects of the physical environment surrounding the delivery of its service—including its facilities, advertising, promotional materials, and so forth—to act as tangible symbols of the quality and reliability of its service offering. Such actions are particularly important for prospector businesses attempting to develop new markets for new service offerings. Because new offerings are both intangible and unfamiliar to most customers, potential buyers have a doubly hard time judging whether the benefits they offer justify their cost.

  The service firm's personnel can also be important tangible symbols of service quality. Everyone who comes in contact with customers should be carefully trained to project an appropriate image, as well as to actually provide a high-quality experience for the customer. This is especially true in differentiated defender businesses where superior employee training and performance can provide a premium image and an important advantage over competitors. Recall, for instance, the effort and resources that American Express devotes to training, measuring, and rewarding the service performance of its employees as a primary element of its strategy for defending its strong position in the highly competitive credit-card industry.

- *Creating a tangible representation of the service.* American Express has done this, for instance, with its prestigious Gold and Platinum Cards.

- *Tying the marketing of services to the marketing of goods.* For example, H&R Block tax preparation services and Allstate Insurance benefit substantially from their association with Sears.

Perishability

Because a service is an experience, it is perishable and cannot be inventoried. Motel rooms and airline seats not occupied, idle telephone capacity, and the unused time of physicians and lawyers cannot be reclaimed. Further, when demand exceeds capacity, customers must be turned away because no backup inventory is available. Thus, service organizations must do everything possible to anticipate peak loads and to fit capacity to demand. Possible approaches to this problem include:

- *Smoothing out the variability in demand.* One way firms attempt to accomplish this is by offering lower prices during off-peak periods, as when hotels offer lower rates on the weekends and theaters charge less for tickets to matinee performances. Other firms advertise extensively to get customers to change their habits, as in the case of the U.S. Postal Service's campaign to encourage early mailing of Christmas cards and packages. And some service firms have added additional services or goods to make more complete use of their facilities and personnel during slow periods, as with the addition of breakfast items at fast-food chains.

- *Lowering fixed costs by making capacity more flexible.* Firms have attempted to accomplish this in a variety of ways, such as training employees to handle multiple tasks, substituting machines for labor (as with automatic teller machines at banks), sharing facilities, equipment, or personnel with other similar service organizations, and using part-time or paraprofessional employees.

Customer contact

The physical presence of the customer is another characteristic of many service organizations. Many services are sold, produced, and consumed almost simultaneously. The amount of customer contact during the production process is especially important because it affects service design, production, and delivery decisions. High-contact service systems are more difficult to manage than low-contact systems because the greater involvement of the customer in the process affects the timing of demand and the nature and quality of the service itself.[32]

Exhibit 3–11 shows how a variety of decisions are influenced by high and low levels of customer contact in a service system. Some of the general conclusions suggested by the exhibit follow.

- There is a high degree of uncertainty in the day-to-day operations of high-contact systems because the customer can disrupt the production system in a variety of ways. For instance, an unexpected need for emergency service from a hospital can overload operating room facilities.

- Rarely does the demand for a high-contact service equal capacity at any one time—not only because of the difficulty of making reliable forecasts, but also because of last-minute changes by the customer, as in the case of cancellations of hotel reservations. Low-contact systems can better match supply and demand by structuring a resource-oriented schedule and lengthening delivery times when necessary.

- It is difficult to set up an efficient production schedule for high-contact services because customers cannot be programmed.

- Because employees interact directly with customers in high-contact service systems, their appearance and behavior can directly affect customer satisfaction with the service.

---

[32]Richard B. Chase, "Where Does the Customer Fit into a Service Operation?" *Harvard Business Review*, November–December 1978, pp. 139–73.

EXHIBIT 3-11

Major Design Considerations in High- and Low-Contact Service Systems

Decision	High-contact system	Low-contact system
Facility location	Operations must be near the customer.	Operations may be placed near supply, transportation, or labor.
Facility layout	Facility should accommodate the customer's physical and psychological needs and expectations.	Facility should enhance production.
Product design	Environment as well as the physical product define the nature of the service.	Customer is not in the service environment so the product can be defined by fewer attributes.
Process design	Stages of production process have a direct immediate effect on the customer.	Customer is not involved in majority of processing steps.
Scheduling	Customer is in the production schedule and must be accommodated.	Customer is concerned mainly with completion dates.
Production planning	Orders cannot be stored, so smoothing production flow results in loss of business.	Both backlogging and smoothing are possible.
Worker skills	Direct work force comprises a major part of the service product and so must be able to interact well with the public.	Direct work force need only have technical skills.
Quality control	Quality standards are often in the eye of the beholder and hence variable.	Quality standards are generally measurable and hence fixed.
Time standards	Service time depends on customer needs, and therefore time standards are inherently loose.	Work is performed on customer surrogates (e.g., forms), and time standards can be tight.
Wage payment	Variable output requires time-based wage systems.	"Fixable" output permits output-based wage systems.
Capacity planning	To avoid lost sales, capacity must be set to match peak demand.	Storable output permits setting capacity at some average demand level.
Forecasting	Forecasts are short term, time-oriented.	Forecasts are long term, output-oriented.

SOURCE: Reprinted by permission of the *Harvard Business Review*. An exhibit from "Where Does the Customer Fit into a Service Operation?" by Richard B. Chase (November–December 1978). Copyright © 1978 by the President and Fellows of Harvard College; all rights reserved.

Variability

A final, closely related characteristic, particularly of high-contact services, has to do with variability, or the difficulty of maintaining quality control. Because of the human element, service quality can vary substantially depending on who provides it and when. In some respects, this can be viewed as a positive opportunity for the service organization. The personal nature of many services enables firms to customize their services and thus attain a better fit with customer needs. For example, travel agencies can prepare special itineraries for individual travelers, and stockbrokers can recommend individualized portfolios for their clients.

On the other hand, variability can lead to inconsistent experiences for the customer and result in dissatisfaction. Variations in quality can be a particularly difficult problem for firms that operate multiple outlets, such as banks, hotels, airlines, and retail chains. Delivering a uniform experience to customers of the Marriott Hotel group is much more difficult than producing and selling Zenith TVs of consistent quality.

To overcome these quality control problems, as well as to increase supplier productivity, Leavitt suggests that firms should attempt to "industrialize" their services.[33] Some means of accomplishing this include:

- *Use of hard technologies.* This involves finding ways to control service production and delivery processes by substituting machinery and/or tools for people where possible. Examples include automatic teller machines, automatic toll collectors, vending machines, and bank cards that enable loans to be preapproved for reliable customers.

- *Use of soft technologies.* This is primarily concerned with improving the quality and consistency of employee performance through the development of standardized job procedures, detailed training, and close supervision. This approach, used by McDonald's, Marriott, H&R Block, and many other firms, helps ensure the delivery of consistently high-quality service regardless of the employee or situation involved.

- *Use of hybrid technologies.* These function by using hard equipment in conjunction with carefully planned job procedures to control service quality and gain efficiency. Leavitt cites as examples specialized, limited-service, fast, low-priced automobile repair businesses such as Midas Muffler and Jiffy-Lube.

Finally, though, it is important to keep in mind that the marketing programs for individual product-market entries within a particular business unit—whether services or goods—may vary a good deal on some or all of the 4 Ps: product, price, promotion, and place of distribution. Within the constraints imposed by the characteristics of the offering and the business's strategy, individual marketing managers usually have a range of strategic options to choose from when developing a marketing plan. The nature of those options, their relative advantages and weaknesses, and the environmental conditions in which each is most appropriate are the focus of the rest of this book.

SUMMARY

To be implemented successfully, the marketing program for a given product-market entry must be compatible with both the internal capabilities, resources, management processes, and procedures of the firm. It should also fit

---

[33]Theodore Leavitt, *The Marketing Imagination* (New York: The Free Press, 1986), pp. 38–61.

with the corporation's higher-level strategies, particularly the competitive strategy of the entry's business unit.

When formulating a business-level strategy, managers must make recommendations about (1) the SBU's objectives and scope, (2) how resources should be allocated across product-markets and functional departments within the SBU, and (3) which competitive strategy the unit should pursue in attempting to build a sustainable competitive advantage in its product-markets. Decisions about an SBU's scope, objectives, and resource deployments are similar to and should be consistent with those made at the corporate level. However, the major question to be addressed by a business-level strategy is, How are we going to compete within our industry? Thus, an SBU's competitive strategy should take into account the unit's unique strengths and weaknesses relative to competitors and the needs and desires of customers in its target markets.

Researchers have identified general categories of business-unit strategies based on observations of how those SBUs compete within their industries. We combined the classification schemes of Porter and Miles and Snow to arrive at a typology of six different business-level competitive strategies: (1) prospector, (2) differentiated analyzer, (3) low-cost analyzer, (4) differentiated defender, (5) low-cost defender, and (6) reactor.

Businesses pursuing a **prospector** strategy are primarily concerned with attaining rapid volume growth through the development and introduction of new products and by attaining a leading share of new markets. This strategy is particularly appropriate for industries in the introductory or early growth stages of their life cycle.

At the other extreme, **defender** businesses are primarily concerned with maintaining an already strong position in one or more major market segments in industries where the technology, customer segments, and competitive structure are all relatively well developed, stable, and mature. Their major objective is usually to gain and sustain a substantial return from their businesses. **Differentiated defenders** try to do this by maintaining an advantage based on either premium product quality or superior customer service. **Low-cost defenders** seek economies of scale, attempt to minimize unit costs in production and marketing, and compete largely on the basis of low price.

The **analyzer** strategies fall in between prospectors and defenders. Such strategies are most commonly found in industries that are in the late growth or early maturity stages of their life cycles where, although the industry is largely developed, some technological changes, shifts in customer needs, or adjustments in competitive structure are still occurring. Because the analyzer is a hybrid strategy, it is difficult to make many generalizations about its implications for the allocation of resources across functional departments or for the design of marketing programs for individual product-market entries within such businesses.

Reactors are businesses that operate without any well-defined or consistently applied competitive strategy. They react to changing circumstances in an ad hoc, unsystematic way. Consequently, they tend not to perform as well on any dimension as units with more consistent strategies, and it is impossible to draw conclusions about how such businesses are likely to market their products.

Most business units incorporate multiple product-market entries. Although those entries often face different market and competitive situations, their marketing programs are all likely to be influenced and constrained by the SBU's overall competitive strategy.

Successful prospector businesses tend to be competent in, and allocate a relatively large proportion of their resources to, functional areas directly related to new-product and market development, such as R&D, product engineering, marketing, sales, and marketing research. Differentiated defenders also spend substantial resources on marketing and sales to maintain a strong product quality or customer service position. But low-cost defenders usually allocate relatively few resources to any of these functions to hold down costs and prices.

The competitive thrust of a business unit's strategy influences and constrains marketing policies and programs, such as the breadth of the product line, pricing policies, and the size of advertising and promotion budgets. Thus, while marketing managers often play a crucial role in formulating the SBU's strategy, that strategy subsequently imposes constraints and direction on the marketer's decisions about the marketing program for a specific product-market entry within the SBU.

Finally, service businesses tend to pursue the same kinds of business-level strategies as goods producers, and those strategies impose the same kinds of influences and constraints on their marketing policies and programs. However, service offerings often have some unique characteristics, including (1) intangibility, (2) perishability, (3) close customer contact, and (4) variability, which can create special marketing and operational challenges.

OPPORTUNITY ANALYSIS

As noted in Section One, in formulating and implementing strategic marketing programs a firm must select target markets that represent attractive opportunities and must have the resources to exploit such opportunities to attain an enduring competitive advantage. Before the firm can develop any such programs, it must analyze the market opportunity, target the markets, and position the products properly. This process is the focus of this section.

The major steps in a market opportunity analysis emphasize that opportunities and threats derive primarily from the external environment, for example, an increase in the size of a particular age group, a new technology that generates a new type of product, or a change in the relative importance of a channel of distribution. Opportunities and threats can also come from within the firm. Examples of internal opportunities are new products from R&D or an ability to lower relative costs. A deteriorating product quality and high turnover in the salesforce represent threats and are strong barriers to profitable growth.[1]

Opportunity analysis focuses on various environmental components in an attempt to identify future opportunities and threats. Thus, in Chapter 4 we examine the firm's macroenvironment to determine what forces and trends might affect the business unit's relevant industries and hence its strategic marketing programs. Since products and markets are constantly changing, it is critical to understand the process by which this occurs over time. This process and its strategic implications are discussed in Chapter 5, "Industry Dynamics and Strategic Change."

The analysis merges the business unit's competitive strengths with information about the market's attractiveness to determine which market segments the business should target and how its product offerings should be positioned in each to gain a competitive advantage. The targeting process is discussed in Chapter 6; market positioning decisions are covered in Chapter 7. An appendix to the text discusses the various sources of market and competitor information.

---

[1]For a discussion of the internal environment analysis that focuses on the organization's financial accomplishments, see John C. Camillus, *Strategic Planning and Management Control* (Lexington, Mass.: D. C. Heath and Company, 1986), p. 71.

Environmental Analysis

THE GREEN LINE OF ENVIRONMENT-FRIENDLY PRODUCTS[1]

The Loblaws supermarket chain, the largest in Canada with 340 stores (and 30 in the United States through the National Tea chain), recently launched the first supermarket line of environment-friendly products packaged under one brand name. Currently, the Green line includes over 100 products, some already best-sellers in their categories. First-year sales were $50 million with margins equal to those of non-Green items in each category.

The line, which features a green label, includes disposable diapers made from nonchlorine-bleached pulp, toilet paper made from recycled paper, phosphate-free detergents, alar-free apple juice, tuna caught without netting dolphins, recycled motor oil, organic fertilizers, rechargeable batteries, and high-efficiency light bulbs.[2] One such light bulb costs about 10 times more than an ordinary bulb but saves about $32 in energy costs over its lifetime, plus the cost of the nine incandescent bulbs it replaces.

The story of how the company developed its Green line is interesting. A high-level Loblaws executive was in England in 1988 when *The Green Consumer Guide* (an environmental handbook that ranks products and retailers on an environmental basis) was published. Out of curiosity, he obtained one. But it wasn't until he learned it was the best-selling book in the United Kingdom that Nichols became interested in its contents.

Canadian polls showed that the environment was the nation's number-one concern, further spurring his interest in a line of environment-friendly products.

---

[1]Carolyn Lesh, "Loblaws," *Advertising Age,* special issue, "The Green Marketing Revolution," January 29, 1991, p. 38.

[2]Ibid.

Five months and more than $8 million later, the new line of competitively priced products was launched in green packaging made from recycled paper.

This case study illustrates the importance of the environment in generating opportunities that affect an organization's objectives, strategies, and action plans. In the supermarket industry, the numerous and diverse players include all corporations that produce products sold through such stores. Both Canadian and U.S. federal and state agencies have enacted legislation pertaining to pollution (including waste disposal), product safety, and proper labeling. And research organizations have developed procedures and new technologies to solve many of the problems associated with clean air and recycling solid waste disposal. The attitudes of many consumers toward the planet's health have changed over the years. Many are now willing to pay more for groceries if it means recyclable packages and to accept a lower standard of living to protect the environment.[3]

In this chapter, we first discuss the elements of the major components of the marketing environment and how changes in each provide companies with opportunities and threats.[4] Second, we discuss the subject of competitor analysis. Finally, we examine the strategic issue management process required to monitor and evaluate environmental factors that may be of importance in targeting certain market segments and in formulating strategic marketing programs.

CRITICAL COMPONENTS OF MARKETING'S MACROENVIRONMENT

Five components of the macroenvironment are critical from a marketing point of view: the physical, demographic/economic, political/legal, technological, and sociocultural environments. These components typically interact. For example, problems in the physical environment (air pollution) lead to legislation (Clean Air Act) that affects the economics of various industries (alternative fuels), stimulating the development of new technologies (catalytic converters), and so on. Changing consumer attitudes support government actions to reduce pollution and lead to demands for even more stringent laws to protect the environment (see Exhibit 4–1). The following section discusses

---

[3]Denise Kalette, "Save the Environment," *USA Today,* April 13, 1990, p. A–1.

[4]Most futurists predict dramatic changes in the years to come. For a sample of their views on what the 1990s will bring, see Frank Snowden Hopkins, "What Futurists Believe"; and Cynthia G. Wagner and Daniel M. Fields, "Future View: The 1990s & Beyond," both in *The Futurist,* November–December 1989, pp. 27 and 29.

EXHIBIT 4-1

Components of the Macroenvironment

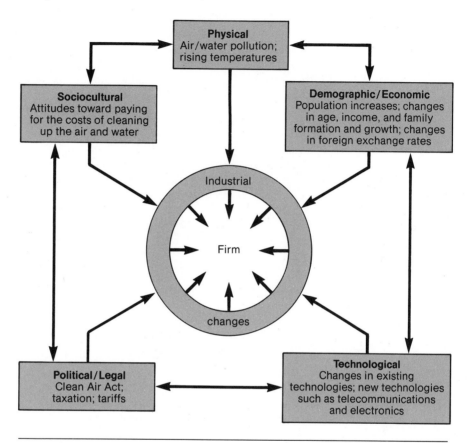

specific aspects of each component and their effects on marketing strategies and programs.

The physical environment[5]

Aside from a growing depletion of many of its valuable resources, there are strong indications that the earth's overall health is declining. Research shows, among other things, that our deserts are growing while our forests are

---

[5]This section is based on the following sources: Lester R. Brown, Christopher Flavin, and Edward C. Wolf, "Earth's Vital Signs," *The Futurist,* July–August 1988, pp. 13–20; Vicky Cahan and Brian Bremmer, "When the Rivers Go Dry and the Ice Caps Melt," *Business Week,* February 13, 1989, p. 96; and David Landes, "Environmental Concerns Catch Up to Business," *USA Today,* May 28, 1989, p. 18. For an interesting discussion of research studies relating to the health of our planet, see Jonathan Weiner, *The Next One Hundred Years* (New York: Bantam Books, 1990).

EXHIBIT   4–2
Business Planning for the Greenhouse Effect

Because of dire predictions about increases in the earth's temperature (the greenhouse effect), more and more companies—especially those in agriculture, forestry, and fishing—are trying to do something about it.

- Archer Daniel Midland, a large grain and barge company operating out of Decatur, Illinois, became concerned about the long-run capability of the Mississippi River to handle its grain barges. In the summer of 1988, the Mississippi's water level dropped so much that barges couldn't move. While this situation was not caused by the greenhouse effect, it did show what a global increase in temperatures could do. The company's response was to purchase a stake in the Illinois Central Railroad, which has track running parallel to the Mississippi.
- Weyerhaeuser Company, a large lumber company, is planting more drought-resistant saplings in case of less rainfall.
- Travelers Insurance is researching models to track storms and their intensity in case global temperatures increase. It is predicted that just a small increase in temperature can lengthen the hurricane season by 20 to 30 days.

SOURCE: Vicky Cahan and Brian Bremmer, "When the Rivers Go Dry and the Ice Caps Melt." Reprinted from February 13, 1989 issue of *Business Week* by special permission, copyright © 1989 by McGraw-Hill, Inc.

shrinking, that more and more lakes are biologically dying, that the quality and quantity of our groundwater is declining, that the ozone layer in the upper atmosphere is thinning, and that the earth may be experiencing a rising temperature.

One of the more frightening scenarios has to do with the projected increase in the earth's mean temperature. The fear is that our heavy use of fossil fuels has and will cause a build-up of carbon dioxide in the atmosphere, resulting in a blanket of gas that traps the sun's radiation (the so-called greenhouse effect). Some scientists consider mean temperature changes of 1.5° and 4.5° F likely over the next 50 to 60 years. If this happens, sea levels would increase, which would inundate many of our coastal cities. It would devastate Asia, for most of its rice is produced on low-lying deltas and flood plains. Further, the rich U.S. midwestern plains and U.S.S.R.'s grain-growing regions would yield substantially fewer crops. Exhibit 4–2 shows how some companies are responding to this potential threat.

Concern about water pollution has caused more and more people to drink bottled water. Sales in the $1.5 billion bottled-water industry are growing 15 percent annually. Many large food and beverage companies, including Beatrice, Coca-Cola, McKesson, G. Heileman Brewing, Nestlés, and Anheuser-Busch, now own bottled-water companies.[6] Stronger clean-air legislation, coupled with the possibility of increased costs of imported oil, have caused automakers to seriously consider the production of cars capable of running on fuels other than gasoline (see Exhibit 4–3). Methanol seems to be the most

---

[6]Alex Beam and Stephen Jones, "Water: Where Profits Could Spring Eternal," *Business Week,* September 15, 1986, p. 75.

EXHIBIT   4-3
Alternative-Fuel Cars

In 1989, Ford showed off a Taurus sedan that can run on methanol, ethanol, and gasoline, and GM has converted its mid-sized Lumina to a flexible-fuel engine. Chrysler Corporation recently introduced a methanol-using LeBaron. One problem with a flexible-fuel vehicle is that both methanol and ethanol provide substantially fewer miles per gallon than gasoline; thus, if drivers want the same driving range, larger fuel tanks will be needed.

SOURCE: "New Push for Alternative Fuels in Autos," *The Wall Street Journal*, June 8, 1989, p. B1.

promising such fuel because its feedstocks of coal or natural gas are plentiful. Ethanol, which is made from corn, is considerably more expensive, but its price may decline when it is made from other plants or even garbage.

The demographic/economic environment

The economy is the most pervasive component of the marketing environment. It is also the most analyzed, although our ability to fully comprehend and forecast changes in the economy remains limited. In an uncertain economic climate, the variables most likely to affect marketing activities are population demographics (particularly changes in age levels), the rate of economic growth, interest rates, currency exchange rates, and international competition.

Demographics

Population evolution is a key environmental factor for marketers. It directly affects consumer markets and influences other economic forces. Despite declining birthrates, the United States is far from experiencing zero population growth. According to the Bureau of the Census, the total U.S. population will grow to nearly 300 million by 2020, compared to 226 million in 1980. The absolute number of annual births should increase as baby boomers enter their childbearing years. U.S. births are expected to reach 4.4 million annually at the height of the new baby boom, compared to 3.6 million in 1980. This should provide a sizable market for environment-friendly diapers (like Loblaws's Green line brand) among families concerned with the environment.

One major demographic force affecting the U.S. economy in the years ahead is the maturing of the baby boomers. This group will be well educated, sophisticated, and relatively well-to-do (see Exhibit 4–4). This demographic trend will offer companies the opportunity to develop new products and services catering to the needs of the aging boomers. Some examples of new-product possibilities include:[7]

[7]Thomas R. King, "Catering to the Maturing Baby-Boom Generation," *The Wall Street Journal, Centennial Edition*, 1989, p. A7. Also, see Judith Waldrop, "Inside America's Households," *American Demographics*, March 1989, p. 20.

EXHIBIT 4-4

Implications of the Graying of America

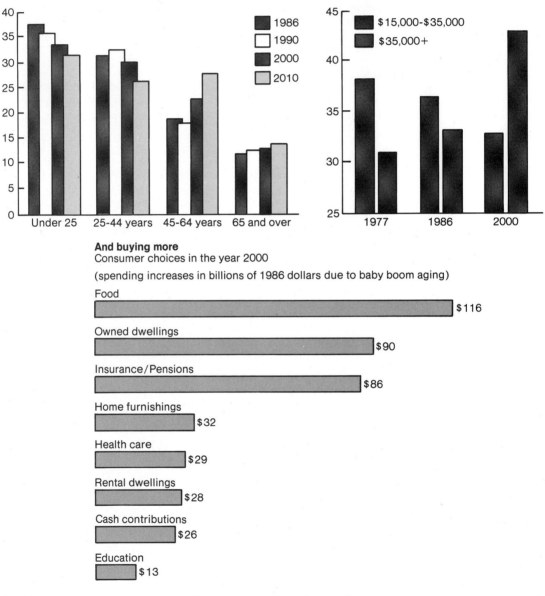

As Americans grow older...
The graying population

(percent of the U.S. population by age group)

- 1986
- 1990
- 2000
- 2010

They'll be wealthier
Household income

(percent of U.S. households;
in 1986 dollars)

- $15,000-$35,000
- $35,000+

And buying more
Consumer choices in the year 2000

(spending increases in billions of 1986 dollars due to baby boom aging)

Food — $116
Owned dwellings — $90
Insurance/Pensions — $86
Home furnishings — $32
Health care — $29
Rental dwellings — $28
Cash contributions — $26
Education — $13

Source: Thomas R. King, "Catering to the Maturing Baby-Boom Generation," *The Wall Street Journal, Centennial Edition,* 1989, p. A7. Based on data prepared by the Institute for the Future and the U.S. Census Bureau.

- Cars with special electronic indicators that alert the driver to the presence of nearby cars.
- Specially designed major appliances with large, easy-to-read knobs.
- High-tech self-monitoring systems that enable people to "test" their health at home.
- Housing systems that provide apartment living with easy access to food and cleaning services for the elderly.
- Drive-in grocery stores.
- Grocery products that restore flavor to foods, to compensate for aging taste buds.

Minorities, especially Hispanics, will become an increasingly important percentage of the U.S. population. Much future U.S. growth will come from immigration, which will further internationalize this country—particularly in such major cities as Los Angeles, San Francisco, Miami, and New York. Products with high ethnic appeal such as food, clothing, and home furnishings will be in strong demand.

Growth

Economic growth is usually measured by the gross national product (GNP), which represents the sum total of all expenditures made on final products. The real annual growth in GNP (corrected for inflation) declined from 4.5 percent in the early 60s to 2.5 percent and less in the late 70s and early mid–80s. GNP is expected to grow at an average of 2.5 percent through the year 2000.[8]

The high economic growth rate following World War II resulted from a number of factors such as a baby boom and an explosion of new technologies. But increased competition from abroad that negatively affected employment, along with higher energy costs, has slowed more recent economic growth. When slow growth is coupled with product maturity, competition heats up. Marketing strategies must be designed with that in mind.

Interest rates

In the early 80s, the U.S. prime interest rate was around 20 percent. Since then it has declined dramatically to around 10 percent, and many economists believe that interest rates will remain relatively low over the next several years. High interest rates adversely affect the market by restricting capital spending and customers' financing capabilities. They particularly affect the demand for consumer durables, such as housing, cars, and heavy appliances.

---

[8]Henry Kaufman, "Fortune Forecast," *Fortune,* December 31, 1990, p. 23.

Currency exchange rates

Fluctuating exchange rates may significantly change the relative price competitiveness of firms that manufacture in different countries. For example, the exchange rate between the U.S. dollar and the Japanese yen changed from 264.45 yen to the dollar on February 13, 1985, to 135.69 in March 1991, a drop of about 50 percent in a little over four years. A weak currency improves a firm's export opportunities; a strong currency places it at a disadvantage. Thus, the fact that the Canadian dollar is weak compared to the U.S. dollar should make it easier for Loblaws to export its line of Green products to the United States.

Given the substantial appreciation of the yen against the dollar—as noted above—Japanese car makers should have nearly doubled their retail prices versus 1985. But the prices of these imports have increased considerably less because the Japanese were fearful of losing market share. The evolution of the exchange rate also pushed the Japanese toward even higher cost effectiveness and the relocation of parts of their production to North America.

International competition

The United States is the largest national market in the world, representing about 25 percent of the total world market for all products and services. In comparison, Japan is the second-largest, with 10 percent of the total world market. The size of the U.S. market makes it a high-priority target for the business firms of most countries, but particularly those of Japan and Western Europe.

Today, about 25 percent of all automobiles sold in the Unites States are from abroad. Japan, in particular, has successfully penetrated the U.S. market with cars, calculators, TVs and radios, motorcycles, binoculars, cameras, and digital watches. But Americans are also familiar with products from Europe, such as Norelco electric shavers (Holland), Volkswagen cars (Germany), Saab cars (Sweden), and Wedgewood china (England).

Businesses in the United States increasingly seek foreign markets. In 1989, over 100 U.S. firms had foreign revenues in excess of $1 billion each. For many of these firms, such as Exxon, Coca-Cola, Colgate-Palmolive, Gillette, and Avon, more than 50 percent of their earnings came from exports.[9]

Both opportunities and threats abound in world trade. Europe's decision to create a truly common market by 1992 with over 300 million consumers has posed a threat to many U.S. companies. The free flow of people, capital, and goods among the nations of the European Economic Community (EEC) may trigger a move to protectionism. If so, U.S. companies already in Europe (such as Ford, GM, IBM) will be better off than those simply exporting to the EEC. Consequently, direct investment in the EEC has increased dramatically. For example, Federal Express has spent $250 million acquiring courier companies in Italy, West Germany, and Holland.

---

[9]"U.S. Firms with the Biggest Foreign Revenues," *Forbes*, July 23, 1990, p. 5.

The political/legal environment

The political/legal environment includes all the factors controlled by public authorities. Its major element is legislation, which defines the regulatory environment within which business must operate. Its key distinctiveness is its ability to impose mandatory constraints on a firm's operations. As with any other external force, the political/legal environment presents strategic opportunities as well as threats to the firm. New regulations or deregulations may open new markets, such as the pollution or energy-control markets. Or the political environment can destabilize an industry and enable the more aggressive firms to improve on their competitive posture. Other elements in the political/legal environment, such as taxes, subsidies, and government contracts, often present opportunities for business firms.

Our review here includes only the major elements of the political/legal environment that have a potential impact on marketing activities: government regulation and deregulation, consumer protection legislation, and other political influences.

Government regulation

The intricacies and sheer number of laws and regulations make it difficult for marketing executives to fully comprehend the regulatory elements that may affect them. This complexity has continually increased, with the federal government creating more than 35 new regulatory agencies since 1950.

A major area of government regulation concerns antitrust legislation, the purpose of which is to maintain and enforce competition. Because marketing activities affect a firm's competitive posture, they are a prime target of antitrust regulations. Firms operating in international markets must also be attentive to antitrust legislation in foreign countries. The antitrust regulations of the EEC are of growing importance. These regulations prohibit agreements between enterprises that restrict or distort competition within the Common Market.

Government deregulation

Government, business, and the general public throughout much of the world have become increasingly aware of the negative effects of overregulation that protects inefficiencies, restricts entry by new competitors, and creates inflationary pressures. A trend started in the United States in the 70s toward a reduction in the administrative and legal barriers to competition—a process called **deregulation**—affects mainly economic regulations controlling the operations of specific industries. Industries that have been deregulated are passenger and cargo airlines, trucking, railroads, telecommunications, banking, and insurance. Markets are now opening up not only in North America and Western Europe but also in Eastern Europe and Asia. Trade barriers that have existed for many decades are crumbling due to political unrest and technological innovation. Many directives for the creation of a single European market deal with the deregulation of a number of industries, including financial services, transportation, and telecommunications.

In discussing the opportunities resulting from deregulation, Bleeke notes that strategies of the firms involved change immediately following deregulation and again about five years later. Thus, the early actions of broad-based competitors include improving pricing capabilities, cutting structural costs, finding new ways to differentiate their services, conserving capital to maintain flexibility, and increasing their marketing skills, especially those relating to new products. Five years later, strategies for the same companies center on fine-tuning pricing capabilities (both offensively and defensively), preempting competitors via strategic alliances, and developing market power (see Exhibit 4–5).[10]

Bleeke goes on to note that the patterns of competition characterizing deregulation in the United States are now occurring in Western Europe:

> The wave of merger, acquisition, and alliance activity that followed U.S. deregulation is also well underway. Air France has acquired control of UTA and Air Inter to become the largest airline in continental Europe. British Airways and KLM are seeking a 20 percent stake in Sabena World Airlines. Similar alliances are emerging in the communications and financial services, suggesting that the powerful series of local oligopolies that characterize the second phase of open-market competition are already developing, even before 1992.[11]

Consumer protection legislation

Consumer protection laws have centered primarily on product safety and information. Although the regulations deal for the most part with consumer goods, they also significantly affect industrial products used in their manufacture. These laws are enforced by more than 50 federal agencies, the most prominent ones being the Food and Drug Administration (FDA) and the Federal Trade Commission (FTC).

The most significant element in the evolution of consumer protection legislation has been the increased recognition of the **strict liability** concept. This makes it possible for a seller to be held responsible for injuries caused by a defective product even though due care was exercised in its preparation and sale. Business firms' responsibilities under strict liability can be substantial: witness the millions of cars that automakers have been forced to recall over the years because of safety-related defects.

Other government influences and actions

There is now a strong and growing public sentiment to do something about air and water pollution, hazardous waste and garbage, and toxic substances. Loblaws's decision to develop and market its Green line of environment-

---

[10]Joel A. Bleeke, "Strategic Choices for Newly Opened Markets," *Harvard Business Review*, September–October 1990, p. 165.

[11]Ibid., p. 165.

EXHIBIT 4-5

After Deregulation, Strategies Change

	Broad-Based Distribution Company	Low-Cost New Entrant	Focused-Segment Marketer	Shared Utility
Key Actions Early On	• Cut costs • Differentiate service • Improve pricing capabilities • Increase marketing, product development • Don't overcommit	• Target the most profitable segments • Eliminate structural costs • Focus on price-sensitive customers and price-oriented advertising • Outsource to limit the scope of operations • Don't grow too fast	• Target nonprice-sensitive segments • Bundle products • Develop customer information systems • Build personal relationships	• Identify separable, scale-intensive functions • Sign up development partners to share costs, provide inputs • Build a core set of clients
Five Years Later . . .	• Develop new oligopolies • Use detailed pricing as a strategic weapon • Preempt competitors via strategic alliances	• Move up the service-price ladder • Identify new niches • Maintain cost advantages • Avoid competing in the core markets of broad-based competitors	• Continue to emphasize early actions • Selectively expand into related segments • Improve customer service • Expand product features to support price	• Become the industry standard by building share • Ensure participation and use by industry players, often by selling minority interests • Move to a high-service, high-price position while increasing customer dependence on the shared utility
Examples	American Airlines Merrill Lynch	Midway Airlines Charles Schwab	Hambrecht & Quist Northern Trust Goldman, Sachs	SABRE SWIFT Telerate Reuters

SOURCE: Joel A. Bleeke, "Strategic Choices for Newly Opened Markets," *Harvard Business Review,* September–October 1990, p. 161.

friendly products resulted largely from the company's awareness of many consumers' strong feelings about the need to protect the environment. The publicity over acid rain, toxic landfills, droughts, the Exxon Valdez oil tragedy and, more recently, Saddam Hussein's dumping of oil into the Persian Gulf has led to a new activism by the general public.

The government has responded by passing a new and much tougher Clean Air Act (1990), which mandates further reductions in pollutants. This dramatically affects producers of automobiles and trucks, farm machinery, gasoline, alternative fuels (coal and natural gas), chemicals, utilities, and smokestack industries in general. Some experts put the annual cost of implementing this bill at $25 billion a year. Ford Motor Company says it could be forced to discontinue its line of full-sized pickup trucks, and oil companies contend they don't know how to produce a gasoline that will burn the required 15 to 20 percent cleaner than current gasolines. The act has revived interest in the production of electric cars.[12] Some states and large municipalities (e.g., Los Angeles) are going farther by targeting such products as chemical coolants used by the air conditioning and refrigeration industries, nonbiodegradable diapers, and nonrecyclable plastics contained in throwaway food containers.[13]

The $25 billion annual cost of the Clean Air Act will provide important opportunities for many firms. For example, the bill's requirement to clean up tail-pipe exhaust will benefit producers of filters and catalytic converters; additives to make gasoline burn cleaner; baking soda, which cleans up sulfur dioxide emission from utility boilers; precious metals used to meet the new exhaust standards; and corn, which is used to make ethanol (a substitute fuel). Unfortunately, the new law will also benefit an industry that has moved overseas—which makes scrubbers or flue-gas desulfurization systems used to reduce acid rain and, in general, clean up emissions from utilities.[14]

In an effort to meet government fuel economy standards, Mercedes Benz is introducing three diesel models after practically eliminating diesels from its U.S. line during recent years. It's clear that Mercedes is concerned that these standards will increase in the future—perhaps to an average of over 40 miles per gallon for a company's annual output by the year 2000. The new diesels won't, however, be sold in California because they can't meet the state's strict emissions standards. See Krystal Miller, "Mercedes to Introduce Three Diesel Models to Help It Meet U.S. Fuel Standards," *The Wall Street Journal,* September 11, 1990, p. A–16.

The technological environment

Technology is the driving force behind the development of many new products and markets, but it is also a major reason for the decline of some products and markets. It can have a substantial impact on an industry's performance; for example, consider the effect of genetic engineering on pharmaceuticals, of transistors on telecommunications, and of plastics on the use of metals.

Dramatic acceleration has occurred in identifying the commercial potential of technological developments. Thus, the time between ideas, invention, and

---

[12]David Woodruff, John Rossant, and Karen Lowry Miller, "GM Drives the Electric Car Closer to Reality," *Business Week,* March 14, 1990, p. 60.

[13]David A. Landes, "Tighter Rules Put Squeeze on Firms," *USA Today,* May 28, 1989, p. 13.

[14]Rose Gutfeld, "For Each Dollar Spent on Cleaner Air Someone Stands to Make a Buck," *The Wall Street Journal,* October 29, 1990, p. A–7.

commercialization has decreased. In particular, new technologies affecting production will be adopted more quickly.[15]

The importance of external technological change

Most companies try to develop new products internally through their R&D departments. But they are often affected by technological innovations that first occurred in other firms, including those outside their industry. U.S. R&D is still the most productive in the world, although in recent years, Japan and, to a lesser extent, West Germany and France have made considerable progress.

Specific signals of technological change include patents, trend analyses of product performance, industrial and governmental research budgets, and economic, political, and social pressures. These need to be carefully scrutinized, or firms may overlook substantial threats and opportunities, as happened in the development of xerography. In the early 1940s, both IBM and Eastman Kodak learned about Chester Carlson's first patent on xerography, but neither company took any significant action. In 1948, the little Haloid Company (now the Xerox Company) held a widely acclaimed demonstration but received no industry reaction. Less than a decade later, however, this form of copying was widely used both in the United States and Europe.

In addition to forwarding the creation of new products, technological developments have an impact on all marketing activities, including *communications,* by making available new media or new selling tools; *distribution,* by opening new channels or modifying the operations and performance of existing outlets; *packaging,* by allowing the use of new materials or designs (e.g., Loblaws launched its environment-friendly products in green packaging made from recycled paper); *marketing research,* by making feasible new data-gathering and analysis techniques; and *marketing decision making,* by offering improved procedures and computerized models.

Intensification of technological development

In the past 10 to 12 years, an amazing number of new technologies have brought such new products as videocassette recorders, compact discs, ever-more-powerful/ever-smaller computers, and highly effective genetically engineered drugs. Many researchers predict that technological progress between now and the year 2000 will be 10 times that experienced during the past decade,[16] much of it will be spurred by the need to find solutions to our environmental problems. Major technological innovations can be expected in a variety of fields, especially in biology, electronics/telecommunications, and manufactured materials.

---

[15]Marvin J. Cetron, Wanda Rocha, and Rebecca Luckens, "Into the 21st Century," *The Futurists,* July–August 1988, p. 30.

[16]Bylinsky, "Technology in the Year 2000," *Fortune,* July 18, 1988, p. 92.

The *biological revolution* is of fairly recent origins. By modifying the hereditary characteristics of bacteria, biologists have opened whole new areas of research concerned with such subjects as enhancing the body's ability to heal itself and the possibility of regrowing whole organs in the body. Plans are under way to map all human genes—some 50,000 to 100,000—by the year 2005. This undertaking would include identifying each gene's function and how each learns how to follow instructions.[17] Anticipated applications of this new technology in the pharmaceutical and agricultural areas include:

- In *pharmaceuticals:* production of pure pharmaceutical substances such as insulin and interferon; production of human growth hormones to cure dwarfism and prevent muscle wastage; and introduction of powerful genetically engineered vaccines to eliminate many infectious diseases, including AIDS.
- In *agriculture:* production of more resistant livestock and new species of animals, more resistant plants, nonpolluting biological pesticides and insecticides, and protein by fermentation of algae or by the action of yeasts on hydrocarbons.

It is still too soon to comprehend all the ethical issues and potential applications of biotechnology. But it will affect other industries in addition to those listed above; and it can be expected to have a deep, long-term impact on our society.

Electronics have played an important role in our society since the 1950s. They were first used in such limited areas as computers, radio, and television. As technology improved, electronics contributed to the development of new products like digital watches, automatic cameras, video games, and microcomputers. By the year 2000, we can expect the following with respect to computers.[18]

- Supercomputers that are 1,000 times more powerful than those of today. They are expected to do at least 4 trillion complex calculations a second.
- Pocket-size computers that will respond to handwritten and human voice commands.
- Electronic storage computers that can store up to 200 novels or nonfiction volumes, any one of which is available on command.
- Increasing use of the computer as an instrument of discovery; for example, simulating how the body reacts to a given disease or how an automobile handles before it is built.
- More effective linkage of computers with other electronic machines; for example, as with medical diagnostic machines.

Without computers, much of the progress in biology, electronics, and the development of new materials would not be possible.

---

[17]Tim Friend, "Gene Project Maps the 'Book of Life'," *USA Today,* October 2, 1989.
[18]Bylinsky, "Technology in the Year 2000," p. 92–6.

EXHIBIT 4–6

Telecommunications and Dow Jones Profits

In recent years, *The Wall Street Journal*'s circulation has declined 7.5 percent, and much the same has happened to advertising lineage. Operating income from the *Journal* and Dow Jones' other business publications—*Barron's* and the *Asian Wall Street Journal*—has dropped 44 percent in the last two years. In contrast, Dow Jones' Information Services, which distributes financial news to desktop terminals, has increased its operating profits 69 percent over the past two years to $70 million. In addition, Dow Jones gets the benefit of its 67 percent equity interest in Telerate—a service that electronically transmits government bond prices to traders. In 1988, Telerate contributed $141 million to Dow's profits. In short, business publications that accounted for some 90 percent of Dow Jones' operating income early in the 1980s now account for only 31 percent.

Source: Alex Taylor, III, "A Tale Dow Jones Won't Tell," *Fortune*, July 3, 1989, p. 100.

Another area of particular importance is the increasing interaction between electronics and communications called *telecommunications*. This interaction allows for an easier transmission of data between persons, computers, and a variety of devices through cables, microwave relays, and satellites. In the near future, we can expect much-improved telephone lines permitting simultaneous transmission of voice, video, and data.[19] For an illustration of how newer developments in telecommunications are affecting the profits of a well-known American corporation, see Exhibit 4–6.

A third megatechnology has to do with such *manufactured materials* as high-performance plastics, which include composites based on carbon fibers, and superconducting ceramics. The two main areas of application for such plastics are in cars and planes. General Motors anticipates that within the next few years 20 percent of its cars will have all-plastic bodies that will reduce weight, thereby increasing fuel economy.

The new ceramics are lighter, stronger, and much more durable than many metals. They are currently used in knives, scissors, batteries, and artificial limbs. Engines and electronics will benefit most from the use of such materials. Nissan, for example, is using a ceramic turbo rotor in its 300ZX sports car because of its ability to tolerate temperatures up to 1500° C without lubrication.

Biomaterials made of plastics, composites, and ceramics are used to replace or augment bodily tissues, organs, and parts. Replacement joints and bone implants are now widely available, as are artificial tendons and ligaments. The implementation of artificial lenses is already widely practiced. Within a few years, synthetic human skin will help heal severe burns.[20]

---

[19]Ibid., p. 96.

[20]Tom Forester, "The Materials Revolution," *The Futurist*, July–August 1988, pp. 13–20.

Marketing strategy for high-technology products

In most cases, the firm should target a limited number of market segments because the new product is likely to have limited appeal, at least initially. Such a strategy enables the firm to focus on a smaller product line, to use specialized distribution with a talented salesforce, and to concentrate on limited but effective vertical trade shows and publications serving the target group. Focus also enables the company to devote its R&D efforts to developing products that serve a precise customer base, lowering relative per-unit costs (via scale and learning effects) at a faster rate than if the company held a smaller share of a broader market. The firm can thus better serve major customers. When a company's resources are targeted in this manner, the cumulative investment in the specific market can be quite large relative to competition—especially large competitors attempting to serve a broad market.

Davidow notes that technology marketing is essentially concerned with direct sales, including postsales service; training and supporting channels of distribution, where appropriate; and customer knowledge, including application support. He reports that in the computer business and related fields it is not uncommon to have companies spend over 20 percent of their revenues on sales, service, and postsales support. In addition, a large amount of money is spent on product documentation.[21]

As a high-technology industry moves into the growth stage it is apt to encounter more consolidation via mergers and acquisitions. It is anticipated that on average 25 biotechnology companies a year will disappear, through merger, acquisition, or failure. By the year 2000, it is expected that more than half the world's 400 biotechnology companies will be gone. New product development is critical, but being first in the market does not guarantee success since followers may develop more effective and/or less expensive entries.[22]

The sociocultural environment

This environment represents the values, attributes, and general behavior of the individuals in a given society, which evolve more slowly than the other environments. Transformations in the structure of a society, in its institutions, and in the distribution of wealth occur gradually in democratic countries. Even so, in recent years we have seen substantial changes in individual values, family structure, minority rights, leisure-time activities, and conservation. These changes have affected the sale of personal consumer products; advertising programs to accommodate more joint decision making; the creation of special marketing programs for minority groups; the popularity of fast-food outlets; and the emergence of more energy-saving, reliable, and longer-lasting products. Two of the more important evolutionary trends have involved individual values and the family structure.

---

[21]William H. Davidow, *Marketing High Technology* (New York: The Free Press, 1986), p. 33.

[22]"Biotechnology," *Chemical Week,* September 27, 1989, p. 31.

The evolution of individual values

North American society has traditionally been characterized by such values as the Puritan ethic of hard work, thriftiness, and faith in others and in institutions. In the 60s, however, a new social force emerged that did not entirely share these values. Instead of leaving the destiny of their country in the hands of their elders and institutions, the young—particularly college students—collectively fought aggressively for causes such as civil rights, the end of the Vietnam war, and individual nonconformism. The young emerged as a new social force, sharing and defending a common set of new values even across national borders. This era is often referred to as the "Age of Us."

More recently, individual values shifted again for a variety of reasons, including "a new sense of lowered expectations, apprehensions about the future, mistrust of institutions, and a growing sense of limits.[23] Thus, individuals are becoming more concerned about self-actualization, or the quality of life, than security. The meaning of work, relations with the opposite sex, and the importance of inner harmony underwent change as more people questioned the traditional ways of defining success.[24] As a consequence of this trend, marriages were postponed, birthrates dropped, divorce rates skyrocketed, and young women in the millions joined the labor force. Increasingly, marketers find that consumers are preoccupied with maintaining economic stability in an environment perceived as hostile. Other changes include more concern about health, the environment (which shows itself in the willingness to support the efforts of manufacturers such as Loblaws, who market environment-friendly products), sexuality, travel, education, creativity, and because of our success in the Persian Gulf war, patriotism. Exhibit 4–7 lists the shift in values occurring in Western societies.[25]

The evolution of family structure

The traditional husband-dominated, closely structured family is less and less typical of our North American society. Children are becoming more autonomous and participate at an earlier age in many family decisions. A more balanced allocation of power between husband and wife has also emerged. This is partly because more women are more independent economically. Working parents' absence from the home has substantially reduced the interactions among family members, eroding cohesiveness. The rising divorce rate has made one-parent households commonplace.

This evolution has considerably changed the buying process for many goods. Often today, all family members influence the purchase of such major durables as housing, cars, furniture, and appliances. The influence of men on

---

[23]Daniel Yankelovich as quoted by Joseph T. Plummer, "Changing Values," *The Futurist,* January–February 1989, p. 8.

[24]Ibid., pp. 8–13.

[25]Also, see Marvin Cetron and Owen Davis, *American Renaissance* (New York: St. Martin's Press, 1989), chap. 18; and Oxford Analytica, *America in Perspective* (Boston, Mass.: Houghton Mifflin Company, 1986), chap. 3.

EXHIBIT 4–7

Shifting Values in the Western World

Traditional values	New values
Self-denial ethic	Self-fulfillment ethic
Higher standard of living	Better quality of life
Traditional sex roles	Blurring of sex roles
Accepted definition of success	Individualized definition of success
Traditional family life	Alternative families
Faith in industry, institutions	Self-reliance
Live to work	Work to live
Hero worship	Love of ideas
Expansionism	Pluralism
Patriotism	Less nationalistic
Unparalleled growth	Growing sense of limits
Industrial growth	Information/service growth
Receptivity of technology	Technology orientation

Developed Western societies are gradually moving away from traditional values and toward the emerging new values being embraced on an ever-widening scale, says author Plummer.

Source: "Changing Values. The New Emphasis on Self-Actualization," *The Futurist,* January–February 1989, p. 15.

food purchases compared with that of women has risen in households where both spouses work outside the home. Consequently, many food firms are redirecting some of their marketing communications from media aimed primarily at women to those appealing to men and children.

Competitive analysis

The competitive environment is typically of more immediate importance to most managers than the other environments discussed thus far and hence is treated as a separate and distinct subject area. More and more U.S. firms are setting up in-house organizations to gather and analyze competitive intelligence. (See Exhibit 4–8 for examples of successful competitive intelligence projects.) Why the recent interest in this subject area? The main reason seems to be that competition has intensified as well as become global. As industries mature and growth slows, increased business can only come from competitors. Thus, companies are forced to pay more attention to strategies designed to exploit their competitors' weaknesses.

Any analysis of the competitive environment must consider two major areas of investigation. The first has to do with industry structure and how the interplay of various competitive forces affect the industry's long-term profitability. The second deals with knowing the competitive position, strategy, and the strengths and weaknesses of a firm's close rivals. This helps the firm to better anticipate what competitors will do in the future and how it

EXHIBIT 4–8

Some Examples of Competitive Intelligence

Americans are beginning to learn from the Japanese that competitive intelligence is critically important and that intelligence gathering should be given a high priority in the organization. More and more U.S. companies are spending an increasing amount of money on competitive intelligence. For example, McDonnell Douglas used such intelligence to proceed with the development of a new prop fan airliner. It did so only after a specially assembled team studied Boeing's finances, R&D commitments, production capacity, and the like before concluding that the rival could not produce such an aircraft as cheaply as could McDonnell Douglas.

Coors wanted back into the wine cooler business despite an earlier failure. An intelligence task force determined that Coors could not compete on price against Gallo because the latter paid less for its grapes. Management reluctantly decided to cancel its plans for another wine cooler entry.

Marriott decided to spend $500 million for a new hotel chain because management was sure it would beat the competition in every respect. It made the decision only after an intelligence team toured the country gathering firsthand information about the various players in the economy hotel segment.

SOURCE: Brian Dumaine, "Corporate Spies Snoop to Conquer," *Fortune,* November 7, 1988, p. 68.

will respond to the competitor's moves. For example, in the highly competitive beer business, Coors keeps track of the activities of five major domestic competitors and four foreign beer companies. Once the company knows what action the competition is taking, it decides what response(s) to make.[26] We are concerned here with the second subject area—**competitor analysis.** Industry structure is discussed in the next chapter.

INDIVIDUAL COMPETITOR ANALYSIS

The major steps in an analysis of individual competitors is shown in Exhibit 4–9. After identifying present and potential close rivals, the analysis consists of examining objectives, strategies, performance to date, and strengths and weaknesses and then predicting the future behavior of each, including the likelihood that each will change its strategy and how it will respond to moves made by others.

Competitor's objectives

Analysis of a competitor's objectives is important for several reasons. It provides insights into whether the competitor is satisfied with its profitability and its current market position and thus how likely it is to retain its present strategy. It helps a firm predict how the competition will respond to changes

---

[26]Cyndee Miller, "Intelligence Systems," *Marketing News,* May 9, 1988, p. 2.

E X H I B I T   4 – 9
Competitor Evaluation Process

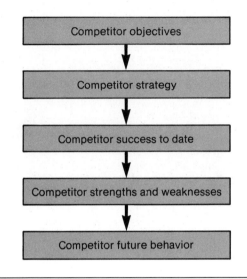

in the environment, such as a sharp decrease in demand. And it is a predictor of how the firm will react to a competitor's particular strategic move.

Objectives usually include more than simply financial goals. Most also include competitive position (market share) and such qualitative objectives as industry leadership in price, product technology, and social responsibility. Managers must know which trade-offs the competitor will make between these and its economic (profitability) objectives during times of stress. For example, at the *business-unit level* managers typically try to get answers to the following questions.[27]

- What are the competitor's financial and market position objectives? How are trade-offs made between these objectives, especially short term versus long term? How does the competitor balance its rate of growth and return on assets managed?

- What are the competitor's apparent expectations for some of its activities, and how do they affect its objectives? Does it think of itself as the market leader? The price leader? The technological leader? Is the competitor, in fact, the leader it perceives itself to be in a given field? What will it pay to remain the leader?

- What incentive and control systems does the competitor use? How do these affect management's response to competitive action?

---

[27]Based on Porter, *Competitive Strategy,* pp. 51–7.

EXHIBIT 4–10
Clorox versus P&G

> Clorox Co. president Jack Collins is upping the ante in his battle with Procter &
> Gamble Co.
>
>   Defending its lead in the $600 million liquid chlorine bleach market, the company has
> begun testing Clorox Lemon Scent liquid chlorine bleach in Houston with TV ad sup-
> port, via Foote, Cone & Belding, San Francisco.
>
>   The move is significant because the product is going head-to-head with a similar new
> P&G product in an anticipated battle between two major household product companies.
>
>   In an interview with *Advertising Age,* Mr. Collins, who is also the marketer's chief
> operating officer, said, "Liquid bleach is our largest brand from the standpoint of volume
> and overall contribution to the company's earnings. Any time a competitor, and espe-
> cially an established, well-respected company like P&G comes in . . . I don't like to use
> the word concern, but it's of keen interest to us."
>
>   Market analysts contend Clorox's Lemon Scent test is a signal to P&G that it will not
> take any challenge to its core business.

SOURCE: Jennifer Pendleton, "Clorox Ups Ante in War with P&G," *Advertising Age,* August 1988, p. 1.

- What is the background of the competitor's key executives? What func-
  tional areas have they managed? What companies have they worked for?
- What successes or failures of consequence has the competitor had re-
  cently? Will these affect future behavior? How?
- Does the competitor have any commitments that may inhibit action?
  (Commitments may or may not be contractual and include licensing,
  debt, and joint ventures.)
- Does the competitor have any regulatory constraints on its behavior?
  (This constraint can be inferred, for example, when a large firm is reluc-
  tant to respond to the price moves made by a small competitor.)

In addition to these, a firm needs to make inquiries about the parent organization since, directly or indirectly, it may impose constraints on the behavior of its SBUs. Thus, the following questions need to be asked at the
corporate level of the competitor:

- What are the parent company's objectives and how important is the SBU
  in helping attain these objectives?
- How successful has the parent been, and how does this affect its reaction
  to the SBU's performance?
- What strategic value does the SBU have in the parent's overall strategy?
  A large and successful parent that has assigned an important strategic
  role to an SBU is likely to react strongly to any action by a competitor
  it perceives as threatening. For an example of such a situation, see Exhibit 4–10.
- What is the economic relationship between the SBU and other SBUs?
  That is, to what extent do they involve shared costs or complementary
  products?

A portfolio analysis of the competitor's company can often provide answers to many of these questions. In particular, such an analysis should reveal how the competitor fits into the overall needs of the parent and how it relates to the firm's other SBUs (as, for example, in the area of shared costs).

Competitor's strategy

This component of the analysis reviews past and present strategies of each major competitor. Past strategies provide insights into failures and reveal how the firm engineered changes, especially in new product-market relationships. Such historical information helps anticipate which strategic marketing programs the competitor might use in the future. For example, Philip Morris has traditionally emphasized programs that stressed heavy brand advertising (to support a desired brand image), low costs, and maximum product availability with its cigarette, beer, and food products—and with considerable success.

Competitor's success to date

The next step is to evaluate how successful the competitor has been in achieving its objectives and carrying out its strategies. Profitability measures may be difficult when the competitor is part of a large corporate entity and even more difficult where specific product-market entries are concerned. It is often possible, however, to obtain reliable estimates of sales and market share even at the segment level from a variety of sources, including syndicated commercial service organizations (see appendix at the end of the text).

Another important indicator is the number of times the competitor has failed or succeeded in recent years. The memory of past successes or failures can affect a competitor's confidence for better or worse. In a similar vein, a firm should examine how the competitor responded over the years to market and industry changes, including strategy moves made by other firms. Was there a response? How quickly? Was it a rational or emotional response? Was it successful?

Competitor's strengths and weaknesses

To a considerable extent, knowledge of a competitor's strengths and weaknesses derives from the previous steps taken in the competitor analysis. This information is important, especially when tied to the competitor's objectives and strategies. Any evaluation of strengths and weaknesses must take into account the relative importance of the major components of the strategic marketing program required to exploit the situation. Ideally, a firm would take advantage of a competitor's weakness using the firm's own strength. For a listing of areas that relate to strengths and weaknesses, see Exhibit 4–11.

EXHIBIT 4-11
Areas Relating to Competitor's Strengths and Weaknesses

Innovation
Technical product/service superiority
New-product capacity
R&D
Technologies
Patents

Manufacturing
Cost structure
Flexible production operations
Equipment
Access to new material
Vertical integration
Workforce attitudes and motivation
Capacity

Finance—access to capital
From net short-term assets
Ability to use debt and equity financing
Parent's willingness to finance

Management
Quality of top and middle management
Knowledge of business
Corporate culture

Strategic goals and plans
Entrepreneurial thrust
Planning/operations system
Loyalty/turnover
Quality of strategic decision making

Marketing
Product quality/reputation
Product characteristics/differentiation
Brand name recognition
Breadth of product line/systems
  capability
Customer orientation
Segmentation/focus
Distribution
Retailer relationships
Advertising/promotion skills
Salesforce
Customer service/product support

Customer base
Size and loyalty
Market share
Growth of segments served

SOURCE: David A. Aaker, *Strategic Marketing Management* (New York: John Wiley & Sons, 1988), p. 84.

Competitor's future behavior

The objective of the analysis thus far has been to assess the competitor's likely future behavior in terms of its objectives and strategies. To develop a response profile for each key competitor, analysts ask the following questions. The answers should help the firm decide which competitors to target within each major segment and which strategies to use.

- How satisfied is the competitor with its current position?
- How likely is the competitor to change its current strategy? What specific changes will it likely make?
- How much weight will the competitor put behind such changes?
- How will other competitors likely respond to these moves? How will those responses affect the competitor initiating the changes?
- What opportunities does the competitor provide its close rivals? Will these opportunities endure for some time or will they close down shortly?
- How effective will the competitor be in responding to environmental change, including moves made by its competitors? Which events and

moves can it respond to well and which poorly? For each event or move, what retaliatory action is most likely?

To answer questions like these requires a great deal of information about present and potential competitors. The appendix at the end of the text discusses not only the major sources of competitive information but provides examples of intelligence gathering as well.

STRATEGIC ENVIRONMENTAL ISSUE MANAGEMENT

Most managers are aware of the importance of environmental analysis but also know the many difficulties involved in making such an analysis operational. They need a system that enables them to identify, evaluate, and respond to environmental issues that may affect the firm's longer-term profitability and market position. One such approach, termed **strategic environmental issue management,** is used by many well-known companies, including Coca-Cola, Bank of America, General Electric, Whirlpool, and Travelers Insurance. Basically, it consists of a four-stage process.[28]

1. *Environmental scanning.* This activity systematically seeks information about the various elements of the environment and detects new developments. It requires special expertise and extensive information systems and is usually performed by a central staff such as a strategic planning service.

2. *Key environmental issue identification.* New environmental developments detected by a scanning system may have a significant impact on some activities of the firm. These are isolated for further consideration. In particular, key issues that have marketing implications are brought to the attention of marketing executives. It is a narrowing process that starts with a mass of data and screens those likely to have an impact on the business.

3. *Impact evaluation.* The managers directly affected evaluate the potential impact of key environmental issues. A key environmental issue may represent a marketing opportunity or threat; managers must ascertain its short- and long-term implications.

4. *Formulation of a response strategy.* Given the foreseeable impact of a key environmental issue, managers must formulate an appropriate response strategy. The set of feasible response strategies includes a status-quo or wait-and-see position if the impact is not sufficiently significant or too uncertain. Issue management does not involve the handling of a crisis, which, by definition, is an event too difficult to predict but that has a great effect on the business. (We discuss this under contingency planning, which is part of the last chapter.)

---

[28]See H. Igor Ansoff, "Strategic Issue Management," *Strategic Management Journal* 1 (1980), pp. 131–48.

Note the different organizational responsibilities for the various stages of the strategic environmental issue management process. Environmental scanning and identifying key issues are done at the corporate level by a special staff. Different functional area managers participate by providing information gathered as part of their normal activities. The output of these two stages are communicated to the appropriate areas of the firm for evaluation.

Impact evaluation and formulation of a response strategy are the responsibility of the executives whose areas may be affected by specific issues. These managers should have the expertise needed to deal with such issues. Moreover, they are the ones who have to live with the consequences of their actions.

Environmental scanning

A business has three ways of organizing its scanning activities: via line managers (as was the case at Loblaws, where Nichols recognized the opportunity of producing an environment-friendly line of products), a strategic planning group, or a special office responsible for such scanning.

If the first alternative is adopted, environmental scanning is more of an ad hoc rather than continuous activity. When either scanning or strategic planning officers are present, the environment is likely to be monitored continuously, and ad hoc studies are made on request from an SBU.[29]

The organization and extent of a firm's scanning activities depend primarily on the complexity and stability of its environment. A firm operating in a complex and dynamic environment is more vulnerable and requires a more complete scanning system than one operating in a relatively simple and static environment.

Key environmental issue identification

In any given period many issues may be detected that could change the environment. Somehow the system must determine (1) the *probability* that an issue can materialize into an opportunity or a threat, and (2) the *degree of impact* it can have on the firm.

Initially, environmental issues are evaluated judgmentally on these two dimensions, using the information available to identify the more important issues. Each issue is then plotted on a opportunity/threat matrix that graphically shows their relative importance. The matrix in Exhibit 4–12 contains four potential events a large electrical utility might have identified in the late 1980s. The probability of each occurring by 1995 was rated, as was its impact on the utility's profitability. Those events having the greatest impact appear in the upper-left box of the exhibit.

---

[29]John C. Camillus, *Strategic Planning and Management Control*, pp. 226–28.

EXHIBIT 4–12

Opportunity/Threat Matrix for Electric Utility Company

		Probability of occurrence	
Level of impact	High →	4	1
	Low →	2	3

1. Fluidized-bed combustion technology, which can remove 95 percent of coal's sulfur without a scrubber, will be available by 1995.
2. Compressed air energy storage technology will become available at an affordable cost for the storage of electricity by 1995.
3. New small modular nuclear reactors that cannot release radioactivity into the environment will be available by 1995.
4. Given present trends in the demand for electricity and the rate at which new capacity is being added, a wave of blackouts can be expected to strike this state by 1995.

The opportunity/threat matrix enables the handling of a large number of events. Indeed, its function is to process events in such a way that management can focus on the most important ones. Thus, events with a high probability of occurring *and* a high impact on the business should be monitored with great care and frequency. Those with a low probability of occurring and a low impact should probably be dropped, at least for the time being. Events with a low probability/high impact should be reexamined at frequent intervals; those with a high probability/low impact should be reexamined less frequently to determine if the impact rating remains basically sound.

Impact evaluation

Determining the impact of a key environmental issue requires answering four basic questions:

1. Does the issue represent an opportunity or a threat to the firm?
2. How significant will its impact be on the operations and performance of the firm?
3. What is the likely timing of its impact?
4. What are the specific marketing areas it will impact?

Analysts can chart the first three considerations for key environmental issues on a graph called an **opportunity/threat profile** (see Exhibit 4–13). The horizontal axis of the graph corresponds to the estimated timing of the environmental event. (The width of the box indicates the extent of uncertainty about the timing.) The vertical axis represents its impact on a performance measure such as profits or market share. (The length of the box indicates the extent of uncertainty about the profit impact.) Environmental issues be-

EXHIBIT 4-13
Opportunity/Threat Profile

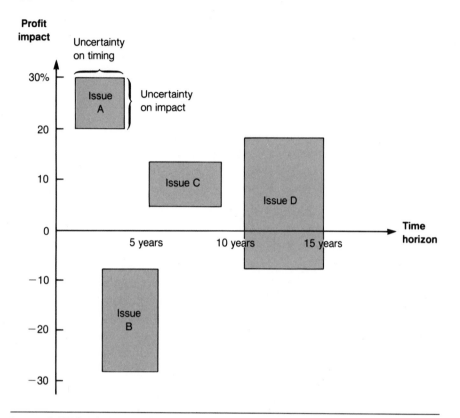

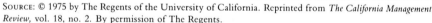

Source: © 1975 by The Regents of the University of California. Reprinted from *The California Management Review,* vol. 18, no. 2. By permission of The Regents.

low the time horizon imply potential losses in performance; those above indicate gains.[30]

In Exhibit 4–13, issues A and C are opportunities, although A is more immediate and significant. Issue B represents a definite threat, but there is substantial uncertainty about its impact level. Issue D is remote in the future, and there is considerable uncertainty concerning both its timing and impact. It could either be a substantial opportunity or have a limited negative effect on the firm's profitability.

It is often desirable to undertake a cross-impact analysis in an effort to forecast the occurrence of an event. For example, will electric cars account

---

[30]The opportunity/threat profile representation was proposed by H. Igor Ansoff, "Managing Strategic Surprise by Response to Weak Signals," *California Management Review,* Winter 1975, pp. 21–33.

for 10 percent of the new cars sold in the United States by the year 2000? The probability of this occurring would then be estimated by considering the simultaneous impact other events would have on this estimate, such as the development of longer-lasting (four versus the present two years) and faster-charging (one hour versus overnight) batteries; lighter-weight cars (one-third as heavy); and that the cost of a gallon of gasoline by the year 2000 would be $1.50 or more (in present dollars).

Of particular interest to the firm is the relative impact of a key environmental issue. That is, within the same industry some firms perceive a given issue as an opportunity and others see it as a threat. For example, the energy crisis provided a major opportunity for Japanese and European automakers to increase their exports of fuel-efficient cars to the United States. It posed a severe threat, however, to U.S. manufacturers of larger, less fuel-efficient cars.

Formulation of response strategies

The expression **response strategy** indicates a response to an environmental issue—one not necessarily undertaken after the event. It includes both reactive and proactive strategies. This assumes a time interval between the identification of a key issue and the event it triggers. A **reactive strategy** is undertaken in response to a major environmental event, often in a crisis situation. A **proactive strategy** is formulated in response to a key environmental issue and in anticipation of its becoming an event; for example, Loblaws's Green line in response to the public's growing concern about the deterioration of the environment.

A proactive strategy is usually more desirable than a reactive one. It avoids making pressure decisions and enables the firm to perform more in-depth analyses. Further, the greater the lead time, the broader the array of options. Reactive strategies benefit from more information being available and consequently less uncertainty about the event.

Exhibit 4–14 discusses and provides examples of six response strategies that can be fashioned in either a reactive or proactive mode. Most marketing strategies are more reactive than proactive; they derive from a set of environmental constraints already defined by management. Many consider adaptation to external forces the essence of the marketing concept. In recent years, however, more writers have advocated that marketing managers emphasize proactive response strategies whenever possible. They suggest changing the context in which the organization operates by extending the firm's influence over the environment. The present movement toward innovative, entrepreneurial management captures the essence of this perspective,[31] as shown in

---

[31]Carl P. Zeithaml and Valarie A. Zeithaml, "Environmental Management: Revising the Marketing Perspective," *Journal of Marketing,* Spring 1984, p. 49.

EXHIBIT 4-14
Response Strategies to Environmental Issues

1. **Opposition strategy:** The effectiveness of this strategy is limited because environmental factors are largely beyond the control of a firm. In some situations, a firm may, however, try to delay, attenuate, or otherwise influence an environmental force. Lobbying and corporate issue advertising are examples of opposition strategy used by some large firms to sensitize the public to their point of view and to influence the evolution of legislation. One example is the National Rifle Association, which opposes gun control legislation.

2. **Adaptation strategy:** Adaptations are often compulsory as, for example, is the case with legislation on product specifications, packaging, and labeling. Choices often exist, however, in the type and extent of adaptation. The danger is that if an adaptation strategy is pursued to the extreme, the environment (not management) sets the pace and scope of strategic change. For example, in response to mandatory fuel economy standards, a major strategy available to auto makers was to downsize existing fleets. This increased gas mileage while avoiding substantial retooling expenses.

3. **Offensive strategy:** Such a strategy uses the environmental issue to improve the firm's competitive position. A key environmental issue may have a destabilizing effect on an industry, which may create opportunities for the more aggressive firms. For example, because of increased cost, federal and state regulation, and risk, the operators of toxic waste dumps have been under economic pressure. Waste Management, Inc., the nation's largest hazardous-waste company which owes much of its success to its large landfill business, is increasingly directing more of its research to innovative disposal methods, including biotechnology.*

4. **Redeployment strategy:** Faced with major environmental issues in one market, a firm may decide to redeploy its resources in other less-exposed areas. For example, tobacco companies such as Philip Morris and R. J. Reynolds have diversified into other consumer goods because of the environmental pressures concerning the health effects of cigarette smoking and the resulting less-attractive long-term prospects of their prime market.

5. **Contingency strategies:** One such strategy decreases the risk of being exposed to potentially harmful environmental events. For example, a search may be launched for substitutes for raw materials with volatile prices.

   Another contingency strategy designs alternative courses of action corresponding to the different possible evolutions of the environment. This involves isolating discrete environmental scenarios the firm may have to face in the future and designing appropriate responses for each. For example, given the possibility that the use of saccharin might be banned in drugs, cosmetics, soft drinks, and food, Plough, Inc., the maker of St. Joseph's Aspirin for Children and Maybelline Cosmetics, developed other sweetening agents that could be substituted for saccharin if necessary.†

6. **Passive strategy:** This strategy calls for not responding to an environmental threat or opportunity. For example, in the early days of modern consumerism, some corporations took major public action to oppose their critics—which only provided greater exposure to the issue and worsened their images. A better alternative would have been not to have taken *any* action until performing more complete analyses and formulating an appropriate response.

*Ken Wells, "Toxic Waste Disposal Firms Enter High Technology Era," *The Wall Street Journal,* October 10, 1987, p. 27.

†See "Drugmakers Seek a Substitute Sweetener," *Business Week,* December 11, 1978, p. 68 D-1.

Nichols's actions in developing a line of Green products in but a few months. In brief, this approach emphasizes that "marketing is a significant force which the organization can call upon to create change and extend its influence over the environment."[32]

SUMMARY

External analysis is concerned not only with the market and the industry but also with the environmental trends affecting them. The deteriorating physical environment is rightly a cause of considerable concern, although the effects may be long term. The demographic/economic environment has the most pervasive impact on marketing. The elements most likely to affect marketing strategies are demographics, economic growth, interest rates, and currency exchange rates. The political/legal environment includes all those factors controlled by authorities. The major factor here is legislation that defines the regulatory environment within which businesses must operate. The influence of the political/legal environment is not necessarily negative—opportunities may also be provided.

Technology can have a substantial impact on the performance and competitive structure of an industry. The pace of technological development has been increasing and promises to become even more intensive in the future. It is difficult to predict the exact timing of a basic discovery. Three technologies having a significant influence on the future of our society are electronics/telecommunications, biology, and manufactured materials.

The sociocultural environment, which evolves slowly, represents the values, attitudes, and general behavior of people in a given society. Some of the more significant trends involve shifts in individual values toward self-realization and fulfillment, recognition of minority rights, changes in family structure, and concern about the environment.

Competitive analysis involves an industry and individual close competitors. Only the latter is discussed in this chapter. The process consists of analyzing present and potential key competitors in an effort to better anticipate their future moves. The major steps in the competitor-evaluation process are the analyses of competitors' objectives, strategies, success to date, and strengths and weaknesses.

Firms should assess the objectives and success to date of a competitor's parent company, the strategic value of the competitor SBU to the parent, and the economic relations between the competitor SBU and other SBUs.

The strategic environmental issue management process consists of scanning the environment, identifying key environmental issues, evaluating their impact, and formulating a response strategy. The latter can be fragmented into six response strategies having to do with opposition, adaptation, offensive action, redeployment, contingency planning, and doing nothing.

---

[32]Ibid.

Industry Dynamics and Strategic Change

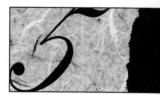

ICE CREAM: A NOT-SO-HOT INDUSTRY[1]

Ice cream was a hot industry through most of the 1980s; but when sales slowed in 1987, it faced significant changes. (See Exhibits 5–1 a and b, which show total ice cream production and dollar sales, 1980–87.) While economy and regular packs selling at $2 and $3 per half gallon still accounted for a majority of the ice cream sold, superpremium varieties provided most of the growth of the 1980s. In 1988 superpremium accounted for 12 percent of all ice cream dollar sales compared to 4.7 percent in 1980. Sales of this type of ice cream grew 14 percent from 1982 through 1987, while all other ice creams had only a 3.2 percent gain (see Exhibit 5–1 c).

But the sales of superpremium ice cream are also slowing, largely because of the competition from substitute products. Thus, super-

premium sales are expected to grow only 5.6 percent over the next several years. The cholesterol problem associated with ice cream—especially superpremium, which has at least 14 percent butterfat compared to 10 percent for economy ice cream—has caused heavy users of ice cream to turn to soft frozen yogurt and low-calorie ice milk. This has forced many established players to start selling these products. Häagen-Dazs (owned by Pillsbury), International Dairy Queen, Inc., and Baskin-Robbins are now also selling frozen yogurt. The latter has introduced yogurt in more than 20 percent of its 2,500 U.S. shops and has even changed the name of these stores to Baskin-Robbins Ice Cream & Yogurt.

Kraft, which owns Dreyer's Grand Ice Cream, Inc., is among

---

[1]Lawrence Ingrassia, "Ice Cream Makers' Rivalry Heating Up," *The Wall Street Journal*, December 21, 1988, p. 31; and Dan Sperling, "The Simple Pleasures of Life: Fake Fat," *USA Today*, February 23, 1990, p. 1A.

EXHIBIT 5-1
Ice Cream Industry Data

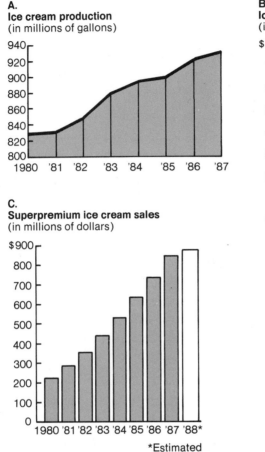

A.
Ice cream production
(in millions of gallons)

B.
Ice cream sales
(in billions of dollars)

C.
Superpremium ice cream sales
(in millions of dollars)

*Estimated

SOURCE: Lawrence Ingrassia, "Ice Cream Makers' Rivalry Heating Up," *The Wall Street Journal*, December 21, 1988, p. B1.

many ice cream producers who have responded to the growing interest in low-fat products by promoting gourmet versions of ice milk. They are even seeking government approval to call such products "light ice cream." Traditionally, ice milk has been a low-priced product with a 2 to 7 percent butterfat content. It developed a bad reputation because of its poor taste and coarse texture. The new gourmet products with 7 percent butterfat and less air content taste better and still have only half the calories of ice cream, but they are more expensive than traditional ice milk products. In the meantime, frozen yogurt has become more and more popular, in part, because today's reformulated yogurt tastes a lot like ice cream.

And yet another substitute

The ice cream industry may be in for yet another jolt with the introduction of Simplesse, a dietary fat substitute. Simplesse is made of egg white and milk protein and became available in the summer of 1990. Since it looks and tastes like ice cream but has none of the dietary problems associated with fat, it is expected to favorably affect the sales of premium ice creams. One serving of Simplesse ice cream will have only 250 calories and 15 grams of fat. Some industry analysts feel that Simplesse will hurt the sales of soft yogurt substantially.

Firms can benefit greatly if they are among the first to identify and adjust to environmental change, particularly when a new product-market entry is involved. Thus, Dreyer's decision to produce a gourmet ice milk to counter the slowdown in sales of superpremium ice cream has resulted in annual sales of about $50 million for such products after only two years. This is in contrast to many competitors who failed to adjust to the inroads made by frozen yogurt and went out of business. For an example of a high-tech product that benefited from early entry, see Exhibit 5–2.

Firms that delay in taking advantage of an environmental opportunity, particularly in product development, frequently find themselves at a disadvantage in a number of areas. The leader's product often becomes the standard against which other products are compared. In addition, the leader may appropriate distribution intermediaries and the essentials of the advertising message. Dreyer's Light may become the industry's standard, and its success will surely make it difficult for followers to obtain strong retail distribution.

There is considerable evidence to suggest that the first businesses to exploit the environmental opportunity of a new product-market tend to retain an advantage over firms that follow, in both higher levels of market share and profitability. One U.S. study of 371 mature consumer goods businesses found that early entrants (pioneers) had an average market share of 29 percent, while early followers had 17 percent and late entrants 12 percent.[2]

It would be a mistake, however, to assume that the simple act of being first leads to a strong advantage over time. A recent study found that since some firms excel at leading and others at following, entry timing depends on the firm's ability to assess its internal skills and resources in light of the market's requirements.[3]

---

[2]William T. Robinson and Claes Fornell, "Sources of Market Pioneering Advantages in Consumer Goods Industries," *Journal of Marketing Research,* August 1985, pp. 305–17.

[3]Michael J. Moore, William Boulding, and Ronald C. Goodstein, " Pioneering and Market Share: Is Entry Time Endogenous and Does It Matter?" *Journal of Marketing Research,* February 1991, p. 97.

EXHIBIT 5-2
Canon Makes Early Entry a Top Priority

In the mid-1980s, Canon's president, Ryuzaburo Kahu, made commercialization a top priority in order the beat the competition to the marketplace with superior new products. The company's objective was to cut product development cost and time in half, partly by involving customers in product testing to discover problems early. The company was successful in cutting time to market by 50 percent, and this made it possible for one division to launch two generations of equipment in the time it took competitors to introduce one. Canon could also offer upgraded versions of each generation every one and a half years, while its toughest competitor took three years. Canon's share of the world market for photolithographic equipment rose from 16 percent in 1978 to 25 percent in 1988. One of its main competitors made little effort to strengthen commercialization capacity and saw its share drop from 51 percent to 23 percent during the same period.

SOURCE: T. Michael Nevens, Gregory L. Summe, and Bro Uttal, "Commercializing Technology: What the Best Companies Do," *Harvard Business Review,* May–June 1990, pp. 154, 169–60.

STRATEGIES OF EARLY VERSUS LATE ENTRANTS

A study by Lambkin revealed that the major differences in entry strategy between pioneers, early followers, and late entrants was in their scale of entry. Pioneers entered their markets on a large scale with a broad product line that was widely distributed and heavily promoted. Compared to pioneers, early followers entered with less breadth to their product line, less market coverage, less promotional support for their product, and fewer customer services. Early followers appeared to rely primarily on price discounting as a basis for competing. Late entrants entered on a small-scale basis, using a niche strategy designed to exploit segments not currently heavily targeted by the major firms.[4] Dreyer's appears to be using a preemptive strategy in its entry into the gourmet ice milk market. From the beginning it has operated on a large-scale basis with a broad line that it promotes extensively.[5] We discuss the strategies of early entrants versus followers in Chapter 8.

In the international arena, some firms have extended the benefits of early entry over long periods by establishing a worldwide network, which results in strong cost advantages through scale and learning effects. For example, German firms have long been international leaders in printing presses and chemicals, while the United States leads in soft drinks, computers, and jet passenger aircraft.[6]

---

[4]Mary Lambkin, "Order of Market Entry and Performance: The Experience of Start-Up Ventures," *The Pimsletter,* no. 41 (Cambridge, Mass.: The Strategic Planning Institute, 1987).

[5]Ingrassia, "Ice Cream Makers' Rivalry Heating Up," p. B1.

[6]Michael E. Porter, *The Competitive Advantage of Nations* (New York: The Free Press, 1990), pp. 64–65.

PRODUCT-MARKET EVOLUTION

Products and markets are constantly evolving, for a variety of reasons. On the product side, the growing commonality of technology increases the difficulty of maintaining strong product differentiation. Also, over time, costs per unit tend to decline because of scale and learning effects. On the market side, demand eventually slows, and consumers become more knowledgeable about the product, forming attitudes about the attractiveness of competing brands. And over time, industry structure and rivalry among established companies change.

These evolutionary forces affect the basic attractiveness of the market and change the requirements for success in the firm's various product-market entries. As a consequence, the business must constantly adjust its objectives, strategies, and marketing programs.

Evolutionary consequences

The management implications of this evolutionary process are threefold.

- At the *portfolio level,* the firm must generate new products or enter new markets to sustain its profitability over time, as has been the case in the ice cream industry—especially with companies producing superpremium ice cream.

- At the *product level,* the objectives and strategy change as the product passes through various evolutionary stages. For example, as the long-distance telephone business matured, cost became the strategic variable. Because MCI paid higher connect charges to local telephone companies, it found itself at a disadvantage against AT&T.[7]

- At the *marketing program level,* the evolutionary process often generates significant changes. Thus, as the market for mainframe computers matured, IBM accelerated its introduction of new models, beefed up its direct sales activities, and was more aggressive about price.[8]

Given the critical importance and complexity of any attempt to anticipate change, a systematic framework is needed to help managers better understand the product-market evolutionary process. This chapter discusses the major components of the evolutionary process: the market, the product, and the competitive (supply-side) environment.

[7]"More Static on the Lines for an Expanding MCI," *Business Week,* November 5, 1984, p. 40.
[8]Standard & Poor's, *Industry Surveys Basic Analysis,* October 1, 1987, p. C79.

THE FRAMEWORK NEEDED TO UNDERSTAND PRODUCT-MARKET EVOLUTION

Specifying a framework for understanding product-market evolution requires that we first define our unit of analysis.[9] The definitional problem here is confounded because products can be summed in different levels of aggregation: industries, product class, product type, and brands.

The problem with using the industry level is that it typically includes an array of noncompeting products. For example, within the automotive industry, is a Ford Fiesta in competition with a BMW? Within the chemical industry, do polymers that substitute for natural materials compete with gasoline additives, dye stuffs, and industrial coatings? Product class suffers from this same type of problem since the products involved may serve diverse markets. For example, the unit sales of ice cream (the product class) increased far less than the sales of superpremium ice cream during the late 1980s.

Nor are brands, which are at the bottom of the aggregation hierarchy, appropriate units of analysis. Their sales are largely a function of management's strategic decisions, marketing expenditures, and competitive action.

Product types are subsets of a product class and contain items that are technically the same, although they may vary in such aspects as appearance and price. We have selected this level as our unit of analysis because product types, while serving different subsets of needs, are often close substitutes for one another. The product-type level of aggregation is considerably more sensitive to environmental changes that lead to opportunities and threats for individual product-market entries.

Categorizing evolutionary forces

The evolution of individual product-markets results from the interplay of numerous forces that can be grouped in many different ways. To simplify our discussion, we focus on three categories of forces—those relating to the market, the product, and the competitive (supply-side) environment. These three forces are mediated by the happenings in the physical, demographic/economic, technological, and political/legal environments in which the business operates. The three sets of forces and the environments within which they operate form the framework we will use to help explain the evolution of product-market relationships. Exhibit 5–3 elaborates this framework.

---

[9]The material in this section owes much to Mary Lambkin and George S. Day, "Evolutionary Processes in Competitive Markets: Beyond the Product Life Cycle," *Journal of Marketing,* July 1989, pp. 4–8.

EXHIBIT　5–3

Framework for Understanding the Evolution of a Product-Market Relationship

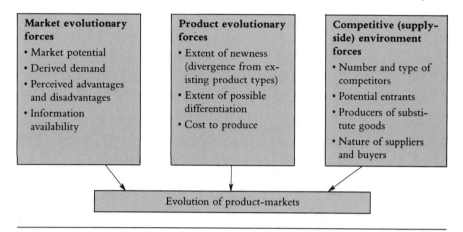

SOURCE: Suggested, in part, by Mary Lambkin and George S. Day, "Evolutionary Processes in Competitive Markets: Beyond the Product-Life Cycle," *Journal of Marketing,* July 1989, pp. 6–7.

THE PRODUCT LIFE CYCLE

The product life cycle is a generalized model of the sales history of a given product category over a long period of time.[10] The concept holds that the product's sales change over time in a predictable way and that products go through a series of five distinct stages: introduction, growth, shakeout, maturity, and decline (see Exhibit 5–4).

Overview of the product life-cycle concept

At the beginning (**introductory stage**), the purchase of a new product is limited, because only a relatively few members of the target market are aware of its existence and its features; further it often lacks easy availability. As more people learn about the product and its features and it becomes more readily available, sales increase at a progressively faster rate (**growth stage**). Growth slows as the number of buyers nears a maximum. Repeat sales then become increasingly more important than trial sales. As both the number of buyers and their purchases stabilize, growth becomes largely a function of population growth as it relates to buyers of a given product type.

---

[10]For a more complete discussion of the product life cycle, see Harper W. Boyd, Jr., and Orville C. Walker, Jr., *Marketing Management: A Strategic Approach* (Homewood, Ill.: Richard D. Irwin, 1990), chap. 8.

EXHIBIT 5-4
Generalized Product Life Cycle

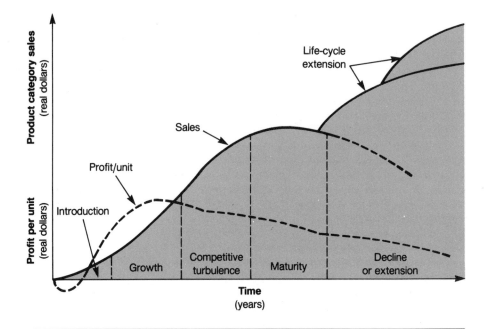

SOURCE: George S. Day, *Analysis for Strategic Market Decisions* (St. Paul: West Publishing, 1986) p. 60.

At the end of the growth period—just before the advent of maturity—the **shakeout** or **competitive turbulence** stage occurs. This is characterized by a rapidly decreasing growth rate that results in strong price competition. Many firms are forced to exit the industry, as was the case with many small sellers of superpremium ice cream. The **mature stage** is reached when the net adoption rate holds steady, that is, when adopters approximate dropouts. When dropouts begin to exceed new first-time users, the sales rate declines and the product is said to have reached its final or **decline stage.**

Life-cycle curves

Many products do not go through the product life-cycle curve shown in Exhibit 5–4 because a high percentage are aborted after an unsatisfactory introductory period. Other products seemingly never die (Scotch whiskey, TVs, automobiles). The shape of the life-cycle curve varies considerably between and within industries. For example, one study identified 12 different types of curves (see Exhibit 5–5).

In general, only one or a very few curves typify an industry. The most common curve is the classical type, followed by the cycle-recycle curve. Consumer durables tend to follow the classical curve, although many major household appliances, such as refrigerators and washing machines, have never

EXHIBIT 5-5

Product Life-Cycle Curves

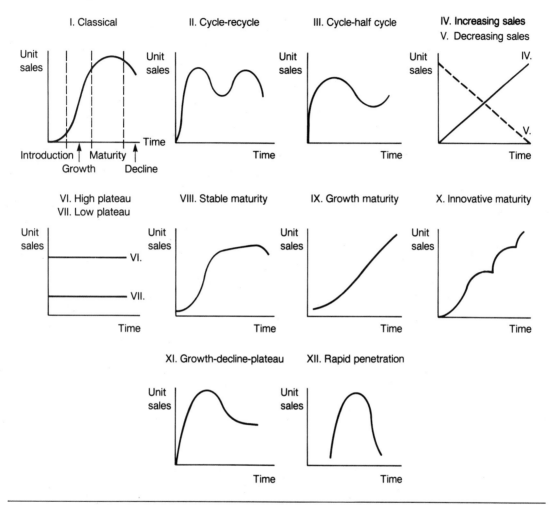

SOURCE: Reprinted from *Marketing in the 80s,* published by the American Marketing Association, 1980. In "Effective Use of Industrial Product Life-Cycle Trends," by John E. Swan and David R. Rink, pp. 198–99.

entered the decline stage. Drug products present the most complex patterns, involving almost all cycles. Even here, however, the cycle-recycle curve seems most common. Industrial products typically follow the pattern of sales depicted by the classical curve. Product life cycles for industrial goods are usually longer than those for consumer goods.[11]

---

[11]Hans B. Thorelli and Stephen C. Burnett, "The Nature of Product Life Cycles for Industrial Goods Businesses," *Journal of Marketing,* Fall 1981, p. 105.

A surge in demand during the mature period—or recycling—can occur for many reasons. These include an increase in the price of a close substitute; a disproportionate increase in the size of a prime market segment caused by demographic shifts or increased purchases by one or more end-user industries; reduced prices resulting from lower raw material costs; the development of new applications (e.g., nylon was first used in parachutes, then women's stockings, and then tires); or a basic shift in derived demand. The latter can result from a change in lifestyle, as has occurred with more women working outside the home. Innovative maturity occurs when new product types or even subtypes introduced within a product class experience considerable sales success (for example, more nutritional and natural fiber ready-to-eat cereals).

Strategic implications of the product life cycle

The product life-cycle model is a framework that signals the occurrence of opportunities and threats in the marketplace and the industry, thereby helping the business change a product's strategic market objective, its strategy, and its marketing program. (See Exhibit 5–6, which summarizes the characteristics of each stage in the product life cycle and the firm's normative responses.)

By matching the entry's market position objective with the investment level required profits, and cash flows associated with each stage in the product life cycle, we can better visualize the interrelationships (see Exhibit 5–7). As would be expected, there is a high correlation between the market and industry characteristics of each stage, the market share objectives, and the level of investment, which, in turn, strongly affects cash flow.

Investment strategy during introductory and growth stages

Because the introduction of a new product requires large investments in product and marketing, most firms sustain a rather sizable short-term loss. As the product moves into the growth stage, sales increase rapidly; hence, substantial investments continue. Profitability is depressed because facilities have to be built in advance to ensure supply. The firm with the largest share during this period should have the lowest per-unit costs due to scale and learning effects. If it chooses to decrease its real price proportionate to the decline in its costs, it dries up the investment incentives of would-be entrants and lower-share competitors. At the same time, it lowers its own profitability and increases its cash flow problems. It has every incentive to hold or increase share during this period and to make the required investments to do so.

The innovating firm's share is likely to erode substantially during the growth stage. Nevertheless, it must still make large investments, for even though it is losing share, its sales are increasing. New entrants and low-share sellers are at a substantial disadvantage here. They must not only invest to accommodate market growth but also to gain market share. If low-share sellers do not gain share, they will continue to be at a cost disadvantage com-

EXHIBIT 5–6

Expected Characteristics and Responses by Major Product Life-Cycle Stages

	Stages in product life cycle				
Stage characteristics	Introduction	Growth	Shakeout	Mature	Decline
Market growth rate (constant dollars)	Moderate	High	Leveling off	Insignificant	Negative
Technical change in product design	High	Moderate	Limited	Limited	Limited
Segments	Few	Few to many	Few to many	Few to many	Few
Competitors	Small	Large	Decreasing	Limited	Few
Profitability	Negative	Large	Low	Large for high market-share holders	Low
Firm's normative responses					
Strategic marketing objectives	Stimulate primary demand	Build share	Build share	Hold share	Harvest
Product	Quality improvement	Continue quality improvements	Rationalize*	Concentrate on features	No change
Product line	Narrow	Broad	Rationalize*	Hold length of line	Reduce length of line
Price	Skimming versus penetration	Reduce	Reduce	Hold or reduce slightly	Reduce
Channels	Selective	Intensive	Intensive	Intensive	Selective
Communications	High	High	High to declining	High to declining	Reduce

*Eliminate weaker items.

EXHIBIT 5–7

Relationship of Strategic Market Position Objective, Investment Levels, Profits, and Cash Flow to Individual Stages in the Product Life Cycle

Stage	Strategic market objective	Investments	Profits	Cash flows
Introduction	For both innovators and followers, accelerate overall market growth and product acceptance through awareness, trial, and product availability	Moderate to high for R&D, capacity, working capital, and marketing (sales and advertising)	Highly negative	Highly negative
Growth	Increase competitive position	High to very high	High	Negative
Shakeout	Improve competitive position	Moderate	Low to moderate	Low to moderate
Mature	Maintain position	Low	High	High
Decline	Harvest	Negative	Low	Moderate

pared to high-share firms. This situation is aggravated as prices decline to a point where low-share firms may not survive the industry shakeout.

Investment strategy during mature and declining stages

As the product enters the mature stage, the larger-share sellers should be able to reap the benefits of their earlier investments. This is particularly so with the leader, who should have lower relative costs. Given that the price is sufficient to keep the higher-cost sellers in business, that growth investments are no longer needed, and that most competitors may no longer be striving to gain share, the leader's profitability and positive cash flow can be substantial. But this is not to suggest that the leader no longer needs to make investments. It would be shortsighted not to make every effort to reduce manufacturing costs by improving the plant and its equipment, standardizing common component parts, and improving the efficiency of marketing and physical logistics. R&D and process engineering expenditures should also be continued at a high level.

The generalized product life-cycle model portrays a profitability trend that peaks during the latter part of the growth stage. This is largely based on price competition resulting from overcapacity. But one study of over 1,000 industrial businesses found that despite declining margins, overall profitability did not decline during maturity. More mature businesses spent less on marketing and R&D and were most likely working with a lower asset base because of depreciation.[12]

In the decline stage, the firm's normative decision is to cease making investments—indeed, cash may be removed from the business if at all possible. But under certain conditions, a firm may increase its investments in a declining market (that is, when several firms exit, leaving one or more enduring segments open).

Product life-cycle limitations

The product life-cycle concept holds a unique position among strategic management theories. Its proponents argue that it provides a framework that prescribes which strategies are most appropriate for each stage of the life cycle, and thus it can be used for allocating resources across the firm's various business units as well as the product-market entries within each unit. But there is little in the way of research findings to support these claims.

The product life cycle's major weakness lies in its normative approach to prescribing strategies based on assumptions about the features or characteristics of each stage. Lambkin and Day argue that there are strong conceptual gaps in the product life-cycle framework. Their major criticisms are summarized below.[13]

---

[12]Ibid., p. 105.

[13]Lambkin and Day, "Evolutionary Processes . . . ," pp. 8–9.

- The life-cycle framework takes little account of how the different competitive positions or resources of competing business units might alter the applicability of the generalized courses of action. Thus, differences between large and small firms, established and new firms, firms entering on their own versus by acquisition, and firms employing different strategies are largely ignored.

- There is no recognition that the strategic window for entry opens at different times for different types of firms.

- The lack of a supply-side (competitive environment) orientation means little or no guidance is provided on when, and why, shakeouts occur and which types of businesses are more apt to survive and prosper.

- The framework does not reflect feedback effects of the choice of strategy on the shape of the growth curve, even though supply-side factors can increase or decrease the rate of growth.

- The inevitability of the one-way direction of the framework (introduction through decline and death) is unwarranted; there is ample evidence that some strategies can successfully rejuvenate and extend a life cycle.

- The environment within which the business operates is not taken into account. For example, the fact that certain environments are more conducive to entry than others is largely ignored.

- The life-cycle concept does not take into account uncertainty about any number of variables regarding emerging markets (e.g., consumer acceptance, size of market long term, and actions of competitors).

Lambkin and Day conclude by suggesting that greater emphasis on supply-side issues can help elucidate the evolution of a product-market. This is especially the case in understanding the dynamics of competitive behavior in evolving market structures.

MARKET EVOLUTION

The product life-cycle concept owes much to the **diffusion of innovation** theory, which seeks to explain adoption of a product or a service over time among a group of potential buyers. Thus initially, lack of awareness limits adoption. As word about the product spreads—partly via satisfied buyers— the product enters the growth stage. When the net adoption rate holds steady, the mature stage is reached; when the rate begins to decline, the product has reached its final or decline stage.

Diffusion theory emphasizes the behavior of individuals, their demographics, and how they respond to various kinds of communication. It does, however, consider product attributes and the competitive environment as determinants of the adoption rate. The theory has been tested extensively with considerable success.

The adoption process

The **adoption process** involves the attitudinal changes experienced by individuals from the time they first hear about a new product or idea until they adopt it. Individuals receive various stimuli about the new product from a variety of sources. These accumulate until consumers respond by either accepting or rejecting the product. As might be expected, not all individuals respond alike—some tend to adopt early, some late, and some never. Thus, the market for a new product tends to be segmented over time.

The five stages in the adoption process include awareness, interest, evaluation, trial, and adoption. Each of these is discussed briefly below.

1. *Awareness stage.* In this stage, the individual is exposed to the new product but does not have full information about it. At this point, the person is only aware of its existence and is not sufficiently motivated to seek information about it.

2. *Interest stage.* Here the individual becomes interested in the new product to the extent of seeking out information about it. He is not yet involved and has only committed to the new idea in a very general way. He has not judged it on the basis of its worth to him personally.

3. *Evaluation stage.* This is sometimes referred to as the mental rehearsal stage. At this point, the individual is mentally applying the new product to his/her own use requirements and anticipating the results. This is a prelude to trying the new product, because if the evaluation is positive, the individual will typically move into the trial stage.

4. *Trial stage.* At this point, the individual actually uses the product, but if at all possible, on a limited basis to minimize the risk involved. But trial is not tantamount to adoption, since only if the use experience is satisfactory will the product stand a chance of being adopted.

5. *Adoption stage.* In this stage, the individual not only continues to use the new product but adopts it in lieu of substitutes. In other words, adoption is complete and continuous.

The rate of adoption

If plotted on a cumulative basis, the percentage of people adopting a new product over time would have a curve like that shown in Exhibit 5–8. Although the curve tends to have the same shape regardless of the product involved, the amount of time required differs among products, often substantially.

The time dimension is a function of the rate at which people in the target group (those ultimately adopting) move through the five stages in the adoption process. Generally speaking, the speed of the adoption process depends on the following factors: (1) the risk (cost of product failure or dissatisfaction), (2) the relative advantage over other products, (3) the relative simplicity of the new product, (4) its compatibility with previously adopted ideas, (5) the extent to which its trial can be accomplished on a small-scale basis, and (6) the ease with which the central idea of the new product can be commu-

E X H I B I T   5 – 8
Percent of People Adopting over Time

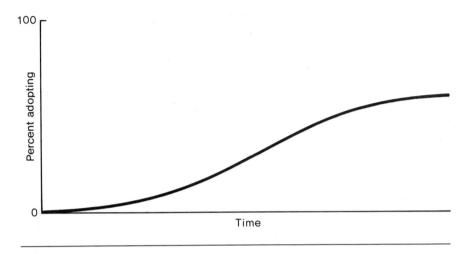

nicated.[14] Some new products move quickly through the adoption process (e.g., a new breakfast cereal), while others take years (e.g., computerized process controls that require a change in manufacturing facilities).

The rate at which a product passes through the adoption process is also a function of the actions taken by the product's supplier. Thus, the diffusion process is faster when there is strong competition among members of the supplier group, when they have favorable reputations, and when they allocate substantial sums to R&D (to improve performance) and marketing (to build awareness).[15]

Adopter categories

People who adopt early differ in a number of ways from those who adopt late. If time of adoption is used as a basis for classifying individuals, five major adopter groups can be distinguished: innovators, early adopters, early majority, late majority, and laggards. (Note that these are different from the five stages of adoption listed above.) Since each category comprises individuals who have similar characteristics and since individuals differ substantially across categories, these adopter groups can and should be considered market segments. Thus, one would use a different set of strategies to market a new product to the early adopter group than to market it to the late majority group. See Exhibit 5–9 for the approximate size of each group.[16]

---

[14]Everett M. Rogers, *Diffusion of Innovations* (New York: The Free Press, 1983).

[15]Thomas S. Robertson and Hubert Gatignon, "Competitive Effects on Technological Diffusion," *Journal of Marketing,* July 1986, pp. 1–12.

[16]Rogers, *Diffusion of Innovations.*

EXHIBIT 5–9
Size of Individual Adopter Group

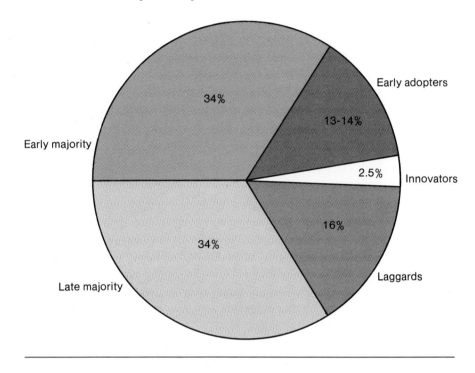

- **Innovators** represent the first 2.5 percent of all individuals who ulti- mately adopt a new product. Such individuals are more venturesome than those who adopt later and are more likely to seek out and experi- ment with new ideas. Usually, they are part of an informal communica- tions network (professional or social or both) that includes other innovators. They tend to have high incomes, which enables them to ac- cept more readily any loss arising from an early adoption.
- **Early adopters** represent the next 13 to 14 percent who adopt the new product. These individuals are more a part of the local scene and are often opinion leaders. They serve as vital links to members of the early majority group because they are not too far removed from them socially. Early adopters participate more in community organizations than do later adopters.
- **Early majority** includes 34 percent of those who adopt. These individ- uals display less leadership than early adopters, but they tend to be active in community affairs, thereby gaining respect from their peers. They do not like to take unnecessary risks and want to be sure that a new product will prove successful before they adopt it.
- **Late majority** represents another 34 percent. Frequently, these individ- uals adopt a new product because they are forced to do so for either

EXHIBIT   5-10

Major Differences between Early and Late Adopters

	Early adopters	Late adopters
Age	Younger	Older
Income	Higher	Lower
Education	Higher and more specialized	Lower and less specialized
Social class	Higher status	Lower status
Occupation	More prestigious	Less prestigious
Media and sources information	Greater exposure to more media; variety of sources of information	Less exposure to fewer media and less variety of sources; more reliance on personal sources
Cosmopolitanism of contacts	More nonlocal contacts	Essentially local contacts

economic or social reasons. They participate in community activities less than the previous groups and only rarely assume a leadership role.

- **Laggards** comprise the last 16 percent of adopters. Of all the adopters, they are the most "local" and may even be isolates. They participate less in community matters than do members of the other groups and stubbornly resist change. In some cases, their adoption of a product may be so late it may already have been replaced by another new product.

Some generalizations about early versus late adopters: the implications for marketing strategy

Exhibit 5–10 indicates the major differences between early and late adopters. Here the category "early adopters" refers to early adopters and early majority, and "late adopters" refers to late majority and laggards. The differences cited in the exhibit are important because they provide guidelines for the construction of strategic marketing programs. In organizational markets, suppliers can identify innovative firms by reputation, profitability, size, and the suppliers' experiences in dealing with them. For example, the early adopters of new model jet aircraft were the larger, faster-growing airlines that had more borrowing capacity than later adopters. Firms that adopt earlier also spend more on R&D and tend to have presidents who are younger and better educated.

As was evident from the discussion of stages in the adoption process, information per se is not usually sufficient for adoption. This is especially true in the case of late adopters. Commercial sources of information (e.g., salespeople and mass media advertising) are important at the outset. However, less commercial and more "professional" sources are sought as validators of the proclaimed merits of the new product—especially during the evaluation stage, which constitutes a mental rehearsal of the consequences of adoption. Advice from opinion leaders appears to be more critical as a legitimatizing agent than as a source of information. A classic study of how doctors reacted to the introduction of a new "miracle drug" found that only 10 percent of them adopted on the basis of data provided by their initial source of information, indicating that data alone will not cause adoption.[17]

Thus, commercial sources are most important at the awareness stage in the adoption process, while personal influence is most important at the evaluation stage. In the interest stage, both are important. In the trial stage, marketers should attempt to make it relatively easy for a prospect to try a product under conditions that minimize risk. Thus, strategic marketing programs can be generated to accommodate the various stages in the adoption process as well as the different adoption audiences.

While the diffusion of innovation theory sheds considerable light on the evolution of a market for a given product-market entry, it is insufficient in and of itself. More and more, marketers recognize that the evolutionary process results from the interaction of many kinds of forces.

PRODUCT EVOLUTION

Our discussion of the diffusion process described the impact of the product and its characteristics on the rate of diffusion; for example, the more complex and expensive the product, the slower the rate.

As product characteristics evolve over time they generate opportunities and threats, which in turn affect product differentiation. This is a key variable in determining the intensity and form of rivalry among existing firms within an industry and the ease of entry into it. The importance of product differentiation over time is further underscored by its prominence in the strategy formulation process. Indeed, Porter cites it as one of three potentially successful generic strategies for a firm to employ in coping with industry's competitive forces.[18]

Product differentiation over time

The PIMS (Profit Impact of Market Strategy) research on competitive strategy has studied how many of a product-market's characteristics, including the rate of innovation, change as the market evolves.[19] As might be expected, innovation diminishes over time. This tendency is revealed in a number of ways (see Exhibit 5–11). First, as the figures clearly show, new product sales as a percentage of total market volume decline from 10.2 percent during the

[17]Frederick E. Webster, Jr., *Industrial Marketing Strategy* (New York: John Wiley & Sons, 1991), pp. 158–74.

[18]Michael E. Porter, *Competitive Strategy* (New York: The Free Press, 1980), p. 35.

[19]The PIMS program was originated in 1972 and has involved data relating to the strategies and financial results of about 3,000 strategic business units from 450 companies for periods from 2 to 12 years. For more information about PIMS, see Robert D. Buzzell and Bradley T. Gale, *The PIMS Principles* (New York: The Free Press, 1987), chap. 3. This section of our discussion is based largely on Chapter 10 of that book. For an interesting discussion of how Japanese executives perceive the validity of PIMS principles, see Masaaky Kotable and Dale F. Durham, with David K. Smith, Jr. and R. Dale Wilson, "The Perceived Veracities of PIMS Strategy Principles in Japan: An Empirical Inquiry," *Journal of Marketing*, January 1991, p. 26.

EXHIBIT 5-11

Market Evolution and Product/Service Innovation

Measures of innovation (averages)	Stage of evolution				
	Growth	Growth maturity	Stable maturity	Declining maturity	Decline
New product sales, percent of market	10.2	5.4	3.5	3.7	2.8
R&D spending, percent of sales	3.1	2.0	1.7	1.7	1.2
Product R&D, percent of total R&D	72%	67%	67%	70%	60%
Percent of markets					
With major changes in technology	49	27	18	21	23
Where new product development takes two years or more					
Industrial	51	43	43	42	28
Consumer	30	28	31	28	27

NOTE: New products (those introduced during the preceding 3 years) are, for the four largest competitors only, expressed as a percentage of those businesses' total sales. (On average, the four largest competitors accounted for 72 percent of total market volume.) R&D expenditures are for the reporting business only.

SOURCE: Adopted with permission of The Free Press, a Division of Macmillan, Inc. from *The PIMS Principles: Linking Strategy to Performance* by Robert D. Buzzell and Bradley T. Gale. Copyright © 1987 by The Free Press.

growth stage of evolution to 5.4 percent during growth maturity, to 3.5 and 3.7 percent during stable maturity and declining maturity, and to 2.8 percent in the decline stage.

A decline in the rate of innovation is also reflected in the amount of monies spent on R&D, as expressed as a percentage of sales. Rates fall from 3.1 percent during the growth period to 2.0 to 1.7 percent during the maturity periods and to only 1.2 percent during the decline phase. A further and important point here is that product R&D declines from 72 percent of total R&D costs during growth to 60 percent during the decline period. Thus, the proportion of the R&D expenditure spent on process (rather than on product) R&D increases over time. This increase reflects a desire to decrease per-unit costs as the product matures.

The percentage of markets experiencing a major change in technology drops from 49 in the growth stage to only 18 to 21 during the stable and declining maturity markets. Twenty-three percent of the markets in a state of decline had a major technological change, indicating that such change is clearly possible and that to assume otherwise is a mistake.

The type and amount of R&D also appear to affect the evolutionary process by increasing the rate and level of diffusion. Robertson and Gatignon show that the more standardized the technology, the higher the diffusion rate. It seems reasonable to assume that the more the industry spends on product

EXHIBIT 5–12

Competitors Become More Alike as Markets Evolve

Measures of competitive differentiation	Stage of evolution				
	Growth	Growth maturity	Stable maturity	Declining maturity	Decline
Product/service differentiation (index)	51	43	42	40	32
Price differentiation (index)	7.0	6.3	6.2	6.0	5.4
Percentage of markets where major competitors have similar product-line breadth	32%	36%	39%	39%	42%
Serve same types of customers	58	60	63	58	69
Have similar number of customers	30	34	36	38	50

SOURCE: Adapted with permission of The Free Press, a Division of Macmillan, Inc. from *The PIMS Principles: Linking Strategies to Performance* by Robert D. Buzzell and Bradley T. Gale. Copyright © 1987 by The Free Press.

R&D, the faster standardization is achieved.[20] Assuming that process R&D leads to lower manufacturing costs, which in turn are translated into lower prices, then the more money spent on this activity the faster the diffusion rate.

Product evolution and competitive differences

Exhibit 5–12 presents several measures prepared by PIMS indicating that the extent of differences between competitors declines over time; that is, competitors become more alike. The index of product differentiation drops substantially (from 51 to 32) from the growth to the decline stage.[21] Given this decline, it is understandable why price differences between competing products also decline.

Other indicators of competitive differentiation present further evidence of a decline over time. Thus, as the market evolves, more major competitors have a similar breadth to their product lines, serve the same types of customers, and have about the same number of customers. These similarities and their consequences are illustrated in the following example:

---

[20]Robertson and Gatignon, "Competitive Effects . . . ," pp. 4–6.

[21]The relative superiority of a company's product was determined by asking managers to rate their product's performance versus that of leading competitors on a scale of 1 to 10 for each product attribute. For further information on how this rating takes place, see Buzzell and Gale, *The PIMS Principles,* chaps. 3 and 6.

EXHIBIT 5-13

The Major Forces that Determine Industry Competition

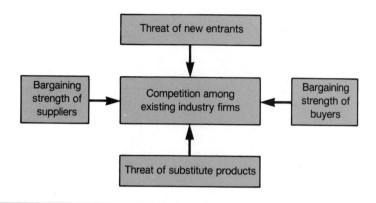

SOURCE: Adapted from Michael F. Porter, "Industry Structure and Competitive Strategy: Keys to Profitability," *Financial Analysts Journal,* July–August 1980, p. 33.

> IBM-compatible PCs and workstations are increasingly incorporating Apple's MacIntosh "graphic-user interface" (until recently an innovative way of presenting information on a computer screen). It is expected that more and more desktop computers will look alike. Apple is responding by bringing out a number of product-line extensions, introducing better software, and increasing its personal selling and support services.[22]

As competitive differentiation declines over time, so do margins and ROI. Margins drop from 30.5 percent during the growth period to 26.0 percent in stable maturity and to 21.8 percent in the decline stage. The decline in ROI is less severe—from 23.8 percent during the growth period to 17.9 percent during the decline period.

COMPETITIVE (SUPPLY-SIDE) ENVIRONMENT EVOLUTION

This part of the evolutionary framework is primarily concerned with supply-side issues; that is, the effect of evolving industry structures on competitive behavior among firms serving much the same market(s). There seems little doubt that an industry's structural attributes affect not only the degree of competitive intensity but the bases of competition as well. Industry evolution can best be judged by analyzing changes that affect the interplay of five competitive forces over time: present competitors, potential competitors, the bargaining power of suppliers and buyers, and substitute products (see Exhibit 5–13).

Collectively these forces determine an industry's long-term attractiveness as measured by return on investment. The mix of forces explains why some

---

[22]Maria Shao and Geoff Lewis, "Apple Turns from Revolution to Evolution," *Business Week,* January 23, 1989, p. 90.

EXHIBIT 5-14

Federal Express Faces New Challenges

Federal Express still dominates the overnight express business it created some 15 years ago, but is facing new challenges—especially from FAX machines and aggressive competitors. The company's glory days of 40 percent annual growth may well be over. Operating profits have gradually declined by one-third over the past several years.

The company's basic business—shipping documents—is saturated and is being challenged by new technology—facsimile machines. In addition, UPS, the giant package-delivery company, is now a viable competitor for the overnight air market segment and has forced Federal to cut prices. UPS is spending hundreds of millions of dollars to buy the technology that will enable it to go head-to-head with Federal—especially with respect to on-call pick-up and continuous tracking.

Federal Express's plan for continued profitability is to place more emphasis on the higher-margin package business, in part, by becoming a just-in-time middleman. Thus, it is managing inventories for high-priced goods at its various sorting hubs using its sophisticated tracking system. For example, Federal warehouses parts for IBM workstations, thereby enabling IBM to cut its delivery costs and begin closing its over-100 parts depots. The company is also betting big on the fast-growing foreign market and recently acquired Flying Tigers, a veteran airfreight carrier serving the international market.

SOURCE: Dean Foust and Resa W. King, "Why Federal Express Has Overnight Anxiety," *Business Week,* November 9, 1987, p. 62; and Larry Reibstein, "Federal Express Faces Challenges to Its Grip on Overnight Delivery," *The Wall Street Journal,* January 8, 1988, p. 1.

industries are consistently more profitable than others and provides insights into what resources are required and which strategies should be adopted if the business is to be successful.

The strength of the individual forces varies from industry to industry and, over time, within the same industry. In the overnight express business, the key forces are present competitors and substitute products (see Exhibit 5–14). In particular, the growth and profitability of Federal Express is affected by UPS and the growing use of FAX machines to transmit documents (substitute product).

Present (existing) competitors

Rivalry occurs among firms that produce products that are close substitutes for each other–especially when one competitor acts to improve its standing or protect its position. Thus, firms are mutually dependent—what one firm does affects others and vice versa. This is certainly the case with Federal Express and UPS, both of which are seeking to enhance their market position by offering new services and lower prices and using new technology.

Ordinarily, profitability decreases as rivalry increases. Competition is greater when:[23]

---

[23]See Michael F. Porter, "Industry Structure and Competitive Strategy: Key to Profitability," *Financial Analysts Journal,* July–August 1980, pp. 30–41.

- **There is high investment intensity; that is, the amount of fixed and working capital required to produce a dollar of sales is large.** High intensity requires firms to operate at or near capacity as much as possible, thereby putting strong downward pressure on prices when demand slackens.[24] Thus, high-investment-intensity businesses such as steel mills, airlines, and ocean transport are, on average, much less profitable than those with a lower level of investment.

- **There are many small firms in an industry or when no dominant firms exist.** Also, when entry into an industry is easy—as is the case with the regional frozen pizza market, where almost anyone with a garage and a freezer can make a frozen pizza.[25]

- **The industry growth rate slows.** This means that a firm's growth can come only by taking sales away from a competitor. This has recently been the case in the overnight, small-package delivery business.

- **There is little product differentiation, since buyer loyalty reduces the likelihood of price reductions.** This has not been the case in the overnight small-package delivery business, since Federal Express has had a differentiated product that only recently has been challenged by UPS, thereby heating up the competition.

- **There is a high cost to changing suppliers (switching costs).** Recently, Roadway Services challenged UPS's dominance of the small package delivery business (nonair) using a lower price. But Roadway "will still have a tough time competing against UPS's untouchable reputation for reliability. Many shipping managers are reluctant to switch to an unproven source. Says one: 'It would take an unbelievable arm-twist to get me to dump UPS.' "[26]

Threat of new entrants

A second driving force affecting competition is the threat of new entrants. This has been the case in recent years in many industries because of international competition, as in the invasion of the United States by Japanese firms producing a variety of home electronics products, automobiles, cameras, and watches. New competitors add new capacity to the industry and bring with them the need to gain market share, thereby making competition more intense. Entry is more difficult under the following conditions:

- **When strong *economies of scale* and *learning effects* are present.** Entry is much more difficult, since it takes time to obtain the volume and learning required to yield a low relative cost per unit. This means that a

---

[24]Buzzell and Gale, *The PIMS Principles,* pp. 109–17.

[25]Julie Liesse Erickson, "Frozen Pizza Makers Feeding on Success," *Advertising Age,* September 28, 1988, p. 8.

[26]Dan Cook, "Two Rivals Disturb United Parcel's 'Sheltered Life,' " *Business Week,* February 11, 1985, p. 34.

new entrant must accept a strong cost disadvantage from the outset and heavily subsidize the new entrant. If firms already present are vertically integrated, it is even more expensive for new firms to enter. Also, if the existing firms share their output with related businesses, the problem of overcoming the cost disadvantage is made more difficult.

- **If the industry has strong *capital requirements* at the outset.** Entry will then be limited to large organizations. UPS is spending hundreds of millions of dollars to buy just the technology that will enable it to compete with Federal Express (in addition to an expensive fleet of jet aircraft and their facilities). Where possible, it might be preferable to acquire an existing competitor, which is what Federal Express did to enter the international market.

- **When strong *product differentiation* exists, since this leads to customer loyalty.** Thus, a new entrant must not only develop a unique product but also spend heavily to develop favorable consumer attitudes toward it. This certainly has been true with Federal Express, which has a unique product with a strong and favorable brand image.

- **If gaining *distribution* is particularly difficult, as is the case in some industries.** Retailers are reluctant to add new brands, given scarcity of shelf space and the capital required for inventory. This is especially true in a mature market. Thus, a retailer carrying the Häagen Dazs line may be reluctant to carry other superpremium brands of ice cream.

- **If a buyer incurs *switching costs* in moving from one supplier to another.** If these involve considerable monies, retraining of personnel, or risk, then the entrant must offer a substantially improved product or a lower cost to get users to switch. UPS, in its efforts to combat the risks associated with switching from Federal Express, priced its service considerably lower.

Bargaining strengths of suppliers

The bargaining power of suppliers over firms in an industry is the third major determinant of industry competition. It is exercised largely through increased prices. And its impact can be significant. This is particularly the case when a limited number of suppliers service a number of different industries. Their power is increased if switching costs and the prices of substitutes are high. Suppliers are especially important when their product is a large part of the buyer's value added—as is the case with metal cans, where the cost of tinplate is over 60 percent of the value added.

Bargaining strength of buyers

An industry's customers constantly look for reduced prices, improved product quality, and added services and thus can affect competition within an industry. Buyers play individual suppliers against one another in their efforts to obtain these and other concessions. This is certainly the case with some large customers in their dealings with Federal Express and UPS.

The extent to which buyers succeed in their bargaining efforts depends on (1) the extent of buyer concentration—a few large buyers that account for a large portion of industry sales facilitate gaining concessions; (2) switching costs—they reduce the buyer's bargaining power; (3) the threat of backward integration—thereby alleviating the need for the supplier; (4) the product's importance to the performance of the buyer's product—the greater the importance the lower their bargaining powers; and (5) buyer profitability—if buyers earn low profits and the product involved is an important part of their costs, then bargaining will be more aggressive.

Threat of substitute products

Substitutes are alternative product types (not brands) that perform essentially the same functions. Examples include gas for electricity, margarine for butter, and plastic for glass or metal containers. Substitute products put a ceiling on the profitability of an industry by limiting the price that can be charged, especially when supply exceeds demand. The ones that offer a significant improvement in price or performance represent a considerable threat, assuming switching cost is not important. Thus, in the metal container industry, aluminum is a substitute for tinplate and constrains the prices charged by tinplate producers.

Changing competition and industry evolution[27]

All five competitive forces discussed above are affected by the passage of time and, therefore, their strength varies as the industry passes from its introductory to growth stage and on to maturity, followed by decline. Competitive forces are apt to be weakest during the fast-growth period and, thus, there are substantial opportunities for gaining market share. During the shakeout period, competitive forces are at their strongest, and many competitors are forced to exit the industry. During industry maturity, competition typically slackens, but only if the industry leader holds a strong relative share position.

Industry evolution and present competitors

The rivalry between established competitors changes as the industry evolves (see Exhibit 5–15). At the outset, rivalry is apt to be low because the industry comprises at best a few firms and often only one. These firms are typically preoccupied with making sure their product design is satisfactory, for success here is imperative.

The low rivalry intensity continues during the growth stage. Here companies can expand their revenues without taking share from competitors. Rivalry becomes more intense during the shakeout period. Companies now compete for market share, because overall growth has slowed.

---

[27]This section owes much to Charles W. L. Hill and Gareth R. Jones, *Strategic Management* (Boston, Mass.: Houghton Mifflin Company, 1989), pp. 75–81.

EXHIBIT 5-15

Extent of Rivalry among Existing Firms by Stage of Industry Evolution

Stage of industry evolution	Extent of rivalry
Introduction	Low
Growth	Low
Shakeout	High
Mature	Low
Decline	High

SOURCE: Adopted from Charles W. L. Hill and Gareth R. Jones, *Strategic Management,* First Edition. Copyright © 1989 by Houghton Mifflin Company. Used with permission.

By maturity, many industries have become oligopolies. It is easier now for companies to recognize their interdependence and to engage in less price competition, except where the leader holds a weak relative share position. For example, Pepsi and Coke account for some 60 percent of the U.S. soft-drink sales (eight companies account for 80 percent); but since they have about the same share of the retail market (the largest segment), the industry experiences considerable price competition. A declining industry usually witnesses a high degree of rivalry, the extent of which depends on the strength of the exit barriers and the rate of decline.

Industry evolution and potential competitors

During the early stages of industry evolution, technology is a major barrier along with scale economies and product differentiation. An existing company can take advantage of high technology barriers to build sales and customer loyalty. This is exactly what Federal Express has done over the years.

As the industry evolves into its growth stage, technology as a barrier to entry declines. Further, scale economies have not yet set in to any great extent, nor has brand loyalty emerged as a strong force. Thus, at this time entry barriers are at their lowest and the danger of entry at its greatest. Entry is made even more attractive because high growth means entrants ordinarily do not provoke retaliation from existing competitors.

Entry barriers increase as the industry passes through the shakeout stage and enters maturity. Firms now focus on reducing costs and developing a favorable brand image. These constitute further entry barriers throughout the mature stage. As the industry enters the decline stage, the threat of entry is further reduced by the industry's low profits. For a summary of how entry barriers change with industry evolution, see Exhibit 5-16.

Other forces and industry evolution

As an industry matures, buyers' bargaining strengths increase at the expense of suppliers. This occurs because as individual companies become larger, they can exercise stronger bargaining power not only because of their size but also in some cases because they can better threaten backward integration. Also,

EXHIBIT 5-16

The Change in Entry Barriers by Different Stages in the
Evolution of the Industry

Entry barriers	Stage of industry evolution				
	Introduction	Growth	Shakeout	Maturity	Decline
Technology	High to medium	Medium to low	Low	Low	Low
Scale economies	Low	Low to medium	Medium to high	Medium to high	Medium to high
Brand loyalty	Low	Low to medium	Medium to high	Medium to high	Medium to high

SOURCE: Charles W. L. Hill and Gareth R. Jones, *Strategic Management*, First Edition. Copyright © 1989 by Houghton Mifflin Company. Used with permission.

the more consolidated an industry, the less buyers and suppliers can maneuver other buyers and suppliers against each other to increase or decrease existing prices. An industry also develops greater protection from substitute products as it moves toward maturity. Scale and learning effects reduce costs while brand loyalty is increased, thereby further eroding the strengths of existing substitute products. But a new substitute product may emerge (such as the development of the FAX machine in the overnight air delivery of documents business) that will strongly affect an industry's evolution.

Industry driving forces

Industries, or subsets thereof, are constantly evolving. Rarely are they static for any length of time. Forces of change are always present, and marketers must identify and understand them to take advantage of them. A change in any of the five forces that determine the nature and scope of industry competition—suppliers, buyers, potential entrants, substitute products, and industry competitors—affects industry structure and hence a firm's strategy and marketing program for a product-market entry. Thus, it is important to look at the forces driving an industry to see how they will affect any of the five competitive forces. Porter identifies a number of such driving forces that to a greater or lesser degree are present in the evolution of any industry.[28]

Changes in the market's long-term growth rate

This is a strong force since it directly affects investment decisions, especially those relating to capacity and growing market share. The rate of change also has a direct bearing on the intensity of competition. Market growth rates are

---

[28]Porter, *Competitive Strategy*, chap. 3.

a function of several forces. First, changing consumer demographics, which affect the demand for consumer goods immediately (e.g., the aging of America has increased the demand for many prescription drugs) and the demand for industrial products longer term. Second, changes in the lifestyle and values of the relevant buyer groups as, for example, occurred in the 1960s and 70s when the American public embraced physical fitness, thereby triggering a stronger demand for all kinds of sports equipment, clothing, and facilities. Third, changes in the price and/or quality of a substitute and/or complementary product (e.g., the growing popularity of the VCR increased the demand for low-rent video tapes). Fourth, penetration (saturation) of a market, which means a leveling off in industry sales. Fifth, product innovation, which can trigger an increase in demand by improving the industry's position with respect to substitute products as, for example, occurred with the formulation of a low-calorie and cholesterol-free margarine versus butter.

Changes in buyer segments

A change in segmentation can occur because the same product is being used by different consumers (e.g., use of personal computers in both business and the home) and/or the same consumers using the product differently (e.g., baking soda being used in baking and as a refrigerator deodorant). The significance of such change lies not only in its impact on demand, but also on its effect on strategic marketing programs. Witness what selling a personal computer to individuals versus businesses meant to IBM in terms of its product's features, servicing, pricing, channels of distribution, sales force, and advertising activities.

Diffusion of proprietary knowledge

Learning about the product's basic technology occurs over time among all industry members. The major issues here are the rate at which such diffusion occurs, the extent to which it enables new firms to enter the industry, and the degree to which products become more alike.

Innovation

Three kinds of innovation individually and collectively represent major forces of change within an industry. These are product innovation, marketing innovation, and process innovation. The first can increase demand and enhance product differentiation, both of which affect entry. Marketing innovations can include the use of new channel intermediaries, new advertising themes and media, and new selling methods (e.g., via telephone). These can affect an industry's structure by increasing demand and affecting scale economies. For example, the use of telephone selling by brokerage firms to enter new geographical markets has increased competition within the financial industry. Changes in manufacturing processes can affect per-unit costs, minimum efficient plant size, desirability of integration, and scale economies.

Product differentiation

Over time, differentiated products tend to become more like commodities, thereby affecting promotional and price elasticity as well as production and distribution costs. Industries vary in the rate at which this trend occurs. Compare, for example, the short time it took digital watches to become like commodities versus personal computers, where individual brands differ substantially from one another after considerable time.

Risk reduction

Emerging industries are characterized by considerable uncertainty with respect to such important factors as ideal product configuration, market size, rate of demand increase, costs, and buyer characteristics. Over time, uncertainties are reduced, and the remaining firms adopt successful strategies that make for increased competition. Risk reduction may make entry easier. For example, once it became evident that there was a large potential market for personal computers, IBM—which had focused heavily on larger machines—entered, changing drastically the industry's structure and the bases of competition.

Changes in costs and efficiency

Scale and learning effects cause per-unit costs to decline. Strong effects make entry more difficult. Changes in the cost of any important industry input, therefore, can affect industry structure. Such changes affect prices, and therefore demand, as well as industry costs. A change in exchange rates can also strongly affect competition.

Entry and exit

Both can be strong forces that can trigger a change in the industry's structure. Entry by large firms that are well established in other industries can bring not only an increase in competition but a change in the way competition is waged. Such was the case when Philip Morris entered the beer industry by buying Miller Brewing Company and introducing a light beer. Exit changes industry structure by enabling the dominant firms to become even more so.

Changes in government policies and regulations

These affect entry, costs, bases of competition, and profitability. Examples include deregulation of the airline and trucking industries, changes in the benefits provided by Medicare, and regulations regarding automobile safety.

Because industries are integrated systems, a change in one industry component is likely to trigger changes in other components, thereby affecting structure. For example, product innovation may increase demand, resulting in increased economies of scale that make entry more difficult, and so on. Such a chain reaction can affect industry structure in many ways.

SUMMARY

Firms benefit greatly if they are among the first to identify and take advantage of environmental change. This is especially true when a new product-market is involved. Early entrants tend to attain higher market share and profitability than later entrants. This is typically accomplished by entering on a large scale with a broad product line that is widely distributed and heavily promoted.

In addition to analyzing the several dimensions of the macroenvironment, firms must also consider the evolution of their product-market entries. A suggested framework for understanding product-market evolution consists of three categories of forces: those relating to the product, the market, and the competitive environment.

The product life cycle is the traditional model used to explain the evolution of product-market entries. Essentially, it is a generalized model of the sales history of a given product category over a long period of time. This concept holds that a product's sales change over time in a predictable way and that the product goes through a series of distinct stages. The product life-cycle concept has been used as a framework that, by signaling the timing of opportunities and threats, prescribes the strategies and marketing programs most appropriate for each stage of the cycle. The major weakness of the concept lies in its normative approach to prescribing strategies based on assumptions concerning the features or characteristics of each stage.

Diffusion theory seeks to explain the adoption process for a given product or idea over time and thus relates directly to market evolution. It emphasizes the behavior of individuals, their demographics, and how they respond to various kinds of communication. The process is defined as the attitudinal changes experienced by individuals from the time they first hear about a new product until they adopt it. It consists of five stages: awareness, interest, evaluation, trial, and adoption. Adopter categories are innovators, early adopters, early majority, late majority, and laggards. There are substantial demographic differences between early and late adopters.

Product evolution is mainly affected by changes in a firm's product differentiation. PIMS research shows that innovation diminishes over time, based on such measures as new product sales as a percentage of that of all firms, monies spent on R&D, a switch from product R&D to process R&D, and the percentage change in markets experiencing a major change in technology. And as time passes, the extent of differences between competitors declines. Competitors become more alike with respect to their product, the breadth of their product line, and the type of customers served.

The competitive environment evolution is mainly concerned with supply-side issues and can best be studied by analyzing changes affecting the interplay of five competitive forces over time: present competitors, potential competitors, bargaining power of buyers and suppliers, and substitute forces. The strength of these individual forces varies from industry to industry and over time within the same industry. Competitive forces are apt to be at their weakest during the fast-growth and mature periods and at their strongest during the shakeout and decline stages. The forces of present and potential competitors are the two most affected by industry evolution.

There are a number of driving forces typically present in the evolution of any industry. These include changes in the market's long-term growth rate, changes in buyer segments, diffusion of proprietary knowledge, changes in costs and efficiency, entry and exit, and changes in government policies and regulations.

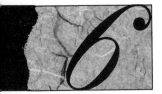

Market Targeting

LADY SMITH HANDGUNS[1]

More women are buying handguns, which is not surprising, given the prevailing crime rates in large U.S. cities. Gallup recently reported that 15.6 million women were considering buying a handgun in the next several years. This represents an increase of almost 100 percent over reports a few years earlier. About 90 percent of the guns to be purchased were for home and personal protection.

Smith & Wesson (S&W), the largest firearms manufacturer in the world, took this information seriously. The company spent over two years researching this emerging market. This included nationwide focus interview groups comprising female gun owners, nonowners, and sporting goods dealers. In addition, information was compiled from over 6,000 female Smith & Wesson owners—one of every 10 S&W buyers is a woman.

From this research the company found out what women wanted in a personal handgun—and S&W did not have an appropriate model to fit these needs. The company sought additional input from dealers before designing the Lady Smith revolvers and the supporting marketing programs. The new guns were a modification of two models in the company's existing line of .38 special revolvers that were easy to operate and packed sufficient power.

The two major areas of improvement were the grip and the trigger. The standard grip did not permit a woman's hand to be adequately positioned for shooting, nor did it permit her to place her finger on the trigger in a way that facilitated an easy straight-through pull. Two new grips that accommodated most hand sizes were developed to eliminate this problem.

---

[1]Based on information provided by Smith & Wesson.

EXHIBIT 6-1

An Excerpt from the Smith & Wesson Brochure on Safety Awareness

If you live in an apartment

If you have the option of living in a building with a doorman, electronic security, or both, take it.

Insist that entries, halls, stairways, elevators, and parking areas be well lighted.

Before you step into an elevator, check out the other occupants. If you feel suspicious, don't get in.

Once you're in an elevator, stand near the control panel—which will usually put you near the door. If a person you find questionable gets on, you can step out just before the doors close. If you're accosted between floors, press all the buttons to give yourself a chance to escape at the next floor—or hit the emergency alarm button.

If your building has a common laundry facility, it should only be accessible from the inside of the building and should be kept locked. Keys should be issued to tenants only. If you use a commercial laundry facility, try to pick one that's attended—or go with a friend—especially if you have to go at night.

SOURCE: Smith & Wesson, "Safety Awareness," pp. 2–3.

Modifications in the trigger pull were also made. The edges on the trigger, cylinder release, and the hammer were rounded for greater shooting ease. A wider hammer and front sight were added and a new frosted stainless finish applied. The two-inch models come standard with rose-laminate stocks, while the three-inch comes with goncalo-alves combat stocks.

Smith & Wesson's research also told them what women wanted to know before they purchased a personal handgun. From these data they designed a Lady Smith information program that included a special 12-page safety-awareness brochure describing how a revolver functions and answering 20 questions typically asked about safety and firearms in the home. It included a toll-free number to call for answers to questions about guns. The safety brochure was designed to make women more aware of potentially dangerous situations, and avoid them. Exhibit 6–1 gives an example of one such situation.

A second part of the Lady Smith program consisted of an advertising schedule in magazines that reached millions of women. These publications included *Ladies' Home Journal, Executive Female, Women's Sports & Fitness,* and *Real Estate Today.* The ads did not show or make any mention of guns. The message clearly concerned safety.

The Smith & Wesson example illustrates the critical role played by three interrelated decisions in the formulation of marketing strategies and the development of marketing programs to accompany them. The first of these decisions concerns **market segmentation**—determining how to divide the market into segments for investing to gain a competitive advantage. In the Smith & Wesson example, the segmentation scheme clearly involved women. Within this group the company probably engaged in additional segmentation using such variables as age, marital status, income, lifestyle, geography, and presence of children.

The second decision has to do with **market targeting**—determining which segments the firm will direct its marketing efforts toward. Smith & Wesson, for example, must have targeted certain women using the kind of variables cited above. Once the targeting decision has been made, marketing managers are faced with the question of how best to **position** the product; for example, selling a revolver to defend one's home and loved ones or as a self-defense instrument carried at all times. This involves designing a marketing program and product that the target segment's customer will perceive as desirable and that will give the firm an enduring advantage over current and potential competitors. These three decisions—market segmentation, market targeting, and positioning—are closely linked and have a strong interdependence. All must be properly made and implemented if the firm is to be successful in exploiting a given product-market relationship (see Exhibit 6–2).

The first two decisions—market segmentation and market targeting—are the focus of this chapter. (Positioning is covered in Chapter 7.) Our concern here is severalfold. First, we examine ways to segment a market. The goal is to segment in ways that will facilitate the formulation of marketing strategies and programs for both consumer and industrial goods. We next discuss the criteria and procedures for evaluating (1) the long-term attractiveness of different market segments and (2) the firm's business strengths and capabilities relative to customer needs and the competitors in each segment. The outcome of this analysis should make it possible for a manager to decide which segments are most attractive.

Market targeting is one of the most important decisions managers make. However large the firm, its resources are usually limited compared to the number of alternative marketing investments available. Thus, a firm must make choices. For a given market, the basic options for marketing investments are expressed in terms of market segments. Even if the firm can afford to serve all segments of a given market, it must determine the most appropriate allocation of its marketing effort across these segments.

Usually the firm must resist the temptation to target too many market segments if it wishes to gain a strong competitive position in some limited areas. Thus, market segmentation and market targeting decisions lie at the heart of the firm's marketing strategy and are two key determinants of its long-run success. Consider the following example:

> In the metal can industry, the sales of Crown Cork & Seal (CC&S) are considerably smaller than those of its much larger rivals. However, over the years it has enjoyed significantly higher annual sales growth, net profit margin, and return on equity than its bigger competitors. It did so by concentrating on

EXHIBIT 6–2
The Market Segmentation, Market Targeting, and Product Positioning Process

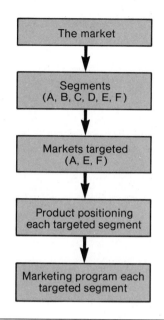

making metal cans for hard-to-hold products such as beer and carbonated soft drinks and aerosol cans. These were the growth segments in which it had special expertise. To better serve these segments, CC&S built small, single-product plants close to its customers instead of large, multiproduct, centralized plants that may have been more efficient.[2]

As the environment and/or the company's resources change over time, a firm may have to adjust its target-market strategy. Smith & Wesson did this when it expanded into a second target market with its new line of Lady Smith handguns. The last section of this chapter, then, examines alternative target-market strategies.

THE NEED TO SEGMENT A MARKET

Because markets are rarely homogeneous in benefits wanted, purchase rates, and price and promotion elasticities, their response rates to products and marketing programs differ. Variations among markets in product preferences, size and growth in demand, media habits, and competitive structures further

---

[2]C. Roland Christensen, Kenneth R. Andrews, Joseph L. Bower, Richard G. Hamermesh, and Michael E. Porter, *Business Policy* (Homewood, Ill.: Richard D. Irwin, 1987), p. 170.

affect the differences in response rates. Thus, markets are complex entities and can be defined (segmented) in a variety of ways. The critical issue is to find an appropriate segmentation scheme that will facilitate market targeting, product positioning, and the development of successful marketing strategies and programs.

Market segmentation

A firm has the option of adopting a market aggregation strategy or a segmentation strategy. Most companies adopt the latter. A market aggregation strategy is appropriate where the total market has few differences in customer needs or desires, especially when the product can be standardized as is sometimes the case internationally. It is also appropriate where it is operationally difficult to develop distinct products or marketing programs to reach different customer segments; that is, not all segmentation schemes are actionable. Because customers and their needs are diverse, relatively few product-markets meet these conditions in our economy; even so, some firms have pursued at least a partial aggregation strategy in recent years. For example, Stouffer's defined two very broad customer segments for its frozen entrees: people who are watching their weight and people who are not. The company treats each group as an aggregate market and does not attempt to segment them any further. Thus, the firm directed a single line of Lean Cuisine products at all weight-conscious adults.

The growing importance of segmentation

Market segmentation has become increasingly important in the development of marketing strategies for four reasons. First, population growth has slowed, and increasingly more product-markets are maturing. This, in turn, has sparked more intense competition as firms seek growth through gains in market share. To survive, firms are forced to pay more attention to the needs and wants of their customers. Not surprisingly, this often results in more sophisticated products, for example, the development of baby diapers tailored for boys or girls. They must identify customer segments with different needs and target segments where they have greater strengths than their competitors.

Second, such social and economic forces as expanding disposable incomes, higher educational levels, and more awareness of the world have produced customers with more varied and sophisticated needs, tastes, and lifestyles than ever before. As Joel Weiner, Senior Vice President for marketing services at Kraft, USA, notes, "The myth of a logical homogenous America is gone. We are a mosaic of minorities. All companies will have to do more stratified or tailored or niche marketing."[3]

Third, new technology such as computer-aided design and manufacturing has enabled firms to customize almost any product "from designer jeans to

---

[3]Zachary Schiller, "Stalking the New Consumer," *Business Week,* August 28, 1989, p. 55.

designer genes. . . . Auto buyers . . . can choose from 300 different types of cars and light trucks, domestic and imported, and get variations within each of those lines."[4]

Finally, many marketing institutions have facilitated the implementation of marketing programs by broadening and segmenting their own services and operations. For example, new advertising media have sprung up to appeal to narrow-interest groups, including special-interest magazines, radio programs, and cable TV channels.

IDENTIFICATION OF MARKET SEGMENTS[5]

The objective of the segmentation process is to divide the market into relatively homogeneous groups of prospective buyers of a good or service with regard to their demand functions. Ideally, the variances within individual groups would be relatively small versus the differences between groups.[6] The process must also describe these groups so that members can be readily identified, the size/value of each group determined, and the differences in customer needs noted. Ideally, the segmentation criteria (called **descriptors**) selected will accomplish these objectives.

We will examine four major categories of descriptors and discuss how they can be used to segment consumer and industrial markets.

Physical descriptors

These describe individual consumers on the basis of such demographics as age, sex, family life cycle, income, occupation, education, geographic locations, and race/ethnic origin. Physical descriptors are used to provide estimates of the size/worth of a given market segment, to select media vehicles (magazines and TV programs) that typically describe their audiences in such terms, and to provide insight into purchasing behavior, as, for example, with products used exclusively by children or by men or by certain professional or ethnic groups.

Physical descriptors are also important in the segmentation of industrial markets, which are dissected in two stages. The first, **macrosegmentation,** divides the market according to the characteristics of the buying organization. Here such descriptors as geographic location, company size, and industrial sector affiliation (SIC) are important. (The international counterpart of the SIC is the trade category code.)

---

[4]Regis McKenna, "Marketing in an Age of Diversity," *Harvard Business Review,* September–October 1988, pp. 88–9.

[5]For a more detailed discussion of this subject, see Harper W. Boyd, Jr., and Orville C. Walker, Jr., *Marketing Management: A Strategic Approach* (Homewood, Ill.: Richard D. Irwin, 1990), chap. 6.

[6]Peter R. Dickinson and James L. Ginter, "Market Segmentation, Product Differentiation, and Marketing Strategy," *Journal of Marketing,* April 1987, p. 1.

The second stage, **microsegmentation,** groups customers by the characteristics of the individuals who influence the purchasing decision; for example, age, sex, and position within the organization. International markets are segmented in a similar hierarchical fashion, starting with countries and followed by groups of individuals or buying organizations. Thus, for example, General Mills and its overseas partner, Nestlé S.A., selected France, Spain, and Portugal as their first target markets for General Mills Golden Grahams and Honey Nut Cheerios because Nestlé has a distribution network in place in those countries.[7]

General behavioral descriptors

These descriptors attempt to provide a better understanding of why and how a customer behaves in the marketplace. The most common behavioral descriptors in consumer markets are **lifestyle** (psychographics) and **social class.** The former groups consumers on the basis of their activities, interests, and opinions (AIOs). The result is an identification of different lifestyle types that are considered representative of different consumer groups. From such information it is possible to infer, on a general basis, what products and benefits would appeal to a particular group, as well as how best to communicate with individuals in the group (see Exhibit 6–3).

Social class

Every society has status groupings based largely on similarities in income, education, and occupation. From these similarities come social attitudes that characterize a particular class. Researchers have documented the values of different social classes in a wide range of areas. Thus, knowing a buyer's social class can help the seller infer certain behavior relevant to the marketing of a given product. For example, the middle classes tend to place more value on education, family activities, cleanliness, and being up-to-date than do lower-class families.

Industrial behavioral descriptors

Purchasing structure and buying situation segmentation descriptors are unique to industrial markets. **Purchasing structure** is the degree to which the purchasing activity is centralized. In a centralized structure the buyer is likely to consider all transactions with a given supplier on a global basis, emphasize cost savings, and minimize risk. In a decentralized situation, the buyer is apt to be more sensitive to the user's need, emphasize product quality and fast delivery, and be less cost conscious.

The **buying situation** descriptor includes three distinct types of situations: straight rebuy, a recurring situation handled on a routine basis; modi-

---

[7]Richard Gibson, "Cereal Venture Is Planning Honey of a Battle in Europe," *The Wall Street Journal,* November 14, 1990, p. 1.

EXHIBIT 6-3

Purchasing Behavior Ascribed to a Self-Admirer

This is one of the more confident types of men, and he knows exactly what he wants. He is body-aware (checks his weight regularly, pays attention to what he eats), the most frequent user of toiletries, and the most keen on running and jogging. He sees himself as gregarious and optimistic for the future. Success is very important to him, and he does not see himself as a tolerant individual—this type of man is self-conscious and wants success. He responds to brands that exude self-confidence and success; for example, "Martini, the right one," and "You get more than a card with American Express" . . .

SOURCE: Bickley Townsend, "Psychographic Glitter and Gold," *American Demographics,* November 1985, p. 23.

fied rebuy, which occurs when some element, such as price or delivery schedules, has changed in a client-supplier relationship; and a new buying situation, which may require the gathering of considerable information and an evaluation of alternative suppliers.

Product-related behavioral descriptors

These descriptors include product usage, loyalty, purchase predisposition, and purchase influence, all of which can be used to segment both consumer and industrial markets. **Product usage** is important because in many markets, a small proportion of potential customers makes a high percentage of all purchases. In industrial markets, the customers are better known, and heavy users, often called *key accounts,* are easier to identify.

With respect to **loyalty**—reflected by the numbers of successive purchases over time—current users can vary considerably in their purchases of a given brand or patronage of a particular supplier. In industrial markets, sellers can often observe this directly; in consumer markets, identifying loyal customers requires market research.

Consumers hold different predispositions toward the purchase of a product. A market segmentation scheme based on product knowledge (are they aware of it?) and **purchase predisposition** can identify the nonusers who are most likely to become future buyers. For example, knowledgeable nonusers who state intentions to buy, say, a high-fiber cereal, are the most likely to become future users. Knowledgeable nonusers who do not intend to buy, on the other hand, would probably represent a low potential.

Market segmentation by sources of **purchase influence** is relevant for both consumer and industrial markets. Many products used by various family members are purchased by the wife; but joint husband-wife decisions are becoming more common. Children's products, prescription drugs, and gifts are clearly influenced by a variety of individuals. In industrial markets, several individuals or organizational units with varying degrees of influence participate in the buying center.

Customer needs

Customer needs are expressed in **benefits sought** from a particular product or service.[8] Individual customers do not have identical needs and thus attach different degrees of importance to the benefits offered by different products. In the end, the product that provides the "best" bundle of benefits—given the customer's particular needs—is mostly likely to be purchased.

Since purchasing is a problem-solving process, consumers evaluate product or brand alternatives on the basis of desired characteristics and how valuable each characteristic is to the consumer (**choice criteria**). Marketers therefore can define segments according to these different choice criteria both in terms of the presence or absence of certain characteristics and the importance attached to each. Firms have typically singled out a limited number of benefit segments to target. Thus, different toothpaste manufacturers have emphasized different benefits, such as decay prevention versus plaque removal. The same is true with automobile companies. For example, the Ford Explorer stresses comfort, safety, and ease of driving.[9]

In industrial markets, customers consider relevant benefits that include product performance in different use situations, on-time delivery, credit terms, economy, spare parts availability, and training. Different customers have different choice criteria. For example, in the office supply market, some industrial buyers want service; others are primarily concerned with cost and credit terms.

Note that benefits sought must be linked to usage situations. There is ample evidence that usage often strongly affects product choice and substitutability.[10] Thus, the appropriateness of product attributes varies across different usage environments. Any attempt to define viable segments must recognize this fact—particularly with consumer goods. For example, the appropriateness of drinking beer versus a soft drink, coffee, or gin and tonic varies substantially across such usage situations as with or after a meal, immediately following work, while watching TV, or at a formal dinner party.

As we move from physical to general behavioral to product-related to customer needs (benefits wanted) descriptors, the implications for the formulation of marketing strategies and programs become more apparent and meaningful. All the various descriptors are important and would be likely used to some extent in the segmentation of a given market. For a summary listing of these various descriptors, see Exhibit 6–4.

---

[8]The importance of benefit segmentation was originally advocated by Russell I. Haley, "Benefit Segmentation: A Decision-Oriented Research Tool," *Journal of Marketing,* July 1968, pp. 30–35.

[9]James B. Treece and Mark Landler, "Beep, Beep, There Goes Ford Explorer," *Business Week,* January 26, 1991, p. 60.

[10]Rajendra K. Srivastava, "Usage Situation Influences on Perceptions of Product Market: Theoretical and Empirical Issues," *Advances in Consumer Research,* ed. Kent Monroe (Chicago: Association for Consumer Research, 1981), pp. 32–37.

EXHIBIT 6-4

Descriptors Used to Segment Consumer and Industrial Markets

	Market type		
	Industrial		
Descriptors	Macro	Micro	Consumer
Physical			
Demographics	—	X	X
Company size	X	—	—
Industrial sector	X	—	—
General behavioral			
Innovative*	—	X	X
Lifestyle	—	—	X
Social class	—	—	X
Purchasing structure	X	—	—
Buying situation	X	—	—
Product-related behavior			
Product usage	X	—	X
Loyalty	X	—	X
Purchase predisposition	—	X	X
Purchase influence	—	X	X
Customer needs	X	—	X

*Adopter group (e.g., innovators, early adopters, and so on).

THE SEGMENTATION PROCESS: SELECTING MEANINGFUL DESCRIPTORS AND DETERMINING DIFFERENCES IN NEEDS ACROSS SEGMENTS

As we have noted, selection of meaningful descriptors in a given market situation is the first step in the market segmentation process. The next step is to determine whether and to what extent there are differences in the needs or benefits being sought by customers in the various segments. The first and second steps in the process are sometimes reversed, however. Thus, a firm first can segment a market on the basis of different benefits sought and then identify it on the basis of physical descriptors.

The segmentation descriptors used should describe the differences in customers' buying behavior in such a way that management can determine which segments require differentiated marketing programs involving different products and marketing mixes. This is why benefits sought and product-specific behavioral variables are particularly useful for answering strategic questions, such as:

- How many distinct product-markets are there within a particular industry? In the handgun industry, there are several distinct segments that have different needs including the military, police, collectors, ordinary citizens, and men and women.
- Which segments represent attractive opportunities in view of the customers' needs and the firm's competitive strengths and weaknesses? Smith & Wesson determined that women wanted/needed guns for protection and that the firm's resources were adequate to develop a program to satisfy this segment and to do so at a profit.
- Which segments are not currently being satisfied and therefore represent opportunities for new-product development? The Smith & Wesson example also applies here.

Benefit segmentation further enhances the resource allocation process by helping the firm better understand the relative standing accorded its product compared to competitors. It also provides insights into the extent to which different segments will respond to various elements in the marketing mix, a critical part of the firm's plan of action.

General behavioral and physical descriptors are useful for answering many of the operational questions that arise when designing a marketing program to reach a particular product-market, such as:

- Which retail outlets or distributors should be included in the distribution channel?
- How should sales territories be designed and how frequently should salespeople call on different customers?
- What advertising media should be used?
- Which promotional appeals should be emphasized?

Marketers thus try to define segments using a combination of benefit, behavioral, and physical factors, even though this often requires the collection of marketing research data and the use of sophisticated statistical analyses.

MARKET ATTRACTIVENESS

Once a firm has identified and described the various segments in a given market, it must determine the attractiveness of each. Relevant factors to consider here pertain to the market, economics and technology, competition, and the general environment. The factors listed in Exhibit 6–5 are illustrative only, although they are the ones most commonly used. A firm undertaking an attractiveness analysis would add or delete factors according to its own needs.

EXHIBIT 6–5
Market Attractiveness Factors

> **Market**
>　Size
>　Growth including stage in product life cycle
>　Market gaps
>　Differentiation possibilities
>　Bargaining power of customers
>　Cyclicality and seasonality
>　Distribution
> **Economic and technological**
>　Investment intensity
>　Industry capacity
>　Technology
>　Barriers to entry and exit
>　Access to supplies
> **Competitive**
>　Competitive structure
>　Competitive groupings
>　Substitute products
>　Price
>　Individual competitor analysis
> **Environmental**

Source: Derek F. Abell and John S. Hammond, *Strategic Market Planning: Problems and Analytical Approaches* (Englewood Cliffs, N.J.: Prentice Hall, Inc., 1979), p. 214; and George S. Day, *Strategic Market Planning* (St. Paul, Minn.: West Publishing Company, 1984), p. 128.

Market factors

Here we are mainly concerned with size, growth, market gaps, product differentiation, bargaining power of customers, seasonality and cyclicality, and distribution. Each of these factors is discussed briefly below.

Size

The size of a market represents its current sales potential. The notion of minimum size is relative to the size of the firm. Large firms generally have higher minimum size requirements than do smaller firms since their opportunity costs (e.g., diverting management time from larger to smaller segments) are higher. For example, IBM could not afford to cover small segments of the computer market, which explains its late entry into both the mini and personal computer markets.

Marketers generally believe that the greater the size of a market segment, the more attractive it is. But this ignores the resources required, including the ability to compete successfully against present and future competitors.

EXHIBIT   6–6

Impact of Growth on Future Sales Potential for a Given Market Segment—
Cumulative Impact of Compounded Growth (in Percent)

Annual growth rate	Increase in market segment size (constant dollars) after		
	5 years	10 years	15 years
2	10.4%	22%	35%
5	28	63	108
10	61	159	318
15	101	305	714
20	149	519	1,441
30	271	1,279	5,019

Some firms may not have the resources required to obtain and hold a viable share of a large market.

Growth

A key attractiveness factor is the market's growth rate, since the cumulative impact of compounded growth on the future sales potential of a given segment can be enormous (see Exhibit 6–6). Growth is important; it gives firms an opportunity to better exploit the experience curve (scale and learning effects) and thus better position themselves on a lower relative per-unit cost basis longer term. The growth analysis should consider the amount of time remaining in this growth stage of the product life cycle. Such information is important, since the stage of the life cycle provides insights into the present and pending opportunities and threats the firm faces in a given segment.

Market gaps

Some market segments are more attractive than others because of the existence of competitive market gaps the firm can exploit. These gaps may result from the low awareness or trial rates of existing brands, customers' dissatisfaction with existing products, lack of needed service, high prices, restricted distribution, or a lack of product availability (e.g., handguns for women).

Product differentiation

Benefits-sought segmentation provides valuable information concerning the opportunities for product differentiation. If existing products are rated poorly against the ideal choice criteria, then a new or modified product possessing the desired characteristics should do well, assuming it is properly priced, readily available, and prospective buyers are made aware of its qualities. Presumably this was the reasoning behind Smith & Wesson's development of its Lady Smith line of handguns. If, on the other hand, all major products are rated highly against the ideal choice criteria, then it will be more difficult to penetrate the segment via product differentiation.

Successful differentiation usually results in above-average industry earnings because it generates brand loyalty and thus a lower sensitivity to price. It also makes it more difficult for competitors to enter a segment. Differentiation is, on average, a faster way to grow market share than is a low-cost/low-price strategy.

Bargaining power of customers

Segments often vary in attractiveness because of servicing costs and customers' bargaining power with respect to price and service. Thus, large buyers typically cost less to service on a per-unit basis because of their bigger orders, direct selling versus use of distributors, and lower shipping costs; but they typically demand lower prices, usually through quantity discounts. Two critical questions are, therefore, What percentage of customers account for two-thirds of segment sales? What percentage will account for two-thirds at some future date?

Seasonality and cyclicality

The extent to which segment sales are seasonal and/or cyclical affects profitability because of the uneven utilization of assets over time, including the cost of capital tied up in inventories. Manufacturers of snowmobiles are a good example of firms affected by such fluctuations.

Distribution

If channels of distribution differ from those used with other segments, the firm may experience difficulty in penetrating the segment of interest. For example, when IBM launched its new personal computer, one of its biggest obstacles was the need to sell it through retail stores versus selling direct to the ultimate user (IBM's standard policy).

Economic and technological factors

These include investment intensity (both plant and working capital), industry capacity, technology requirements, barriers to entry and exit, and access to supplies.

Investment intensity and industry capacity

High-investment-intensity businesses tend to have low average profitability because of the pressure to operate at high levels of capacity.[11] This, in turn, forces a decline in prices when the demand for industry output slackens and

---

[11] Robert D. Buzzell and Bradley T. Gale, *The PIMS Principles* (New York: Free Press, 1987), chap. 7.

capacity utilization declines. Such high-investment industries as steel, aluminum, commodity chemicals, color printing, and paper are forced at times during slack periods to accept orders that yield below break-even margins but still make some contribution to fixed costs.

Overcapacity is particularly disruptive when products are not differentiated and product choice depends heavily on price. If demand is cyclical, the firm's capacity limits the sales it can make during the peak demand period. This in turn forces a firm aspiring to a leadership position to invest heavily in large, modern plants. Sometimes a firm is willing to expand its facilities even if the forecasted demand does not warrant it in order to discourage others from also expanding or to inhibit entry. Perhaps this was part of the thinking of the executives of Wheeling-Pittsburgh Steel Company when they committed several hundred million dollars during the early 1980s to construct several production facilities that employed the latest technology, even though the steel industry was substantially depressed.[12]

Industry undercapacity may offer a firm a unique opportunity, assuming demand continues and possibly increases, other firms respond inadequately in building new facilities or expanding present ones, and strong experience effects are present.

Technology

This factor can affect product features or the production process. In either case it is an important consideration in determining the attractiveness of a given segment. Technological change can be viewed either positively (an opportunity) or negatively (a threat), depending on the technological experience and expertise of the firm involved. With respect to product features, the firm needs to anticipate what changes are likely to occur in the ways consumers will want to be serviced. Will delivery times be shorter? Will the need for postpurchase service change?

Entry barriers

A firm entering a segment for the first time must consider the barriers to entry as well as the reaction of present competitors. The major entry barriers include product differentiation, access to distribution channels, experience effects that place the new entrant at a cost disadvantage, and the costs of switching from one supplier to another. Strong retaliation from existing competitors can be expected if there is a lack of product differentiation, slow growth, high investment is required, and high exit costs.

Access to suppliers

Being unable to obtain a reliable source of supply for needed raw materials and components makes a segment less attractive to enter or penetrate further. Also, a firm must determine the strength of suppliers in dealing with

---

[12]Leslie W. Rue and Phyllis G. Holland, *Strategic Management* (New York: McGraw-Hill Book Company, 1989), pp. 845–49.

the industry. This is especially important where the supplier's product is differentiated and an important part of the finished product (e.g., electric motors).

Access to cheap raw materials can provide a substantial cost advantage. For example, Fort Howard Paper is the only major papermaker to rely on recycled pulp. While the finished product is not so high in quality as paper from virgin wood, Fort Howard's lower cost gives it a competitive edge in toilet paper and other price-sensitive paper products used in hotels, restaurants, and office buildings.

Competitive factors

These are among the most important factors to consider in assessing the attractiveness of a particular segment. Factors concerned with competitive structures, different groups of competitors, the effects of substitute products, and individual competitors are discussed below.

Competitive structure

A market structure can be described as *open* if the segment is not adequately served by any firm, as was the case with Smith & Wesson when they introduced their Lady Smith line. The competitive structure is *disaggregated* if many firms serve the segment without any one of them dominating it or *concentrated* if a small number of firms account for a large proportion of sales. An example of a disaggregate structure is the dental equipment and supplies industry, which has only 500 small, privately owned companies, of which about 75 percent have fewer than 20 employees. An example of a concentrated structure is the carbonated soft-drink industry, which is dominated by two players—Pepsi and Coke.

Entry costs and competitive reactions are likely to be greatest when firms seek to enter a concentrated market. A disaggregated structure often offers opportunities to develop a competitive advantage through economies of scale in marketing and/or production, since competitive reactions are likely to be dispersed and hence less effective. Open structures are easier to penetrate, as has often been the case in the dental equipment and supplies industry. However, the lack of competition may be the result of limited size or limited attractiveness of other criteria.

Competitive groupings

Established firms servicing a given segment often emphasize different marketing mixes (e.g., product features, price, technological innovation, physical logistics including channels, personal selling, and advertising). Thus, firms with a similar mix should be grouped together, since this is the only way the entry firm can identify its competitors and understand what is required to be successful. For example, major tire companies (eight account for about 95 percent of the tires produced in the United States) vary in the way they service the premium radial passenger car replacement segment. They also differ with respect to the product features emphasized, price and warranties, distribution (some have their own retail outlets), and advertising (both message content and weight).[13]

Substitute products

These products limit the price a firm can charge. The more attractive a given substitute (based on price performance), the more difficult it is for firms to raise prices. Indeed, the improvement of a substitute product's price performance relative to the industry affects not only the attractiveness rating but the kind of product strategy to employ. For example, Polaroid has been hurt by the growing availability of instantly developed color film.

Prices

The extent to which industry prices are expected to decline (in constant dollars) is an important consideration. Price trends can be predicted to some extent based on industry structure, investment intensity, differentiation opportunities, entry/exit barriers, and experience effects. The hotel/motel industry, for example, is experiencing increased price competition as more and more of its heavy hitters move into the budget segment (Quality Inns, Holiday Corp., and Marriott).[14]

Individual competitor analysis

Firms should evaluate each present and potential major competitor's objectives, strategies, and strengths and weaknesses. An analysis of existing competitors' performances to date is also important. And, finally, firms need to ask, What behavior can be expected from each competitor in the future?

Environmental Factors

The environmental factors to consider vary by industry and country. Generally speaking, the demographic/economic environment, technology, the regulatory situation, social attitudes, and unionization are always important factors to analyze. In the late 1970s, Daimler-Benz—which dominated the high-priced luxury European-style automobile market segment with its Mercedes line—decided to target the U.S. lower-priced luxury European car segment dominated by BMW. Other competitors included Volvo and Audi. Management felt its overall image was an advantage in targeting this market. It chose to target the fast-growing 25-to-44-age group in the United States and positioned its new baby Benz, the 190, to attract young, first-time buyers

---

[13]William H. Newman, James P. Logan, and W. Harvey Hegarty, *Strategy* (Cincinnati, OH: Southwestern Publishing Co., 1989), pp. 52–54.

[14]Tom Ichniowski, "Hey, Little Spender, Have These Motels Got a Deal for You," *Business Week,* November 2, 1987, p. 63.

of Mercedes. It spent about $1 billion to develop the 190, an expenditure justified by its sales over the years.[15]

Regulation

Government regulation and deregulation can provide opportunities and threats to a firm. The regulatory climate can be severe (e.g., toxic chemicals) to relatively mild (men's clothing), and it can apply to production or marketing or both (pharmaceuticals). Regulations may affect the product (safety), price (controls), channels of distribution (no full-line forcing or tying agreements), and promotion (limited TV advertising availability). Ordinarily, heavy regulation, or the likelihood of such occurring, makes a segment less attractive. Sometimes a firm can turn a threat into an opportunity. For example, a firm producing infants' nightwear correctly forecasted government action requiring the use of nonflammable material and gained market share by meeting the requirements ahead of schedule.

Social attitudes

Many, if not most, established firms will not enter a market if there is any likelihood of social disapproval. For example, some U.S. companies have refused to sell their products to South Africa because of the pressure from antiapartheid groups. Many analysts would not view the domestic beer industry favorably because of the widespread trend toward fitness and the strong campaign against drunk driving.

Unionization

Some companies will not enter an industry that is heavily unionized. They feel that unions dampen productivity and flexibility, thus lowering profitability. If, however, a firm can find a way to gain an advantage in cost by hiring at lower than the going rate, substantial profits can result.

BUSINESS STRENGTHS

In addition to market attractiveness, the firm must consider its own resources before deciding which segment(s) to target. This requires an evaluation of the firm's competitive strengths and weaknesses relative to the segment's unique requirements. The business-strength factors typically included in any such analysis are grouped by market position, economic/technology position, capabilities, and interaction with other segments (see Exhibit 6–7). Some factors in the first two groups are applicable to only those situations where the firm already has an entry.

---

[15]Thomas F. O'Boyle, "Small Luxury Car Is Success for Daimler," *The Wall Street Journal,* September 19, 1986, p. 24.

EXHIBIT 6-7
Business Strength Factors

> **Market position trends**
>> Sales and share data for total market and segment—
>> company and major competitors
>> Relative share data
>> Product/service differentiation
>> Distribution
>
> **Economic/technology position trends**
>> Relative per unit costs
>> Capacity utilization
>> Technology position—product and manufacturing
>
> **Capabilities**
>> Financial
>> Product development
>> Manufacturing
>> Distribution, including channels and physical logistics
>> (product availability)
>> Salesforce
>> Advertising
>
> **Interaction with other segments**

Market position

The factors here provide the basis for a review and analysis of the entry's present market position. The review starts by setting forth the entry's market and profitability objectives, the date (year) they were adopted, and the strategy followed. The latter includes a discussion of the strategy elements (product features, product line, channels, personal selling, and advertising) that form the essence of the strategic plan. It is important to provide information that explains why changes occurred in market demand (e.g., a lowering of price), company sales and share (entry of a new and strong competitor), and the sales and share of individual major competitors (introduction of new products). Any failures here with respect to new-product development, product quality, product availability, price, personal selling, advertising, and service should be noted. An analysis of the entry's current market position will ordinarily include a considerable amount of trend data. Examples are:

1. Industry sales data in both dollars and units for the total market (total color TV sets for the United States) and the segment (small-screen second sets).

2. Segment's share of total market by dollars and units.

3. Company sales and market share of total market and segments in both dollars and units, plus similar information for each major competitor.

4. Relative share of the total market and segment in dollars and units.

5. Product/service differentiation as evidenced by changes in the rate new customers are attracted and retention of old customers (loyalty).

6. The proportion of distribution outlets (retailers and distributors) stocking the product versus major competitors. Firms should weigh the outlets by their relative importance; for example, distribution in 10 percent of the stores doing 65 percent of the sales of the relevant product class.

Economic/technology

The firm's position here is assessed on the basis of costs, capacity utilization, and R&D and engineering capabilities. Costs are considered on a relative per-unit basis and, as noted earlier, are usually inversely related to the firm's cumulative relative share position. Since Smith & Wesson had the largest share of the handgun market in the United States and since the new Lady Smith line was essentially a modification of its existing line, the company had every reason to believe it would have the lowest per-unit cost in servicing the women's market even after competitors entered. The firm's cost position is especially important with undifferentiated products.

High capacity utilization is an important determinant of profitability, especially when fixed investment is high. If the firm has overcapacity, it ordinarily will seek increased sales, and thus, an entry in a growth market has the resources to cope with the other market factors (e.g., competition).

Capabilities

The firm's capabilities, or strengths and weaknesses, in a given segment derive essentially from its financial and management resources. The importance of financial resources is obvious, especially so when exploitation of a given market opportunity requires large and continuous expenditures (a strong market growth situation coupled with high plant investments).

Product and new-product development

If the firm segments its market on the basis of benefits sought, it should have considerable knowledge about what target consumers want or expect in the product. For an existing product, such segmentation would reveal how well the firm's product matched up to the segment's choice criteria versus competition. Assuming such data are available from the segmentation process, the firm should know what, if anything, it needs to do to make a closer fit between the product and the ideal product.

If a new product is involved, the firm must make certain it has the skills required to commercialize the product concept under consideration.[16] Product quality and its maintenance are a critical part of the commercialization process. Quality can be defined and differentiated in many different ways:

---

[16]For more on new-product development, see Glen L. Urban, John R. Hauser, and Nikhilesh Dholakia, *Essentials of New Product Management* (Englewood Cliffs, N.J.: Prentice Hall, Inc., 1987).

performance, features, reliability, conformance to specifications, durability, source ability, and esthetics. Companies will ordinarily do better to focus on a limited number of quality dimensions rather than to seek high performance on most or all of them.[17] Paccar has emphasized reliability and durability in its trucks to such an extent that it has been able to command a price premium over competitors.[18]

Distribution

The ability to give the target market access to the product is a considerably important business strength. In some cases it may be possible to use a firm's existing distribution network and even enhance its overall importance in so doing. When it is necessary for the channel members to provide superior customer services, the firm's ability to develop the appropriate channel design and to manage it over time becomes critical.

It may be desirable to integrate forward to develop a channel structure that best fits the firm's product-market strategy. This has been the case with Firestone's MasterCare Service Centers and Goodrich's Tire Centers. A firm's channel structure can be an enduring competitive advantage, as in Coke's and Pepsi's franchise networks.

Salesforce

A dedicated salesforce can make the difference between success or failure in many situations, especially with industrial goods.

The success of the salesforce depends heavily on how well it is integrated with the other elements in the marketing mix. Thus, for example, when the parent company of Wilkinson Sword USA withdrew advertising support of its razor blades to focus its resources on the European market, the company's U.S. market share dropped from over 7 percent to less than 1 percent. This was due in part to the company's use of manufacturers' reps and brokers who could not maintain distribution through drugstores and supermarkets without such help. When Wilkinson restored its consumer advertising *and* switched to a company salesforce, market share rebounded quickly to 3.5 percent.[19]

Advertising

Marketing consists of far more than developing a good product, offering it to the target market at the right price, and making it readily available. A company, especially one selling consumer goods, must be able to communi-

---

[17]For a thorough discussion of quality, see David A. Garvin, *Managing Quality* (New York: The Free Press, 1988).

[18]Newman et al., *Strategy,* p. 103.

[19]Rayna Skolnik, "The Birth of a Salesforce," *Sales & Marketing Management,* March 16, 1986, pp. 42–44.

cate a considerable amount of information about itself, including its products, its price structure, and its distribution structure, to a variety of audiences. The ability to properly position a product in the mind of target consumers often requires considerable skills. An example is Gallo's classic promotion featuring Frank Bartles and Ed Jaymes. Gallo launched its brand into first place in the wine cooler category by declining to link this entry with their then low-price image and, instead, developing a fictional company managed by two folksy country bumpkins.[20]

Interaction with other segments

Any evaluation of market opportunities cannot be conducted without considering the firm's activities in other market segments. The presence of the firm in one segment may help or hinder its position—currently or in the future—in other segments. Certainly this is true with respect to economies of scale and learning effects that can occur in all parts of the business, including manufacturing, engineering, marketing, and general management. Joint effects between segments often occur with military and government contracts, which allow companies the technology and scale effects that permit them to enter the commercial sector. Thus, for example, the French Telecommunications authority ordered 300,000 terminals from Alcatel, a French electronics company, as part of a project to provide 30 million telephone subscribers with a free terminal to replace the telephone directory by 1992. The initial order of 300,000 units gave Alcatel the necessary economies of scale to become a strong contender in the low-cost domestic home market segment as well as in the export market.[21]

Other kinds of synergy relating to marketing involve the salesforce (it may be easier to sell a full line than a partial one), distribution intermediaries who may wish to buy more from a given supplier, and image transfer. The latter can be positive or negative. For example, high-fashion designers and expensive perfume markets have long hesitated to enter the mass clothing and cosmetics markets because of the negative effect such action could possibly have on their core businesses. Positive image transfer is critical when a company expands its product line to enter a new segment using the same company or brand name.

MATCHING BUSINESS STRENGTHS AND MARKET ATTRACTIVENESS

The process considered here seeks a structure in which a firm's business strengths are matched with market attractiveness to yield an assessment of the firm's competitive position (see Exhibit 6–8). The analysis is done on an

---

[20]Jaclyn Fierman, "How Gallo Crushes the Competition," *Fortune*, September 1, 1986, p. 31.
[21]"France: An Export Flood of Low-Cost Terminals," *Business Week*, May 11, 1981, p. 18.

EXHIBIT 6–8

Process of Matching Business Strengths with Market Attractiveness to Determine Company's Competitive Position in a Given Market Segment

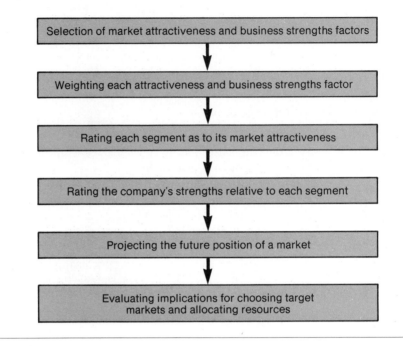

| Selection of market attractiveness and business strengths factors |
| Weighting each attractiveness and business strengths factor |
| Rating each segment as to its market attractiveness |
| Rating the company's strengths relative to each segment |
| Projecting the future position of a market |
| Evaluating implications for choosing target markets and allocating resources |

individual product-market basis and uses a business strength/market attractiveness matrix that can function with either a present or a new entry.

Which attractiveness and strength factor to use is very much an individual company choice; thus, there is considerable variation in the factors used between companies. For example, access to raw materials is critical to a petroleum company but not to a semiconductor firm. What is important is that the factors be strongly related to the dimension they are assigned to measure.

Assigning factor weights

A numerical weight is assigned to each factor to indicate its relative importance. For example, a large food company assigned the weights indicated in Exhibit 6–9. (Note that weights were assigned only to groups of factors although individual factors were taken into account in so doing.) One way of assigning weights to business strengths is to ask, "What are the critical success determinants with respect to this particular market?" This can best be answered in terms of a given mix of strategy elements. Identification of this

EXHIBIT 6-9

Examples of Weights and Ratings Accorded Market Attractiveness and Business Strength Factors by Large Packaged Food Company

Attractiveness			
Factor group	Weight	Rating*	Total
Market	50	8	400
Economic/technology	20	9	180
Competition	20	9	180
Environment	10	10	100
Total	100	36	860

$$\text{Attractiveness rating} = \frac{860}{100} = 86$$

Business Strengths			
Factor group	Weight	Rating*	Total
Market position	20	9	180
Economic/technology	20	8	160
Capabilities	50	9	450
Interaction with other segments	10	10	100
Total	100	36	890

$$\text{Business strength rating} = \frac{890}{100} = 89$$

*0-10 rating scale

mix is helpful in assigning weights to business strength factors and evaluating competitors. For example, Smith & Wesson was greatly concerned with the rate of growth in the women's handgun segment, the kinds of products needed, and the firm's ability to design and market them.

Assessing the segment's attractiveness and the company's business strengths

This step requires that each market segment and business strength factor be evaluated (rated) as to its attractiveness. This can be done on a scale of 0-10. In the case of our large packaged food products company example (see Exhibit 6-9), the market received an attractiveness rating of 86 and a business strengths rating of 89. On the basis of these scores, management considered its competitive position to be very strong. Exhibit 6-10 shows a matrix of the two ratings, which would indicate that management should strongly consider making the necessary investment to seek, or maintain, a strong (high-share) market position.

EXHIBIT 6-10

Matrix Showing Package Food Company's Competitive Position
in a Given Segment Based on a Matching of Business
Strengths and Market Attractiveness

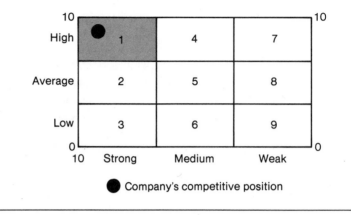

● Company's competitive position

Projecting the future position of a market

Forecasting a market's future is more difficult and more speculative than assessing its current state. Managers should first determine how the market's attractiveness is likely to change over the next three to five years. The starting point for this assessment is the product-market evolution analysis discussed in Chapter 5, including consideration of possible shifts in customer needs and behavior, the entry or exit of competitors, and changes in their strategies. Managers must also address several broader issues, such as possible changes in product or process technology, shifts in the economic climate, the impact of social or political trends, and shifts in the bargaining power or vertical integration of customers.

Managers must next determine how the business's competitive position in the market is likely to change, assuming that it responds effectively to projected environmental changes but does not undertake any initiatives requiring a change in basic strategy. The expected changes in both market attractiveness and competitive position can then be plotted on the matrix in the form of a vector (arrow) that reflects the direction and magnitude of the expected changes.

Evaluating implications for choosing target markets and allocating resources

Managers should only consider a market to be a desirable target if it is strongly positive on at least one of the two dimensions of market attractiveness and potential competitive position and at least moderately positive on

EXHIBIT 6 – 11

Implications of Alternative Positions within the Market Attractiveness/Business Position Matrix for Target Market Selection, Strategic Objectives, and Resource Allocation

Competitive position

	Strong	Medium	Weak
High	**DESIRABLE POTENTIAL TARGET** **Protect position** • Invest to grow at maximum digestible rate • Concentrate on maintaining strength	**DESIRABLE POTENTIAL TARGET** **Invest to build** • Challenge for leadership • Build selectively on strengths • Reinforce vulnerable areas	**Build selectively** • Specialize around limited strengths • Seek ways to overcome weaknesses • Withdraw if indications of sustainable growth are lacking
Medium	**DESIRABLE POTENTIAL TARGET** **Build selectively** • Emphasize profitability by increasing productivity • Build up ability to counter competition	**Manage for earnings** • Protect existing strengths • Invest to improve position only in areas where risk is low	**Limited expansion or harvest** • Look for ways to expand without high risk; otherwise, minimize investment and focus operations
Low	**Protect and refocus** • Defend strengths • Seek ways to increase current earnings without speeding market's decline	**Manage for earnings** • Protect position • Minimize investment	**Divest** • Sell when possible to maximize cash value • Meantime, cut fixed costs and avoid further investment

(Market attractiveness — vertical axis)

SOURCES: Adapted from material found in G. S. Day, *Analysis for Strategic Market Decisions* (St. Paul: West Publishing Co., 1986), p. 204. D. F. Abell and J. S. Hammond, *Strategic Market Planning: Problems and Analytical Approaches* (Englewood Cliffs, N.J.: Prentice Hall, 1979) and S. J. Robinson, R. E. Hitchens, and D. P. Wade, "The Directional Policy Matrix: Tool for Strategic Planning," *Long Range Planning* 11 (1978), pp. 8–15.

the other. In Exhibit 6–11 this includes markets positioned in any of the three cells in the shaded upper-left corner of the matrix. However, a business may decide to enter a market that currently falls into one of the middle cells if: (1) managers believe that the market's attractiveness or their competitive strength is likely to improve over the next few years; (2) they see such markets as stepping-stones to entering larger, more attractive markets in the future; or (3) where shared costs are present, thereby benefiting another entry.

The market attractiveness/business position matrix offers general guidance for strategic objectives and allocation of resources for segments currently targeted and suggests which new segments to enter. Exhibit 6–11 summarizes generic guidelines for strategic objectives and resource allocations for markets in each of the matrix cells. The general thrust of these guidelines is that managers should concentrate resources in attractive markets where the business is securely positioned, use them to improve a weak competitive position in attractive markets, and disengage from unattractive markets where the firm enjoys no competitive advantages.

TARGETING STRATEGIES

A number of strategies can help guide a manager's choice of target markets. Three of the more common of these are **mass-market, niche-market,** and **growth-market** strategies.

Mass-market strategy

A business can pursue a mass-market strategy in two ways. First, it can ignore any segment differences and design a single product and marketing program that will appeal to the largest number of consumers. This is often referred to as **undifferentiated marketing,** the primary objective of which is to capture sufficient volume to gain economies of scale and a cost advantage. This strategy requires substantial resources, including production capacity, and good mass-marketing capabilities. Consequently, it is favored by larger business units or by those whose parent corporation provides substantial support. For example, when Honda first entered the American and European motorcycle markets, it targeted the high-volume segment consisting of buyers of low-displacement, low-priced cycles. Honda subsequently used the sales volume and scale economies it achieved in that mass-market segment to help it expand into smaller, more specialized segments of the market.

A second approach to the mass market is to design separate products and marketing programs for the different segments. This is called **differentiated marketing.** For example, Marriott did this with its various hotel chains. Although such a strategy can generate more sales than an undifferentiated strategy, it also increases costs in product design, manufacturing, inventory, and marketing, especially promotion.

Niche-market strategy

This market strategy involves serving one or more segments that, while not the largest, consist of substantial numbers of customers seeking somewhat specialized benefits from the product or service. Such a strategy is designed to avoid direct competition with larger firms that are pursuing the bigger segments. It may not require maximum cost efficiencies because it enables the business to differentiate itself using a specific technical or marketing advantage. For example, IC Industries, Inc. is exporting its best selling line of Mexican food to selected European countries.[22]

Growth-market strategy

Businesses pursuing a growth-market strategy target one or more fast-growth segments, even though they may not currently be very large. This strategy is most compatible with an objective emphasizing future volume growth rather than short-term profits or ROI. It is a strategy often favored by smaller competitors to avoid direct confrontations with larger firms while building volume and share for the future. However, such a strategy usually requires strong R&D and marketing capabilities to identify and develop products appealing to newly emerging user segments, plus the resources to finance rapid growth. Digital Equipment (DEC) has successfully pursued this strategy in the minicomputer systems, such as engineering workstations for computer-assisted design activities.

The problem, however, is that fast growth, if sustained, attracts large competitors. This happened to DEC when IBM entered the minicomputer business. The goal of the defender (DEC) is to have developed an enduring competitive position via its products, service, distribution, and costs by the time competitors enter.

SUMMARY

This chapter focused on two interrelated decisions that constitute the first steps toward the formulation of a strategic marketing program for a product-market entry—market segmentation and market targeting. A company must follow either a market aggregation or a market segmentation strategy. Market aggregation strategy is appropriate when most customers have similar needs and desires. When customers are more diverse, however, a single standardized product and marketing program does not appeal to those who need or want something different. Segmentation has become increasingly popular because it reflects the realities faced by firms in most markets.

The process of segmenting markets involves describing the characteristics of customers and identifying the different needs or benefits sought by those customers. The variables used to explain the differences in product purchases across segments are called descriptors. Generic descriptors are relevant for both consumer and industrial markets. The more commonly used ones include benefits sought, product usage, loyalty, purchase predisposition, purchase influence, innovativeness, and geographical location.

---

[22]Joan S. Lublin, "U.S. Firms Find Europe's Huge Markets Hardly a Piece of Cake," *The Wall Street Journal*, May 15, 1990, p. 31.

Segmentation descriptors specific to consumer markets include age, sex, family life cycle, income, occupation, culture, and lifestyle. Industrial markets need to be segmented in two stages. Macrosegmentation divides the market according to the organizational characteristics of the customer. Microsegmentation groups customers by the characteristics of the individuals who influence the purchasing decision. Product usage and geographical locations are examples of macrosegmentation descriptors; purchase influence, loyalty, and area of expertise are microsegmentation descriptors. To be effective and useful, the chosen segmentation scheme must meet four criteria: adequate size, measurability, accessibility, and differential response to marketing variables.

Market targeting uses a market attractiveness/business position matrix as an analytical framework to help managers decide which market segments to target and how to allocate resources and marketing efforts. In applying such a matrix, the manager must first identify a relevant set of variables underlying the attractiveness of alternative market segments. This typically involves selecting variables related to four broad sets of factors: market factors, economic and technological factors, competitive factors, and environmental factors. Similarly, the manager must select a relevant set of variables to judge the firm's relative competitive position within the market segment. These competitiveness variables typically include items related to market position factors, economic and technological factors, the business's capabilities, and interactions or synergies across multiple target markets.

After managers have weighted these factors according to their relative importance, they can rate the attractiveness of alternative market segments and the strength of the firm's competitive position within each of those segments.

They can then test the validity of the combined ratings with a market attractiveness/business position matrix that shows the implications of alternative positions in the matrix. Because a firm or business unit has limited resources, however, it often identifies more attractive potential target markets than it is capable of pursuing. Consequently, a firm must develop a targeting strategy to guide managers' choices of alternative target markets in a manner consistent with corporate objectives, resources, and competitive strengths. The most common targeting strategies include mass-market, niche-market, and growth-market strategies.

Positioning Decisions

THE FORD EXPLORER VERSUS THE JEEP CHEROKEE

For years Jeep dominated the market for four-wheel-drive vehicles. Its four-door Cherokee enjoyed strong success during the 80s, partly because it became popular with many Yuppies who used it as a family vehicle. During this period few competitors entered this market, and the products of those that did were not well received. For example, General Motors entered two four-door models—the Chevrolet Blazer and GMC Jimmy. Neither, however, provided the space expected of a four-door, since both were designed as two-door models and then modified to add two more doors.

The Ford Explorer, introduced in 1990 to replace the Bronco II, did what no other brand had been able to do: outsell the Jeep Cherokee. During the second half of 1990 (July–December) Explorer outsold Cherokee nearly 2 to 1 (113,560 units versus 61,536). Unit sales of Jeep fell 21 points during 1990.

The reason for this success lies in Ford's realization that a lot more women were buying or influencing the purchase of off-road vehicles. Accordingly, Ford designed the Explorer as a spacious four-door vehicle. Compared with Cherokee, it has 8.5 more cubic feet of cargo space, more shoulder room (1.8 inches in the front and 2.6 inches in back), more headroom (1.6 inches in the front and 1.0 inches in the rear), and more leg room (1.3 inches in both front and rear).[1]

In addition to space, the Explorer makes driving a lot easier. To switch from two-wheel to four-wheel drive requires only the press of a button,

---

[1]James B. Treece and Mark Landler, "Beep, Beep! There Goes Ford's Explorer," *Business Week,* January 28, 1991, pp. 60–61; and Bob Plunkett, "Exploring Today's 4 × 4's," *Arkansas Gazette,* July 7, 1990, pp. G1 and G5.

even when driving. This is not the case with Cherokees, where drivers have to use a lever resembling a parking lever to make the change. The Explorer also has safety features not found in many off-road vehicles; for example, head restraints and rear shoulder belts.

Ford's top-of-the-line Explorer is a deluxe Eddie Bauer Signature series four-door 4 × 4 with leather interior, premium captain's chairs divided by a console, and a wrapped, quick-action steering wheel. Its price is about $4,500 less than a comparable Cherokee. Compared to the Explorer, the Cherokee looks dated—the last major overhaul of its vintage styling was 1984.

Explorer's advertising emphasizes its unique features—its comfort and safety—and encourages drivers to exercise their curiosity, to explore new territory. To many families, it's the best four-door off-road driving machine suited for city life.

As the above case demonstrates, the success, or lack thereof, of a product offering within a chosen target market depends on how well it is positioned within that market; that is, how well it is perceived to perform relative to competitive offerings and customers' needs in the target segment. Also, successful positioning depends on how consistent the company is in adhering to the ideal positioning requirements. Positioning, therefore, has to do with the perceived fit between a particular product offering and the target market. The concept must be defined relative to two entities—competitive offerings and consumer needs.

This chapter is concerned with answering the critical question, How can a business position its offering so that customers in the target market perceive it as providing the desired benefits, thereby giving it an advantage over current and potential competitors? Thus, the choice of a market position is a strategic decision with implications not only for how the firm's product or service should be designed, but for the design of the other elements of the marketing program associated with that program as well.[2] For example:

Ford's attempt to position its Explorer as both a compatible family car and a road vehicle was clearly reflected in its advertising, which stated: "Curiosity runs in your family. It always has. That's why you're always searching for the new or unexpected. Explorer from Ford is just what you had in mind. Four-door Explorer [is] an unexpected combination of comfort and versatility. It offers more total room for people and cargo than any vehicle in its class."[3]

---

[2]For a discussion of how marketing-mix elements can and do affect the position of a brand, see Russell S. Winer and William L. Moore, " Evaluating the Effects of Marketing Mix Variables on Brand Positioning," *Journal of Advertising Research,* February–March 1989, pp. 39–45.

[3]Treece and Landler, "Beep, Beep!", p. 61.

In this chapter, we first cover physical versus perceptual positioning then discuss the major steps in the positioning process, including the criteria for identifying attractive positions in a given target market and the alternative positioning strategies a business might pursue.

PHYSICAL PRODUCT POSITIONING

One way to assess the current position of a product offering relative to competitors is on the basis of how the various offerings compare on some set of objective, physical characteristics. For example, media often compared Explorer and Cherokee on price, appearance, braking systems, horsepower, comfort, roominess, turning radius, and safety features. (For other examples of important physical characteristics in several product categories, see Exhibit 7–1.)

In many cases, a physical product positioning analysis can provide useful information to a marketing manager, particularly in the early stages of identifying and designing new-product offerings. This was probably the case with Ford in launching its Explorer, since it was an immediate success.

To be meaningful, the physical characteristics used to make the comparison should be significant to the potential buyer. Managers can make inferences about the criteria customers use in purchase decisions. These inferences can be based on experience or marketing research. The characteristics of competitive offerings can usually be evaluated with considerable precision, since they can be directly observed and measured. In any case, managers must note that some physical characteristics change in importance over time—for example, gas mileage for cars.

Value of physical product positioning

Despite being based primarily on technical rather than on market data, physical product positioning can be an essential step in undertaking a strategic marketing analysis. This is especially true with the competitive offerings of many industrial goods and services, which buyers typically evaluate on the basis of such characteristics. In addition, it contributes to a better marketing R&D interface by determining key physical product characteristics, helps define the structure of competition by revealing the degree to which the various brands compete with one another, and may indicate the presence of meaningful product gaps (the lack of products having certain physical characteristics), which, in turn, may reveal opportunities for a new product entry.

Internal versus external physical positioning strategies

If a firm already has a product line, its new-product physical positioning strategy is best described in terms of its existing line. This reflects an *internal* positioning strategy, of which there are three main types: product-line filling, product-line stretching, and product-line extension.

EXHIBIT 7–1
Examples of Some Important Physical Characteristics in
Several Product Categories

Product categories	Physical characteristics
Executive airplanes	Price, speed, power, capacity, comfort, range, minimum field length for landing and takeoff, maneuverability, maintenance requirements, and operating costs
Computers	Price, memory size, cycle time, number of registers, maximum number of channels, direct memory access speed, software availability, reliability, and costs of maintenance and service
Cars	Price, power, mileage, range, maximum speed, acceleration, length, width, number of seats, safety, reliability, and optional features
Electric drills	Price, maximum power output, stall torque, noise level, speed, and weight
Credit cards	Annual charge, interest rate, retail coverage, protection against theft, and secondary services provided

1. *Product-line filling.* This consists of filling an internal gap within the existing line.
2. *Product-line stretching.* This involves adding new items at either end of the existing product line. This is essentially an incremental strategy; thus, the costs and risks incurred are substantially less than those of introducing a new and different product. For example, McDonnell Douglas, a U.S. airplane manufacturer, introduced several large versions of its original DC-9 model.
3. *Product-line extensions.* This strategy consists of introducing new products that differ significantly from those in the existing line. For example, McDonnell's introduction of its L-1011 three-engine plane was substantially different from its DC line.

A physical product positioning strategy may also be defined relative to competitive offerings, as opposed to the firm's own product line. There are two types of *external* physical product positioning strategies: differentiation and imitative. In a **differentiation strategy,** the new product differs significantly from existing products in the market. Because of its distinctiveness, the new product limits the impact of competitive reactions based on price and promotion.

When there are no significant opportunities for physical differentiation and the more attractive market segments have been successfully penetrated, a business may have little choice but to opt for an **imitation strategy,** (sometimes referred to as a head-on strategy) by introducing a new product that is similar to one or more existing competitive offerings.

An imitation strategy is risky, for it is often difficult to get consumers to believe that a new but similar product is better than an established one. Further, competitors are likely to react strongly to such a strategy. But it may be effective if the targeted competitors are vulnerable in their financial resources, image, and/or distribution. Thus, before adopting an imitation strategy, a firm should investigate the vulnerability of different competitors on aspects other than the product's physical specifications. Examples of firms that have adopted an imitation strategy include E. & J. Gallo Winery, in their move into the more prestigious and profitable varietal wines, and McDonald's, which has been testing a way to get into the pizza market by focusing on how long people typically wait for a pizza. (McDonald's test market ads promise no more than a 5½-minute wait, which is made possible by using a new super-fast oven developed specially for the company.)[4]

Limitations of physical positioning

A simple comparison of only the physical dimensions of alternative offerings usually does not provide a complete picture of relative positions, however. This is because positioning ultimately takes place in customers' minds. Even though a product's physical characteristics, package, brand name, price, and ancillary services can be designed to achieve a particular position in the market, customers may attach less importance to some of those characteristics, or perceive them differently, than the firm expects. Also, customers' attitudes toward a product are often based on social or psychological attributes not amenable to objective comparison, such as perceptions of the product's esthetic appeal, sportiness, or status image (e.g., the modern look of Explorer versus the dated look of Cherokees).

Al Ries and Jack Trout—two advertising executives who popularized the concept of positioning—note, positioning has more to do with how the product is positioned in the consumer's mind than with the product per se.[5] Consequently, *perceptual positioning analyses*—whether aimed at discovering opportunities for new-product entries or at evaluating and adjusting the position of a current offering—require marketing research about the perceptions and attitudes of customers and potential customers. The remainder of this chapter is concerned with this type of positioning analysis.

PERCEPTUAL PRODUCT POSITIONING

As noted above, physical product positioning is flawed by its failure to explicitly consider the consumer. Consumers know very little about the essential physical attributes of many products, especially those involving the household, and even if they did, they would not understand them well enough to use as a basis for choosing between competitive offerings. (For an outline of the differences between physical and perceptual product positioning

---

[4]Richard Gibson, "McDonald's Fires Fast Pitch at Pizza Buffs," *The Wall Street Journal,* August 28, 1989, p. B4.

[5]Al Ries and Jack Trout, *Positioning: The Battle for Your Mind* (New York: McGraw-Hill, 1982).

EXHIBIT   7-2
Comparison of Physical and Perceptual Analyses

Physical positioning	Perceptual positioning
• Technical orientation	• Consumer orientation
• Physical characteristics	• Perceptual attributes
• Objective measures	• Perceptual measures
• Data readily available	• Need marketing research
• Physical brand properties	• Perceptual brand positions and positioning intensities
• Large number of dimensions	• Limited number of dimensions
• Represents impact of product specs and price	• Represents impact of product specs, price, and communication
• Direct R&D implications	• R&D implications need to be interpreted

analyses, see Exhibit 7–2.) Many consumers often do not want to be bothered by information about a product's physical characteristics; they are not buying these physical properties but rather the benefits they provide. While the physical properties of a product definitely influence the benefits provided, a consumer can typically better evaluate a product on the basis of what it *does* than what it *is*. Thus, for example, a headache remedy is judged on how quickly it brings relief, a toothpaste on the freshness of breath provided, a beer on its taste, and a vehicle on how comfortably it rides.

The evaluation of many products is subjective, because it is influenced by many factors other than physical properties, including the way products are presented, past experience with them, and the opinion of other people. Thus, physically similar products may be perceived as being different because of different histories, names, and advertising campaigns. For example, despite their similarities in taste and appearance, Coke led Pepsi 100 to 1 in total sales at the time Pepsi won the legal right to use "cola" in its name. Three advertising agencies worked for 30 years to gain a respectable share for Pepsi; but it was not until one of them came up with a campaign built around "think young" and the "Pepsi generation" that a significant market share was achieved.

Dimensions on which consumers perceive competitive offerings

Consumers perceive competitive offerings on various dimensions, which can be classified as follows:

1. *Simple physically based attributes.* These are directly related to a single physical dimension such as price, power, or size. While there is a direct correspondence between a physical dimension and a perceptual attribute, an analysis of the consumers' perception of products on these attributes

may unveil some phenomena of interest to a marketing strategy. Two cars with estimated gasoline mileage of 23.2 and 25.8 miles per gallon may be perceived as having similar gasoline consumption.

2. *Complex physically based attributes.* Because of the presence of a large number of physical characteristics, consumers may use composite attributes to evaluate competitive offerings. The development of such summary indicators is usually subjective because of the relative importance attached to different cues. Examples of composite attributes are the efficiency of a computer system, roominess of a car, and the economy of a major electrical appliance.

3. *Essentially abstract attributes.* Although these perceptual attributes are influenced by physical characteristics, they are not related to them in any direct way. Examples include bodiness of a beer, sexiness of a perfume, and prestige of a car. All of these attributes are highly subjective and difficult to relate to physical characteristics other than by experience.

While all perceptual attributes have a subjective component, its importance varies across consumer and product classes. Thus, it can be argued that consumers familiar with a given product class are apt to rely more on physical characteristics and less on perceptual attributes than consumers who are less familiar with that product class. It can also be argued that perceptual product positioning is essential for nondurable consumer goods, less important for consumer durables (e.g., off-road vehicles versus coffee), and of little value for many industrial goods.

Even though there is considerable truth in the above statements, there is still a strong need to consider perceptual attributes in formulating a market strategy for most products. One reason is the similar physical characteristics of more and more products within product classes. This increases the importance of other, largely subjective dimensions; for example, the quality of postpurchase service for an industrial product. Further, because many industrial buyers tend to minimize perceived risk in their purchasing decisions, these subjective attributes assume increased importance.

The positioning process

The process of determining the perceived positions of a set of product offerings and evaluating strategies for positioning a new entry or repositioning an existing one involves the steps outlined in Exhibit 7–3. After managers have selected a relevant set of competing offerings (step 1), they must identify a set of critical or determinant product attributes (step 2).

Step 3 involves collecting information from a sample of customers about their perceptions of the various offerings; and in the fourth step, researchers analyze this information to determine the intensity of a product's current position in customers' minds (does it occupy a predominant position?).

In step 5, managers analyze the location in the **product space** of the product's position relative to those of competing products. They then ascertain the customers' most preferred combination of determinant attributes, which

EXHIBIT 7-3

Steps in the Positioning Process

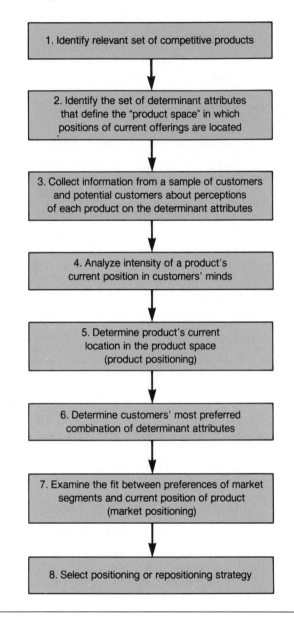

1. Identify relevant set of competitive products

2. Identify the set of determinant attributes that define the "product space" in which positions of current offerings are located

3. Collect information from a sample of customers and potential customers about perceptions of each product on the determinant attributes

4. Analyze intensity of a product's current position in customers' minds

5. Determine product's current location in the product space (product positioning)

6. Determine customers' most preferred combination of determinant attributes

7. Examine the fit between preferences of market segments and current position of product (market positioning)

8. Select positioning or repositioning strategy

requires the collection of further data (step 6). This allows an examination of the fit between the preferences of a given target segment of customers and the current positions of competitive offerings (step 7). And finally, in step 8, managers examine the degree of fit between the positions of competitive products and the preferences of various market segments as a basis for choos-

EXHIBIT 7–4

Product Category and Brand Positioning

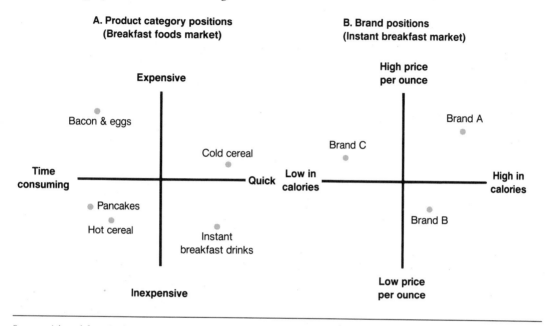

SOURCE: Adapted from Paul S. Busch and Michael J. Houston, *Marketing: Strategic Foundations* (Homewood, Ill.: Richard D. Irwin, 1985), p. 430.

ing a successful strategy for positioning a new entry or for repositioning an existing product.

A discussion of each of these steps takes up the remainder of this chapter.

IDENTIFYING A RELEVANT SET OF COMPETITIVE PRODUCTS (STEP 1)

A positioning analysis takes place at either the **product category** or the **brand level.** A positioning analysis at the product category level examines customers' perceptions about types of products they might consider as substitutes to satisfy the same basic need. Suppose, for example, that a company is considering introducing a new instant breakfast drink.[6] The new product would have to compete with other breakfast foods, such as bacon, eggs, and breakfast cereals. To understand the new product's position in the market, the manager could obtain customer perceptions of the new-product concept relative to likely substitute products on various critical determinant attributes. Part A of Exhibit 7–4 shows a product positioning map constructed from

---

[6]Adapted from Paul S. Busch and Michael J. Houston, *Marketing: Strategic Foundations* (Homewood, Ill.: Richard D. Irwin, 1985), pp. 429–30.

such information. The two attributes defining the product space in this instance were price and convenience of preparation. The proposed new drink occupies a distinctive position relative to the other alternatives because customers perceive it as a comparatively low-cost, convenience breakfast food.

Once competitors introduce similar brands into the same product category, a marketer needs to find out how a brand is perceived compared to its competitors. Thus, Part B of Exhibit 7–4 shows the results of a positioning analysis conducted at the brand level. It summarizes customer perceptions concerning three existing brands of instant breakfast drinks. Notice, however, that two different attributes define the product space in this analysis: relative price per ounce and calorie content. This brand-level analysis is very useful for helping marketers understand a brand's competitive strengths and weaknesses in the marketplace and for determining whether the brand should be repositioned to differentiate and strengthen its position. The danger in conducting only a brand-level positioning analysis, though, is that it can overlook threats from possible substitutes in other product categories.

IDENTIFYING DETERMINANT ATTRIBUTES (STEP 2)

Positioning can be based on a product feature, customer benefit, use or application, and/or a surrogate. Features and benefits are often referred to collectively as attributes and are directly related to the product per se. Features are often used in physical product positioning, a subject discussed earlier. Examples of positioning based on benefits include Volvo, which has over the years emphasized safety and durability largely via ads showing how well Volvos survive car crashes; Ford's Explorer, with claims of more total room for people and cargo than any vehicle in its class; Sony's Handycam (CCD-TR5), marketed as being "convenient to pack and carry on a vacation"; Norelco, promising a "close, comfortable shave"; and the Corporate Card from American Express, advertised as providing "preferential treatment for America's best."

Many products have based their positioning efforts on use or application. This is often the case in attempts to expand the market during the mature stage of the product life cycle. Examples include Campbell's positioning many of its soups for use in other foods, sauces, and dips; Arm & Hammer baking soda, which has been successfully positioned as a food ingredient and an odor destroying product in refrigerators; and Alka Seltzer, advertised as a cure for a hangover and as providing relief from colds.

Crawford reports that the use of surrogates as a positioning base (which implies desirable features or benefits) represents about a third of all positionings attempts, and this percentage is growing. A surrogate is a reason other than one involving product features why the company's product is best. The reason for the popularity of using surrogates is that it does not provide "specific reasons *why* the product is better . . . the listener or viewer has to provide those. And, the theory says, if the surrogate is good, the listener will bring favorable attributes to the product. . . . The system is efficient because

EXHIBIT 7-5

Meaning of Various Surrogates and Examples of Each

Nonpareil	— Because the product has no equal . . . it is the best (e.g., Jaguar).
Parentage	— Because of who makes or sells it. This can be done by *brand* (Cadillac, Jeep Cherokee), *company* (Hewlett Packard), or *person* (Gore Vidal's novel, *Hollywood*).
Manufacturer	— Because of how the product was made. This includes *process* (Anheuser Busch), *ingredients* (Sea-Island cotton boxer shorts by the Green Pond Company), and *design* (Mercedes Benz's engineering).
Target	— Because the product was made especially for people/companies like you. There are four ways to implement such a surrogate strategy: *end use* (John Hancock Life Insurance, "accumulate savings for college tuition"); *demographic* (American Airlines and the business traveler); *psychographic* (Michelob Light, "for the people who want it all"); and *behavioral* ("only Nordic Track gives you a total-body workout").
Rank	— Because it is the best-selling product ("Today, Digital has the largest data network in the world, serving over 100,000 people at nearly 500 sites." Or, "The Ford Explorer is the number-one selling vehicle in its class").
Endorsement	— Because people or organizations you respect say it's good ("Motor Trend's Car of the Year . . . the 1990 Lincoln Town Car" or the automotive magazine *Four Wheeler*'s proclamation of the Explorer as "the best vehicle in its class").
Experience	— Because of our long history we can do it best ("We're not the best because we're the oldest—we're the oldest because we're the best"— Cunard).
Competitor	— Because it is just like another product, one you respect ("if you've been thinking about buying a Mercedes, you'd do well to consider a Volvo 760").

SOURCE: Adapted from C. Merle Crawford, *New Products Management,* 2nd ed. (Homewood, Ill.: Irwin, 1987), pp. 397–99.

a one-sentence statement of surrogate positioning lets the listener bring perhaps four or five attributes to the product; the next listener can bring a different set, and so on."[7]

Surrogates in use today are (in order of their popularity) nonpareil, parentage, manufacture, target, rank, endorsement, experience, and competitor. A brief description and examples of each are presented in Exhibit 7–5. The claim in each example would be that "our product is better than or different from the others. . . ."[8]

Theoretically, consumers can use a large number of attributes to evaluate products and brands, but the number actually influencing a consumer's choice is normally small. Consumers can first consider only those attributes they are aware of—the **salient attributes.** But the *importance* attached to those salient attributes by consumers often varies. For instance, while the

---

[7]C. Merle Crawford, *New Products Management,* 2nd ed. (Homewood, Ill.: Irwin, 1987), p. 397.

[8]Ibid., p. 397.

brands of soap or shampoo provided by a hotel may be a salient attribute for many consumers when evaluating hotels, most are unlikely to attach a great deal of importance to it when deciding which hotel chain to patronize. Further, an important attribute may not greatly influence a consumer's preference if he or she perceives all the alternatives to be about equal on that dimension. As another example, deposit safety is an important attribute to consider when choosing a bank; but most consumers perceive all banks to be about equally safe. Consequently, deposit safety is not a **determinant attribute.** It does not play a major role in helping customers to differentiate among the alternatives and determine which bank they prefer.

Marketers should use only determinant attributes, then, to define the product space in a positioning analysis. The question is, How can a marketer find out which product dimensions are determinant attributes? The answer depends on the analytical technique the marketer uses. Choosing an appropriate statistical technique (the next step in the planning process) can help the marketer determine which of the important attributes are truly determinant in guiding customers' choices.

DETERMINING CONSUMERS' PERCEPTIONS (STEP 3)

Marketers can use several techniques to collect and analyze customers' perceptions about the competitive positions of alternative products or brands. These include factor analysis, discriminant analysis, multiattribute compositional models, and multidimensional scaling. Each of these analytical techniques and their advantages and disadvantages is described in an appendix to this chapter.

ANALYZING THE INTENSITY OF A PRODUCT'S CURRENT POSITION (STEP 4)

The position of a brand may not exist in the minds of consumers or may vary in intensity. Often, the awareness set for a given product class is three or less brands, even though the number of available brands is greater than 20. Thus, many if not most brands have little or no position in the minds of many consumers. For example, in the last ten or so years, over 200 new soft drinks have been introduced, most of which were not noticed or remembered by consumers.

A brand that is not known by a consumer cannot, by definition, occupy a position in that consumer's mind (see Exhibit 7–6). Thus, the first step in acquiring an intense position for a brand is to build brand awareness. There are different degrees of awareness corresponding to different positioning intensities, which can be assessed using the following measurements:

1. *Unaided brand recall.* This is obtained by simply asking a consumer to name the brands he or she knows in a given product class under limited

EXHIBIT 7-6

Mercury Cars Strive for Brand Recognition

"The good news is Mercury doesn't have a bad reputation or bad presence," says one Lincoln-Mercury dealer. "The bad news is it doesn't have much presence, period." Originally, Mercury's mission was to offer stylish cars with more comfort and power than those under the Ford label. But over the years most of Mercury's models were essentially "me-too" copies of Fords. Mercury "got lost under the Ford umbrella." In 1988 Mercury sold about 500,000 cars or 4.8 percent of total cars sold in the United States.

Despite a "brand" campaign started in 1983, a Cougar (one of Mercury's better selling models), which differs significantly in features and styling from Ford's Thunderbird, and several distinct vehicles of its own, Mercury still lacks a clearly defined image. In 1989, Mercury placed last in "brand power," which measures such things as recognizability and cachet among domestic cars. Another survey showed that 76 percent of consumers didn't recognize the symbol Mercury adopted in 1984, a stylized "M" in a circle that many dealers say reminds them of a "flying hockey stick."

People do remember the Cougar cat that appeared in 1966 but was dropped in 1979. Dealers have been instrumental in reviving the cat, but this requires considerable care. The old symbol (a cougar which lounged majestically next to the cars) might remind people of the old Mercurys and scare away the younger buyers. The new cat jumps, turns, and stops quickly to reflect the agile motion of the brand's newer cars.

SOURCE: Melinda G. Guiles, "Ford's Mercury Line Strives to Establish a Firm Identity," *The Wall Street Journal,* April 4, 1989, p. B1.

and controlled time conditions. The brands here do not all have the same positioning intensity, since some are easily and quickly recalled while others are recalled only after some delay.

2. *Aided brand recall.*   This measure is obtained by submitting a list of brands from a given product class to a consumer and asking him or her to indicate the ones known. It is likely that the consumer will only vaguely recall some of the brands under these circumstances.

3. *Spontaneity of brand recall.*   The order in which brand names are given in unaided recall can be used as a measure of brand spontaneity. Thus, the first brand named is the one recalled most spontaneously and is a better predictor of positioning intensity than the other two measures of brand awareness.

Strengths of mental association with a brand name

Awareness is necessary for a brand to have an intense positioning, but the brand also needs to be strongly associated with a number of concepts related to the purchase decision. There are two important types of association that affect the positioning intensity of a brand:

1. *Association between a brand and a product class.*   This refers to the association(s) made by a consumer between a product class, usage situation, or specific problem, and a given brand. When thinking about a product class, consumers usually recall a name—Coca-Cola for soft drinks, Smirnoff for

vodka, Xerox for photocopiers, or IBM for computers. The image of a ladder can represent the associations between a product class and brand names. The brand name at the top of the ladder is the one most strongly associated with the product class. In car rentals this is likely to be Hertz, followed by Avis and National.

2. *Association between a brand and specific attributes.* The positioning intensity of a brand also depends on its association with properties that are relevant in a purchasing situation. For example, most toothpastes have a positive effect on decay prevention when used regularly. Many have similar fluoride ingredients and have been endorsed by the American Dental Association. But Crest is probably the brand most strongly associated with decay prevention. Other brands have not been able to create such an intense position.

An intense position can best be obtained by developing a strong association between a brand and a very limited number of attributes (two or three maximum). For example, Pacific Southwest Airlines (PSA), in their efforts to gain an increased share of the San Francisco–Los Angeles traffic market, centered on price and "friendliness." Everything they did, from their advertising to the smile painted on their airplanes, was intended to create a strong association between PSA and friendliness.

Marketing opportunities in gaining positioning intensity

In situations where one brand dominates a product class in the minds of consumers, the main opportunity for competitors lies in obtaining the second or third position. Competing head-on against the leading brand by presenting the challenger as a better choice on attributes associated with the dominant brand is usually ineffective. A better option is to concentrate on an attribute not strongly associated with the dominant brand, presenting the challenger as a feasible substitute for certain situations. Avis developed a successful positioning strategy based on these principles. Presenting itself as the number-two in car rentals, the company advertised "we try harder." In so doing it positioned itself as an alternative to the unnamed firm in car rentals, Hertz, on the basis of service. Avis hoped to, and did, gain some consumers from Hertz as well as from the smaller car-rental firms. They did not explicitly try to dislodge Hertz on all dimensions. Rather, they acknowledged their number-two position and focused on a single attribute, service. More recently, Avis has provided a rationale as to why it tries harder; namely, because many workers own company stock.

Constraints imposed by an intense position

Although marketers should seek an intense position for their brands, they should also keep in mind that attaining such a position can impose some constraints on future strategies. If shifts in the market environment should cause customers to reduce the importance they attach to a current determinant attribute, marketers may have difficulty repositioning a brand with an intensely perceived position on that attribute. This problem has plagued Sears for a number of years. Because of the prosperity and sophisticated tastes of the baby-boom generation, Sears has attempted to trade up many of its soft goods and fashion lines. But this has been difficult to accomplish because of the firm's strongly perceived position as a low-priced mass merchandiser.

The second threat concerns the dilution of an existing intense position. For example, British Leyland was formed through a series of mergers involving a number of British car manufacturers. For years, the company did not have a clear identity because it was new and it distributed a variety of brands, including Rover, Triumph, and Austin-Morris. Indeed, most Europeans had difficulty recalling spontaneously any British car manufacturer since once-strong brand names such as Austin and Morris had lost their identity and meaning.

Another danger associated with an intensely positioned brand is the temptation to overexploit that position by using the brand name on line extensions and new products. The danger here is that the new products may not fit the original positioning and the brand's strong image may become diluted. Scott Paper provides an example of the problems caused by diluting a brand's position with new products. After achieving a strong position in the toilet tissue market with its Scott brand, the firm introduced a variety of other paper products with such names as ScotTowels, ScotTissue, Scottkins, and Babyscott. None of these new products achieved a strong position of its own and only served to dilute the positioning intensity of the Scott brand name. Procter & Gamble took advantage of this to capture the number-one share in the toilet tissue market with its Charmin brand. As Trout and Ries point out, shoppers could write Charmin, Kleenex, Bounty, and Pampers on their shopping lists and know exactly what products they were going to get; but Scott on a shopping list has no meaning.[9]

ANALYZING THE PRODUCT'S CURRENT RELATIVE POSITION (STEP 5)

How does a marketer know if a brand occupies a strong position on a particular attribute? The only way to find out is to collect information through marketing research and analyze it using the techniques discussed earlier. An example of what can be done with such information is shown in Exhibit 7–7. It shows the results of discriminant analysis of a sample of consumers' ratings of a number of automobile brands on several attributes. The analysts designated the two underlying determinant attributes as "conservative/appeals to older people" versus "spirited/sporty/appeals to young people" and "practical/affordable" versus "classy/distinctive looking." Since the attributes the analysts chose for consumers to use in rating the brands influenced these dimensions, the real meaning of the results may be open to question.

---

[9]Ries and Trout, *Positioning*.

EXHIBIT 7–7

Product Positioning Map of Selected Automobile Brands

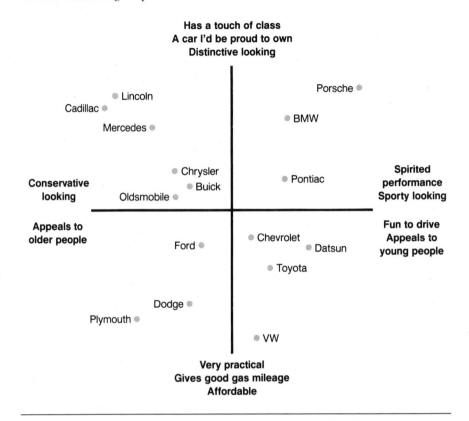

Source: John Koten, "Car Makers Use 'Image' Map as Tool to Position Products," *The Wall Street Journal,* March 22, 1984, p. 31.

Some brands—such as Porsche and Volkswagen—occupy relatively isolated positions away from any of the other brands included in the analysis; others occupy positions relatively close together in consumers' minds, such as Oldsmobile, Buick, and Chrysler. Because brands positioned near one another are considered by consumers to be relatively similar, the degree of substitutability and the intensity of competition between such brands is likely to be greater than for those that occupy widely divergent positions. Consequently, the perceived similarity between Oldsmobile and Buick in consumers' minds is a problem for General Motors because it suggests that those two divisions of the company are waging a marketing war more against each other than the competition.

Competitive gaps

The product positioning analysis in Exhibit 7–7 also provides useful information about possible opportunities for the development of a new brand or for repositioning an existing brand by differentiating it more clearly. Market-

EXHIBIT 7-8

Dutch Boy Repositions Itself to Reach Upscale,
Fashion-Oriented Consumers

Sherwin Williams has targeted its Dutch Boy brand on a younger (18–34 age group), more fashion-oriented market segment that accounts for nearly 38 percent of all paint purchased in the United States. The company believes that consumers in this group are not yet loyal to a particular brand and, thus, represent an untapped market. While the traditional selling points of paint—"scrubability," durability, and one-coat coverage—are important attributes, Dutch Boy is emphasizing fashion and overall finished appearance of the painted surface.

From 1984–88, the company redesigned the packaging, merchandising, and color system in its attempt to reposition the brand in the hope of giving retailers something more than price to sell. To carry out this repositioning, Dutch Boy has tripled its annual ad expenditures over those of any previous year.

Source: Cyndie Miller, "Dutch Boy Repositions Itself to Reach Upscale, Fashion-Oriented Consumers," *Marketing News*, July 4, 1988, p. 1.

ers can accomplish this by examining the positioning map for competitive gaps, or empty spaces where no existing brand is currently located. For instance, there is such a gap in the "affordable/appeals to young people" in the lower-right quadrant of the map. Such a gap may represent an opportunity for acquiring a distinctive position by developing a new entry that is perceived to offer good performance and sporty styling at a low price or by repositioning an existing brand along those attributes. (See Exhibit 7–8 for an example of repositioning.) Of course, such gaps may exist simply because a particular position is either impossible for any brand to attain because of technical or marketing constraints or undesirable in the sense that very few customers would purchase a brand with that particular set of attributes.

Limitations of product positioning analysis

The analysis depicted in Exhibit 7–7 is usually referred to as *product positioning* because it indicates how alternative products or brands are positioned relative to one another in customers' minds. The problem with this analysis, though, is that it does not tell the marketer which positions are most appealing to customers. For existing brands, such attractiveness can be inferred from current sales volumes and market shares. The position occupied by the share leader is obviously more appealing to more customers than the positions occupied by lesser brands. But this analysis fails to answer two important questions:

1. Is there one or more "open" positions—gaps in the competitive map where no current product or brand is located—that would be even more attractive to customers and provide a competitive advantage for a new brand or for an existing brand that could be repositioned to occupy that location?

2. Do customers in different market segments prefer products or brands with different attributes and positions?

To answer such questions, analysts must explicitly measure customers' preferences and locate them in the product space along with their perceptions of the current positions of existing brands. This is commonly called a **market positioning analysis.**

DETERMINING CUSTOMERS' MOST PREFERRED COMBINATION OF ATTRIBUTES (STEP 6)

There are several ways analysts can measure customer preferences and include them in a positioning analysis. For instance, survey respondents can be asked to think of the ideal product or brand within a product category—a hypothetical brand possessing the perfect combination of attributes (from the customer's viewpoint). Respondents could then rate their ideal product and existing products on a number of attributes. Then analysts could use discriminant or factor analysis to plot the position of ideal points and existing brands within the same product space. An alternative approach is to ask respondents to not only judge the degree of similarity among pairs of existing brands but to also indicate their degree of preference for each brand on a rating scale. Multidimensional scaling techniques can then locate the respondents' ideal points relative to the positions of the various existing brands on the product space map.

Whichever approach is used, the result will look something like Exhibit 7–9, which shows a hypothetical cluster of ideal points for one segment of automobile consumers. As a group, this customer segment (which presumably can afford to buy a luxury car) would seem to prefer BMW to any other brand on the map, because the closer the position of a given brand to a customer's ideal point, the greater the probability that the customer will prefer and purchase that brand. However, there are several reasons why not all customers in this segment are likely to purchase a BMW the next time they buy a car. First, the ideal points of some customers are actually closer to the Porsche brand. These customers will slightly prefer Porsche to BMW. Also, customers whose ideal point is equidistant between the two brands are likely to be relatively indifferent in their choice of which brand to purchase. Finally, customers may sometimes purchase brands somewhat farther away from their ideal—particularly when buying low-involvement nondurable goods or services to assess the qualities of new brands, to reassess older brands from time to time, or just for the sake of variety.

DEFINING MARKET POSITIONING AND MARKET SEGMENTATION (STEP 7)

An important criterion for defining market segments is differences in the benefits sought by different customers. Because differences between customers' ideal points reflect variations in the benefits they seek, a market po-

E X H I B I T 7 – 9

Market Positioning Map of Selected Automobile Brands with the Ideal Points of a Segment of Automobile Customers

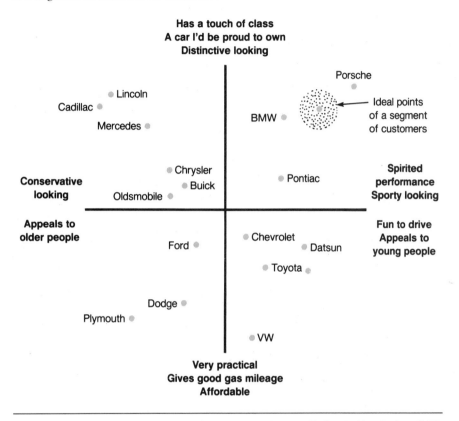

SOURCE: Adapted from John Koten, "Car Makers Use 'Image' Map as Tool to Position Products," *The Wall Street Journal*, March 22, 1984, p. 31.

sitioning analysis can simultaneously identify distinct market segments as well as the perceived positions of different brands. When customers' ideal points cluster in two or more locations on the product space map, the analyst can consider each cluster a distinct market segment.[10] For analytical purposes, each cluster is represented by a circle that encloses most of the ideal points for that segment; the size of the circle reflects the relative proportion of customers within a particular segment. Exhibit 7–10 groups the sample of re-

---

[10]When using preference data to define market segments, however, the analyst should also collect information about customers' demographic characteristics, lifestyle, product usage, and other potential segmentation variables. This enables the analyst to develop a more complete picture of the differences among benefit segments. Such information can be useful for developing advertising appeals, selecting media, focusing personal selling efforts, and designing many of the other elements of a marketing program that can be effective in appealing to a particular segment.

EXHIBIT   7–10
Market Positioning Map of Selected Automobile Brands

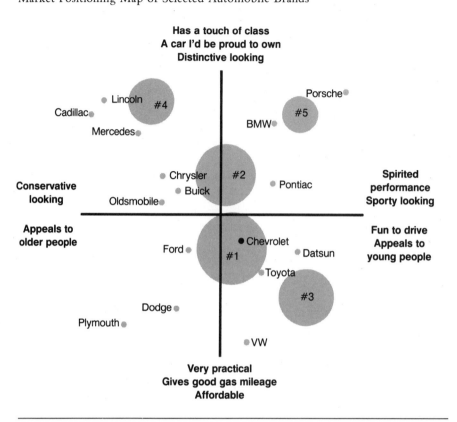

SOURCE: Adapted from John Koten, "Car Makers Use 'Image' Map as Tool to Position Products," *The Wall Street Journal*, March 22, 1984, p. 31.

spondents in our automobile example into five distinct segments on the basis of hypothetical clusters of ideal points. Segment 1 contains the largest proportion of customers; segment 5 the smallest.[11]

---

[11]The map in Exhibit 7–10 shows five distinct preference segments but only one set of perceived product positions. The implication is that consumers in this sample were similar in the way they perceived existing brands but different in the product attributes they preferred. This is the most common situation; customers tend to vary more in the benefits they seek than in how they perceive available products or brands. Sometimes, however, various segments may perceive the positions of existing brands quite differently. They may even use different determinant attributes in assessing these positions. Under such circumstances, a marketer might construct a separate market positioning map for each segment. For example, in a study of the positioning of different pharmaceutical brands, researchers discovered that two segments of doctors differed dramatically in their perceptions of the side effects of various brands as well as in their preferences for those brands. See Lester A. Neidell, "The Use of Nonmetric Multidimensional Scaling in Marketing Analysis," *Journal of Marketing*, October 1969, pp. 37–43.

By examining the preferences of customers in different segments together with their perceptions of the positions of existing brands, analysts can learn much about (1) the competitive strength of different brands in different segments, (2) the intensity of the rivalry between brands in a given segment, and (3) the opportunities for gaining a differentiated position within a specific target segment. For example, BMW occupies a strong and relatively unchallenged competitive position among consumers in segment 5. Chevrolet, Ford, and Toyota appear to have an intense rivalry for the preferences of many consumers in segment 1. On the other hand, none of the brands occupies a strongly attractive position with respect to the preferences of customers in segment 3. This segment may represent a good opportunity for the development of a new brand or the repositioning of an existing brand. For example, even though customers in segment 3 are probably splitting their purchases between Toyota, Datsun (Nissan), and VW, a new brand positioned more closely to the ideal points of customers in the segment would likely take sales from all of those brands. Analysts could estimate the sales volume such a new brand would generate by examining the current volume of purchases of the existing brands by segment 3 customers and the distances between the average ideal point of segment 3 customers and the positions of an existing and a new brand.[12]

SELECTING POSITIONING STRATEGIES (STEP 8)

The final decision about where to position a new brand or whether to reposition an existing one should be based on both the market targeting analysis discussed in an earlier chapter and the results of a market positioning analysis. The position chosen should match the preferences of a particular market segment and take into account the current positions of competing brands. It should also reflect the current and future attractiveness of the target market (its size, expected growth, and environmental constraints) and the relative strengths and weaknesses of competitors. Such information, together with an analysis of the costs required to acquire and maintain these positions, allows an assessment of the economic implications of different market positioning strategies.

Sales potential of market positions

The sales level of a brand is affected by many things, some of which are controlled by the firm (product, price, promotion, and distribution) and some that are not (competitive activities and the environment's evolution).

[12]Some sophisticated statistical techniques have recently been developed for making more precise forecasts of the sales volumes likely to be generated by new brands. For a technical review of such techniques, see Richard Schmalensee and Jacques-Francois Thisse, "Perceptual Maps and the Optimal Location of New Products," technical working paper, report 86–103 (Cambridge, Mass.: The Marketing Institute, 1986).

EXHIBIT 7–11
Perceptual Map of Sales Potential for Two Positions

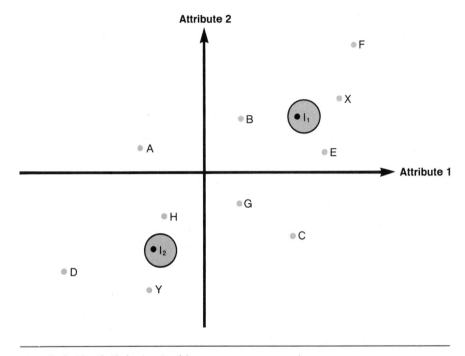

Note: Circles identify ideal points 1 and 2.

All of these influence elements of the consumer's purchasing process, such as awareness, purchase intent, and search for the product. The **purchase intent share** represents the percentage of consumers who intend to buy a specific brand before actually searching for it. It is one of the most important indicators of the likely success of a given product and integrates all those factors that influence the perceived qualities of a product.

Analysts can estimate the purchase intent share a brand could acquire in a segment (assuming a certain positioning strategy) from the positions of existing brands and the preferences of consumers in the segments. In a perceptual map obtained via multidimensional scaling, the purchase intent is related to the inverse of the distance of the brand's position from the ideal point.

The estimation of the sales potential of two positions is illustrated in Exhibits 7–11 and 7–12. Two segments are considered, with the size of the second being about half the size of the first. The overall market is currently dominated by three brands—E, H, and B, with brands E and B strongly positioned in segment 1 and H in segment 2. The firm owning brand B is considering the introduction of a new brand and, as a first step, evaluates the marketing potential of two positions, X and Y. They correspond to a reinforcement of the firm's position in segment 1 and a penetration of segment 2, respectively.

EXHIBIT 7–12

Illustration of Purchase Intent Shares before and after Introduction
of New Product (in Percent)

		A	B	C	D	E	F	G	H	New brand X or Y
Current	Segment 1	3.9	24.0	6.4	1.3	38.1	12.2	9.6	4.4	---
	Segment 2	11.1	4.5	5.9	14.0	2.9	1.4	10.3	49.9	---
	Total	6.3	17.5	6.2	5.5	26.4	8.6	9.8	19.6	---
With X	Segment 1	2.9	18.0	4.8	1.0	28.6	9.2	7.2	3.3	25.0
	Segment 2	10.9	4.4	5.8	13.7	2.9	1.4	10.1	48.9	1.9
	Total	5.6	13.5	5.1	5.2	20.0	6.6	8.2	18.5	17.3
With Y	Segment 1	3.8	23.4	6.3	1.3	37.2	11.9	9.4	4.3	2.4
	Segment 2	8.0	3.3	4.2	10.1	2.1	1.0	7.4	36.0	27.8
	Total	5.2	16.7	5.6	4.2	25.5	8.3	8.7	14.9	10.9

Existing brands columns A–H; New brand column X or Y.

The estimates made in Exhibit 7–12 assume that the new brand—X or Y—will obtain adequate awareness and distribution. Brand X is expected to gain a 17.3 purchase intent share, of which about one-third would come from the cannibalization of brand B. The firm's total purchase intent share is expected to increase from 17.5 percent to 30.8 percent. Brand Y would cannibalize brand B less, but the expected purchase intent share of Y is only 10.9 percent because of the smaller size of segment 2 and the strong position of brand H in this segment. The expected increase in total purchase intent share would be greater for brand X than Y despite its higher degree of cannibalization.

Evaluations of the sales potential of alternative positions should consider the more pertinent market dynamics. These include:

1. *Growth of market segments.* The current sales potential of a position close to the ideal point may be limited. If the segment's growth rate is higher than the market growth rate, the cumulative sales potential of this segment may be substantial. Acquiring a position in this segment while its size is limited will generally be easier than later on.

2. *Evolution of segments' ideal points.* Brands should be positioned on the evolutionary path of a segment's ideal point to enjoy an increasing market share. For instance, the then relatively small Levi Strauss Company met with big success when teenage boys and girls of the 60s decided to express their freedom by wearing jeans.

3. *Changes in positioning intensity.* An existing brand with low positioning intensity may have a favorable position in one segment. In this case, the firm marketing this brand should try to increase its positioning intensity, which will increase the brand's penetration and reduce the sales potential of other positions.

4. *Evolution of existing brands' positions.*   The shifts in the positions of existing brands may be difficult to predict, but their evolution can be anticipated. For example, in recent years both GM and Ford have emphasized greater quality (reliability) in their cars.

5. *Emerging attributes.*   The long-term sales potential of a brand will consequently be affected not only by its position on the current determinant attributes but by its position on emerging attributes. In the last decade, the increasing determinance of gasoline mileage in the car industry and of caloric contents in the food market have had a significant impact on the sales potential of brands in these two product classes.

6. *Development of new segments.*   The number of consumers with similar needs distinct from the rest of the market may increase to the point where some firms consider them a separate segment. The emergence of new segments will create new opportunities but may also weaken the sales potential of existing brands.

7. *Introduction of new brands.*   The introduction of new brands by competitors is often unpredictable. The analysis of a product space from a competitor's point-of-view gives an indication of moves that competitors could consider.

Market positioning strategies

Formulating a market positioning strategy consists of selecting and defining a market position the firm plans to occupy in reaching its marketing objectives. This requires estimates of the economic potential of alternative positions, which are based largely on an analysis of the sales potential of each position and the investments required to occupy the targeted position.

A systematic analysis of a large number of positions must be developed for each alternative position. An approach that better exploits management's experience and induces strategic thinking consists of selecting a limited number of options based on a qualitative anticipation of competitive and market dynamics. Analysts can then evaluate these options quantitatively while still keeping in mind the underlying strategic issues. The eight market position strategies described below are relevant to a large number of situations.

1. *Monosegment positioning.*   As the name suggests, monosegment positioning involves developing a product and marketing program tailored to the preferences of a single market segment. Continuing with our automotive example, for instance, a firm might attempt to position its brand within the circle representing the ideal points of customers in segment 3. Successful implementation of such a strategy would give the brand an obvious advantage within the target segment. However, it would not generate many sales from customers in other segments with divergent preferences. This strategy thus is best used in conjunction with the mass-market targeting strategy discussed earlier.

2. *Multisegment positioning.*   This consists of positioning a product in such a way as to attract consumers from different segments (as witness the posi-

tion of Datsun (Nissan) between segments 1 and 3 in Exhibit 7–10). It provides a larger market for the product and, as long as the individual segments are not served by "tailored" competitive brands, may yield high sales. This is an attractive strategy since it provides higher economies of scale, requires smaller investments, and avoids dispersion of managerial attention. It is particularly appropriate when individual segments are small, as is generally the case in the early stages of the product's life cycle.

3. *Standby positioning.* It may not be in the best interest of a firm to switch from a multisegment positioning strategy to a monosegment strategy (assuming the use of several brands, each positioned to serve the needs of only one segment) even if it increases total market share. The lower sales volume per brand may cause a reduction in total contribution despite an increase in overall sales volume. In such a case, the firm may decide to implement a monosegment positioning strategy only when forced to do so. In order to minimize response time the firm prepares a standby plan specifying the product(s) and their attributes as well as details of the marketing program(s) that would be used to position the new product(s).

4. *Imitative positioning.* This is essentially the same as a head-on strategy described earlier, where a new brand targets a position similar to that of an existing successful brand. In following this strategy, the firm hopes that a certain proportion of the current brand's customers will switch to the new brand. While an imitative positioning strategy does result in a direct confrontation, it may be an appropriate strategy if the imitative firm has a distinctive advantage beyond positioning, such as better access to channels of distribution or a more effective salesforce.

5. *Anticipatory positioning.* A firm may position a new brand in anticipation of the evolution of a segment's needs. This is particularly appropriate when the new brand is not expected to have a fast acceptance, and market share will build as the needs of consumers become more and more aligned with the benefits being offered. At its best, this strategy enables a firm to preempt a market position that may have a substantial long-term potential. At its worst, it may cause the firm to face a difficult economic situation for an extended period, if the needs of a segment do not evolve as expected. For example, when Seymour Cray began developing the Cray-1 supercomputer in 1972, marketing research suggested that the total market would only absorb about 90 such computers. But Cray was right in assuming that when firms and government agencies realized the advantages of such high-performance machines, they would find new uses for them and demand would continue to expand.[13]

6. *Adaptive positioning.* This consists of periodically repositioning a brand to follow the evolution of the segment's needs.

7. *Defensive positioning.* When a firm occupies a strong position in a market

---

[13]Tom Alexander, "Cray's Way of Staying Super-Duper," *Fortune*, March 18, 1985, pp. 66–76.

segment with a single brand, it is vulnerable to imitative positioning strategies. The firm may preempt competitive strategies by introducing an additional brand in a similar position for the same segment. This will reduce immediate profitability; but it may allow the firm to better protect itself against competitors in the long term. Procter & Gamble has followed such a positioning strategy over the years in a number of product categories; for example, the firm has seven brands of laundry detergents, such as Tide and Bold, several of which occupy similar positions in consumers' minds.

8. *Stopgap positioning.*   Although a given market position may not be currently attractive, consumer preferences or technology may evolve in such a way that it becomes attractive. A firm may, therefore, decide to make a limited investment in a new brand in a given position to obtain market share, technical experience, and an early lead on competition.

SUMMARY

Positioning is concerned with how well the product performs relative to competitive offerings and the needs (benefits sought) of one or more targeted market segments. There are two types of positioning—one based on the physical product, the other on the market's perception of the product. The former depends primarily on technical versus market data; but it still represents an important step in the formulation and implementation of marketing strategy because it facilitates the interface between marketing and R&D, forces management to discriminate between selected physical characteristics, helps in identifying key competitors, and may reveal important product gaps.

If a firm already has a product line, its new-product positioning strategy can be described in terms of its existing line. This reflects an internal positioning strategy, of which there are three main types—product-line filling, product-line stretching, and product-line extension. A product positioning strategy that considers competitive factors represents an external positioning strategy, of which there are two types—differentiation and imitative.

Physical product positioning is flawed by its failure to explicitly consider the consumer. For many products, consumers know very little about the physical characteristics, and even if they did, they would not understand them well enough to use them as a basis for selecting one brand over another. Thus, consumers perceive competitive offerings using various dimensions, which can be classified as simple physically based attributes, complex physically based attributes, or essentially abstract attributes.

To determine which positioning strategy to adopt, a firm must proceed through the eight steps in the positioning process. These are (1) identify a relevant set of competitive products, (2) identify the set of determinant attributes that define the product space in which positions of current offerings are located, (3) collect data from a sample of customers and potential customers about perceptions of each product on the determinant attributes, (4) analyze the intensity of a product's current position in the customer's minds, (5) determine the product's current location in the product space (product positioning), (6) determine customers' most preferred combination of determinant attributes, (7) examine the fit between preferences of market segments and the current position of the product (market positioning), and (8) select a positioning or repositioning strategy. The latter consists of such common strategies as those concerned with a monosegment, multiple segments, a standby position, an imitative position, an anticipatory position, an adaptive position, a defensive position, and a stopgap position.

APPENDIX: STATISTICAL TECHNIQUES USED TO ANALYZE CONSUMERS' PERCEPTIONS ABOUT THE COMPETITIVE POSITIONS OF ALTERNATIVE PRODUCTS OR BRANDS[14]

Factor analysis

To employ factor analysis, the analyst must first identify the salient attributes consumers use to evaluate products in the category under study. The analyst then collects data from a sample of consumers concerning their ratings of each product or brand on all attributes. The factor analysis program then determines which attributes are related to the same underlying construct ("load" on the same factor). The analyst uses those underlying constructs or factors as the dimensions for a product space map, and the program indicates where each product or brand is perceived to be located on each factor.

Discriminant analysis

Discriminant analysis requires the same input data as factor analysis. The discriminant analysis program then determines consumers' perceptual dimensions on the basis of which attributes best differentiate, or discriminate, among brands. Once again, those underlying dimensions can be used to construct a product space map; but they are usually not so easily interpretable as the factors identified through factor analysis. Also, as with factor analysis,

---

[14]For a more technical discussion of how these techniques work, the data that must be collected as inputs for the different analyses, and their statistical strengths and weaknesses, see Harper W. Boyd, Jr., Ralph Westfall, and Stanley F. Stasch, *Marketing Research* (Homewood, Ill.: Irwin, 1989), chaps. 16 and 17. For extensive critical reviews of past marketing applications of these different approaches, see John R. Hauser and Frank S. Koppleman, "Alternative Perceptual Mapping Techniques: Relative Accuracy and Usefulness," *Journal of Marketing Research,* November 1979, pp. 495–506; and John W. Keon, "Product Positioning: TRINODAL Mapping of Brand Images, Ad Images, and Consumer Preference," *Journal of Marketing Research,* November 1983, pp. 380–92. Also see Paul E. Green, J. Douglas Carroll, and Stephen M. Goldberg, "A General Approach to Product Design Optimization via Conjoint Analysis," *Journal of Marketing,* Summer 1981, pp. 17–37; Michael R. Hagerty, "Improving the Predictive Power of Conjoint Analysis," *Journal of Marketing Research,* May 1985, pp. 168–84; Thomas W. Leigh, David M. McKay, and John O. Summers, "Reliability and Validity of Conjoint Analysis and Self-Explicated Weights," *Journal of Marketing Research,* November 1984, pp. 456–63; and Paul E. Green, "Hybrid Models for Conjoint Analysis: An Expository Review," *Journal of Marketing Research,* May 1984, pp. 184–93.

the underlying dimensions may be more a function of the attributes used to collect consumer ratings than of the product characteristics that consumers actually consider to be most important.

Conjoint measurement

Conjoint measurement determines which combination of a limited number of attributes consumers most prefer. The technique is helpful for identifying appealing new-product designs and important points that might be included in a product's advertising. Although it can provide some insights about consumer preferences, it cannot provide information about how consumers perceive the positioning of existing products in relation to product dimensions. In other words, it is not very useful for product positioning analysis because it does not show how similar two products are perceived to be on underlying determinant attributes.

Multidimensional scaling

Unlike the other techniques where the underlying dimensions identified depend on the attributes supplied by the researcher when collecting data, multidimensional scaling produces dimensions based on consumer judgments about the similarity of, or their preferences for, the actual brands. These underlying dimensions are thought to be the basic attractive dimensions that consumers actually use to evaluate alternative brands in the product class. Multidimensional scaling programs that use data on similarities construct geometrically spaced maps on which the brands perceived to be most similar are placed close together. Those that use consumer preferences produce joint space maps that show consumer ideal points and then position the most preferred brands close to those ideal points.

Unfortunately, the underlying dimensions of the maps produced by multidimensional scaling can be difficult to interpret. Also, the dimensions identified are only those that already exist for currently available brands. This makes the technique less useful for investigating new-product concepts that might involve new characteristics. Finally, the technique is subject to statistical limitations when the number of alternative brands being investigated is small. As a rule of thumb, such techniques should only be applied when at least eight or more different products or brands are being examined.

Marketing Strategies for New-Market Entries

GEO. A. HORMEL & COMPANY: FROM BACON TO SPAM TO TOP SHELF[1]

When asked to name the most innovative developers of new products and new markets, most people would think of high-tech firms like 3M, Apple, or Micro-Soft. Few would come up with a meat processor. Yet, throughout its 100-year history, Geo. A. Hormel & Company has been one of the most prolific and successful developers of new products in the food industry.

The firm began in 1890 when George Hormel started making sausage to sell in his meat market in Austin, Minnesota. The firm's tradition of new-product development began in 1895 with George's introduction of Hormel's Sugar-Cured Pig Back Bacon, a product now commonly known by the more appetizing name of Canadian bacon.

Hormel's long string of new-product successes really got rolling after George's son, Jay, took over in the 1920s. The firm was a pioneer in canning meats, becoming the first U.S. producer of canned hams in 1927. Jay also introduced Dinty Moore stew and Hormel chili to the American palate. But probably his most famous, and most maligned, invention was Spam. Despite all the jokes associated with the product, Spam recently celebrated its 50th anniversary, holds a 75 percent share of the spiced-ham market, produced an estimated $150 million in sales in 1990, and—believe it or not—continues to grow.

[1]This example is based on material found in Jane Simon, "From Spam to Fish, Hormel Expands," *Compass Readings,* September 1990, pp. 26–32; and *Geo. A. Hormel & Company 1991 Annual Report* (Austin, Minn.: Geo. A. Hormel & Company, 1991).

Looking for the "point of difference"

In recent years, Hormel has focused even more effort on developing unique products for consumer markets. The firm's mission is "To be a leader in the food field with highly differentiated quality products that attain optimum share of market while meeting established objectives." Consistent with that mission, the company has moved away from producing basic commodity-like meat products, such as bacon and ham. Several years ago, for instance, it closed its Austin slaughterhouse and leased the plant to Quality Pork Processors, Inc., which in turn buys the hogs, slaughters them, and sells the meat to Hormel. Thus, Hormel avoids the cost of a labor-intensive meat packing operation but still maintains some control over the quality of the meat the company buys.

Over the past decade, Hormel has sought increased volume growth and profitability by developing high value-added products that fit newly emerging consumer preferences and lifestyles. As Richard Knowlton, the firm's CEO, puts it, "We have tried to transform the company into a food company with less and less dependence on red meat, . . . and we've tried to meet the need for foods that take less preparation time." The firm's basic strategy is to develop differentiated products by designing in features that consumers want but other companies do not offer. "We look to the market and ask, What could be competitive?" says Knowlton. "What would be original? That's our main key in every-

thing we do—to look for the point of difference, and if we can't bring forth a point of difference, then we don't go to the party."

Modifying existing products and entering new markets

In some cases, Hormel achieved a point of difference by making only relatively minor modifications to some of its old familiar products. The company's Light & Lean wiener, a hot dog that is 90 percent fat free, is one example. Another is the firm's Frank 'N Stuff wieners. To differentiate the product from the 30 or so other brands of hot dogs on the market, Hormel designed, built, and patented a system to insert a tunnel of chili or cheese inside every wiener.

In other instances, Hormel's product introduction efforts have taken the company into product categories new to the company but relatively familiar to consumers. Several years ago, for example, the firm acquired and expanded Chicken By George—a line of packaged chicken breasts marinated in eight different flavors that was developed by TV personality Phyllis George. The line represented Hormel's first entry into the already well-developed brand-name poultry market.

Developing innovative products

At the other extreme, some of Hormel's recent new-product development efforts have been so innovative they established a whole new product category in the grocery store:

microwave prepared meals. The firm's first entry in this area was Top Shelf, a line of 13 shelf-stable dinner entrees such as Italian-style lasagna and beef stroganoff with noodles. The products' taste equals that of high-quality frozen dinners, but Top Shelf doesn't require refrigeration or use preservatives. Unlike frozen food, which has a shorter shelf life, Top Shelf is guaranteed fresh for 18 months and can be microwaved in its container in about two minutes. Since its introduction in 1986, Top Shelf has steadily gained consumer acceptance, with sales for the line reaching an estimated $100 million in 1990. Recently, Hormel has further expanded the shelf-stable microwave meal category with its Micro Cup and Kids Kitchen product lines and microwave versions of its best-selling

Dinty Moore stew and Hormel chili.

A successful repositioning

Hormel's aggressive product and market development efforts over the past decade have successfully repositioned the company and helped it attain substantial volume growth and profitability. In 1980, 70 percent of the firm's sales were from commodity meat products; but by 1990, 70 percent of sales were generated by value-added prepared foods with wider profit margins and higher growth potential. As a result, the firm posted earnings increases in 9 out of 10 years during the 1980s, and net earnings for 1990 reached a record $77 million, more than a 10 percent increase over the previous year.

SOME ISSUES CONCERNING NEW-MARKET ENTRY STRATEGIES

What is a "new" product?

Hormel's approach to securing volume and profit growth illustrates several important points about new-product and market development, each of which is explored later in this chapter. First, a firm's new-market entries can involve products that differ in their degree of newness from the perspective of both the company and its customers. Top Shelf, for example, involved a shelf-stable food technology that was new to both the company and its customers. On the other hand, Hormel's foray into prepared poultry products with its Chicken By George line involved products that were new to the firm but not to its customers, since other manufacturers already offered similar products. Finally, the development of Light & Lean wieners involved manufacturing technology, marketing, and distribution efforts that were old hat for the company. But those efforts resulted in the first low-fat hot dogs on the market, a new product that appealed to many health-conscious consumers.

This chapter focuses on marketing objectives and programs appropriate for introducing and developing markets for offerings that are *new to the target customers.* We examine programs that firms who are **pioneers,** or first entrants, into a particular product-market might use. Later entrants can also face difficulties in developing and introducing their own versions of a product. But given that the challenge facing such **followers** is essentially to capture market share in the face of established competitors, we will postpone our discussion of marketing programs appropriate for later entrants until the next chapter, when we examine share-building strategies.

What are the objectives of new product-market development?

While Hormel pursues a variety of different approaches to new-market development, all have the common objective of increasing the firm's future sales volume and profitability. However, different approaches can achieve a variety of secondary objectives as well. Developing new-user segments for an existing product, for instance, can reduce unit costs and increase the product's profitability. Similarly, major product improvements or line extensions—such as Hormel's introduction of Frank 'N Stuff and Light & Lean wieners— can help protect a firm's market share in a product category in the face of increasing competition. This suggests that top management must establish explicit objectives for new-market entries in a firm's various business units to provide useful guidelines for choosing appropriate development strategies. A later section of this chapter discusses some objectives that new entries can achieve and the conditions under which various objectives are appropriate.

Should a firm be a pioneer or a follower?

Finally, the development of new-market entries can be both expensive and risky. Hormel will not disclose the total development cost of its Top Shelf line, but no doubt it was enormous. The firm spent more than $1 million just for two pieces of specialized testing equipment to conduct research for product and package development, and a large team of R&D, production, and marketing people spent four years readying the line for introduction. And there was no guarantee that grocery stores would distribute or consumers would accept Top Shelf's unique new form.

This raises an intriguing strategic question: Is it better for a firm to be the pioneer in developing and introducing a new product—as Hormel was with Top Shelf—or to be a follower who watches other innovators bear the risks of product failure and marketing mistakes before joining the battle with its own entry? Before discussing alternative marketing programs pioneers might use to penetrate and develop new markets, we turn to this more basic strategic issue and examine the conditions in which pioneer and follower strategies each have the greatest probability of long-term success.

HOW NEW IS "NEW"?

A survey of the new-product development practices of 700 U.S. corporations conducted by the consulting firm of Booz, Allen & Hamilton found that the products introduced by those firms in the five-year period from 1976 to 1981 were not all equally "new." The study identified six categories of new products based on their degree of newness as perceived by both the company and the target customers. These categories are discussed below and diagrammed in Exhibit 8–1, which also indicates the percentage of new entries falling in each category during the five-year study period. Notice that only 10 percent of all new-product introductions fell into the new-to-the-world category.[2]

- *New-to-the-world products*—True innovations that are new to the firm and create an entirely new market (10 percent).
- *New product lines*—A product category that is new for the company introducing it, but not new to customers in the target market because of the existence of one or more competitive brands (20 percent).
- *Additions to existing product lines*—New items that supplement a firm's established product line. These items may be moderately new to both the firm and the customers in its established product-markets. They may also serve to expand the market segments appealed to by the line (26 percent).
- *Improvements in or revisions of existing products*—Items providing improved performance or greater perceived value brought out to replace existing products. These items may present moderately new marketing and production challenges to the firm; but unless they represent a technologically new generation of products, customers are likely to perceive them as similar to the products they replace (26 percent).
- *Repositionings*—Existing products that are targeted at new applications and new market segments (7 percent).
- *Cost reductions*—Product modifications providing similar performance at lower cost (11 percent).

A product's degree of newness to the company, its target customers, or both help determine the amount of complexity and uncertainty involved in the engineering, operations, and marketing tasks necessary to make it a successful new entry. It also contributes to the amount of risk inherent in those tasks.

Introducing a product that is new to both the firm and target customers requires the greatest expenditure of effort and resources. It also involves the greatest amount of uncertainty and risk of failure due to the lack of information and experience with the technology and the target customers.

---

[2]*New Products Management for the 1980s* (New York: Booz, Allen & Hamilton, 1982).

EXHIBIT 8 – 1

Categories of New Products Defined according to Their Degree of Newness to the Company and Customers in the Target Market

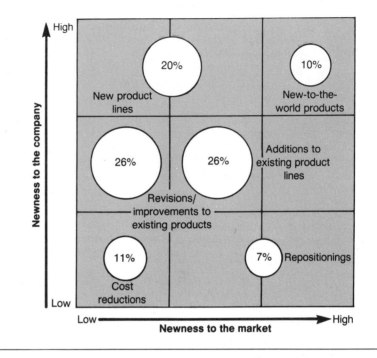

Source: *New Products Management for the 1980s* (New York: Booz, Allen & Hamilton, 1982).

Products new to target customers but not new to the firm (such as line extensions or modifications aimed at new customer segments or repositionings of existing products) are often not very innovative in design or operations; but they may present a great deal of marketing uncertainty. The marketing challenge here—as with new-to-the-world products—is to build **primary demand,** making target customers aware of the product and convincing them to adopt it. We investigate this marketing problem in this chapter.

Finally, products new to the company but not to the market (such as new product lines, line extensions, product modifications, and cost reductions) often present fewer challenges for R&D and product engineering. The company can study and learn from earlier designs or competitors' products. However, these products can present major challenges for process engineering, production scheduling, quality control, and inventory management. Once the company introduces such a product into the market, its primary marketing objective is to build selective demand and capture market share, convincing customers the new offering is better than existing competitive products. We discuss marketing programs a firm might use to accomplish these objectives in Chapter 9.

EXHIBIT 8-2

Strategic Objectives Attained by Successful New-Market Entries

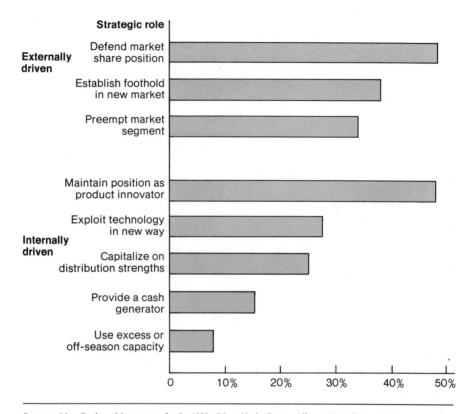

SOURCE: *New Products Management for the 1980s* (New York: Booz, Allen & Hamilton, 1982), p. 11.

OBJECTIVES OF NEW-PRODUCT AND MARKET DEVELOPMENT

The primary objective of most new-product and market development efforts is to secure future volume and profit growth. This has become more crucial in recent years. As we saw in Chapter 5, rapidly advancing technology, shifting customer needs and preferences, and more intense global competition have led to shorter product life cycles. Thus, a steady flow of new products and the development of new markets, including those in foreign countries, are essential for the continued growth of most firms.

The Hormel case illustrates, however, that individual development projects may also accomplish a variety of other strategic objectives. When asked what strategic role their most successful recent new entry served, the respondents in the Booz, Allen & Hamilton survey mentioned eight different strategic objectives. Exhibit 8–2 lists these objectives and the percentage of respondents that mentioned each one. The exhibit also indicates which objectives focused on external concerns, such as defending market share, and which

EXHIBIT 8-3

Types of New-Market Entries Appropriate for Different Strategic Objectives

Objective	New entry
Maintain position as a product innovator	New-to-the-world products; improvements or revisions to existing products
Defend a current market-share position	Improvements or revisions to existing products; additions to existing product line; cost reductions
Establish a foothold in a future new market; preempt a market segment	New-to-the-world products; additions to existing product line; repositionings
Exploit technology in a new way	New-to-the-world products; new product line; additions to or revisions of existing product line
Capitalize on distribution strengths	New-to-the-world products; new product line; additions to or revisions of existing product line
Provide a cash generator	Additions to or revisions of existing product line; repositionings; cost reductions
Use excess or off-season capacity	New-to-the-world product; new product line

were driven by a desire to improve or build on the firm's internal strengths. Most respondents indicated their new entry helped accomplish more than one objective.

Exhibit 8–3 shows that different types of new entries are appropriate for achieving different strategic objectives. For example, if the objective is to establish a foothold in or preempt a new-market segment, the firm must introduce a product that is new to that market, although it may not be entirely new to the company. On the other hand, if the objective is to improve cash flow by adding another cash generator, simple line extensions or product modifications—particularly those that reduce unit costs—may do the trick.

The business's objective for its new entries influence the kind of entry strategy it should pursue and the marketing and other functional programs needed to implement that strategy. For instance, if a business pursues a prospector strategy and its objectives are to maintain a position as a product innovator and establish footholds in a variety of new product-markets, it should attempt to be the pioneer in as many of those markets as possible. And as we saw in Chapter 3, successful implementation of such a strategy requires the business to be competent in and devote substantial resources to R&D, product engineering, marketing, and marketing research.

On the other hand, if the business is primarily concerned with defending an already strong market-share position, it may prefer to be a follower. Usually entering new product-markets only after an innovator, a follower relies on superior quality, better customer service, or lower prices to offset the pioneer's early lead. Such a strategy requires fewer investments in R&D and product development, but marketing and sales still are critical in implementing it effectively. A more detailed comparison of these alternative new-market entry strategies—pioneer versus follower—is the focus of the next section of this chapter.

MARKET ENTRY STRATEGIES: PIONEERS VERSUS FOLLOWERS

Even though IBM is one of the world's premier high-tech companies, it usually has not been a pioneer in the sense of being the first to enter new markets. For example, IBM did not enter the personal computer (PC) market until after several other firms, including Apple and Tandy, had already established substantial sales volumes. But as a follower, IBM developed an improved product design offering superior performance. It also had vast financial resources to support extensive advertising and promotional efforts; in addition, it had established a reputation for reliability and customer service. Consequently, IBM captured a commanding share of the PC market within a year of its entry.

On the other hand, IBM appears committed to a pioneering entry strategy in a few product categories with high potential for future growth, such as computer-integrated manufacturing systems. Which of the two entry strategies makes the most sense? Or do both entry strategies have particular advantages under different conditions?

Pioneer strategy

Conventional wisdom holds that although they take the greatest risks and probably experience more failures than their more conservative competitors, successful pioneers are handsomely rewarded. It is assumed competitive advantages inherent in being the first to enter a new product-market can be sustained through the growth stage and into the maturity stage of the product life cycle, resulting in a strong share position and substantial returns. This is particularly true when the pioneer gains patent protection for the new product.

One study of a cross section of industries with mature industrial products provides some support for this view. The study's findings, summarized in Exhibit 8–4, indicate that surviving pioneers in a product category held an average market share of 30 percent when their industries reached maturity. This compared to average shares of 21 percent for followers and 15 percent for late entrants.[3] Further support is provided by the PIMS data base, an ongoing repository of information collected from nearly 3,000 SBUs in 450 companies. Of the SBUs currently holding the leading market share in their

---

[3]William T. Robinson, "Market Pioneering and Sustainable Market Share Advantages in Industrial Goods Manufacturing Industries," working paper, Purdue University, 1984. Also see William T. Robinson and Claes Fornell, "Sources of Market Pioneer Advantages in Consumer Goods Industries," *Journal of Marketing Research* 22 (1985), pp. 305–17; and William T. Robinson, "Sources of Market Pioneer Advantages: The Case of Industrial Goods Industries," *Journal of Marketing Research* 25 (1988), pp. 87–94.

EXHIBIT   8–4
Average Market Shares at Industry Maturity of Firms
Pursuing Different Market Entry Strategies

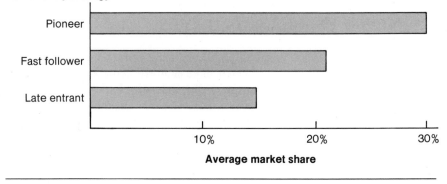

Market entry strategy

SOURCE: Based on material in William T. Robinson, "Market Pioneering and Sustainable Market Share Advantages in Industrial Goods Manufacturing Industries," working paper, Purdue University, 1984.

industries, 70 percent report being "one of the pioneers" in the industry. In contrast, only 40 percent of those SBUs with less than a leading market share report being an industry pioneer.[4]

Of course, volume and market share are not the only dimensions by which analysts measure success. Unfortunately, there is currently almost no evidence concerning the effect of the timing of a firm's entry into a new market on its ultimate profitability in that market or the value generated for shareholders.[5] There are many examples, though, of businesses that are profitable even though they were not pioneers and do not hold leading market shares. For instance, Compaq has done very well in the PC market by offering computers with features that market-leader IBM could not match, such as portability and more power.

Potential pioneering advantages

Some of the potential sources of advantage available to pioneers are briefly summarized in Exhibit 8–5 and discussed below.[6]

---

[4]Robert D. Buzzell and Bradley T. Gale, *The PIMS Principles: Linking Strategy to Performance* (New York: Free Press, 1987), p. 183.

[5]Marvin B. Lieberman and David B. Montgomery, "First-Mover Advantages," *Strategic Management Journal* 9 (1988), pp. 41–59; and Michael J. Moore, William Boulding, and Ronald C. Goodstein, "Pioneering and Market Share: Is Entry Time Endogenous and Does It Matter?" *Journal of Marketing Research* 28 (1991), pp. 97–104.

[6]The following discussion expands on material found in George S. Day, *Analysis for Strategic Market Decisions* (St. Paul, Minn.: West Publishing, 1986), pp. 99–106; Michael E. Porter, *Competitive Advantage* (New York: Free Press, 1985), pp. 181–91; and Marvin B. Lieberman and David B. Montgomery, "First-Mover Advantages," *Strategic Management Journal* 9 (1988), pp. 41–58.

E X H I B I T 8 - 5

Potential Advantages of Pioneer and Follower Strategies

Pioneer	Follower
• First choice of market segments and positions	• Ability to take advantage of pioneer's positioning mistakes
• Pioneer defines the "rules of the game"	• Ability to take advantage of pioneer's product mistakes
• Distribution advantages	
• Economies of scale and experience	• Ability to take advantage of pioneer's marketing mistakes
• High switching costs for early adopters	• Ability to take advantage of the latest technology
• Possibility of preempting scarce resources	• Ability to take advantage of pioneer's limited resources

1. *First choice of market segments and positions.* The pioneer has the opportunity to develop a product offering with attributes most important to the largest segment of customers, or to promote the importance of attributes that favor its brand. Thus, the pioneer's brand can become the standard of reference customers use to evaluate other brands. This can make it more difficult for followers with me-too products to convince existing customers that their new brands are superior to the older and more familiar pioneer. If the pioneer has successfully tied its offering to the choice criteria of the largest group of customers, it also becomes more difficult for followers to differentiate their offerings in ways that are attractive to the mass-market segment. They may have to target a smaller peripheral segment or niche instead.

2. *The pioneer defines the "rules of the game."* The pioneer's actions on such variables as product quality, price, distribution, warranties, postsale service, and promotional appeals and budgets set standards that subsequent competitors must "meet or beat." If the pioneer sets those standards high enough, it can raise the costs of entry and perhaps preempt some potential competitors.

3. *Distribution advantages.* The pioneer has the most options in designing a distribution channel to bring the new product to market. This is particularly important for industrial goods where, if the pioneer exercises its options well and with dispatch, it should end up with a network of the best distributors. This can exclude later entrants from some markets. Distributors are often reluctant to take on second or third brands. This is especially true when the product is technically complex and the distributor must carry large inventories of the product and spare parts and invest in specialized training and service.

   For consumer packaged goods, it is more difficult to slow the entry of later competitors by preempting distribution alternatives. Nevertheless, the pioneer still has the advantage of attaining more shelf facings at the outset of the growth stage. By quickly expanding its product line follow-ing an initial success, the pioneer can appropriate still more shelf space, thereby making the challenge faced by followers even more difficult.

4. *Economies of scale and experience.*   Being first means the pioneer can gain accumulated volume and experience and thereby lower per-unit costs at a faster rate than followers. This advantage is particularly pronounced when the product is technically sophisticated and involves high development costs or when its life cycle is likely to be short with sales increasing rap-idly during the introduction and early growth stages.

   As we shall see later, the pioneer can deploy these cost advantages in a number of ways to protect its early lead against followers. One strategy is to lower price, which can discourage followers from entering the market because it raises the volume necessary for them to break even. Or the pioneer might invest its savings in additional marketing efforts to expand its penetration of the market, such as heavier advertising, a larger sales-force, or continuing product improvements or line extensions.

5. *High switching costs for early adopters.*   Customers who are early to adopt a pioneer's new product may be reluctant to change suppliers when com-petitive products appear. This is particularly true for industrial goods where the costs of switching suppliers can be high. Compatible equip-ment and spare parts, investments in employee training, and the risks of lower product quality or customer service make it easier for the pioneer to retain its early customers over time.

   In some cases, however, switching costs can work against the pioneer and in favor of followers. A pioneer may have trouble converting cus-tomers to a new technology if they must bear high switching costs to abandon their old way of doing things. Pioneers in the manufacture of ethanol, for instance, have had a difficult time convincing car owners to modify their engines to be able to use ethanol instead of gasoline. Once the pioneer has persuaded early adopters to change technologies, however, their costs of switching to a follower's brand within the new product cat-egory may be relatively low.

6. *Possibility of preempting scarce resources and suppliers.*   The pioneer may be able to negotiate favorable deals with suppliers who are eager for new business or who do not appreciate the size of the opportunity for their raw materials or component parts. If later entrants subsequently find those materials and components in short supply, they may be con-strained from expanding as fast as they might like or be forced to pay premium prices.

Not all pioneers reap the benefits of their advantage

The evidence suggests that these advantages can help a pioneer gain and maintain a competitive edge in a new market, but not all pioneers are suc-cessful at doing so. For one thing, some pioneers fail during the introductory stage of the product life cycle. Others disappear during the shakeout that typically occurs later in the growth period. As we discuss in the next section, in some cases—particularly when the pioneer is pursuing a prospector business strategy—a withdrawal during the shakeout period may be intentional and strategically planned. In other cases, it is simply the result of failure due to inadequate resources, poor product design, or marketing mistakes.

Even when the pioneer survives the shakeout period, it is not always able to convert its initial advantage into a continuing position of share leadership. The pioneer may lack the resources to keep up with rapid growth in the market or the competencies needed to maintain its early lead in the face of a competitive onslaught by strong followers. This was the case, for instance, in the personal computer market during the 1980s. Even though early entrants like Commodore, Tandy, and Apple survived and, in some cases, prospered, follower IBM stood high above the rest as the industry share and profit leader at the end of the decade.

Follower strategy

In many cases a firm becomes a follower by default. It is simply beaten to a new product-market by a quicker competitor. But even when a company has the capability of being the first mover, the above observations suggest there may be some advantages to letting other firms go first into a product-market. Let the pioneer shoulder the initial risks while the followers observe their shortcomings and mistakes. Possible advantages of such a follower strategy are briefly summarized in Exhibit 8–5 and discussed below.

1. *Ability to take advantage of the pioneer's positioning mistakes.* If the pioneer misjudges the preferences and purchase criteria of the mass-market segment or attempts to satisfy two or more segments at once, it is vulnerable to the introduction of more precisely positioned products by a follower. By tailoring its offerings to each distinct segment, the follower(s) can successfully encircle the pioneer.

2. *Ability to take advantage of the pioneer's product mistakes.* If the pioneer's initial product has technical limitations or design flaws, the follower can benefit by overcoming these weaknesses. Even when the pioneering product is technically satisfactory, a follower may gain an advantage through product enhancements. For example, Compaq captured a substantial share of the commercial PC market by developing faster and more portable versions of IBM's original machine.

3. *Ability to take advantage of the pioneer's marketing mistakes.* If the pioneer makes any marketing mistakes in introducing a new entry, it opens opportunities for later entrants. This observation is closely related to the first two points, yet goes beyond product positioning and design to the actual execution of the pioneer's marketing program. For example, the pioneer may fail to attain adequate distribution, spend too little on introductory advertising, or use ineffective promotional appeals to communicate the product's benefits. A follower can observe these mistakes, design a marketing program to overcome them, and successfully compete head-to-head with the pioneer. As detailed in Exhibit 8–6, for instance, follower Sharp

EXHIBIT 8–6

How a Follower Captured the Leading Share of the Fax Market

Like the TV and the VCR, the fax (facsimile machine) is another Western invention the United States surrendered to Japan. Xerox produced the world's first commercially successful fax in 1970, and several other American companies, like Burroughs and 3M, quickly followed. But while the pioneers concentrated on selling sophisticated equipment to large companies, Sharp and other Japanese manufacturers attacked the low end of the market. Sharp invaded the industry in 1984 with a no-frills $2,000 machine, less than half the price of anything else available. The company distributed its machine through its established office dealer network, which meant a mobilization of 2,000 salespeople. Other companies used expensive direct-sales forces and could afford a battalion of 90 troops at most. As Allen Mahmarian, Sharp's general manager, points out, "We had a minimal product lineup but the right distribution channel." Sharp was also the first to establish a home office products division to sell faxes and other merchandise through retailers. As shown in the chart below, by 1989 Sharp had raced past Ricoh and Canon to grab the leading position in the industry with a 21 percent market share.

1982		1986		1988	
Company	Market share	Company	Market share	Company	Market share
Xerox	30%	Ricoh	16%	Sharp	21%
Exxon	24%	Canon	13%	Murata	15%
Burroughs	17%	Pitney Bowes	12%	Canon	11%
3M	14%	Sharp	10%	Ricoh	10%
Matsushita	6%	Fujitsu	7%	Pitney Bowes	6%

SOURCE: Frederick H. Katayama, "Who's Fueling the Fax Frenzy?" *Fortune*, October 23, 1989, pp. 151–156. © 1989 The Time Inc. Magazine Company. All rights reserved.

captured a leading share of the fax market by focusing on low-end products and developing a more extensive distribution system than the early industry leaders.

4. *Ability to take advantage of the latest technology.* In industries characterized by rapid technological advances, followers can possibly introduce products based on a superior, second-generation technology and thereby gain an advantage over the pioneer. And the pioneer may have difficulty reacting quickly to such advances if it is heavily committed to an earlier technology. Consumer popularity of the newer VHS format, for instance, gave followers in the videocassette recorder market an advantage over pioneer Sony, who was locked in to the less popular Beta format.

5. *Ability to take advantage of pioneer's limited resources.* If the pioneer has limited resources for production facilities or marketing programs, or fails to commit sufficient resources to its new entry, followers willing and able to outspend the pioneer experience few enduring constraints. For example, Minnetonka, Inc. was the pioneer in several health and beauty-aid product categories with brands like Softsoap liquid soap and Cheque-Up plaque fighting toothpaste. But with annual sales of only about $150 million, the

firm could not maintain its leading share position in these markets. Companies like Procter & Gamble and Colgate-Palmolive introduced competing brands with advertising and promotion budgets much larger than Minnetonka could match.

Determinants of success for pioneers and followers

Our discussion suggests that a pioneering firm stands the best chance for long-term success in market-share leadership and profitability when (1) the new product-market is insulated from the entry of competitors, at least for a while, by strong patent protection, proprietary technology (e.g., a unique production process), or substantial investment requirements; or (2) the firm has sufficient size, resources, and competencies to take full advantage of its pioneering position and preserve it in the face of later competitive entries. Indeed, some recent evidence suggests that organizational competencies, such as R&D and marketing skills, not only affect a firm's success as a pioneer, they may also influence the company's decision about whether or not to be a pioneer in the first place. Firms that perceive they lack the competencies necessary to sustain a first-mover advantage may be more likely to wait for another company to take the lead and enter the market later.[7]

Polaroid Corporation is a pioneer that profited from the first kind of situation. Strong patent protection enabled the firm to grow from an entrepreneurial start-up to a $1.6 billion company with little direct competition. Kodak, the only firm that attempted to challenge Polaroid in the instant photography business, dropped out of the industry after losing a patent infringement suit in 1985. Consequently, Polaroid could grow and profit by introducing a steady but narrowly focused stream of product improvements, and by supporting those products with only modest advertising and promotion. However, the firm's insulated market situation led it to focus largely on the instant photography business rather than expanding into other technologies or product-markets. As a result, the firm's primary concern now is that instant photography is declining as consumers shift their purchases to products based on newer technologies, such as video recorders.[8]

McDonald's is an example of a pioneer that has succeeded by aggressively building on the foundations of its early advantage. Although the firm started small as a single hamburger restaurant, it used the franchise system of distribution to rapidly expand the number of McDonald's outlets with a minimum cash investment. That expansion plus stringent quality and cost controls, relatively low prices made possible by experience curve effects, heavy advertising expenditures, and product-line expansion aimed at specific market segments (such as Egg McMuffin for the breakfast crowd and salads for health and diet-conscious adults) have all enabled the firm to maintain a

---

[7]Moore, Boulding, and Goodstein, "Pioneering and Market Share . . . "
[8]"Polaroid's Spectra May Be Losing Its Flash," *Business Week,* June 29, 1987, p. 31.

EXHIBIT 8-7
Marketing Strategy Elements Pursued by Successful Pioneers,
Fast Followers, and Late Entrants

These marketers . . .	are characterized by one or more of these strategy elements:
Successful pioneers	• Large entry scale • Broad product line • High product quality • Heavy promotional expenditures

Successful fast followers	• Larger entry scale than the pioneer
	• "Leapfrogging" the pioneer with superior:
	  product technology
	  product quality
	  customer service

Successful late entrants	• Focus on peripheral target markets or niches

commanding 40 percent share of the fast-food hamburger industry—more than double the share of Burger King, its largest competitor.[9]

On the other hand, a follower will most likely succeed when there are few legal, technological, or financial barriers to inhibit entry and when it has sufficient resources and competencies to overwhelm the pioneer's early advantage. IBM exploited such a situation in the personal computer industry where it competed with a quality product and extensive software, extensive advertising, a strong salesforce, and an excellent reputation for reliability and good customer service. IBM quickly captured more than half the worldwide PC market,[10] although its market share has been eroded somewhat in recent years by low-cost clones.

A study conducted across a broad range of industries in the PIMS data base supports these observations.[11] The study's findings are briefly summarized in Exhibit 8–7 and discussed in more detail below.

The study found that regardless of the industry involved, pioneers who maintained their preeminent position well into the market's growth stage had supported their early entry with the following marketing strategy elements:

- *Large entry scale*—Successful pioneers have sufficient capacity, or can expand quickly enough, to pursue a mass-marketing strategy, usually on a national rather than a local or regional basis. Thus, they can expand their volume quickly and achieve the benefits of experience curve effects before major competitors can challenge them.

[9]"McWorld?" *Business Week,* October 13, 1986, pp. 78–86.

[10]"Who's Afraid of IBM?" *Business Week,* June 29, 1987, pp. 68–74.

[11]Mary L. Coyle, "Competition in Developing Markets: The Impact of Order of Entry," unpublished doctoral dissertation, University of Toronto, 1986.

- *Broad product line*—Successful pioneers quickly add line extensions or modifications to their initial product to tailor their offerings to specific market segments. This reduces their vulnerability to later entrants who might differentiate themselves by targeting one or more peripheral markets. After introducing its Top Shelf line, for instance, Hormel quickly added Micro Cup and Kids Kitchen products as well as microwave versions of Dinty Moore stew and Hormel chili to strengthen its position in the new microwave prepared meals category.

- *High product quality*—Successful pioneers offer a high-quality, well-designed product from the beginning, thus removing one potential source of differential advantage for followers. Competent engineering, thorough product and market testing before commercialization, and good quality control are all important to the continued success of pioneers.

- *Heavy promotional expenditures*—Relatively high advertising and promotional expenditures as a percentage of sales are characteristic of the marketing programs of pioneers who continue to be successful. Initially, the promotion helps to stimulate awareness and primary demand for the new product category, build volume, and reduce unit costs. Later, this promotion helps build selective demand for the pioneer's brand and reinforces loyalty as new competitors enter.

The same study found that the most successful fast followers tend to have the resources to enter the new market on a larger scale than the pioneer. Consequently, they can quickly reduce their unit costs and offer lower prices than incumbent competitors. Some fast followers achieve success, however, by leapfrogging earlier entrants by offering a product with more sophisticated technology, better quality, or superior service (like IBM in the PC market). As mentioned, followers in high-tech industries have the potential advantage of being able to utilize the second generation of technology to develop products technically superior to the pioneer's. As we shall see in the next chapter, however, the success of such a leapfrog strategy depends heavily on the speed and effectiveness of the follower's product development process.[12]

Finally, the study found that some late followers also achieve substantial profits by avoiding direct confrontation with established competitors and targeting peripheral markets. They offer products tailored to the needs of smaller market niches and support them with high levels of customer service.

A more detailed discussion of the marketing strategies appropriate for followers is presented in the next chapter. Followers typically enter a market after it has entered the growth stage of its life cycle, and they start with low market shares relative to the more established pioneer. Consequently, the

[12]Ralph E. Gomory, "From the 'Ladder of Science' to the Product Development Cycle," *Harvard Business Review,* November–December 1989, pp. 99–105.

next chapter's examination of strategies for low-share competitors in growth markets is relevant to both fast followers and late entrants. The remainder of this chapter concentrates only on the strategic marketing programs that pioneers in new product-markets might successfully pursue.

STRATEGIC MARKETING PROGRAMS FOR PIONEERS

The preceding discussion suggests that the ultimate success of a pioneering strategy depends on the nature of the demand and potential competitive situation the pioneer encounters in the market and on the pioneer's ability to design and implement an appropriate strategic marketing program. The empirical evidence suggests that a pioneer's long-term success in continued share leadership and profitability depends on the firm's ability to implement and maintain a **mass-market penetration** marketing strategy. This strategy aims at convincing as many potential customers as possible to adopt the new product quickly to drive down unit costs and build a large contingent of loyal customers before competitors enter the market. The ultimate objective of such a strategy is to capture and maintain a commanding share of the total market for the new product. It tends to be most successful when entry barriers inhibit or delay the entry of competitors, thus allowing the pioneer more time to build volume, lower unit costs, and establish a loyal customer base, or when the pioneer has resources or competencies that most potential competitors cannot match.

Exhibit 8–8 presents a detailed listing of specific circumstances favoring the use of a mass-market penetration strategy. Keep in mind, though, that while these conditions favor a mass-market strategy compared to one of the alternatives, they do not necessarily guarantee its success. Much depends on how effectively the firm implements the strategy. Also, it is highly unlikely that all of the listed conditions will exist simultaneously in any single product-market.

Note that barriers to entry can result from a number of factors, including patent protection for the pioneer's technology, limited supply of materials or components, substantial investment requirements, or the lack of resources required to enter the market on a major scale.

The successful implementation of a mass-market penetration strategy requires several competencies, including product engineering and marketing skills and the financial and organizational resources necessary to expand capacity in advance of demand. In some cases, though, a smaller firm with limited resources can successfully employ a mass-market penetration strategy if the market has a protracted adoption process and slow initial growth. Slow growth can delay competitive entry because fewer competitors are attracted to a market with questionable future growth. This allows the pioneer more time to expand capacity. For example, while Medtronic introduced heart pacemakers in 1960, it took nearly a decade for cardiologists to embrace the new technology in large numbers. Consequently, even though Medtronic was a small entrepreneurial firm, it could keep pace with the slow rate of volume growth and expand its capacity and product line sufficiently to maintain a leading position in the pacemaker industry.[13]

Even when a new product-market expands quickly, however, it may still be possible for a small firm with limited resources to be a successful pioneer. In such cases, though, the firm must define success in a more limited way. Instead of pursuing the objective of capturing and sustaining a leading share of the entire market, it may make more sense for such firms to focus their efforts on a single market segment. This kind of **niche penetration** strategy can help the smaller pioneer gain the biggest bang for its limited bucks and avoid direct confrontations with bigger competitors.

As Exhibit 8–8 suggests, a niche penetration strategy is most appropriate when the new market is expected to grow quickly and there are a number of different benefit or applications segments to appeal to. It is particularly attractive when there are few barriers to the entry of major competitors and when the pioneer has only limited resources and competencies to defend any advantage it gains through early entry.

Stouffer provides an example of this strategy. As the first to introduce high-quality, relatively expensive frozen entrees, the firm focused solely on the upscale, working adult segment of the market. Stouffer threw all available resources into expanding variety within the product line, consumer advertising, and trade promotion to obtain adequate shelf space; and the company concentrated all those efforts on the upscale singles segment. Stouffer has never attempted to expand into the higher-volume (but lower-margin) "quick, low-cost meals for the family" segment dominated by Swanson's (a division of Campbell).[14]

Some pioneers may intend to pursue a mass-market penetration strategy when introducing a new product or service, but end up implementing a niche penetration strategy instead. This is particularly likely when the new market grows faster or is more fragmented than the pioneer expects. Facing such a situation a pioneer with limited resources may decide to concentrate on holding its leading position in one or a few segments rather than spreading itself too thin developing unique line extensions and marketing programs for many different markets, or going deep into debt to finance rapid expansion.

For example, Progressive—a property and casualty insurer that was one of America's fastest-growing companies during the last half of the 1980s—prospered by developing insurance policies for high-risk drivers. It succeeded by developing an extensive data base on the personalities, lifestyles, and driving habits of various high-risk groups. Then, by differentiating between, for instance, bartenders and rock musicians, the firm priced policies to match the underwriting risk. But Progressive ran into trouble in 1988 after a plunge

[13]David H. Gobeli and William Rudelius, "Managing Innovation: Lessons from the Cardiac-Pacing Industry," *Sloan Management Review*, Summer 1985, pp. 29–43.
[14]Kevin Higgins, "Meticulous Planning Pays Dividends at Stouffers," *Marketing News*, October 28, 1983, pp. 1, 20.

EXHIBIT 8-8

Marketing Strategies for New-Product Pioneers

Situational variables	Alternative marketing strategies		
	Mass-market penetration	Niche penetration	Skimming; early withdrawal
Market characteristics	• Large potential demand	• Large potential demand	• Limited potential demand
	• Relatively homogeneous customer needs	• Fragmented market; many different applications and benefit segments	• Customers likely to adopt product relatively slowly; long adoption process
	• Customers likely to adopt product relatively quickly; short diffusion process	• Customers likely to adopt product relatively quickly; short adoption process	• Early adopters willing to pay high price; demand is price inelastic
Product characteristics	• Product technology patentable or difficult to copy	• Product technology offers little patent protection; easily copied or adapted	• Product technology offers little patent protection; easily copied or adapted
	• Components or materials difficult to obtain; limited sources of supply	• Components or materials easy to obtain; many sources of supply	• Components or materials easy to obtain; many sources of supply
	• Complex production process; substantial development and/or investment required	• Relatively simple production process; little development or additional investment required	• Relatively simple production process; little development or additional investment required
Competitor characteristics	• Few potential competitors	• Many potential competitors	• Many potential competitors

into trucking and transportation insurance. "We thought we were better than we really were," says CEO Peter H. Lewis. "We jumped into new markets and put on too much business too fast—our organization and support systems couldn't handle it." To get back on track, the firm refocused its efforts on its original market niche and put its more aggressive expansion program on hold, at least for a while.[15]

Even when a firm has the resources to sustain a leading position in a new product-market, it may choose not to. Competition is usually inevitable; and prices and margins tend to drop dramatically after followers enter the market. Therefore, some pioneers opt to pursue a **skimming** strategy while planning an early withdrawal from the market. This involves setting a high price and engaging in only limited advertising and promotion to maximize per-unit profits and recover the product's development costs as quickly as possible. At

[15]William E. Sheeline, "Avoiding Growth's Perils," *Fortune*, August 13, 1990, pp. 55–58.

EXHIBIT 8–8 *(concluded)*

Situational variables	Alternative marketing strategies		
	Mass-market penetration	**Niche penetration**	**Skimming; early withdrawal**
Firm characteristics	• Most potential competitors have limited resources and competencies; few sources of differential advantage	• Some potential competitors have substantial resources and competencies; possible sources of differential advantage	• Some potential competitors have substantial resources and competencies; possible sources of differential advantage
	• Strong product engineering skills; able to quickly develop product modifications and line extensions for multiple market segments	• Limited product engineering skills and resources	• Strong basic R&D and new-product development skills; a prospector with good capability for continued new-product innovation
	• Strong marketing skills and resources; ability to identify and develop marketing programs for multiple segments; ability to shift from stimulation of primary demand to stimulation of selective demand as competitors enter	• Limited marketing skills and resources	• Good sales and promotional skills; able to quickly build primary demand in target market; perhaps has limited marketing resources for long-term market maintenance
	• Sufficient financial and organizational resources to build capacity in advance of growth in demand	• Insufficient financial or organizational resources to build capacity in advance of growing demand	• Limited financial or organizational resources to commit to building capacity in advance of growth in demand

the same time, the firm may work to develop new applications for its technology or the next generation of more advanced technology. Then when competitors enter the market and margins fall, the firm is ready to cannibalize its own product with one based on new technology or to move into new segments of the market.

The 3M Company is a master of the skimming strategy. According to one 3M manager, "We hit fast, price high (full economic value of the product to the user), and get the heck out when the me-too products pour in." The new markets pioneered by the company are often smaller ones of $10 million to $50 million; and the firm may dominate them for only about five years or so. By then, it is ready to launch the next generation of new technology or to move the old technology into new applications.[16] An example of 3M's approach is described in Exhibit 8–9.

---

[16]George S. Day, *Analysis for Strategic Marketing Decisions* (St. Paul, Minn.: West Publishing Company, 1986), pp. 103–4.

EXHIBIT 8-9

3M's Skimming Strategy in the Casting Tape Market

3M developed the first water-activated synthetic casting tape to set broken bones in 1980, but by 1982 eight other companies had brought out copycat products. 3M's R&D people retreated to their labs and developed and tested 140 new versions in a variety of fabrics. In 1983, the firm dropped the old product and introduced a technically superior version that was stronger, easier to use, and commanded a premium price.

SOURCE: Christopher Knowlton, "What America Makes Best," *Fortune*, March 28, 1988, p. 45. © 1988 The Time Inc. Magazine Company. All rights reserved.

As Exhibit 8–8 indicates, either small or large firms can use strategies of skimming and early withdrawal. But it is critical that the company have good R&D and product development skills so it can produce a constant stream of new products or new applications to replace older ones as they attract heavy competition. Also, since a firm pursuing this kind of strategy plans to remain in a market only short term, it is most appropriate when there are few barriers to entry, the product is expected to diffuse rapidly, and the pioneer lacks the capacity or other resources necessary to defend a leading share position over the long haul.

Objectives of alternative pioneer strategies

Exhibit 8–10 outlines the short-term, intermediate-term, and long-term objectives that pioneers should focus on when pursuing mass-market, niche penetration, or skimming strategies.

The ultimate long-term objective of a mass-market penetration strategy is to maximize ROI. But to accomplish this, the firm must seek in the intermediate term to gain and hold a leading share of the new product-market throughout its growth and perhaps to even preempt competitors from entering the market. Thus, the short-term objective should be to maximize the number of customers adopting the new product as quickly as possible.

The short-, intermediate-, and long-term objectives of a niche penetration strategy are largely the same as those of a mass-market penetration strategy. The one essential difference is that a firm pursuing a niche strategy tries to capture and maintain a leading share of a more narrowly focused market segment rather than diffusing its limited resources across the entire market.

Finally, since businesses pursuing a skimming strategy usually expect to leave the market eventually, they have no long-term objectives. Therefore, their intermediate-term objective is to maximize returns before competitors enter the market. When increasing competition begins to reduce profit margins, firms pursuing this strategy typically license the product to another firm, introduce a new generation of products, or move to other markets or product categories. Thus, the short-term objective should be to gain as much volume as possible while simultaneously maintaining high margins to recoup development expenses and to generate profits quickly.

EXHIBIT 8-10
Objectives of Strategic Marketing Programs for Pioneers

Strategic objectives	Alternative strategic marketing programs		
	Mass-market penetration	Niche penetration	Skimming; early withdrawal
Short-term objectives	• Maximize number of triers and adopters in total market; invest heavily to build future volume and share.	• Maximize number of triers and adopters in target segment; limited investment to build volume and share in chosen niche.	• Obtain as many adopters as possible with limited investment; maintain high margins to recoup product development and commercialization costs as soon as possible.
Intermediate-term objectives	• Attempt to preempt competition; maintain leading share position even if some sacrifice of margins is necessary in short-term as new competitors enter.	• Maintain leading share position in target segment even if some sacrifice of short-term margins is necessary.	• Maximize ROI; withdraw from market when increasing competition puts downward pressure on margins.
Long-term objectives	• Maximize ROI	• Maximize ROI	• Withdraw

Marketing program components for a mass-market penetration strategy

As mentioned, the short-term objective of a mass-market penetration strategy is to maximize the number of customers adopting the firm's new product as quickly as possible. This requires a marketing program focused on (1) *aggressively building product awareness and motivation to buy* among a broad cross section of potential customers and (2) *making it as easy as possible for those customers to try the new product,* on the assumption that they will try it, like it, develop loyalty, and make repeat purchases. Exhibit 8–11 outlines a number of marketing program activities in each of the 4Ps that might help increase customers' awareness and willingness to buy, or improve their ability to try the product. This is by no means an exhaustive list; nor do we mean to imply that a successful pioneer must necessarily engage in all of the listed activities. Marketing managers must develop programs combining activities that fit both the objectives of a mass-market penetration strategy and the specific market and potential competitive conditions the new product faces.

EXHIBIT 8–11

Components of Strategic Marketing Programs for Pioneers

Strategic objectives and tasks	Alternative strategic marketing programs		
	Mass-market penetration	Niche penetration	Skimming; early withdrawal
Increase customers' awareness and willingness to buy	• Heavy advertising to generate awareness among customers in mass market; broad use of mass media.	• Heavy advertising directed at target segment to generate awareness; use selective media relevant to target.	• Limited advertising to generate awareness, particularly among least price sensitive early adopters.
	• Extensive salesforce efforts to win new adopters; possible use of incentives to encourage new-product sales.	• Extensive salesforce efforts focused on potential customers in target segment; possible use of incentives to encourage new-product sales to target accounts.	• Extensive salesforce efforts, particularly focused on largest potential adopters; possible use of volume-based incentives to encourage new-product sales.
	• Advertising and sales appeals stress generic benefits of new-product type.	• Advertising and sales appeals stress generic benefits of new-product type.	• Advertising and sales appeals stress generic benefits of new-product type.
	• Extensive introductory sales promotions to induce trial (sampling, couponing, quantity discounts).	• Extensive introductory sales promotions to induce trial, but focused on target segment.	• Limited use, if any, of introductory sales promotions; if used, they should be volume-based quantity discounts.
	• Move relatively quickly to expand offerings (line extensions, multiple package sizes) to appeal to multiple segments.	• Additional product development limited to improvements or modifications to increase appeal to target segment.	• Little, if any, additional development within the product category.

Increasing customers' awareness and willingness to buy

Obviously, heavy expenditures on advertising, introductory promotions such as sampling and couponing, and personal selling efforts can all increase awareness of a new product or service among potential customers. This is the critical first step in the adoption process for a new entry. The relative importance of these promotional tools varies, however, depending on the nature of the product and the number of potential customers. For instance, personal selling efforts are often the most critical component of the promotional mix for highly technical industrial products with a limited potential customer base. Media advertising and sales promotion are usually more useful for building awareness and primary demand for a new consumer good among customers in the mass market. In either case, when designing a mass-market

EXHIBIT   8 – 1 1   *(concluded)*

Strategic objectives and tasks	Alternative strategic marketing programs		
	Mass-market penetration	Niche penetration	Skimming; early withdrawal
Increase customers' ability to buy	• Offer free trial, liberal return, or extended warranty policies to reduce customers' perceived risk of adopting the new product.	• Offer free trial, liberal return, or extended warranty policies to reduce target customers' perceived risk of adopting the new product.	• Offer free trial, liberal return, or extended warranty policies to reduce target customers' perceived risk of adopting the new product.
	• Penetration pricing; or start with high price but bring out lower-priced versions in anticipation of competitive entries.	• Penetration pricing; or start with high price but bring out lower-priced versions in anticipation of competitive entries.	• Skimming pricing; attempt to maintain margins at level consistent with value of product to early adopters.
	• Extended credit terms to encourage initial purchases.	• Extended credit terms to encourage initial purchases.	• Extended credit terms to encourage initial purchases.
	• Heavy use of trade promotions aimed at gaining extensive distribution.	• Trade promotions aimed at gaining solid distribution among retailers or distributors pertinent for reaching target segment.	• Limited use of trade promotions; only as necessary to gain adequate distribution.
	• Offer engineering, installation, and training services to increase new product's compatibility with customers' current operations to reduce "switching costs."	• Offer engineering, installation, and training services to increase new product's compatibility with customers' current operations to reduce "switching costs."	• Offer limited engineering, installation, and services necessary to overcome customers' objections.

penetration marketing program, firms should broadly focus promotional efforts to expose and attract as many potential customers as possible before competitors show up.

Firms might also attempt to increase customers' willingness to buy their products by reducing the risk associated with buying something new. This can be done by letting customers try the product without obligation, as when car dealers allow potential customers to test drive a new model, or by committing to liberal return or extended warranty policies for the product. When Lee Iacocca took over Chrysler, for instance, he decreed that all new car models should be introduced with the longest warranty in the industry to overcome the low-quality image of Chrysler products.

Finally, a firm committed to mass-market penetration might also broaden its product offerings to increase its appeal to as many market segments as possible. This helps reduce its vulnerability to later entrants who could focus on specific market niches. Firms can accomplish such market expansion through the rapid introduction of line extensions, product modifications, and additional package sizes.

Increasing customers' ability to buy

For customers to adopt a new product and develop loyalty toward it, they must be aware of the item and be motivated to buy. But they must also have the wherewithal to actually purchase it. Thus, to capture as many customers in as short a time as possible, it usually makes sense for a firm pursuing mass-market penetration to keep prices low (penetration pricing) and perhaps offer liberal financing arrangements or easy credit terms during the introductory period.

Another factor that can inhibit customers' ability to buy is a lack of product availability within the distribution system. Thus, extensive personal selling and trade promotions aimed at gaining adequate distribution are usually a critical part of a mass-market penetration marketing program. Such efforts should take place before the start of promotional campaigns to ensure that the product is available as soon as customers are motivated to buy it.

A highly technical new product's incompatibility with other related products or systems currently used can also inhibit customers' purchases. For example, some businesses were reluctant to buy Apple's early Macintosh computers because they had large investments in IBM software that could not be used with the Apple system, and their employees had to be retrained to use the new system. In other words, a new product's lack of compatibility with other elements of an existing system can result in high switching costs for a potential adopter. The pioneer might reduce those costs by designing the product to be as compatible as possible with related equipment. It might also offer engineering services to help make the new product more compatible with existing operations, provide free installation assistance, and conduct training programs for the customer's employees.

Marketing program components for a niche penetration strategy

Because short-, intermediate-, and long-term objectives are similar for niche and mass-market companies, the marketing program elements a niche penetrator pursues are also likely to be similar to those for a mass-marketing penetration strategy. However, the niche penetrator should keep all its marketing efforts clearly focused on the target segment to gain as much impact as possible from a limited budget. This point is clearly evident in the outline of program components in Exhibit 8–11. For example, although a niche penetrator strategy calls for the same advertising, sales promotion, personal selling, and trade promotion activities as a mass-market program, the former should use more selective media, call schedules, and channel designs to precisely direct those activities toward the target segment.

Marketing program components for a skimming strategy

As Exhibit 8–11 suggests, one major difference between a skimming strategy and a mass-market strategy involves pricing policies. A relatively high price is appropriate for a skimming strategy to increase margins and revenues, even though some price-sensitive customers may be reluctant to adopt the product at that price.[17] This also suggests that introductory promotional programs might best focus on customer groups who are least sensitive to price and most likely to be early adopters of the new product. This can help hold down promotion costs and avoid wasting marketing efforts on less profitable market segments. Thus, in many consumer goods businesses, skimming strategies focus on relatively upscale customers, since they are often more likely to be early adopters and less sensitive to price.

Another critical element of a skimming strategy is the nature of the firm's continuing product development efforts. A pioneer that plans to leave a market when competitors enter should not devote much effort to expanding its product line through line extensions or multiple package sizes. Instead, it should concentrate on the next generation of technology or on identifying new application segments; in other words, preparing its avenue of escape from the market.

Now that we have examined some strategies a pioneer might follow in entering a new market, we are left with two important strategic questions. The pioneer is by definition the early share leader in the new market; hence the first question is, What adjustments in strategy might be necessary for the pioneer to *maintain its leading share position* after competitors arrive on the scene? The second is, What strategies might followers adopt *to take business away from the early leader and increase their relative share position* as the market grows? These two strategic issues are the focus of the next chapter.

SUMMARY

Not all new products are equally new. Only about 10 percent of the new product introductions made by U.S. companies involve new-to-the-world products. Many new entries, such as line extensions or modifications, are new to the customers in the target market but are relatively familiar to the company. Other new entries, like new-product lines, extensions of an existing line, or cost reductions, may be quite new to the company but not to the target customers. The firm that introduces products new to the target market must *build primary demand* by making potential customers aware of the new product and stimulating their willingness and ability to buy.

The primary objective of most new-market entries is to secure future volume and profit growth for the firm. However, individual market development efforts often accomplish a variety of secondary objectives as well:

---

[17]This assumes that demand is relatively price inelastic. In markets where price elasticity is high, a skimming price strategy may lead to lower total revenues due to its dampening effect on total demand.

maintaining the firm's position as a product innovator, defending a current market-share position in an industry, establishing a foothold in a future new market, preempting a market segment, or exploiting technology in a new way. Top management must clearly specify the new-market entry objectives for each SBU. If a prospector SBU's new-entry objectives are to maintain a position as a product innovator and establish footholds in many new markets, for example, its most appropriate new-entry strategy is to be the *pioneer,* or first entrant, in as many new product-markets as possible. But if the SBU is primarily concerned with defending a strong market-share position in its industry, it might adopt a *follower* strategy whereby it enters new product-markets later and relies on superior product quality, better customer service, or lower prices to offset the pioneer's early lead.

Both pioneer and follower new-market entry strategies offer unique potential sources of competitive advantage. A pioneering strategy is most likely to lead to long-term share leadership and profitability when the new market is insulated from the entry of competitors by patent protection for the pioneer's product, proprietary technology, or other barriers or when the pioneer has sufficient marketing resources and competence to maintain its early lead in the face of competitive attacks. Pioneers are most likely to maintain their early market-share lead when they can enter the new market on a large scale, quickly add line extensions, offer and sustain high product quality, and support their product introduction with heavy promotional expenditures. Followers are most successful when they can enter the market on a larger scale and attain lower per-unit costs than the pioneer or when they can leapfrog the pioneer by offering a superior product or better service.

Alternative strategic marketing programs that are appropriate for a pioneer include a *mass-market penetration* strategy, a *niche penetration* strategy, or a *skimming* strategy. A mass-market penetration strategy aims at getting as many potential customers as possible to try the new product and develop brand loyalty before competitors can enter. The pioneer must maximize customers' *awareness* of the new product and attempt to increase their *willingness* and *ability to buy.* Because the necessary actions require substantial resources, a mass-market strategy is most appropriate for larger businesses or when barriers slow competitive entry.

Pioneers with limited resources are better off adopting a niche penetration strategy. The marketing objectives and actions involved in a niche strategy are similar to those of mass-market penetration, but they focus on a smaller segment of customers where fewer resources are needed to defend the pioneer's early lead.

Finally, some technological leaders, particularly those pursuing a prospector business strategy, may prefer to enter many new markets, attain as much profit as possible before competitors enter, and then withdraw as competition increases and margins erode. A skimming strategy incorporating relatively high prices and low marketing expenditures is appropriate for such businesses.

Strategies for Growth Markets

CONNER PERIPHERALS: AMERICA'S FASTEST-GROWING COMPANY[1]

Conner Peripherals—a maker of compact hard disk drives for personal computers—was the fastest-growing major manufacturing firm in America during the last half of the 1980s, as measured by average annual percentage increases in sales. After its inception in 1986 the firm's sales grew explosively, reaching an estimated $1.1 billion in sales and $80 million in earnings for 1990. The company has also showered its shareholders with wealth. The stock, which went public in April 1988 at $8 a share, reached nearly $30 by July 1990.

Each of Conner's hard disk drives is smaller than a paperback book and is built to nest within a personal computer, endowing the machine with elephantine memory: It can store 1.5 billion bits of information and retrieve any of them, on aver-age, in 25 one-thousandths of a second. While many other firms make similar products, Conner has achieved its phenomenal growth with a strategy emphasizing close-to-the-customer marketing, rapid product development, and smart manufacturing. And Conner's strategy has enabled it to capture more than a 12 percent share of the rapidly growing compact hard disk industry even though the firm was a relatively late entrant.

Finis F. Conner, the cofounder and CEO of Conner Peripherals, is an industrial engineer who was working as an electronics salesman in 1979 when he foresaw that future computers would need to hold more information than could squeeze onto a floppy disk. Until then, the smallest hard disk drives were 8-inch models used with minicomputers.

[1]This case example is based largely on material found in Andrew Kupfer, "America's Fastest-Growing Company," *Fortune,* August 13, 1990, pp. 48–54.

Conner proposed to build a much more compact 5¼-inch version. He took his idea to Al Shugart, an engineer who had developed the first small floppy disk drives. Together they founded Seagate Technology and pioneered the compact hard disk industry.

Conner was in charge of marketing at Seagate and ran the company with Shugart and three partners. By 1984, the firm achieved revenues of $344 million, but Conner found himself at odds with his partners. Intent on building sales of their main product, they refused to develop innovative new disk drives that Conner had brashly promised to customers. After months of infighting, Conner cashed in his share of Seagate—worth about $15 million—and quit.

In December 1985, Conner got a phone call from John Squires, a disk drive engineer in Colorado. When Conner arrived in Denver, Squires handed him a prototype drive that to the entrepreneur's experienced eye was a winner. It was far more compact than Seagate's drives, with a disk only 3½ inches in diameter, and it promised to be much faster at retrieving data. Squires wanted money and the use of Conner's name, which had credibility in the industry. But Conner says he had no wish to be a mere spectator: "I told Squires I wouldn't go along unless I could set the strategy and have control over the rate at which we grew." The engineer readily agreed.

The competitive situation

The compact disk drive industry had become crowded by 1986, with more than 70 companies clawing for $1.2 billion of business. But Seagate Technology, the industry pioneer, continued to prosper and maintain its leading market-share position with a low-cost competitive strategy—supplying high volumes of standard disk drives at low margins. Seagate and other commodity manufacturers faced a risk, however, because they had to invest a lot of money in plants and production equipment—investments that fast-changing technology or more efficient competitors could render worthless.

A number of industry followers, such as Maxtor and Quantum, pursued a different competitive strategy. They sought to differentiate their products by staying on the leading edge of technology. They raced to develop the smallest, fastest drives, selling them to computer makers at premium prices. The risk they faced was new-product failure—spending money on R&D for products that might not find a buyer.

Conner Peripherals' strategy

From the start, Conner Peripherals pursued a prospector strategy aimed at achieving differentiation by introducing a steady flow of new products at the cutting edge of technology. But to avoid some of the development risks inherent in such a strategy, Conner also adopted a philosophy of "sell, design, build." To marry itself to customers and justify R&D expense, the company won't engineer a new product unless a major customer—such as Compaq—has already promised to buy it. Each new Conner disk drive is a premium-priced product engineered to specifications negotiated by a Conner sales engineer with Compaq or some other key customer.

To help its production people quickly gear up to produce large quantities of each new product, Squires and his designers try to keep their innovations simple, altering only one or two features at a time. The firm has also designed as much flexibility as possible into its manufacturing operation. Forgoing the cost advantages of making its own components, the company buys nearly all of its parts from others. It also leases the factory space it needs to assemble and test its drives.

Conner Peripherals' approach has helped hold down the firm's capital investment: For every dollar in plant and equipment, the firm produces $7.17 in sales, compared with $3.59 for Seagate. It has also given the company flexibility to respond to shifts in market needs and stay one technological jump ahead of compet-

itors. In 1988, for example, it was able to quickly pounce on the fastest-growing market segment, disk drives for laptop and notebook computers.

Conner Peripherals' strategy has been so successful that in a mere four years the firm vaulted from a late entrant to the number two market share in the compact disk drive industry. Seagate, meanwhile, has managed to maintain its leading position in the industry with sales in fiscal 1990 of $2.4 billion. But the inflexibility of Seagate's low-cost strategy has cost the firm both in relative market share and profitability. The firm failed to anticipate how quickly customers would shift from 5¼-inch drives, its standard, to smaller sizes. Consequently, the company spent heavily in 1987 to expand its production lines for the larger units and took a $53 million loss in September 1988 as it wrote off part of its investment.

STRATEGIC ISSUES IN GROWTH MARKETS

Seagate's experience in the compact hard disk drive market, where increasingly intense competition has eroded its leading market-share position and profitability, is common. As we discussed in Chapter 5, product-markets in the growth stage of their life cycles are usually characterized by the entry of many competitive followers. Both conventional wisdom and the various portfolio models suggest there are advantages in quickly entering—and investing heavily to build share in—growth markets. But a market is neither inherently attractive nor unattractive simply because it promises rapid future growth. Managers must consider how the market and competitive situation are likely to evolve and whether their firms can exploit the rapid growth opportunities to establish a competitive advantage. The next section of this chapter examines both the market opportunities and the competitive risks often found in growing product-markets.

The primary strategic objective of the early share leader, usually the market pioneer, in a growth market is **share maintenance.** From a marketing view, the firm must accomplish two important tasks: (1) retain repeat or replacement business from its existing customers, and (2) continue to capture the major portion of sales to the growing number of new customers entering the market for the first time. The leader might use any of several marketing strategies to accomplish these objectives. It might try to build on its initial scale and experience advantages to achieve low-cost production and reduce its prices, as Seagate did in the compact disk drive industry. Alternatively, the leader might focus on rapid product improvements, expand its product line to appeal to newly emerging segments, and increase its marketing and sales efforts. The third section of this chapter explores strategic marketing programs—both defensive and offensive—that leaders might use to maintain market share in the face of rapid market growth and increasing competition.

A challenger's strategic objective in a growth market is usually to *build its share* by expanding its sales faster than the overall market growth rate. Firms do this by stealing existing customers away from the leader or other competitors, capturing a larger share of new customers than the market leader, or both. Once again, challengers might use a number of strategies to accomplish these objectives. These include developing a superior product technology; differentiating through rapid product innovations or line extensions, as illustrated by Conner Peripherals; offering lower prices; or focusing on market niches where the leader is not well established, as Conner did in the laptop and notebook segment of the computer industry. The fourth section details these and other **share-growth** strategies that market challengers use under different conditions.

The success of a firm's strategy during the growth stage is a critical determinant of its ability to reap profits, or even survive, as a product-market moves into maturity. Unfortunately, the growth stage is often short; and increasingly rapid technological change and market fragmentation are causing it to become even shorter in many industries.[2] This shortening of the growth stage concerns many firms—particularly late entrants or those who fail to acquire a substantial market share—because as growth slows during the transition to maturity, there is often a shakeout of marginal competitors. In the personal computer industry, for example, there were an estimated 150 manufacturers and another 300 or so firms producing add-on products, software, services, and support in 1982.[3] As the industry growth rate began to slow during 1984–85, a majority of those firms—including some very large companies like Texas Instruments—failed, abandoned the industry, or were acquired by their larger competitors. Thus, when choosing marketing strategies

[2]Hans B. Thorelli and S. C. Burnett, "The Nature of Product Life Cycles for Industrial Goods Businesses," *Journal of Marketing,* Fall 1981, pp. 102–7.

[3]"The Coming Shakeout in Personal Computers," *Business Week,* November 22, 1982, pp. 72–78.

for competing in a growing product-market, managers should keep at least one eye on building a competitive advantage that the business can sustain after growth slows and the market matures.

OPPORTUNITIES AND RISKS IN GROWTH MARKETS[4]

Why are followers attracted to rapidly growing markets? Conventional wisdom suggests such markets present attractive opportunities for future profits because:

- It is easier to gain share when a market is growing.
- Share gains are worth more in a growth market than in a mature market.
- Price competition is likely to be less intense.
- Early participation in a growth market is necessary to make sure that the firm keeps pace with the technology.

While generally valid, each of these premises may be seriously misleading for a particular business in a specific situation. Many followers attracted to a market by its rapid growth rate are likely to be shaken out later when growth slows, either because the preceding premises did not hold or they could not exploit growth advantages sufficiently to build a sustainable competitive position. By understanding the limitations of the assumptions about growth markets and the conditions under which they are most likely to hold, a manager can make better decisions about entering a market and the kind of marketing strategy likely to be most effective in doing so.

Gaining share is easier

The premise that it is easier for a business to increase its share in a growing market is based on two arguments. First, there may be many potential new users who have no established brand loyalties or supplier commitments and who may have different needs or preferences than earlier adopters. Thus, there may be gaps, or undeveloped segments in the market. It is easier, then, for a new competitor to attract those potential new users than to convert customers in a mature market. Second, established competitors are less likely to react aggressively to market-share erosion as long as their sales continue to grow at a satisfactory rate.

There is some truth to the first argument. It usually is easier for a new entrant to attract first-time users than to take business away from entrenched competitors. To take full advantage of the situation, however, the new entrant

---

[4]For a more extensive discussion of the potential opportunities and pitfalls of rapidly growing markets, see David A. Aaker and George S. Day, "The Perils of High-Growth Markets," *Strategic Management Journal* 7 (1986), pp. 409–21; and George S. Day, *Analysis for Strategic Market Decisions,* (St. Paul, Minn.: West Publishing Company, 1986), chap. 4.

must be able to develop a product offering that new customers perceive as more attractive than other alternatives, and it must have the marketing resources and competence to effectively persuade them of that fact. This can be difficult, especially when the pioneer has had months or years to influence potential customers' decision criteria and preferences.[5] It took Apple, for instance, three years and millions of dollars in marketing effort to overcome IBM's superior brand reputation and capture a relatively modest 7.5 percent share of the commercial PC market with its more user-friendly Macintosh machines.[6]

The notion that established competitors are less likely to react to share losses so long as their revenues are growing at an acceptable rate is more tenuous. It overlooks the fact that those competitors may have higher expectations for increased revenues when the market itself is growing. Capital investments and annual operating budgets are usually tied to those sales expectations; therefore, competitors are likely to react aggressively when sales fall below expected levels, whether or not their absolute volumes continue to grow. This is particularly true given that increased competition will likely erode the leader's relative market share, even though its volume may continue to increase. As illustrated by the hypothetical example in Exhibit 9–1, the leader's market share might drop from a high of 100 percent at the beginning of the growth stage to 50 percent by the maturity stage, even though the firm's absolute volume shows steady growth.

Industry leaders often react forcefully when their sales growth falls below industry levels and their relative market share begins to decline. For example, IBM's objective for the PC market during the 1980s was to equal or exceed the growth rate for the overall market. Thus, when the entry of lower-priced IBM-clones and Apple's new Macintosh knocked IBM's sales growth below the industry rate and reduced its relative market share in the middle of the decade, IBM took aggressive action—such as reducing prices and introducing the more technically advanced PS/2 line—even though the firm's absolute sales volume was still increasing.[7]

Share gains are worth more in growth markets

The premise that share gains are more valuable when the market is growing stems from the expectation that the earnings produced by each share point continues to expand as the market expands. The implicit assumption in this argument, of course, is that the business can hold its relative share as the market grows. The validity of such an assumption depends on a number of factors, including:

---

[5]Gregory S. Carpenter and Kent Nakamoto, "Consumer Preference Formation and Pioneering Advantage," *Journal of Marketing Research*, August 1989, pp. 285–98.

[6]"Apple's Comeback," *Business Week*, January 19, 1987, pp. 84–89.

[7]"Who's Afraid of IBM?" *Business Week*, June 29, 1987, pp. 68–74.

EXHIBIT 9-1

Market Shares of the Leader and Followers over the
Life Cycle of a Hypothetical Market

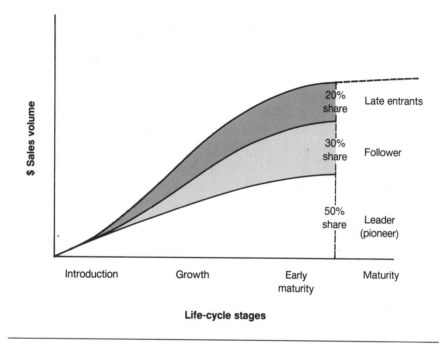

SOURCE: Adapted from George S. Day, *Analysis for Strategic Market Decisions* (St. Paul: West Publishing, 1986), p. 100.

- *Future changes in technology or other key success factors.* If the rules of the game change, the competencies a firm relied on to capture share may no longer be adequate to maintain that share. For instance, Sony was the pioneer and early share leader in the videocassette recorder industry with its Betamax technology. But Matsushita's longer-playing and lower-priced VHS format equipment ultimately proved much more popular with consumers, captured a commanding portion of the market, and dethroned Sony as industry leader.

- *Future competitive structure of the industry.* The number of firms that ultimately decide to compete for a share of the market may turn out to be larger than the early entrants anticipate, particularly if there are few barriers to entry. The sheer weight of numbers can make it difficult for any single competitor to maintain a substantial relative share of the total market.

- *Future fragmentation of the market.* As the market expands, it may fragment into numerous small segments, particularly if potential customers have relatively heterogeneous functional, distribution, or service needs. When such fragmentation occurs, the market in which a given competitor competes may shrink as segments are splintered away.

In addition to these possible changes in future market conditions, a firm's ability to hold its early gains in market share also depends on how it obtained them. If a firm captures share through short-term promotions or price cuts that competitors can easily match and that may tarnish its image among customers, its gains may be short-lived.

Price competition is likely to be less intense

In many rapidly growing markets, demand exceeds supply. The market exerts little pressure on prices initially; the excess demand may even support a price premium. Thus, early entry provides a good opportunity for a firm to recover its initial product development and commercialization investment relatively quickly. New customers may also be willing to pay a premium for technical service as they learn how to make full use of the new product. In contrast, as the market matures and customers gain more experience, the premium a firm can charge without losing market share slowly shrinks; it may eventually disappear entirely.[8]

However, this scenario does not hold true in every developing product-market. If there are few barriers to entry or if the adoption process is protracted and new customers enter the market slowly, demand may not exceed supply—at least not for very long. Also, the pioneer, or one of the earliest followers, might adopt a penetration strategy and set its initial prices relatively low to move quickly down the experience curve and discourage other potential competitors from entering the market.

Early entry is necessary to maintain technical expertise

In high-tech industries, early involvement in new-product categories may be critical for staying abreast of technology. The early experience gained in developing the first generation of products and in helping customers apply the new technology can put the firm in a strong position for developing the next generation of superior products. Later entrants, lacking such customer contact and production and R&D experience, are likely to be at a disadvantage.

There is substantial wisdom in these arguments. Sometimes, however, an early commitment to a specific technology can turn out to be a liability. This is particularly true when multiple unrelated technologies might serve a market or when a newly emerging technology might replace the current one. Once a firm is committed to one technology, adopting a new one can be difficult. Management is often reluctant to abandon a technology in which it

---

[8]Irwin Gross, "Insights from Pricing Research," *Pricing Practices and Strategies* (New York: The Conference Board, 1979).

EXHIBIT 9-2

Medtronic's Commitment to an Old Technology Cost It Sales and Market Share

The dangers inherent in being overly committed to an early technology are demonstrated by Medtronic, Inc., the pioneer in the cardiac pacemaker industry. Medtronic was reluctant to switch to a new lithium-based technology that enabled pacemakers to work much longer before being replaced. As a result, several Medtronic employees left the company and founded Cardiac Pacemakers Inc. to produce and market the new lithium-based product. They quickly captured nearly 20 percent of the total market. And Medtronic saw its share of the cardiac pacemaker market fall rapidly from nearly 70 percent to 40 percent.

SOURCE: Daniel H. Gobeli and William Rudelius, "Managing Innovation: Insights from the Cardiac-Pacing Industry," *Sloan Management Review,* Summer 1985, pp. 29–43.

has made substantial investments, and it might worry that a rapid shift to a new technology will upset present customers. As a result, early commitment to a technology has become increasingly problematic because of more rapid rates of technological change. This problem is dramatically illustrated by the experience of Medtronic, Inc., as described in Exhibit 9–2.

GROWTH-MARKET STRATEGIES FOR MARKET LEADERS

For the share leader in a growing market, of course, the question of the relative advantages versus risks of market entry is moot. The leader is typically the pioneer, or at least one of the first entrants, who developed the product-market in the first place. Its strategic objective is to maintain its leading relative share in the face of increasing competition as the market expands. Share maintenance may not seem like a very aggressive objective, because it implies the business is merely trying to stay even rather than forge ahead. But two important facts must be kept in mind. First, the dynamics of a growth market—including the increasing number of competitors, the fragmentation of market segments, and the threat of product innovation from within and outside the industry—make maintaining an early lead in relative market share very difficult. The continuing need for investment to finance growth, the likely negative cash flows that result, and the threat of governmental antitrust action can make it even more difficult.[9] For example, 31 percent of the 877 market-share leaders in the PIMS data base experienced losses in relative share, as shown in Exhibit 9–3. Note, too, that leaders are especially likely to suffer this fate when their market shares are very large.

[9]Robert D. Buzzell and Bradley T. Gale, *The PIMS Principles: Linking Strategy to Performance* (New York: Free Press, 1987), pp. 188–90.

EXHIBIT 9–3

The Proportion of Market Leaders in the PIMS Data Base Who
Lost Market Share, by Size of Their Initial Share

Leader's initial market share	Percent losing share
Under 20%	16%
20–29	24
30–39	34
40–49	41
Over 50	45
All leaders	31

SOURCE: Adapted from Robert D. Buzzell and Bradley T. Gale, *The PIMS Principles: Linking Strategy to Performance* (New York: Free Press, 1987), p. 188.

Second, a firm can maintain its current share position in a growth market only if its sales volume continues to grow at a rate equal to that of the overall market, enabling the firm to stay even in *absolute* market share. It may, however, be able to maintain a *relative* share lead even if its volume growth is less than the industry's.

Marketing objectives for share leaders

Share maintenance for a market leader involves two important marketing objectives. First, the firm must *retain its current customers,* ensuring that those customers remain brand loyal when making repeat or replacement purchases. This is particularly critical for firms in consumer nondurable, service, and industrial materials and components industries where a substantial portion of total sales volume consists of repeat purchases. Second, the firm must *stimulate selective demand among later adopters* to ensure that it captures a large share of the continuing growth in industry sales.

In some cases the market leader might pursue a third objective: stimulating primary demand to help speed up overall market growth. This can be particularly important in product-markets where the adoption process is protracted because of the technical sophistication of the new product or high switching costs for potential customers.

The market leader is the logical one to stimulate market growth in such situations; it has the most to gain from increased volume, assuming, of course, that it can maintain its relative share of that volume. However, expanding total demand—by promoting new uses for the product or stimulating existing customers' usage and repeat purchase rates—is often more critical near the end of the growth and early in the maturity stages of a product's life cycle. Consequently, we discuss marketing actions appropriate to this objective in the next chapter.

Marketing actions and strategies to achieve share-maintenance objectives

A business might take a variety of marketing actions to maintain a leading share position in a growing market. Exhibit 9–4 outlines a lengthy, though by no means exhaustive, list of such actions and their specific marketing objectives. Because share maintenance involves multiple objectives, and different marketing actions may be needed to achieve each one, a strategic marketing program usually integrates a mix of the actions outlined in the exhibit.

Not all of the actions summarized in Exhibit 9–4 are consistent with one another. It would be unusual, for instance, for a business to invest heavily in new-product improvements and promotion to enhance its product's high-quality image and simultaneously slash prices, unless it was trying to drive out weaker competitors in the short run with an eye on higher profits in the future. Thus, the activities outlined in Exhibit 9–4 cluster into five internally consistent strategies that a market leader might employ, singly or in combination, to maintain its leading share position: a **fortress** or **position defense strategy**, a **flanker strategy**, a **confrontation strategy**, a **market expansion** or **mobile strategy**, and a **contraction** or **strategic withdrawal strategy.** Exhibit 9–5 diagrams this set of strategies. It is consistent with what a number of military strategists and some marketing authorities have identified as common defensive strategies.[10] To think of them as strictly defensive, though, can be misleading. Companies can use some of these strategies offensively to preempt expected future actions by potential competitors. Or they can use them to capture an even larger share of future new customers.

Which, or what combination, of these five strategies is most appropriate for a particular product-market depends on (1) the market's size and its customers' characteristics; (2) the number and relative strengths of the competitors or potential competitors in that market; and (3) the leader's own resources and competencies. Exhibit 9–6 outlines the situations in which each strategy is most appropriate and the primary objectives for which they are best suited.

Fortress or position defense strategy

The most basic defensive strategy is to continually strengthen a strongly held current position—to build an impregnable fortress capable of repelling attacks by current or future competitors. This strategy is nearly always at least a part

---

[10]For a detailed discussion of these strategies in a military context, see Carl von Clausewitz, *On War* (London: Routledge and Kegan Paul, 1908); and B. H. Liddell-Hart, *Strategy* (New York: Praeger, 1967). For a related discussion of the application of such strategies in a business setting, see Philip Kotler and Ravi Singh Achrol, "Marketing Warfare in the 1980s," *Journal of Business Strategy,* Winter 1981, pp. 30–41.

EXHIBIT 9-4

Marketing Actions to Achieve Share-Maintenance Objectives

Marketing objectives	Possible marketing actions
Retain current customers by:	
• Maintaining/improving satisfaction and loyalty	• Increase attention to quality control as output expands. • Continue product modification and improvement efforts to increase customer benefits and/or reduce costs. • Focus advertising on stimulation of selective demand; stress product's superior features and benefits; reminder advertising. • Increase salesforce's servicing of current accounts; consider formation of national or key account representatives for major customers; consider replacing independent manufacturer's reps with company salespeople. • Expand postsale service capabilities; develop or expand company's own service force, or develop training programs for distributors' and dealers' service people; expand parts inventory; consider development of customer service hotline.
• Encourage/simplify repeat purchase	• Expand production capacity in advance of increasing demand to avoid stockouts. • Improve inventory control and logistics systems to reduce delivery times. • Continue to build distribution channels; use periodic trade promotions to gain more extensive retail coverage and maintain shelf-facings; strengthen relationships with strongest distributors/dealers. • Consider negotiating long-term requirements contracts with major customers. • Consider developing automatic reorder systems for major customers.
• Reduce attractiveness of switching	• Develop a second brand or product line with features or price more appealing to a specific segment of current customers (*flanker strategy*). • Develop multiple-line extensions or brand offerings targeted to the needs of several user segments in the market (*market expansion, mobile strategy*). • Meet or beat lower prices or heavier promotional efforts by competitors —or try to preempt such efforts by potential competitors—when necessary to retain customers and when lower unit costs allow (*confrontation strategy*).
Stimulate selective demand among later adopters by:	
• Head-to-head positioning against competitive offerings or potential offerings	• Develop a second brand or product line with features or price more appealing to a specific segment of potential customers (*flanker strategy*). • Make product modifications or improvements to match or beat superior competitive offerings (*confrontation strategy*). • Meet or beat lower prices or heavier promotional efforts by competitors when necessary to retain customers and when lower unit costs allow (*confrontation strategy*). • When resources are limited relative to competitor's, consider withdrawing from smaller or slower growing segments to focus product development and promotional efforts on higher potential segments threatened by competitor (*contraction or strategic withdrawal strategy*).
• Differentiated positioning against competitive offerings or potential offerings	• Develop multiple-line extensions or brand offerings targeted to the needs of various potential user applications, or geographical segments within the market (*market expansion or mobile strategy*). • Build unique distribution channels to more effectively reach specific segments of potential customers (*market expansion or mobile strategy*). • Design multiple advertising and/or sales promotion campaigns targeted at specific segments of potential customers (*market expansion or mobile strategy*).

EXHIBIT   9–5

Strategic Choices for Share Leaders in Growth Markets

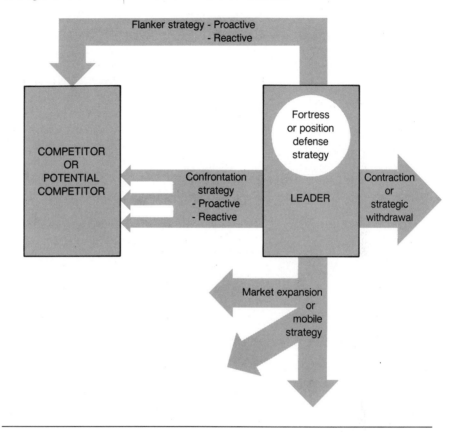

SOURCE: Adapted from P. Kotler and R. Singh, "Marketing Warfare in the 1980s," *Journal of Business Strategy,* Winter 1981, pp. 30–41.

of a leaders' share-maintenance efforts. By shoring up an already strong position, the firm can improve the satisfaction of current customers while increasing the attractiveness of its offering to new customers with needs and characteristics similar to those of earlier adopters.

Strengthening the firm's current position, then, makes particularly good sense when current and potential customers have relatively homogeneous needs and desires and the firm's offering already enjoys a high level of awareness and preference in the mass market. In some homogeneous markets, a well-implemented position defense strategy may be all that is needed for share maintenance. This is particularly true if the leader commands more R&D and marketing resources and competencies than its current or potential competitors. Firms in this fortunate position have the luxury of taking a wait-and-see attitude when a competitor attacks. Their position may be strong and appealing enough that they need not respond directly to aggressive competitors by changing their products, cutting prices, or increasing promotional

EXHIBIT 9–6
Marketing Objectives and Strategies for Share Leaders
in Growth-Market Situations

Situational variables	Fortress or position defense	Flanker	Confrontation	Market expansion or mobile	Contraction or strategic withdrawal
Primary objective	Increase satisfaction, loyalty, and repeat purchase among current customers by building on existing strengths; appeal to late adopters with same attributes and benefits offered to early adopters.	Protect against loss of specific segment of current customers by developing a second entry that covers a weakness in original offering; improve ability to attract new customers with specific needs or purchase criteria different from those of early adopters.	Protect against loss of share among current customers by meeting or beating a head-to-head competitive offering; improve ability to win new customers who might otherwise be attracted to competitor's offering.	Increase ability to attract new customers by developing new product offerings or line extensions aimed at a variety of new applications and user segments; improve ability to retain current customers as market fragments.	Increase ability to attract new customers in selected high-growth segments by focusing offerings and resources on those segments; withdraw from smaller or slower growing segments to conserve resources.
Market characteristics	Relatively homogeneous market with respect to customer needs and purchase criteria; strong preference for leader's product among largest segment of customers.	Two or more major market segments with distinct needs or purchase criteria.	Relatively homogeneous market with respect to customer's needs and purchase criteria; little preference for, or loyalty toward, leader's product among largest segment of customers.	Relatively heterogeneous market with respect to customer's needs and purchase criteria; multiple product uses requiring different product or service attributes.	Relatively heterogeneous market with respect to customer's needs and purchase criteria and growth potential; multiple product uses requiring different product or service attributes.

budgets. This was the situation enjoyed by H. J. Heinz in the ketchup market, as described in Exhibit 9–7 on p. 274.

Most of the marketing actions listed in Exhibit 9–4 as being relevant for retaining current customers might be incorporated into a position defense strategy. Anything the business can do to improve customer satisfaction and loyalty and encourage and simplify repeat purchasing should help the firm protect its current customer base and make its offering more attractive to new customers. Some of the specific actions appropriate for accomplishing these two objectives are discussed in more detail below.

EXHIBIT   9–6   *(concluded)*

Situational variables	Fortress or position defense	Flanker	Confrontation	Market expansion or mobile	Contraction or strategic withdrawal
Competitors' characteristics	Current and potential competitors have relatively limited resources and competencies.	One or more current or potential competitors with sufficient resources and competencies to effectively implement a differentiation strategy.	One or more current or potential competitors with sufficient resources and competencies to effectively implement a head-to-head strategy.	Current and potential competitors have relatively limited resources and competencies, particularly with respect to R&D and marketing.	One or more current or potential competitors with sufficient resources and competencies to present a strong challenge in one or more growth segments.
Firm's characteristics	Current product offering enjoys high awareness and preference among major segment of current and potential customers; firm has marketing and R&D resources and competencies equal to or greater than any current or potential competitor.	Current product offering perceived as weak on at least one attribute by a major segment of current or potential customers; firm has sufficient R&D and marketing resources to introduce and support a second offering aimed at the disaffected segment.	Current product offering suffers low awareness, preference and/or loyalty among major segment of current or potential customers; firm has R&D and marketing resources and competencies equal to or greater than any current or potential competitor.	No current offerings in one or more potential applications segments; firm has marketing and R&D resources and competencies equal to or greater than any current or potential competitor.	Current product offering suffers low awareness, preference, and/or loyalty among current or potential customers in one or more major growth segments; firm's R&D and marketing resources and competencies are limited relative to those of one or more competitors.

Actions to improve customer satisfaction and loyalty

The rapid expansion of output necessary to keep up with a growth market can often lead to quality control problems for the market leader. As new plants, equipment, and personnel are quickly brought on-line, bugs can suddenly appear in the production process. Thus, the leader must

EXHIBIT 9-7
H. J. Heinz—The Defensive Advantage of a Strong Competitive Position

H. J. Heinz, the share leader in the ketchup industry, provides an example of a firm with such a strong competitive position that it could weather a direct attack without altering its basic strategy or marketing program. In the mid-1960s, Heinz had strengthened its leading share position in the ketchup market to 27 percent largely through emphasis on high product quality and heavy consumer advertising. Hunt's, with a 19 percent share, decided to directly attack the leader with a combination of new pizza and hickory flavors that it hoped would appeal to specific segments of ketchup users, heavy trade allowances to retailers to capture more shelf space, a price cut to 70 percent of Heinz's price, and an increase in its advertising budget to twice the amount spent by Heinz.

Heinz's position was so strong, however, that Hunt's expensive attack failed to make any inroads into the leader's market share, even though Heinz did not bother to react to the attack. Heinz did not cut prices, increase advertising, or trade allowances, or develop any line extensions. Yet when the dust settled, Heinz's share had increased to about 40 percent of the market. Hunt's share also increased somewhat but entirely at the expense of smaller regional brands.

Heinz's strategy continues to be one of strengthening its current position in existing product categories by carefully controlling costs and quality and by using its high margins to support advertising and promotional efforts as necessary to maintain consumer awareness and preference. The company's product development efforts are mostly directed at new markets—such as instant baby food and frozen entrees—rather than toward line extensions or multiple brand offerings in its established markets.

SOURCE: "The H. J. Heinz Company (A)," Harvard Business School Case 9–569–011 M 357; and Bill Saporito, "Heinz Pushes to Be the Low-Cost Producer," *Fortune*, June 24, 1985, pp. 44–54.

pay particular attention to quality control during this phase. Most customers have only limited, if any, positive past experiences with the new brand to offset their disappointment when a purchase does not live up to expectations.

Perhaps the most obvious way a leader can strengthen its position is to continue to modify and improve its product. This can reduce the opportunities for competitors to differentiate their products by designing in features or performance levels the leader does not offer. The leader might also try to reduce unit costs to discourage low-price competition.

The leader should take steps to improve not only the physical product but customers' perceptions of it as well. As competitors enter or prepare to enter the market, the leader's advertising and sales promotion emphasis should shift from stimulating primary demand to building selective demand for the company's brand. This usually involves creating appeals that emphasize the brand's superior features and benefits. While the leader may continue sales promotion efforts aimed at stimulating trial among later adopters, some of those efforts might be shifted toward encouraging repeat purchases among existing customers. For instance, it might include cents-off coupons inside the package to give customers a price break on their next purchases of the brand.

For industrial goods, some salesforce efforts should shift from prospecting for new accounts to servicing existing customers. Firms that relied on independent manufacturer's reps to introduce their new product might consider replacing them with company salespeople to increase the customer-service orientation of their sales efforts. Firms whose own salespeople introduced the product might reorganize their salesforces into specialized groups focused on major industries or user segments. Or they might assign key account representatives to service their largest customers.

Finally, a leader can strengthen its position as the market grows by giving increased attention to postsale service. Rapid growth in demand can not only outstrip a firm's ability to produce a high-quality product, it can also overload the firm's ability to service customers. Obviously, this can lead to a loss of existing customers as well as negative word-of-mouth that might inhibit the firm's ability to attract new users. Thus, the growth phase often requires increased investments to expand the firm's parts inventory and hire and train service personnel and dealers.

Actions to encourage and simplify repeat purchasing

One of the most critical actions a leader must take to ensure that customers continue buying its product is to maximize its availability. It must reduce stock-outs on retail store shelves or shorten delivery times for industrial goods. To do this, the firm must invest in plant and equipment to expand capacity in advance of demand; and it must implement adequate inventory control and logistics systems to provide a steady flow of goods through the distribution system. The firm should also continue to build its distribution channels. It must seek more extensive representation in retail outlets and more shelf-facings in each store, or in the case of industrial goods, it must gain representation by the best distributors or dealers in each market area. These actions not only increase the product's availability, they can also help reduce competitive threats by making it more difficult for later entrants to gain an adequate share of limited shelf space or distributor support.

Some market leaders, particularly in industrial goods markets, can take more proactive steps to turn their major customers into captives and help guarantee future purchases. For example, a firm might negotiate requirements contracts or guaranteed price agreements with its customers to ensure their loyalty and preempt competitors. It may have to offer concessions to win such agreements, however. These can involve substantial risks for the firm if future market conditions are likely to be volatile. A less risky method of tying major customers to a supplier is for the selling firm to provide a computerized reorder system or channel information system. American Hospital Supply was one of the earliest adopters of this approach, as described in Exhibit 9–8.

Flanker strategy

One shortcoming of a fortress strategy is that a challenger might simply choose to bypass the leader's fortress and try to capture territory where the

E X H I B I T   9 – 8
American Hospital Supply's Computerized Reorder System

In the mid-1970s, American Hospital Supply, a major wholesaler of medical supplies, offered to install the industry's first computer order terminals in the stockrooms of major hospitals. Because hospitals were accustomed to ordering supplies from salespeople making regular rounds, they at first accepted the system only as a hedge against emergencies. But stock clerks found the terminals more convenient than waiting for a salesperson to call; and they turned to American Hospital for everything from tongue depressors to blood analyzers. Rival distributors filed an antitrust suit, claiming the system represented an attempt to establish exclusive supply arrangements with major hospitals, but they lost the suit on appeal. By the mid-1980s, American Hospital had become a $3.4 billion-a-year operation and was purchased in a friendly acquisition for nearly $4 billion by drug maker Baxter Travenol.

SOURCE: Peter Petre, "How to Keep Customers Happy Captives," *Fortune*, September 2, 1985, pp. 42–46.

leader has not yet established a strong presence. This can represent a particular threat when the market is fragmented into major segments with different needs and preferences and the leader's current brand does not meet the needs of one or more of those segments. A competitor with sufficient resources and competencies can develop a differentiated product offering to appeal to the segment where the leader is weak and thereby capture a substantial share of the overall market.

To defend against an attack directed at a weakness in its current offering (its exposed flank), a leader might develop a second brand (a flanker or fighting brand) to compete directly against the challenger's offering. This might involve trading up, where the leader develops a high-quality brand offered at a higher price to appeal to the prestige segment of the market. Honda did this with the development of the Acura. The new brand served not only to penetrate the higher-priced segment of the market, it also helped Honda hold on to former Accord owners who were beginning to trade up to more expensive European brands as they got older and earned higher incomes.

More commonly, though, a flanker brand is a lower-quality product designed to appeal to a low-price segment to protect the leader's primary brand from direct price competition. Pillsbury's premium-quality Hungry Jack brand holds the major share of the refrigerated biscuit dough market; however, a substantial number of consumers prefer to pay less for a somewhat lower-quality biscuit. Rather than conceding that low-price segment to competitors, or reducing Hungry Jack prices and margins in an attempt to attract price-sensitive consumers, Pillsbury introduced Ballard, a low-priced flanker brand.

A flanker strategy is always used in conjunction with a position defense strategy. The leader simultaneously strengthens its primary brand while introducing a flanker to compete in segments where the primary brand is vulnerable. This suggests that a flanker strategy is only appropriate when the firm has sufficient resources to develop and fully support two or more entries. After all, a flanker is of little value if it is so lightly supported that a competitor can easily wipe it out.

Finally, a flanker strategy can be either proactive or reactive. The leader might introduce a flanker in anticipation of a competitor's entry, either to establish a strong position before the competitor arrives or to dissuade the competitor from entering. In some cases, however, the leader does not recognize the severity of the threat until a competitor has already begun to enjoy a measure of success. Pillsbury did not develop its Ballard brand, for instance, until after a number of low-priced regional private labels began capturing significant chunks of the market.

Confrontation strategy

Suppose a competitor chooses to attack the leader head-to-head and attempts to steal customers in the leader's main target market. If the leader has established a strong position and attained a high level of preference and loyalty among customers and the trade, it may be able to sit back and wait for the competitor to fail, as Heinz did when Hunt's attacked its ketchup. In many cases, though, the leader's brand is not strong enough to withstand a frontal assault from a well-funded, competent competitor. Even mighty IBM, for instance, lost 20 market-share points in the commercial PC market during the mid-1980s to competitors like Compaq—whose machines cost about the same but offered features or performance levels that were better—and to the clones who offered IBM-compatible machines at much lower prices.

In such situations, the leader may have no choice but to confront the competitive threat directly. If the leader's competitive intelligence is good, it may decide to move proactively and change its marketing program before a suspected competitive challenge occurs. A confrontational strategy, though, is more commonly reactive. The leader usually decides to meet or beat the attractive features of a competitor's offering—by making product improvements, increasing promotional efforts, or lowering prices—only after the challenger's success has become obvious.

Simply meeting the improved features or lower price of a challenger, however, does nothing to reestablish a sustainable competitive advantage for the leader. And a confrontation based largely on lowering prices creates an additional problem of shrinking margins for all concerned. Unless decreased prices generate substantial new industry volume and the leader's production costs fall with that increasing volume, the leader may be better off responding to price threats with increased promotion or product improvements while trying to maintain its profit margins. Evidence also suggests that in product-markets with high repeat purchase rates or a protracted diffusion process, the leader may be wise to adopt a penetration pricing policy in the first place. This would strengthen its share position and may preempt low-price competitors from entering.[11]

---

[11]Robert J. Dolan and Abel P. Jewland, "Experience Curves and Dynamic Demand Models: Implications for Optimal Pricing Strategy," *Journal of Marketing,* Winter 1981, p. 52.

The leader can avoid the problems of a confrontation strategy by reestablishing the competitive advantage eroded by challengers' frontal attacks. However, this may require large new investments to develop a new generation of products that offer expanded benefits to customers. This was the approach taken by IBM when it introduced its technically advanced line of PS/2 personal computers to recapture some of the market share it had lost to the low-priced clones.

Market expansion or mobile strategy

A market expansion or mobile strategy is a more aggressive and proactive version of the flanker strategy. Here the leader defends its relative market share by establishing positions in a number of different market segments. This strategy's primary objective is to capture a large share of new customer groups who may prefer something different than the firm's initial offering, protecting the firm from future competitive threats from a number of different directions. Such a strategy is particularly appropriate in fragmented markets if the leader has the resources to undertake multiple product development and marketing efforts.

The most obvious way a leader can implement a market expansion strategy is to develop line extensions, new brands, or even alternative product forms utilizing similar technologies to appeal to multiple market segments. For instance, although Pillsbury holds a strong position in the refrigerated biscuit dough category, biscuit consumption is concentrated among older, more traditional consumers in the south. To expand its total market, gain increased experience curve effects, and protect its overall technological lead, Pillsbury developed a variety of other product forms that use the same refrigerated dough technology and production facilities but appeal to different customer segments. The expanded line includes crescent rolls, Danish rolls, and soft breadsticks.

A less expensive way to appeal to a variety of customer segments is to retain the basic product but vary other elements of the marketing program to make it relatively more attractive to specific users. Thus, a leader might create specialized salesforces to deal with the unique concerns of different user groups. Or it might offer different ancillary services to different types of customers or tailor sales promotion efforts to different segments. This approach is becoming particularly popular in consumer package goods industries with substantial regional differences in customer tastes and preferences. Campbell Soup, for instance, has created regional product managers in some of its major product categories and given them their own promotional budgets to create campaigns tailored to the specific preferences and competitive challenges in their areas of the country.[12]

---

[12]"Marketing's New Look," *Business Week,* January 26, 1987, pp. 64–69.

Contraction or strategic withdrawal

In some highly fragmented markets, a leader may be unable to defend itself adequately in all segments. This is particularly likely when newly emerging competitors have more resources than the leader. The firm may then have to reduce or abandon its efforts in some segments to focus on areas where it enjoys the greatest relative advantages or that have the greatest potential for future growth. Even some very large firms may decide that certain segments are not profitable enough to continue pursuing. For example, IBM made an early attempt to capture the low end of the home hobbiest market for personal computers with the introduction of the PC Jr. But the firm eventually abandoned that effort to concentrate on the more lucrative commercial and education segments.

SHARE-GROWTH STRATEGIES FOR FOLLOWERS

Marketing objectives for followers

Not all late entrants to a growing product-market have illusions about eventually surpassing the leader and capturing a dominant market share. Some competitors, particularly those with limited resources and competencies, may simply seek to build a small but profitable business within a specialized segment of the larger market that earlier entrants have overlooked. As we saw in Chapter 8, this kind of *niche strategy* is one of the few entry options that small, late entrants can pursue with a reasonable degree of success.[13] If a firm can successfully build a profitable business in a small segment while avoiding direct competition with larger competitors, it can often survive the shakeout period near the end of the growth stage and remain profitable throughout the maturity stage.

On the other hand, many followers—particularly larger firms entering a product-market shortly after the pioneer—have more grandiose objectives. They often seek to displace the leader or at least to become a powerful competitor within the total market. Thus, their major marketing objective is to attain *share growth,* and the size of the increased relative share such challengers seek is usually substantial. It is rarely less than 50 percent of its current share and more often about a 100 percent to 150 percent increase.[14] The rationale for such aggressive goals is the expected relationship between market share and unit costs in the short run and between share and ROI over the longer term. General Electric, for instance, has adopted a formal policy of not competing in any business where it does not have or can reasonably expect to attain, a leading position.

[13]Mary L. Coyle, "Competition in Developing Markets: The Impact of Order of Entry." Unpublished doctoral dissertation, University of Toronto, 1986.

[14]Charles W. Hofer and Dan Schendel, *Strategy Formulation: Analytical Concepts* (St. Paul, Minn.: West Publishing Co., 1978), p. 163.

E X H I B I T   9 – 9
Marketing Actions to Achieve Share-Growth Objectives

Marketing objectives	Possible marketing actions
Capture repeat/replacement purchases from current customers of the leader or other target competitor by:	
• Head-to-head positioning against competitor's offering in primary target market	• Develop products with features and/or performance levels superior to those of the target competitor.
	• Draw on superior product design, process engineering, and supplier relationships to achieve lower unit costs.
	• Set prices below target competitor's for comparable level of quality or performance, but only if low-cost position is achieved.
	• Outspend the target competitor on promotion aimed at stimulating selective demand:
	Comparative advertising appeals directed at gaining a more favorable positioning than the target competitor's brand enjoys among customers in the mass market.
	Sales promotions to encourage trial if offering's quality or performance is perceptibly better than target competitor's, or induce brand switching.
	Build more extensive and/or better trained salesforce than target competitor's.
	• Outspend the target competitor on trade promotion to attain more extensive retail coverage, better shelf space, and/or representation by the best distributors/dealers.
	• Outperform the target competitor on customer service:
	Develop superior production scheduling, inventory control, and logistics systems to minimize delivery times and stockouts.
	Develop superior postsales service capabilities; build a more extensive company service force, or provide better training programs for distributor/dealer service people than target competitor.
	• If resources are limited, engage in one or more of the preceding actions (e.g., an advertising blitz, sales or trade promotions) on a sporadic basis in selected territories (*guerrilla attack strategy*).

Marketing actions and strategies to achieve share growth

A challenger with visions of taking over the leading share position in an industry has two basic strategic options, each involving somewhat different marketing objectives and actions. Where the share leader and perhaps some other early followers have already penetrated a large portion of the potential market, a challenger may have no choice but to *steal away some of the repeat purchase or replacement demand from the competitors' current customers.* As Exhibit 9–9 indicates, the challenger can attempt this through marketing activities that give it an advantage in a head-to-head confrontation with a target competitor. Or it can attempt to leapfrog over the leader by developing a new generation of products with enough benefits to induce customers to trade in

EXHIBIT 9–9 *(concluded)*

Marketing objectives	Possible marketing actions
• Technological differentiation from target competitor's offering in its primary target market	• Develop a new generation of products based on different technology that offers a superior performance or additional benefits desired by current and potential customers in the mass market (*leapfrog strategy*).

	• Build awareness, preference, and replacement demand through heavy introductory promotion:
	    Comparative advertising stressing product's superiority.
	    Sales promotions to stimulate trial or encourage switching.
	    Extensive, well-trained salesforce; heavy use of product demonstrations in sales presentations.

	• Build adequate distribution through trade promotions and dealer training programs.
Stimulate selective demand among later adopters by:	
• Head-to-head positioning against target competitor's offering in established market segments	• See preceding actions.
• Differentiated positioning focused on untapped or underdeveloped segments	• Develop a differentiated brand or product line with unique features or price that is more appealing to a major segment of potential customers whose needs are not met by existing offerings (*flanking strategy*). or
	• Develop multiple line extensions or brand offerings with features or prices targeted to the unique needs and preferences of several smaller potential applications or regional segments (*encirclement strategy*).
	• Design advertising, personal selling, and/or sales promotion campaigns that address specific interests and concerns of potential customers in one or multiple underdeveloped segments to stimulate selective demand.
	• Build unique distribution channels to more effectively reach potential customers in one or multiple underdeveloped segments.
	• Design service programs to reduce the perceived risks of trial and/or solve the unique problems faced by potential customers in one or multiple underdeveloped segments (e.g., systems engineering, installation, operator training, or extended warranties).

their existing brand for a new one. Secondarily, such actions may also help the challenger attract a larger share of late adopters in the mass market.

If the market is relatively early in the growth phase and no previous entrant has captured a commanding share of potential customers, the challenger can focus on *attracting a larger share of potential new customers* who enter the market for the first time. This may also be a viable option when the overall market is heterogeneous and fragmented and the current share leader has established a strong position in only one or a few segments. In either case, the primary marketing activities for increasing share via this approach should aim at *differentiating* the challenger's offering from those of existing competitors

EXHIBIT 9–10

Strategic Choices for Challengers in Growth Markets

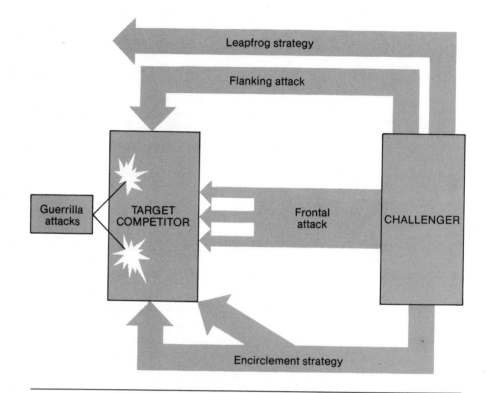

Source: Adapted from P. Kotler and R. Singh, "Marketing Warfare in the 1980s." Reprinted with permission from *Journal of Business Strategy*, Winter 1981, pp. 30–41. Copyright © Warren, Gorham & Lambert, Inc., 210 South Street, Boston, MA 02111. All rights reserved.

by making it more appealing to new customers in untapped or underdeveloped segments of the market.

Once again, Exhibit 9–9's list of possible marketing actions for challengers is not exhaustive; and it contains actions that do not always fit well together. The activities that do fit tend to cluster into five internally consistent strategies that a challenger might use singly or in combination to secure growth in its relative market share. As Exhibit 9–10 indicates, these five share-growth strategies are: *frontal attack, leapfrog strategy, flanking attack, encirclement,* and *guerrilla attacks.* Many of these strategies are mirror images of the share-maintenance strategies discussed earlier.

Which, or what combination, of these five strategies is best for a particular challenger depends on market characteristics, the existing competitors' current positions and strengths, and the challenger's own resources and competencies. The situations in which each of the five strategies is likely to work best are briefly outlined in Exhibit 9–11 on pp. 284–85 and discussed in greater depth in the following sections.

Deciding who to attack

When more than one competitor is already established in the market, a challenger must decide which competitor, if any, to target. There are several options:

- *Attack the market-share leader within its primary target market.* As we shall see, this typically involves either a *frontal assault* or an attempt to *leapfrog* the leader through the development of superior technology or product design. It may seem logical to try to win customers away from the competitor with the most customers to lose, but this can be a dangerous strategy unless the challenger has superior resources and competencies that can be converted into a sustainable advantage. In some cases, however, a smaller challenger may be able to avoid disastrous retaliation by confronting the leader only occasionally in limited geographic territories through a series of *guerrilla attacks.*

- *Attack another follower who has an established position within a major market segment.* This also usually involves a *frontal assault,* but it may be easier for the challenger to gain a sustainable advantage if the target competitor is not as well established as the market leader in the minds and buying habits of customers.

- *Attack one or more smaller competitors who have only limited resources.* Because smaller competitors usually hold only a small share of the total market, this may seem like an inefficient way to attain substantial share increases. But by focusing on several small regional competitors one at a time, a challenger can sometimes achieve major gains without inviting retaliation from stronger firms. For example, by first challenging and ultimately acquiring a series of smaller regional manufacturers, Borden has managed to capture the leading share of the fragmented domestic pasta market.

- *Avoid direct attacks on any established competitor.* In fragmented markets in which the leader or other major competitors are not currently satisfying one or more segments, a challenger is often best advised to "hit 'em where they ain't." This usually involves either a *flanking* or an *encirclement* strategy, with the challenger developing differentiated product offerings targeted at one large or several smaller segments in which no competitor currently holds a strong position.

Deciding which competitor to attack necessitates a comparison of relative strengths and weaknesses, a critical first step in developing an effective share-growth strategy. It can also help limit the scope of the battlefield, a particularly important consideration for challengers with limited resources.

Frontal attack strategy

Where the market for a product category is relatively homogeneous, with few untapped segments and at least one well-established competitor, a firm wanting to capture an increased market share may have little choice but to

EXHIBIT 9-11

Marketing Objectives and Strategies for Challengers in Growth-Market Situations

Situational variables	Sharegrowth strategies				
	Frontal attack	**Leapfrog**	**Flank attack**	**Encirclement**	**Guerrilla attack**
Primary objective	Capture substantial repeat/replacement purchases from target competitor's current customers; attract new customers among later adopters by offering lower price or more attractive features.	Induce current customers in mass market to replace their current brand with superior new offering; attract new customers by providing enhanced benefits.	Attract substantial share of new customers in one or more major segments where customer's needs are different from those of early adopters in the mass market.	Attract a substantial share of new customers in a variety of smaller, specialized segments where customers' needs or preferences differ from those of early adopters in the mass market.	Capture a modest share of repeat/replacement purchases in several market segments or territories; attract a share of new customers in a number of existing segments.
Market characteristics	Relatively homogeneous market with respect to customers' needs and purchase criteria; relatively little preference or loyalty for existing brands.	Relatively homogeneous market with respect to customers' needs and purchase criteria, but some needs or criteria not currently met by existing brands.	Two or more major segments with distinct needs and purchase criteria; needs of customers in at least one segment not currently met by existing brands.	Relatively heterogeneous market with a number of small, specialized segments; needs and preferences of customers in some segments not currently satisfied by competing brands.	Relatively heterogeneous market with a number of larger segments; needs and preferences of customers in most segments currently satisfied by competing brands.

tackle a major competitor head-on. Such an approach is most likely to be successful when most existing customers do not have strong brand preferences or loyalties and when the challenger's resources and competencies, particularly in marketing, R&D, and production, are greater than the target competitor's. But even superior resources are no guarantee of success when a challenger's frontal assault strategy merely imitates the target competitor's, as P&G discovered when it attacked Maxwell House in the coffee market. Exhibit 9–12 describes P&G's experience.

To successfully implement a frontal attack, a challenger must find one or more ways to achieve a sustainable advantage over the target competitor. As

EXHIBIT 9–11 *(concluded)*

Situational variables	Sharegrowth strategies				
	Frontal attack	**Leapfrog**	**Flank attack**	**Encirclement**	**Guerrilla attack**
Competitor's characteristics	Target competitor has relatively limited resources and competencies, particularly in marketing and R&D; would probably be vulnerable to direct attack.	One or more current competitors have relatively strong resources and competencies in marketing, but relatively unsophisticated technology and limited R&D competencies.	Target competitor has relatively strong resources and competencies, particularly in marketing and R&D; would probably be able to withstand direct attack.	One or more competitors have relatively strong marketing, R&D resources and competencies, and/or lower costs; could probably withstand a direct attack.	A number of competitors have relatively strong marketing, R&D resources and competencies, and/or lower costs; could probably withstand a direct attack.
Firm characteristics	Firm has stronger resources and competencies in R&D and marketing and/or lower operating costs than target competitor.	Firm has proprietary technology superior to that of competitors; firm has necessary marketing and production resources to stimulate and meet primary demand for new generation of products.	Firms' resources and competencies are limited, but sufficient to effectively penetrate and serve at least one major market segment.	Firm has marketing, R&D, and production resources and competencies necessary to serve multiple smaller segments; firm has decentralized and adaptable management structure.	Firm has relatively limited marketing, R&D, and/or production resources and competencies; firm has decentralized and adaptable management structure.

EXHIBIT 9–12
P&G's Frontal Assault on Maxwell House

The dangers of launching a frontal assault with a me-too product and marketing program are illustrated by P&G's experience in the coffee market. P&G attacked General Food's Maxwell House coffee with Folger's, a brand that lacked the superior quality that P&G usually builds into its products. Maxwell House, tough to the last drop, fought back with increased advertising and consumer and trade promotions. Although Folger's managed to capture 25 percent of the coffee market, most of its gains were taken from smaller brands. And after seven years of battle, Folger's still had not achieved acceptable levels of profitability.

SOURCE: Michael E. Porter, "How to Attack the Industry Leader," *Fortune*, April 29, 1985, pp. 153–66.

discussed earlier, such an advantage is usually based on attaining lower costs or a differentiated position in the market. If the challenger has a cost advantage, it can cut prices to lure away the target competitor's customers—as a number of the clone manufacturers did to IBM in the commercial PC market—or it can maintain a similar price but engage in more extensive promotion.

Challenging a leader solely on the basis of low price is a highway to disaster, however, unless the challenger really does have a sustainable cost advantage. Otherwise, the leader might simply match the lower prices until the challenger is driven from the market. The problem is that initially a challenger is often at a cost *disadvantage* due to the experience curve effects established competitors have accumulated. The challenger must have offsetting advantages like superior production technology, established relations with low-cost suppliers, the ability to share production facilities or marketing efforts across multiple SBUs, or other sources of synergy before a low-price assault makes sense.

A similar caveat applies to frontal assaults based solely on heftier promotional budgets. Unless the target competitor's resources are substantially more limited than the challenger's, it can retaliate against any attempt to win away customers through more extensive advertising or attractive sales and trade promotions.

One possible exception to this limitation of greater promotional effort is the use of a more extensive and better trained salesforce to gain a competitive advantage. A knowledgeable salesperson's technical advice and problem-solving abilities can add additional value to a firm's product offering, particularly in newly developing high-tech industries.

In general, the best way for a challenger to effectively implement a frontal attack is to differentiate its product or associated services in ways that better meet the needs and preferences of many customers in the mass market. If the challenger can support those meaningful product differences with strong promotion or an attractive price, so much the better; but usually the unique features or services offered are the foundation for a sustainable advantage. Thus, Compaq achieved a measure of success in its battles with IBM by developing a variety of product offerings with features, such as portability, that were unavailable on comparable IBM equipment or that delivered better performance for the same price. Compaq also made extensive use of marketing research to stay in close touch with changing customer needs. And it invested a relatively large percentage of revenues in R&D and in strategic alliances with suppliers such as Conner Peripherals to produce a continuing stream of product modifications and improvements.

Variables that might limit the competitor's willingness or ability to retaliate can also improve the chances for success of a frontal attack. The industry leader, for instance, may be reluctant to retaliate aggressively against a direct attack for fear of violating antitrust laws. This has continually restrained IBM's competitive behavior in both domestic and foreign computer markets. Similarly, a target competitor with a reputation for high product quality may be loath to cut prices in response to a low-price competitor for fear of cheapening its brand's image. And a competitor pursuing high ROI or cash flow objectives may be reluctant to increase its promotion or R&D expenditures in the short run to fend off an attack.[15]

Leapfrog strategy

A challenger stands the best chance of attracting repeat or replacement purchases from a competitor's current customers when it can offer a product that is attractively differentiated from the competitor's offerings. The odds of success might be even greater if the challenger can offer a far superior product based on advanced technology or a more sophisticated design. This is the essence of a leapfrog strategy. It is an attempt to gain a significant advantage over the existing competition by introducing a new generation of products that significantly outperform or offer more desirable customer benefits than existing brands. Conner Peripherals' development of a steady stream of smaller, faster, and more technically advanced hard disk drives is a good example of a leapfrog strategy.

In addition, such a strategy often inhibits quick retaliation by established competitors. Firms that have achieved some success with one technology—or that have committed substantial resources to plant and equipment dedicated to a current product, as was the case with Seagate—are often reluctant to switch to a new one because of the large investments involved or a fear of disrupting current customers.

On the other hand, a leapfrog strategy is not viable for all challengers. To be successful, the challenger must have technology superior to that of established competitors as well as the product and process engineering capabilities to turn that technology into an appealing product. Also, the challenger must have the marketing resources to effectively promote its new products and convince customers already committed to an earlier technology that the new product offers sufficient benefits to justify the costs of switching. Conner Peripherals has attempted to avoid this problem by working closely with potential customers to design new disk drives to be used as components in their future product lines rather than trying to convince them to switch to Conner's drives for use in their existing models.

Unfortunately, Conner's approach will not work in industries in which customers do not introduce new product lines or engage in replacement purchases as quickly as they do in the computer industry. Thus, to speed up the replacement process, the challenger might have to develop sales promotion or customer service programs aimed at reducing customer's switching costs. For instance, Polaroid ran a promotional program that offered buyers a $20

---

[15]For a more extensive discussion of factors that can limit a leader's willingness or ability to retaliate against a direct attack, see Michael E. Porter, *Competitive Advantage* (New York: Free Press, 1985). chap. 15.

trade-in on any old camera, whether it worked or not, toward the purchase of its new Spectra camera. For industrial goods, the offer of systems engineering services or product features that help potential customers integrate the new technology with their existing equipment and processes can encourage them to switch suppliers. Apple, for example, worked feverishly to develop its open Macintosh II system that could use IBM software. This product modification enabled old IBM customers to preserve their earlier investments in IBM software while switching to the more user-friendly Macintosh hardware.

Flanking and encirclement strategies

The military historian Liddell-Hart, after analyzing battles ranging from the Greek Wars to World War I, determined that only 6 out of 280 victories were the result of a frontal attack.[16] He concluded that it is usually wiser to avoid attacking an established adversary's point of strength and to focus instead on an area of weakness in his defenses. This is the basic premise behind flanking and encirclement strategies. They both seek to avoid direct confrontations by focusing on market segments whose needs are not being satisfied by existing brands and where no current competitor has a strongly held position.

Flank attack

A flank attack is appropriate when the market can be broken into two or more large segments, when the leader and/or other major competitors hold a strong position in the primary segment, and when no existing brand fully satisfies the needs of customers in at least one other segment. A challenger may be able to capture a significant share of the total market by concentrating primarily on one large untapped segment. This usually involves developing product features or services tailored to the needs and preferences of the targeted customers, together with appropriate promotional and pricing policies to quickly build selective demand. Japanese auto companies, for instance, first penetrated the U.S. car market by focusing on the low-price segment where domestic manufacturers' offerings were limited. Domestic car manufacturers were relatively unconcerned by this flanking action at first. They failed to retaliate very aggressively because the Japanese were pursuing a segment which they considered to be rather small and unprofitable. History proved them wrong.

In some cases, a successful flank attack need not involve unique product features. Instead, a challenger can sometimes meet the special needs of an untapped segment by providing specially designed customer services or distribution channels. One major reason for the success of L'eggs pantyhose, for instance, was that it was the first brand to be distributed through an extensive

---

[16]B. H. Liddell-Hart, *Strategy* (New York: Praeger, 1967), p. 163.

EXHIBIT 9–13

Apple's Encirclement Strategy

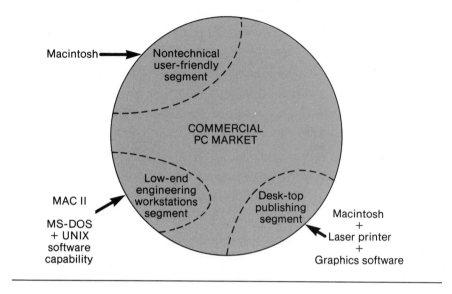

channel of convenience goods retailers, such as grocery and drug stores, instead of more fashionable department and clothing stores. The greater shopping convenience provided by this new distribution channel appealed strongly to the growing segment of working women.

Encirclement

An encirclement strategy involves targeting several smaller untapped or underdeveloped segments in the market simultaneously. The idea is to surround the leader's brand with a variety of offerings aimed at several peripheral segments. This strategy makes most sense when the market is fragmented into many different applications segments or geographical regions with somewhat unique needs or tastes.

Once again, this strategy often involves developing a varied line of products with features tailored to the needs of different segments. For example, Apple originally developed the Macintosh in an attempt to attract the less technically sophisticated customers in the commercial PC market who desired a user-friendly computer. But as Exhibit 9–13 illustrates, the company then developed the desktop publishing segment by bringing out a high-quality laser printer to supplement the Macintosh system and by encouraging software producers to develop the sophisticated graphics software desired by customers in that application segment. Subsequently, Apple attacked the low-priced end of the market for engineering workstations by developing the more powerful Macintosh II and giving it the capability of handling the UNIX software popular for engineering applications. In some cases, though, minor variations in customer services, promotional appeals, or distribution channels may be all that is required to capture various specialized segments.

Guerrilla attack

When well-established competitors already cover all major segments of the market and the challenger's resources are relatively limited, flanking, encirclement, or all-out frontal attacks may be impossible. In such cases, the challenger may be reduced to making a series of surprise raids against its more established competitors. To avoid massive retaliation, the challenger should use such guerrilla attacks sporadically, perhaps in limited geographic areas where the target competitor is not particularly well entrenched.

A challenger can choose from a variety of means for carrying out guerrilla attacks. These include sales promotion efforts—such as coupon drops and merchandising deals (send in three box tops and receive a magic decoder ring)—local advertising blitzes, and even legal action. Short-term price reductions through sales promotion campaigns are a particularly favored guerrilla tactic in consumer goods markets. They can target specific customer groups in limited geographic areas; they can be implemented quickly; and they are often difficult for a larger competitor to respond to, because that firm's higher share level means that a given discount will cost it more in absolute dollars.[17]

In some cases, the ultimate objective of a series of guerrilla attacks is not so much for the challenger to build its own share as it is to prevent a powerful leader from further expanding its share or engaging in aggressive actions that would be costly for the followers to respond to. Lawsuits brought against the leader by several smaller competitors over a range of activities can effectively slow down the leader's expansionist tendencies by diverting some of its resources and attention.

Empirical evidence

Several empirical studies conducted with the PIMS data base provide empirical support for many of the managerial prescriptions discussed.[18] These studies compare businesses that achieved high market shares during the growth stage of the product life cycle, or that increased their market shares over time,

---

[17]A. L. Stern, "New Marketing Game: Stealing Customers," *Dun's Business Month,* February 1985, pp. 48–50.

[18]Robert D. Buzzell and Frederik D. Wiersema, "Successful Share-Building Strategies," *Harvard Business Review,* January–February 1981, pp. 135–43; Carl R. Anderson and Carl P. Zeithaml, "Stages of the Product Life Cycle, Business Strategy, and Business Performance," *Academy of Management Journal,* March 1984, pp. 5–25; and Robert D. Buzzell and Bradley T. Gale, *The PIMS Principles: Linking Strategy to Performance* (New York: Free Press, 1987), chap. 9.

EXHIBIT 9-14

Strategic Changes Made by Challengers that Gained versus Lost Market Share

Strategic changes	Share-gaining challengers	Share-losing challengers
Relative product quality scores	+1.8	−0.6
New products as a percent of sales	+0.1	−0.5
Relative price	+0.3	+0.2
Marketing expenditures (adjusted for market growth)		
Salesforce	+9.0%	−8.0%
Advertising		
Consumer products	+13.0%	−9.0%
Industrial products	−1.0	−14.0
Promotion		
Consumer products	+13.0%	−5.0%
Industrial products	+7.0	−10.0

Source: Adapted from Robert D. Buzzell and Bradley T. Gale, *The PIMS Principles: Linking Strategy to Performance* (New York: Free Press, 1987), p. 190.

with low-share businesses. As shown in Exhibit 9–14, the marketing programs and activities of businesses that successfully achieved increased market share differed from their less successful counterparts in the following ways:

- Businesses that increased the quality of their products relative to those of competitors achieved greater share increases than businesses whose product quality remained constant or declined.

- Share-gaining businesses typically developed and added more new products, line extensions, or product modifications to their line than share-losing businesses.

- Share-gaining businesses tended to increase their marketing expenditures faster than the rate of market growth. Increases in both salesforce and sales promotion expenditures were effective for producing share gains in both consumer and industrial goods businesses. Increased advertising expenditures were effective for producing share gains primarily in consumer goods businesses.

- Surprisingly, there was little difference in the relative prices charged between firms that gained and those that lost market share.

These findings are consistent with many of our earlier observations. For instance, they underline the folly of launching a frontal attack solely on the basis of lower price. Unless the challenger has substantially lower unit costs or the leader is inhibited from cutting its own prices for some reason, the challenger's price cuts are likely to be retaliated against and will, therefore, generate few new customers. On the other hand, frontal, leapfrog, flanking, or encirclement attacks based on product improvements tailored to specific segments are more likely to succeed, particularly when the challenger supports those attacks with substantial promotional efforts.

Regardless of the strategies pursued by market leaders and challengers during a product-market's growth stage, the competitive situation often changes as the market matures and its growth rate slows. As fewer new customers enter the market, competition to retain repeat business from current customers and to strengthen share position by winning other firm's customers becomes more intense. This change in market and competitive conditions often leads to a shakeout within the industry, with less profitable firms either withdrawing from the market or being acquired by stronger firms. Such changes also usually require the remaining competitors to adjust their objectives and to develop new strategic marketing programs to achieve them. In the next chapter, we examine the environmental changes that occur as a market matures and the marketing strategies that firms might use to adapt to those changes.

SUMMARY

Both conventional wisdom and the various portfolio models suggest that firms gain advantages by quickly entering, and investing heavily to build share in, growth markets. Among the premises on which the early, aggressive pursuit of growing markets is based are (1) it is easier to gain share when a market is growing, (2) share gains are worth more when total volume is expanding rather than stable, (3) price competition is likely to be less intense in growing markets since demand often exceeds supply, and (4) early experience gained in developing products and applications for a growth market can give a firm the technical expertise needed to keep up with advancing technology.

Although true in general, each of these premises is not always valid for every firm in every situation. Thus, a market does not always represent an attractive opportunity for a business simply because it promises rapid future growth. Managers must consider how the market and competitive situations are likely to evolve and whether their firms can exploit the market's rapid growth to establish a sustainable competitive advantage.

The primary strategic objective of the early share leader, typically the market pioneer, in a growth market is *share maintenance*. From a marketing view, the firm must accomplish two important tasks: (1) retain repeat or replacement business from its existing customers, and (2) continue to capture the major portion of sales to the growing number of new customers entering the market for the first time. Among the marketing strategies a firm might use either singly or in combination to maintain a leading share position are (1) a fortress or position defense strategy, (2) a flanker strategy, (3) a confrontation strategy, (4) a market expansion or mobile strategy, and (5) a contraction or strategic withdrawal strategy.

A challenger's strategic objective in a growth market is usually to *build its share* by expanding its sales faster than the overall market growth rate. It can accomplish this by stealing existing customers away from other competitors, capturing a larger share of new customers than the market leader, or both. Possible share-growth strategies include (1) a frontal attack, (2) a leapfrog strategy, (3) a flanking attack, (4) encirclement, and (5) guerrilla attacks.

Strategies for Mature and Declining Markets

ALCOA: A HEAVYWEIGHT MANUFACTURER OF A LIGHTWEIGHT COMMODITY[1]

How do you take an old company in a mature and highly cyclical commodity industry and dunk it in the Fountain of Youth? In the 1970s and 1980s, many corporate leaders would have prescribed diversification: Harvest the commodity business, move to the high end of the market, send merger and acquisitions people out to nab some high-growth businesses, and emerge so different that, in time, you change your name—say, from U.S. Steel to USX.

The 102-year-old Aluminum Company of America—better known as Alcoa—is taking a different path. Although world demand for aluminum has grown at an annual rate of only 3 percent in recent years, Alcoa is seeking substantial new volume growth and profitability within its traditional industry.

To accomplish this, the firm transformed its internal culture to lower costs, improve product quality and customer service, and become a more formidable global competitor. At the same time, it launched aggressive R&D and marketing efforts aimed at stimulating greater demand for aluminum in its traditional, and some very nontraditional, markets.

Pursuing higher quality and lower costs

When Paul O'Neill became Alcoa's CEO in 1987, one of his first acts was to review all customer contracts and evaluate Alcoa's competitive position with respect to both quality and cost product by product. But his first priority was safety. This may seem curious given that Alcoa

---

[1]This case example is based largely on material found in Thomas A. Stewart, "A New Way to Wake Up a Giant," *Fortune*, October 22, 1990, pp. 90–103.

already had the best safety record in the industry. But by focusing on safety, Alcoa's new boss unlocked the whole tool chest associated with total quality management. Says O'Neill: "You can't get safety unless you really understand your processes." And understanding production and other operating processes is also a critical first step for finding ways to improve quality and lower costs.

By putting safety first, O'Neill encouraged employees to develop a larger view of their jobs and to start thinking like managers. Specially trained teams of workers now observe other employees to help them find new ways to improve the safety, efficiency, and effectiveness of their jobs. And the firm's managers have also been trained to focus more attention on safety and quality. Finally, the firm backed all these efforts to change employee attitudes and behavior with a six-year, $1 billion-plus plant modernization program.

These actions have already had a major impact on the quality of Alcoa's products and services. For instance, the firm makes beverage-can sheet within a tolerance of 0.0002 inches—a standard so high that five Japanese canmakers now buy their aluminum sheet from Alcoa.

One major step Alcoa took to improve its costs was to aggressively expand its recycling operation. Compared with starting from bauxite ore, recycling aluminum takes 10 percent of the labor and capital and 5 percent of the energy. The firm's 2,400 recycling centers paid $232 million for 17.1 billion used beverage cans in 1989, supplying one-seventh of its primary aluminum needs.

The focus on higher quality and lower costs has had other positive consequences, including savings from reduced inventories equal to half the cost of the company's modernization drive and an almost 50 percent increase in capacity. As a result, the firm was able to reduce its long-term debt by 58 percent in 1988 and 1989, and the combined profit for those two years was more than double the total of the eight previous years.

Stimulating future growth

Although Alcoa's focus on higher quality and lower costs has strengthened its competitive position and profitability, aluminum remains a mature and highly cyclical industry. Instead of pursuing revenue growth through diversification into unrelated businesses, however, Alcoa is attempting to revitalize the aluminum industry. The firm is aggressively expanding into underdeveloped markets for its existing products, seeking ways to encourage current customers to use more aluminum, and developing new uses for the metal that will create new and, it is hoped, less cyclical markets.

Increased penetration of underdeveloped markets

Alcoa's most immediate growth opportunities are international. Aluminum demand is growing fastest in Europe and the Pacific Rim. In Asia, for instance, only one out of every three beverage cans is aluminum—a far cry from the metal's 32-to-1 dominance in the U.S. market. Thus, Alcoa has put high priority on expanding its aluminum fabrication overseas. In 1989, for example, the company announced a joint venture with Kobe Steel, a leading Japanese metals company, to build a factory that will roll Alcoa ingot into can sheet for the Asian market.

Increasing aluminum use among existing customers

Over the years 1987–89, Alcoa increased its R&D budget by 50 percent. A major part of the firm's increased research activity was aimed at finding ways to enable current customers, particularly those in the automobile and can industries, to increase their use of aluminum. The metal has 97 percent of the U.S. beer and soda can business, for instance, but it claims less than 9 percent of food cans. Until recently, the industry was unable to make a food can rigid enough and cheap enough to beat steel. But Alcoa has developed new alloys, a ribbed can wall, and a patented electrocoating process that it thinks will lick the problem. Thus, the company and two partners are building a 100,000-square-foot plant capable of making 300 million cans a year, enough to

increase U.S. aluminum food can production by 12 percent.

The automotive industry also offers opportunities for extending the use of aluminum. Exhibit 10–1 discusses some of the ways Alcoa and other firms are attempting to develop and promote increased usage in that industry.

Expanding into new markets

Finally, Alcoa is concentrating the rest of its R&D and marketing efforts on developing new products for new types of customers. In 1990, for instance, the firm opened a new factory that takes it into the esoteric business of electronic packages. These are ceramics made from alumina—produced in refining bauxite into aluminum—and baked into wafers an inch square and only a few thousandths of an inch thick. In a computer, they act like transformers to amplify and send information coded on a microchip. The market for such packages, already worth several billion dollars annually, is growing 20 to 30 percent a year. While it is dominated by Japanese high-tech companies like Kyocera, Alcoa believes its knowledge of alumina gives it a potential competitive advantage that will enable the firm to grab a billion-dollar share by 1995.

STRATEGIC ISSUES IN MATURE AND DECLINING MARKETS

Many managers, particularly those in marketing, seem obsessed with growth. Their objectives tend to emphasize annual increases in sales volume, market share, or both. But the biggest challenge for managers in most U.S.

EXHIBIT 10-1

Getting Ready for the Aluminum Lizzie: Efforts to Increase
Auto Manufacturers' Use of Aluminum

Think car buyers are hanging back? It took Jaguar just half an hour to unload every one
of its new all-aluminum XJ220 supercars. True, only 350 will be built for 1992 delivery.
But then, these babies cost $600,000.

What aluminum does for high-performance cars like the XJ220, whose staggering cost
only minimally reflects its metal content, it can also do for your ordinary sedan. The
reason: At half the weight of steel, aluminum gives a big boost to fuel economy and efficiency. With soaring oil prices bringing renewed pressure for better gas mileage, Peter
Bridenbaugh, head of R&D for Alcoa, suggests carmakers have two options: "They can
either make cars so small you zip them on in the morning, or they can lightweight
them."

The average North American–made car weighs in at 3,100 pounds, only 157 of which
are aluminum. By the year 2000 that share should rise to at least 250 pounds or, in the
most optimistic estimate, a glittering 600 pounds.

To replace steel entirely, aluminum carmakers have had to develop alloys and manufacturing processes that match steel's strength and crashworthiness. Honda's new Acura
NSX sports car, the first all-aluminum mass production auto (yours for $60,000), relies
on a new method of spot welding and a design that eliminates joint fatigue. Alcan uses
powerful adhesives on its Jaguar. Both cars employ a variation of traditional unit-body
construction.

Alcoa takes a more radical approach to what it calls the "aluminum-intensive vehicle." Its AIV, being developed with Audi, uses castings and extrusions to make a space
frame—a skeleton from which other body parts hang. In addition to a 250- to 300-pound
weight reduction (more with aluminum hang-ons), the space frame, by cutting in half the
number of parts, promises savings in tooling costs that would more than compensate for
aluminum's higher price. It would also make it easier to design and build a wider variety
of cars.

SOURCE: Adapted from Thomas A. Stewart, "A New Way to Wake Up a Giant," *Fortune,* October 22,
1990, p. 98.

companies over the next decade will be running businesses that compete in
markets that grow slowly, if at all. The majority of products, like aluminum,
are currently in the mature or decline stage of their life cycle. Their marketing managers face the task of developing strategic marketing programs for
stable or declining markets.

But the situation is not always as depressing as it sounds, as Alcoa's recent
performance confirms. In many cases, managers can find opportunities to
earn substantial profits, and even increase volume in such markets.

Issues during the transition to market maturity

A period of competitive turbulence almost always accompanies the transition
from market growth to maturity in an industry. This period often begins
after approximately half the potential customers have adopted the product
and the rate of sales growth starts to decline. As growth slows, many competitors find they have excess production capacity. Competition becomes

more intense as firms battle to increase volume, cover high fixed costs, and maintain profitability.

Such transition periods are commonly accompanied by a **shakeout,** during which weaker businesses fail, withdraw from the industry, or are acquired by other firms. The shakeout period is pivotal in influencing a brand's continued survival and the strength of its competitive position during the later maturity and decline stages of the life cycle. The next section of this chapter examines some common strategic traps that can threaten a product's survival in an industry shakeout.

Issues in mature markets

As a market matures, total volume stabilizes; replacement purchases rather than first-time buyers account for the vast majority of that volume. A primary marketing objective of all competitors in mature markets, therefore, is simply to hold their existing customers—to sustain a meaningful competitive advantage that will help ensure the continued satisfaction and loyalty of those customers. Thus, a product's financial success during the mature life-cycle stage depends heavily on the firm's ability to achieve and sustain a lower delivered cost or some perceived product quality or customer service superiority.

Some firms tend to passively defend mature products while using the bulk of the revenues produced by those items to develop and aggressively market new products with more growth potential. This can be shortsighted, however. All segments of a market and all brands in an industry do not necessarily reach maturity at the same time. Aging brands like Jell-o, Johnson's baby shampoo, and Arm & Hammer baking soda experienced sales revivals in recent years because of creative marketing strategies. Thus, a share leader in a mature industry might build upon a cost or product differentiation advantage and pursue a marketing strategy aimed at increasing volume by promoting new uses for an old product or by encouraging current customers to buy and use the product more often. A later section of this chapter examines basic business strategies necessary for survival in mature markets and marketing strategies a firm might use to extend a brand's sales and profits.

Issues in declining markets

Eventually, technological advances; changing customer demographics, tastes, or lifestyles; and development of substitutes result in declining demand for most product forms and brands. As a product starts to decline, managers face the critical question of whether to divest or liquidate the business. Unfortunately, firms sometimes support dying products too long at the expense of current profitability and the aggressive pursuit of future breadwinners.

An appropriate marketing strategy can, however, produce substantial sales and profits even in a declining market. If few exit barriers exist, an industry leader might attempt to increase market share via aggressive pricing or promotion policies aimed at driving out weaker competitors. Or it might try to consolidate the industry by acquiring weaker brands and reducing overhead by eliminating excess capacity and duplicate marketing programs. Alternatively, a firm might decide to harvest a mature product by maximizing cash flow and profit over the product's remaining life. The last section of this chapter discusses specific marketing strategies for gaining the greatest possible returns from products approaching the end of their life cycle.

SHAKEOUT: THE TRANSITION FROM MARKET GROWTH TO MATURITY

Characteristics of the transition period

The transition from growth to maturity typically begins when the market is still growing but the rate of growth starts to decline, as shown in Exhibit 10–2. This declining growth either sparks or occurs simultaneously with other changes in the market and competitive environment. Such changes include the appearance of excess capacity, increased intensity of competition, increased difficulty of maintaining product differentiation, worsening distribution problems, and growing pressures on costs and profits. Weaker members of the industry often fail or are acquired by larger competitors during this shakeout stage.

Excess capacity

During a market's growth stage, manufacturers must usually invest heavily in new plant, equipment, and personnel to keep up with increasing demand. Some competitors fail to anticipate the transition from growth to maturity, however, and their expansion plans eventually overshoot market demand. Thus, excess production capacity often develops at the end of the growth stage. This leads to an intense struggle for market share as firms seek increased volume to hold down unit costs and maintain profit margins.

More intense competition

The intensified battle for increased volume and market share at this stage often leads to price reductions and increased selling and promotional efforts. Firms modify products to appeal to more specialized user segments, make deals to produce for private labels, and take other actions that lower per-unit revenues, increase R&D and marketing costs, and put pressure on profit margins.

Difficulty of maintaining differentiation

As an industry's technology matures, the better and more popular designs tend to become industry standards, and the physical differences among brands become less substantial. The popularity of the VHS format among videocassette recorder customers, for example, eventually made it the industry

EXHIBIT   10–2
The Transition or Shakeout Stage of the Generalized Product Life Cycle

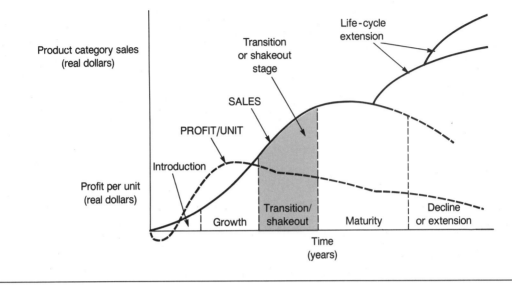

Source: Reprinted with permission from p. 60 of *Analysis for Strategic Market Decisions,* by George S. Day, copyright © 1986 by West Publishing Company. All rights reserved.

standard, and Sony's alternative Beta format largely disappeared from the market. This decline in differentiation across brands often leads to a weakening of brand preference among consumers and makes it more difficult for even the market leaders to command premium prices for their products.[2] Such problems have been magnified in recent years as consumers have become more demanding and more willing to objectively evaluate alternatives rather than rely on heavily advertised brand names or past loyalty. As one advertising executive warns, "The savvy shoppers of the early 1980s have been reborn in 1990 as leaner, meaner, more cynical individuals. They are saying to manufacturers, 'Show me what you've got before you earn my trust.' "[3]

Diminishing product differentiation can also increase costs as firms seek differentiation in other ways, such as through improved service. As the products and prices offered by competing suppliers become more similar, many purchasing agents become increasingly concerned with service and its impact on their firm's costs. For instance, they may demand a higher level of delivery reliability (as in just-in-time [JIT] deliveries) to help reduce their cost of capital tied up in inventory.

---

[2]Joel Dean, "Pricing Policies for New Products," *Harvard Business Review,* November–December 1976, pp. 141–53.

[3]Faye Rice, "How to Deal with Tougher Customers," *Fortune,* December 3, 1990, p. 40.

Distribution problems

During an industry's transition from growth to maturity, channel members often become more assertive in ways particularly detrimental to smaller-share competitors. As sales growth slows, for example, retailers may reduce the number of brands they carry to reduce inventory costs and space requirements. Much the same can happen at the wholesale/distributor level. Because any reduction in product availability has serious repercussions for a manufacturer, low-share firms often must offer additional trade incentives simply to hold their distribution coverage during this period.

Pressures on prices and profits

Prices typically decrease and margins get squeezed during shakeout, which increases the industry's instability and volatility. Given their higher per-unit costs, smaller-share businesses often operate at a loss during transition. Some are ultimately forced to leave the industry. This is particularly likely with commodity-type products, when few unique market niches exist in which the firm can maintain a competitive advantage and when heavy investments in fixed assets are required and experience curve effects are high.

Firms that enter the transition period with high relative market shares are more likely to survive. Even these firms may experience a severe drop in profits, however. As the shakeout proceeds, the shares held by firms exiting the industry pass to the surviving firms, increasing their volumes and lowering per-unit costs. This does not necessarily mean, though, that the leaders' market shares remain stable after shakeout. One study indicates that larger firms tend to lose share during market maturity because they fail to maintain their cost advantage.[4] We will discuss this danger in more detail later in this chapter.

Strategic traps during the transition period

A business's ability to survive the transition from market growth to maturity also depends to a great extent on whether it can avoid some common strategic traps.[5] Four such traps are summarized in Exhibit 10–3 and discussed below.

The most obvious trap is simply the *failure to recognize the events signaling the beginning of the shakeout period*. The best way to minimize the impact of slowing growth is to accurately forecast the slowdown in sales and hold the firm's production capacity to a sustainable level. For both industrial and consumer durable goods markets, models can forecast when replacement sales will begin to outweigh first-time purchases, a common signal that a market is

---

[4]Robert D. Buzzell, "Are There 'Natural' Market Structures?" *Journal of Marketing,* Winter 1981, pp. 42–51.

[5]For a more detailed discussion of these traps, see Michael E. Porter, *Competitive Strategy* (New York, Free Press, 1980), pp. 247–49.

EXHIBIT 10-3

Four Common Strategic Traps Firms Can Fall Into during the Shakeout Period

1. Failure to anticipate transition from growth to maturity.
   - Firms may make overly optimistic forecasts of future sales volume.
   - As a result, they expand too rapidly and production capacity overshoots demand as growth slows.
   - Their excess capacity leads to higher costs per unit.
   - Consequently, they must cut prices or increase promotion in an attempt to increase their volume.
2. No clear competitive advantage as growth slows.
   - Many firms can succeed without a strong competitive advantage during periods of rapid growth.
   - However, firms that do not have the lowest costs or a superior offering in terms of product quality or service can have difficulty sustaining their market share and volume as growth slows and competition intensifies.
3. Assumption that an early advantage will insulate the firm from price or service competition.
   - In many cases, technological differentials become smaller as more competitors enter and initiate product improvements as an industry approaches maturity.
   - If customers perceive that the quality of competing brands has become more equal, they are likely to attach greater importance to price or service differences.
   - Failure to detect such trends can cause an early leader to be complacent and slow to respond to competitive threats.
4. Sacrificing market share in favor of short-run profit.
   - A firm may cut marketing or R&D budgets or forgo other expenditures in order to maintain its historical level of profitability even through industry profits tend to fall during the transition period.
   - This can cause long-run erosion of market share and further increases in unit costs as the industry matures.

beginning to mature.[6] But in consumer nondurable markets—particularly those where growth slows because of shifting consumer preferences or the emergence of substitute products—the start of the transition period can be nearly impossible to predict.

A second strategic trap is for a business to *get caught in the middle during the transition period without a clear strategic advantage.* A business may survive and prosper during the growth stage even though it has neither differentiated its offering from competitors nor attained the lowest cost position in its industry. But during the transition period, such is not the case.

A third trap is the *failure to recognize the declining importance of product differentiation and the increasing importance of price or service.* Businesses that have built their success on technological superiority or other forms of product differentiation often disdain aggressive pricing or marketing practices even though

---

[6]For a description of one such model used by a major manufacturer, see Stephen B. Lawton and William H. Lawton, "An Autocatalytic Model for the Diffusion of Educational Innovations," *Educational Administration Quarterly,* Winter 1979, pp. 19–46.

such differentiation typically erodes as markets mature. As a result, such firms may delay meeting their more aggressive competitors head-on and end up losing market share.

Why should a firm not put off responding to the more aggressive pricing or marketing actions of its competitors? Because doing so may lead to a fourth trap—*giving up market share too easily in favor of short-run profit.* Many businesses try to maintain the profitability of the recent past as markets enter the transition period. They usually do this at the expense of market share or by forgoing marketing, R&D, and other investments crucial for maintaining future market position. While some smaller firms with limited resources may have no choice, this tendency can be seriously shortsighted, particularly if economies of scale are crucial for the business's continued success during market maturity.

BUSINESS STRATEGIES FOR MATURE MARKETS

The maturity phase of an industry's life cycle is often depicted as one of stability characterized by few changes in the market shares of leading competitors and steady prices. The industry leaders, because of their low per-unit costs and little need to make any further investments, enjoy high profits and positive cash flows. These cash flows are harvested and diverted to other SBUs or products in the firm's portfolio that promise greater future growth.

Unfortunately, this conventional scenario provides an overly simplistic description of the situation businesses face in most mature markets. For one thing, it is not always easy to tell when a market has reached maturity. Variations in brands, marketing programs, and customer groups can mean that different brands and market segments reach maturity at different times.

Further, as the maturity stage progresses, a variety of threats and opportunities can disrupt an industry's stability. Shifts in customer needs or preferences, product substitutes, increased raw material costs, changes in government regulations, or factors such as the entry of low-cost foreign producers or mergers and acquisitions can threaten individual competitors and even throw the entire industry into early decline. Consider, for example, the competitive position of Timex, a brand that dominated the low-price segment of the American watch market in the 1970s. First the appearance of imported digital watches and later a shift in consumer preferences toward more fashionable and prestigious brands buffeted the firm and eroded its market share.

On the positive side, such changes can also open new growth opportunities in mature industries. Product improvements (such as the development of high-fiber nutritional cereals), advances in process technology (e.g., the creation of minimills for steel production), falling raw materials costs, increased prices for close substitutes, or environmental changes (e.g., the increased demand for storm windows in the energy crisis of the 1970s and early 80s) can all provide opportunities for a firm to dramatically increase its sales and profits. An entire industry can even experience a period of renewed growth.

Discontinuities during industry maturity suggest that it is dangerously shortsighted for a firm to simply milk its cash cows.[7] Even industry followers can substantially improve volume, share, and profitability during industry maturity if they can adjust their marketing objectives and programs to fit the new opportunities that arise.[8] Thus, success in mature markets requires two sets of strategic actions: (1) the development of a well-implemented business strategy to sustain a competitive advantage, and (2) flexible and creative marketing programs geared to pursue growth or profit opportunities as conditions change in specific product-markets.

Strategies for maintaining competitive advantage

As discussed in Chapter 3, both *analyzer* and *defender strategies* may be appropriate for units with leading, or at least a profitable, share of one or more major segments in a mature industry. Analyzers and defenders are both concerned with maintaining a strong share position in established product-markets. But analyzers also do some product and market development to avoid being leapfrogged by competitors with more advanced products or being left behind in new applications segments. On the other hand, defenders may initiate some product improvements or line extensions to protect and strengthen their position in existing markets, but they spend relatively little on new-product R&D. Thus, an analyzer strategy is most appropriate for developed industries that are still experiencing some technological change and may have opportunities for continued growth, such as the computer and commercial aircraft industries. The defender strategy works best in industries where the basic technology is not very complex or is unlikely to change dramatically in the short run, as in the food industry.

Both analyzers and defenders can attempt to sustain a competitive advantage in established product-markets through *differentiation* of their product offering (either on the basis of superior quality or service) or by maintaining a *low-cost* position. Evidence suggests the ability to maintain either a strongly differentiated or a low-cost position continues to be a critical determinant of success throughout both the transition and the maturity stage. One study examined the competitive strategies pursued by the two leading firms (in terms of return on investment) in eight mature industries characterized by slow growth and intense competition. In each industry, the two leading firms offered either the lowest relative delivered cost or high relative product differentiation. In most cases, an industry's ROI leader opted for one of the strategies, while the second-place firm pursued the other. For example, Exhibit 10–4 shows the competitive positions and ROI obtained by firms in the

---

[7]Buzzell, "Are There 'Natural' Market Structures?"

[8]Cathy Anterasian and Lynn W. Phillips, "Discontinuities, Value Delivery, and the Share-Returns Association: A Re-Examination of the 'Share-Causes-Profits' Controversy," Distributed working paper, (Cambridge, Mass.: Marketing Science Institute, April 1988).

EXHIBIT   10-4

The Strategic Competitive Positions and Return on Investment
Percentages of Firms in the U.S. Heavy-Duty Truck Industry

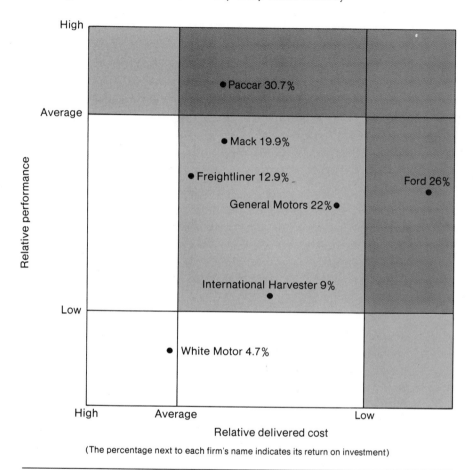

(The percentage next to each firm's name indicates its return on investment)

SOURCE: William K. Hall, "Survival Strategies in a Hostile Environment," *Harvard Business Review*, September–October 1980, p. 81.

heavy-truck industry. Paccar, the ROI leader, offered the most highly differentiated (in terms of good performance) product in the industry; while number two Ford had the lowest relative delivered cost. Generally, it is difficult for a business to pursue both low-cost and differentiation strategies at the same time. The low margins generated by a low-cost strategy usually cannot support efforts to maintain high differentiation over time.[9] Keep in mind,

----

[9]William K. Hall, "Survival Strategies in a Hostile Environment," *Harvard Business Review*, September–October 1980, pp. 75–85.

though, that a firm may have two or more SBUs focused on different industry segments or product-markets, and each SBU may pursue a different strategy. For instance, Daimler Benz has the lowest cost position in the European truck market but offers a highly differentiated automotive line in export markets.

Methods of differentiation

Differences in product designs, features, or performance are not the only ways a business can differentiate its offering. Customer service can also effectively help maintain an advantage over competitors.

Dimensions of product quality[10]

To attain a sustainable competitive advantage in product quality, a firm must understand what *dimensions customers perceive to underlie differences in quality* across products. One authority has identified eight such dimensions of product quality. These are summarized in Exhibit 10–5 and discussed below.

European manufacturers of prestige automobiles, such as Mercedes-Benz and Porsche, have emphasized the first dimension of product quality—**functional performance.** These automakers have designed cars that provide excellent performance on such attributes as handling, acceleration, and comfort. Volvo, on the other hand, has emphasized and aggressively promoted a different quality dimension—**durability** (and the related attribute of safety). A third quality dimension, **conformance to specifications,** or the absence of defects, has been a major focus of the Japanese automakers. It has also been the primary focus of Alcoa's quality improvement program. Until recent years, American carmakers relied heavily on broad product lines and a wide **variety of features,** both standard and optional, to offset their shortcomings on some of the other quality dimensions.

The **reliability** quality dimension can refer to the consistency of performance from purchase to purchase or to a product's uptime, the percentage of time that it can perform satisfactorily over its life. Tandem Computers has maintained a competitive advantage based on reliability by designing computers with several processors that work in tandem, so that if one fails, the only impact is the slowing of low-priority tasks. IBM cannot match Tandem's reliability because of its commitment to an operating system not easily adapted to the multiple-processor concept. Consequently, Tandem has maintained a strong position in market segments consisting of large-scale computer users—such as financial institutions and large retailers—for whom system downtime is particularly undesirable.

The quality dimension of **serviceability** refers to a customer's ability to obtain prompt and competent service when the product does break down.

---

[10]The following discussion is based on material found in David A. Aaker, *Strategic Market Management,* 2nd ed., (New York: John Wiley & Sons, Inc., 1988), chap. 11.

EXHIBIT 10–5

Dimensions of Product Quality

• Performance	How well does the washing machine wash clothes?
• Durability	How long will the lawn mower last?
• Conformance with specifications	What is the incidence of product defects?
• Features	Does an airline flight offer a movie and dinner?
• Reliability	Will each visit to a restaurant result in consistent quality? What percentage of the time will a product perform satisfactorily?
• Serviceability	Is the product easy to service? Is the service system efficient, competent, and convenient?
• Fit and finish	Does the product look and feel like a quality product?
• Brand name	Is this a name that customers associate with quality? What is the brand's image?

SOURCE: Adapted from David A. Garvin, "What Does 'Product Quality' Really Mean?" *Sloan Management Review,* Fall 1984, pp. 25–43, by permission of the publisher. Copyright © 1984 by the Sloan Management Review Association. All rights reserved.

For example, Caterpillar Tractor has long differentiated itself with a parts and service organization dedicated to providing "24-hour parts service anywhere in the world."

Many of these quality dimensions can be difficult for customers to evaluate, particularly for consumer products. As a result, consumers often generalize from quality dimensions that are more visual or qualitative. Thus, the **fit and finish** dimension can help convince consumers that a product is of high quality. They tend to perceive attractive and well-designed products as generally high in quality, as witnessed by the success of the Krups line of small appliances. Similarly, the **quality reputation of the brand name,** and the promotional activities that sustain that reputation, can strongly influence consumers' perceptions of a product's quality. In pursuing a differentiation strategy based on quality, then, a business must understand what dimensions or cues customers use to judge quality and pay attention to the seemingly less important but more visible attributes of the product.

Dimensions of service quality

One series of studies of customer perceptions of service quality in industries such as retail banking and appliance repair identified a number of quality dimensions, five of which are summarized in Exhibit 10–6.[11]

The quality dimensions listed in Exhibit 10–6 apply specifically to service businesses, but most of them are also relevant for judging the service component of a product offering. This pertains to both the objective performance

---

[11]Valarie A. Zeithaml, A. Parasuraman, and Leonard L. Berry, *Delivering Quality Service: Balancing Customer Perceptions and Expectations.* (New York: Free Press, 1990).

EXHIBIT   10-6

Dimensions of Service Quality

• Tangibles	Appearance of physical facilities, equipment, personnel, and communications materials
• Reliability	Ability to perform the promised service dependably and accurately
• Responsiveness	Willingness to help customers and provide prompt service
• Assurance	Knowledge and courtesy of employees and their ability to convey trust and confidence
• Empathy	Caring, individualized attention the firm provides its customers

SOURCE: Valarie A. Zeithaml, A. Parasuraman, and Leonard L. Berry, *Delivering Quality Service: Balancing Customer Perceptions and Expectations* (New York: Free Press, 1990), p. 26.

dimensions of the service delivery system—such as its **reliability** and **responsiveness**—as well as to elements of the performance of service personnel, such as their **empathy** and level of **assurance.**

The results of a number of surveys suggest that customers perceive all five dimensions of service quality to be very important regardless of the kind of service being evaluated. As Exhibit 10–7 indicates, customers of four different kinds of services gave reliability, responsiveness, assurance, and empathy mean importance ratings of more than 9 on a 10-point rating scale. And though the mean ratings for tangibles were somewhat lower in comparison, they still fell toward the upper end of the scale, ranging from 7.14 to 8.56.

The same respondents were also asked which of the five dimensions they would chose as being the most critical in their assessment of service quality. Their responses—which are also shown in Exhibit 10–7—suggest that reliability is the most important aspect of service quality to the greatest number of customers. The key to a differentiation strategy based on providing superior service, then, is to meet or exceed target customers' service quality expectations and to do it more consistently than competitors. The problem is that sometimes managers underestimate the level of those customer expectations, and sometimes those expectations can be unrealistically high. Therefore, a firm needs to clearly identify target customers' desires with respect to service quality and to clearly define and communicate what level of service they intend to deliver. When this is done, customers have a more realistic idea of what to expect and are less likely to be disappointed with the service they receive.

The major factors that determine a customer's expectations and perceptions concerning service quality—and five "gaps" that can cause unsatisfactory service delivery—are outlined in Exhibit 10–8 on page 310 and discussed next.

1. *Gap between the customer's expectations and the marketer's perceptions.* Managers do not always have an accurate understanding of what customers want or how they will evaluate a firm's service efforts. The first

EXHIBIT 10-7

Perceived Importance of Service Quality Dimensions in Four Different Industries

	Mean importance rating on 10-point scale*	Percentage of respondents indicating dimension is most important
Credit-card customers (*n* = 187)		
Tangibles	7.43	0.6
Reliability	9.45	48.6
Responsiveness	9.37	19.8
Assurance	9.25	17.5
Empathy	9.09	13.6
Repair-and-maintenance customers (*n* = 183)		
Tangibles	8.48	1.2
Reliability	9.64	57.2
Responsiveness	9.54	19.9
Assurance	9.62	12.0
Empathy	9.30	9.6
Long-distance telephone customers (*n* = 184)		
Tangibles	7.14	0.6
Reliability	9.67	60.6
Responsiveness	9.57	16.0
Assurance	9.29	12.6
Empathy	9.25	10.3
Bank customers (*n* = 177)		
Tangibles	8.56	1.1
Reliability	9.44	42.1
Responsiveness	9.34	18.0
Assurance	9.18	13.6
Empathy	9.30	25.1

*Scale ranges from 1 (not at all important) to 10 (extremely important).

SOURCE: Valarie A. Zeithaml, A. Parasuraman, and Leonard L. Berry, *Delivering Quality Service: Balancing Customer Perceptions and Expectations* (New York: Free Press, 1990), p. 27.

step in providing good service, then, is to collect information—either through customer surveys, evaluations of customer complaints, or other methods—to determine what service attributes customers consider important.

2. *Gap between management perceptions and service quality specifications.* Even when management has a clear understanding of what customers want, it might not translate that understanding into effective operating standards. A firm's policies concerning customer service may be unclear, poorly communicated to employees, or haphazardly enforced. Unless a firm's

EXHIBIT 10-8

The Determinants of Perceived Service Quality

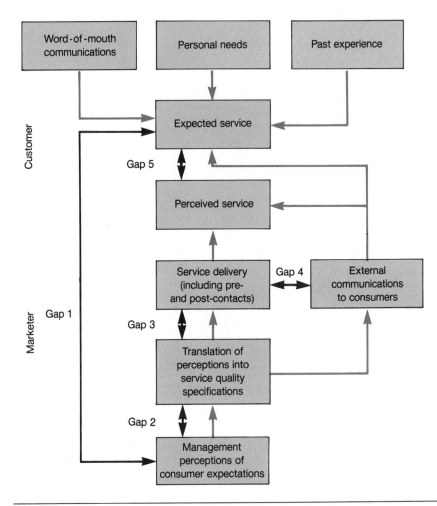

SOURCE: Adapted from Valarie A. Zeithaml, A. Parasuraman, and Leonard L. Berry, *Delivering Quality Service* (New York: Free Press, 1990), p. 46.

employees know what the company's service policies are and believe that management is seriously committed to those standards, their performance may fall short of desired levels.

3. *Gap between service quality specifications and service delivery.* Lip-service by management is not enough to produce high-quality service. High standards must be backed by the programs, resources, and rewards necessary to enable and encourage employees to deliver good service. Employees must be provided with the training, equipment, and time necessary to

deliver good service. Their service performance must be measured and evaluated. And good performance must be rewarded by making it part of the criteria for pay raises or promotions, or by other more direct inducements, to motivate the additional effort that good service requires.

4. *Gap between service delivery and external communications.* Even good service performance may disappoint some customers if the firm's marketing communications cause them to have unrealistically high expectations. If the photographs in a vacation resort's advertising and brochures make the rooms look more spacious and luxurious than they really are, for instance, first-time customers are likely to be disappointed no matter how clean those rooms are kept by the resort's staff.

5. *Gap between perceived service and expected service.* This results when management fails to close one or more of the other four gaps. It is this difference between a customer's expectations and his or her actual experience with the firm that leads to dissatisfaction.

The above discussion suggests a number of actions marketers can take to close the possible gaps and improve customer satisfaction with a company's services. Achieving and sustaining high levels of service quality can present some difficult implementation problems, however, because it often involves the coordination of efforts of many different employees from different departments and different levels of the organization. We will examine some of these problems, and ways managers can attempt to resolve them, in more detail in Chapter 12.

Methods for maintaining a low-cost position

Moving down the experience curve is the most commonly discussed method for achieving and sustaining a low-cost position in an industry. But a firm does not necessarily need a large relative market share to implement a low-cost strategy. The small clone manufacturers in the PC industry, for instance, found other ways to hold their costs well below those of the industry leaders. Other means for obtaining a sustainable cost advantage include producing a no-frills product, creating an innovative product design, finding cheaper raw materials, automating production, developing low-cost distribution channels, and reducing overhead.[12]

A no-frills product

A direct approach to obtaining a low-cost position involves simply removing all frills and extras from the basic product or service. Thus, Suzuki cars, warehouse furniture stores, legal services clinics, and grocery stores selling

---

[12]For a more detailed discussion of these and other approaches for attaining a low-cost position, see Aaker, *Strategic Market Management,* chap. 12.

canned goods out of crates all offer lower costs and prices than their competitors. This lower production cost is often sustainable because established differentiated competitors find it difficult to stop offering features and services their customers have come to expect. However, those established firms may lower their own prices in the short run—even to the point of suffering losses—in an attempt to drive out a no-frills competitor that poses a serious threat. This was the response of the major airlines to inroads made by People Express. Thus, a firm considering a no-frills strategy needs the resources to withstand a possible price war.

Innovative product design

A simplified product design and standardized component parts can also lead to cost advantages. In the office copier industry, for instance, Japanese firms overcame substantial entry barriers by designing extremely simple copiers, with a fraction of the number of parts compared to those of market-leading Xerox.

Cheaper raw materials

A firm with the foresight to acquire or the creativity to find a way to use relatively cheap raw materials can also gain a sustainable cost advantage. For example, Fort Howard Paper has achieved an advantage by being the only major papermaker to rely exclusively on recycled pulp. While the finished product is not so high in quality as paper from virgin wood, Fort Howard's lower cost gives it a competitive edge in the price-sensitive commercial market for toilet paper and other such products used in hotels, restaurants, and office buildings.

Innovative production processes

Although low-cost defender businesses typically spend little on *product R&D,* they often continue to devote substantial sums to *process R&D.* Innovations in the production process, including the development of automated or computer controlled processes, can help them sustain cost advantages over competitors.

In some labor-intensive industries, a business can achieve a cost advantage, at least in the short term, by gaining access to inexpensive labor. This is usually achieved by moving all or part of the production process to countries with low wage rates, such as Taiwan, Korea, or Mexico. Unfortunately, because such moves are relatively easy to emulate, this kind of cost advantage may not be sustainable.

Low-cost distribution

When distribution accounts for a relatively high proportion of a product's total delivered cost, a firm might gain a substantial advantage by developing lower-cost alternative channels. Typically, this involves eliminating, or shifting to the customer, some of the functions performed by traditional channels in return for a lower price. In the PC hardware and software industries, for example, mail-order discounters can offer lower prices because they have fewer fixed costs than the retail stores with which they compete. However, they also do not provide technical advice or postsale service to their customers.

Reductions in overhead

Successfully sustaining a low-cost strategy requires that the firm pare and control its major overhead costs as quickly as possible as its industry matures. Indeed, many U.S. companies learned this lesson the hard way during the 1980s when high costs of old plants, labor, and large inventories left them vulnerable to more efficient foreign competitors and to corporate raiders.

Business strategy and performance

Analyzer, and particularly defender, businesses are mostly concerned with protecting their existing positions in one or more mature market segments and maximizing profitability over the remaining life of those product-markets. Thus, financial dimensions of performance, such as return on investment and cash flow, are usually of greater interest to such businesses than more growth-oriented dimensions, like volume increases or new-product success. Businesses can achieve such financial objectives by either successfully differentiating their offerings or by maintaining a low-cost position.

Today's customer is willing to pay more to get better quality. Respondents in a 1988 Gallup survey said they would be willing to pay 67 percent more than the $300 base price of a TV, 42 percent above the $400 list price of a dishwasher, and 21 percent more than the $12,000 sticker price of a car to get better quality products.[13] This, together with the fact that improved quality often lowers manufacturing costs, means that firms with the highest-quality goods and services obtain higher average pretax returns on investment across all types of industries than businesses with average- or below-average-quality offerings.[14] This positive relationship between quality differentiation and ROI appears to hold true regardless of a business's market share or investment intensity.[15] In other words, a business need not limit its focus to the relatively small "snob-appeal" segment of the market to make money with a high-quality strategy. Good products and good service can have mass appeal, as the Japanese automakers have demonstrated.

Alternatively, low-cost producers can also prosper in mature markets. In all eight industries studied by Hall, for example, one of the two businesses with the highest ROIs in each industry was the firm with the lowest delivered

---

[13]Rice, "How to Deal with Tougher Customers," p. 40.

[14]To refresh your memory concerning the evidence of a positive relationship between relative quality and ROI performance, return to Exhibit 3–9 in Chapter 3.

[15]Robert Jacobson and David A. Aaker, "The Strategic Role of Product Quality," *Journal of Marketing,* October 1987, pp. 31–44.

cost position in that industry.[16] And, because factors other than the experience curve affect a business's unit costs, a firm does not necessarily have to be a market-share leader to successfully implement a low-cost strategy.

The major lesson to be learned, then, is that the choice between a differentiation or a low-cost business strategy is not the critical determinant of success in mature markets. What is critical is that *one or the other* strategy be chosen, clearly defined, and well implemented. The businesses with the poorest financial performance during industry maturity, and those most vulnerable to environmental changes and threats, are those *without any consistent strategy.* They fail to provide either a differentiated offering or lower costs than their competitors.

MARKETING STRATEGIES FOR MATURE MARKETS

Marketing objectives

Since markets can remain in the maturity stage for decades, milking or harvesting mature product-markets by maximizing short-run profits usually makes little sense. Pursuing such an objective typically involves substantial cuts in marketing and R&D expenses, which can lead to premature losses of volume and market share and lower profits in the longer term. The business should strive during the early years of market maturity to *maximize the flow of profits over the remaining life of the product-market.* Thus, the most critical marketing objective is to *maintain and protect the business's market share.* In a mature market where few new customers buy the product for the first time, the business must continue to win its share of repeat purchases from existing customers.

Market maturity is defined by a flattening of the growth rate. In some instances growth slows for structural reasons, such as the emergence of substitute products or a shift in customer preferences. Marketers can do little to revitalize the market under such conditions. But in some cases a market only *appears* to be mature because of the limitations of current marketing programs, such as target segments that are too narrowly defined or limited product offerings. Here, more innovative or aggressive marketing strategies might successfully extend the market's life cycle into a period of renewed growth, as previously illustrated in Exhibit 10–2. Thus, *stimulating additional volume growth* can be an important secondary objective under such circumstances, particularly for industry share leaders because they often can capture a relatively large share of any additional volume generated.

A firm might pursue several different marketing objectives to squeeze additional volume from a mature market. First, they can try to *increase the product's penetration* in one or more existing market segments by converting current nonusers into users. The firm usually does this by modifying the

---

[16]Hall, "Survival Strategies in a Hostile Environment," pp. 75–85.

product offering to enhance its value to those potential customers. In a second approach, the firm *increases the amount used by current customers* through marketing actions that increase their frequency of use or promote new ways to use the product. Finally, the firm might try to *expand into underdeveloped market segments* by moving into new geographic areas (say, global marketing) or by developing a flanker brand or producing for private labels to appeal to more price-sensitive segments.

Marketing actions and strategies for maintaining current market share

In Chapter 9, we saw that holding current customers was an important marketing objective for maintaining market share in a growth market. A number of the share-maintenance marketing strategies discussed in that chapter continue to be relevant as markets mature. The appropriateness of those various strategies for a specific business unit depends, however, on whether it is a share leader in its industry or a smaller competitor.

Strategies for share leaders

For leading firms with a strong competitive position, perhaps the most obvious strategy is to continue to protect and strengthen that position through a **fortress defense.** Recall that such a strategy involves two sets of marketing actions: those aimed at improving customer satisfaction and loyalty, and those intended to encourage and simplify repeat purchasing.

Differentiated defender businesses can maintain and improve customer satisfaction and loyalty by continuing to pay strict attention to quality control and by making reasonable R&D expenditures for product improvements. Advertising should also continue to inform customers about product improvements and keep the brand name fresh in their memories. Thus, while the physical appearance of BMW's automobiles did not change dramatically throughout the 1980s, the firm made hundreds of technical improvements, such as antilock brakes. BMW heavily promoted those improvements as part of a campaign to enhance the firm's high-quality image.

A firm should also continually strengthen customer service. For consumer goods, this might involve ongoing incentive and training programs for retail dealers or the expansion of company-owned service centers. An industrial goods firm might switch to more direct channels of distribution to gain better control over inventories, delivery times, and customer relations. It might also organize its salesforce into specialized groups focused on servicing major industries or applications segments, as IBM has done in the commercial PC market. Or it might develop national or key account executives to concentrate on servicing its largest customers.

For low-cost defenders, implementing a fortress defense largely means a continuing search for ways of maintaining a low delivered cost position within the industry. The bulk of their R&D expenditures should focus on process improvements to increase production efficiency. Such businesses can

EXHIBIT   10-9
Low Costs Allow Greater Market Expenditures at Heinz

> The H. J. Heinz Company worked diligently during the early 1980s to become the low-cost producer in a number of food categories. Between 1980 and 1985, the firm increased its gross profit rate (i.e., sales less the cost of goods) from 35.2 percent to 38.1 percent of sales, generating about $115 million in additional gross profit. About half of that came from lower costs and the rest from price increases. Heinz plowed 60 percent of the proceeds back into marketing, mostly for increased advertising and promotion. As a result, the firm has maintained a commanding lead in many of its mature markets. For instance, Heinz holds more than a 50 percent share of the ketchup and frozen french fries markets.

SOURCE: Bill Saporito, "Heinz Pushes to Be the Low-Cost Producer," *Fortune*, June 24, 1985, pp. 44.

also look for ways to increase the efficiency of their sales and distribution systems (e.g., telemarketing for smaller accounts or the use of manufacturer's reps in territories with low sales potential) and to reduce overhead.

However, a low-cost strategy does not necessarily mean the firm must always compete by offering the lowest prices. It might maintain prices at competitive levels and use some of its higher margins to support continued advertising and promotion programs aimed at preserving customer loyalty and stimulating repeat purchases. The H. J. Heinz Company provides an example of this approach, as described in Exhibit 10–9.

Regardless of its competitive strategy, a share leader in a mature market should always seek ways to simplify and encourage repeat purchasing by current customers. Maintenance of the firm's distribution coverage is critical here. Businesses might also attempt to tie up major customers by offering long-term requirements contracts, just-in-time (JIT) delivery agreements, or computerized reorder systems like the one American Hospital Supply developed for its major hospital customers.

When confronted by aggressive low-cost competitors, a share leader may have no choice but to adopt either a **confrontation** or a **flanker strategy** to preserve its market share. In the airline industry, for instance, the major carriers confronted the low-price, no-frills challenge of People Express by matching the firm's low prices on directly competing routes. Even though the major lines lost money on those routes, their ability to subsidize those losses with income from other less competitive routes and their greater financial resources eventually enabled them to drive People Express into bankruptcy.

Strategies for low-share competitors

Small-share businesses can earn substantial profits in mature markets by focusing on marketing strategies that avoid prolonged direct confrontations with share leaders, such as a niche strategy or a guerrilla attack. A **niche strategy** can be particularly effective when the target segment is too small to appeal to larger competitors or when the small firm can establish a strong differential advantage and brand preference among customers in the segment.

For instance, even in an era when many people were reducing their alcohol consumption and turning to lighter beverages such as white wine, Jim Beam maintained a very profitable share of the small but loyal segment of bourbon drinkers. The family-run operation maintained product quality by remaining faithful to the traditional production methods handed down for generations. It promoted its quality image with $10 million of annual advertising focused on the target segment of bourbon drinkers through ads in carefully selected magazines. The company also avoided any attempts to diversify or expand its product line into areas that might lead to direct confrontations with the larger competitors in the liquor industry. As a result, Jim Beam earned about $40 million on sales of $250 million in 1985.[17]

When the market is more homogeneous, or when one of the industry's larger competitors dominates all segments, a small-share firm may have little choice but to engage in a **guerrilla attack strategy.** The small-share firm launches sporadic raids against the customers of its more established competitors to preserve or even marginally increase its limited share of the mature market. To avoid massive retaliation, such raids should be of limited duration and directed against limited geographic areas. Local advertising blitzes, particularly regional sales promotion efforts such as coupon drops and merchandising deals, are effective tools for implementing such a guerrilla attack.[18]

Marketing actions and strategies for extending volume growth

Even when total industry sales volume has been stagnant for a while, there may still be opportunities for a firm, particularly a share leader, to precipitate a renewed spurt of growth through aggressive marketing actions. A firm might use three different strategies, either singly or in combination, to do so: an **increased penetration strategy,** an **extended use strategy,** and a **market expansion strategy.** Exhibit 10–10 summarizes the environmental situations where each of these strategies is most appropriate and the objectives each is best suited for accomplishing. Exhibit 10–11 on page 319 outlines some specific marketing actions a firm might employ to implement each of the strategies. We discuss them in more detail in the following paragraphs.

Increased penetration strategy

The total sales volume produced by a target segment of customers is a function of (1) the number of potential customers in the segment, (2) the product's penetration of that segment, that is, the proportion of potential customers who actually use the product, and (3) the average frequency with which customers consume the product and make another purchase. Where usage frequency is quite high among current customers but only a relatively small portion of all potential users actually buy the product, a firm might

---

[17]Jaclyn Fierman, "How to Make Money in Mature Markets," *Fortune,* November 25, 1985, pp. 46–53.

[18]A. L. Stern, "New Marketing Game: Stealing Customers," *Dun's Business Month,* February 1985, pp. 48–50.

EXHIBIT 10–10

Situational Determinants of Appropriate Marketing Objectives and Strategies for Extending Growth in Mature Markets

Situational variables	Growth-extension strategies		
	Increased penetration	**Extended use**	**Market expansion**
Primary objective	Increase the proportion of users by converting current nonusers in one or more major market segments.	Increase the amount of product used by the average customer by increasing frequency of use or developing new and more varied ways to use the product.	Expand the number of potential customers by targeting underdeveloped geographic areas or applications segments.
Market characteristics	Relatively low penetration in one or more segments (i.e., low percentage of potential users have adopted the product); relatively homogeneous market with only a few large segments.	Relatively high penetration but low frequency of use in one or more major segments; product used in only limited ways or for special occasions; relatively homogeneous market with only a few large segments.	Relatively heterogeneous market with a variety of segments; some geographic areas, including foreign countries, with low penetration; some product applications underdeveloped.
Competitor characteristics	Competitors hold relatively small market shares; comparatively limited resources or competencies make it unlikely they will steal a significant portion of converted nonusers.	Competitors hold relatively small market shares; comparatively limited resources or competencies make it unlikely their brands will be purchased for newly developed uses.	Competitors hold relatively small market shares; have insufficient resources or competencies to preempt underdeveloped geographic areas or applications segments.
Firm characteristics	A market share leader in the industry; has R&D and marketing competencies to produce product modifications or line extensions; has promotional resources to stimulate primary demand among current nonusers.	A market share leader in the industry; has marketing competencies and resources to develop and promote new uses.	A market share leader in the industry; has marketing and distribution competencies and resources to develop new global markets or applications segments.

aim at increasing market penetration. It is an appropriate strategy for an industry's share leader because such firms can more likely gain and retain a substantial share of new customers than smaller firms with less well-known brands.

The secret to a successful increased penetration strategy lies in discovering why nonusers are uninterested in the product. Very often the product does not offer sufficient value from the potential customer's point of view to justify the effort or expense involved in buying and using it. One obvious solution to such a problem is to enhance the product's value to potential customers by adding features or benefits, usually via line extensions.

EXHIBIT 10–11
Possible Marketing Actions for Accomplishing Growth-Extension Objectives

Marketing strategy and objectives	Possible marketing actions
Increased penetration	
Convert current nonusers in target segment into users	• Enhance product's value by adding features, benefits, or services.
	• Enhance product's value by including it in the design of integrated systems.
	• Stimulate additional primary demand through promotional efforts stressing new features or benefits:
	Advertising through selected media aimed at the target segment.
	Sales promotions directed at stimulating trial among current nonusers (e.g., tie-ins with other products).
	Some sales effort redirected toward new account generation; perhaps by assigning some sales personnel as account development reps or by offering incentives for new account sales.
	• Improve availability by developing innovative distribution systems.
Extended use	
Increase frequency of use among current users	• Move storage of the product closer to the point of end use by offering additional package sizes or designs.
	• Encourage larger volume purchases (for nonperishable products):
	Offer quantity discounts.
	Offer consumer promotions to stimulate volume purchases or more frequent use (e.g., multipack deals, frequent flier programs).
	• Reminder advertising stressing benefits for a variety of usage occasions.
Encourage a wider variety of uses among current users	• Develop line extensions suitable for additional uses or applications.
	• Develop and promote new uses for the basic product.
	Include information about new applications/recipes on package.
	Develop extended use advertising campaign, particularly with print media.
	Communicate new application ideas through sales presentations to current customers.
	• Encourage new uses through sales promotions (e.g., tie-ins with complementary products).
Market expansion	
Develop differentiated positioning focused on untapped or under-developed segments	• Develop a differentiated flanker brand or product line with unique features or price that is more appealing to a segment of potential customers whose needs are not met by existing offerings (*see flanker strategy in Chapter 9*).
	<div align="center">or</div>
	• Develop multiple line extensions or brand offerings with features or prices targeted to the unique needs and preferences of several smaller potential applications or regional segments (*see encirclement strategy in Chapter 9*).
	• Consider producing for private labels.
	• Design advertising, personal selling, and/or sales promotion campaigns that address specific interests and concerns of potential customers in one or multiple underdeveloped segments to stimulate selective demand.
	• Build unique distribution channels to more effectively reach potential customers in one or multiple underdeveloped segments.
	• Design service programs to reduce the perceived risks of trial and/or solve the unique problems faced by potential customers in one or multiple underdeveloped segments (e.g., systems engineering, installation, operator trailing, extended warranties).

Another way to add value to a product is to design and sell integrated systems that help improve the basic product's performance or ease of use. Both Apple and IBM, for instance, offer entire computer systems, which integrate the computer with software, disk drives, printers, and so on, for both individual and commercial users. Such capability gives these firms an advantage in attracting relatively uninformed buyers intimidated by the prospect of buying many individual pieces of equipment and trying to hook them all together.

A firm may also enhance a product's value by offering services that improve its performance or ease of use for the potential customer. Since it is unlikely that people who do not know how to knit will ever buy yarn or knitting needles, for example, most yarn shops offer free knitting lessons.

Product modifications or line extensions will not, however, attract nonusers unless the enhanced benefits are effectively promoted. For industrial goods, this may mean redirecting some sales efforts toward nonusers. The firm may offer additional incentives for new account sales or assign specific salespeople to call on targeted nonusers and convert them into new customers. For consumer goods, some combination of advertising to stimulate primary demand in the target segment and sales promotions to encourage trial, such as free samples or tie-in promotions with complementary products that nonusers currently buy, can be effective. In some cases, informative advertising can convert nonusers into customers without having to modify the product, especially when potential customers hold misconceptions or unjustifiably negative attitudes about the product. America's pork producers, for instance, have attempted to persuade health- and diet-conscious consumers to eat pork by promoting some cuts as relatively low in fat and calories and by positioning pork as the "other white meat."

Finally, some potential customers may be having trouble finding the product due to limited distribution, or the product's benefits may simply be too modest to justify much purchasing effort. In such cases, expanding distribution or developing more convenient and accessible channels may help expand market penetration. Thus, Alcoa's joint venture with Kobe Steel aims to increase the availability of low-cost, high-quality sheet aluminum so that the metal can capture a larger proportion of the Asian beverage-can market. Similarly, few travelers are so leery of flying that they would go through the effort of calling an insurance agent to buy an accident policy for a single flight. But the sales of such policies are greatly increased by making them conveniently available through vending machines located in airport terminals.

Extended use strategy

Some years ago, the manager of General Foods' Cool Whip frozen dessert topping discovered through marketing research that nearly three-fourths of all households used the product, but the average consumer used it only four times per year and served it on only 7 percent of all toppable desserts. In situations of good market penetration but low frequency of use, an extended use strategy may effectively increase volume. This was particularly true in the

Cool Whip case; the relatively large and homogeneous target market consisted for the most part of a single mass-market segment. Also, General Foods held nearly a two-thirds share of the frozen topping market; and it had the marketing resources and competencies to capture most of the additional volume that an extended use strategy might generate.

One effective approach for stimulating increased frequency of use is to move product inventories closer to the point of use. This approach works particularly well with low-involvement consumer goods. Marketers know that most consumers are unlikely to expend any additional time or effort to obtain such products when they are ready to use them. If there is no Cool Whip in the refrigerator when the consumer is preparing dessert, for instance, he or she is unlikely to run to the store immediately and will probably serve the dessert without topping.

One obvious way to move inventory closer to the point of consumption is to offer larger package sizes. The more customers buy at one time, the less likely they are to be out of stock when a usage opportunity arises. This approach can backfire, though, for a perishable product or one that consumers perceive to be an impulse indulgence. Thus, most superpremium ice creams, such as Hägen-Dazs, are sold in small pint containers; most consumers want to avoid the temptation of having large quantities of such a high-calorie indulgence too readily available.

The design of a package can also help increase use frequency by making the product more convenient or easy to use. Examples include single-serving packages of Jell-O pudding to pack in lunches, packages of paper cups that include a convenient dispenser, and frozen-food packages that can go directly into a microwave oven.

Various sales promotion programs also help move inventories of a product closer to the point of use by encouraging larger volume purchases. Marketers commonly offer quantity discounts for this purpose in selling industrial goods. For consumer products, multi-item discounts or two-for-one deals serve the same purpose. Promotional programs also encourage greater frequency of use and increase customer loyalty in many service industries. Consider, for instance, the frequent flier programs offered by major airlines.

Sometimes the product's characteristics inhibit customers from using it more frequently. If marketers can change those characteristics, such as difficulty of preparation or high calories, a new line extension might encourage customers to use more of the product or to use it more often. Microwave waffles and low-calorie salad dressings are examples of such line extensions. For industrial goods, however, firms may have to develop new technology to overcome a product's limitations for some applications. Thus, Alcoa and other aluminum producers are working with automakers to discover new alloys and manufacturing methods that will make aluminum a more viable alternative to steel for car frames and body parts.

Finally, advertising can sometimes effectively increase use frequency by simply reminding customers to use the product more often. For instance, General Foods conducted a reminder campaign for Jell-O pudding that featured Bill Cosby asking, "When was the last time you served pudding, Mom?"

Another approach for extending use among current customers involves finding and promoting new functional uses for the product. Jell-O gelatin is a classic example, having generated substantial new sales volume over the years by promoting the use of Jell-O as an ingredient in salads, pie fillings, and other dishes.

Firms promote new ways to use a product through a variety of methods. For industrial products, firms send technical advisories about new applications to the salesforce to present to their customers during regular sales calls. For consumer products, new use suggestions or recipes may be included on the package or in an advertising campaign. Sales promotions, such as including cents-off coupons in ads featuring a new recipe, encourage customers to try a new application. To reduce costs, two or more manufacturers of complementary products sometimes cooperate in running such promotions. A recent ad promoting a simple Italian dinner, for instance, featured coupons for Kraft's Parmesan cheese, Pillsbury's Soft Breadsticks, and Campbell's Prego spaghetti sauce.

In some cases, slightly modified line extensions might encourage customers to use the product in different ways. Thus, Kraft introduced a jalapeño-flavored Cheese-Whiz in a microwavable container and promoted the product as an easy-to-prepare topping for nachos.

Market expansion strategy

In a mature industry with a fragmented and heterogeneous market where some segments are less well developed than others, a market expansion strategy may generate substantial additional volume growth. Such a strategy aims at gaining new customers by targeting new or underdeveloped geographic markets (either regional or foreign) or new customer segments. Once again, share leaders tend to be best suited for implementing this strategy. But even smaller competitors can employ such a strategy successfully, as illustrated by the Baldor Company described in Exhibit 10–12.

Pursuing market expansion by strengthening a firm's position in new or underdeveloped **domestic geographic markets** can lead to experience curve benefits and operating synergies. The firm can rely on largely the same expertise and technology, and perhaps even the same production and distribution facilities, it has already developed. Unfortunately, domestic geographic expansion is often not viable in a mature industry because the share leaders usually have attained national market coverage. Smaller regional competitors, on the other hand, might consider domestic geographic expansion a means for improving their volume and share position. However, such a move risks retaliation from the large national brands as well as from entrenched regional competitors in the prospective new territory.

To get around the retaliation problem, a regional producer might try to expand through the acquisition of small producers in other regions. This can be a viable option when (1) the low profitability of some regional producers enables the acquiring firm to buy their assets for less than the replacement cost of the capacity involved, and (2) synergies gained by combining regional

EXHIBIT 10–12

Surviving a Decade of Foreign Competition in a Mature Industry

> For the past decade, the U.S. electric motor industry has experienced poor sales. But unlike such big boys as General Electric, Reliance Electric, and Emerson Electric, a relatively small Fort Smith (Arkansas) company—Baldor—has emerged with record sales and profits as well as a higher market share. Since 1985, the company's sales have increased by 40 percent to an all-time high of $243 million while profits rose 53 percent. Baldor survived and prospered by identifying undeveloped segments of potential industrial users and engineering highly specialized high-quality motors to meet the needs of those new market niches.
>
> For example, Baldor turns out explosion-proof motors for mining and gas applications, lint-proof motors for the textile industry, heart pumps for hospitals, large motors for the windshield wipers on battleships, and really big motors to roll steel. Such motors, while not sold in large quantities, do sell at premium prices. The company continues to explore new markets such as a "fitness" motor to turn jogger's treadmills and a wash-down motor that will survive dousings with the hot soapy waters used in canning mushrooms.

SOURCE: Alan Farnham, "Baldor's Success: Made in the U.S.A.," *Fortune,* July 17, 1989, p. 101.

operations and the infusion of resources from the acquiring firm can improve the effectiveness and profitability of the acquired producers. For example, Heileman Brewing Company grew from the 31st largest brewer of beer in the mid-1960s to the fourth largest by the mid-1980s through the acquisition of nearly 30 regional brands. Heileman took control of strong regional brands such as Old Style, Carling, and Rainier, but because it had no dominant national brand it avoided antitrust opposition to its acquisition program. After acquisition, Heileman maintained the identity of each brand, increased its advertising budget, and expanded its distribution by incorporating it into the firm's distribution system in other regions. As a result, Heileman achieved a strong earnings record for two decades.

For share leaders in a mature domestic market, less-developed markets in foreign countries usually present the most viable opportunities for geographic expansion. Firms can accomplish this kind of **global marketing** in a variety of ways, from simply using agent middlemen to developing joint ventures (such as the one between Alcoa and Kobe Steel) to establishing wholly owned subsidiaries in foreign markets. However, because of differences in the social, political, and competitive environments across nations, firms may need to modify their strategic marketing programs. Because the issues involved are both crucial and complex, the next chapter is devoted to a discussion of global marketing strategies.

In a different approach to market expansion, the firm identifies and develops entirely **new customer** or **application segments.** Sometimes the firm can effectively reach new customer segments by simply expanding the distribution system without changing the product's characteristics or the other marketing-mix elements. A sporting goods manufacturer that sells its products to consumers through retail stores, for instance, might expand into the commercial market consisting of schools and amateur and professional sports teams by establishing a direct salesforce.

In most instances, though, developing new market segments requires modifying the product to make it more suitable for the application or to provide more of the benefits desired by customers in the new segment. For example, Alcoa has invested millions in both product and process R&D to develop its ability to produce high-quality alumina ceramic electronic packages suitable for use in the computer industry.

One danger in investing heavily to develop new customer or application segments is that other competitors might ultimately reap the lion's share of the benefits. This is especially true when the product involved is hard to differentiate. For example, Inco, the leading producer of nickel, developed a variety of new uses for nickel during the 1960s and 1970s, including applications in stainless steel for automobiles and appliances. But the additional market growth stimulated by these new applications attracted a number of new competitors. Inco was vulnerable to the lower prices offered by many of these competitors and its market share slipped sharply.[19] Thus, a market expansion strategy is most suitable when the firm can be reasonably certain of maintaining a competitive advantage in the newly developed segments.

One final possibility for market expansion is to produce **private-label brands** for large retailers such as Sears or Safeway. Firms whose own brands hold relatively weak positions and who have excess production capacity find this a particularly attractive option. Private labeling allows such firms to gain access to established customer segments without making substantial marketing expenditures, thus increasing the firm's volume and lowering its per-unit costs. However, since private labels typically compete with low prices and their sponsors usually have strong bargaining power, producing private labels is often not a very profitable option unless a manufacturer already has a relatively low-cost position in the industry. It can also be a risky strategy, particularly for the smaller firm, because reliance on one or a few large private-label customers can result in drastic volume reductions and unit-cost increases should those customers decide to switch suppliers.

STRATEGIES FOR DECLINING MARKETS

Most products eventually enter a decline phase in their life cycles. As sales decline, excess capacity once again develops. As the remaining competitors fight to hold volume in the face of falling sales, industry profits erode. Consequently, conventional wisdom suggests that firms should either divest declining products quickly or harvest them to maximize short-term profits. Not all markets decline in the same way or at the same speed, however; nor

---

[19]"Inco: Guarding Its Edge in Nickel while Starting to Diversify Again," *Business Week,* June 9, 1980, pp. 104–6.

do all firms have the same competitive strengths and weaknesses within those markets. Therefore, as in most other situations, the relative attractiveness of the declining product-market and the business's competitive position within it should dictate the appropriate strategy.

Relative attractiveness of declining markets

Although U.S. high school enrollment declined by about 2 million students from its peak in 1976 through the end of the 1980s, Jostens, Inc.—the leading manufacturer of class rings and other school merchandise—achieved annual increases in revenues and profits every year during that period. One reason for the firm's success was that it saw the market decline coming and prepared for it by improving the efficiency of its operations and developing marketing programs that were effective at persuading a larger proportion of students to buy class rings.[20]

Jostens' experience shows that some declining product-markets can offer attractive opportunities well into the future, at least for one or a few strong competitors. In other product-markets, the potential for continued profits during the decline stage is dismal. The acetylene industry offers a good example of an unattractive declining market. Acetylene, a gas used for welding and other high-temperature applications, is rapidly being replaced by ethylene and other substitutes. Because acetylene is a commodity product with high fixed manufacturing costs, the remaining producers have engaged in protracted price wars in an attempt to hold volume. Rapidly declining volumes and low profits have driven most acetylene producers to seek ways of abandoning the industry as quickly as possible.[21]

Three sets of factors help determine the relative attractiveness of declining product-markets from a strategic point of view: **conditions of demand,** including the rate and certainty of future declines in volume; **exit barriers,** or the ease with which weaker competitors can leave the market; and factors affecting the **intensity of future competitive rivalry** within the market. The impact of each of these sets of variables on the attractiveness of declining market environments is summarized in Exhibit 10–13 and discussed below.

Conditions of demand

Demand in a product-market declines for a number of reasons. Technological advances produce substitute products (such as electronic calculators for slide rules), often with higher quality or lower cost. Demographic shifts lead to a shrinking target market (for example, baby foods). Customers' needs, tastes,

[20]Fierman, "How to Make Money in Mature Markets," p. 47.

[21]This example, as well as much of the following discussion, is based on material found in Kathryn Rudie Harrigan and Michael E. Porter, "End-Game Strategies for Declining Industries," *Harvard Business Review,* July–August 1983, pp. 111–20. Also see Kathryn Rudie Harrigan, *Strategies for Declining Businesses* (Lexington, Mass.: D. C. Heath, 1980).

EXHIBIT   10-13

Factors Affecting the Attractiveness of Declining Market Environments

	Environmental attractiveness	
Factors	**Hospitable**	**Inhospitable**
Conditions of demand		
Speed of decline	Very slow	Rapid or erratic
Certainty of decline	100% certain, predictable patterns	Great uncertainty, erratic patterns
Pockets of enduring demand	Several or major ones	No niches
Product differentiation	Brand loyalty	Commodity-like products
Price stability	Stable, price premiums attainable	Very unstable, pricing below costs
Exit barriers		
Reinvestment requirements	None	High, often mandatory and involving capital assets
Excess capacity	Little	Substantial
Asset age	Mostly old assets	Sizable new assets and old ones not retired
Resale markets for assets	Easy to convert or sell	No markets available, substantial costs to retire
Shared facilities	Few free-standing plants	Substantial and interconnected with important businesses
Vertical integration	Little	Substantial
Single-product competitors	None	Several large companies
Rivalry determinants		
Customer industries	Fragmented, weak	Strong bargaining power
Customer switching costs	High	Minimal
Diseconomies of scale	None	Substantial penalty
Dissimilar strategic groups	Few	Several in same target markets

SOURCE: Kathryn Rudie Harrigan and Michael E. Porter, "End-Game Strategies for Declining Industries," *Harvard Business Review,* July–August 1983, p. 117.

or lifestyles change (the falling consumption of beef). Finally, the cost of inputs or complementary products rises and shrinks demand (the effects of rising gasoline prices on sales of recreational vehicles).

The cause of a decline in demand can affect both the rate and the predictability of that decline. A fall in sales due to a demographic shift, for instance, is likely to be gradual, whereas the switch to a technically superior substitute can be abrupt. Similarly, the fall in demand as customers switch to a better substitute is predictable, while a decline in sales due to a change in tastes is not.

As Exhibit 10–13 indicates, both the rate and certainty of sales decline are demand characteristics that affect a market's attractiveness. A slow and gradual decline allows an orderly withdrawal of weaker competitors. Overcapacity does not become excessive and lead to predatory competitive behavior, and the competitors who remain are more likely to make profits than in a quick or erratic decline. Also, when most industry managers believe market decline is predictable and certain, reduction of capacity is more likely to be orderly than when they feel substantial uncertainty about whether demand might level off or even become revitalized. For instance, because the market for high school class rings is largely shaped by demographic trends, Jostens and its competitors could accurately forecast a decline in future market potential. This not only gave Jostens time to develop an aggressive marketing strategy to improve its market share during the decline period, but it also lowered the odds that smaller competitors would stay in the industry because of false expectations of future growth.

Of course, not all segments of a market decline at the same time nor at the same rate. The number and size of enduring niches or pockets of demand and the customer purchase behavior within them also influence the continuing attractiveness of the market. When the demand pockets are large or numerous and the customers in those niches are brand loyal and relatively insensitive to price, competitors with large shares and differentiated products can continue to make substantial profits. For example, even though the market for cigars has been shrinking for years, there continues to be a sizable number of smokers who prefer premium-quality cigars. Those firms with well-established positions at the premium end of the cigar industry have continued to earn above-average returns.

Exit barriers

The higher the exit barriers, the less hospitable a product-market will be during the decline phase of its life cycle. When weaker competitors find it hard to leave a product-market as demand falls, excess capacity develops and firms engage in aggressive pricing or promotional efforts to try to prop up their volume and hold down unit costs. Thus, exit barriers lead to competitive volatility.

Once again, Exhibit 10–13 indicates that a variety of factors influence the ease with which businesses can exit an industry. One critical consideration involves the amount of highly specialized assets. Assets unique to a given business are difficult to divest because of their low liquidation value. The only potential buyers for such assets are other firms who would use them for a similar purpose, which is unlikely in a declining industry. Thus, the firm may have little choice but to remain in the business or to sell the assets for their scrap value. This option is particularly unattractive when the assets are relatively new and not fully depreciated.

Another major exit barrier occurs when the assets or resources of the declining business intertwine with the firm's other business units, either through shared facilities and programs or through vertical integration. Exit from the declining business might shut down shared production facilities, lower salesforce commissions, damage customer relations, and increase unit costs in the firm's other businesses to a point that damages their profitability.

Emotional factors can also act as exit barriers. Managers often feel reluctant to admit failure by divesting a business even though it no longer produces acceptable returns. This is especially true when the business played an important role in the firm's history and it houses a large number of senior managers.

Intensity of future competitive rivalry

Even when substantial pockets of continuing demand remain within a declining business, it may not be wise for a firm to pursue them in the face of future intense competitive rivalry. In addition to exit barriers, other factors also affect the ability of the remaining firms to avoid intense price competition and maintain reasonable margins: size and bargaining power of the customers who continue to buy the product; customers' ability to switch to substitute products or to alternative suppliers; and any potential diseconomies of scale involved in capturing an increased share of the remaining volume.

Divestment or liquidation

When the market environment in a declining industry is unattractive or a business has a relatively weak competitive position, the firm may recover more of its investment by selling the business in the early stages of decline rather than later. The earlier the business is sold, the more uncertain potential buyers are likely to be about the future direction of demand in the industry and thus the more likely that a willing buyer can be found. Thus, Raytheon sold its vacuum-tube business in the early 1960s even though transistors had just begun replacing tubes in radios and TV sets and there was still a strong replacement demand for tubes. By moving early, the firm achieved a much higher liquidation value than companies that tried to unload their tube-making facilities in the 70s when the industry was clearly in its twilight years.[22]

Of course, the firm that divests early runs the risk that its forecast of the industry's future may be wrong. Also, quick divestment may not be possible if the firm faces high exit barriers, such as interdependencies across business units or customer expectations of continued product availability. By planning early for departure, however, the firm may be able to reduce some of those barriers before the liquidation is necessary.

---

[22]Harrigan and Porter, "End-Game Strategies," p. 114.

Marketing strategies for remaining competitors

Conventional wisdom suggests that a business remaining in a declining product-market should pursue a harvesting strategy aimed at maximizing its cash flow in the short run. But such businesses also have other strategic options. They might attempt to maintain their position as the market declines, improve their position to become the profitable survivor, or focus efforts on one or more remaining demand pockets or market niches. Once again, the appropriateness of these strategies depends on factors affecting the attractiveness of the declining market and on the business's competitive strengths and weaknesses. Exhibit 10–14 summarizes the situational determinants of the appropriateness of each strategy. Some of the marketing actions a firm might take to implement them are discussed below and summarized in Exhibit 10–15 on page 331.

Harvesting strategy

The objective of a harvesting, or milking, strategy is to generate cash quickly by maximizing cash flow over a relatively short term. This typically involves avoiding any additional investment in the business, greatly reducing operating (including marketing) expenses, and perhaps raising prices. Since the firm usually expects to ultimately divest or abandon the business, some loss of sales and market share during the pursuit of this strategy is likely. The trick is to hold the business's volume and share declines to a relatively slow and steady rate. A precipitous and premature loss of share would limit the total amount of cash the business could generate during the market's decline.

A harvesting strategy is most appropriate for a firm holding a relatively strong competitive position in the market at the start of the decline and a cadre of current customers likely to continue buying the brand even after marketing support is reduced. Such a strategy also works best when the market's decline is inevitable but likely to occur at a relatively slow and steady rate and when rivalry among remaining competitors is not likely to be very intense. Such conditions help enable the business to maintain adequate price levels and profit margins as volume gradually falls.

Implementing a harvesting strategy means avoiding any additional long-term investments in plant, equipment, or R&D. It also necessitates substantial cuts in operating expenditures for marketing activities. This often means that the firm should greatly reduce the number of models or package sizes in its product line in order to reduce inventory and manufacturing costs.

The business should improve the efficiency of sales and distribution. For industrial goods, a business might establish minimum-order quantities to avoid the high processing and delivery costs associated with small purchases. It could service its smaller accounts though a telemarketing system rather than through its field salesforce; or assign its smaller customers to agent middlemen. For consumer goods, the business might move to a more selective distribution system by concentrating its efforts on the larger retail chains.

EXHIBIT 10–14

Situational Determinants of Appropriate Marketing Objectives and Strategies for Declining Markets

	Strategies for declining markets			
Situational variables	**Harvesting**	**Maintenance**	**Profitable survivor**	**Niche**
Primary objective	Maximize short-term cash flow; maintain or increase margins even at expense of a slow decline in market share.	Maintain share in short term as market declines, even if margins must be sacrificed.	Increase share of the declining market with an eye to future profits; encourage weaker competitors to exit.	Focus on strengthening position in one or a few relatively substantial segments with potential for future profits.
Market characteristics	Future market decline is certain, but likely to occur at a slow and steady rate.	Market has experienced recent declines, but future direction and attractiveness are currently hard to predict.	Future market decline is certain, but likely to occur at a slow and steady rate; substantial pockets of demand will continue to exist.	Overall market may decline quickly, but one or more segments will remain as demand pockets or decay slowly.
Competitor characteristics	Few strong competitors; low exit barriers; future rivalry not likely to be intense.	Few strong competitors, but intensity of future rivalry is hard to predict.	Few strong competitors; exit barriers are low or can be reduced by firm's intervention.	One or more stronger competitors in mass market, but not in the target segment.
Firm's characteristics	Has a leading share position; has a substantial proportion of loyal customers who are likely to continue buying brand even if marketing support is reduced.	Has a leading share of the market and a relatively strong competitive position.	Has a leading share of the market and a strong competitive position; has superior resources or competencies necessary to encourage competitors to exit or to acquire them.	Has a sustainable competitive advantage in target segment, but overall resources may be limited.

The firm would substantially reduce consumer advertising and promotion expenditures, usually to the minimum level necessary to retain adequate distribution. Finally, the business should attempt to maintain or perhaps even increase its price levels to increase margins. A classic example of a harvesting strategy is that of Chase & Sandborn coffee, as described in Exhibit 10–16 on page 332.

Maintenance strategy

In markets where future volume trends are highly uncertain, a business with a leading share position might pursue a strategy aimed at maintaining its

EXHIBIT 10–15
Possible Marketing Actions Appropriate for Different Marketing Strategies in Declining Markets

Marketing strategy and objectives	Possible marketing actions
Harvesting strategy	

Maximize short-term cash flow; maintain or increase margins even at the expense of market share decline.	• Eliminate R&D expenditures and capital investments related to the business.
	 • Reduce marketing and sales budgets.
	    Greatly reduce or eliminate advertising and sales promotion expenditures, with the possible exception of periodic reminder advertising targeted at current customers.
	    Reduce trade promotions to minimum level necessary to prevent rapid loss of distribution coverage.
	    Focus salesforce efforts on attaining repeat purchases from current customers.
	 • Seek ways to reduce production costs, even at the expense of slow erosion in product quality.
	 • Raise price if necessary to maintain margins.

Maintenance strategy	
Maintain market share for the short term, even at the expense of margins	• Continue product and process R&D expenditures in short term aimed at maintaining or improving product quality. • Continue maintenance levels of advertising and sales promotion targeted at current users. • Continue trade promotion at levels sufficient to avoid any reduction in distribution coverage. • Focus salesforce efforts on attaining repeat purchases from current users. • Lower prices if necessary to maintain share, even at the expense of reduced margins.
Profitable survivor strategy	

Increase share of the declining market; encourage weaker competitors to exit.	• Signal competitors that firm intends to remain in industry and pursue an increased share.
	    Maintain or increase advertising and sales promotion budgets.
	    Maintain or increase distribution coverage through aggressive trade promotion.
	    Focus some salesforce effort on winning away competitors' customers.
	    Continue product and process R&D to seek product improvements or cost reductions.
	 • Consider introducing line extensions to appeal to remaining demand segments.
	 • Lower prices if necessary to increase share, even at the expense of short-term margins.
	 • Consider agreements to produce replacement parts or private labels for smaller competitors considering getting out of production.

Niche strategy	
Strengthen share position in one or a few segments with potential for continued profit.	• Continued product and process R&D aimed at product improvements or modifications that will appeal to target segment(s). • Consider producing for private labels in order to maintain volume and hold down unit costs. • Focus advertising, sales promotion, and personal selling campaigns on customers in target segment(s); stress appeals of greatest importance to those customers. • Maintain distribution channels appropriate for reaching target segment; seek unique channel arrangements to more effectively reach customers in target segment(s). • Design service programs that address unique concerns/problems of customers in target segment(s).

EXHIBIT 10–16

Chase & Sandborn's Harvesting Strategy

> In 1879, Chase & Sandborn was the first U.S. company to sell roasted coffee in sealed cans. The company became part of Standard Brands and dominated the coffee industry during the 1920s and 30s largely through heavy expenditures on radio advertising. After World War II, however, the slowing growth of coffee consumption, the development of instant coffee, and large and aggressive new competitors like General Foods' Maxwell House brand made Chase & Sandborn reluctant to continue the large marketing expenditures necessary to hold its market share. Consequently, it adopted a harvesting strategy. Advertising and promotional expenditures were gradually cut, and eventually stopped, while the brand's share slowly eroded. Finally, Standard Brands merged with Nabisco in 1981, and the coffee business was sold to a small Miami firm for $15 million.

Source: David Aaker, *Strategic Market Management,* 2nd ed. (New York: John Wiley & Sons, 1988), p. 284.

market share, at least until the market's future becomes more predictable. In such a maintenance strategy, the business continues to pursue the same strategy that brought it success during the market's mature stage. This approach often results in reduced margins and profits in the short term, though; because firms usually must reduce prices or increase marketing expenditures to hold share in the face of declining industry volume. Thus, a firm should consider share maintenance an interim strategy. Once it becomes clear that the market will continue to decline, the business should switch to a different strategy that will provide better cash flows and return on investment over the market's remaining life.

Profitable survivor strategy

An aggressive alternative for a business with a strong share position and a sustainable competitive advantage in a declining product-market is to invest enough to increase its share position and establish itself as the industry leader for the remainder of the market's decline. This kind of strategy makes most sense when the firm expects a gradual decline in market demand or when substantial pockets of continuing demand are likely well into the future. It is also an attractive strategy when a firm's declining business is closely intertwined with other SBUs through shared facilities and programs or common customer segments.

A strong competitor can often improve its share position in a declining market at relatively low cost because other competitors may be harvesting their businesses or preparing to exit. The key to the success of such a strategy is to encourage other competitors to leave the market early. Once the firm has achieved a strong and unchallenged position, it can switch to a harvesting strategy and reap substantial profits over the remaining life of the product-market.

A firm might encourage smaller competitors to abandon the industry by being visible and explicit about its commitment to become the leading survivor. It should aggressively seek increased market share, either by cutting prices or by increasing advertising and promotion expenditures. It might also introduce line extensions aimed at remaining pockets of demand to make it more difficult for smaller competitors to find profitable niches. Finally, the firm might act to reduce its competitors' exit barriers, making it easier for them to leave the industry. This could involve taking over competitors' long-term contracts, agreeing to supply spare parts or to service their products in the field, or to provide them with components or private-label products. For instance, large regional bakeries have encouraged grocery chains to abandon their own bakery operations by supplying them with private-label baked goods.

The ultimate way to remove competitors' exit barriers is to purchase their operations and either improve their efficiency or remove them from the industry to avoid excess capacity. With continued decline in industry sales a certainty, smaller competitors may be forced to sell their assets at a book-value price low enough for the survivor to reap high returns on its investment. For example, White Consolidated Industries purchased a number of appliance brands such as Kelvinator, Philco, Westinghouse, and Frigidare from firms that were strongly motivated to exit the sagging appliance industry. By paying favorable prices for each operation, streamlining their product lines, and improving the efficiency of their manufacturing and distribution operations, White captured the third leading market share in the appliance industry.

Niche strategy

Even when most segments of an industry are expected to decline rapidly, a niche strategy may still be viable if one or more substantial segments will either remain as stable pockets of demand or decay slowly. The business pursuing such a strategy should have a strong competitive position in the target segment or be able to build a sustainable competitive advantage relatively quickly to preempt competitors. This is one strategy that even smaller competitors can sometimes successfully pursue, because they can focus the required assets and resources on a limited portion of the total market. The marketing actions a business might take to strengthen and preserve its position in a target niche are similar to those discussed earlier concerning niche strategies in mature markets.

SUMMARY

An industry's transition from growth to maturity begins when approximately half the potential customers have adopted the product and, while sales are still growing, the rate of growth begins to decline. As growth slows, some competitors are likely to find themselves with excess production capacity. Other changes in the competitive environment, including a reduction in the degree of differentiation across brands and increased difficulty in maintaining adequate distribution, occur at about the same time. As a result, competition becomes more intense with firms either cutting prices or increasing their marketing expenditures as they battle to increase volume, cover high fixed costs, and maintain profitability.

This transition period is usually accompanied by a shakeout as weaker competitors fail or leave the industry. A number of strategic mistakes, or traps, increase the likelihood that a firm will be forced out of an industry during the transition period. These traps include (1) a failure to recognize that the market is becoming mature, (2) the lack of a clearly defined competitive strategy, (3) a failure to recognize the declining importance of product differentiation and the increasing importance of price and service, and (4) a tendency to sacrifice market share in favor of maintaining short-term profits.

Success during the maturity stage of a product-market's life cycle requires two sets of strategic actions. First, managers should work to maintain and strengthen either the differentiation of the firm's offerings on quality and/or service dimensions or its position as a low-cost competitor within the industry. The second strategic consideration during the maturity stage is to develop meaningful marketing objectives and a marketing strategy appropriate for achieving them. Since maturity can last for many years, the most critical marketing objective is to maintain and protect the business's market share. For share leaders, some variation of the fortress defense, confrontation, or flanker strategies discussed in Chapter 9 are often appropriate for achieving that objective. Smaller competitors, on the other hand, may have to rely on a niche or guerrilla attack strategy to hold their position.

Since different market segments may mature at different times and environmental conditions can change over the mature phase of a product's life, firms often find opportunities to extend the growth of seemingly mature product-markets. Thus, an important secondary objective for firms in many mature markets is to stimulate additional volume growth. Among the marketing strategies firms might use to accomplish that objective are an increased penetration strategy, an extended use strategy, or a market expansion strategy focused on developing either new geographic territories (including global markets) or new applications segments.

Conventional wisdom suggests that declining products should either be divested or harvested to maximize short-term profits. However, some declining product-markets remain attractive enough to justify more aggressive marketing strategies. The attractiveness of such markets is determined by three sets of factors: (1) conditions of demand, including the rate and certainty of future declines in volume; (2) exit barriers, or the ease with which weaker competitors can leave the market; and (3) factors affecting the intensity of future competitive rivalry. When a declining product-market is judged to offer continuing opportunities for profitable sales, managers might consider one of several strategic alternatives to divestment or harvesting. Those alternative strategies include a maintenance strategy, a profitable survivor strategy, and a niche strategy.

International Marketing Strategy

P&G'S INTERNATIONAL DIVISION: A REAL WINNER[1]

In the second quarter of 1989, Procter & Gamble (P&G) reported a 25 percent increase in profits, primarily due to the strength of its overseas operations. In fiscal 1988, international sales reached $7 billion, representing 36 percent of the company's total sales of $19.3 billion. Sales were up 18 percent over 1987, and company officials predicted that they would be half of total revenues in the not-too-distant future.

Much of the growth in foreign sales resulted from efforts over the years to overcome trade barriers and cultural differences in selling the company's basic products such as diapers and detergents overseas. In 1989, P&G marketed over 160 brands in 140 countries, with two-thirds of its sales coming from 24

brands including Pampers (diapers), Crest (toothpaste), and Head and Shoulders (shampoo). In 1991, the company purchased two of Revlon's beauty businesses—Max Factor and Betrix—for $1.14 billion. These and earlier acquisitions (especially Richardson-Vicks, maker of Oil of Olay and Cover Girl) have made P&G a global player in personal-care items. P&G's latest acquisitions had sales of about $800 million in 1990, with some 80 percent of them coming from overseas.

Many of P&G's early problems overseas occurred in Japan, which it entered in 1972 in an effort to obtain a share of the diaper and detergent businesses. By 1982, the company's accumulated losses in Japan were over $200 million, mainly because of

[1]Based on Laurie Freeman and Laurel Wentz, "P&G on a Roll Overseas," *Advertising Age,* June 27, 1988, p. 30; Alicia Swasy, "After Early Stumbles, P&G Is Making Inroads Overseas," *The Wall Street Journal,* February 6, 1989, p. B1, and Chris Wloszcyna, "P&G See Beauty in World Markets," *USA Today,* April 11, 1991, p. 3B.

P&G's failure to understand what Japanese consumers wanted. For example, the original P&G diaper sold in Japan was a bulky, shapeless version of the U.S. Pampers brand. But the Japanese preferred cloth diapers until KAO introduced a thin disposable diaper that provided superior comfort and absorbency and was better adapted to the shortage of space in Japanese homes and shops. It took P&G years to overcome the resulting setback, even though the company soon brought out its own sleek superabsorbent product.

Another similar occurrence in Japan involved Cheer laundry detergent, which was first promoted as being effective in all water temperatures. The problem was that most Japanese didn't care about all-temperature washing since they washed their clothes in cold water. And if much fabric softener was added to the water, Cheer didn't generate many suds. After reformulating the product and undertaking an expensive ad campaign, Cheer sales became "respectable." Detergents still, however, represent a difficult product category in Japan for P&G, given the strength of KAO's Attack brand—a superconcentrated detergent containing an enzyme that removes dirt from cotton fibers.

In Europe, P&G's biggest problem was that its liquid laundry detergents were not well adapted to the local washing machines, which had dispensers only for powdered detergents. The eventual solution was the use of a plastic "dosing ball" (supplied with each bottle) that is filled with detergent and used with a load of clothes. The company now enjoys a 50 percent share of the European liquid-detergent market.

As the P&G case illustrates, the internationalization of competition has become one of the most important challenges facing most firms today. Since the late 70s, international trade has grown at an annual rate of 6.8 percent and is expected to sustain a 10 percent growth rate during the 90s. This figure doesn't include the output of the increasing number of firms who produce their goods overseas rather than exporting from their home country.[2] This growth, coupled with an array of new international competitors, has caused a basic change in the nature and scope of the global competitive environment. See Exhibit 11–1 on the importance of international trade to U.S. firms.

The question now facing large segments of American business is, What is the best way to compete in this new world order? The process involved is similar to that used for marketing domestic products. But some important differences affect a business's international marketing objectives, marketing

---

[2]Stanley Reed, William Glasgall, and William J. Holstein, "Seeking Growth in a Smaller World," *Business Week,* October 1989, p. 94.

EXHIBIT 11-1

Importance of International Trade to U.S. Business

International trade has become increasingly important to American business. Foreign revenues of the 100 largest U.S. multinationals totaled over $553 billion in 1989 and is expected to grow dramatically during the 1990s. A number of firms derive more than 50 percent of their earnings from overseas. For example, 80 percent of Coke's operating earnings comes from abroad, and its biggest profit center is not the United States but Japan. Such firms as Exxon, Mobil, IBM,* Dow Chemical, and Hewlett-Packard typically generate more profits abroad than domestically, some with even fewer assets employed overseas than in the United States.† Even so, the United States is one of the smaller exporting nations on the basis of the ratio of imports to GNP (10 percent); Japan is at 13 percent, and Australia, 19 percent.

Small and medium-size companies are also finding overseas markets an important source of growth and profits. For example, the POM company of Russellville, Arkansas, which manufactures coin-operated parking meters, is bigger abroad than domestically. In 1981, the company began exporting meters to newly industrialized countries experiencing crowded urban streets. POM now holds a world market share of 42 percent.‡

American firms face increasingly strong competition from such foreign companies as Toyota, Nissan, Siemens, Nestlé, Mitsubishi, Imperial Chemical Industries, Nippon Steel, and Uni-Lever. Despite their considerable domestic success, U.S. firms like General Motors, Kentucky Fried Chicken, Campbell Soup, and P&G have encountered sales and profitability problems in marketing their products abroad.

* Michael J. McCarthy, "As a Global Marketer, Coke Excels by Being Tough and Consistent," *The Wall Street Journal*, December 19, 1989, p. A1.

† "The 100 Largest U.S. Multinationals," *Forbes*, July 23, 1990, pp. 362–65.

‡ Christopher Knowlton, "The New Export Entrepreneurs," *Fortune*, June 6, 1988, p. 87. © 1988 The Time Inc. Magazine Company. All rights reserved.

strategies, market entry strategies, and product marketing programs. Exhibit 11–2 presents the issues firms need to address in developing and implementing an international marketing strategy. This chapter is organized around a discussion of these issues.

THE INTERNATIONAL BUSINESS ENVIRONMENT

Strong environmental differences between countries present a rich opportunity for international firms to develop strategy options. To select and prioritize target markets, firms must analyze these different environments. An obvious but frequently overlooked factor is a country's physical environment, including its geographical location. Extreme hot or cold temperatures, high humidity, unusual amounts of snow and rain, and even an overabundance of sand (as in the Middle East) can lead not only to needed differences in products but also to the demand for a given product. For example, vehicles operating in Africa experience severe climate-related maintenance problems unless certain safeguards are taken, such as rustproofing and the use of heavy-duty electrical systems.

E X H I B I T   1 1 – 2

Issues to Be Addressed in Developing and Implementing
an International Marketing Strategy

- **International business environment—physical, legal, economic, political, cultural, and competitive**
    Issues: What is the relative attractiveness of each country? What opportunities are present? What threats exist? What are the major differences between each overseas market and the home market?
- **International marketing objectives—other than profitability**
    Issues: What does a company hope to achieve by going overseas other than increase its profitability? How important is it to protect *market leadership*? To benefit from *scale economies*? To *service* customers who have moved overseas?
- **Selecting export target markets**
    Issues: What candidate product(s) should be selected? What countries are most attractive and where does the firm have strong relative business advantages? Which countries should be targeted and in what order?
- **Alternative overall strategies**
    Issues: What are the characteristics of a global high-share strategy? A global niche strategy? A national high-share strategy? A niche strategy? Under what conditions would each of the above strategies be used?
- **Market entry strategies**
    Issues: What are the major ways by which a firm can enter a foreign country? Within each of these ways, there are a variety of specific entry modes—What are they and under what set of conditions should each be used?
- **International marketing mix**
    Issues: To what extent can a firm standardize its marketing plan across countries? Under what conditions should it market the same product to all countries? Why do the other elements in the marketing mix tend to be localized?
- **Exporting services**
    Issues: What kinds of services has the United States exported? What has happened to the value of these exports?

Countries differ in the demand for particular products not only because of their physical environments, but also because of their legal, economic, political, cultural, competitive, and infrastructure environments. These differences are far greater than those existing among geographical segments within the United States.

Legal environment

Trade regulations can raise a firm's cost per transaction directly or indirectly by increasing the legal hurdles to entry. Countries have long enacted certain trade regulations to protect local industries, provide income, and inhibit the flow of foreign exchange. Such regulations include **tariffs,** which impose a tax on imported goods; **quotas,** which limit the number of units or the value of specific goods that can be imported in a given time period; and

EXHIBIT 11-3

Examples of Trade Barriers to American Products
and Annual Sales Lost by United States

Product	Countries	Barrier	Sales lost by U.S. annual, estimated
Grain	European Community	Price supports, variable duties	$2.0 billion
Soybeans	European Community	Price supports	$1.4 billion
Rice	Japan	Ban	$300 million
Beef	European Community	Ban on growth hormones in livestock	$100 million
Commercial aircraft	Britain, France, W. Germany, Spain	Subsidies to Airbus Industries	Over $850 million
Telecommunications equipment	European Community, S. Korea	Standards stacked against imports	No estimate
Telecommunications satellites	Japan	Ban on import by government agencies	No estimate
Pharmaceuticals	Argentina, Brazil	No patent protection	Over $110 million
Videocassettes, films	Brazil	Requirements to subsidize and market local films	Over $40 million
Computer software	Thailand	Poor patent protection	No estimate

SOURCE: Rahul Jacob, "Export Barriers the U.S. Hates Most," *Fortune,* February 27, 1989, p. 89. © 1989 The Time Inc. Magazine Company. All rights reserved.

embargoes, which ban the import of certain goods—as, for example, from South Africa.

Indirect legal or quasilegal barriers to trade include customs and administrative entry procedures, such as tariff classifications and documentation requirements, and restrictions on the quality, packaging, and labeling of goods that may enter a country. Other barriers include government participation in trade, such as procurement policies and export subsidies, and charges on imports, such as credit discriminations, import deposit requirements, and administrative fees.[3] (For examples of export barriers particularly worrisome to the United States, see Exhibit 11–3.)

---

[3]A. D. Cao, "Non-Tariff Barriers to U.S. Manufactured Exports," *The Columbia Journal of World Business,* Summer 1980, p. 94.

EXHIBIT 11-4

Beyond 1992—a Super Europe

There is the prospect of a super Europe by the beginning of the 21st century, which would link two dozen European nations with a population of over half a billion people. This would go far beyond the 13-nation economic union of 1992 and would add not only those nations comprising the European Free Trade Association (Iceland, Norway, Sweden, Finland, Switzerland, and Austria) but such Eastern European countries as East Germany, Poland, Czechoslovakia, Hungary, and Yugoslavia. And some analysts are not ruling out the addition of Romania and Bulgaria. Eastern Europe represents a total market of some 136 million people with a hunger for Western products. Already such well-known U.S. companies as General Electric, Colgate-Palmolive, P&G, Gillette, General Motors, Estée Lauder, and Ralston Purina either have invested or are considering investing in one or more Eastern European countries.

SOURCE: Andrew Clark, "Super Europe," *World Monitor,* September 1989, p. 16; and Laurel Wentz, "Eastern Europe Beckons," *Advertising Age,* November 20, 1989, p. 1.

Following World War II, the United States and 22 other countries sought to liberalize trade by reducing tariffs through the General Agreement on Tariffs and Trade (GATT). Today the average tariff is about 8 percent in the United States, 10 percent in Western Europe, and 11 percent in Japan—compared to 50 percent and more for these countries before World War II.

Some countries have even banded together to form economic communities to reduce tariffs. The best known of these, the European Economic Community (EEC or the Common Market), was formed to eliminate trade barriers between member nations and generally to encourage economic integration. By 1992, the last trade barriers within the EEC are scheduled to be eliminated, resulting in a unified market of over 300 million consumers. (See Exhibit 11–4 for a brief discussion on the possibilities of an even larger Europe by the end of the 1990s.) By 1992, the EEC will have to decide what approach to adopt regarding the rest of the world. Will it encourage protectionism? This question is being raised by many large multinational companies throughout the world.[4] Since P&G already has a strong presence in Europe, it is not likely to be affected by whatever policy the EEC adopts.

Economic, political, and cultural environments

These three environments strongly affect whether a company should target a country and if so, how the company should do business there. The **economic environment** primarily affects the demand for a particular product. Thus, it is important for marketers to know about such economic measures as per capita income and the distribution of income (the purchasing

---

[4]Richard I. Kirkland, Jr., "Outsider's Guide to Europe in 1992," *Fortune,* October 24, 1988, p. 121.

power of various consumer groups). A country's stage of economic development greatly affects its purchasing power and income distribution.

Firms must consider the stability of a country's **political environment** both short and long term. Some U.S. companies have suffered considerable losses from political instability in such countries as Iraq, Chile, Iran, Lebanon, and Libya. In addition, the extent to which a country relies on centralized planning and government ownership is likely to affect an importer's freedom in pricing, distribution, and advertising.

In some cases, a company may still consider it worthwhile to export goods to a country experiencing considerable political instability, such as Iran, Argentina, and Libya. Ordinarily, a company would do so via export marketing rather than by direct investment.

A country's **cultural environment**—its system of values, beliefs, and norms—strongly affects the way firms market their goods, as in P&G's experience in Japan. This is particularly true in communication. People from Western nations tend to be verbal; people from Eastern nations tend to be nonverbal. Thus, the latter believe people will understand via nonverbal cues—they don't have to be told. For example, a Japanese who responds to an American businessperson by smiling and nodding is not saying "yes" to a proposal but rather "I understand what you're saying—please continue."[5]

Competitive and infrastructure environments

Knowledge about the **competitive environment** of a particular country is important because it is likely that substantial differences exist among the various target countries. Companies must tailor marketing programs to accommodate these different competitive conditions. For example, Nestlé was able to obtain a 60 percent market share for its instant coffee in Japan, in part because of weak domestic competition. This is in contrast to the United States, where Nestlé is in competition with two strong companies (General Foods and P&G) and holds less than a 30 percent share.[6] One reason Coke does so well overseas is that Pepsi is not a strong competitor in Europe and Japan.

Differences in the **infrastructure environment** of target countries may, to some extent, force companies to individualize marketing programs. Particularly important here are the local transport system, media (to be discussed later in this chapter), and channels of distribution. The latter is critical and includes the physical handling of goods and the buying and selling of them among channel members, producers, and consumers. There are considerable

---

[5]Warren J. Keegan, *Global Marketing Management* (Englewood Cliffs, N.J.: Prentice Hall, 1989), chap. 4.

[6]Hirotaka Takeuchi and Michael E. Porter, "Three Roles of International Marketing in Global Strategy," in *Competition in Global Industries,* ed. Michael E. Porter (Boston: Harvard Business School Press, 1986), p. 114.

EXHIBIT 11–5
The Japanese Distribution System—Biggest Obstacle Facing American Exporters

According to a study by the American Chamber of Commerce in Japan, almost 48 percent of home electronics in Japan are sold through exclusively affiliated stores, and 99 percent of cars are distributed through exclusive dealerships. Only Japanese products carry the guarantee of being returned to the wholesaler if they don't sell; imports don't. Through such arrangements, Japanese manufacturers keep 1.6 million retailers in business. The United States, with 25 times the area and twice the population, has only 1.4 million retailers.

The Japanese retailer survives this inefficiency by charging the world's highest prices. A recent survey by the Japanese and U.S. governments found 84 of 122 items priced in both countries were excessively expensive in Japan, including food, wine, cosmetics, bed linens, golf clubs, and sparkplugs. One problem imported products face is the high markup the complex Japanese distribution system adds to the final retail price, as shown in the example of an imported necktie.

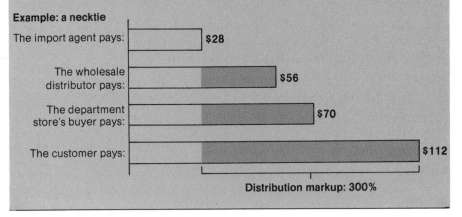

Example: a necktie

The import agent pays: $28

The wholesale distributor pays: $56

The department store's buyer pays: $70

The customer pays: $112

Distribution markup: 300%

SOURCE: Elaine Kurtenback, "Trade Friction Worse than Ever with Japan," *Arkansas Gazette,* December 4, 1989, p. C1.

differences among countries in the availability of certain channels and in the functions performed, how well they are performed, and at what cost. (See Exhibit 11–5 for the situation in Japan.) As a result, some companies use vastly different channels abroad than at home. For example, P&G uses mass merchandising in the United States and Europe but sells door-to-door in many developing countries.

INTERNATIONAL MARKETING OBJECTIVES

A company's profitability objectives for its foreign trade are essentially the same as for its domestic market. They include return on investment, return on assets managed, marginal contribution, cash flow, and market share.

EXHIBIT 11-6
Transnational Strategy Saves Ford

No company was hit harder in the early 80s by the tide of Japanese imports into the United States than Ford. What saved it was its leadership position in the European market. It gave Ford the profits and the cash flow that pulled it through the dismal years. And because the dollar bought so much in Europe in those years, Ford could develop there the new models for the American market that now have made Ford highly profitable again in the United States and a serious contender for the domestic leadership it held 60 years ago. GM, though twice Ford's size, is essentially a one-country company—and is still floundering.

SOURCE: Peter F. Drucker, "The Transnational Economy," *The Wall Street Journal,* August 25, 1987, p. 26. Reprinted by permission.

These economic objectives are typically specified for each foreign country and vary from country to country depending on the local environment, including the strength of local competitors.

Protecting market leadership

Some companies have no alternative but to seek a strong international presence if they are to protect their leadership position at home. This requires the firm to attain and hold leadership positions in the major developed markets—the United States, Western Europe, and Japan, The reason for this is that

> the developed world has become one in terms of technology. All developed countries are equally capable of doing everything, doing it well, and doing it equally fast. All developed countries also share instant information. Companies can therefore compete just about anywhere the moment economic conditions give them a substantial price advantage. In an age of sharp and violent currency fluctuations, this means a leader must be able to innovate, to produce, and to market in every area of the developed world—or else be defenseless against competition should foreign-exchange rates sharply shift.[7] (See Exhibit 11–6.)

Thus, some companies go international to defend themselves against global competitors who are constantly looking for vulnerability. Competitors can attack by reducing prices in large markets, the cost of which is subsidized by profits generated elsewhere in the world. If the defending company is solely a domestic player, it must respond by cutting price on its entire volume, while the aggressor has to do so on just part of its total sales.

---

[7]Peter F. Drucker, "The Transnational Economy," *The Wall Street Journal,* August 25, 1987, p. 26.

To prevent such attacks, or minimize their impact, a firm must have the capacity to strike back in markets where the aggressor is vulnerable. For example, in the 1970s Michelin used resources generated in Europe to attack the American market. Goodyear, a major U.S. competitor, could have responded by lowering prices; but because of its large U.S. share, it had much more to lose than Michelin. Instead, it chose to strike back in Europe, the major source of Michelin's cash flows. In so doing, Goodyear slowed Michelin's penetration of the U.S. market.[8]

Economic reasons

Companies also seek foreign sales to benefit from scale economies. This is particularly the case when such economies depend on volumes greater than those provided by the home market (e.g., production of jet airliners). Indeed, a firm may have no alternative if it is to remain cost competitive and retain its position within its industry.

Other economic reasons may also prompt a company to export. One is a comparative advantage in factor cost or quality tied to the production of a given product. Thus, the firm's location in countries possessing such advantages is critical to its world position. For example, the relatively low cost of quality labor in Japan and, more recently, in South Korea, Singapore, and Taiwan has given these countries an economic advantage over the United States in the production of certain goods (shipbuilding, textiles, consumer electronics, and certain automobile models).

Other sources of global competitive advantage include logistical economies of scale (Japan's use of specialized ocean-going bulk carriers to transport raw materials), R&D (pharmaceuticals, jet engines, computers), and marketing.[9] An example of the latter is Honda, which dominated the U.S. motorcycle market by convincing large numbers of Americans that riding motorcycles is fun and that its product was better than those of competitors. Honda did this by investing heavily in advertising, consumer promotions, trade shows, and a network of some 2,000 dealers.[10]

To compete effectively in the global arena, a company must be able to incur heavy fixed costs. Increasingly the international environment is a fixed-cost game because

> As automation has driven the labor content out of production, manufacturing has increasingly become a fixed cost activity and because the cost of developing breakthrough ideas and turning them into marketable products has skyrocketed, R&D has become a fixed cost, too. . . . In much the same way, building and maintaining a brand name is a fixed cost. In many products a

[8]Gary Hamel and C. K. Prahalad, "Do You Really Have a Global Strategy?" *Harvard Business Review,* July–August 1985, pp. 139–48. Also, see Craig M. Watson, "Counter-competition Abroad to Protect Home Markets," *Harvard Business Review,* January–February 1982, p. 40.

[9]Michael E. Porter, *Competitive Strategy* (New York: Free Press, 1980), chap. 13.

[10]Thomas Hout, Michael E. Porter, and Eileen Rudden, "How Global Companies Win Out," *Harvard Business Review,* September–October 1982, pp. 98–108.

brand name has no value at all if brand recognition falls below certain levels. . . . The past decade has seen a comparable movement toward fixed costs in sales and distribution networks.[11]

This increase in the importance of fixed costs requires that managers pay greater attention to increasing marginal contribution via expanding sales. For many companies this means entering overseas markets and/or expanding their position in them in an effort to amortize their fixed costs over a larger sales base.[12]

Other reasons

But there are still other reasons a firm may go overseas. One is the desire to service customers who are doing so. Thus, in the 1950s and 1960s, many U.S. advertising agencies set up offices in Europe to service their American clients who were exporting there. Japanese automobile companies with manufacturing facilities in the United States have encouraged some of their parts suppliers to do the same. Firms also enter overseas markets to earn foreign exchange and, in some cases, are subsidized by their governments to do so. Other reasons include countering demographic trends and disposing of excess goods. The marketing of U.S.-produced baby food to Central America because of declining U.S. birthrates is an example of this.

SELECTING TARGET MARKETS

We are concerned here with the selection of *export* target countries since ordinarily firms don't target a country for *investment* entry until after they have exported to it.[13] The investment entry decision requires the consideration of many additional factors and hence involves a more complex process. In either case, however, the selection of overseas target markets follows essentially the same procedure as for domestic markets (discussed in Chapter 5). As would be expected, targeting overseas markets is more difficult in part because of a lack of readily available information and management's bias for its own experiences and knowledge as a basis for decisions.

At the outset the firm must select the appropriate product to export—one with a strong likelihood of acceptance by the international marketplace. The profile of the ideal product would emphasize such factors as probability of market acceptance, availability from the firm's existing production facilities, ease in marketing, and profit potential. Further, the product must possess

---

[11]Kenichi Ohmae, "The Global Logic of Strategic Alliances," *Harvard Business Review,* March–April 1989, p. 146.

[12]Ibid.

[13]For more details on the process by which target markets are selected, see Franklin R. Root, *Entry Strategies for International Markets* (Lexington, Mass.: D. C. Heath and Company, 1987), chap. 2.

sufficient advantages to obtain a satisfactory market share of whatever foreign markets are targeted. This means the product has to carry a low relative price or have features that differentiate it from competitive products.

After selecting the product candidate, the firm identifies countries that are most attractive (have a high potential) and offer strong business advantages relative to competition. This requires a procedure that includes a matrix using the two summary ratings of market attractiveness and business strengths as a way of ranking target markets.

PRODUCT STRENGTH VERSUS GEOGRAPHIC EXPANSION

For many companies, the targeting problem must consider the trade-offs between product strength (share within country) and geographic expansion.[14] The decline of mobility barriers (e.g., in Europe) while offering opportunities for geographic expansion, presents greater competitive threats. At the corporate level, the firm manages a portfolio of products and geographic markets. Its main axes of **product strength** (share within country) and **geographic coverage** (number and size of country) must be managed in a balanced way. If the firm invests too much in attempting to gain product strength, it will miss some international opportunities; if it invests too much in geographic expansion, it may underinvest in products and weaken its competitive position.

The emphasis placed on developing product strength versus geographic coverage depends on the firm's current position relative to competition. Gogel and Larréché suggest the use of an International Competitive Posture Matrix with the two dimensions of product strength and geographic coverage as a way of plotting competitors, which are categorized in four groups—kings, barons, crusaders, and commoners—as follows:

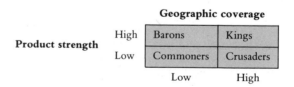

Kings are companies in the strongest position with both wide geographic coverage and a strong product portfolio. If they selectively expand the latter through internal development or acquisition, kings can obtain important leverage because of their geographic coverage. *Barons* have a strong position

---

[14]This section is based on Robert Gogel and Jean-Claude Larréché, "The Battlefield for 1992: Product Strength and Geographic Coverage," *European Management Journal* 7, no. 2 (1989) pp. 132–40.

in a limited number of countries and thus can expand in other countries or in new product areas. They are attractive as a possible acquisition.

Crusaders have geographic coverage but lack consistently strong product positions. They are highly vulnerable to an increasing level of competition. Their challenge is to consolidate their product position through internal development and/or acquisition or even to disinvest in order to focus on a narrower product portfolio. *Commoners* have a relatively weak position in both geographic coverage and product strength. They have benefited from strong mobility barriers and hence are most vulnerable to decreasing barriers. Before expanding geographically, commoners must strengthen their product positions by divesting to build share of selected products or by developing niche strategies.

Product strength and geographic coverage compete for resources but also support each other. Each provides a leveraging effect on the other. But product strength typically deserves the highest priority, for it is not only the basis for expansion but the best defense against increasing competition.

GLOBAL VERSUS NATIONAL MARKETING STRATEGIES

Firms can use two major kinds of marketing strategies to compete in the international arena—global and national.[15] Global strategy is concerned with opportunities and threats on a world basis. Hence, a firm adopting a global strategy must develop a set of competitive strengths that will enable it to compete successfully against other international firms. These strengths include (1) scale effects that reduce unit costs below those of national firms; (2) the ability to transfer ideas, experience, and know-how from one country to another; (3) global recognition of brand names and a reputation for quality that makes it easier to introduce new products; (4) the ability to shift resources across countries to reduce risks; and (5) access to such place economies as low-cost labor and raw materials.

National strategies, in contrast, are based on a more localized presence—that is, on the firm's operations in a defined national environment. The firm's success lies in its national performance, or its market share. National strategies are not undertaken solely by local companies. Multinationals may permit their subsidiaries considerable freedom in formulating their strategies. In other situations, a company's strategy may center primarily on the home market while viewing overseas operations as secondary.

Global strategies

The success of a global strategy depends largely on the extent to which the product—and to a lesser extent the marketing program—can be standardized

---

[15]This section is based in part on James C. Leontiades, *Multinational Corporate Strategy* (Lexington, Mass.: D. C. Heath and Company, 1985), chap. 5.

across countries. Levitt and, more recently, Ohmae have been articulate advocates for what they refer to as a *standardization strategy*.[16] Both see standardization as the wave of the future because of the growing worldwide homogenization of needs, which leads to substantial economies of scale and results in lower prices.

The growing convergence of consumer needs and preferences is attributed to the influences of mass communications, including the viewing of the same TV programs, live broadcasts, and news programs. Ohmae refers to this as the "California-ization of needs." Regardless of their nationality, consumers in western Europe, Japan, and the United States "increasingly receive the same information, seek the same kinds of lifestyles, and desire the same kinds of products. They all want the best products available at the lowest prices possible. Everybody, in a sense, wants to live—and shop—in California."[17]

The nature of the product, or the extent to which it can be standardized, is a major factor in a firm's decision to adopt a global strategy. As might be expected, industrial goods lend themselves more to a global strategy than do consumer goods. This is especially the case with high-tech products such as computers, airplanes, medical electronic equipment, and robotics.

Durable consumer goods, (e.g., TVs, VCRs, cameras, and automobiles) offer a better opportunity for standardization than nondurables, which are more apt to be affected by the local culture. Food, clothing, personal-care items, household cleaners, and confections, for example, traditionally have not been considered good candidates for a global (standardization) strategy. But even here there is evidence that tastes are becoming more common across countries:

> Coffee is sneaking up on tea as a favorite drink in Japan, and U.S.-style frozen dinners have become a hit in Europe. While these products have to be fine-tuned to local tastes, the companies that win the global battle will be those that can support costly advertising and R&D—and get maximum mileage from their brands—by selling similar products worldwide.[18]

Standardization is also more feasible when the product can be positioned in overseas markets the same way it is in the home market. For example, Tang was positioned as an orange juice substitute in the United States, but this was not possible in France, where orange juice is not considered a part of the breakfast meal.[19]

---

[16]Theodore Levitt, "The Globalization of Marketing," *Harvard Business Review*, May–June 1983, pp. 92–102; and Kenichi Ohmae, "The Global Logic of Strategic Alliances," *Harvard Business Review*, March–April 1989, pp. 143–52.

[17]Ohmae, "The Global Logic of Strategic Alliances," p. 144.

[18]Shawn Tully, "Nestlé Shows How to Gobble Markets," *Fortune*, January 16, 1989, p. 74.

[19]Subhash C. Jain, "Standardization of International Marketing Strategy," *Journal of Marketing*, January 1989, p. 73.

Global high-share versus global niche strategies

Leontiades notes that there are two major types of global strategy—those involving high market share and those concerned with a global niche. Such firms as Sony, Honda, Ford, IBM, Electrolux, and SKF pursue a high-share strategy. Such a strategy is characterized by:

1. A drive for a strong international market-share position.
2. Products with a high degree of international standardization.
3. A marketing program—especially price, product line, and advertising—geared to the mass market.
4. Large expenditures on design and R&D relative to the industry's norm. Because of the large volume of sales, these costs on a unit basis are low.
5. The use of regional production facilities or a rationalized global network designed to reduce logistics costs.

These characteristics, individually and collectively, make it difficult for firms in the same industry who use a national strategy to compete. As noted earlier in this chapter, the growing effectiveness of firms adopting a global strategy has had a strong impact on many industry structures. For example, the U.S. television industry has been decimated by Japanese firms that have adopted a high-share global strategy.

Because of the enormous resources required to implement a high-share global strategy, many firms opt for some type of specialization, focusing on a global niche. Such strategies can take many forms, including specialization by technology (genetic engineering), product (low-cost motor cars), geography (exporting only to England), market segment (designer apparel), and stage of production (components versus final assembly).

Global niche strategies are characterized by a product line that is relatively insensitive to price competition, avoids direct competition with global high-share competitors, uses alliances to reduce research costs, is capable of entering new markets, has a narrow product-market scope, and takes advantage of possible tie-ins with products offered by large competitors (such as equipment that is plug-compatible with IBM computers). An example is the joint venture purchase by General Mills and Nestlés of a larger U.K. breakfast cereal operation to obtain entry into one of the world's biggest cereal-eating countries, Great Britain. Subsequently, the joint venture decided to build the U.K. acquisition's shredded-wheat business versus importing a General Mills product, which would be a new-market entry. The venture wanted to build growth with a local product, then expand its operations there.[20]

---

[20]Richard Gibson, "Cereal Venture Is Planning Honey of a Battle in Europe," *The Wall Street Journal,* November 14, 1990, p. B1.

National strategies

A national strategy—sometimes called a *localization* strategy—is based on the premise that products and programs must be adapted to the needs and wants of individual countries because of their environmental, especially cultural, differences. Critics of the global-type strategies argue that because most marketing activities are situation specific, marketing programs—especially advertising—cannot be sufficiently standardized to gain a competitive advantage in the form of lower costs.[21] P&G adjusts its products and marketing programs to country-specific markets whenever it is expedient to do so.

National high-share versus national niche strategies

Companies adopting a national high-share strategy must achieve high volume and low relative costs to be successful. Even so, the firm remains vulnerable to companies following a similar strategy at the global level. To protect themselves, national companies must, whenever possible:

1. Exploit and do everything possible to maintain existing legal trade barriers, especially tariffs and quotas.
2. Enhance their ability to respond to consumer preferences, especially regarding certain product features.
3. Lobby aggressively for the continuance of government purchasing arrangements that give preferences to national companies.
4. Provide a fast response to changes in local conditions, especially in the form of new or modified products.

National niche strategies are the same as global niche strategies except they apply at the national or local level. They seek to take advantage of some form of specialization in a narrow market segment to defend against both national and global competitors. Typically, the target market is too small to be of interest to the global competitor and perhaps even to large national companies.

Using both global and national strategies

Many companies use a combination of global and national strategies. Some firms use a global strategy in parts of the world while pursuing a national strategy elsewhere because some countries and some products are more receptive to global strategies than others. Global strategies are directed at

> those national product-markets that are large and have low barriers to foreign products and companies. They are also likely to comprise the center of world demand, particularly in the newer, more technologically intensive products.

[21]Joanne Lipman, "Marketeers Sour on Global Sales Pitch Harvard Guru Makes," *The Wall Street Journal,* May 12, 1988, p. 1.

For example, Japan, the United States, and the member countries of the European community account for over 75 percent of total world demand for integrated circuits. Securing a position as a global competitor will require active participation in one, and very likely more than one, of these national markets.[22]

Companies adopting global strategies are not likely to target seriously countries with high barriers and small national product-markets. However, given the long-term trend in declining trade barriers coupled with economic growth, more companies will likely adopt global strategies.

Much the same reasoning for the use of a mix of global and national strategies applies to adopting a standardized or a localized marketing program. It does not have to be an either/or proposition—there can be degrees of standardization just as there can be degrees of localization. What is important is management's global orientation, which reflects itself in

> a marketing plan that strives for standardization whenever it is cost and culturally effective. This might mean a company's global marketing plan has a standardized product but country-specific advertising or a standardized theme in all countries with country or cultural-specific appeals. . . . In other words . . . where feasible in the marketing mix, efficiencies of standardization are sought. Whenever cultural uniqueness dictates the need for adaptation of the product, its image, and so on, it is accommodated.[23]

In the final analysis, if a firm's upper-level managers are not strongly oriented toward doing business on a global basis, a nationalized strategy is most apt to emerge. This is particularly the case when the headquarters/subsidiary relationship is loosely defined. The more a firm delegates decision making, the less likely it will adopt a global strategy. Such delegation is most apt to occur with decisions pertaining to price, advertising, and channels of distribution.

MARKET ENTRY STRATEGIES

Once a firm decides to sell its goods in a particular country, it must decide which entry strategy to use.[24] A company can enter a foreign country in three major ways. One is to export goods manufactured outside the target country. A second is to transfer the technology and skills necessary to produce and market the goods to an organization in the foreign country through licensing

[22]Leontiades, *Multinational Corporate Strategy*, p. 57.

[23]Philip R. Cateora, *International Marketing*, 7th ed., (Homewood, Ill.: Richard D. Irwin, 1990), chap. 4.

[24]This section is based on Franklin R. Root, *Entry Strategy for International Markets* (Lexington, Mass.: D.C. Heath and Company, 1987), chaps. 1, 2, 3, and 5; and David A. Aaker, *Strategic Market Management* (New York: John Wiley & Sons, 1988), chap. 16.

EXHIBIT 11–7
Classification of Major Entry Modes

Export entry modes
    Indirect
    Direct agent/distributor
Contractual entry modes
Licensing	Management contracts
Franchising	Turkey construction contracts
Technical agreements	Contract manufacture
Service contracts	Coproduction agreements

Investment entry modes
    Sole venture: new establishment
    Sole venture: acquisition
    Joint venture: new establishment acquisition

SOURCE: Adapted from Franklin R. Root, *Entry Strategies for International Markets* (Lexington, Mass.: D. C. Heath & Company, 1987), p. 6.

or other contractual agreements. Finally a firm might transfer manufacturing and marketing resources through direct investment in a foreign country. Since services cannot be produced independently of consumption, a service company must use the second or third way to enter a foreign country. These three types of entry break down into a number of different modes, as shown in Exhibit 11–7.

Exporting

Exporting is the simplest way to enter a foreign market because it involves the least commitment and risk. Manufacturing remains in the home country, and the firm may not even modify the product for export. Export may be **passive** and sporadic, mainly involving the firm's surpluses, or **active,** with regular shipments to one or more countries.

Exporting can be direct or indirect. **Indirect exporting** involves less investment and risk than any other strategy, since the firm makes no investment in an overseas salesforce; rather, it relies on the expertise of domestic international middlemen: **export merchants,** who buy the product and sell it overseas for their own account; **export agents,** who sell on a commission basis; and **cooperative organizations,** which export for several producers, especially those selling farm products.

Sellers begin using **direct exporting** when they have enough business abroad to warrant investing in marketing activities. Direct exporting involves using foreign-based distributors/agents or setting up operating units in the foreign country in the form of branches or subsidiaries. (See Exhibit 11–8 for an example.) Exporting is a viable entry strategy for a small firm with limited resources or under conditions of considerable political risk, a small foreign market, or where there is little or no political pressure to manufacture locally.

EXHIBIT 11-8

Selling Athletic Socks to the Japanese

Price apart, the goods most likely to be warmly received by foreigners are those considered distinctive for their innovation, quality, or technology. But as Thorneburg Hosiery discovered, even humble socks can meet such criteria. The $10 million company in Statesville, North Carolina, makes a line of athletic socks designed and padded for specific sports such as tennis and jogging. Thorneburg has been exporting to Canada since 1983, but in 1987 it launched an all-out effort to get its socks abroad.

After resolving to target Europe and the Far East, President Lynn Moretz flew to Munich for the August sporting goods trade show. Like many exporters starting out, Thorneburg chose to rely on established distribution channels. Moretz set up a booth, hung up his socks, and began chatting with distributors. The Japanese showed particular enthusiasm for the company's cushiony footwear, turning the socks inside out to examine the stitching. Before long, five Japanese distributors were competing to represent the product. Negotiations took a relatively brief four months. In January, the company awarded the contract to a Swiss-owned Japanese distributor, Liebermann Waelchli, after being won over by a marketing plan featuring a product giveaway. Moretz raves about the agreement: "More than 125 million people on an island just a bit bigger than the state of North Carolina. . . . You can almost whisper the name of your product and pretty soon everybody knows it." With a $300,000 initial order on the books, Moretz anticipated sales in Japan alone to exceed $1 million in the first year.

SOURCE: Christopher Knowlton, "The New Export Entrepreneurs," *Fortune,* June 6, 1988, pp. 90–91. © 1988 The Time Inc. Magazine Company. All rights reserved.

Contractual entry modes

Nonequity contractual arrangements involve the transfer of technology and/or human skills to an entity in a foreign country. In **licensing** arrangements, a firm offers the right to use its intangible assets (technology, know-how, patents, company name, trademarks) in exchange for royalties or some other form of payment. Licensing is less flexible than exporting and a firm has less control over a licensee than over its own exporting or manufacturing abroad. Licensing is particularly appropriate, however, when the market is unstable and the licensing firm would have financial and marketing problems in penetrating the foreign market.

Franchising is similar to but different than licensing, especially in motivation, services rendered, and duration. It grants the right to use the company's name, trademarks, and technology. Also, the franchisee typically receives help in setting up the franchise, its organizational structure, and its marketing. Franchising has been an attractive way for U.S. firms, especially service firms, to penetrate foreign markets at low cost and to couple their skills with local knowledge and entrepreneurial spirit.

By the end of 1989, some 450 American franchisors were operating overseas, up 37 percent over five years ago.[25] Fast-food companies have been

[25]Richard Kirkland, Jr., "The Bright Future of Service Exports," *Fortune,* June 8, 1987, p. 32. Also, see Joann S. Lubin, "For U.S. Franchisers, a Common Tongue Isn't a Guarantee of Success in the U.K.," *The Wall Street Journal,* August 16, 1988, p. 18.

especially aggressive globally. For example, McDonald's, Pizza Hut, Burger King, and Kentucky Fried Chicken have substantial overseas investments. ServiceMaster launched over 500 home-cleaning franchises in Japan, in addition to winning contracts to do the housekeeping for 40 hospitals.[26]

Other contractual entry modes have increased in prominence in recent years, especially with developing and communist countries. **Contract manufacturing** is similar to licensing and involves sourcing a product from a manufacturer located in a foreign country for sale there or elsewhere. It is most attractive when the local market is small, export entry is blocked, and a quality licensee is not available.

A **turnkey construction contract** requires that the contractor make the project operational (up and running) before releasing it to the owner or, in some cases, provide services (such as worker training) after the project is completed. Such contracts involve considerable risks. **Management contracts** give a company the right to manage the day-to-day operations of a local company. They are used primarily in conjunction with a turnkey operation or a joint venture agreement.

Industrial cooperation agreements (ICAs) include all kinds of contract arrangements between a Western company and an organization in a communist country. The most common types of ICAs are licensing technical assistance agreements and turnkey projects. Another type of ICA is **coproduction,** where a Western company provides technology know-how and components in return for a share of the output that it agrees to market in the West. ICA agreements often call for the Western company to accept payment in the form of locally produced goods. This is referred to as **countertrade** and may comprise as much as 10 percent of all world trade. It is discussed under the marketing-mix section later in this chapter.

ICA agreements in the form of joint ventures are becoming more common in the Soviet Union. By mid-1989, over 350 joint ventures had been signed between Russia and Western companies. Since then, however, the number has slumped badly due to uncertainty about the future of the Soviet economy.[27]

Investment overseas

Firms can enter overseas markets through joint ventures or sole ownership. **Joint venture** involves an ownership arrangement between, say, a U.S. firm and one in the host country to produce and/or market goods in a foreign market. The extent of ownership for the U.S. firm can vary from small to 50 percent. Joint ventures have more risk and less flexibility than either exporting or licensing. Xerox provides an excellent example of a successful joint venture strategy. In the 1950s, the then small Haloid-Xerox Company formed a 50 percent joint venture with Rank in the U.K. Named Rank

---

[26]Michael Selz, "Overseeing Overseas: Franchisers Go Abroad," *The Wall Street Journal,* November 21, 1989, p. B1.

[27]Ann Reilly Dowd, "U.S. Business Leery of Soviet Trade," *Fortune,* July 2, 1990, pp. 11, 12.

Xerox, it was to sell copiers worldwide except in the United States and Canada. In 1962, Rank Xerox entered into a 50 percent partnership with Fuji to sell copiers in the Far East. Thus, the small Haloid-Xerox Company was able to secure international coverage much faster than it could have if it relied on its own resources.

In recent years, joint ventures have become increasingly popular as a way to avoid quotas and import taxes and to satisfy government demands of local production. For example, Brazil has an 85 percent local content requirement for automobile production. Joint ventures also have the advantage of sharing the investment costs and gaining local marketing expertise.

Increasingly, globalization demands alliances, a form of joint venture. They are the only way most companies have of servicing companies in the triad of the United States, Western Europe, and Japan because of the almost prohibitive cost of maintaining superiority in the several technologies most products require, the change from a variable cost to a fixed-cost environment, and the increasing number of giant competitors.[28] The growing convergence of consumer needs facilitates these arrangements. American companies, in their search for new markets and technology, formed over 2,000 alliances in the 1980s with European countries alone.[29] Exhibit 11–9 gives an example of an alliance between a U.S. and a Japanese company.

Marketers encounter a number of problems in their joint ventures, as, for example, when changes in one partner's product-market portfolio make the joint venture less attractive to the other. The lack of flexibility may be especially difficult if one partner later wants to adopt a global strategy of direct investment to control all manufacturing and marketing. If the results of a joint venture disappoint one of the parties, its commitment to making the venture successful may weaken. For example, when Mitsubishi became disappointed in the sales of its cars through Chrysler dealers, it set up its own dealers to handle sales of its other models in the United States.

A **sole ownership** investment entry strategy involves setting up a production subsidiary in a foreign country. Ordinarily, the subsidiary makes its own operating decisions, with the parent company providing the finances, R&D, product specifications, and production technology. Direct investment usually allows the parent company to retain total control of the overseas operation and avoids the problems of shared management and loss of flexibility. Firms using a direct investment strategy extensively include General Motors, Procter & Gamble (as we have already noted), General Foods, Hewlett-Packard, and General Electric. Many of the same reasons for using joint ventures apply to direct investments.

High risks can be associated with direct investment. Such risks are classified as *macro,* which affect the total country, and *micro,* which affect only some industries. Macro risks include changes in the political and economic environments ranging from armed revolution (as in Iran) to high inflation (as in

[28]Ohmae, "The Global Logic of Strategic Alliances," pp. 144–48.
[29]Louis Kraar, "Your Rivals Can Be Your Allies," *Fortune,* March 27, 1989, p. 61.

EXHIBIT 11-9
The Ford and Mazda Alliance

The relationship with Mazda, formed two decades ago when Ford felt the need for a Japanese connection after it was caught napping by that country's auto blitz, is more fruitful than ever. Among other things, the two companies make components and design cars for each other. Mazda created the Mercury Tracer, which Ford assembles in Mexico, and the Ford Probe, which Mazda built in Flat Rock, Michigan. Reversing roles, Ford will supply Mazda with a sporty compact utility vehicle to sell in North America in the next few years.

Since 1985, the two companies have been engaged in the biggest joint venture in Detroit's history—the 1991 Ford Escort. Mazda engineered the inside of the car while Ford styled the outside. The two companies collaborated so well that the Escort will arrive on time and within its $2 billion budget and may, indeed, be the global car.

This partnership also gives Ford extra thrust in fast-growing Asian markets, where the U.S. automaker's line includes its own versions of Mazdas. Moreover, Mazda brought Ford into South Korea. . . . Already the South Koreans are among the lowest-cost producers of small cars, including the Ford Festiva sold in this country. That model comes from Kia Motors, a Korean automaker long associated with Mazda and now 10-percent-owned by Ford. In the future, Kia may be able to develop new products that Ford's own engineers are too busy to handle and provide a way into the elusive China market.

SOURCE: Louis Kraar, "Your Rivals Can Be Your Allies," *Fortune*, March 27, 1989, p. 67; and James B. Treece and Amy Borus, "How Ford and Mazda Shared the Driver's Seat," *Business Week*, March 26, 1990, p. 94.

Argentina). A change in market attractiveness is an example of micro risk. Despite these risks, direct investments are accelerating. Executives everywhere have concluded that to capture customers who demand constant innovation and rapid, flexible response, they must make major overseas investments.

Sequential strategies

A company can follow a number of routes or paths in becoming a worldwide marketer.[30] By *route* we mean the order in which the firm enters foreign markets. Japanese companies provide an illustration of different global expansion paths. The most common expansion route involves moving from Japan to developing countries to developed countries. They used this path, for example, with automobiles (Toyota), consumer electronics (National), watches (Seiko), cameras (Minolta), and home appliances, steel, and petrochemicals. This routing reduced manufacturing costs and enabled them to gain marketing experience. In penetrating the U.S. market, the Japanese obtained further economies of scale and gained recognition for their products, which would make penetration of European markets easier.

---

[30]The contents of this section derive largely from Somkid Jatusripitak, Liam Fahey, and Philip Kotler, "Strategic Global Marketing: Lessons from the Japanese," *Columbia Journal of World Business,* Spring 1985, pp. 47–53.

This sequential strategy succeeded: by the early 1970s, 60 percent of Japanese exports went to developed countries—more than half to the United States. Japanese motorcycles dominate Europe, as do its watches and cameras. Its cars have been able to gain a respectable share in most European countries.

A second type of *expansion path* has been used primarily for high-tech products such as computers and semiconductors. For the Japanese it consists of first securing their home market and then targeting developed countries. Japan largely ignored developing countries in this strategy because of their small demand for high-tech products. When demand increased to a point where developing countries became "interesting," Japanese producers quickly entered and established strong market positions using price cuts of up to 50 percent.

INTERNATIONAL MARKETING MIX

Here again the major question is, To what extent can firms standardize the elements of the marketing plan? Standardization is greatest for product features, branding, and packaging because of the substantial savings in manufacturing costs. One study involving the marketing of consumer package goods to lesser developed countries showed that while changes relating to such factors as measurement units, labeling, and usage instructions were relatively common, over two-thirds of all products retained their physical features.[31] Firms also use similar distribution channels whenever possible to capitalize on the experience gained in serving a particular channel system.

Pricing tends to be localized because of differences in both manufacturing and marketing costs, taxes, and the prices of competitive products. Cultural and language differences frequently require firms to adapt advertising messages to local conditions. Media allocations vary substantially among countries because of vast differences in media availability and, in the case of print media, the quality of reproduction.

Product strategy

Regardless of whether a company adopts a standardized or a localized international marketing strategy for its products, it must make sure the products are of the highest quality, since "the pursuit of quality is no longer voluntary. If U.S. industry expects to win . . . more customers and market share, it has no choice but to improve its products. For the customer, quality is irresistible. For industry, it is essential."[32]

---

[31]J. S. Hill and R. R. Still, "Adapting Products to LDC Tastes," *Harvard Business Review,* March–April 1984, pp. 92–101.

[32]Christopher Knowlton, "What America Makes Best," *Fortune,* March 28, 1988, p. 53. This article lists the 100 products that America makes best.

A company has three major product options, based on the extent to which it modifies the product's physical dimensions. These are:

1. *Market the same product to all countries (a "world" product).*   This strategy requires that the physical product sold in each country be the same except for labeling and the language used in the product manuals. It assumes customer needs are essentially the same across national boundaries or can be made the same by offering a quality product at a relatively low price resulting from scale effects. This strategy can be successful when products are not culture-sensitive and economies of scale are significant (e.g., jet aircraft engines, basic steel, chemicals, plastics, and memory chips).

2. *Adapt the product to local conditions.*   This strategy keeps the physical product essentially the same. Only modifications that represent a small percentage of total costs are permitted, such as changes in voltage, packaging, and color. Examples include computers, copiers, over-the-road construction equipment, cars, calculators, and motorcycles. P&G reformulated its Cheer detergent in Japan to counter differences in the way they wash clothes.

3. *Develop a country-specific product.*   In this situation, the physical product is substantially altered (affects a significant part of total costs) across countries or groups of countries. Such a strategy is common with packaged food and personal-care items.

Producing a world product is not easy; it requires setting standards that reflect the conditions under which the product is used. The standards developed from U.S.-use conditions may not produce a product acceptable to the rest of the world; hence the need for marketing research. (For an example of adapting a product to the environments of target markets, see Exhibit 11–10.)

Market segmentation can be used to facilitate the sale of physically similar products worldwide. This can be accomplished in two ways. The first involves selling to much the same segment in each country—for example, the high-income segment for expensive cars. A second approach calls for targeting diverse groups across countries using essentially the same physical product. Thus, the Canon AE-1 camera targeted young replacement buyers in Japan, upscale first-time buyers of this type of camera in the United States, and older and more knowledgeable replacement buyers in Germany. Once these segments were identified, Canon proceeded to develop a marketing program for each country.[33]

Pricing

Companies find it difficult to adopt a standardized pricing strategy across countries because of fluctuating exchange rates; differences between countries

---

[33]Based on Keegan, *Global Marketing Management,* chap. 13.

EXHIBIT 11–10
Boeing's Rescue of the 737

Boeing designed its 737 to compete with McDonnell Douglas's DC-9; but its late entry into the market was not altogether successful. In the mid-70s the company was about to phase the 737 out but decided to give it one more chance. Boeing turned to engineer Bob Norton to save the plane. Norton decided to target the Mideast, Africa, and South America. This required adapting the 737 to the aviation environment of the Third World.

The major problems were that the runways in developing countries were too short and too soft because they were asphalt rather than cement, and pilots came in too hard, causing more wear and tear on the planes. Boeing redesigned the wings to permit shorter landings, added thrust to the engines for quicker takeoffs, redesigned the landing gear, and used low-pressure tires to make the plane stick to the ground when it touched down. Recently the Boeing 737 became the best-selling commercial jet in history.

SOURCE: Condensed from Andrew Kupfer, "How to Be a Global Manager," *Fortune*, March 14, 1988, p. 52. © The Time Inc. Magazine Company. All rights reserved.

in costs, competition, and demand; conflicting governmental tax policies plus governmental controls (such as dumping and price ceilings); and other factors such as transportation costs, differences in channels of distribution, and global buyers who demand equal price treatment regardless of location. Much also depends on the firm's objective in its various markets—for example, penetration pricing versus market holding.

Countertrade transactions have increased in importance in recent years. Basically, the four types of countertrade are *barter, compensation packages, counterpurchase, and buy-backs.*[34] **Barter** involves a direct exchange of goods between two or more parties. The seller must be able to sell the bartered goods at a price sufficient to compensate for those traded to the other party. An example is trading Yugoslavian hams for commercial aircraft. **Compensation packages** involve some combination of products and cash, like selling machine tools to Yugoslavia and getting 25 percent cash and the remainder in work shoes.

Counterpurchase, the most popular form of countertrade, involves two contracts. First, the seller agrees to sell a product at a fixed price for cash, conditional on the seller agreeing to buy the goods from the buyer over some future period of time for all or part of the sale. The second condition gives the seller time to sell the goods and thus makes this transaction preferable over barter. A **buy-back agreement** involves selling products used to produce other goods (e.g., a production system). The seller agrees to buy a certain amount of the output, and this is applied as a partial payment to the sale amount.

[34]Stephen S. Cohen and John Zysman, "Counter-trade, Offsets, Barter, and Buybacks," *California Management Review*, Winter 1886, pp. 41–56.

Channels

Two major types of international channel alternatives are available to a domestic producer.[35] The first is the use of domestic middlemen who provide marketing services from their domestic base. They are convenient to use because of their proximity, but suffer from their lack of knowledge about a foreign market and their inability to provide the kinds of representation offered by foreign-based middlemen.

Foreign middlemen

In contrast to dealing with domestic middlemen, a manufacturer may decide to deal directly with middlemen in foreign countries, which shortens the channel and brings the manufacturer closer to the market. A major problem is that because of their distance, foreign middlemen are difficult to control.

The functions of both foreign agents and merchant middlemen are similar to those of American middlemen. There is, however, considerable variation among foreign middlemen across countries as to how well they perform various functions. Further, in some countries (particularly those in Southeast Asia), a small number of large, powerful middlemen dominate trade. This means a manufacturer must either transfer control of its product to such middlemen or set up its own system.

Retail structures in foreign countries vary tremendously because of differences in the cultural, economic, and political environments. European retailing seems to be following a path similar to that pioneered by the United States in store size, self-service, discounting, automation, and direct marketing. Even so, the average size store is still small by U.S. standards, which makes it difficult to sell to them directly. Japanese "papa-mama" stores control some 56 percent of Japan's retail sales (U.S. mom-and-pops account for 3 percent). They keep prices high, limit selection, and minimize their purchases of foreign goods.[36]

Channel problems

Although the problems encountered by a manufacturer in establishing and maintaining a channel system overseas are similar to those experienced domestically, there are some important differences.

1. The kind of channel needed may not be available because of the country's low level of economic development (such as lack of refrigeration) or the presence of only state-controlled middlemen.

---

[35]This section and the next have benefited from Cateora, *International Marketing,* chap. 17; and Louis W. Stern and Adel I. El-Ansary, *Marketing Channels* (Englewood Cliffs, N.J.: Prentice Hall, 1988), chaps. 12, 14.

[36]Damon Darlen, " 'Papa-mama' Stores in Japan Wield Power to Hold Back Imports," *The Wall Street Journal,* April 14, 1988, p. 1.

2. Existing middlemen have already been appropriated by other manufacturers (particularly local ones) via various arrangements, including financial, and the exclusive use of private labels. This has often been the case with Japan.

3. A channel, once set up, may be difficult to change because of strong barriers to the termination of a relationship. In some countries, such as Norway, it is illegal to do so without evidence of incompetency. In some of the lesser-developed countries, terminating a powerful middleman can result in reprisals, including being barred from the marketplace.

4. Control is yet another problem. An international marketer will almost always use a variety of channel systems to penetrate and service its various markets, no two of which are identical. The problems of controlling this varied set of distribution systems are so numerous that many companies use a contractual entry mode (licensing or franchising) whenever possible to facilitate control.

Despite these problems, international middlemen have not only increased in number, they have also become more adept at fulfilling their functions. Even so, the establishment and maintenance of an effective and efficient overseas distribution network remains one of the biggest challenges the international marketer faces.

Promotion

Advertising is extremely difficult to standardize across countries primarily because prospective consumers for a given product live in very different social, economic, and political environments. Exhibit 11–11 enumerates how the different types of environments affect promotion. Standardization is particularly difficult with message construction, where differences in product knowledge, benefit expectations, buying motives, and languages make the use of a standardized message across countries almost impossible. Even when the primary benefits remain intact across national boundaries, language differences can make the transferability of an advertising message difficult.

Traditional beliefs and contemporary behavior patterns inhibit message transferability. In some cases, the target audience may even be ignorant of a product's benefits. For example, Polaroid's Swinger, an inexpensive camera and the company's first entry into France, experienced difficulty because the concept of instant photography was unknown there. Further barriers to transferring the creative presentation intact include culture (response to humor based on exaggeration), competitive conditions (strong versus weak competitors), and execution (poor color reproduction in print ads). Even Coca-Cola, which has been cited as a prime example of standardized advertising, is now using considerable local flavor in its worldwide campaign.[37]

---

[37]Julie Skeer Hill and Joseph M. Winski, "Good-bye Global Ads," *Advertising Age,* November 16, 1987, p. 22.

EXHIBIT 11–11
How Different Kinds of Environments Affect Promotion across Countries

Type of environment	Examples of effect
Social	Languages, culture, religion, and lifestyles vary substantially across most countries. For example, because attitudes differ regarding cleanliness, Gillette promotes its razors, deodorants, and other men's grooming products differently in the developing countries than in the United States.
Economic	Because of substantial variations in standards of living across countries as well as the distribution of wealth within countries, demand for a particular product varies, as does the way a product is perceived. For example, cameras are considered a reasonably standard item in developed countries. Not so in the developing countries, however.
Political	Some countries prevent the importation of some U.S. products under any condition. Political control also determines what products can be advertised (pharmaceuticals, alcohol, airlines, and candy are forbidden in some Arabic countries); what media can be used (no TV advertising is permitted in Scandinavia); and what can be said about products (comparative advertising is not allowed in Germany).

Another difficulty in standardizing advertising has to do with the media. Although much the same media types exist around the world, the extent to which prospective consumers are exposed to each type varies considerably. Thus, while most Americans, British, and Europeans own TVs, such is not the case in the developing countries, and even when it is, the media's availability may be severely restricted. Italy, for example, limits a TV commercial to 10 showings a year with no two exposures within a 10-day period. West Germany severely limits the amount of TV advertising time. And even though the volume of sales promotions is increasing in Europe, there is still a large number of national regulations that stunt the growth of Pan-European promotions. It's not yet clear whether the situation will be reversed when the EEC's trade barriers fall in 1992.[38] Billboards and movies are important media in the developing countries where high illiteracy exists.

EXPORTING SERVICES

America is the world's largest exporter of private services—$113.9 billion in 1989 versus imports of $85.7 for a surplus of $28.2 billion. It is also the world's largest importer of services. Most forecasters expect both the exports and imports of services to increase dramatically during the 1990s. America's strengths in selling private services abroad lie largely in international trans-

---

[38]David Murrow, "Europe Remains Myriad Bag," *Advertising Age,* August 7, 1989, p. 45.

port (travel, passenger fares, freight, port service), which has benefited from
the weak dollar, thereby encouraging foreign travel in the United States; royalties and license fees, which are an important means of transferring technology and marketing expertise (e.g., franchises); and management skills
relating to such industries as education, health care, financial services, insurance, telecommunications, and business, professional, and technical services
(e.g., advertising, computer and data-processing services, legal, engineering,
and management).[39]

McDonald's and other U.S. franchisors have expanded overseas at an ever-
increasing rate. International sales now account for about 30 percent of
McDonald's total revenues from over 2,000 units located around the world,
including a wildly successful one in Moscow. [40] Direct mail, telephone marketing, marketing research, advertising, and head-hunting are other kinds of
services American firms export successfully. International growth in financial
services has been extensive, but Americans are experiencing difficulties here
because four of the world's largest banks and four of the six largest securities
houses are Japanese.[41]

American service firms are experiencing increased competition. The Japanese, having passed us in the international lending area, are now moving
aggressively into construction, hotels, and travel services. European service
companies are acquiring more and more U.S. companies: for example, U.K.-
based Blue Arrow PLC acquired Manpower, Inc. (Milwaukee, Wisconsin), a
leading supplier of temporary help.

SUMMARY

International marketing has become increasingly important to U.S. firms in
recent years. International sales provide an important source of profits, but
they are also critical for some firms' survival because of their impact on both
scale effects and the ability to retaliate against competitive attacks without
lowering profits drastically in the home market. International marketing follows many of the same principles as domestic marketing. There are, however,
major differences between countries and the development of strategy options
and marketing programs built on these differences.

In considering which foreign markets to target, a firm must analyze each
country's physical, legal, economic, political, cultural, competitive, and infrastructure environments. Legal barriers come in a variety of forms, including
tariffs and embargoes. There are also a variety of indirect legal barriers. The
other environments affect demand as well as targeting, product positioning,
and the development of marketing programs. The latter depends heavily on

[39]Anthony J. Dilullo and Obie G. Whichard, "U.S. International Sales and Purchases of Services," *Survey of Current Business,* September 1990, pp. 57–72.
[40]Kirkland, "Entering a New Age," pp. 32–38.
[41]Ibid.

the major marketing-mix elements, all of which are strongly affected by the various environments.

Reasons for entering into overseas markets include economies of scale that extend beyond the size of the home market, defending against a global competitor, and satisfying customers going international. International trade strategies revolve for the most part around either localization or standardization. The extent to which a firm opts for one or the other strategy depends heavily on the product involved. Products that enjoy strong experience effects and are not highly culture-bound are candidates for standardized marketing. Achieving a commanding world competitive position involves low-cost manufacturing and a well-integrated distribution system.

Market entry strategies include exporting, both direct and indirect; contractual, including licensing, franchising, and a variety of other types of agreements; and investment, which can be via joint or sole venture. Companies can mix these to service different overseas markets.

As in the formulation of an international strategy, the major question regarding the international marketing mix is, To what extent can it be standardized across countries? Standardization is greatest in product features, branding, and packaging because of manufacturing scale effects. Firms use similar channels whenever possible, but prices tend to be localized because of differences in cost and competition. Typically, advertising messages need to be adapted to local conditions.

The United States is the largest exporter of services in the world and is particularly strong in international transport and franchising.

IMPLEMENTATION AND CONTROL

Implementing Business and Marketing Strategies

REORGANIZING IBM[1]

Why would the world's fifth-largest industrial corporation—earning more than $6 billion in net profits on annual sales over $60 billion—find itself going through hard times? That is exactly the position IBM found itself in during the late 1980s.

During the first half of the 1980s, "Big Blue" enjoyed tremendous success, generating average annual volume increases of 15 percent and huge profits. Much of this profit came from its commanding market share for large mainframe computers. And much of its growth was generated by selling them in foreign markets. IBM was one of the first truly global U.S. corporations, selling its computers in 130 different countries. By 1985 international operations accounted for 40 percent of its sales volume.

Personal computers also showed rapid sales growth during this period. IBM was not a pioneer in the PC market, but it was a fast-follower with strong advantages in one major customer segment—business users. Giving individual managers their own PCs did not really catch on until IBM entered the market in 1981, promoted the idea through its huge direct salesforce and an extensive advertising campaign, and persuaded software companies to develop new programs, such as Lotus 1–2–3®, for business applications. By 1983, IBM had captured an estimated 50 percent share of the U.S. commercial PC market, and the market was growing at an annual 40 percent rate.

Flushed with their great success through the first half of the 1980s,

[1]This example is based on material found in Carol J. Loomis, "IBM's Big Blues: A Legend Tries to Remake Itself," *Fortune*, January 19, 1987, pp. 34–54; and Joel Dreyfuss, "Reinventing IBM," *Fortune*, August 14, 1989, pp. 30–39.

IBM's executives predicted it would grow into a $100 billion company by 1990. However, those managers fell victim to their own past success. To defend their strong position, enhance productivity, and reduce risks, top management imposed centralized organization structures and controls. A corporate management board of 18 senior executives handed down decisions from world headquarters in Armonk, New York, on everything from advertising campaigns to R&D allocations for specific products.

IBM spent billions during the 1980s on new plants and processes to improve productivity to match its Japanese competitors. But it had difficulty turning its R&D investments into successful new products. Centralized management and tight controls contributed to its product and market development problems. Decision makers lost touch with customer needs and preferences. Product development times lengthened. And many of the resulting new products—such as the PC Jr., a personal computer for the home market—were unexciting and middle-of-the-road. As John Akers, IBM's current CEO, acknowledges, "We didn't want to tamper with success. We decided to be careful instead of aggressive."

A changing environment leads to a change in strategy

As IBM's bureaucratic management structure focused on defending past successes, the firm's environment changed rapidly and in unexpected ways. Major customers turned from the big mainframes that were IBM's bread and butter (see Exhibit 12–1) to networks of smaller but ever more powerful minicomputers and PCs. At the same time, with rapid technological advances and aggressive product development, smaller competitors like Digital Equipment, Compaq, and Apple gained substantial shares of the minicomputer and PC markets; and they developed promising new niches such as desktop publishing and markets for laptop computers and technical workstations. Also, in spite of the firm's efforts to improve productivity, small offshore manufacturers sold IBM-compatible clones at prices far below IBM's.

The upshot of all this environmental turbulence was that IBM's worldwide share in both the mini- and microcomputer (PC) markets fell below 20 percent by 1984; and by 1986 its annual growth rate had sagged to an anemic 2.8 percent. Critics wondered whether a giant enterprise with more than 385,000 employees could keep pace with rapidly changing customer demands and technological advances in a marketplace teeming with small, nimble competitors.

In 1985, John Akers, the new CEO, began moving the firm away from heavy reliance on conservative, defender competitive strategies that protected existing positions in established product-markets. He urged the firm's managers to pursue more aggressive and innovative prospector strategies, at least in those product categories and market segments with high potential for future growth. To take fuller advantage of IBM's incomparable strengths in technical R&D, Akers encouraged his managers to pay closer attention to customer needs and desires, reduce product development times, improve

EXHIBIT   12–1

Big Blue's Ups and Downs

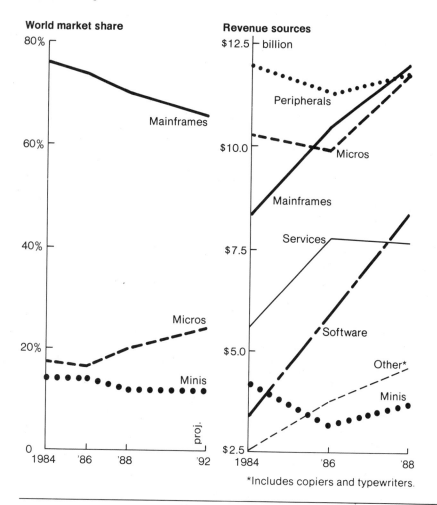

World market share

Revenue sources

*Includes copiers and typewriters.

SOURCE: Annex Research, as reported in Joel Dreyfuss, "Reinventing IBM," *Fortune,* August 14, 1989, p. 33.

the innovativeness and quality of new products and services, and take more risks in pursuing high-potential products and markets.

Organizational changes aimed at implementing the new strategy

The new CEO realized, however, that simply proclaiming a new strat-egy did not guarantee the firm's managers and employees could or would effectively implement it, especially since it required actions inconsistent with deeply en-trenched attitudes and procedures. Consequently, Akers began reorganizing IBM's structure, policies, and procedures to make them more compatible with the new strategy.

Structural changes

To speed up the firm's response to market opportunities and competitive threats, Akers decentralized the organization, reorganizing IBM USA into seven autonomous business units focused on PCs, mainframes, minicomputers, communications, microchip manufacturing, programming and service, and software, with an eighth unit to handle marketing for all the others. The SBU general managers negotiate their business plans with Akers and the management board once a year and then run their units with a minimum of interference. This reorganization pushed more decisions down to lower levels where managers are closer to their markets. It reduced the time needed for approval of new products and gave operating managers more flexibility to launch innovative programs.

The reorganization also enabled the firm to focus more on potential growth areas by dedicating separate SBUs to those businesses. For instance, the 30,000-employee unit that develops new software is now the fastest-growing part of IBM. Similarly, the service division is building on its tremendous experience base to increase its share of the $100 billion computer users spend each year on programming and maintenance services. To accomplish this goal, policies now allow IBM's 29,000 service people to be more responsive to a wide range of customer needs. They can now service other brands, tie them to IBM equipment, or recover lost data after a disaster. IBM currently holds about a 9 percent share of the market for maintenance and service; and every percentage point of additional share translates into about $1 billion in new revenue.

Policy and procedural changes

The company made policy and procedural changes to speed up new-product development and make it more responsive to customer needs. Development teams incorporate managers from a variety of functional areas, including marketing, software, and service divisions, to help ensure that new equipment meets customer requirements. And customers themselves are brought into the development process at various stages. During the development of the new AS/400 minicomputer, for instance, an advisory council of customers evaluated plans and made suggestions. Before IBM introduced the AS/400 to the market, potential buyers tested 1,700 of them; the company then made further refinements in response to their suggestions. These new procedures enabled the company to move the AS/400 from prototype to the marketplace in less than two years and resulted in the most successful new-product launch in IBM's history. In the first year, the company sold more than 25,000 of the machines,—worth an estimated $3 billion.

Marketing and sales changes

Marketing also plays an expanded role in the new IBM. Consolidation into an autonomous division has given the firm's marketing managers more flexibility and authority to design coordinated marketing strategies that cut across related products and markets. Marketing also plays a crucial role in collecting and analyzing information on customer needs and competitor actions for all the other product and service divisions.

Consistent with its expanded strategic role, marketing has also received more resources—in particular, a greatly expanded salesforce. Decentralization enabled IBM to reduce middle management and staff personnel and thereby cut overhead costs. However, the firm has a longstanding policy of not laying off employees. Therefore, it induced 6,500 employees to retire early and moved another 20,000 from administrative jobs into the salesforce, where they could increase the firm's contacts with its customers, especially smaller accounts that had received little attention in the past.

IBM also reorganized its salesforce along industry lines. This further enabled salespeople to become more familiar and maintain closer contact with customers in specific applications segments. For example, one sales group focuses on finance and brokerage firms in New York; another concentrates on the automobile manufacturers in Detroit. And the compensation system was also changed to motivate salespeople to attend to a customer's total needs. IBM salespeople are now rewarded on the basis of the total revenue they generate, whether it comes from the sale of equipment, software, services, or even networks that include other companies' products.

Into the 90s

The ongoing reorganization of IBM has involved so many sweeping changes in the firm's structure, policies, and procedures that one analyst refers to it as "the most radical cultural change in IBM's history." Most important, it is beginning to produce the kind of performance improvements that Akers envisioned when he developed the new competitive strategy. A string of successful new products and the aggressive development of new market segments helped push the firm's growth rate back up to 8 percent as the firm entered the 1990s.

ISSUES IN THE IMPLEMENTATION OF BUSINESS AND MARKETING STRATEGIES

The recent changes at IBM illustrate a point mentioned in Chapter 3: a business's success is determined by two aspects of strategic fit. First, its competitive and marketing strategy must fit the needs and constraints of the external market and competitive environment. Second, the business must be able to effectively implement that strategy; its internal structure, policies, procedures, and resources must fit the demands of the strategy. As Exhibit 12–2 indicates, when a business cannot effectively implement its chosen strategy— even when that strategy is very appropriate for the circumstances it faces— trouble is likely to ensue. Worse, management may conclude the strategy was not appropriate after all, switch to a less desirable strategy, and ultimately

EXHIBIT 12-2

The Combined Effects of Strategy Selection and Implementation

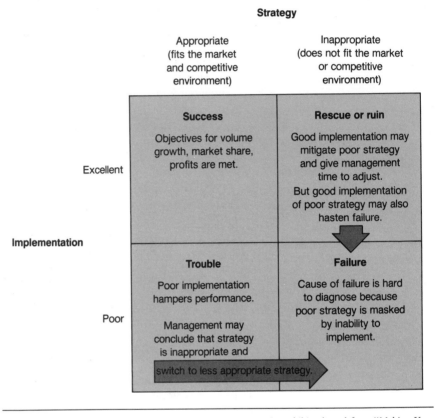

SOURCE: Reprinted by permission of the *Harvard Business Review*. An exhibit adapted from "Making Your Marketing Strategy Work," by Thomas V. Bonoma, March–April 1984. Copyright © 1984 by the President and Fellows of Harvard College; all rights reserved.

depress the business's performance even further. On one hand, excellent execution may offset the negative effects of a poorly conceived strategy. But on the other, good implementation of the wrong strategy can speed the business along the road to failure.

Most of this book has focused on analyzing the external environment and developing marketing strategies that effectively fit the environment a business and its product-market entries face. In this chapter we turn our attention to questions of organizational fit—the fit between a business's strategies and the organizational structures, policies, processes, and plans necessary to implement those strategies. Four major sets of internal variables affect a business's ability to implement particular strategies:

- The fit between the marketing strategies pursued in individual product-markets and the firm's higher-level corporate and business strategies.

- Administrative relationships between the SBU and corporate headquarters.

EXHIBIT 12–3

Factors Affecting the Implementation of Business and Marketing Strategies

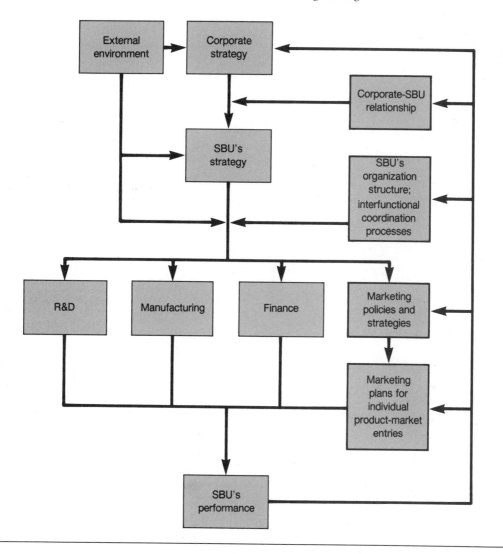

- The SBU's organization structure and coordination mechanisms, including such variables as the technical competence of the various functional departments within the SBU, the manner in which resources are allocated across functions, and the mechanisms used to coordinate and resolve conflicts among the departments.
- The contents of a detailed marketing action plan for each product-market entry.

These four sets of variables are diagrammed in Exhibit 12–3 and serve as a framework for the remainder of our discussion.

EXHIBIT 12-4

The Fit between Business Strategies, the Environment, and SBU Objectives

Situational variables and objectives	Business strategies			
	Prospector	Analyzer	Differentiated defender	Low-cost defender
Industry environment	Industry in the introductory or growth stage of its life cycle; relatively few competitors; technology still evolving.	Industry in growth or early maturity stage of its life cycle; substantial competition; technological advances or new-product applications still possible.	Industry in maturity or decline stage of its life cycle; substantial competition; technology is mature, but new applications may still be possible.	Industry in maturity or decline stage of its life cycle; substantial competition; technology is mature, but new applications may still be possible.
Appropriate SBU objectives	High increases in sales volume and market share; relatively large proportion of volume from new products and markets; relatively low ROI and cash flow.	Moderate increases in volume and share; some volume from new products and markets; moderate levels of ROI and cash flow.	Low increases in sales volume and market share; relatively little volume from new products, but some volume may be gained from new customers or markets; high ROI and cash flow.	Low increases in sales volume and market share; relatively little volume from new products or markets; moderate to high ROI and cash flow.

RELATIONSHIPS BETWEEN BUSINESS AND MARKETING STRATEGIES

As discussed in Chapter 3, generic business-level strategies define how an SBU intends to compete in its industry. Exhibit 12–4 reviews the kinds of industry environments and the SBU objectives most appropriate for the pursuit of prospector, analyzer, differentiated defender, and low-cost defender strategies. Remember, though, that some businesses fail to develop any clearly defined or consistent competitive strategy. Such businesses are referred to as *reactors* because their competitive posture tends to change sporadically in response to the actions of other firms or environmental threats. Because it is impossible to generalize about how to effectively implement a strategy that does not exist or that changes from day to day, we will say no more about reactors in the rest of this chapter.

An SBU may comprise a number of product-markets, each facing different demand and competitive situations. It is thus somewhat risky to generalize about what marketing policies and strategies at the product-market level best fit different business strategies. Still, an SBU's strategy does set a general direction for the types of markets to target, the way to compete in those markets, and the objectives to pursue. Also, an SBU strategy should reflect the general market and competitive conditions it faces within its industry. Therefore, a well-conceived competitive strategy should provide a foundation for and strongly influence an SBU's general policies concerning such marketing program elements as relative product quality, service levels, price, and promotional intensity.

More specifically, the marketing programs for individual product-market entries within a business unit should be consistent with that unit's competitive strategy and overall marketing policies as well as with the market and competitive circumstances those entries face. For example, Pillsbury's prepared dough SBU competes as a differentiated defender in a mature portion of the food industry. The marketing strategies for virtually all of the SBU's core brands, such as Hungry Jack biscuits and Pillsbury Crescent rolls, involve a combination of (1) a fortress defense strategy relying on high product quality, premium price, and extensive distribution to maintain share, (2) the development of flanker brands to protect against low-priced regional competitors, and (3) extended use strategies to increase volume among current users. Such marketing programs are all consistent with the SBU's differentiated defender competitive strategy and its leading share position.

We discussed the marketing policies that are most appropriate for businesses pursuing prospector, analyzer, differentiated defender, and low-cost defender competitive strategies in Chapter 3. Subsequently, in Chapters 8, 9, and 10,[2] we examined a number of specific marketing programs firms might use to implement different competitive strategies under specific market and competitive conditions. To refresh your memory, Exhibit 12–5 summarizes some of the basic relationships among business-level competitive strategies, marketing policies, and strategic marketing programs.

Once again, we can conclude from the relationships outlined in Exhibit 12–5 that while marketing managers often play a primary role in formulating an SBU's overall competitive strategy,[3] once that strategy is in place it constrains the kinds of marketing policies that are appropriate for the SBU to adopt. Those policies—together with the market and competitive situation the business faces and the objectives inherent in its strategy—also limit the range of marketing strategies appropriate for the individual product-market entries within the SBU. Thus, effective implementation of a particular business strategy also involves the implementation of a specific set of marketing policies and strategies. And the organizational structures, policies, and processes necessary for the effective implementation of a given competitive strategy—as discussed in the next two sections—also facilitate the implementation of the marketing policies and programs incorporated within that strategy.

---

[2]While we have briefly discussed many of the specific actions involved in each of the program elements of various marketing strategies in previous chapters, space limitations and the broad strategic, rather than operational, focus of this book prevented us from covering many specific executional issues in much detail. For a more in-depth examination of executional issues, see Thomas V. Bonoma, *The Marketing Edge: Making Strategies Work* (New York: Free Press, 1985).

[3]George S. Yip, "The Role of Strategic Planning in Consumer-Marketing Businesses," Working paper #84–103 (Cambridge, Mass.: Marketing Science Institute, 1984).

EXHIBIT 12-5

The Fit between Business Strategies and Marketing Programs

Appropriate marketing policies and strategies	Business strategies			
	Prospector	Analyzer	Differentiated defender	Low-cost defender
Product and service policies	Broad, technically sophisticated product lines; moderate to high quality and levels of service, especially sales engineering services.	Moderately broad and technically sophisticated product lines; service levels and quality indeterminant.	Relatively narrow but high quality and technically sophisticated product lines; high quality and levels of service.	Narrow, less technically sophisticated product lines; relatively low levels of quality and service.
Price policy	Relatively high prices.	Relatively high prices.	Relatively high prices.	Relatively low to competitive prices.
Distribution policies	Little forward vertical integration; relatively high trade promotion expenses as a percent of sales.	Degree of forward vertical integration indeterminant; moderate to high trade promotion expenses as a percent of sales.	Relatively high degree of forward vertical integration; low trade promotion expenses as a percent of sales.	Degree of forward vertical integration indeterminant; low trade promotion expenses as a percent of sales.
Promotion policies	High advertising, sales promotion, and salesforce expenditures as a percent of sales.	Moderate advertising and sales promotion expenditures as a percent of sales; salesforce expenditures indeterminant.	Relatively low advertising and sales promotion expenditures as a percent of sales; high salesforce expenditures as a percent of sales.	Low advertising, sales promotion, and salesforce expenditures as a percent of sales.
Common marketing strategies	Mass-market penetration; niche penetration; skimming and early withdrawal; market expansion; encirclement.	Flanker strategy; market expansion; leapfrog strategy; encirclement; guerrilla attack.	Fortress defense; confrontation; flanker strategy; increased penetration; extended use; market expansion; profitable survivor strategy; maintenance strategy; niche strategy.	Fortress defense; confrontation; profitable survivor strategy; maintenance strategy; niche strategy; harvesting strategy.

ADMINISTRATIVE RELATIONSHIPS AND STRATEGY IMPLEMENTATION[4]

In organizations consisting of multiple divisions or SBUs, the administrative relationships between the unit and corporate headquarters influence the ability

---

[4]Much of the discussion in this section is based on material found in Orville C. Walker, Jr. and Robert W. Ruekert, "Marketing's Role in the Implementation of Business Strategies: A Critical Review and Conceptual Framework," *Journal of Marketing,* July 1987, pp. 15–33.

of the SBU's managers, including its marketing personnel, to implement specific competitive and marketing strategies successfully. Indeed, as a study of the performance of 69 business units in 12 different industries concluded, "Corporate managers can have as much impact on a business unit's performance by attending to its administrative ties to headquarters as they can by managing according to detailed strategic portfolio analyses."[5]

Three aspects of the corporate-business unit relationship can affect an SBU's success in implementing a particular competitive strategy.

1. The degree to which the unit's managers have the **autonomy** to make decisions independent of other parts of the company, particularly the home office.
2. The degree to which the unit **shares functional programs and facilities,** including marketing programs such as a common salesforce or promotional programs, with other SBUs in a search for corporate synergies.
3. The manner in which the corporation **evaluates and rewards** the performance of the SBU's managers.

Exhibit 12–6 summarizes how these variables relate to the successful implementation of different business strategies. We discuss the rationale underlying these relationships below. Note, however, that analyzer strategies are not included in the following discussion. Because analyzers incorporate some elements of both prospector and defender strategies, the administrative arrangements appropriate for implementing an analyzer strategy typically fall somewhere between those best suited for the other two types. To simplify the following discussion, then, we will focus only on the polar types—prospector, differentiated defender, and low-cost defender strategies.

Business-unit autonomy

Prospector business units likely perform better on the critical dimensions of new-product success and increased volume and market share when organizational decision making is relatively decentralized and the SBU's managers have substantial autonomy to make their own decisions. There are several reasons for this. First, more decentralized decision making allows the managers closest to the market, who should be first to recognize new opportunities, to make more major decisions on their own. Greater autonomy also enables the SBU's managers to be more flexible and adaptable. It frees them from the restrictions of standard procedures imposed from above, allows them to make decisions with fewer consultations and participants, and disperses power. All of these help produce quicker and more innovative responses to environmental opportunities. Thus, IBM recently granted greater autonomy to the managers of its various business divisions to help improve the speed and innovativeness of their responses to the rapidly changing environment of the computer industry.

---

[5]Richard G. Hamermesh and Roderick E. White, "Manage beyond Portfolio Analysis," *Harvard Business Review*, January–February 1984, pp. 103–9.

EXHIBIT 12-6

Administrative Factors Related to the Successful Implementation of Business Strategies

Administrative factor	Type of business strategy		
	Prospector	Differentiated defender	Low-cost defender
SBU autonomy	Relative high level of autonomy is positively related to new-product success and volume and market share performance.	Moderate level of autonomy is related to high levels of ROI and market share maintenance.	Relatively low autonomy is related to high ROI and cash flow performance.
Shared programs and synergy	Relatively little synergy; SBU's volume and market share performance likely to be best when it shares few marketing, R&D, or manufacturing programs or facilities with other SBUs; an exception may be the sharing of distribution channels among consumer goods businesses.	Little synergy in areas central to SBU's differential advantage (e.g., R&D, marketing); programs in such areas should not be shared in order to preserve flexibility; sharing of programs or facilities in other functional areas may improve efficiency and ROI performance.	High levels of synergy; ROI performance is likely to be best when marketing, R&D, and manufacturing programs or facilities are shared with other SBUs.
Evaluation and reward systems	The greater the proportion of SBU managers' compensation accounted for by incentives based on unit's sales or share growth, the better the unit's performance.	The greater the proportion of SBU managers' compensation accounted for by incentives based on unit's profit or ROI, the better the unit's performance.	The greater the proportion of SBU managers' compensation accounted for by incentives based on unit's profit or ROI, the better the unit's performance.

SOURCE: Adapted from Orville C. Walker, Jr., and Robert W. Ruekert, "Marketing's Role in the Implementation of Business Strategies," *Journal of Marketing,* July 1987, p. 31.

On the other hand, low-cost defender SBUs often perform better on their critical dimensions of ROI and cash flow by keeping managers on a tight leash and giving them relatively little decision-making autonomy. For a low-cost strategy to succeed, the SBU must pay close attention to operational details, including the relentless pursuit of cost economies and productivity improvements through standardizing components and processes, routinizing procedures, and integrating functional activities across units. Such efficiencies are more likely to be attained when decision making and control are relatively centralized.

The relationship between autonomy and the ROI performance of differentiated defenders is more difficult to predict. On one hand, such businesses defend existing positions in established markets and their primary objective is ROI rather than volume growth. Thus, the increased efficiency and tighter control associated with relatively low autonomy should lead to better performance. On the other hand, such businesses can maintain profitability only if they continue to differentiate themselves by offering superior products and services. As customers' wants change and new competitive threats emerge, the greater flexibility and market focus associated with greater autonomy may allow these businesses to more successfully maintain their differentiated positions and higher levels of ROI over time. These arguments suggest that the relationship between autonomy and performance for differentiated defenders may be mediated by the level of stability in their environments and by the proportion of offensive or proactive marketing strategies they employ. Units operating in relatively unstable environments and pursuing more proactive marketing programs (such as extended use or market expansion strategies) likely perform better when they have relatively greater autonomy.[6]

Shared programs and facilities

Firms face a trade-off when designing strategic business units. An SBU should be large enough to afford critical resources and to operate on an efficient scale, but it should not be so large that its market scope is too broad or that "it is inflexible and does not respond quickly to customer needs, to the tactics of competition, and to its unique market opportunities."[7] Some firms attempt to avoid this trade-off between efficiency and adaptability by designing relatively small, narrowly focused business units, but then having two or more units share functional programs or facilities, such as common manufacturing plants, R&D programs, or a single salesforce. These firms believe that the managers of such narrowly defined SBUs can stay in close contact with their customers and competitive environments while the sharing of programs simultaneously provides increased economies of scale and synergy across units.

Recent evidence suggests, however, that sharing resources across SBUs reduces their flexibility and innovativeness.[8] This poses a particular problem for prospector business units. Suppose, for instance, a business wants to introduce a new product but it shares a manufacturing plant and a salesforce with other SBUs. The business would have to negotiate a production schedule for the new product, and it may not be able to produce sufficient quantities as quickly as needed if other units sharing the plant are trying to maintain sufficient volumes of their own products. It may also be difficult to train salespeople on the new product or to motivate them to reduce the time spent on established products in order to push the new item. When Frito-Lay introduced Grandma's soft cookies, for instance, they relied on their 10,000 salty-snack route salespeople to attain supermarket shelf space for the new

---

[6]Ibid.

[7]E. Raymond Corey and Steven H. Star, *Organization Strategy: A Marketing Approach* (Boston: Division of Research, Graduate School of Business, Harvard University, 1971), p. 9.

[8]Robert W. Ruekert and Orville C. Walker, Jr., "The Sharing of Marketing Resources across Strategic Business Units: The Effect of Strategy on Performance," *Review of Marketing 1990* (Chicago: American Marketing Association, 1990).

line. But because those salespeople were paid a commission based on their total sales revenue, they were reluctant to take time away from their profitable salty-snack lines to sell the new cookies. The resulting lack of strong sales support contributed to Grandma's failure to capture a sustainable share of the packaged-cookie market. Thus, prospector SBUs likely perform better on their primary objectives of new-product success, volume, and share growth when they are relatively self-contained and share few functional programs or facilities with other units.

One exception to this generalization, though, may be sharing sales and distribution programs across consumer package-goods SBUs. In such cases, a prospector's new product may have an easier time obtaining retailer support and shelf space if it is represented by salespeople who also sell established brands to the same retail outlets. For prospectors producing consumer durables or industrial goods, however, functional independence generally facilitates good performance. That is why successful prospector businesses—like most of the business divisions at the 3M Company—control their own R&D budgets, manufacturing facilities, salesforces, and marketing programs.

On the other hand, the increased efficiencies gained through sharing functional programs and facilities often boost the ROI performance of low-cost defender SBUs. Also, the inflexibility inherent in sharing is usually not a major problem for such businesses because their markets and technologies tend to be mature and relatively stable. Thus, Heinz, the cost leader in a number of food categories, uses a single salesforce to represent a wide variety of products from different business units when calling on supermarkets.

The impact of shared programs on the performance of differentiated defenders is more difficult to predict. However, such businesses must often modify their products and marketing programs in response to changing customer desires or competitive actions to maintain their competitive advantage and profitability over time. Thus, greater functional independence in areas directly related to the SBU's differential advantage—such as R&D, sales, and marketing—tends to be positively associated with the long-run ROI performance of such businesses, particularly for SBUs pursuing proactive strategies such as extended use or market expansion. But greater sharing of facilities and programs in less crucial functional areas, such as manufacturing or distribution, may also help improve their efficiency and short-run ROI levels.

Evaluation and reward systems

Corporate executives periodically compare measures of each SBU's performance to its planned objectives as a means of evaluating and controlling the actions of that unit's managers. The SBU's managers, in turn, are often motivated to achieve their planned objectives by bonuses or other financial incentives tied to their unit's performance. Such incentives are most commonly related to some aspect of the SBU's short-run financial performance, such as unit profits or ROI. Incentive performance also often determines which business-unit managers will win promotions. Those managers typically remain in one position for only three to five years. These facts suggest that the most commonly used evaluation and reward systems encourage SBU managers to concentrate on short-run returns and adopt policies that may discourage innovation, the acceptance of risk, and the aggressive pursuit of growth for future returns.[9]

Reliance on evaluation and reward systems geared to short-run financial performance poses no major problems in SBUs pursuing defender strategies where most markets are stable and mature and where ROI and cash flows are the most important performance objectives. Such incentive systems are likely to be counterproductive, though, when an SBU pursues a prospector strategy requiring some level of risk taking and innovativeness in the short term to achieve long-run success. In such businesses, evaluation and reward systems based on an increase in sales volume or market share or on the percentage of volume generated by new products (say, products introduced within the last five years) more likely motivate managers to engage in aggressive and innovative courses of action. Thus, 3M—a firm with a long history of successful new-product innovation—has an executive incentive system based, in part, on volume generated by new products. Because many firms incorporate both prospector and defender SBUs, however, it is increasingly common for large corporations to adopt evaluation and reward systems based on some combination of volume and profitability.[10]

ORGANIZATIONAL STRUCTURE, PROCESSES, AND STRATEGY IMPLEMENTATION

Implementing any business strategy requires the performance of a number of different functions. But different strategies emphasize different ways to gain a competitive advantage. Thus, a given functional area may be key to the success of one type of strategy but less critical for others. For instance, competence in new-product R&D is critical for the success of prospector business but less so for a low-cost defender.

Regardless of their relative importance, though, the firm must coordinate all functional efforts. The inevitable conflicts that develop between functional departments must be resolved before any strategy can be successful. And once again, different organizational structures and conflict resolution mechanisms are appropriate for businesses pursuing different strategies.

Successful implementation of a given strategy, then, is more likely when the business has the **functional competencies** demanded by its strategy and supports them with substantial **resources** relative to competitors, is **organized** suitably for its technical, market, and competitive environment, and has developed appropriate **mechanisms for coordinating efforts and**

[9]Alfred Rappaport, "Executive Incentives vs. Corporate Growth," *Harvard Business Review*, July–August 1978, pp. 81–88. Also see David Norburn and Paul Miller, "Strategy and Executive Reward: The Mis-Match in the Strategic Process," *Journal of General Management* 6 (1981), pp. 17–27.

[10]Norburn and Miller, "Strategy and Executive Reward." Also see Bernard J. Jaworski, "Toward a Theory of Marketing Control: Environmental Context, Control Types, and Consequences," *Journal of Marketing*, July 1988, pp. 23–39.

EXHIBIT 12–7
Organizational and Interfunctional Factors Related to the Successful
Implementation of Business Strategies

	Type of business strategy		
Organizational factor	**Prospector**	**Differentiated defender**	**Low-cost defender**
Functional competencies of the SBU	SBU will perform best on critical volume and share growth dimensions when its functional strengths include marketing, sales, product R&D, and engineering.	SBU will perform best on critical ROI dimension when its functional strengths include sales, financial management and control, and those functions related to its differential advantage (e.g., marketing, product R&D).	SBU will perform best on critical ROI and cash flow dimensions when its functional strengths include process engineering, production, distribution, and financial management and control.
Resource allocation across functions	SBU will perform best on volume and share growth dimensions when percent of sales spent on marketing, sales, and product R&D are high, and when gross fixed assets per employee and percent of capacity utilization are low relative to competitors.	SBU will perform best on the ROI dimension when percent of sales spent on the salesforce, gross fixed assets per employee, percent of capacity utilization, and percent of sales devoted to other functions related to the SBU's differential advantage are high relative to competitors.	SBU will perform best on ROI and cash flow dimensions when marketing, sales, and product R&D expenses are low, but process R&D, fixed assets per employee, and percent of capacity utilization are high relative to competitors.

resolving conflicts across functional departments. Exhibit 12–7 summarizes the relationships between these organizational structure and process variables and the performance of different generic business strategies.

Functional competencies and resource allocation

Strategic considerations

We saw in Chapter 3 that competence in marketing, sales, product R&D, and engineering are all critical to the success of prospector businesses because

EXHIBIT 12-7
(concluded)

Organizational factor	Type of business strategy		
	Prospector	Differentiated defender	Low-cost defender
Decision-making influence and participation	SBU will perform best on volume and share growth dimensions when managers from marketing, sales, product R&D, and engineering have substantial influence on unit's business and marketing strategy decisions.	SBU will perform best on ROI dimension when financial managers, controller, and managers of functions related to unit's differential advantage have substantial influence on business and marketing strategy decisions.	SBU will perform best on ROI and cash flow when controller, financial, and production managers have substantial influence on business and marketing strategy decisions.
SBU's organization structure	SBU will perform best on volume and share growth dimensions when structure has low levels of formalization and centralization, but high level of specialization.	SBU will perform best on ROI dimension when structure has moderate levels of formalization, centralization, and specialization.	SBU will perform best on ROI and cash flow dimensions when structure has high levels of formalization and centralization, but low level of specialization.
Functional coordination and conflict resolution	SBU will experience high levels of interfunctional conflict; SBU will perform best on volume and share growth dimensions when participative resolution mechanisms are used (e.g., product teams).	SBU will experience moderate levels of interfunctional conflict; SBU will perform best on ROI dimension when resolution is participative for issues related to differential advantage, but hierarchical for others (e.g., product managers, product improvement teams, etc.).	SBU will experience low levels of interfunctional conflict; SBU will perform best on ROI and cash flow dimensions when conflict resolution mechanisms are hierarchical (e.g., functional organization).

SOURCE: Adapted from Orville C. Walker, Jr., and Robert W. Ruekert, "Marketing's Role in the Implementation of Business Strategies," *Journal of Marketing*, July 1987, p. 31.

those functions play pivotal roles in new-product and market development. However, competence in these key functional areas will do an SBU little good, and will be hard to maintain, unless the business unit also supports them with adequate physical, financial, and human resources. Thus, prospectors likely perform better on their new-product success and volume and share-growth objectives when they support these key functions with budgets set at a larger percent of sales than their competitors'. For instance, Johnson & Johnson—a firm respected for its high rate of new-product innovation—

spent over $600 million annually, or about 8 percent of sales, on R&D in the late 1980s. This was about double the average for all U.S. companies and five times the amount the firm had spent 10 years earlier.[11]

Marketing, sales, and R&D managers are also closest to the changes occurring in a business's market, competitive, and technological environments. Therefore, in prospector SBUs the greater the input and influence those managers have in making strategic decisions, the more successful the SBU is likely to be over time. This argues that "bottom-up" strategic planning systems—where analyses and recommendations from lower-level product and functional managers initiate the planning process—are particularly well suited to prospector businesses operating in unstable environments.[12] And when lower-level managers in such businesses are not given the freedom to initiate or modify their own programs, they are less likely to respond effectively to environmental changes. For example, a recent study found that British firms characterized by highly centralized, "top-down" strategic planning processes were plagued by a lack of flexibility and inhibited from responding quickly to changing market needs or environmental conditions. As a result, firms like British Petroleum and Cadbury suffered setbacks in their expansion strategies.[13]

In low-cost defender businesses, on the other hand, those functional areas most directly related to operating efficiency—such as financial management and control, production, process R&D, and distribution or logistics—play the most crucial roles in enabling the SBU to attain good ROI performance. Consequently, executives from those departments should have substantial influence on the strategic decisions made within such SBUs. Also, "top-down," centralized planning systems tend to be more appropriate for low-cost defenders operating in relatively stable environments.

Because of the relatively stable, mature markets most low-cost defenders face, high expenditures on marketing, sales, and product R&D activities are not so critical for maintaining their competitive position. To be successful, such businesses must employ their resources efficiently and work to improve their efficiency even further. Thus, the best-performing low-cost defenders spend a relatively large percentage of revenues on process R&D to further improve production efficiency, have high fixed assets per employee (i.e., replace labor with more efficient capital equipment whenever possible), and operate their plants at near capacity.

Because differentiated defenders need to attain high returns on their established products, functional areas related to efficiency—particularly financial management, control, and production—are also critical for their success.

---

[11]Kenneth Labich, "The Innovators," *Fortune,* June 6, 1988, p. 52.

[12]To refresh your memory concerning the benefits of "top-down" versus "bottom-up" planning, see our discussion of formal planning systems in Chapter 1. Also see George S. Day, *Strategic Market Planning: The Pursuit of Competitive Advantage* (St. Paul, Minn.: West Publishing, 1984), chap. 2.

[13]Michael Goold and Andrew Campbell, "Many Best Ways to Make Strategy," *Harvard Business Review,* November–December 1987, p. 72.

Similarly, such units also seek to improve efficiency by investing in process R&D, making needed capital investments, and maintaining a high level of capacity utilization. But because they must also maintain their differential advantage over time, functional departments related to the source of that advantage—the salesforce and product R&D for SBUs with a technical product advantage, or marketing and distribution for SBUs with a customer service advantage—are also critical for the unit's continued success. Consequently, those departments need substantial resources, and their managers should play a strong role in strategic decision making within the business unit.

Additional considerations for service organizations

Given that service organizations pursue the same kinds of business-level competitive strategies as goods producers, they must meet the same functional and resource requirements to implement those strategies effectively. However, service organizations—and manufacturers that provide high levels of customer service as part of their product offering—often need some additional functional competencies because of the unique problems involved in delivering quality service.

This is particularly true for services involving high customer contact. Because the sale, production, and delivery of such services occur almost simultaneously, close coordination between operations, sales, and marketing is crucial. Also, since many different employees may be involved in producing and delivering the service—as when thousands of different cooks prepare Big Macs at McDonalds outlets around the world—production planning and standardization can reduce variations in quality from one transaction to the next. Similarly, detailed policies and procedures for dealing with customers are necessary to reduce variability in customer treatment across employees. All of this suggests that personnel management—particularly the activities of employee selection, training, motivation, and evaluation—is an important adjunct to the production and marketing efforts of high-contact service organizations.

Competence in personnel management is even more crucial for service businesses pursuing prospector strategies—and perhaps also for defenders and analyzers who differentiate their offerings on the basis of good service—than for those focused primarily on efficiency and low cost. In prospector service organizations, employees often play a critical role in identifying potential new service offerings and in introducing them to potential customers. Consequently, the effective implementation of such a strategy requires employees with superior communication and social skills and necessitates frequent employee retraining and performance feedback. As Exhibit 12–8 indicates, for instance, banks pursuing a prospector strategy not only have more branches and engage in more market scanning, advertising, and new-service development than those with other types of competitive strategies; they also devote more effort to screening potential employees and providing training and support after they are hired.

EXHIBIT   12-8

Importance of Functional Activities across Banks
Pursuing Different Competitive Strategies

	Type of competitive strategy			
Functional Activity	Prospector (n = 54)	Analyzer (n = 87)	Defender (n = 157)	Reactor (n = 31)
Market scanning	.36*	.28	.24	.22
New-service development	.57	.52	.45	.39
Distribution intensity (branch offices)	1.27	.30	.04	.55
Advertising	.23	.17	.15	.17
Personnel management				
Screening	.23	.14	.14	.08
Support	.68	.63	.64	.46

*With the exception of distribution intensity, all scores reflect CEOs' judgments concerning the frequency or intensity with which his or her bank engages in the activity. Measures are expressed in terms of the proportion of aggregate points to the total points available for the scale, so that possible values for each activity range from 0 to 1.

SOURCE: Adapted from Daryl O. McKee, P. Rajan Varadarajan, and William M. Pride, "Strategic Adaptability and Firm Performance: A Market-Contingent Perspective," *Journal of Marketing,* July 1989, p. 28.

Organizational structures

Three structural variables—formalization, centralization, and specialization—are important in shaping both an SBU's and its marketing department's performance within the context of a given competitive strategy. **Formalization** is the degree to which formal rules and standard policies and procedures govern decisions and working relationships. **Centralization** refers to the location of decision authority and control within an organization's hierarchy. In highly centralized SBUs or marketing departments, only one or a few top managers hold most decision-making authority. In more decentralized units, middle- and lower-level managers have more autonomy and participate in a wider range of decisions. Finally, **specialization** refers to the division of tasks and activities across positions within the organizational unit. A highly specialized marketing department, for instance, has a large number of specialists, such as market researchers, advertising managers, and sales promotion managers, who direct their efforts to a narrowly defined set of activities.

High levels of formalization and centralization together with low levels of specialization likely promote relatively efficient performance within an SBU or its marketing department.[14] The top business-unit or marketing manager can use his or her centralized authority to steer a common direction for the unit and keep overt conflicts to a minimum. Formal rules and procedures help

---

[14]Robert W. Ruekert, Orville C. Walker, Jr., and Kenneth J. Roering, "The Organization of Marketing Activities: A Contingency Theory of Structure and Performance," *Journal of Marketing,* Winter 1985, pp. 13–25.

routinize activities and hold down risks and administrative costs. The relatively small number of specialists also helps make such units more cost efficient. Such highly structured businesses should perform well on ROI and cash flow dimensions, making them particularly appropriate for SBUs pursuing low-cost defender strategies.

But highly structured business units and marketing departments are unlikely to be very innovative or quick to adapt to changing environmental circumstances. Adaptiveness and innovativeness are enhanced when (1) decision-making authority is decentralized, (2) managerial discretion and informal coordination mechanisms replace rigid rules and policies, and (3) more specialists operate within the unit. Thus, prospector business units and their marketing departments likely perform better on their critical new-product development and volume and share-growth dimensions when they are decentralized, have little formalization, and are highly specialized.

Differentiated defenders must be efficient to achieve high ROIs but adaptable enough to maintain their differential advantage as the environment changes. Thus, they likely perform best over time when their organization structures incorporate moderate levels of formalization, centralization, and specialization. Those departments most directly related to the source of a differentiated defender's competitive advantage (sales, marketing, and R&D), however, should be less highly structured than those more crucial for the efficiency of the unit's operations (production and logistics).

To achieve different levels of formalization, centralization, and specialization, an SBU or functional department must be designed in different ways and incorporate different types of managerial positions. Thus, the above discussion of structural variables has practical implications for designing an appropriate organization chart for a business pursuing a particular strategy. Before we discuss those implications, though, we must first examine some of the issues involved in coordinating activities and resolving the conflicts that develop across the functional departments within the SBU.

Interfunctional coordination and conflict resolution mechanisms

Levels of interfunctional conflict

Because of their broad product-market domains and their emphasis on new-product and market development, prospector businesses often have a high degree of complexity and uncertainty in their operations. Their functional managers must make unfamiliar decisions about how to adapt to new environments. Such complex and unfamiliar situations can result in substantial interfunctional conflict, particularly among departments that play interdependent roles in helping the business to adapt to new market and technological opportunities, such as marketing, sales, R&D, and production.[15]

---

[15]Robert W. Ruekert and Orville C. Walker, Jr., "Interactions between Marketing and R&D Departments in Implementing Different Business Strategies," *Strategic Management Journal* 8 (1987), pp. 233–48.

On the other hand, low-cost defenders commonly operate in more narrowly defined domains and in more mature, stable environments. They usually have clearly defined operating procedures for holding down costs through routinization. Consequently, though functional managers may chafe under the rules and restrictions imposed by top management, low-cost defender businesses likely have less interfunctional conflict across departments than businesses pursuing other strategies.

Conflict resolution mechanisms

Regardless of its competitive strategy, every business has some degree of conflict among its functional departments. How can managers resolve those conflicts? While there are many variations, conflict resolution mechanisms fit into two broad categories. The first is a **hierarchical approach,** whereby top managers impose a solution, either by adhering to formal rules and operating procedures or by judging on a case-by-case basis. The second is a **participative approach,** in which the parties themselves are expected to work out a mutually acceptable solution.[16] New-product development teams, such as those recently formed at IBM, are examples of the participative approach in practice.

Hierarchical resolution mechanisms are efficient because they reduce the amount of time and effort necessary to reach a decision, and they help ensure consistency in the relations across functional departments over time. Such efficiency and routinization are particularly helpful for low-cost defender businesses.

Participative approaches are less efficient because the parties involved typically require more time to work out their differences. But they often lead to a fuller understanding of, and more innovative solutions to, problems that cut across functional departments. They are particularly appropriate for uncertain, nonroutine situations that call for innovative, adaptive actions[17]—situations most commonly faced by prospector businesses.

Once again, since differentiated defenders (and analyzers) need both efficiency and adaptiveness to maintain their differential advantage and profitability, some combination of resolution mechanisms is appropriate. Moderate use of participative methods can resolve conflicts among those areas directly involved in preserving the SBU's differential advantage. A greater reliance on rules, standard procedures, or top-management fiat can deal with disputes in other operational areas.

---

[16]John McCann and Jay R. Galbraith, "Interdepartmental Relations," *Handbook of Organizational Design,* vol. 2, ed. Paul C. Nystrom and William Starbuck (New York: Oxford University Press, 1981), pp. 60–84.

[17]Ibid.

EXHIBIT 12–9

Functional Organization of an SBU and Its Marketing Department

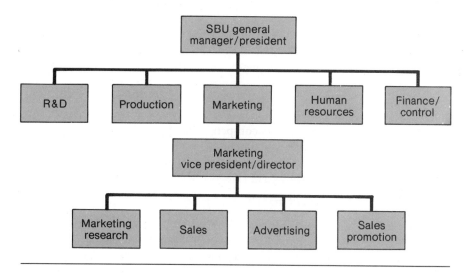

Alternative organizational designs

Several common organizational designs incorporate differences in both the structural variables (formalization, centralization, and specialization) and in the mechanisms for resolving interfunctional conflicts discussed above. These include (1) functional, (2) product management, (3) market management, and (4) various types of matrix organizational designs.[18]

Functional organizations

The functional form of organization, as diagrammed in Exhibit 12–9 for both business-unit and marketing department levels, is the simplest and most bureaucratic design. At the SBU level, managers of each functional department, such as production or marketing, report to the general manager. Within the marketing department, managers of specific marketing activity areas, such as sales, advertising, or marketing research, report to the marketing vice president or director. At each level, the top manager coordinates the activities of all the functional areas reporting to him or her, often with heavy reliance on standard rules and operating procedures. Thus, this is the most centralized and formalized organizational form, and it relies primarily on hierarchical

---

[18]Barton Weitz and Erin Anderson, "Organizing and Controlling the Marketing Function," in *Review of Marketing, 1981,* ed. Ben M. Enis and Kenneth J. Roering, (Chicago: American Marketing Association, 1981), pp. 134–42.

mechanisms for resolving conflicts across functional areas. Also, because top managers perform their coordination activities across all product-markets in the SBU, there is little specialization by product or customer type.

These characteristics make the functional form both simple and efficient. It is particularly appropriate for businesses whose products or markets are few and similar in nature or those operating in relatively stable and predictable environments. Thus, functional organization structures are common among small entrepreneurial start-up firms producing only one or two products or services; they are also appropriate for low-cost defender SBUs attempting to maximize their efficiency and profitability in mature or declining industries. For instance, Ingersol-Rand—a low-cost manufacturer of low-tech air compressors and air-driven tools such as jackhammers—uses a functional structure to organize most of its divisions.

Product management organizations

When an SBU has a relatively complex environment and a large number of product-market entries, the simple functional form of organization is inadequate. A single manager finds it difficult to stay abreast of or to coordinate functional activities across a variety of different product-markets. One common means of dealing with this problem is to adopt a product management organization structure. As Exhibit 12–10 illustrates, this form adds an additional layer of managers to the marketing department, usually called product managers, brand managers, or marketing managers, each of whom has the responsibility to plan and manage the marketing programs and to coordinate the activities of other functional departments for a specific product or product line.

A product management structure decentralizes decision making while increasing the amount of product specialization within the SBU. If the product managers are also given substantial autonomy to develop their own marketing plans and programs, this structure can also decrease the formalization within the business. Finally, although the product managers are responsible for obtaining cooperation from other functional areas both within and outside the marketing department, they have no formal authority over these areas. They must rely on persuasion and compromise—in other words, more participative methods—to overcome conflicts and objections when coordinating functional activities. These factors make the product management form of organization less bureaucratic than the functional structure. It is more appropriate, then, for businesses pursuing differentiated defender and analyzer strategies, particularly when they operate in industries with complex and relatively unstable market and competitive environments.

Businesses that enact flanker, mobile, market penetration or expansion marketing strategies as their industries mature often end up with a number of different brands in the same product category. In some cases, the firm aims the different brands at different market segments; but the brands may also be direct competitors. To coordinate marketing strategies and allocate resources across some related brands, a product management organization typically in-

EXHIBIT   12–10

A Marketing Department with a Product Management Organization

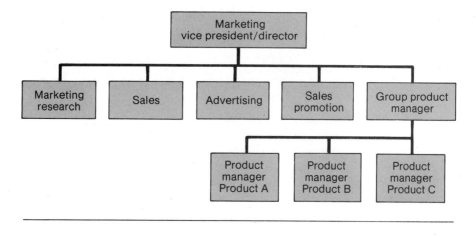

cludes one or more "group" or "category" marketing managers, as shown
in Exhibit 12–10, on the level immediately above the product managers.

Product management organizations have a number of advantages, including (1) the ability to identify and react more quickly to the threats and opportunities individual product-market entries face, (2) improved coordination
of functional activities within and across product-markets, and (3) increased
attention to smaller product-market entries that might be neglected in a functional organization. Consequently, about 85 percent of all consumer goods
manufacturers use some form of product management organization.[19]

Despite its advantages, a product management organization has shortcomings. Although the product manager must rely on persuasion, compromise,
and other more participative conflict resolution and coordination methods to
develop effective programs for his or her product, such coordination does not
always happen. The product manager may pay too little attention to the advice or concerns of managers in other functional departments, or the market,
competitive, or technological environments surrounding the product may be
too complex for a single manager to cope with. Furthermore, such systems
can increase the amount of instability in management ranks because product
management is often the training ground for top management. Thus, successful product managers at firms like P&G or General Mills are often promoted to larger-volume products or higher positions in the organization's
hierarchy—and unsuccessful product managers are often dismissed—after
spending only a year or two managing a given brand. This rapid turnover

[19]Richard T. Hise and J. Patrick Kelly, "Product Managers on Trial," *Journal of Marketing,*
October 1978, pp. 28–33; Also see Jacob M. Duker and Michael V. Laric, "The Product Manager: No Longer on Trial," in *The Changing Marketing Environment,* ed. Kenneth Bernhardt
et.al. (Chicago: American Marketing Association, 1981), pp. 93–96.

EXHIBIT 12-11
Frito-Lay Installs Regional Managers

> Frito-Lay set up a regional organization (six zones) in 1986 to implement local and regional trade and consumer promotions. In June 1989 the company—a division of PepsiCo and the nation's leading marketer of salty-snack foods—created four business areas that replaced the six zones. Each business area is headed by a vice president/general manager. This move will put more senior management in the field and consolidate responsibility for sales, promotion, advertising, and, possibly, even production within each area. Each vice president will report to the Frito-Lay senior vice president/marketing and sales at headquarters. This latest organization is motivated by the desire to get closer to the trade and consumers with an organization that can respond quickly and decisively to regional competition.

SOURCE: Jennifer Lawrence, "Frito Reorganizes," *Advertising Age,* June 26, 1989, p. 4.

can lead to a short-term orientation for the product manager, a lack of continuity in marketing programs over time, and perhaps repetition of past mistakes. As a result of these potential shortcomings, some SBUs have modified the product management form of organization in recent years. We examine two major types of modifications, market management and matrix organizations, next.

Market management organizations

In some industries, an SBU may market a single product to a large number of different markets where customers have very different requirements and preferences. A product manager may be unable to understand all of those markets well enough to develop and coordinate effective programs for each one. In such situations, an SBU might turn to a market management structure in which product managers are replaced with market managers responsible for planning and coordinating programs for one or more products aimed at a particular market segment. Pepsi-Cola, for instance, is sold through restaurants, fast-food outlets, and supermarkets. The syrup needed to make Pepsi is sold direct to institutions such as Kentucky Fried Chicken and Taco Bell. But marketing Pepsi to consumers for home consumption involves the use of franchised bottlers who process and package the product and distribute it to supermarkets. The intermediaries and marketing activities involved in selling to the two markets are so different that it makes sense to have a separate market manager in charge of each.

Recently, some SBUs have adopted a combination of product and regional market management organizational structures. A product manager has overall responsibility for planning and implementing a national marketing program for the product; but several market managers are also given some authority and an independent budget to work with salespeople and develop promotion programs geared to a particular user segment or geographic market. This kind of decentralization, or **regionalization,** of market decision making has become a common organizational response by consumer products companies to increased geographic segmentation and the growing power of regional

EXHIBIT 12–12

One Example of a Matrix Organization: Product Teams

Products	Functional departments					
	Product manager	Marketing research	Advertising	Production	R&D	Finance
Product A			(Team for product A)			
Product B						
Product C						

retailers. Campbell Soup Company was one of the first companies to add regional marketing managers to its organization,[20] but a number of other major firms, including Kraft, General Foods, and P&G, have since followed Campbell's lead. Another example, Frito-Lay's recent addition of regional managers, is described in Exhibit 12–11.

Matrix organizations

A business facing an extremely complex and uncertain environment may find a matrix organization appropriate. The matrix form is the least bureaucratic or centralized and the most specialized type of organization. It brings together two or more different types of specialists within a participative coordination structure. One example is the product-market form of organization that some businesses (such as the textile fibers unit at Du Pont) use to bring together product and market managers. The product managers plan the sales and profits of a particular product and develop advertising, promotion, and pricing policies. They contact the market managers to determine sales estimates for their product in each market. The market managers develop specific customer segments, identify new products or line extensions to fit the needs of their customers, and sell existing products to their markets.

Another matrix form of organization gaining increased popularity is the product team. As illustrated in Exhibit 12–12, a team of representatives from a number of functional areas can be assembled for each product or product line. As a group, the team must agree on a business plan for the product and ensure the necessary resources and cooperation from each functional area. This kind of participative decision making can be very inefficient; it requires a good deal of time and effort for the team to reach mutually acceptable decisions and gain approval from all the affected functional areas. But once reached, those decisions are more likely to reflect the expertise of a variety of

---

[20]"Marketing's New Look," *Business Week*, January 26, 1987, pp. 64–69.

functional specialists, to be innovative, and to be quickly and effectively implemented. Thus, the matrix form of organization particularly suits prospector businesses and the management of new-product development projects within analyzer or differentiated defender businesses, as was the case with IBM's development of its successful AS/400 minicomputer.

Matrix organizations such as product teams are particularly well suited for rapidly changing competitive situations that demand creative and innovative decisions. This helps account for the popularity of this organizational form among advertising agencies. Most large agencies assign a team of functional specialists to a client's account. The team is typically led by an account representative or manager; but it also includes members from several other functional departments. A typical account team includes one or more creative people (whose work is supervised by an art director in their own functional department), a media planner, buyers for print and broadcast media, and perhaps a marketing research person and an accountant to coordinate billing and keep an eye on the account's budget.

MARKETING ACTION PLANS

Despite the ritualistic overtones that accompany the preparation of any formal written plan, most firms feel that "unless all the key elements of a plan are written down . . . there will always be loopholes for ambiguity or misunderstanding of strategies and objectives, or of assigned responsibilities for taking action."[21] Thus, preparation of written plans is a key step in ensuring the effective execution of a strategy because it spells out what actions are to be taken, when, and by whom.

Each functional department within a business—and perhaps even different areas within a functional department (e.g., sales and marketing research within the marketing department)—prepares an annual plan detailing its intended role in carrying out the business's strategy. Our concern here, however, is with the annual marketing plan for a specific product-market entry. Much of this book has focused on the planning process, the decisions that must be made when formulating a marketing strategy, and the kinds of market, competitive, and environmental analyses that managers might engage in to help make those decisions. Consequently, our focus here is on what the plan should include and how its content should be organized and presented to best ensure that the firm effectively carries out the strategy for a product-market entry.

As you might expect, marketing plans across companies vary a good deal in content and organization.[22] In general, however, most annual marketing plans follow a format similar to that summarized in Exhibit 12–13. Although

---

[21]David S. Hopkins, *The Marketing Plan* (New York: The Conference Board, 1981), p. 2.

[22]The results of a survey conducted with a broad sample of companies from different industries concerning the contents of their marketing plans, and a number of examples of plan formats used by different types of firms, are presented in David S. Hopkins, *The Marketing Plan*.

EXHIBIT 12–13

Contents of an Annual Marketing Plan

Section	Content
I. Executive summary	Presents a short overview of the issues, objectives, strategy, and actions incorporated in the plan and their expected outcomes for quick management review.
II. Current situation	Summarizes relevant background information on the market, competition, past performance of the product, and the various elements of its marketing program (e.g., distribution, promotion, etc.), and trends in the macroenvironment.
III. Key issues	Identifies the main opportunities and threats to the product that the plan must deal with in the coming year, and the relative strengths and weaknesses of the product and business unit that must be taken into account in facing those issues.
IV. Objectives	Specifies the goals to be accomplished in terms of sales volume, market share, and profit.
V. Marketing strategy	Summarizes the overall strategic approach that will be used to meet the plan's objectives.
VI. Action plans	This is the most critical section of the annual plan for helping to ensure effective implementation and coordination of activities across functional departments. It specifies: • What specific actions are to be taken, • Who is responsible for each action, • When the action will be engaged in, and • How much will be budgeted for each action.
VII. Projected profit-and-loss statement	Presents the expected financial payoff from the plan.
VIII. Controls	Discusses how the plan's progress will be monitored; may present contingency plans to be used if performance falls below expectations or the situation changes.

most plans offer an executive summary to facilitate a quick management review, the first substantive section is usually a brief analysis of the current situation. This section reviews the history of the brand and its marketing program and examines relevant trends in the target market, the competitive situation, and the broader macroenvironment. Next, the key issues the brand will face during the planning period—including potential threats, competitive weaknesses, and possible opportunities for additional growth or profitability—are outlined.

Given the brand's recent performance, its current market and competitive situation, and the key issues to be dealt with, management can set specific objectives for the coming year. These should include both the financial objectives for the brand as well as the marketing objectives, such as sales volume and market-share goals, that must be met to achieve the desired financial outcomes.

Because there may be a number of different ways to accomplish the objectives, the plan must specify the overall marketing strategy the firm will pursue. That strategy is then broken down into more specific action plans for the coming period. These action plans are the most important part of the whole document for ensuring proper execution. They detail the specific activities the firm will undertake to implement the brand's marketing strategy, who is responsible for each action, when it will be undertaken, and how much is to be spent on each activity.

Given the brand's performance objectives and the expenses involved in its action plans, analysts can develop a budget. This budget is essentially a projected profit-and-loss statement that top management reviews for approval or modification.

The final section of the plan specifies how the brand's progress will be monitored and controlled over the course of the year. It might also include some contingency plans the business can implement if threats or opportunities emerge during the planning period. Many of the issues and methods involved in controlling strategic marketing programs are discussed in the next chapter.

For the interested reader, the kinds of information that might be included in each section of the annual marketing plan are discussed in more detail in the Appendix following this chapter. That discussion is further illustrated with the contents of a recent annual marketing plan for a Pillsbury refrigerated dough product.

SUMMARY

For a business to be successful it must not only have competitive and marketing strategies that fit the demands of the external market and competitive environment, but it must also implement those strategies effectively. The business's internal structure, resources, policies, procedures, and plans must fit the demands of its strategies. This chapter examined four aspects of organizational fit that are critical for effective implementation: (1) the compatibility of strategies at different levels within the business, (2) the administrative relationships between the SBU and corporate headquarters, (3) the organization structure of the SBU and its interfunctional coordination mechanisms, and (4) annual marketing plans that detail the specific actions necessary to execute strategy in each of the SBU's product-markets.

Both the broad marketing policies guiding the development of marketing plans for individual product-markets and the specific marketing strategies pursued within those product-markets should be consistent with the SBU's overall competitive strategy. Thus, higher-level strategies and policy decisions often place some constraints on a manager's freedom of action in designing a marketing program for an individual product-market entry.

Administrative relationships between an SBU and its corporate headquarters can influence its ability to implement different business and marketing strategies. Prospector businesses perform best when their managers have substantial autonomy to make independent decisions, when SBUs share few functional programs or facilities, and when evaluation and reward systems are primarily based on growth dimensions of performance such as increases in sales volume or market share. On the other hand, low-cost defender businesses perform best when their managers are relatively tightly controlled, when SBUs substantially share functional programs and facilities, and when evaluation and reward systems focus primarily on financial dimensions of performance.

The SBU's organizational structure and the processes it uses to coordinate functional activities and resolve conflicts across departments also influence its ability to implement different strategies. Prospector businesses perform best when their structures feature low centralization and formalization, high specialization, and participative methods of interfunctional coordination and conflict resolution. Consequently, matrix forms of organizational design, such as interfunctional product teams or product and market management structures, are particularly well suited to such businesses. At the other extreme, low-cost defenders perform best when their structures provide high centralization and formalization, relatively little specialization, and hierarchical methods of coordination. Highly structured and bureaucratic organizational designs, such as those organized along functional lines, are most appropriate for businesses pursuing low-cost defender strategies. While the product management form of organization is most commonly used, especially in consumer products businesses, it is most appropriate for businesses pursuing differentiated defender and analyzer strategies.

Finally, a detailed annual marketing plan for each product-market entry within the business unit facilitates strategy implementation. Such plans should contain (1) an executive summary, (2) a discussion of the current market and competitive situation and the product's past performance, (3) a summary of the key issues facing the product, (4) the objectives for the coming year, (5) the overall marketing strategy, (6) action plans detailing the specific activities involved in carrying out the strategy, (7) a projected profit-and-loss statement, and (8) a summary of how the business will monitor and control the plan's performance. A detailed set of action plans are particularly crucial for effective implementation because they describe exactly what is to be done, by whom, when, and how much is to be spent on each activity.

APPENDIX: THE CONTENTS OF THE ANNUAL MARKETING PLAN

To illustrate the kinds of information that might be included in each section of the annual marketing plan for a product-market entry, Appendix Exhibit 12A–1 summarizes a recent plan for a Pillsbury refrigerated bread dough, one of the smaller product lines within the firm's differentiated defender prepared dough products business unit. The plan's contents are discussed in the following sections.[1]

---

[1]While this example is based on the material contained in an actual marketing plan for a Pillsbury product, the name of the brand and some of the specific numbers included in this example have been disguised in order to protect proprietary information.

EXHIBIT 12A–1

Summary of an Annual Marketing Plan for a Refrigerated Bread Dough Product

I. Analysis of current situation
A. Market situation
- The total U.S. market for dinner breadstuffs is enormous, amounting to about 10.5 billion servings per year.
- Specialty breads, such as whole grain breads, are growing in popularity, largely at the expense of traditional white breads.
- Pillsbury's share of the total dinner breadstuffs market, accounted for by several brands including Crescent rolls as well as refrigerated bread dough, is small, amounting to only about 2 percent of the total dollar volume.
- Since its introduction several years ago, refrigerated bread dough (RBD) has been able to achieve only low levels of penetration (only about 15 percent of all households have used the product) and use frequency (nearly two-thirds of the product's volume comes from light users who buy only one or two cans per year).
- RBD consumption is concentrated in the northern states and during the fall and winter months (about 75 percent of volume is achieved from September through February).
- Marketing research results suggest consumers believe RBD is relatively expensive in terms of price/value compared to alternative forms of dinner breadstuffs.

B. Competitive situation
- RBD's share of the total dinner breadstuffs category is likely to remain low because of the wide variety of competing choices available to consumers.
- The largest proportion of volume within the category is captured by ready-to-eat breads and rolls produced by supermarket chains and regional bakeries and distributed through retail grocery stores.
- RBD's major competition within the refrigerated dough category comes from other Pillsbury products, such as Crescent rolls and Soft Breadsticks.
- There are currently no other national competitors in the refrigerated bread dough category; but Merico, a small regional producer, was recently acquired by a major national food manufacturer. Evidence suggests Merico may be preparing to introduce a competing product line into national distribution at a price about 10 percent lower than Pillsbury's.

C. Macroenvironmental situation
- Changes in American eating habits may pose future problems for dinner breadstuffs in general, and for RBD in particular:
    More meals are being eaten away from home, and this trend is likely to continue.
    People are eating fewer starchy foods.
    While total volume of dinner breadstuffs did not fall during the early 1980s, neither did it keep pace with population growth.
- Increasing numbers of women working outside the home, and the resulting desire for convenience, may reduce consumers' willingness to wait 30 minutes while RBD bakes, even though the dough is already prepared.
- Because RBD does not use yeast as a leavening agent, Food and Drug Administration regulations prohibit the company from referring to it as "bread" in advertising or package copy, even though the finished product looks, smells, and tastes like bread.

D. Past product performance
- While sales volume in units increased only slightly from 1986 to 1987, dollar volume increased by 24 percent due to a price increase taken in early 1987.
- The improvement to gross margin from 1986 to 1987 was even greater than the price increase due to an improvement in manufacturing costs.
- The improvement in gross margin, however, was not sufficient to produce a positive net margin due to high advertising and sales promotion expenditures aimed at stimulating primary demand and increasing market penetration of RBD.
- Consequently, while RBD showed improvement from 1986 to 1987, it was still unable to make a positive contribution to overhead and profit.

EXHIBIT 12A–1
(*continued*)

II. Key issues
A. Threats
- Lack of growth in the dinner breadstuffs category suggests the market is mature and may decline in the future.
- The large variety of alternatives available to consumers suggests it may be impossible for RBD to substantially increase its share of the total market.
- Potential entry of a new, lower-priced competitor poses a threat to RBD's existing share and may result in lower margins if RBD responds by reducing its price.

B. Opportunities
- The largest percentage of RBD volume accounted for by light users suggests an opportunity of increasing volume among current users by stimulating frequency of use.
- Trends toward increased consumption of specialty breads suggests possible line extensions, such as whole wheat or other whole grain flavors.

C. Strengths
- RBD has a strong distribution base, with shelf facings in nearly 90 percent of available retail outlets.
- RBD sales have proved responsive to sales promotion efforts (e.g., cents-off coupons), primarily by increasing purchases among existing users.
- The fact that most consumers who try RBD make repeat purchases indicates a high level of customer satisfaction.

D. Weaknesses
- RBD sales have proved unresponsive to advertising. Attempts to stimulate primary demand have not been able to increase market penetration.
- Consumer concerns about RBD's price/value place limits on ability to take future price increases.

III. Objectives
A. Financial objectives
- Achieve a positive contribution to overhead and profit of $4 million in current year.
- Reach the target level of an average of 20 percent return on investment over the next five years.

B. Marketing objectives
- Maintain market share and net sales revenues at previous year's levels.
- Maintain current levels of retail distribution coverage.
- Reduce marketing expenditures sufficiently to achieve profit contribution objective.
- Identify viable opportunities for future volume and profit expansion.

IV. Marketing strategy
- Pursue a **maintenance strategy** aimed at holding or slightly increasing RBD volume and market share primarily by stimulating increased frequency of use among current users.
- Reduce advertising aimed at stimulation of primary demand/penetration and reduce manufacturing costs in order to achieve profit contribution objective.
- Initiate development and test marketing of possible line extensions to identify opportunities for future volume expansion.

V. Marketing action plans
- Improve the perceived price/value of RBD by maintaining current suggested retail price at least through the peak selling season (February). Review the competitive situation and the brand's profit performance in March to assess the desirability of a price increase at that time.
- Work with production to identify and implement cost savings opportunities that will reduce manufacturing costs by 5 percent without compromising product quality.
- Maintain retail distribution coverage with two trade promotion discount offers totaling $855,000; one offered in October–November to support peak season inventories, and another offered in February–March to maintain inventories as volume slows.
- Reduce advertising to a maintenance level of 1,100 gross ratings points during the peak sales period of September to March. Focus copy on maintaining awareness among current users.

continues

EXHIBIT   12A-1
(*concluded*)

> • Encourage greater frequency of use among current users through three sales promotion events, with a total budget of $748,000, that will stimulate immediate purchase:
>> One free-standing insert (FSI) coupon for 15 cents off next purchase to appear in newspapers on September 19.
>> One tear-off offer (buy three, get one free) placed in retailers' shelves during November.
>> A $1 refund with proof of purchase offer placed in women's service books (i.e., women's magazines like *Good Housekeeping*) during March.

Analysis of the current situation

This section of the plan summarizes relevant background information drawn from a detailed analysis of target customers, competitors, and macroenvironmental variables. It also reviews the recent performance of the product on such dimensions as sales volume, margin, and profit contribution. This information provides the foundation for identifying the key issues—the threats and opportunities—the product must face in the coming year.

Market situation

Here data on the target market are presented. The section should discuss total market size and growth trends, along with any variations across geographic regions or other market segments. It might also present marketing research information concerning customer perceptions (e.g., awareness of the brand) and buying behavior trends (e.g., market penetration, repeat purchase rate, heavy versus light users). As Exhibit 12A–1 indicates, for instance, this section of the plan for Pillsbury's refrigerated bread dough (RBD) includes not only data about the size of the total market for dinner breadstuffs and the company's market share; it also points out the low penetration and use frequency of RBD among potential users.

Competitive situation

This section identifies and describes the product's major competitors in terms of size, market share, product quality, marketing strategies, and other relevant factors. It might also discuss the likelihood that other potential competitors will enter the market in the near future and the possible impact of such entry on the product's competitive position. Note, for instance, that while other Pillsbury brands are the primary competitors for RBD in the refrigerated dough category, the potential entry of a new low-cost competitor could dramatically change the competitive situation.

The macroenvironmental situation

This section describes broad environmental occurrences or trends that may affect the product's future. The issues mentioned here include any relevant

EXHIBIT 12A-2

Historical and Projected Financial Performance of
Refrigerated Bread Dough Product

Variable	1986	1987	Percent change 1986–87	Projected 1988	Percent change 1987–88
Sales volume (cases)	2,290M	2,350M	+3%	2,300M	(2%)
Net sales ($)	17,078M	21,165M	+24	21,182M	0
Gross margin ($)	6,522M	10,767M	+65	11,430M	+5
Gross margin/net sales	38%	51%	—	54%	—
Advertising and sales promotion ($)	11,609M	12,492M	+6	6,100M	(51)
Advertising & sales promotion/gross margin	178%	116%	—	53%	—
Net margin ($)	(5,087M)	(1,725M)	—	5,330M	—
Net margin/net sales	—	—	—	25	—
Product contribution ($)	(6,342M)	(3,740M)	—	4,017M	—

economic, technological, political/legal, or social/cultural changes. As Exhibit 12A–1 indicates, for example, lifestyle trends leading to more meals being eaten away from home and increased desires for convenience pose a threat to future demand for Pillsbury's RBD.

Past product performance

This part of the situation analysis discusses the product's performance on such dimensions as sales volume, margins, marketing expenditures, and profit contribution for several recent years. This information is usually presented in a table, such as the one shown in Appendix Exhibit 12A–2. As the table indicates, even though reduced manufacturing costs improved RBD's gross margin, high advertising and sales expenditures prevented the product from making a positive contribution to overhead and profit in 1987.

Key issues

After analyzing the current situation, the product manager must identify the most important issues facing the product in the coming year. These typically represent either threats to the future market or financial performance of the product or opportunities to improve those performances. This section should also highlight the product's strengths and weaknesses in responding to future threats and opportunities. Some of the key threats and opportunities Pillsbury's RBD faces, together with the product's major strengths and weaknesses, are summarized in section II of Exhibit 12A–1.

Objectives

Information about the current situation, the product's recent performance, and the key issues to be addressed can now serve as the basis for setting specific objectives for the coming year. Managers must specify two types of objectives. **Financial objectives** provide goals for the overall performance of the brand and should reflect the objectives for the SBU as a whole and its competitive strategy. Those financial goals must be converted into **marketing objectives** that specify the changes in customer behavior and levels of performance of various marketing program elements necessary to reach the product's financial objectives.

The major financial and marketing objectives for Pillsbury's RBD are summarized in section III of Exhibit 12A–1. Note that while sales volume and market share are not expected to increase, the product is expected to make a $4 million contribution to overhead and profit through additional cost reductions.

Marketing strategy

Because there may be a number of different ways to achieve the objectives specified in the preceding section, the manager must now specify the overall marketing strategy to be pursued. It is likely to be one, or a combination of several, of the strategies discussed in earlier chapters of this book. Keep in mind, though, that the marketing strategy selected must not only fit the product's situation and objectives, it must also be consistent with the overall competitive strategy of the business unit.

The RBD product manager recommended the unit pursue a maintenance strategy during 1988. The intense competitive situation, uncertainty over the possible entry of Merico, and the past inability of primary demand advertising to increase market penetration all suggest that it would be difficult to expand RBD's market by simply doing "more of the same." Consequently, the recommended strategy seeks to maintain, or slightly increase, RBD volume and market share primarily by stimulating repeat purchases among current customers. The business will rely on reductions in advertising expenditures and continued improvements in manufacturing costs to help the brand achieve its profit contribution objective. In addition, the manager recommended the development and test marketing of several line extensions (e.g., whole wheat and a French-style loaf) in 1988 in an attempt to identify viable opportunities for future volume expansion.

Action plans

The action plan is the most crucial part of the annual marketing plan for ensuring proper execution. This section lists the specific actions necessary to implement the strategy for the product and clearly states who is responsible for each action, when it will be done, and how much is to be spent on it. Of course, the plan should include actions requiring the cooperation of other functional departments only after the product manager has contacted the departments involved, worked out any potential conflicts, and received assurances of support.

Some of the action programs specified for RBD in 1988 are outlined in section V of Exhibit 12A–1. It is also common practice to display an events calendar detailing when each promotional action is scheduled for the coming year.

Projected profit-and-loss statement

The action plan includes a supporting budget that is essentially a projected profit-and-loss statement. On the revenue side, it forecasts next year's sales volume in units and dollars. On the expense side, it reflects manufacturing, distribution, and marketing costs associated with the planned actions. Higher levels of management then review and possibly modify this budget. Once approved, the product's budget serves as a basis for the plans and resource allocation decisions of other functional departments within the SBU, such as manufacturing and purchasing. The projected financial results of RBD's 1988 annual plan are summarized in the last column of Exhibit 12A–2.

Controls

The final section of the plan outlines the controls management will use to monitor the brand's progress during the year. The objectives and budget are usually broken down by quarter to allow management to review the results for each period and, if necessary, make adjustments to the plan during the year to achieve the annual objectives. This section might also specify contingency plans the business can implement if specific threats or opportunities should occur during the year. The RBD product manager, for instance, recommended that the firm make no change in price or promotion programs during 1988 even if Merico should enter the national market. The rationale was that it would need time to assess the magnitude of Merico's potential threat and to determine the most appropriate response.

Controlling Marketing Strategies and Programs

CONTROLS PAY OFF AT WAL-MART[1]

Wal-Mart, a discount general merchandise retailer, is America's most admired retailer and ranks sixth on the list of the most admired large U.S. companies. Founded only 25 years ago, Wal-Mart had sales in 1990 of $32.6 billion, which made it the nation's largest retailer ahead of both Kmart ($31 billion) and Sears ($26.6 billion). In April 1991, the United Shareholders Association said Wal-Mart was the company that did best for its shareholders over the past 10 years, providing them with an average annual return of 44.4 percent.

At the end of April 1991, the company operated 1,591 Wal-Mart stores (including five supercenters), 178 Sam's Clubs, and four Hyper-marts, which are five-acre "malls without walls." Sam's, with annual sales of over $7 billion, targets small businesses and low-risk households. It operates on gross margins of 9 to 10 percent and stocks only about 3,500 items versus nearly 50,000 for a Discount City store.

Total square footage of retail space, as of April 30, 1991, was 133 million versus 110 million a year ago. Management has an aggressive plan for new store and club growth during 1991. It plans to add 165 to 175 Wal-Mart stores, 25 to 27 Sam's Clubs, 3 to 4 Supercenters, and one Hypermart. The firm plans to enter seven new states with Wal-Mart stores and four with Sam's Clubs. In moving ever closer to its objec-

[1]Based on a case written by Clark Lawrence of the College of Business, University of Arkansas at Little Rock, in 1983 and revised in 1986; Wal-Mart's 1988, 1990, 1991 *Annual Report;* and First Quarter 1991 Financial Report; John Huey, "Wal-Mart—Will It Take Over the World?" *Fortune,* January 30, 1989, p. 52; Sarah Smith, "America's Most Admired Corporations," *Fortune,* January 29, 1990, p. 53; Bill Saporito, "Retailing's Winners and Losers," *Fortune,* December 18, 1989, p. 69; and "Briefly . . . ," *USA Today,* April 10, 1991, p. 28.

tive of not having a single operating unit that has not been updated in the past seven years, the firm anticipates 70 to 80 relocations or expansions and 88 refurbishings and remodels during 1991. In support of this expansion, it planned to open three new 1 million square foot plus distribution centers in calendar 1991.[2]

A major reason for Wal-Mart's success is its ability to control cost. Despite the substantial increase in the number of stores and wholesale clubs it operates and the start-up of its Hypermarts, its cost of sales has increased only 1.7 percentage points over 1986. This was due largely to the cost of sales in Sam's units, which as a percent of sales is considerably higher than in the Discount City stores because of a lower markup. Reductions in operations, selling, and general administrative costs lowered overall expenses 1.3 percentage points from 1986. As a result, the company experienced record profits of $1.291 billion in 1990, an increase of 20 percent over 1989.

Wal-Mart's management emphasizes frugality, illustrated by the fact that its corporate headquarters in Bentonville, Arkansas, is often mistaken for a warehouse. Management regularly emphasizes that money is not well spent if it does not foster growth or lower costs. Wal-Mart is unique in the way it controls not only its expenses (down to a given department at the individual store level) but its merchandising activities as well. The essence of the company's success lies in its ability to

couple state-of-the-art computer communications technology with hands-on management.

All of the company's regional vice presidents live in or near Bentonville. Every Monday they and other management personnel, often including Sam Walton and David Glass, president and chief executive officer, fly via corporate turboprops to stores in the various regions. There they talk with store managers, employees ("associates"), and customers. On Friday they return to Bentonville to share their findings with headquarters personnel and prepare for a Saturday merchandise meeting attended by the regional vice presidents, the chairman or vice chairman, the president, and 100 or more other employees.

These are no-holds-barred sessions concerned with moving merchandise. The participants use printouts of inventory levels and sales of key items. *Fortune* describes one such meeting, just before Christmas 1988, as follows:

> For three hours, the managers pore over the printout. One is concerned that Wal-Mart has priced children's corduroy jeans at $3, while Kmart is promoting them at two for $5; this is corrected. CEO Glass worries that a certain video game isn't moving in stores he has visited this week, and he wants orders put off; the buyers have beaten him to it. Then a discussion ensues over knives, which the printout shows are heavily stocked in Wal-Mart's distribution centers. Quickly a senior manager orders a Christmas-gift knife display.[3]

[2]*Wal-Mart Annual Report, 1990*, p. 3.
[3]Huey, "Wal-Mart—Will It Take Over the World?" p. 54.

These and similar decisions will reach all store managers by the following Monday at the latest. The company communicates all this by phone but can use its satellite system if necessary. This system's basic function is to transmit store data to the central computer, handle requests for credit-card approval from all stores, and track distribution activities. This communication network also informs managers at the individual store level how well their sections did the previous week and how they compare with similar sections in other stores. Managers seek causes for both good and bad performances. A department or section that consistently performs better than average receives monetary rewards and recognition. Management talks to units doing less well in an effort to find out why and how to correct the problem.

Wal-Mart has mastered distribution technology to a point where a store should never be out of stock. Doing that better than its rivals, the company generates 9 percent more sales per square foot than them and hence turns its inventories faster. This means less borrowing to carry inventories and hence lower interest payments (over $200 million less than Kmart). By carefully controlling other expenses, Wal-Mart is able to operate with a gross margin of 23 percent (versus Kmart's 28 percent) and still yield a net profit of 4.2 percent of sales compared to an industry average of 2.9 percent.[4] Exhibit 13–1 presents Wal-Mart's net income from 1983–89 as compared to its primary competitors.

The marketing management process consists of setting objectives, formulating strategies, implementing a plan of action, devising and controlling procedures, and reappraising the results. In the control and reappraisal step, the firm monitors the extent to which it is achieving its objectives. If not, at this step the firm determines whether the reason lies in the environment, the strategies employed, the action plans, the way the plans were implemented, or some combination thereof. Thus, the control and reappraisal step is diagnostic, serving to start the marketing management process anew.

Control processes differ at each organizational level. Thus, corporate management is concerned with how well its various SBUs are performing relative to the opportunities and threats each faces and the resources given them. Control here would be environmentally oriented and, hence, strategic in nature. In addition, corporate management is concerned with how well each SBU is performing in its various functional areas. At the SBU level, concern is primarily with the unit's own strategy, especially as it pertains to its individual product-market entries. We will concentrate mainly on this latter organizational level since it constitutes the bulk of any control system.

---

[4]Saporito, "Retailing's Winners and Losers," pp. 72, 76.

EXHIBIT 13-1

Merchandise Net Income of Wal-Mart, Kmart,
J.C. Penney, and Sears, 1983–89* ($ millions)

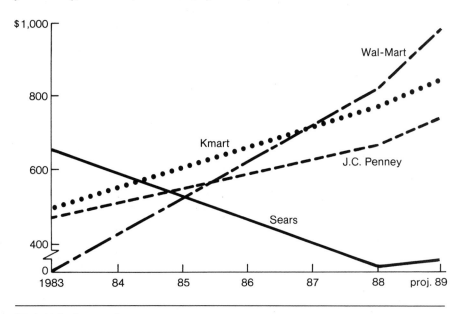

*Excludes foreign operations.

SOURCE: John Huey, "Wal-Mart—Will It Take Over the World?" *Fortune,* January 30, 1989, p. 56. © 1989
The Time, Inc., Magazine Company. All rights reserved.

In this chapter, we first discuss the control process and then examine strategic controls. Next, we discuss controls pertaining to individual product-market entries, particularly their competitive position, their adherence to plan (including budget and share determinants), and the efficiency with which marketing manages its resources. The chapter ends with a discussion of global marketing control, marketing audits, and marketing decision support systems.

THE CONTROL PROCESS

Regardless of the organization level involved, the control process is essentially the same. It consists essentially of setting performance standards, specifying and obtaining feedback data, evaluating it, and taking corrective action (see Exhibit 13–2). Although the staff organization is largely responsible for generating the control data, the line organization administers the control process. Certainly, this is the case with Wal-Mart, as seen,in the involvement of regional vice presidents, district managers, store managers, and department heads in obtaining and processing control data as well as taking corrective action.

EXHIBIT 13-2
The Control Process

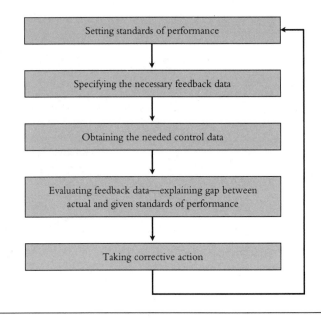

Setting standards of performance

The standards of performance we are most concerned about derive largely from the objectives and strategies set forth at the SBU and individual product-market entry levels. These generate a series of performance expectations for profitability (return on equity or return on assets managed), market share, and sales. At the product-market level, standards of performance also include sales and market-share determinants such as percent effective distribution, relative shelf facings, awareness, consumers' attitude change toward a given product attribute, and the extent of price parity. And, finally, budget line items having to do with expenses such as the salesforce (salary payments) and advertising (cost of a specific campaign) serve as cost controls and standards of performance. Without a reasonable set of performance standards, managers could not know what results are being obtained, the extent to which they are satisfactory, or why they are or are not satisfactory.

To be of any value, performance standards must be measurable; further, they must be tied to some specific time periods, particularly so when they concern a management compensation system (see Exhibit 13–3). Generally speaking, control systems at the product-market level operate on a monthly, quarterly, and annual basis, with the monthly and quarterly data cumulated to present a current picture and to facilitate comparisons with prior years. In recent years, the trend has been for control systems to operate over shorter periods (weekly and even daily) and for control data to be more quickly available. Wal-Mart's inventory-control system, for example, provides instanta-

EXHIBIT 13-3

Strategic Control at General Electric

While General Electric monitors the performance of its individual business units on such traditional criteria as profitability, cash flow, market share, and technological position, it is concerned about tailoring the compensation to fit the situation. Thus, in the words of Jack Welch, chairman and CEO of General Electric, "we let every business come up with its own pay plan. It can create bonus plans in any way that makes sense. We're doing all kinds of exciting things to reward people for their contributions, things we've never done before. For example, we now give out $20 to $30 million in management awards every year—cash payments to individuals for outstanding performance."

SOURCE: Noel Tichy and Ram Charan, "Speed, Simplicity, Self-Confidence: An Interview with Jack Welch," *Harvard Business Review,* September–October 1989, pp. 112–20.

neous up-to-date data. Strategic control tends to operate over longer periods of time.

Of particular importance is whether the business unit as a whole and its individual product-market entries have set forth milestone measures to achieve. For example, in a three-year strategy plan, a given SBU might have such 18-month milestones as sales at an annual rate of $36 million, profits of $6.2 million, and a return on assets managed of 14.5 percent. At the product-market entry level, milestones include such measures as product sales by segments, marginal contribution, and operating margins. At the marketing functional area level, examples of milestone measures for a consumer good are level of awareness, trial, and repeat purchases among members of the target audience, and percent of stores stocking (weighted by sales).

Profitability analysis

Regardless of the organizational level, control involves some form of profitability analysis. In brief, **profitability analysis** requires that analysts determine the costs associated with specific marketing activities to find out the profitability of such units as different market segments, products, customer accounts, and distribution channels (intermediaries). Wal-Mart does this at department and store levels as well as for individual lines of goods within a department. More and more, management is attempting to obtain profitability measures for individual products in their various markets.

Profitability is probably the single most important measure of performance, but it has limitations. These are (1) many objectives can best be measured in nonfinancial terms (e.g., maintaining marketing share); (2) profit is a short-term measure and can be manipulated by taking actions that may prove dysfunctional longer term (e.g. reducing R & D expenses); and (3) profits can be affected by factors over which management has no control (e.g., the weather).[5]

---

[5]For further discussion, see John C. Camillus, *Strategic Planning and Management Control* (Lexington, Mass.: D. C. Heath & Company, 1986), pp. 170–73.

EXHIBIT 13–4

Finding Product or Entry Profitability with Full Costing and
Marginal Contributions Methods ($000)

	Full costing	Marginal contribution
Net sales	$5,400	$5,400
Less: Cost of goods sold—includes direct costs (labor, material, and production overhead)*	3,800	3,800
Gross margin	$1,600	$1,600
Expenses		
Salesforce—includes direct costs (commissions) plus indirect costs (sales expenses, sales management overhead)†	$ 510	$ 450
Advertising—includes direct costs (media, production) plus indirect costs (management overhead)	215	185
Physical logistics—includes direct costs (transportation) plus indirect costs (order processing, warehousing costs)	225	190
Occupancy—includes direct costs (telephone) plus indirect costs (heat/air, insurance, taxes, building maintenance)	100	25
Management overhead—includes direct costs (product/brand manager and staff) plus indirect costs (salaries, expenses, occupancy costs of SBU's general management group)	180	100
Total	$1,230	$ 950
Profit before taxes	$ 370	
Contribution to fixed costs and profits		$ 650

*Production facilities dedicated to a single product.
†Multiproduct salesforce.

Analysts have the option of using direct or full costing in determining the profitability of a product or market segment. In **full costing,** analysts assign both direct, or variable, and indirect costs to the unit of analysis. **Indirect costs** involve certain fixed joint costs that cannot be linked directly to a single unit of analysis. For example, the costs of occupancy, general management, and the management of the salesforce are all indirect costs for a multiproduct company. Those who use full costing argue that only by allocating all costs to a product or a market can they obtain an accurate picture of its value.

Direct costing involves the use of contribution accounting. Those favoring the **contribution margin** approach argue there is really no accurate way to assign indirect costs. Further, because indirect costs are mostly fixed, a product or market may make a contribution to profits even if it shows a loss. Thus, even though the company must eventually absorb overhead, the contribution method clearly indicates what is gained by adding or dropping a product or a customer. Exhibit 13–4 shows an example of full and direct costing. The difference in the results obtained is substantial—$370,000 using full costing versus $650,000 with the contribution method.

EXHIBIT 13-5

Effect of $300,000 Increase in Sales Resulting from Increased Sales Commissions and Expenses of $35,000 (Same data as in Exhibit 4)

Net sales	$5,700
Less: direct costs (29.62%)	4,012
	$1,688
Expenses	
Sales commissions and expenses	$ 485
Advertising	185
Physical logistics	190
Occupancy	25
Management	100
	$ 985
Contribution to overhead and profits	$ 703
Increase in profit (before tax) = $703 − $650 = $53	

Contribution analysis is helpful in determining the yield derived from the application of additional resources (for example, to certain sales territories). Using the data in Exhibit 13–5, we can answer the question, "How much additional profit would result from a marginal increase in sales of $300,000— assuming the gross margin remains at 29.62 percent and the only cost is $35,000 more in sales commissions and expenses?" As Exhibit 13–5 shows, the answer is a profit increase before taxes of $53,000.

Specifying and obtaining feedback data

Once a company has established its performance standards, its next step is to develop a system that provides usable and timely feedback data on actual performance. In most cases someone must gather and process considerable data to obtain the performance measures, especially at the product-market level. Analysts obtain feedback data from a variety of sources, including company accounting records and syndicated marketing information services such as A. C. Nielsen. The sales invoice is the basic internal source of data because it provides a detailed record of each transaction. Invoices are the basis for measuring profitability, sales, and various budget items. They also provide data for analysis of the geographic distribution of sales and customer accounts by type and size.

The remaining source, and typically the most expensive and time consuming, involves undertaking one or more marketing research projects to obtain needed information. In-house research projects are apt to take longer and be more expensive than using an outside syndicated service. But there may be no alternative, as, for example, in determining awareness and attitude changes. Exhibit 13–6 gives an example of how Wal-Mart uses in-house-generated marketing research to help maintain its low-price image.

EXHIBIT   13-6

Wal-Mart Uses Marketing Research to Maintain Price Image

Wal-Mart makes every effort to keep its regular everyday prices lower than competitors on a set of critical products. These "image items" are thought to be the basis of a customer's perception of how expensive a store is. Every few weeks Wal-Mart undertakes research to determine the prices charged by Kmart, Target, and Magic-Mart for these identical items. The company then makes sure that Wal-Mart has the lowest price. Even management—including Sam Walton—has been known to do comparison shopping.

SOURCE: Case prepared by Clark Lawrence, College of Business, University of Arkansas at Little Rock, 1986.

Evaluating feedback data

Management evaluates feedback data to find out why the business unit or entry did or did not perform as expected; that is, why there was a deviation from plan. Wal-Mart does this by sending its regional vice presidents into the field on a regular basis to learn firsthand what's going on and why.

Typically, managers must use a variety of information to determine what the company's performance should have been under the actual market conditions that existed when the plan was executed. In some cases this information can be obtained in measured form; examples include a shift in personal disposable income (available from government sources), a change in the demand for a given product type (obtained in the process of measuring market share), the impact of a new brand on market share (reported by a commercial source), or a change in price by a major competitor (see Exhibit 13–6). Often, however, the explanation may rest on inferences drawn from generalized data, as would be the case in attributing poor sales performance to an improvement in a competitor's salesforce.

Taking corrective action

The last step in the control process concerns prescribing the needed action to correct the situation. At Wal-Mart, this is partly accomplished at the Saturday breakfast meeting, when managers decide what actions to take to solve selected problems. Success here depends on how well managers carry out the evaluation step. When linkages between inputs and outputs are clear, managers can presume a causal relationship and specify appropriate action. For example, assume that inputs consisted of an advertising schedule that specified the frequency to air a given TV message. The objective was to change attitudes about a given product attribute (the output). If the attitude change did not occur, remedial action would start with an evaluation of the firm's advertising effort, particularly the advertising message and how frequently it was run.

But in most cases it is difficult to identify the cause of the problem. Almost always, an interactive effect exists among the input variables. For example, advertisers can rarely separate the effects of the message, media, frequency of exposure, and competitive responses in an attempt to determine advertising effects. Even if the company could determine the cause of a problem in a reasonably unambiguous way, it faces the difficulty of prescribing the appropriate action to take. Most control systems are "based on the assumption that corrective action is *known* should significant variations arise. Unfortunately, marketing is not at a stage where performance deviations can be corrected with certainty."[6]

As we have seen throughout this text, marketing management finds it difficult to perceive and formulate problems and to make decisions. There are many reasons for this, including the need to deal with the firm's external environment—something over which no executive has control. Further, because of delayed responses and carry-over effects, marketing executives find it difficult to predict outcomes for both the short and long terms. In addition, there are myriad ways to solve a marketing problem. And for each alternative, it is possible to vary the intensity with which specific resources are applied, making the problem that much more difficult to solve from an efficiency point of view.

Sometimes the outcome is greater or better than management had planned; for example, when sales and market share exceed the schedule. In such cases, the marketers still need an evaluation to find out why such a variance occurred. Perhaps a more favorable environment evolved because demand was greater than expected and a major competitor failed to take advantage of it. Or perhaps the advertising message was more effective than expected. These different "reasons why" would call for different marketing responses to hold what had been obtained and to exploit the favorable situation.

We now turn our attention to strategic control, which very much concerns both corporate and SBU-level management.

STRATEGIC CONTROL

Strategic control is concerned with monitoring and evaluating a firm's SBU-level strategies (see Exhibit 13–7 for the kinds of questions this type of control system is designed to answer). Such a system is difficult to implement because there is usually a substantial amount of time between strategy formulation and when a strategy takes hold and results are evident. Since both the external and internal environments are constantly evolving, strategic control must provide some way of correcting the firm's thrust if new information about the environment and/or the firm's performance so dictates. Inevitably, much of this intermediate assessment is based on information about the marketplace and the results obtained from the firm's marketing plan.[7]

---

[6]Bernard J. Jaworski, "Toward a Theory of Marketing Control: Environmental Context, Control Types, and Consequences," *Journal of Marketing,* July 1988, p. 24.

[7]Leslie W. Rue and Phyllis G. Holland, *Strategic Management* (New York: McGraw Hill, 1989), chap. 1.

EXHIBIT 13-7

Examples of Questions a Strategic Control System Should Be Able to Answer

> 1. What changes in the environment have negatively affected the current strategy (e.g., interest rates, government controls, or price changes in substitute products)?
> 2. What changes have major competitors made in their objectives and strategies?
> 3. What changes have occurred in the industry in such attributes as capacity, entry barriers, substitute products?
> 4. What new opportunities or threats have derived from changes in the environment, competitors' strategies, or the nature of the industry?
> 5. What changes have occurred in the industry's key success factors?
> 6. To what extent is the firm's current strategy consistent with the preceding changes?

Traditionally, the marketing control system as part of the marketing plan is highly structured, emphasizes the short term, and relies almost exclusively on financial or market-based performance measures. Such a system works best over short periods of time, in a relatively stable environmental setting, and when the duties of the managers involved are programmable. Its effectiveness is often limited by its failure to include environmental considerations.[8] For an illustration of the importance of considering environmental events, see Exhibit 13–8 on pages 416–17.

To implement strategic control, a company identifies the strategy's more important assumptions (planning premises) and monitors them using updated information. Typically a company will set up periodic intervals at which to review strategy using new information. At the product-market entry level, many companies mandate an annual strategy review. Reviews can be triggered, however, by an unusual environmental happening (e.g., action by competitors).

Identifying key variables

The key variables (measures of the assumptions or planning premises) to monitor are of two types—those concerned with external forces and those with the effects of certain actions taken by the firm to implement the strategy. The former includes changes in the various components of the external environment; for example, changes in long-term demand, the advent of new technology, a change in governmental legislation, actions by a competitor, union difficulties, and threats pertaining to a critical supplier. Examples of the latter type (actions by the firm) include the firm's advertising objectives, which are based on assumptions about an improvement in consumer attitudes toward the product's characteristics, or the monies spent on merchandising

---

[8]Jaworski, "Toward a Theory of Marketing Control," p. 23.

to improve product availability. Exactly which variables to monitor is a company-specific decision, but in general, monitoring should focus on variables most likely to change and substantially affect the company's future position within its industry group.[9]

Key variables to monitor should be identified during the strategic planning process, when managers are more acutely aware of the assumptions they are making in their strategy formulation. Inevitably, monitoring involves predicting what impact the change in one or more variables will have on the viability of the current strategy; that is, can the strategy still achieve the firm's profitability and market position objectives within the original time and cost constraints?

Assigning probabilities and rank ordering the critical assumptions

This step consists of assigning probabilities of being right to the critical assumptions. Firms must also consider the consequences of these probabilities being wrong. Thus, they must examine assumptions that have a low probability of being wrong but that could affect the firm strongly (e.g., gas shortages on the demand for large-size, luxury automobiles).

By categorizing assumptions by their importance, the extent to which they are controllable, and the confidence management has in them, the firm establishes the basis for rank ordering them and drafting the contingency plan. Ordinarily, these criteria will have screened out those assumptions that need not be included—those with a low impact on objectives and those for which there is a high confidence. However, the firm should monitor assumptions relating to uncontrollable events if they strongly affect the entry's strategic objectives, because the firm can react to them. For example, if the assumption about the rate of market growth is wrong, the firm can either slow or increase its marketing investments.

Tracking and monitoring

The next step is to specify what information, or measures, are needed to determine whether the implementation of the strategic plan is on schedule—and if not, why. The firm can use the control plan as an early-warning system as well as a diagnostic tool. If, for example, the firm has made certain assumptions about the rate at which market demand will increase, it should monitor industry sales on a regular basis. If it has made assumptions about advertising and its effect on attitudes, it would likely use measures of awareness, trial, and repeat buying. In any event, the firm must closely examine relevancy, accuracy, and cost of obtaining the needed measures.

---

[9]William H. Newman, James P. Logan, and W. Harvey Hegart, *Strategy* (Cincinnati, Oh.: South-Western Publishing, 1989), chap. 23.

EXHIBIT 13-8

An Example of the Use of Environment Measures in a Strategic Control System

Hulbert and Toy contend that most firms have not related marketing control procedures to such key strategy parameters as market share, market size, and market growth. They propose a strategic framework for marketing control that evaluates marketing performance and includes **variance decomposition,** which attempts to isolate the causes for the deviations from plans. An example of their control procedure featuring an analysis of Product Alpha is shown in Tables A and B below.

The unfavorable variance in contribution of $100,000 could develop from either the differences between planned and actual quantities and/or contribution per unit. The former could be due to differences between planned and actual market size and market share or penetration.

TABLE A
Operating Results for Product Alpha (000)

Item	Planned	Actual	Variance
Revenues			
Sales (pounds)	20,000	22,000	+2,000
Price per pound ($)	$0.50	$0.4773	$-0.227
Revenues	$10,000	$10,500	+$500
Total market (pounds)	40,000	50,000	+10,000
Market share	50%	44%	-6%
Costs			
Variable cost per pound ($)	$0.30	$0.30	—
Contribution			
Per pound ($)	$0.20	$0.1773	-$0.0227
Total ($)	$4,000	$3,900	-100

Thus, the potential sources of the $100,000 are the differences between planned and actual market size, market share, and price/cost per unit. The variance decomposition of each of these three variables makes it possible to determine the origin of the variances.

The conclusions of the analysis showed:

1. The favorable volume variance of $400,000 was caused by two larger variances canceling each other out—one positive and one negative, but neither desirable. By not achieving the planned share of market, the firm lost $600,000 in profit contribution. The loss of market share may have been due to poor planning and/or execution.
2. The $1 million positive contribution variance compensated for the unfavorable share variance because the market turned out to be much larger than forecasted. This represents a forecasting error.

Strategy reassessment

This can take place at periodic intervals—for example, quarterly or annually. If such is the case, the firm would evaluate its performance to date along with major changes in the external environment. Or it can use the control system to alert management of a significant change in either or both its external/internal environments. This involves setting "triggers" to signal an immediate need to reassess the viability of the firm's strategy. It requires a specifi-

EXHIBIT 13–8
(concluded)

3. The danger signal, strategywise, is clear—as the largest competitor, the company lost market share in a fast-growth market.
4. The final variance component is the unfavorable price variance of −$500,000. To what extent did this lower price level expand the total market? Was the failure to hold price at the planned level a failure in tactics or planning, that is, inaccurate forecasts?

Hulbert and Toy conclude that this analysis "has limited potential for diagnosing the causes of problems. Rather, its major benefit is in the *identification* of areas where problems may exist. Determining the factors which have actually caused favorable or unfavorable variances requires the skill and expertise of the manager."

TABLE B
Variance Decomposition Analysis for Product Alpha

$$\text{Market volume variance} = \begin{pmatrix} \text{Actual total} \\ \text{market} \\ \text{units} \end{pmatrix} - \begin{pmatrix} \text{Planned total} \\ \text{market} \\ \text{units} \end{pmatrix} \times \begin{pmatrix} \text{Planned} \\ \text{market} \\ \text{share} \end{pmatrix} \times \begin{pmatrix} \text{Planned} \\ \text{contribution} \\ \text{per unit} \end{pmatrix}$$

$$= (50,000,000 - 40,000,000) \times (.50) \times (.20) \qquad = \quad \$1,000,000$$

$$\text{Company volume variance} = \begin{pmatrix} \text{Actual} \\ \text{sales} \\ \text{in units} \end{pmatrix} - \begin{pmatrix} \text{Planned} \\ \text{sales} \\ \text{in units} \end{pmatrix} \times \begin{pmatrix} \text{Planned} \\ \text{contribution} \\ \text{per unit} \end{pmatrix}$$

$$= (22,000,000 - 20,000,000) \times (.20) \qquad = \quad \$\ 400,000$$

$$\text{Company share variance} = \begin{pmatrix} \text{Actual} \\ \text{market} \\ \text{share} \end{pmatrix} - \begin{pmatrix} \text{Planned} \\ \text{market} \\ \text{share} \end{pmatrix} \times \begin{pmatrix} \text{Actual total} \\ \text{market} \\ \text{in units} \end{pmatrix} \times \begin{pmatrix} \text{Planned} \\ \text{contribution} \\ \text{per unit} \end{pmatrix}$$

$$= (.44 - .50) \times (50,000,000) \times (.20) \qquad = \ -\$\ 600,000$$

$$\text{Contribution variance} = \begin{pmatrix} \text{Actual} \\ \text{contribtion} \\ \text{per unit} \end{pmatrix} - \begin{pmatrix} \text{Planned} \\ \text{contribution} \\ \text{per unit} \end{pmatrix} \times \begin{pmatrix} \text{Actual} \\ \text{sales} \\ \text{in units} \end{pmatrix}$$

$$= (.1773 - .20) \times (22,000,000) \qquad = \ -\$\ 500,000$$

$$\text{Total variance} = \begin{matrix} \text{Market} \\ \text{volume} \\ \text{variance} \end{matrix} + \begin{matrix} \text{Company} \\ \text{volume} \\ \text{variance} \end{matrix} + \begin{matrix} \text{Company} \\ \text{share} \\ \text{variance} \end{matrix} + \begin{matrix} \text{Contribution} \\ \text{variance} \end{matrix}$$

$$= \$1,000,000 + \$400,000 - \$600,000 - \$500,000 \qquad = \quad \$\ 300,000$$

SOURCE: Reprinted from *Journal of Marketing,* published by the American Marketing Association, "Strategic Framework for Marketing Control," by James M. Hulbert and Norman E. Toy, April 1977, p. 13.

cation of both the level at which an alert will be called and the combination of events that must occur before the firm reacts. For example, total industry sales of 10 percent less than expected for a single month would not likely trigger a response, whereas a 25 percent drop would. Or a firm may decide the triggering would occur only after three successive months in which a difference of 10 percent occurred. Therefore, the firm must define triggers precisely and assign responsibility for responding to the alarm signals.

PRODUCT-MARKET ENTRY CONTROL

Having discussed strategic control, the primary concern of corporate and SBU top management, we turn our attention to product-market entry control systems. These systems are designed to ensure that the company achieves the sales, profits, and other objectives set forth in its annual product-market entry action plans. In the aggregate, these plans represent the SBUs' short-term planning efforts, which specify how resources will be allocated across products and markets. These entry plans include a line-item budget and detail the actions required of each organizational unit both inside and outside the marketing department to attain certain financial and competitive position objectives. In this section, we discuss competitive position control, adherence to plan (both budget and sales/share determinants), and sales analysis.

Because budgets project revenues and expenses for a given time period, they are a vital part of the firm's planning and control activities. They provide the basis for a continuous evaluation and comparison of what was planned with what actually happened. In this sense, budgeted revenues and profits serve as objectives against which to measure performance in sales and profits as well as actual costs.

Budget analysis requires that managers continuously monitor marketing expenses to make certain that the company does not overspend in its effort to reach its objectives. They also evaluate the magnitude and pattern of deviations from the target ratios. Before taking corrective action, managers may need to disaggregate the data to help isolate the problem. For example, if total commissions as a percent of sales are out of line, analysts need to specify them for each sales territory and product (when possible) to help determine exactly where the problem lies.

Sales/share determinants

Sales and market share are a function of a number of primary determinants. For a consumer product these include effective distribution, relative price, attitude change toward one or more salient product characteristics relative to competition, and shelf facings. These, in turn, are a function of secondary determinants such as number and frequency of sales calls, trade deals, and the effectiveness of the advertising message with a given reach and frequency schedule. These determinants form a hierarchy of objectives ensuring that strategy is elaborated in specific measurable actions. Thus, the action plan provides the basis for the operational control system.

An analysis of the share determinants should provide insights into presumed linkages between the firm's inputs and outputs; for example, number and frequency of sales calls and effective distribution. This, in turn, leads to a better understanding of the firm's marketing efficiency. Is the salesforce making as many calls per day as expected—and the right number of calls on target accounts to obtain a certain level of distribution?

Marketing research is usually required to ascertain the extent to which determinants are being attained. For example, a change in awareness and attitudes toward certain product characteristics would require the use of certain messages and an ad schedule with a certain reach and frequency. Interviewers would need to question the targeted audience to determine the message's success in communicating the desired information. Analysts could use data from syndicated research services to obtain estimates of frequency of exposure and reach of the media vehicles used.

Sales analysis

A firm's marketing department routinely undertakes a **sales analysis** to learn about opportunities and problems relating to individual products as well as to a variety of marketing activities. The general procedure is to break down aggregate sales data into certain categories such as products, end-user customers, channel intermediaries, sales territories, and order size. Analysts then compare the data to other internal and external data.

The objective of a sales analysis is to find areas of strengths and weakness; for example, products producing the greatest and least volume, customers accounting for the bulk of the revenues, and salespersons and territories performing the poorest. Thus, one of the more important benefits of even the most primitive sales analysis lies in identifying products, territories, and customers that account for the bulk of the company's sales. Such information enables a company to concentrate its resources where they provide the best yield.

Sales analysis recognizes that aggregate sales and cost data often mask the real situation sufficiently to allow a misdiagnosis of the real problem. For example, a firm marketing a line of male toiletries experienced an overall increase in dollar sales of 12 percent. In analyzing this increase, company executives were surprised to learn that the increase came primarily from two new products. Indeed, without the new products, overall sales would have declined 3 percent despite an inflationary factor of over 5 percent. Sales analyses not only help to evaluate and control marketing efforts, they help management better formulate objectives and strategies and administer such nonmarketing activities as production planning, inventory management, and facilities planning.

Units of analysis

An important decision in designing the firm's sales analysis system concerns which units of analysis to use—that is, what levels of aggregation are important? Most companies assemble data in the following groupings:

- Geographical areas—regions, counties, and sales territories.
- Product, package size, and grade.
- Customer—by type and size.
- Channel intermediary—such as type and/or size of retailer.
- Method of sale—mail, phone, channel, or direct.
- Size of order—less than $10, $10–$25, and so on.

These breakdowns are not mutually exclusive. Most firms perform sales analyses hierarchically; for example, by county within a sales territory within a sales region. Further, they usually combine product and account breakdowns with a geographical one; say, the purchase of product X by large accounts located in sales territory Y, which is a part of region A. Only by conducting a sales analysis on a hierarchical basis using a combination of breakdowns can analysts be at all sure that they have made every reasonable attempt to locate the opportunities and problems facing their firms. We discuss the different kinds of sales analyses briefly in the following sections.

Sales analysis evaluation systems

The two major evaluation systems are a simple sales analysis and a comparative one. In a **simple sales analysis,** the data are listed in tabular form with no effort to compare the figures against any standard, while the **comparative analysis**—as its name implies—uses comparisons between the facts and some set of standards.

Consider, for example, the data in Exhibit 13–9. A simple sales analysis would be restricted to the data in column 1, which suggests that White, who sold the most, was the best salesperson and Finch, who sold the least, was the worst. But a comparative analysis uses a performance standard such as a sales quota (column 2). It determines individual performance by dividing actual sales by the sales quota (column 4). On this basis, White was not the best salesperson but the worst, with a performance index of 77 percent. Burrows's over-quota performance was best with an index of 104 percent. Other possible standards to use include last year's sales, average sales of the past three years, and forecasted sales.

Sales analysis sources of information

Once managers have determined what comparisons to make, they must choose which sources of information to use. Invoices are the major source because they contain data that form the essence of any sales analysis. Sometimes the firm needs to add further information about the customer, such as size, type of business, and chain or independent. Other information sources include sales staff call reports and expense accounts, credit memos for returns and allowances, service costs for products under warranty, and data from syndicated subscription research firms.

Sales analysis by territory

The first step in a sales territory analysis is to decide which geographical control unit to use. The county is the typical choice since it can be combined into larger units such as sales territories and also represents the smallest geographical unit for which many data items are available, such as population, employment, income, and retail sales. Analysts can compare actual sales by county against a standard such as the market potential or last year's sales

EXHIBIT 13-9

Sales Analysis Based on Selected Sales Territories

Sales territory	Salesperson	(1) Company sales 1990	(2) Sales quota 1990	(3) Overage, underage	(4) Percent of potential performance
1	Barlow	$552,630	$585,206	− $ 32,576	94%
2	Burrows	470,912	452,800	+ 18,112	104
3	White	763,215	981,441	− 218,226	77
4	Finch	287,184	297,000	− 9,816	96
5	Brown	380,747	464,432	− 83,685	82
6	Roberts	494,120	531,311	− 37,191	93
7	Macini	316,592	329,783	− 13,191	96

adjusted for inflation. They can single out territories that fall below standard for special attention. Is competition unusually strong? Has less selling effort been expended there? Is the salesforce weak? Studies dealing with such questions as these help a company improve its weak areas and exploit its stronger ones.

Exhibit 13–9 also illustrates a comparative sales territory analysis. It shows that only one territory out of seven exceeded its 1990 quota or standard of performance. The amount of sales over quota was only $18,112. The other six territories accounted for a total of $394,685 under quota. Territory 3 alone accounts for 55 percent of the total loss. The sales and the size of the quota in this territory suggest the need for further breakdowns, especially by accounts and products. Such breakdowns may reveal that the firm needs to allocate more selling resources to this territory. In any event, the company needs to improve its sales primarily in territories 3 and 5. If it can reach its potential in these two territories, overall sales would increase by $301,911, assuming that the quotas set are at all valid.

Sales analysis by product

Over time, a company's product line tends to become overcrowded and less profitable unless management takes strong and continuous action to eliminate no-longer-profitable items. By eliminating weak products and concentrating on strong ones, a company can increase its profits substantially. Before deciding which products to abandon, management must study such variables as market-share trends, contribution margins, scale effects, and the extent to which a product is complementary with other items in the line.

A product sales analysis is particularly helpful when combined with account size and sales territory data. Using such an analysis, managers can often pinpoint substantial opportunities and develop specific tactics to take advantage of them. For example, one firm's analysis revealed that sales of one of its highest-margin products were down in all of their New England sales territories. Further investigation showed that a regional producer was aggressively promoting a recently modified product with reduced prices. An analysis of the competing product revealed questionable reliability under certain operating conditions. The salesforce used this information to turn around the sales problem.

Sales analysis by order size

Sales analysis by order size may identify which dollar-size orders are not profitable. For example, if some customers frequently place small orders that require salesforce attention and need to be processed, order picked, and shipped, a problem of some importance likely exists. Using cost accounting data, managers can determine if such orders incur a loss.

Analysis by order size locates products, sales territories, and customer types and sizes where small orders prevail. Such an analysis may lead to setting a minimum order size, charging extra for small orders, training sales reps to develop larger orders, and dropping some accounts. An example of such an analysis involved a nationwide needlework product distributor, which found that 28 percent of all its orders were $10 and under. A study revealed that the average cost of servicing such an order was $12.82. The analysis also showed that the company did not break even until the order size reached $20. Based on these findings, the company installed a $35 minimum order, charged a special handling fee of $7.50 on all orders below $35, and alerted its field sales reps and telephone salespeople to the problem. The company generated $52,000 more in profits before taxes during the first year it operated with these new rules.

Sales analysis by customer

Analysts use procedures similar to those described earlier to analyze sales by customers. Such analyses typically show that a relatively small percentage of customers account for a large percentage of sales. For example, the needlework products distributor found that 13 percent of its accounts represented 67 percent of its total sales. Frequently, a study of sales calls show that the salesforce spends as much time with the small accounts as with the larger ones. Shifting some of this effort to the larger accounts may well increase sales.

Adherence to plan control

Because budgets project revenues and expenses for a given time period, they are a vital part of the firm's planning and control activities. They provide the basis for a continuous evaluation and comparison of what was planned with what actually happened. In this sense, budgeted revenues and profits serve as objectives against which to measure performance in sales, profits, and actual costs.

Budget analysis requires that managers continuously monitor marketing expenses to make certain the company does not overspend in its effort to reach its objectives. They also evaluate the magnitude and pattern of deviations from the target ratios. Before taking corrective action, managers may need to disaggregate the data to help isolate the problem. For example, if total commissions as a percent of sales are out of line, analysts need to analyze them by each sales territory and product to determine exactly where the problem lies.

GLOBAL MARKETING CONTROL

Thus far we have been concerned with the various types and levels of control systems of a company operating nationally. Maintaining control over global marketing activities is more difficult than with domestic marketing, primarily because the company operates in a number of countries, each presenting a unique set of opportunities and threats. This makes it difficult to monitor simultaneously a variety of environments and to prescribe corrective action on an individual country basis where appropriate. Differences in language and customs, accentuated by distance, further compound the control problem.

Keegan recommends that global companies use essentially the same control system format for both their domestic and foreign operations.[10] Report frequency and extent of detail would vary by the subsidiary's size and environmental uncertainties. The great advantage of using a single system is that it facilitates comparisons between operating units and communications between home office and local managers.

The extent of control exercised over an overseas subsidiary is largely a function of its size; differences in the environment, including its stability; and the extent to which the company employs a standardized rather than a localized strategy.[11] The larger a company's international operation, the greater the likelihood that staff personnel specializing in control activities will be on site, making the control system more elaborate and precise in its operation. Small overseas operations tend to involve fewer specialists and a less intensive control system.

Another factor affecting the control system is the extent to which environmental differences exist. Ordinarily, the greater the differences between the home country and the foreign subsidiary, the more decision-making authority is delegated. For example, a U.S. subsidiary in England would likely be given less autonomy than one in Brazil. Large multinationals compensate for

---

[10]Warren J. Keegan, *Global Marketing Management* (Englewood Cliffs, N.J.: Prentice Hall, 1989), chap. 4.

[11]Ibid.

these differences by clustering countries with similar environments into regions that have sufficient revenues to permit the use of a headquarters staff.
When considerable environmental instability is present, it is difficult to employ a formal control system; the tendency is to delegate to local management
the authority to make certain kinds of decisions without review and approval
by the home office.

A third major factor affecting the international control system is the extent
to which a standardized strategy is used. The more standardized the strategy,
especially with respect to the product, the greater the degree of control exercised over many activities, including purchasing raw materials and determining components, manufacturing, and quality specifications. Ordinarily,
control over marketing activities is less stringent than with manufacturing.

Other factors affecting control are the success of the subsidiary (the greater
the success, the less the home office interference); the physical distance sepa-
rating the home office and the subsidiary (the greater the distance, the less
frequently the subsidiary will be visited by home office personnel); and the
availability of a satisfactory communication system in a subsidiary (the more
primitive the system, the less control can be exercised). Rapidly improving
voice and data communication systems throughout the world are fast negat-
ing this constraint.

THE MARKETING AUDIT

Marketing audits, a different type of control activity than anything we have
discussed this far, are growing more popular, especially for firms with a variety of SBUs that differ in their market orientation.

The marketing audit involves a comprehensive review of the company's
total marketing efforts cutting across all products and business units. Our
concern here is at the individual SBU level. Such an audit covers both the
SBU's objectives and strategy and its plan of action for each product-market
entry. It provides an assessment of each SBU's current overall competitive
position as well as that of its individual product-market entries. It requires an
analysis of each of the marketing-mix elements and how well they are being
implemented in support of each entry. The audit must take into account the
environmental changes that can affect the SBU's strategy and product-market
action programs.

Types of audits

Audits are normally conducts for such areas as the SBU's marketing environment, objectives and strategy, planning and control systems, organization,
productivity, and individual marketing activities such as sales and advertising.
These areas are shown in Exhibit 13–10 with examples of the kinds of data
needed and serve as the basis for the discussion that follows.

EXHIBIT 13–10

Major Areas Covered in Marketing Audit and Questions
concerning Each for a Consumer Goods Company

Audit area	Examples of questions to be answered
Marketing environment	What opportunities and/or threats derive from the firm's present and future environment; that is, what technological, political, and social trends are significant? How will these trends affect the firm's target markets, competitors, and channel intermediaries? Which opportunities/threats emerge from within the firm?
Objectives and strategy	How logical are the company's objectives given the more significant opportunities/threats and its relative resources? How valid is the firm's strategy, given the anticipated environment, including the actions of competitors?
Planning and control system	Does the firm have adequate and timely information about consumers' satisfaction with its products? With the actions of competitors? With the services of intermediaries?
Organization	Does the organization structure fit the evolving needs of the marketplace? Can it handle the planning needed at the individual product/brand level?
Marketing productivity	How profitable are each of the firm's products/brands? How effective are each of its major marketing activities?
Marketing functions	How well does the product line meet the line's objectives? How well do the products/brands meet the needs of the target markets? Does pricing reflect cross elasticities, experience effects, and relative costs? Is the product readily available? What is the level of retail stockouts? What percent of large stores carry the firm's in-store displays? Is the salesforce large enough? Is the firm spending enough on advertising?

- The **marketing environment audit** requires an analysis of the firm's present and future environment with respect to its demographic/economic, technological, political, social, and competitive components. The intent is to identify the more significant trends to see how they affect the firm's customers, competitors, channel intermediaries, and suppliers.

- The **objectives and strategy area audit** call for an assessment of how appropriate these internal factors are, given current major environmental trends and any changes in the firm's resources.

- The unit's **planning and control system area audit** evaluates the adequacy of the systems that develop the firm's product-market entry action plans and the control and reappraisal process. The audit also evaluates the firm's new-product development procedures.

- The **organization area audit** deals with the formal overall structure (can it meet the changing needs of the marketplace?); how the marketing department is organized (can it accommodate the planning requirements of the firm's assortment of brands?); and the extent of synergy between the various marketing units (are there good relations between sales and merchandising?).

- The **marketing productivity area audit** evaluates the profitability of the company's individual products, markets (including sales territories), and key accounts. It also studies the cost effectiveness of the various marketing activities.

- The **marketing functions area audit** examines, in depth, how adequately the firm handles each of the marketing-mix elements. Questions relating to the *product* concern the attainability of the present product-line objectives, the extent to which individual products fit the needs of the target markets, and whether the product line should be expanded or contracted. *Price* questions have to do with price elasticity; experience effects, relative costs, and the actions of major competitors; and consumers' perceptions of the relationship between a product's price and its value. *Distribution* questions center on coverage, functions performed, and cost effectiveness. Questions about *advertising* focus on advertising objectives and strategies, media schedules, and the procedures used to develop advertising messages. The audit of the salesforce covers its objectives, role, size, coverage, organization, and duties plus the quality of its selection, training, motivation, compensation, and control activities.

Recently, a more focused type of audit has been suggested for consumer goods companies. It involves the **product manager.** Since these managers have a great deal to do with the success or failure of individual products, higher-level managers are, or should be, concerned whether product managers are channeling their efforts in the best ways possible. Quelch and colleagues suggest an audit process that gets product managers to talk about what they're doing versus what they *ought* to be doing. (See Exhibit 13–11 for a listing of interview subjects.)[12] Respondents should also be asked to rate the extent to which various support groups, such as marketing research and management information systems, are helpful. Based on their research, these authors concluded product managers spend too much time on routine matters such as those relating to promotion execution and too little on product design and development.

DECISION SUPPORT SYSTEMS (DSSs)

The final section of this chapter deals with the use of computer technology (both hardware and software) to make control possible as a more-or-less continuous day-in, day-out activity. In recent years, a new generation of

---

[12]John A. Quelch, Paul W. Farris, and James M. Oliver, "The Product Manager Audit," *Harvard Business Review*, March–April 1987, p. 30.

EXHIBIT 13–11

Suggested Interview Subjects in a Product Manager Audit

1. What percent of your time do you actually spend on each activity?
2. Rate how you like each of these activities (like, neutral, dislike, not applicable).
3. Rate the degree to which you expect to be supported in each activity (neither encouraged nor supported, officially encouraged but resources I need are inadequate, financial and technical resources I need are available but the time is not, financial and technical resources are available and I have enough time).
4. Rate the degree to which you expect to be rewarded for each activity (excellent performance is assumed and not rewarded, while failure to perform well gets me in trouble; excellent performance wins me a pat on the back but doesn't help me get a raise, a promotion, or more responsibility; excellence performance leads to one or more of these rewards).
5. What percent of your time would you ideally spend on each activity to build the business?
6. If you could free 10 hours each week of what is now busywork, to which activities would you reallocate them?
7. Rank the top five activities in which you would like training or coaching to help you do your job even better and prepare you for a higher-level job.

SOURCE: Reprinted by permission of *Harvard Business Review*. "The Product Management Audit (1 of 2 Ideas for Action)," by John A. Quelch, Paul W. Farris, and James M. Oliver (March–April 1987). Copyright © 1987 by the President and Fellows of Harvard College; all rights reserved.

management information systems (MIS)—**decision support systems (DSS)**—has been developed to help managers analyze control-oriented data. Originally, MIS procedures led to the presentation and analysis of a regular series of reports to assist marketing decision making. It required an evaluation of each manager's needs, capabilities, and decision-making style. Because it was extremely difficult to gain any consensus about what data were wanted, how they should be analyzed and presented, and with what frequency, almost no report formats satisfied all users. Developers were forced to use compromise reports that rarely satisfied anyone. Or they had to tailor the system to meet the unique needs of each manager, an expensive and time-consuming task.

Another problem with MIS involved the dynamics inherent in the operations of such a system. New product-market entries, changes in competitors, realignment of sales territories, and changing managers necessitated a great deal of reprogramming. This, too, required considerable time and effort.

DSSs attempt to bypass these problems by designing systems that permit each user to manipulate the data to conduct any analysis desired—from simply adding a set of numbers to a sophisticated statistical analysis. A DSS uses dialogue systems that permit managers to explore the data banks using system models to generate reports for their specific needs. Managers can query the computer and, based on the answer, ask another question. This can be done at a terminal rather than asking for a computer printout. For example, a marketing manager who notes that sales are down in a given region can ask the computer whether sales for the product type are down, if the company's

E X H I B I T   1 3 – 1 2

Glaxo's Multimillion Dollar Marketing Decision Support System

> Glaxo, Inc., is a pharmaceutical maker located in the Research Triangle Park, North Carolina. The company spends about $2 million annually on its sales and marketing decision support system including those monies spent on hardware, software, and operating personnel. According to Donald Rao, Glaxo's manager of market analysis and decision support, the company's return on investment has been substantial since the system was developed in 1987.
>
> Mr. Rao bases his claim on a consultant's study of the system, which showed that Glaxo had realized significant cost savings and productivity gains since its product managers started using the system. For example, with more detailed data available on physicians in Glaxo's sales territories, product managers were able to allocate product samples (which involves large expenditures) more accurately. Since the system also provided easier and faster access to data, the product managers were able to save valuable time in searching for information.

SOURCE: Tom Eisenhart, "Where's the Payoff?" Reprinted with permission from *Business Marketing,* June 1990, p. 46. Copyright © Crain Communications, Inc. All rights reserved.

brand is losing share and if so, to which competitors, or if the decline is confined to a specific type of retailer.

DSSs are highly flexible and action-oriented. They enable managers to follow their instincts in solving a problem and to do so on-line. (For an example of a marketing decision support system, see Exhibit 13–12.) Serving the needs of different managers, they are more adaptable to the changing environment. In brief,

> Decision support systems are small-scale interactive systems designed to provide managers with flexible, responsive tools that act, in effect, as a staff assistant, to whom they can delegate more routine parts of their job. DSSs support, rather than replace, a manager's judgment. They do not impose solutions and methods, but provide access to information, models, and reports, and help extend the manager's scope of analysis.[13]

Marketing decision support system (MDSS) elements

These systems contain a number of elements that can be classified in various ways. After noting that "data collection, recording, analysis, and interpretation are all implied within a marketing information system," Parasuraman describes a marketing information system as being comprised of a data collection system, data bank, data input and retrieval system, models/techniques system, and information dissemination system.[14] (See Exhibit 13–13 for an elaboration of these five elements.)

---

[13]Peter G. W. Keen and M. S. Scott Morton, *Decision Support Systems: An Organizational Perspective* (Reading, Mass.: Addison-Wesley, 1978), p. 1.

[14]A. Parasuraman, *Marketing Research* (Reading, Mass.: Addison-Wesley, 1986), p. 20.

EXHIBIT   13–13

Description of Marketing Information System Elements

Description of marketing information system elements	
Data collection system	A set of capabilities for continuously monitoring a firm's internal and external environments and extracting relevant marketing data from them
Data bank	A repository for data collected from within and outside a firm
Data input and retrieval system	A set of capabilities for transferring the collected data to the data bank and for locating and extracting needed data from the data bank
Models/techniques system	A set of frameworks, procedures, and tools for manipulating data so as to obtain useful information
Information dissemination system	A set of capabilities for generating reports from the information obtained and relaying them to appropriate marketing decision makers

Source: Figure is adapted from William G. Ouchi, *Theory Z,* appearing in A. Parasuraman, *Marketing Research* (Reading, Mass.: Addison-Wesley, 1986), p. 20. © 1986 by Addison-Wesley Publishing Co., pp. 58–71, 78, and 79. Reprinted by permission.

Clearly one of the most important elements in these systems has to do with the collection of strategic intelligence that drives the firm's planning and control processes, including providing the inputs for the strategy analysis models. Of particular importance here is monitoring the environment—especially inputs concerned with both the competitive and customer environments. (For a discussion of sources of competitive information, see the appendix at the end of this text.) When merged with data from within the firm, such information helps management to make effective decisions in a variety of marketing areas such as price, channels, advertising, and, especially, new products.

A MDSS can, therefore, support all aspects of decision making in marketing, including problem identification, selecting the appropriate data to work with, specifying and evaluating alternative courses of action, and quantifying the results obtained. Marketing offers considerable opportunities for the use of an MDSS because of its lack of structure in most decision-making situations—as contrasted, for example, to a procurement/inventory system.

Marketing models

Another important area has to do with models that are designed specifically for use by a particular company, or industry, in solving a problem of recurring nature, such as allocation of sales resources. Indeed, sales and product analysis are an integral part of most MDSSs. Typically, such systems enable managers to analyze the sales (in dollars and/or units) of individual products by various breakdowns, as we discussed earlier.

Day argues that the most useful models for making market strategy decisions, particularly those involving the evaluation and selection of strategy options, are those used to provide conditional sales forecasts. Such models attempt to forecast sales in dollars and units as well as market share, making different assumptions about the strategy employed, the competition, and the environment. Such models facilitate an analysis that seeks to determine which factors, both inside and outside of the firm, have the greatest impact on sales.[15]

Future of MDSSs

To date, the systems described above have been used primarily by large companies operating in such industries as retailing, banking, brokerage, airlines, and pharmaceuticals. Such companies have spent large sums of money to develop transactional data bases. This is not to suggest that many firms are not using some kind of a system—typically a data base consisting of sales transactions tied to certain classification data concerned with the buyer's characteristics, time period, sales representative, channel involved, and so on. (For a description of a transactional system in action, see Exhibit 13–14.)

There are a number of reasons why more companies have not progressed further in developing the more sophisticated systems. A major one has to do with the risk involved in making a large investment given the difficulty of estimating the return. A closely related problem is that the success of such a system depends heavily on the decision-making capabilities of the user—"The tools don't make decisions. . . . If you put MDSS in the hands of lousy decision makers, you get lousy decisions."[16] Yet another factor inhibiting the adoption of MDSSs is that most strategic decisions are long term, and, therefore, the decision maker may not know if the decision was correct for several years. Further complicating the situation, any number of factors beyond the decision maker's control typically influence the outcome. Not surprisingly, many marketers believe that the benefits derived from an MDSS are more at the short-term operation level versus the strategic level.[17]

But there is reason to believe that an increasing number of companies will adopt more sophisticated MDSSs during the 1990s. First and foremost, companies are increasingly asking their managers to make bigger, more complex decisions more quickly because, in large part, of increased global competition. Thus, MDSSs will become a critically needed resource—especially those that enable marketers to correlate large quantities of external data with sales and company decision areas such as those relating to price and promotion.

---

[15]George S. Day, *Analysis for Strategic Market Decisions* (St. Paul, Minn.: West Publishing Company, 1986), pp. 225–30. For a discussion of marketing areas that lend themselves to MDSSs and models within each, see William R. Dillon, Thomas J. Madden, and Neil H. Firtle, *Marketing Research in a Marketing Environment* (Homewood, Ill.: Richard D. Irwin, 1987), pp. 744–59.

[16]Eisenhart, "Where's the Payoff?", p. 47.

[17]Ibid.

EXHIBIT 13–14
Using an Information System to Make Supermarkets More Efficient

The increasing use of scanners at the checkout counters has generated the development of management information systems that have affected management decision making dramatically. Basically four steps are involved in such systems:

Step 1: Raw data flow from stores and warehouses to a mainframe computer, usually at chain headquarters. Included are sales records from checkout stands and data on product delivery schedules, energy use, and the amount of time products spend in chain warehouses before they're shipped to stores.

Step 2: The numbers are crunched to help make better decisions about what products to sell, how to display them, and how to make their storage and delivery more efficient. Headquarters can determine which brands of soap make the most money, for example, and cut back on the least profitable ones. Or it can use computer-projected cost estimates to gauge how profitable a new brand of soap might be. The numbers might also suggest whether products should be delivered directly to stores or go to a central warehouse first.

Step 3: Headquarters sends its recommendations back to the store and to warehouse managers and their assistants. Sometimes called "Plan-A-Grams," these instructions include detailed schematics of every shelf, showing the store managers where to display each of the up to 17,000 products sold in large supermarkets. The plan may even recommend prices for these goods.

Step 4: Headquarters also gives or sells the numbers generated in Step 1 to manufacturers, which may subsequently modify their products. For instance, the numbers may tell a soap maker that its products would sell better if they were packaged differently.

The above steps fail to reveal the interactive potential between management and the system. For example, by proper querying of the system one chain regularly determines what brands to carry, what prices to charge, and how much shelf space to provide for its many thousands of items carried by each of its 65 stores.

SOURCE: Gary Geipel, "At Today's Supermarket, the Computer Is Doing It All," *Business Week,* August 11, 1986, p. 64.

For managers who make decisions with customers at the global level, a MDSS that facilitates group decision making is a necessity. These systems enable a group of users in a conference room or in different locations to access and work with the same data simultaneously.

Furthermore, interactive personal computer hardware with more storage ability, when coupled with more user-friendly software, will make the use of MDSSs faster and less expensive. One group of experts predicts that in the not-too–distant future "desktop computers will be as powerful as today's supercomputers, and supercomputers will run at speeds over a thousand times faster than those of today. Computer chips now with one million processing elements will have more than one billion."[18] Given these trends, there is every reason to be optimistic about a growing interest in MDSSs during the 1990s; further, the new or modified systems will be better able to determine

[18]Linda M. Applegate, James I. Cash, Jr., and D. Quinn Mills, "Information Technology and Tomorrow's Manager," *Harvard Business Review,* November–December 1988, p. 132.

what responses can be obtained with what kinds of inputs; for example, what level of awareness resulted from expenditures of x dollars on advertising?

SUMMARY

Marketing control and reappraisal is the final step in the marketing strategy process. Highly diagnostic, it starts the marketing management process anew. Marketing controls are necessary if the company is to operate profitably; and yet many, if not most, companies have poor control procedures. Much of the problem is a failure to set measurable objectives. When this is coupled with a weak plan of action, it becomes almost impossible to set up an effective control system.

Different control processes correspond to the organizational levels involved; that is, corporate, SBU, and product-market entry. Regardless of level, the control process sets standards of performance, specifies and obtains feedback data, evaluates it, and takes corrective action. It is difficult in most cases to identify the exact cause of marketing problems and hence to take effective corrective action.

Control typically involves some form of profitability analysis. In these analyses, managers determine the costs associated with specific marketing activities to find out the profitability of such units of analysis as different market segments, products, customer accounts, and channel intermediaries. In performing such investigations, analysts have the option of using direct or full costing to determine the unit's profitability. In full costing, they assign both direct and indirect costs. Direct costing uses contribution accounting and is favored by those who argue that there is no really accurate way to assign indirect costs. It is also helpful in doing a marginal analysis study.

Strategic control is concerned with the opportunities and threats pertaining to each SBU and their product-market entries and with the strategies adopted to exploit them. A strategic control system should provide data to help answer questions about changes in the environment, strategies of major competitors, and the maturity of the industry—especially those changes in the industry's key success factors. From these answers, marketers can identify new opportunities and threats and determine whether the current strategy is still viable.

Product-market entry control is concerned with the product's competitive position, its sales/share determinants, and sales analyses. The first has to do with such key parameters as market share, market size, and market growth. It is important to determine whether any deviation from plan is caused by errors in forecasting or errors in management. Control systems are primarily concerned with the extent to which the plan is adhered to, especially the budget. It is also important to determine whether the sales/share determinants have been attained.

Sales analysis involves dividing aggregate sales data into certain breakdowns such as those having to do with products, end-user customers, channel intermediaries, sales territories, and order size. Then analysts make comparisons against other data. The objective of such analysis is to find areas of strengths and weaknesses—products, territories, and customers that account for the bulk of the revenues. Sales analysis recognizes that aggregate sales and cost data may mask the situation sufficiently for a misdiagnosis of the problem. The two major evaluation systems are simple and comparative sales analyses.

The marketing audit is the mechanism by which corporate management evaluates the company's total marketing effort. It involves an SBU's objectives, strategy, plan of action, and personnel. It provides an assessment of each SBU's present competitive position and insights into its marketing strengths and weaknesses.

Control over a firm's international operations is a difficult undertaking largely because of the number of different environments present. A firm should use the same control system for its international operations as it does for its domestic ones. The extent of control exercised over overseas units varies, depending on the unit's size, whether a standardized or a localized marketing strategy is used, and the extent of environmental differences, coupled with the magnitude of risk present.

Marketing decision support systems provide managers with flexible, responsive tools that help them do a faster and better job of problem solving. Such systems are comprised of a data collection system, a data bank, a data input and retrieval system, a models/techniques system, and an information dissemination system. The outlook for greater use of these systems over the next decade is considered excellent, given that managers are being asked to make bigger and more complex decisions, the global nature of competition, and more powerful personal computers.

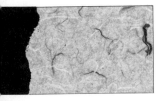

Card Wars: Competition Heats Up in the Credit-Card Industry[1]

As discussed in Chapter 1, American Express's success at gaining and maintaining a preeminent position in the credit-card industry by offering exceptional service, and at achieving growth through internal innovation, illustrated the importance of clearly defined and well-implemented marketing strategies in today's economy. As the 1990s began, however, credit-card competition became even more intense. A number of new players introduced new cards (e.g., Sears' Discover card) or began offering credit cards in conjunction with their nonfinancial services (e.g., AT&T's Universal Visa and Master-Card). And established card issuers, like Citicorp and Chemical Bank, began offering additional services and reducing their interest rates on unpaid balances to attract and hold more Visa and MasterCard users.

In spite of the increased competition, American Express's Travel Related Services Division continues to grow and prosper. The actions the division has taken to maintain its market position, and those the new entrants have pursued in their attempts to capture a viable share of the credit-card market, reflect a number of the major themes emphasized throughout this book, including:

- Careful monitoring of and quick reactions to changes and trends in the environment, particularly those involving customers and competitors.
- Development of well-defined corporate, business-level, and marketing strategies that fit the firm's environment and its internal capabilities and are consistent with one another.
- Creation of marketing strategies targeted at clearly defined market segments.

---

[1]The following discussion is based on material found in Bill Saporito, "Melting Point in the Plastic War," *Fortune*, May 20, 1991, pp. 71–78.

- Planning marketing programs in which all of the four Ps are consistent with the target customers' desires and the business's competitive strategy and that establish an advantage over competitive offerings.
- Ensuring effective implementation of marketing strategies and programs through an appropriate allocation of resources and the careful coordination of marketing actions with those of other functional departments.

Not surprising, the above list looks suspiciously like a capsule summary of the steps in the process of formulating and implementing a marketing strategy that we outlined in Chapter 1. A brief examination of some of the new credit-card competitors' actions in each of these areas, and American Express's reactions to them, will serve as a final review and reaffirmation of the importance of that process.

Market opportunity analysis

Because American Express's green, gold, and platinum cards require customers to pay their entire balance every month, the company makes money on them in only two ways: annual fees charged to customers and the so-called discounts collected from merchants, a charge that has historically amounted to from 2.5 to 4.5 percent of each transaction. All other credit cards, including AmEx's Optima card, add a third important source of income: interest on customers' unpaid balances. New competitors, then, were drawn to the industry at the start of the 1990s partly because of simple economics. The cost of money had fallen to about 8 percent while the major banks were charging their credit-card customers an average of 19.5 percent interest on their unpaid balances.

Market analysis convinced many firms of the potential for substantial additional growth, which in turn affected the intensity of competition. For one thing, penetration of the traditional consumer market remained relatively low, particularly among more moderate-income, price-sensitive consumers. Also, 19 million American businesses spend $120 billion annually on business travel and entertainment, but by 1991 the credit-card companies had signed up only about a third of the companies with more than 100 employees and even fewer small businesses to use corporate cards. Finally, markets for consumer credit cards are much less developed in most other countries than in the United States, offering tremendous potential for global expansion.

Well-defined and integrated strategies

Changes in corporate strategies also spurred the entry of new firms into the credit-card industry. A number of nonfinancial organizations pursued corporate growth and diversification strategies that carried them into financial service businesses. For example, Sears added stock and real estate brokerage businesses to its Allstate insurance subsidiary during the 1980s so it could offer a wide range of financial services to its retail customers. Those moves, together with the fact that millions of people already had credit accounts at

Sears' retail stores, made the development of the Discover card a logical extension of Sears' corporate growth strategy.

Other firms outside of the financial services industry, such at AT&T, were attracted to credit cards because of extensive credit and collections departments with huge data bases of customers' credit information. Such firms could also "bundle" their cards with discounts on their other products or services. For instance, AT&T offered a 10 percent discount on long-distance phone calls to early customers of its Universal card.

Careful market targeting

The newer entrants in the credit-card wars did not simply try to steal existing customers from established card companies by attacking head-on. Instead, most targeted market segments where credit-card use had traditionally been relatively low and designed card features and services to increase their penetration of those target segments. In Sears' case, for example, a large portion of its retail charge customers consisted of moderate-income families who were reluctant to use credit cards because of high annual fees and interest charges. Sears designed the Discover card to appeal to such consumers by charging no annual fee and offering rebates of 1 percent of the purchase price of items charged on the card.

American Express, on the other hand, has continued to target the more upscale segments of the market, emphasizing the prestige and excellent service that accompany its cards. But to protect its customer base against possible inroads from increasingly aggressive competitors, it introduced the Optima card as a flanker brand in 1987. As we saw in Chapter 1, Optima is offered as an add-on that enables existing AmEx cardholders to charge items they don't want to put on their green card and pay for promptly without having to resort to using another company's card. To offset the low-price appeals of competitors like Sears and AT&T, AmEx charges a relatively low 16.25 percent interest on Optima card balances.

Integrated marketing programs

Many of the new competitors in the credit-card industry not only have sufficiently deep pockets to entice customers with lower fees and interest rates, they also have the market resources and skills to effectively promote, distribute, and service their cards. AT&T, for example, introduced its Universal card with promotional pieces included with the monthly bills mailed to its long-distance customers. It also spent $30 million in the first year on a media advertising campaign designed to make consumers aware that they have broad choices in fees, interest charges, and services when selecting a credit card. As a result, the firm attracted 4.7 million customers with $1.7 billion in card balances in its first year of operation. Exhibit E–1 shows how AT&T's performance stacks up against the other top-10 credit-card issuers. Note, however, that the exhibit does not include the American Express green card or other cards that must be paid in full every month.

E X H I B I T   E-1

How the Top-10 Credit-Card Issuers Stack Up

Issuer	Credit-card balances	Number of accounts
	(in billions)	*(in millions)*
Citicorp	$31.7	22.5
Sears Discover	$11.5	22.9
Chase Manhattan	$9.4	10.0
First Chicago	$7.1	7.2
MBNA America	$6.8	5.3
Bank of America	$6.7	6.1
AmEx Optima	$6.0	2.5
Bank of New York	$3.9	3.2
Manufacturers Hanover	$3.5	3.4
AT&T Universal	$1.7	4.7

SOURCE: RAM Research's Bankcard Update Barometer, cited in Bill Saporito, "Melting Point in the Plastic War," *Fortune*, May 20, 1991, p. 72.

About half the customers attracted by the AT&T Universal card in its first year did not use a credit card previously, but the other half switched from one of the more expensive bank cards. Indeed, banks have suffered most from the aggressive pricing practices of their new nonfinancial competitors, with the nonbanks increasing their market share from 5 percent in 1986 to 19 percent by 1991. The move toward no annual membership fees has been particularly bad for banks, which recently have depended on card fees for as much as 60 percent of their income. Consequently, banks like Citicorp have adjusted their marketing strategies to convince customers that their fees continue to be worth it. Citicorp has added additional features, like a low-price guarantee on all purchases made with their card, and has improved customer services through actions such as the addition of toll-free, 24-hour customer service phone lines.

Implementation—a source of problems for some competitors

As discussed in Chapter 1, American Express constantly monitors customer purchase trends and behavior patterns to spot market opportunities and encourages its marketing managers to be innovative in developing new products and services to exploit those opportunities. The firm also encourages, trains, and rewards personnel in all its functional departments to improve customer service. Such actions are essential for enabling American Express to effectively implement its strategy of differentiation on the basis of superior service and prestige and for achieving its growth objectives through new-product development. And effective implementation has continued to pay dividends, with AmEx recording an additional 9 percent growth in cardholders in 1990 despite the increased competition.

Not all of the new credit-card competitors have been as successful at implementing their strategies as American Express, however. AT&T, for example, was not prepared for the rapid growth generated by its marketing program for its Universal Card. When the firm began getting 800,000 calls a month from potential new customers, it had to draft senior executives to help man the phone lines. At one point it even ran out of plastic cards. The firm eventually had to slow the business down in order to manage it. It stopped mass-media advertising before the end of its first-year campaign, and at the end of that year it announced that all subsequent members would have to pay a $20 annual fee, receive no long-distance discounts, and pay a higher interest rate than charter members. Thus, implementation problems are likely to hold the firm's volume and market share below the levels it might otherwise have reached.

The recent experiences of AT&T, American Express, and their competitors suggest an obvious conclusion: making a living in the credit-card business has gotten tough and is likely to be even tougher in the future. As more competitors crowd into the market, the big players will protect their share even more aggressively. And as the industry's growth eventually slows, some marginal firms likely will be shaken out. That is why most analysts say that if you want to compete in this industry, don't bring your credit cards. Bring cash—and lots of it. More important, bring an outstanding marketing team, a responsive customer service organization, and some information-processing genius. Continued success in the credit-card business will require increasingly creative competitive strategies, the identification of new target markets based on a clear understanding of customers needs and preferences, and innovative, effectively implemented marketing programs. Of course, while this is a good formula for success in the credit-card industry, it also provides a succinct summary of what this book has been all about.

Major Sources of Competitive Intelligence and the Marketplace

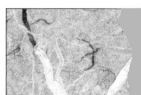

Competitive intelligence is primarily intelligent reading. A surprising amount of detail about a competitor's objectives, strategies, and tactics is available from public sources. Admiral Ellis Zacharias, Deputy Chief of Naval Intelligence during World War II, said that 95 percent of all necessary intelligence, corporate or military, can be found in the public arena.[1] Harold Geneen, the past CEO of ITT, had a research staff that was often referred to facetiously as being little more than "Value Line and a Xerox machine." But Geneen, never overlooking the available 95 percent that Zacharias referred to, believed that "the highest art of professional management requires . . . the temerity, intelligent curiosity, guts, and/or plain impoliteness, if necessary, to be sure that what you do have is indeed what we will call an 'unshakable fact.' "[2]

There is considerable evidence that it pays a firm to continuously monitor its competitive environment. One research study found that successful firms tend to monitor relevant environments more than do their competitors.[3] Another study, concerned with turnaround situations, found that a downturn problem was caused by the failure of the firm's scanning system to identify major environmental changes that negated the effectiveness of its present strategy.[4] As competition increases, more and more companies will use in-house organizations to gather and evaluate competitive intelligence (see Exhibit 1) and the marketplace systematically.

---

[1]Ellis Zacharias, *Secret Missions: The Story of an Intelligence Officer* (New York: Putnam, 1946), pp. 117–18.

[2]Robert J. Schoenberg, *Geneen* (New York: W.W. Norton & Co., 1985), pp. 191, 193.

[3]As cited in David B. Montgomery and Charles B. Weinberg, "Toward Strategic Intelligence Systems," *Journal of Marketing,* Fall 1979, p. 47.

[4]D.E. Schendel, G.R. Patten, and J. Riggs, "Corporate Turnaround Strategies: A Study of Profit, Decline, and Recovery," *Journal of General Management* 3 (Spring 1976).

EXHIBIT 1

George Smiley Joins the Firm

> They prefer to be called "competitor analysts." But whatever the euphemism, a growing number of professionals are taking corporate sleuthing out of the back alley and into the boardroom. Companies snoop on their rivals to see how products are made or to learn their plans for expansion. Methods run from scouring public documents to scavenging through trash barrels in search of confidential memos. Many companies hire private consultants for fees ranging from $10,000 to upward of $100,000. Others attend seminars to learn the craft themselves. Eighty percent of the Fortune 1,000 companies now maintain in-house snoops, according to the Society of Competitor Intelligence Professions.

SOURCE: "George Smiley Joins the Firm," *Newsweek,* May 2, 1988, p. 46.

Why this recent interest in this subject area? The main reason seems to be that competition has intensified as well as become global. As industries mature and growth slows, increased business can only come from competitors' shares. Thus, companies are forced to pay more attention to designing strategies to exploit their competitors' weaknesses.

The primary purpose of this appendix is to discuss the more important sources of information that facilitate analyses about key competitors and their industry. This should make it easier for firms to monitor the several environmental forces (e.g., economic, technological, political, and social) that impact competitors and their reaction to them. It should also help firms in targeting markets and allocating resources across geographic, demographic, and lifestyle groups.

This appendix is organized primarily around the major types of sources. The first section is concerned with computer data bases and the second with sources that provide information about individual companies, including what companies say about themselves (e.g., annual reports) and the financial data provided by such sources as Moody's and Standard & Poor's. These are followed by a discussion of the main sources of information about individual industries. The third section targets other sources of information about companies and industries, such as business journals, investment houses, and market studies. Next, there is a section concerned with how to get information on subsidiaries and private companies. The last section deals with how to evaluate the information obtained from the various sources.

COMPUTER DATA BASES

In recent years, computer data bases have become increasingly useful in analyzing competitors and market conditions. Readily accessible data bases, often computerized versions of print sources, make information on companies and industries available quickly and in a variety of forms. One of the greatest contributions of on-line files is the presence of the full text of many publications, especially newsletters, which have been difficult to obtain in the past. In the last three years, a number of these on-line resources and others have also appeared in CD-ROM (compact disk-read only memory) format.

Several large vendors of data base resources have integrated many files into one system, thereby simplifying the computer search procedure. The largest of these is DIALOG Information Services, Inc., in Palo Alto, California, which, for a modest annual fee, provides access to some 320 business data bases containing more than 175 million records. Records or units of information range from a directory of companies and associations to an in-depth financial statement for a particular company to the complete text of a journal article. A typical 10-minute search costs from $5.00 to $16.50, not including off-line print charges.

Other data base vendors are also useful for business intelligence.

- *Dow Jones News/Retrieval* (Princeton, N.J.) offers 50 data bases giving access to up-to-the-minute business and financial information, including stock quotations, from domestic and foreign sources.

- *I.P. Sharp* (Toronto, Ont.) hosts public data bases that provide a variety of time series data for Canada, the United States, the United Kingdom, Australia, Singapore, Germany, Europe, and some international trends.

- *Newsbank* (New Canaan, N.J.), in its section called *Business Newsbank,* indexes 30,000 articles per year on large and small businesses, companies, products, and people, from 500 newspapers and local business journals. *Newsbank* produces its *Electronic Index* in paper and on CD-ROM and provides the text of the articles in an accompanying microfiche set that goes back to 1985.

- *Newsnet* (Bryn Mawr, Pa.) mounts the full text of 420 different newsletters and other specialized business publications.

- *NEXIS* (Dayton, Oh.), one of several large data bases from Mead Data Central, Inc., provides full-text access to 350 major newspapers, magazines, newswires, and newsletters.

- *VU/TEXT* (Philadelphia, Pa.) produces a full text data base of approximately 50 national and regional newspapers; it also provides summaries from trade and business journals and newsletters.

There are several excellent directories that identify data bases by subject or vendor and describe their services, including *Computer-Readable Data Bases* (5th ed., Detroit: Gale Research, 1989); *Directory of On-line Data Bases* (New York: Cuadra/Elsevier, semiannually since 1979); *Federal Data Base Finder* (2d ed., Chevy Chase, Md.: Information USA, 1987); and *Information Industry Directory,* formerly *Encyclopedia of Information Systems and Services* (11th ed., Detroit: Gale Research, 1991).

The following sections of this appendix will mention automated resources along with traditional print sources.

COMPANY INFORMATION

At the outset, the firm should identify which competitors, both present and potential, to target for surveillance or investigation. Ordinarily it will target only key competitors, which usually means obtaining information on a relatively few firms. Assuming that the firm also monitors its relevant industries on a regular basis, it should pick up any moves of significance by nontargeted competitors (e.g., new entrants), which it can then investigate further if desired.

While almost all information about a close rival is potentially useful, most firms are particularly concerned about data pertaining to the competitor's objectives, strategy, success to date, and strengths and weaknesses at the SBU level. Such information is also helpful at the product-market entry level, although here firms are likely to be more interested in market-oriented data such as those concerned with sales and market share by segment, customer loyalty, and advertising and salesforce activities. These will be discussed in a later section of this appendix.

Information about the physical dimensions and performance of a competitor's product is considerably important, particularly in the case of a new product. Firms can readily obtain product information from such secondary sources as catalogs, brochures, repair manuals, and advertisements. Trade shows can also be important sources of information (see Exhibit 2 for what one researcher has to say about their value). Competitors' products can also be tested in a laboratory or under simulated use conditions. In some cases, firms use bench marking or "reverse engineering" to determine precisely the content of a competitor's product. For example, in developing its Taurus and Sable cars, Ford tore down some 50 mid-size cars, including the Honda Accord and Toyota Corolla. It did so in an effort to find features that it could incorporate in its new cars.[5] General Motors takes competitors' cars apart and displays the components in a large enclosed area that thousands of employees visit. Xerox also disassembles competitors' products for study.[6] Salespersons provide an excellent—indeed, many say the best—way of getting answers to many questions about competitors since they can often find out from their customers.

Annual reports and SEC filings

One of the most important sources of information about a company is the company itself. This is particularly the case with publicly held companies, since they are required to issue regular statements about their performance and plans. The most formal of these are the annual report to the stockholders

[5]Russell Mitchell, "How Ford Hit the Bull's Eye with Taurus," *Business Week,* June 30, 1986, pp. 69–70.

[6]"George Smiley Joins the Firm," *Newsweek,* May 2, 1988, p. 46.

EXHIBIT 2
Trade Shows Open Season on Competitors

Trade shows are vital sources of competitor information. Ironically, as hard as a competitor will try to mask its marketing strategies during the course of a year, it will try just as hard to reveal as much as possible about a new product while attending a trade show.

Trade shows are notorious for talkative salespeople, piles of literature, and lots of real-life products to see, examine, and try out. It is also the best place to gather a quick and fairly accurate idea of the market, its dynamic growth prospects and trends.

What can you learn from a trade show? An awful lot. You can identify new products, determine if your competitor has shifted strategies, determine if there has been a price point spread, find out if some company has emerged as a major influence in the market, learn whether an old product has suddenly sprouted new product features, ascertain what a company's upcoming promotional activities will look like, find out about the latest industry rumors, identify industry leaders, and examine the strengths and weaknesses of a competitor's product line.

Source: Leonard M. Fuld, *Competitor Intelligence* (New York: John Wiley & Sons, 1985) pp. 376–77. Copyright © 1985 by John Wiley & Sons, Inc. Reprinted by permission.

and the annual 10-K and quarterly 10-Q reports filed with the Securities and Exchange Commission (SEC). Other statements issued sporadically throughout a year are filings with the SEC, a prospectus for a new debt issue, press releases, new-product announcements, and even want ads. Companies are also required to file a constant stream of reports with other state and federal governmental agencies. The state filings can be particularly informative about small publicly held companies, private companies, or specific plants or locations with a larger company.

In recent years, annual reports have become more elaborate as a greater number of companies use them to communicate with their stockholders. The annual report is often dismissed as a glossy bit of puffery about a given company. It does, however, include the required financial statements and related disclosures packaged in ways that can tell a lot about how well the company and its products are doing.

A firm should analyze a competitor's annual reports over several years to detect important trends such as those having to do with the competitor's financial well-being, its revenues and earnings from each of its various business segments, its cash flow relative to its present and projected growth, and whether it has overcome past financial problems. Such information should provide insights into whether the competitor's objectives, strategies, and financial resources are in harmony.

Most informed users of annual reports pay particular attention to footnotes, which often contain some of the most important information in the report (e.g., that which explains any unusual gains or losses in this year's change in operating income). Reading the letter from the chairman and comparing it to prior years is especially helpful, since this is where top management summarizes what they feel are the most important successes and failures of the past year. This letter should provide the analyst with insights into how satisfied or dissatisfied management is with the company's recent progress. Usually, the letter will discuss their expectations about the future.

Company business segments

Annual reports must provide information about the operating revenues and income of each of the company's major lines of business (see Exhibit 3). Similar information is required for each major geographical division if the company operates outside of the United States. Practically speaking, this means that some annual reports include valuable information about individual business units, including market share. For example, Philip Morris reports sales and operating income for its U.S. cigarette business, its international cigarette business, its food business, Miller Brewing Company, and its financial services and real estate businesses.

Some companies' annual reports even reveal share data and future product-market strategy. For example, in its 1990 annual report the Coca-Cola Company indicated that its soft-drink unit case sales increased 7 percent to 9.4 billion unit cases, or almost 226 billion servings. Company share of worldwide soft-drink sales increased to a new high of 44 percent, with a U.S. share of 41 percent and an international share of 46 percent, four times that of any competitor. The report then provided 1990 share results by selected countries as well as unit case results. For example, Coke's share of carbonated soft-drink unit case sales was 42 percent for the European community, with a percent share of 42 in Germany, 32 in Great Britain, and 37 in France. For Latin America, Coke had an overall share of 52 percent, with a percent share of 59 in Brazil, 42 in Columbia, and 51 in Mexico.

Coke's future strategy for its soft-drink business unit calls for growing that unit through its traditional bottler system, but where necessary, taking ownership positions in bottling, canning, and distribution operations around the world. The report discusses the actions Coke took in 1990 and what it plans to do in 1991 by geographical section. Thus, vending continues to be a priority in Europe, with 16,000 new vending machines installed in France and 10,000 in Great Britain in 1990. In West Germany, Coke consolidated 64 bottling operations into 37 manufacturing and distribution units and has assigned a priority to increasing distribution efficiencies.[7]

A company's 10-K report requires considerable financial data, including audited balance sheets, three-year audited statements of income and changes in financial condition, and five-year selected information on sales and operating revenue, income or loss from continuing operations, long-term obligations, and cash dividends declared. Additional items are required that can increase an understanding of the firm's financial position, including the effects of inflation and changing prices. Projections of future sales and profits may or may not be included.

---

[7]The Coca-Cola Company, *1990 Annual Report*.

EXHIBIT 3

Sales and Operating Profits of General Electric's Key Businesses for 1990

The 1990 General Electric annual report disclosed earnings of $4.303 billion on revenues of $58.4 billion. Earnings per share grew 11 percent and return on equity was up slightly to 20.2 percent. The report provided revenues and operating profits for the years 1986–90 for each of GE's key business units. These were aerospace, aircraft engines, appliances, financial services, industrial and power systems, lighting, medical systems, NBC, plastics, communications and services, electrical distribution and control, motors, and transportation systems.

The report discussed the major factors affecting the sales and operating profits of each individual key business unit. For example, it noted that 1990 aircraft engine sales of $7.558 billion were up 10 percent over 1989 because of strong commercial shipments. Operating profits of 1.263 billion was about 20 percent over 1989. New orders of $8.2 billion were received during 1990, up 4 percent. The backlog of unfilled orders as of December 31, 1990, stood at $13.2 billion, of which about 40 percent was scheduled for competition in 1991.

SOURCE: General Electric Company, *Annual Report*, December 31, 1990.

In addition to the above, the 10-K requires a breakout of the firm's principle products and services, markets, and methods of distribution. A statement of sales and net income for each line that accounted for 10 percent or more of total sales or pretax income is required for each of the three past years. While such information often appears in the annual report, the 10-K often reports it in more detail.

The 10-K also reports backlog and fulfillment expectations, raw material availability, number of employees, importance of patents, licenses and franchises, and estimated cost of research. Many such data are not readily available from the annual reports, nor does the SEC require such additional information as location and character of a company's physical properties, pending legal proceedings, principal security holders, high and low sales prices of securities, and remuneration of directors and officers.

When a company is involved in a merger or acquisition, it must file a separate report with the SEC that details the purposes of the offer and the source and amount of the funds required. Considerable information is also available from the reports required when a company issues additional securities.

The Federal Trade Commission also requires numerous reports, especially for regulated industries. Further, whenever a company is involved in antitrust or restraint-of-trade suits, extensive data are usually available, as was the case with both IBM and AT&T in recent years. Because of the large number of regulatory agencies, the amount of specialized information available from the government is extensive. *How to Find Information about Companies: The Corporate Intelligence Source Book* (8th ed., Washington, D.C.: Washington Researchers, Ltd., 1991) is both an excellent listing of governmental agencies charged with overseeing business and a guide to securing the information they gather (see Exhibit 4).

EXHIBIT 4

Federal Government Employee as a Source of Information

> "People in the federal government are absolutely incredible sources. . . . There are five or six people studying the alcohol industry. In another office, they have been collecting specific statistics on sales in robotics or gene splicing. They often spend their lives studying a topic and the highlight of their day is when you call and ask for information."

SOURCE: A statement made by Leila K. Knight, president of Washington Researchers, contained in an article by Kathleen Behof, "The Right Way to Snoop on the Competition," *Sales and Marketing Management,* May 1988, p. 47.

Washington Researchers publish other helpful volumes as well. These include several that focus on sources of information:

- *How to Find Business Intelligence in Washington* (10th ed., 1990)
- *How to Find Company Intelligence in Federal Documents* (4th ed., 1990)
- *How to Find Company Intelligence in State Documents* (12th ed., 1990)
- *How to Find Company Intelligence in Libraries* (4th ed., 1990)
- *How to Find Company Intelligence On-Line* (4th ed., 1990)
- *How to Find Financial Information about Companies* (1990)

Several more concentrate on particular topics:

- *How to Find Information about Acquisition Candidates* (3rd ed., 1990)
- *How to Find Information about Companies in Telecommunications, Data Processing, and Office Automation* (1987)
- *How to Find Information about Divisions, Subsidiaries, and Products* (2nd ed., 1990)
- *How to Find Information about Executives* (3rd ed., 1990)
- *How to Find Information about Foreign Firms* (3rd ed., 1990)
- *How to Find Information about Japanese Companies and Industries* (1987)
- *How to Find Information about Private Companies* (3rd ed., 1990)
- *How to Find Information about Service Companies* (3rd ed., 1990)
- *How to Find Information on Emerging Technologies* (2nd ed., 1990)

Sources of data contained in annual reports and SEC reports

Annual reports and SEC reports are available from the company itself. They are also available in one of two microfiche collections—*Disclosure* by Disclosure, Inc., and *Q-File* by Q-Data, Inc. SEC reports that are too new to be in the microfiche collections can be obtained from either the company or located in the *Disclosure* computer data base. They can also be obtained from the SEC itself, although generally this is a slow way of getting them.

The microfiche collections usually do not contain the most up-to-date reports and might not have the current year's annual report until near the end of the year. They will have, however, the annual reports and SEC filings since 1966 for *Disclosure* and 1978 for *Q-File,* which can be a valuable source of background on a company. A comparison of the various reports and actual performances for the years can reveal, for example, if the company generally overstates or understates its performance or expectations. It can also show how often a company misses its projections or how well it has foreseen and reacted to the major trends in its industry, or the world.

The *Disclosure* data base is built from financial information from the SEC reports, the president's letter and management discussion from annual reports, and some information from proxy statements such as the listing of the companies' directors, their ages, and their remuneration. It covers the last five years' annual reports and the most recent two quarterly statements. The data base is not the ideal way to get these reports, however, because it deletes much of the text and all of the illustrations in the annual report.

Financial data sources

There are two major reporting services that reprint the basic financial data and some of the discussion from the annual reports and SEC filings: Moody's and Standard & Poor's. Each service has a weekly newsletter that passes on some of the other news a company releases about itself such as product announcements, acquisitions, and personnel changes. Moody's *Manuals,* published since 1913, covers 20,000 organizations in five groups: industrials, transportation, bank and finance, public utilities, and municipalities. A newer series begun in 1983 covers international companies. John Moody started his publication when the financial markets existed largely to track railroad stocks and bonds. Henry Varnum Poor, the publisher of the largest information service about these stocks at the time, gave his blessing to his upstart competitor on the promise that Moody would not cover the railroads in his publication. In 1941, Poor merged with Standard Statistics Company, publisher of another stock-watching service, to produce Standard & Poor's Corporation Records, which now covers 9,000 publicly held corporations arranged alphabetically in seven volumes.

Since companies pay to have their financial information reported, each of the above services arranges company sketches by the length of coverage paid for, with the most extensive coverage placed first. The full treatment includes several years of financial data, the president's letter to the stockholders, and a section on corporate background prepared by the publisher. Moody's has traditionally emphasized the bond market, and its corporate background sections reflect that emphasis with more historical information, particularly about a company's debt load. Standard & Poor's sections on corporate background reflect a bent toward the stock market by emphasizing information on current operations.

In addition to the text, each service gives a letter grade or rating to the companies' stocks or bonds. These ratings, particularly Standard & Poor's for stocks and Moody's for bonds, are extremely influential in the financial markets and can determine the extent of a company's access to funds in the stock or bond markets. Both publishers provide indexes to their services that list subsidiaries with a reference to the entry for the appropriate parent company. It is wise to check a company that is not listed in the main listing in these supplementary indexes to make sure it is not a subsidiary.

Value Line Investment Survey (New York: Value Line) is among the most well-known and available sources of background information on companies. It differs from the other sources cited in this section in that it is not a summary of the financial data released by the company. Value Line, Inc., is an independent investment service that analyzes some 1,700 companies in over 92 industries. For each company, it prepares a page of information including a graph of the stock's activity, a short essay on the company's business moves and prospects, and Value Line's own recommendation as to whether to buy or sell the stock. The publication groups the companies by industry, and a one or two-page analysis of the industry precedes each grouping.

Financial ratios

These are used to compare a company's financial data with those from other companies in the same industry. Variations will show the company's performance versus that of the industry. There are three major sources of industrywide financial ratios. The three sources differ in the industries they cover, the particular ratios provided, and most important, the sources used for their information. Dun & Bradstreet's *Industry Norms and Key Business Ratios* (Parsippany, N.J.: D&B, annually since 1982) provides statistics taken from the financial statements of over one million companies. The information comes directly from the companies themselves. In turn, Dun & Bradstreet processes it for use by companies. The emphasis here is on speed and key information for use in business decisions, not historical, complete, or absolutely accurate information. The ratios appear in brief form in the November issue of Dun & Bradstreet's *Business Month.*

Robert Morris & Associates' *Annual Statement Studies* (Philadelphia: RMA, annually since 1964) is almost synonymous with financial ratios. The service gathers information from bank loan applications and processes it for use by bank loan officers. It provides about 40 financial statistics on slightly over 300 industries. For each industry, the publication groups companies by their size of assets, providing more precise groupings for comparison. There are five years of historical statistics as well.

The *Almanac of Business and Industrial Financial Ratios* (Englewood Cliffs, N.J.: Prentice Hall, annually since 1971) by Leo Troy is the most scholarly of the three sources. Dr. Troy takes his information from the tax returns released by the IRS. He gives much more detail about far fewer industries, 181 in all, but the trade-off is that the information is several years old by the time the IRS has processed and released it.

In addition, the *Disclosure* data base lists 32 annual performance ratios covering the last three years.

Business directories

There are several business directories designed to provide only the sparest of background information on a company, such as its address, phone number, chief officers, product line, sales, and number of employees. The two mainstays in this market are Dun & Bradstreet's Million Dollar Directory and Standard & Poor's Register of Corporations. Tri-net, Inc., has recently placed two new entries in the market with its computer data bases, *Trinet Establishment Database* and *Trinet Company Database.* The establishment data base covers all public and private business "establishments" with over 20 employees, giving the basic directory information with the addition of a share figure that shows the company's sales as a percent of the total SIC code sales. It is important to remember, however, that when an establishment produces two or more products, the SIC data are based on the principal product determined on the volume of sales. Thus, the data on the primary product are inflated, but even so such share data can be useful in determining how much a particular plant or location of a major company is contributing to that company.

Dun & Bradstreet also produces an on-line equivalent to the *Million Dollar Directory,* as well as two other on-line directory files, *D&B—Dun's Market Identifiers,* which lists over two million private and public U.S. companies with five or more employees, and *D&B—Dun's Electronic Yellow Pages,* a listing of eight million business and business professionals in the United States. Standard & Poor's data bases include the *S&P Register—Corporate,* 45,000 public and private businesses (95 percent in the U.S.) and *S&P Corporate Descriptions,* more detailed descriptions of 11,000 public U.S. companies.

In recent years, more and more information about the competitive environment has become available. The federal government, in particular, has become an increasingly important source of strategic information primarily because of the Freedom of Information Act (FOIA), which makes it possible for any individual to obtain copies of any documents, files, or records in the possession of a federal agency or department. Requests must be granted or denied within 10 working days to prevent noncompliance by delay. The FOIA allows companies greater access to a large variety of data, including those pertaining to the government (e.g., bidding on government contracts and government procurement policies) and to a company's competitors. A classic example, and one of the few published, has to do with the Air Cruisers Company, which received approval from the Federal Aviation Administration (FAA) for its 42-person inflatable life raft designed for use by commercial aircraft. Switlik Parachute Company used an FOIA request to obtain information about the performance tests and construction design of this raft, saving them time and money in designing and testing a similar product with which it secured a lucrative European contract in competition with Air Cruisers.[8]

---

[8]Burt Schorr, "How Law Is Being Used to Pry Business Secrets from Uncle Sam's Files," *Wall Street Journal,* May 9, 1977, p. 1, 26.

All departments and agencies of the executive branch have published regulations governing their FOIA compliance. A specific agency's rules can be located using the index to the *Code of Federal Regulations* (Washington, DC: Office of the Federal Register) under "Information availability." The names and phone numbers of agency and department contacts for FOIA requests, including those of oversight committees, may be found in many directories, including the *Washington Information Directory* (Washington, D.C.: Congressional Quarterly, annually since 1975).

INDUSTRY INFORMATION

It is difficult to define an industry on the basis that all products produced are close substitutes for one another. Such is usually not the case because of the presence of market segments and their need for different benefit bundles. Thus, it is not always clear what firms compete in a given industry. It is imperative, therefore, that the analyst understand the boundaries of the industry being studied, especially so in relation to industry data. Different sets of industry data likely use different industry definitions, making it difficult to reconcile differences in the data sets.

Information pertaining to the five competitive forces discussed in Chapter 5—existing competitors, potential competitors, the bargaining power of customers and suppliers, and substitute products—is important, particularly trend data. Thus an industry evaluation typically includes an analysis of the industry's growth rate by major segments or strategic groups; changes in buyer segments; changes in product or manufacturing process technology; new products; changes in the relative importance of channel intermediaries, including the emergence of new ones; and changes in government policies and regulations.

Regular industry reports

A basic source of information on industries is Standard & Poor's *Industry Surveys,* a series of 22 pamphlets covering that number of industry groupings. In 20–30 pages, the *Industry Surveys* cover the current view of trends, both inside and outside the industry, that are likely to affect it. The *Industry Surveys* reflect Standard & Poor's usual interest in current operating information and the stock market. For each industry, it singles out the leading products and lists the top publicly held companies in that industry. The surveys are updated once each year, with a four-page current analysis for each grouping revised every quarter. For example, the September 1989 update on the toy industry reported in some detail on the growing importance of brand loyalty, the dramatic and continuing sales revival of traditional toys, the reasons why such sales successes were occurring, the growing concentration of the toy industry, the attempts being made by managers to lengthen product life cycles and expand successful product lines, and the revival of video games. Other sections of the report discussed how leisure industries benefited from economic growth, movie attendance, the growth in the television industry, sales of compact discs, the economics of the casino industry, lodging occupancy, retrenchment in the restaurant industry, sporting goods sales by product categories, new photographic products, and the industry's financials.

Another prominent industry source is the U.S. government, which publishes its own annual survey of industries called the *U.S. Industrial Outlook*. The government's reports are varied (covering 350 industries), and most are relatively short 4–15 pages). Generally speaking, these reports mention few companies and products by name. The strength of the government's industry reports is information on the larger economic trends affecting an industry, including world production and shipments, sources and amounts of raw materials, and five-year economic projections. For an industry dependent on raw materials or regulated by the government, this is an extremely important source. It is weaker on retail or service industries, but even so it is an important counterbalance to Standard & Poor's emphasis on companies listed on U.S. stock exchanges. The *U.S. Industrial Outlook* is often the first place to provide a hint of the presence of foreign competition in an industry. It also cites research done on an industry by government agencies. Furthermore, each report ends with the name and phone number of the person(s) responsible for the information who may be contacted for more detailed or recent information.

For example, the 1991 *Outlook* discusses the entertainment industry in seven pages. There are sections for motion pictures, music, and home entertainment. Each section gives income and production statistics and an analysis of international competitiveness. Motion pictures, for instance, are one of this country's most successful exports, contributing $4 billion each year to the balance of trade. Music, while doing well financially, faces serious problems with a lack of copyright protection in many foreign countries. With the exception of the United Kingdom, however, videotape players and videotapes are found in very few European or Japanese households, a disadvantage for U.S. exporters of feature films. Finally, in each part a paragraph predicts the outlook for 1991 and long-term prospects. A list of six references concludes each section. The entry for computer industry and software occupies 27 pages and covers the same general areas for such products as supercomputers, mainframes, workstations, magnetic and optical disc storage, printers, local area networks, software, artificial intelligence, and others. This report gives the names and market shares of several domestic and foreign firms for various products.

The *Current Industrial Reports* (Washington, D.C.: Bureau of the Census) provides reasonably current data on the production, inventories, and orders of some 5,000 products that represent 40 percent of all U.S. manufacturing. Such reports are helpful in determining the total industry sales and market share for a target company. Thus, if analysts know a company's production, they can estimate its share from the industry's total production. They can also determine which products are the best sellers in an industry segment. The reports appear monthly, quarterly, or yearly, depending on the industry being studied. The standard directory for identifying international companies and their affiliates or subsidiaries is *Principal International Businesses* (Parsippany, N.J.: Dun & Bradstreet, annually since 1974). This lists the name, address, names of executives, products, and sales figures for 55,000 companies in 140 countries. Dun & Bradstreet also publishes four volumes of *Who Owns Whom,* one for North America, one for the United Kingdom and the Republic of Ireland, one for Continental Europe, and one for Australasia and the Far East. Other D&B directories include *Key British Enterprises,* listing 21,000 British companies; *Canadian Key Businesses,* with 14,000 major Canadian companies; *Dun's Latin America's Top 25,000 Companies, Europe's Top 15,000 Companies,* and *Asia's Top 7,500 Companies.*

For information on industries and markets, two federal government publications are helpful. *Foreign Economic Trends and Their Implications for the United States* (Washington, D.C.: Department of Commerce) is published semi-annually. It contains a series of 130 brief country-by-country reports that offer a current or potential market for U.S. goods. It is prepared by U.S. embassies. *Overseas Business Reports* (Washington, D.C.: Department of Commerce) has been published annually since 1962. This is a series of reports on over 100 countries titled "Marketing in . . . ." Each report (about 30 pages) discusses the foreign trade outlook, the economy, the government, distribution channels, transportation, credit, trade regulations, and investment.

In addition, *Predicasts Worldcasts* (Cleveland, Oh.: Predicasts, annually since 1972) provides four annual reports (one issued each quarter) that feature long-range statistical forecasts for industries outside of the United States. Finally, *The Europa World Year Book* (London: Europa Publications; formerly *Europa Year Book*) has been published annually since 1926. For each of the 144 countries, it provides a profile, statistical tables on major commodities and the general economy, and the addresses of embassies, trade and professional associations, and media and industrial organizations. A number of other tools referring to foreign and international companies and industries are mentioned elsewhere in this appendix.

Industry trade associations and trade journals

For the best listing of associations, the analyst is referred to the *Encyclopedia of Business Information Sources* (6th ed., Detroit: Gale Research, 1986). Organized by industry, the *Encyclopedia* gives associations and trade journals, statistical sources, data bases, and handbooks that apply to that industry. Analysts can take the names of the associations given in the *Encyclopedia* and look them up in the *Encyclopedia of Associations* (24th ed., Detroit: Gale Research, 1990), which gives address, phone number, name of executive director or secretary, and a paragraph-long description of the association, its committees, and its members. The *Encyclopedia of Associations* is updated annually whereas the *Encyclopedia of Business Information Sources* is updated only every few years or so. Trade associations can provide tremendous amounts of information on an industry, including financial ratios, annual outlook, and detailed listings of firms active in the industry. In using information from a trade association, analysts must be careful to determine the extent to which the association's membership is representative of the total industry.

Many trade journals publish annual surveys on the state of the industry. Two publications list these surveys: *Guide to Special Issues and Indexes of Peri-*

odicals (New York: Special Libraries Association, 1985) and *Special Issues Index* (Westport, Conn.: Greenwood Press, 1982). A more recent listing appears in *Special Issues* (Wilmette, Ill.: Standard Rate and Data Service, 1989), which appears five times a year. These guides list the issue that usually includes the survey and the price for it. Special issues sell for as little as $7 to $15 but are usually worth much more in terms of the information provided.

Finally, analysts may need a list of all the companies in an industry. The best source is *Ward's Business Directory* (Detroit: Gale Research, annually since 1989), which comes out in four volumes: Vol. 1—*U.S. Largest Private Companies plus Selected Public Companies;* Vol. 2— *U.S. Private Companies Up to $11 Million in Sales;* Vol. 3—*U.S. Private and Public Companies;* and Vol. 4—*U.S. Private and Public Companies Ranked by Industry.* This last volume is the most valuable for business intelligence. A similar volume, *Dun's Business Rankings* (Parsippany, N.J.: D&B, annually since 1982), ranks 7,500 companies, both public and private, in 151 industry categories and within states. *Fortune, Forbes,* and *Business Week,* to name a few, also publish rankings of companies by industry. The main drawback with these lists is that they do not include private companies or subsidiaries.

OTHER SOURCES OF COMPANY, INDUSTRY, AND MARKET INFORMATION

The sources discussed thus far provide regularized information about specific companies and industries and are readily available. We now turn our attention to a miscellaneous array of sources that collectively represent a powerful source of information about companies and industries. The more important categories here are business periodicals, investment house reports, and market studies. Each of these is discussed briefly in this section.

Business periodicals

There is a large and varied collection of publications, including such traditional business journals and magazines as *Fortune, Business Week,* and *Forbes;* such trade journals as *Progressive Grocer* and *Advertising Age;* and such specialized publications as *Production and Inventory Management.* All of these periodicals are potentially important sources of information, although the more general and trade types of magazines are likely to be the most useful (see Exhibit 5).

Several indexes to these publications exist. The single most useful for competitive intelligence is the *Predicasts F&S Index: United States:* Predicasts, Inc., annually since 1965. While the index covers some of the more traditional business publications such as *Forbes, Fortune,* and *Business Week,* it concentrates more on trade papers like the *Wall Street Transcript, Progressive Grocer,* and *Advertising Age.* Each issue of the index has two parts—the first lists articles about industries, the second about companies, including private

EXHIBIT 5
McDonald's Attacks Its Competition

In the February 26, 1990, issue of *Fortune,* an article appeared entitled "Big Mac Attacks with Pizza." This was a report on how McDonald's plans to increase its sales in the face of increased competition and a slowing in the sales of fast-food outlets. Its strategy is essentially to use new products to lure people into its outlets. The company's third attempt to enter the pizza market may well be successful "if the results of its seven-month market test in Evansville, Indiana, and Owensboro, Kentucky, are anything to go on." And, McDonald's is debating other dinnertime gambits, including meals served in a basket (instead of wrapped in paper) and a smiling hostess to greet you or serve you a second cup of coffee. Also under consideration are even more menu items identified only as "secret stuff." One educated guess: more seafood.

companies and subsidiaries. The publishers have tried a couple of things to make this index more useful than a standard bibliography. First, for each article the compilers give a one-sentence statement of the main point of the article instead of its title. Second, many of the articles are marked by a black dot indicating that, in the opinion of Predicasts, this is a "key article." The marking system makes it possible to skim through several years of the index, picking only the key articles, and compile quickly a bibliography on a company or industry. *Predicasts F&S Index: International* has been published since 1968, and *Predicasts F&S Index: Europe* has been available since 1978. The on-line PTS files, as they are called, provide the same information in computerized form.

Business Periodicals Index is the traditional index for business publications such as *Forbes, Fortune, Business Week, Harvard Business Review, Nation's Business,* and *Dun's Business* and more specialized journals such as *Production and Inventory Management, Academy of Management Journal,* and *Journal of Marketing Research.* The index alphabetically lists articles about companies, industries, and all the various topics associated with doing business. Although the coverage here is not limited to companies or even industries, it is important to check *Business Periodicals Index* because of the many different publications it includes. It is also the place to look for articles on any topics that come up in the research. For example, a competitor might announce that it is instituting a materials requirement planning (MRP) system. *Business Periodicals Index* will list articles about that and other inventory and materials flow systems. This index, for 1983 to the present, is available on-line and in CD-ROM.

The latest index is *Business Index,* a new development in both form and content. On one microfilm cassette it lists articles appearing in five years of journals instead of the traditional one year at a time. The cassette is mounted on a reader that is very easy to use. However, the coverage is a bit uneven; the listing includes a smattering of the common business journals mixed with a selection of the trade journals. There seems to be no logic behind the particular choices. Unlike the other indexes, though, this one includes the *Wall Street Transcript,* indexed in *Predicasts F&S Index.*

E X H I B I T   6

Top Confectionery Companies: Performance and Prospects in Europe

For 35 of Europe's leading confectionery firms, *E.R.C. Statistics* provides an in-depth corporate analysis, a market profile on a country-by-country basis, and an assessment of current position and capacity to compete in the future. Particulars include financial highlights, manufacturing and subsidiary operations, strength of brands, market strategies, advertising and promotion, examination of current areas of strength and weakness, and much more. Among the companies included: Alivar SpA, Bassett Foods PLC, Cadbury Schweppes PLC, Campbell Soup Co., Chocolaterie Cantalou SA, Oy Karl Fazer AB, P. Ferrero & C SpA, Freia A/S, General de Confiteria, General Foods, Haribo GmbH & Co. KG, Huhtamaki Oy, Jacobs Suchard, Marabou AB, Mars Inc., Nestle SA, Nora Industrier, Red Band Venco Confectionery BV, Alfred Ritter Schokoladenfabrik GmbH, August Storck KG, Trebor Group Ltd., United Biscuits (Holdings) PLC, Van Melle NV, Wm. Wrigley Jr. Co., others. (850 pages)

E1650 . . . . August 1989 . . . . $10,000

SOURCE: *International Catalog of Business Reports* (Off-the-Shelf Publications, Inc., Commack, New York, 1989).

Investment house reports

Investext, a computer data base, includes over 10,000 reports prepared annually by over 300 analysts with investment banking firms. It can be searched using various approaches to locate a report or even a specific page within a report. *CIRR/Corporate & Industry Research Reports* is a microfiche collection of the complete reports published by JA Micropublishing, Inc. Investment house reports are often highly prized as the statements of people who know in detail the companies and industries they follow.

An example is a March 1989 report on Philip Morris Companies, Inc., listed in the October 1989 issue of the *International Catalog of Business Reports* (Off-the-Shelf Publications, Inc., of Cammack, New York). This report "discusses cigarette pricing and profitability, the sound merging of Kraft and General Foods, the outlook for Miller (beer), and the company's interest in geographic segmentation. Estimates from 1987–93 are supplied for flow of funds, revenues by product line, operating income by product line, domestic unit cigarette sales by brand, Miller Brewing barrelage by brand and U.S. region." This same source also lists a large number of domestic and foreign industry studies (see Exhibit 6 for an example of an international study).

There are a great number of other automated indexes to business literature. The directories of data bases listed earlier can provide the names and descriptions of many more.

Biographical sources

Information on corporate executives may also be useful in predicting competitor strategies. The names of corporate executives and directors can be located in any of the directories mentioned earlier. Basic sources of biographical information include:

- *Who's Who in America* (Chicago: Marquis Who's Who Inc., annually since 1900), also available on-line,
- *Who's Who of American Women* (Chicago: Marquis Who's Who Inc., biennally since 1959),
- *Who's Who in Finance and Industry* (Chicago: Marquis Who's Who Inc., annually since 1972), formerly *World's Who's Who in Finance and Industry* (1936–1971), and
- *Current Biography* (New York: H.W. Wilson, since 1940, monthly with annual cumulations).

In addition, Standard & Poor's offers a data base, *S&P Register—Biographical,* that gives biographical data on key executives. Finally, many of the data bases of newspaper files and newsletters provide information on executives in smaller companies.

Patent information

For many companies, patent applications and awards provide important information about corporate strategy and successes. The official record of patent applications and grants is the *Official Gazette of the U.S. Patent and Trademark Office* (Washington, D.C.: Government Printing Office), begun in 1872 and issued weekly. Since 1975, the *Gazette* has been published in two volumes, one for patents and the other for trademarks.

Data bases that index patents and trademarks include:

- *Claims/U.S. Patents,* covering general, chemical, electrical, and mechanical U.S. patents,
- *Claims/Comprehensive,* indexing 1.7 million U.S. patents issued since 1950,
- *Inpadoc/Family and Legal Status,* indexing 13 million patents from over 500 countries,
- *World Patent Index,*
- *Trademarkscan—Federal,* and
- *Trademarkscan—State.*

Market studies

This section is concerned primarily with sources that concentrate on markets and/or the marketing activities of competitors. There are two major sources dedicated to locating studies that have been done. The first is a computer data base, *PTS PROMT,* produced by Predicast, Inc., the publishers of the *Predicasts F&S Index. PROMT* (Predicasts Overviews of Marketing and Technology) covers marketing in the broad sense of anything affecting the market for products, including new technology, mergers and acquisitions, market data, and new products. The data base lists journal articles, newspaper articles, and special studies of foreign countries. *PTS Marketing and Advertising Reference Service, PTS Product Announcements/Plus,* and *PTS Newsletter Database* offer other information about markets and products.

The print volume *FINDex: The Director of Market Research, Reports, Studies, and Surveys* and its on-line equivalent *FINDEX* describe industry and market studies that are commercially available from U.S. and other marketing research firms at a cost of anywhere from $20 to $20,000. Studies by such well-known firms as Nielsen and Frost & Sullivan are listed here. *FINDex*'s bimonthly information catalog typically lists over 600 new publications in some 30 industries, including company reports for Wall Street.

Market statistics

For plain statistics on markets, there are three major sources. The oldest, *American Statistics Index* (Washington, D.C.: Congressional Information Service, monthly with annual cumulations since 1973), indexes statistics published by all U.S. government agencies. Perhaps more useful for business purposes is its companion title, *Statistical Reference Index* (Washington, D.C.: CIS, monthly with annual cumulations since 1980), which indexes statistics gathered by state agencies, associations, commissions, and other private sources. *Index to International Statistics* (Washington, D.C.: CIS, monthly with annual cumulations since 1983) provides access to figures collected by foreign and international groups.

These indexes come in two parts, one an index and the other, an abstract. The abstracts are arranged by organization or government body producing the statistics and cover both one-time and serial publications. The indexing is specific enough to get the user to a particular table within a publication, not just to the general publication itself.

For a statistical overview of the United States' geographical markets, a major source is the *Survey of Buying Power* from *Sales & Marketing Management.* The *Survey* gives a statistical profile of the population and the sales of various retail businesses for each county and metropolitan area in the United States (see Exhibit 7). The statistics are also broken down by Arbitron's *Areas of Dominant Influence* for TV markets, by zip code, and by newspaper markets. *Sales & Marketing Management* also publishes the *Survey of Industrial Purchasing Power,* a survey by county of the industries there and the dollar sales they account for. The *Survey of Buying Power* appears in the July (part I) and October (part II) issues of *Sales & Marketing Management;* the *Survey of Industrial Purchasing Power* in the April issue. CACI (with offices in Fairfax, Virginia, and London, England) offers a source book that contains demographics and buying power for every zip code for 1989 and forecasts for 1994. Similar information is available from CACI's source book of county demographics and the source book of city demographics.

The Consumer Research Center of the Conference Board regularly publishes studies concerned with consumer expenditures. These are based on the

EXHIBIT 7

Listing of Key Demographic Statistics Available from the 1990 *Survey of Buying Power, Part 1*

- Total population
- Percent of U.S. population
- Median age
- Percent of population by age group
    - 18–24
    - 25–34
    - 35–49
    - 50+
- Total households
- Total retail sales
- Retail sales by store group
    - Food stores
    - Eating and drinking places
    - General merchandise
    - Furniture/furnishings/appliances
    - Automotive
    - Drug stores
- Effective buying income (EBI)
- Median household (EBI)
- Percent of households by EBI group:
    - $10,000–$19,999
    - $20,000–$34,999
    - $35,000–$49,999
    - $50,000 and over
- Buying power index (BPI)

Census Bureau's annual *Current Population Survey.* A recent report entitled *How Consumers Spend Their Money* (1989) presents detailed information on the purchase of over 160 products and services by 11 household characteristics such as age, household size and composition, education, occupation, income, religion, and race. Another recent study—undertaken jointly with the U.S. Bureau of the Census—takes a close look at the upscale market in the United States; that is, 25 million households with about $200 billion in combined discretionary income. Data consists mainly of the number of households by selected demographic characteristics possessing discretionary income and the amount thereof (see Exhibit 8). Older titles include *Midlife and Beyond: The $800 Billion Over-50 Market* (1985), *Baby Boomers at Midpassage* (1987), and *Households and Income by Selected Characteristics* (1987). In a somewhat similar manner, Standard Rate & Data Service, Inc., and National Demographic & Lifestyles, Inc., published a report entitled *The 1989 Lifestyle Market Analysis,* which provides detailed information on U.S. demographics and lifestyles by selected geographical breakdowns. The lifestyle data consists

EXHIBIT 8

Number and Percent of U.S. Households with Discretionary Income by Age Groups

| | Households with discretionary income | | | | | | |
| | Households | | Average income | | Spendable discretionary income | | |
	Number (thousands)	Proportion of households	Before taxes	After taxes	Aggregate (billions)	Average	Per capita
Total	25,292	30.7	36,954	26,962	193.3	7,644	2,661
Under 25 years	1,170	18.2	27,128	20,857	5.4	4,612	1,979
25 to 29 years	2,633	27.7	31,980	23,890	14.2	5,383	1,856
30 to 34 years	3,017	31.3	35,819	25,946	19.4	6,433	2,045
35 to 39 years	2,466	30.9	41,565	29,504	18.9	7,646	2,109
40 to 44 years	2,175	33.5	44,455	31,475	18.3	8,429	2,249
45 to 49 years	2,216	35.7	46,106	32,665	20.3	9,177	2,573
50 to 54 years	2,455	37.8	44,362	31,442	21.6	8,810	2,700
55 to 59 years	2,662	39.5	41,726	29,379	23.9	8,963	3,488
60 to 64 years	2,111	35.4	36,022	26,127	17.8	8,428	3,703
65 years and over	4,388	25.9	25,817	21,014	33.6	7,646	4,118

SOURCE: A Marketer's Guide to Discretionary Income (New York: The Conference Board, 1989).

of an analysis of household participation in over 50 lifestyle activities (see Exhibit 9).

The Bureau of Labor Statistics conducts an ongoing consumer expenditures survey that collects data relating to family expenditures for goods and services used in everyday living. This survey consists of two parts—a quarterly interview with each consumer unit in the sample and a diary or record-keeping survey. The former collects data on major items of expense that respondents can recall for three months or longer. The diary survey asks respondents to report all expenditures made during their two-week participation. Survey results are available in a variety of forms, including tapes. They include tabulations of average annual expenditures by type of expenditure arranged by such characteristics as income, age, region and family size. For example, the mean expenditure for electricity by all consumer units in 1988 was $708.82, for telephone $537.04, babysitting $71.51, sofas $68.18, clocks $4.96, men's sportscoats $16.80, and health insurance $474.39. The survey results also show the percent of units making a given type of expenditure.

Finally, some of the general business directories can be useful for generating a list of industrial clients or prospects. *Ward's Business Directory* lists companies geographically by zip code, making it possible to find prospects in certain areas of the country rather than in certain industries. Dun & Bradstreet's *Million Dollar Directory* and Standard & Poor's *Register of Corporations* also list companies by zip code.

EXHIBIT 9

Number of Households Engaged in Various Activities by Five Major Categories for
Salt Lake City, Utah—1989

The good life activities	Households	Percent	Index
Attend cultural/ Arts events	114,334	19.4	**123**
Career-oriented activities	71,311	12.1	100
Community/Civic activities	73,669	12.5	99
Fashion, clothing	68,365	11.6	90
Fine art/Antiques	58,346	9.9	95
Foreign travel	72,490	12.3	98
Gourmet cooking/ Fine foods	81,330	13.8	81
Home furnishing/ Decorating	129,068	21.9	104
Money-making opportunities	55,399	9.4	100
Real estate investments	33,004	5.6	84
Stock/Bond investments	67,186	11.4	94
Wines	52,452	8.9	81

High-tech activities	Households	Percent	Index
Electronics	56,578	9.6	114
Home video games	74,847	12.7	118
Personal/Home computers	136,140	23.1	142
Photography	136,729	23.2	114
Science fiction	54,810	9.3	124
Science/New technology	57,167	9.7	120
Stereo/Records/ Tapes	264,618	44.9	107
VCR recording/ Viewing	241,044	40.9	106
Watching cable TV	207,451	35.2	87

Sports/leisure activities	Households	Percent	Index
Bicycling frequently	106,672	18.1	115
Boating/Sailing	90,760	15.4	121
Bowling	88,992	15.1	101
Golf	136,140	23.1	130
Physical fitness/ Exercise	209,219	35.5	111
Running/Jogging	78,973	13.4	118
Snow skiing frequently	119,049	20.2	240
Tennis frequently	40,076	6.8	103
Walking for health	228,668	38.8	100
Watching sports on TV	221,596	37.6	101

Outdoor activities	Households	Percent	Index
Camping/Hiking	287,603	48.8	220
Fishing frequently	195,075	33.1	140
Hunting/Shooting	165,607	28.1	180
Motorcycles	69,543	11.8	171
Recreational vehi- cles/4–WD	99,011	16.8	210
Wildlife/ Environmental	101,958	17.3	109

Domestic activities	Households	Percent	Index
Automotive work	107,262	18.2	127
Avid book reading	241,044	40.9	107
Bible/Devotional reading	129,657	22.0	127
Coin/Stamp collecting	49,505	8.4	105
Collectibles/ Collections	56,578	9.6	88
Crafts	184,467	31.3	119
Crossword puzzles	81,920	13.9	70
Current affairs/ Politics	92,528	15.7	98
Entering sweepstakes	84,277	14.3	98
Gardening	230,436	39.1	118
Grandchildren	123,174	20.9	109
Health foods/ Vitamins	84,866	14.4	103
Home workshop	146,748	24.9	111
Household pets	179,162	30.4	101
Needlework/ Knitting	136,729	23.2	123
Self-improvement	127,300	21.6	136
Sewing	144,980	24.6	131
Shopping by catalog	124,942	21.2	84
Veterans benefits/ Programs	24,163	4.1	84
Mean number of interests		10.4	113

SOURCE: *The Lifestyle Market Analyst* 1991, published by Standard Rate and Data Service with National Demographics and Lifestyles, (NDL).

Commercial research sources

The increased demand for marketing data in recent years has stimulated large numbers of companies to collect and sell marketing information.[9] There are two kinds of such companies—those that do research on specific problems faced by their clients, and those that collect selected marketing data on a continuous basis and sell it by subscription. Our concern here is with the latter, as they relate to consumer products.

A number of syndicated sources provide continuous data on consumer purchases. Such data are important with respect to all types of marketing problems and particularly so for identifying competitors and evaluating their marketing activities. They also provide industry sales by segments as well as share data. Purchase data are obtained from consumer panels, retail stores, or warehouse withdrawals.

The Nielsen ScanTRACK service consists of two major components—a national retail store panel and a national household panel. The first is comprised of a national sample of over 3,000 scanner-equipped stores that provide a complete record of their sales. Essentially, these records provide information on an item-by-item basis concerning the sales of any product that bears a Universal Product Code (UPC) symbol. The service is strongly oriented toward packaged food and household items; hence, the store sample is skewed toward supermarkets. Other kinds of stores, including convenience, discount, drug, and department stores, are represented in sufficient numbers to permit reporting of product sales by store type.

Total sales of a given product class can be determined from store records, as well as sales of individual brands (and hence market share), sales of various package sizes, price paid for each brand (including the use of coupons), and brand penetration among retailers. Nielsen also records how much in-store display activity a brand receives and the extent of retailer advertising support of a brand. Such data are available at the national level and for the top 50 markets or by a client's sales regions (see Exhibit 10 for examples of the kinds of questions data from a national retail store panel can answer).

The second part of the ScanTRACK service consists of a national panel of households that is representative of all U.S. households. Panelists use a hand-held scanner to record all of their purchases via the Universal Product Code regardless of the type of store in which the purchases were made. (See Exhibit 11 for examples of the kinds of questions the data from a consumer panel can answer). Panelists in the larger media markets are metered for their TV viewing using people meters that record what programs are viewed and for how long. Thus, the individual commercials embedded in the programs viewed can be linked to a household's purchasing behavior. Purchase and

---

[9]For a profile of each of the top marketing research firms, see Jack Honomichi, "The Honomichi 50," *Marketing News,* May 28, 1990. Also see "*Advertising Age*'s Annual Ranking of Media, Marketing Agencies, and Research Companies," *Advertising Age,* December 24, 1990, p. 12.

EXHIBIT 10

Examples of Questions Data from a National Retail Store Panel Can Answer

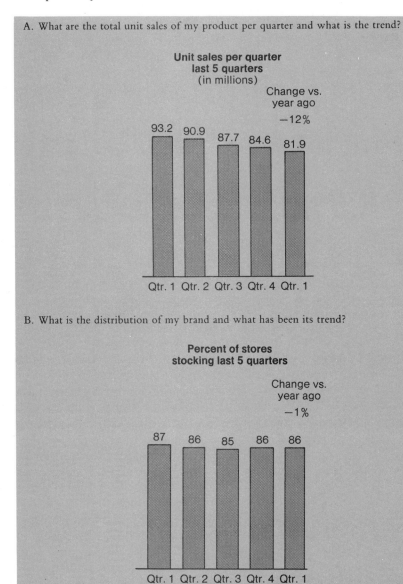

A. What are the total unit sales of my product per quarter and what is the trend?

**Unit sales per quarter
last 5 quarters
(in millions)**

Change vs.
year ago
−12%

93.2 90.9 87.7 84.6 81.9

Qtr. 1 Qtr. 2 Qtr. 3 Qtr. 4 Qtr. 1

B. What is the distribution of my brand and what has been its trend?

**Percent of stores
stocking last 5 quarters**

Change vs.
year ago
−1%

87 86 85 86 86

Qtr. 1 Qtr. 2 Qtr. 3 Qtr. 4 Qtr. 1

C. What are the market shares of major brands fourth quarter this year versus same period last year?

This year	Last year
Our brand, 30%	Our brand, 25%
Brand A, 20%	Brand A, 18%
Brand B, 15%	Brand B, 20%
Brand C, 10%	Brand C, 15%
All others, 25%	All others, 22%

Note: All the above data can be shown by leading markets, clients' sales regions, and type and size of store.

E X H I B I T   1 1

Examples of the Kinds of Questions Data from a Consumer Panel Can Answer

A. What percent of households buy this type product and what is the trend?

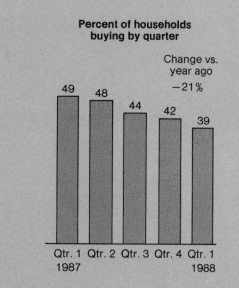

Percent of households buying by quarter

Change vs. year ago
−21%

49   48   44   42   39

Qtr. 1   Qtr. 2   Qtr. 3   Qtr. 4   Qtr. 1
1987   1988

B. What is the demographic profile of the buyers of my brand versus those of leading competitors?

Total annual family income	Distribution of purchases			
	Our brand	Brand A	Brand B	Total category
Under $15,000	26%	18%	20%	22%
$15,000–25,000	40%	52%	53%	48%
$25,000 & over	34%	30%	27%	30%

C. How loyal are the buyers of my brand versus those of competitors?

Number of times same brand purchsed out of last 4 purchases	Percent households purchasing		
	Our brand	Brand A	Brand B
0 of 4	20%	15%	18%
1 of 4	23%	18%	22%
2 of 4	28%	29%	25%
3 of 4	18%	30%	25%
4 of 4	11%	8%	10%

EXHIBIT 12

Of households viewing the TV programs in which our commercials are shown, what percent are buying our brand and what are their average per-household dollar purchases? How does this compare with those who do not view these same TV programs?		
	Past three months	
	View our programs	**Do not view our programs**
Percent households buying our brand	62%	52%
Average per-household dollar purchases during past three months	$18.92	$16.21

viewing behavior is reported by various demographic breakdowns. This integrated (single source) information system provides insights into retail sales, who buys, and the effect of advertising and promotion on purchasing behavior (see Exhibit 12).

The NPD Group provides both custom research and syndicated tracking services. The latter are based on diary panel data provided by demographically balanced samples of U.S. households and audits of leading retailers. Data are provided for the following industries:

1. *Food consumption/away-from-home eating.* The former tracks in-home preparation and consumption of all foods and beverages while the latter tracks meals bought at restaurants.
2. *Softgoods.* This panel tracks mainly apparel and household textile purchases.
3. *Petroleum/automotive.* This service tracks petroleum products and automotive parts and services.
4. *Toys/games/books.* Diary data provide the input for tracking toys, games, and children's books and book sets.
5. *Sporting goods.* Retail audits provide retail sales data on selected sporting goods categories.
6. *Consumer electronics.* This tracking service offers retail audit data on selected consumer electronic items.

For an example of expenditures of the kind of data such syndicated tracking services provide, see Exhibit 13, which shows the distribution of expenditures for toys by major categories.

Own marketing research studies

Yet another way of obtaining information about competitors and the industry involved is for a company to undertake its own specific marketing research studies. These are usually done in an effort to help management set objectives

EXHIBIT 13

Distribution of Dollar Expenditures of Toys in 1988 by Category

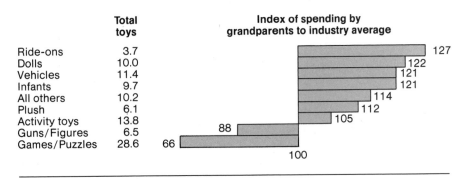

	Total toys	Index of spending by grandparents to industry average
Ride-ons	3.7	127
Dolls	10.0	122
Vehicles	11.4	121
Infants	9.7	121
All others	10.2	114
Plush	6.1	112
Activity toys	13.8	105
Guns/Figures	6.5	88
Games/Puzzles	28.6	66

SOURCE: The NPD Group, Inc., *NPD Insights,* vol. 1 (September 1989), p. 4.

and formulate strategies, develop action plans, and monitor both the company's and competitors' activities.

Almost all manufacturing companies of any size do marketing research on competitive products, market potential, market share, sales analysis, and forecasting. Industrial goods companies do more business trend studies and ecological impact studies than consumer goods companies, while the latter do more research on new products, advertising, and consumer promotions.

GETTING DATA FROM PRIVATE COMPANIES AND SUBSIDIARIES—A SPECIAL PROBLEM

Getting information from private companies, subsidiaries, or separate locations within a larger company, particularly if they are small, can present a real challenge. If there is a parent company, the subsidiary or location might be covered in the reports on the parent. Two sources discussed earlier are particularly helpful with these "problem" companies. These are the *Predicasts F&S Index* and the *Trinet Establishment Database.* The Predicasts F&S Index is the place to start to find any published reports on such companies.

In many cases, however, just verifying that the company exists and finding out what it does is the problem. Several of the major business directories can be of help in this situation. One of the best and most widely available directories is the *Thomas Register of American Manufacturers* published in 25 volumes. The first 16 volumes alphabetically list the companies participating in this service and arrange them by product; 2 volumes give brief profiles of the companies; and the last 7 reprint the complete catalogs of those companies. There is also a trade-name index that can be very useful for small companies where it is common to confuse the name of the product and the company.

The listing will give the company's address and phone number, a code for asset size, the products it makes, and its officers' names. A check under product name(s) will produce a listing of other companies making a similar product and therefore competing with the firm under study. If the company has paid for it, *Thomas* will reprint the company's entire catalog, an excellent source of information on the company and its line of goods.

As already noted, Dun & Bradstreet produces a general business directory, the *Million Dollar Directory*. It is a five-volume alphabetical listing of businesses in the United States with a net worth of $500,000 or more. The listings again include address, phone number, and officers, but also gives a sales figure, number of employees, and the Standard Industrial Classification numbers for the primary industries the company is in. *Ward's Business Directory*, also previously mentioned, reports minimal information on thousands of private companies.

Another Dun and Bradstreet publication, *America's Corporate Families,* is useful for identifying subsidiary companies. It has two volumes, the first listing 9,000 U.S. parent companies and 45,000 subsidiaries or divisions and the second giving 1,700 U.S. parent companies with 13,000 foreign subsidiaries and 2,500 foreign parents with 6,000 U.S. subsidiaries. Another publication, *Directory of Corporate Affiliations* (Skokie, Ill.: National Register Publishing, annual), records 5,000 parent and 40,000 affiliate companies, both public and private.

Leonard Fuld's *Competitor Intelligence: How to Get It; How to Use It* (New York: John Wiley & Sons, 1985) concentrates on creative techniques for locating information on smaller, more elusive companies. He makes a particularly good case for using the state filings, discussed earlier, and also has some excellent ideas for using trade directories and other sources. Fuld emphasizes the usefulness of filings with state governments required under the Uniform Commercial Code (UCC) for all commercial loans. A bank granting a commercial loan is required to file a UCC form stating what was purchased with the money, making these forms an excellent way to keep track of a competitor's addition to its asset base.

EVALUATING COMPETITIVE INFORMATION

The collection and use of competitive information inevitably produces an evaluation problem. This includes determining the relevancy of the data to the organization, its reliability, and its accuracy. Relevancy involves determining who in the company needs what data when. Reliability is concerned with evaluating the source or agency involved with the collection and/or dissemination of the data. Essentially, analysts determine reliability on the basis of previous experience with a specific source; thus, it is particularly important when a given source (e.g., an investment house or the company's own salesforce) is used repeatedly. Accuracy, or validity, has to do with the likely correctness of the data. Analysts can assess accuracy by the research methods used to collect the data, comparing it with other data and the extent to which it "makes sense."

Commercial data

Although commercial agencies that sell data on a regular (subscription) basis may not have the user's specific problem in mind when they collect data, they do so for a particular purpose such as measuring industry sales, providing market share data for specific products, measuring brand loyalty, and so on. Such information can be very helpful in evaluating a company's marketing activities, both short and long run, versus selected competitors. This is particularly true for consumer goods.

In the purchase of such data, the analyst must be certain that it is accurate enough for the purposes at hand. Such an evaluation is easier to make than with most secondary data because detailed information about the research design, the sampling methodology, and the data collection methods can be readily obtained. In some cases, similar data can be purchased from two or more sources that differ in collection methods. For example, radio and television audiences are measured using such different techniques as audiometers, telephone calls, self-administered diaries, and recall interviews. The buyer of such data must evaluate the reliability of these data collection methods in the context of the usage to which the data will be put.

Most continuous subscription services are operated by competent technicians who employ sound sampling and data collection techniques. However, even the best of these organizations are limited by financial considerations, and all are hampered by the difficulties inherent in collecting data from consumers, retailers, and wholesalers. For these reasons, analysts who use such data need to evaluate carefully that service and the data provided, keeping in mind how the data will be used.

When trend data are involved, the data must use the same units of measurement year in and year out and must come from the same sampling universe of interest. Other criteria to use regardless of whether trend data are involved are:

1. *Data collection methods.* If the analyst cannot find out what procedures were used to collect the data, then he/she should be hesitant in using it. Too often, this lack of disclosure is used to cover up the use of inadequate research methods. When the methodology is obtained, the analyst should examine it in detail. For example, if a sample was used, the analyst should ask, Was it selected objectively? Was it large enough, particularly for the subsamples? Was it selected from the universe of interest?

2. *Who collects the information—and why?* An organization that collects and publishes data as its major business activity is likely to furnish reliable data since the organization's success depends on satisfying its clients with accurate data. The ability of the organization to obtain the wanted information is critical. This often is a function of authority and prestige. The government (e.g., the Securities and Exchange Commission and the Bureau of the Census) can obtain more accurate information than a private

firm. Further, it is important to know the capabilities and motivation of the individuals responsible for the data collection. Reputation, training, and experience are all important considerations in assessing the reliability of an "expert."

3. *General evidence of careful work.* An important point of evaluation is the general evidence that the data have been collected and processed carefully. Is the information presented in a well-organized manner? Are the data consistent? Are the conclusions supported by the data?

4. *Conflicting data.* If several sources of data are available, the data can be submitted to a "quality-control analysis." After dividing the data into "good" and "bad" categories on the basis of criteria like those discussed above, the analyst can run correlations on points of interest between the two groups. Internal consistency is also an important consideration here.

THE SAMAR CASE

Introductory Note

T he strategic allocation of marketing resources is one of the most important areas of business strategy. In many situations prompted by deteriorating financial results, threats of hostile take-overs, mergers or leveraged management buy-outs, companies have been able to make strategic turnarounds increasing both their short-term and long-term profitability significantly. Very often dramatic reallocation of marketing resources is at the heart of these strategic turnarounds.

While the SAMAR case describes a fictitious company, its development has been inspired by situations of such strategic turnaround. It does not go in depth into marketing mix decisions, but centers on the allocation of marketing resources between products and segments. It offers an opportunity to apply many concepts covered in all four sections of the book, including:

- Economies of scale and experience effects
- Market share and profitability
- Industry dynamics and the product life cycle
- Competitive analysis
- Portfolio strategies
- Market targeting and positioning

- Strategies for growth, mature and declining markets
- New entry strategies
- The strategic marketing decision process
- Marketing control
- Illustration of a marketing support system.

The accompanying SAMAR simulation gives the case a dynamic dimension. It shows all the importance of the exploitation of time in strategy and the unavoidable conflict between short-term and long-term considerations. Furthermore, it provides a motivating and competitive environment conducive to the acquisition of a strategic mind.

SAMAR: Strategic Allocation of Marketing Resources

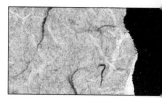

In early January 1991 Ken Smith had just joined SAMAR, a diversified industrial company, as the new Vice President of Marketing of its Zompert division. The division manufactured and commercialized three products, Z38, Z56, and Z75, and R&D planned to make new models available in the coming years. The present document summarizes the information that Smith gathered during his first week with SAMAR.

Ken Smith's challenge

The total marketing budget for the first six months of 1991 was around $4.4 million and was to cover all marketing activities, including salesforce, sales support, and technical support for all three Zompert products. The marketing budget authorized for a given six-month period depended on the financial performance of the division. Smith had, however, received assurance that it would not fall below $3 million. The maximum authorized budget he could expect in a particularly profitable situation was $10 million.

Smith's major objective was to *maximize the cumulative net contribution* generated by his division over the next five-year planning horizon, 1991–1995. His main concern was the *allocation of marketing resources across the product line.* He was particularly concerned that this allocation may have been far from optimum in the past. With the forthcoming potential introduction of new products, he also anticipated the risk of scarce marketing resources being distributed too thinly across too many products.

This case has been developed by Jean-Claude Larréché, Professor at INSEAD, to illustrate strategic marketing allocation issues. It represents a simulated environment developed on the basis of actual business situations and of the MARKOPS simulation.

SAMAR's simulation

SAMAR had developed a software tool that represented a realistic simulation of the operations of the Zompert division. It simulates six-month periods of operations, including expected market and competitive reactions to SAMAR's marketing plans.

Exhibit 1 contains the report of the simulation at the end of Period 0, when Smith took over at the end of 1990. Exhibit 2 contains the report of the simulation in Period 10 under the "status quo" scenario, that is, if no changes are made in the operations of the division for the next five years. These projected results were not very encouraging, and Smith felt compelled to make a number of moves to improve the forecasted situation. Exhibits 3 and 4 contain graphs of the anticipated evolution of the net contribution, the Zompert market size, and the four Zompert market segments under the status quo scenario. Instructions for the SAMAR software appear in Exhibit 5.

The Zompert market

The key characteristic of a Zompert segment was its swotage (measured in swots). The market was composed of four distinct segments corresponding to different swotage levels:

Segment	Swotage range	Description
A	More than 70 swots	High end
B	Between 50 and 70 swots	Upper-middle range
C	Between 30 and 50 swots	Lower-middle range
D	Less than 30 swots	Low end

Profitability was currently greater at the high end of the Zompert market, but growth was higher at the low end of the market.

SAMAR was in competition with three other diversified industrial companies: ATOPRO, KENETEC, and PITBIOX. Each competitor had different products and different positions in the various market segments:

Market segment	SAMAR	ATOPRO	KENETEC	PITBIOX
A	SAMZ75	—	KENZ78	—
B	SAMZ56	ATOZ60	KENZ65	—
C	SAMZ38	ATOZ32	—	PITZ45
D	—	ATOZ17	KENZ25	PITZ28
				PITZ15

The name of each product was composed of the first three letters of the supplying firm (e.g., ATO for ATOPRO), "Z" for Zompert, and the swotage level (e.g., 60 swots for ATOZ60).

Zompert production

Production capacity of a given Zompert model could be increased in multiples of 50,000 units. Building new or additional capacity took six months. Consequently, increases in production capacity has to be requested six months before they can be used.

The total manufacturing cost of a Zompert can be broken down into fixed and variable components. Assuming that the production capacity for a given product was fully used, the fixed and variable manufacturing costs represented 20 percent and 80 percent of total manufacturing costs, respectively.

Fixed manufacturing costs increased with production capacity, but less than proportionately less because of scale economies. Assuming full capacity usage, the fixed manufacturing cost per unit produced would, therefore, decrease at higher capacity levels. Similarly, the unit variable manufacturing cost also decreased for higher capacity levels. In addition, sustained cumulative production of a given product over time resulted in decreased fixed and variable manufacturing costs due to learning effects. The fixed manufacturing cost for a given production capacity was, however, the same if this capacity was fully or only partially used. As a result, these various factors (higher capacity levels, sustained cumulative production, and efficient use of full capacity) could drive total unit manufacturing costs down over time.

Financial issues

The financial statement for the Zompert division is contained in the Product Contribution section of the simulation report, illustrated in Exhibit 1. Sales minus cost of goods sold (computed on the basis of unit variable manufacturing cost) provided a contribution figure before marketing costs (CBM). Marketing resources corresponded to expenditures on salesforce, sales support, and technical support that must be covered by the authorized marketing budget. In addition to marketing resources, total marketing expenditures (TME) included costs associated with credit, inventories, and marketing administration.

The credit cost was a financial charge (at a 5.5 percent rate per six-month period) for the sales outstanding on the basis of 90-day customer credit terms. The inventory cost represented financial and warehouse charges and was computed as 7.5 percent of the average value of the inventory level maintained during a six-month period. The marketing administration cost was composed of a fixed component ($600,000 for each product) and a variable component (2 percent of sales).

Contribution before marketing (CBM) minus total marketing expenditures (TME) provides contribution after marketing (CAM). CAM minus fixed manufacturing costs gives the product contribution for a given Zompert model. Adding this product contribution for each model gives the net contribution for the division in a given period. Eventually, an exceptional cost might be subtracted from this net contribution if a product were withdrawn from the line and if stocks from this product needed to be disposed of. This exceptional cost is computed as 10 percent of the value of the inventory to be disposed of.

New products

The SAMAR R&D department was currently working on two new Zompert models. Their characteristics were:

Swotage level	22	82
Unit variable manufacturing cost	$28	$105
Fixed manufacturing cost	$352,000	$1,312,000

The unit variable and fixed manufacturing costs were estimated on the basis of a fully used 50,000 unit capacity. They obviously varied for different capacity and usage levels, as discussed previously. Both products are available from R&D at the start of Period 3, that is, production capacity could first be built in Period 3. A new product could consequently first be commercialized in the next six-month period, Period 4, that is, in the second half of 1992. Because of limited marketing resources, Smith has decided to introduce only one of these two products over the next 10 periods.

Competition was also expected to introduce new products. The current estimation of competitive product introductions made by the marketing staff and taken into account in the simulation was:

Period	Competitive product introduction
3	PITZ41
4	KENZ81
5	ATOZ22
6	PITZ59
7	KENZ22
8	ATOZ39

The impact of these new competitive products is shown under the status quo scenario in the simulation report shown in Exhibit 2.

Effective marketing impact

The minimum marketing budget required to support a Zompert model is $90,000. Experience in the Zompert market had shown, however, that for a product to make a significant impact in the market required total marketing resources in the order of $3 million per period. This level was only indicative and obviously depended on other factors, such as product quality, targeted segment, or unit price. It clearly showed, however, that with a total marketing budget of between $3 million and $10 million, courageous resource allocation decisions had to be made between products. These resources would be allocated across various marketing activities, such as salesforce, sales support, and technical support, under direct marketing efforts and through independent distributors. Smith thought that, in the planning stage at least, he should concentrate on the allocation of resources *between* products rather than on more tactical decisions for specific products.

Strategic marketing resources allocation

On the basis of the inputs from his marketing staff and the projected outcome of a status quo strategy for 1995, Smith quickly saw the need to develop a new strategic marketing perspective for the Zompert division. He realized that a major issue was the allocation of marketing resources between existing Zomperts and subsequently the amount of support available to introduce new products. Some of the questions that came to mind were: Had SAMAR sufficient resources to support three products on the Zompert market effectively? What segments of the Zompert market should be more attractive for SAMAR given the current situation and expected market and competitive conditions? What market-share objectives could reasonably be reached? What level of resources could be generated by existing products and used to finance the introduction of a new one?

Mr. Smith decided to address the following three issues separately:

- *Which of the existing products should receive the highest marketing investment priority?* This product should be the one that offered the strongest long-term potential. Smith thought that at least one existing product should achieve a leading position to later become a key source of funds for new-product introductions. This product should, at least in the short term, be allocated a higher proportion of available marketing resources to achieve such a strong competitive position.

- *What strategy to adopt for the other two existing products?* On the basis of the information available, Smith did not believe the remaining two products could be allocated sufficient resources to gain a strong competitive position. He wondered what role they should play in the product line, if they could remain profitable without substantial marketing support, or if they should be withdrawn from the market.

- *What strategy to adopt for a new product introduction?* While the current R&D projects offered two interesting product options, Smith thought that only one of them could be introduced effectively in the market given the resources that existing products could generate. The key questions in his mind were: Which new product should be introduced? At what time should it be introduced? And with which strategy?

EXHIBIT 1
Situation at the End of Period 0

```
-------------------------- DECISIONS --------------------------

SAMAR                  Period  0        SAMZ38    SAMZ56    SAMZ75


Production   Capacity increase              0         0         0

             Production level             200        70        50


Marketing    Manuf. sel. price  $          95       129       188

             Mktg. resources            1000      1100       900
```

```
----- SALES & PRODUCTION INFORMATION ------

SAMAR                  Period  0        SAMZ38    SAMZ56    SAMZ75

Unit sales             Units            200        70        43


M. S. P.               $                 95       129       188


$ sales                             19000      9030      8079

Production capacity    Units            200       100        50
Production level       Units            200        70        50
Unit variable manuf. cost  $            40        64        92
Unit contribution      $                55        65        96
Lost sales             Units            39        10         0
Ending inventory       Units             0         0         7
```

EXHIBIT 1

(continued)

```
---------------    P R O D U C T    C O N T R I B U T I O N    ----------------

SAMAR        Period    0              SAMZ38      SAMZ56      SAMZ75     TOTAL

Sales                KS               19000        9030        8079      36109
Cost of goods sold   KS                7993        4513        3948      16455
CBM                  KS               11007        4517        4131      19655

Mktg. resources      KS                1000        1100         900       3000
Credit cost          KS                 515         245         219        979
Inventory cost       KS                   0           0          24         24
Marketing admin.     KS                 980         781         762       2522
TME                  KS                2495        2126        1905       6526

CAM                  KS                8512        2391        2226      13129
Fixed manuf. cost    KS                1998        1612        1148       4759
Prod. contribution   KS                6513         779        1078       8370

Exceptional cost/profit  (KS) ......................................         0
Net contribution   (KS) ............................................      8370

Budget available next period (KS) ..................................      4448
```

```
-----------------    C U M U L A T I V E    R E S U L T S    -----------------

SAMAR
                                     SAMZ38      SAMZ56      SAMZ75     TOTAL
Period    0

Sales   KS                           19000        9030        8079      36109
CGS     KS                            7993        4513        3948      16455
CBM     KS                           11007        4517        4131      19655

MR      KS                            1000        1100         900       3000
CC      KS                             515         245         219        979
INV     KS                               0           0          24         24
ADM     KS                             980         781         762       2522
TME     KS                            2495        2126        1905       6526

CAM     KS                            8512        2391        2226      13129
FMC     KS                            1998        1612        1148       4759
PC      KS                            6513         779        1078       8370

Exceptional cost/profit  (KS) .......................................        0
Net contribution   (KS) .............................................     8370
```

EXHIBIT 1
(continued)

```
----------    P R O D U C T   S A L E S   I N F O R M A T I O N   -----------
```

SAMAR Period 0	Segment	Product Sales U	Product Sales $	Production Capa K U	Level K U
SAMZ38	C	200	19000	200	200
SAMZ56	B	70	9030	100	70
SAMZ75	A	43	8079	50	50
ATOZ17	D	301	12044	300	300
ATOZ32	C	29	2330	50	30
ATOZ60	B	155	22298	150	150
KENZ25	D	245	14705	250	250
KENZ65	B	37	5925	50	40
KENZ78	A	159	31018	150	150
PITZ15	D	166	5817	250	160
PITZ28	D	92	5949	100	90
PITZ45	C	155	16600	150	150

```
-----   P R O D U C T   M A R K E T   S H A R E   I N F O R M A T I O N   -----
```

SAMAR Period 0	Segment	Segment M.S. % U	Segment M.S. % $	TOTAL M.S. % U	TOTAL M.S. % $
SAMZ38	C	52.0	50.1	12.1	12.4
SAMZ56	B	26.7	24.2	4.2	5.9
SAMZ75	A	21.3	20.7	2.6	5.3
ATOZ17	D	37.5	31.3	18.2	7.9
ATOZ32	C	7.7	6.1	1.8	1.5
ATOZ60	B	59.1	59.9	9.4	14.6
KENZ25	D	30.5	38.2	14.8	9.6
KENZ65	B	14.2	15.9	2.3	3.9
KENZ78	A	78.7	79.3	9.6	20.3
PITZ15	D	20.7	15.1	10.1	3.8
PITZ28	D	11.4	15.4	5.5	3.9
PITZ45	C	40.3	43.8	9.4	10.9

E X H I B I T   1

(continued)

```
---------------  P R O D U C T    P O S I T I O N I N G  -----------------

   SAMAR                                              Period :   0

user price ($)                                     Name    $/swot

  195 +                             KL          A:ATOZ17   2.35
  180 +                                         B:PITZ15   2.33
  165 +                       J                 C:KENZ25   2.40
  150 +                    I                    D:PITZ28   2.32
  135 +                 H                       E:ATOZ32   2.47
  120 +                                         F:SAMZ38   2.50
  105 +              G                          G:PITZ45   2.38
   90 +          F                              H:SAMZ56   2.30
   75 +        E                                I:ATOZ60   2.40
   60 +      CD                                 J:KENZ65   2.45
   45 +    A                                    K:SAMZ75   2.51
   30 +    B                                    L:KENZ78   2.50
   15 +
    0 +-+-+-+-+-+-+-+-+-+-+-+-+-+-+-+-+-+-+-
      0  1  2  3  4  5  ·6  7  8  9
         swotage (*10 swots)
```

```
-----------  C O M P E T I T I V E    I N F O R M A T I O N  -------------

SAMAR
Period    0        Segment       User price $       Marketing ,resources K$

   SAMZ38           C                 95                 1000
   SAMZ56           B                129                 1100
   SAMZ75           A                188                  900

   ATOZ17           D                 40                 1083
   ATOZ32           C                 79                  280
   ATOZ60           B                144                 2076

   KENZ25           D                 60                 1709
   KENZ65           B                159                  737
   KENZ78           A                195                 3181

   PITZ15           D                 35                  904
   PITZ28           D                 65                  745
   PITZ45           C                107                 1351
```

EXHIBIT 1
(concluded)

```
-------------------- M A R K E T    F O R E C A S T -------------------

          ---------- Results period  0 ----------   Forecast  period  1
SAMAR
          Market      Market      Market      Market      Market      Market
          volume      growth      value       growth      volume      growth
          K   U       %   U       K   $       %   $       K   U       %   U
```

SAMAR	Market volume K U	Market growth % U	Market value K $	Market growth % $	Market volume K U	Market growth % U
Segment A	202	11.7	39098	9.9	216	6.9
Segment B	262	9.9	37253	10.5	281	7.1
Segment C	385	5.3	37930	6.7	405	5.2
Segment D	804	16.0	38515	13.5	913	13.6
TOTAL	1653	11.8	152795	10.1	1815	9.8

EXHIBIT 2

Situation at the End of Period 10 under the "Status Quo" Scenario

```
-------------------------- D E C I S I O N S -----------------------------

SAMAR                 Period  10            SAMZ38      SAMZ56      SAMZ75


Production   Capacity increase KU                0           0           0

             Production level   KU             200          70          50


Marketing    Manuf. sel. price  $               95         129         188

             Mktg. resources   K$             1000        1100         900
```

```
-----  S A L E S  &  P R O D U C T I O N  I N F O R M A T I O N  ------

SAMAR                 Period  10            SAMZ38      SAMZ56      SAMZ75


Unit sales            K Units                   64          51          22


M. S. P.              $                          95         129         188


$ sales               K$                       6109        6516        4144


Production capacity    K Units                  200         100          50
Production level       K Units                  200          70          50
Unit variable manuf. cost  $                     38          61          88
Unit contribution          $                     57          68         100
Lost sales             K Units                     0           0           0
Ending inventory       K Units                  824         119         223
```

EXHIBIT 2
(continued)

```
---------------  P R O D U C T   C O N T R I B U T I O N  ----------------

SAMAR      Period  10              SAMZ38     SAMZ56     SAMZ75     TOTAL

Sales              K$               6109       6516       4144      16769
Cost of goods sold K$               2442       3083       1930       7456
CBM                K$               3667       3433       2214       9313

Mktg. resources    K$               1000       1100        900       3000
Credit cost        K$                166        177        112        455
Inventory cost     K$               2155        502       1375       4032
Marketing admin.   K$                722        730        683       2135
TME                K$               4043       2509       3070       9622

CAM                K$               -376        923       -856       -309
Fixed manuf. cost  K$               1884       1520       1083       4487
Prod. contribution K$              -2261       -597      -1939      -4796

Exceptional cost/profit  (K$) ......................................          0
Net contribution  (K$) .............................................      -4796

Budget available next period (K$) ..................................       3000
```

```
------------------  C U M U L A T I V E   R E S U L T S  ------------------

SAMAR
                                SAMZ38     SAMZ56     SAMZ75     TOTAL
Period  10

Sales   K$                      130673      83917      61427     276018
CGS     K$                       53555      40628      29222     123405
CBM     K$                       77118      43290      32205     152613

MR      K$                       11000      12100       9900      33000
CC      K$                        3544       2276       1666       7487
INV     K$                        7642       1880       7271      16792
ADM     K$                        9213       8278       7829      25320
TME     K$                       31399      24534      26666      82599

CAM     K$                       45719      18756       5539      70014
FMC     K$                       21217      17114      12193      50525
PC      K$                       24502       1641      -6654      19489

Exceptional cost/profit  (K$) ......................................          0
Net contribution  (K$) .............................................      19489
```

EXHIBIT 2

(continued)

```
----------- P R O D U C T   S A L E S   I N F O R M A T I O N  ------------
```

SAMAR Period 10	Segment	Product Sales K U	Product Sales K $	Production Capa K U	Level K U
SAMZ38	C	64	6109	200	200
SAMZ56	B	51	6516	100	70
SAMZ75	A	22	4144	50	50
ATOZ17	D	272	8991	950	270
ATOZ22	D	880	38703	850	850
ATOZ39	C	120	10777	150	120
ATOZ60	B	218	28304	300	210
KENZ22	D	308	14162	350	320
KENZ65	B	10	1510	50	10
KENZ78	A	61	10782	200	60
KENZ81	A	101	20135	100	100
PITZ28	D	25	1367	100	30
PITZ41	C	465	39962	500	460
PITZ45	C	19	1872	200	40
PITZ59	B	50	6450	50	50

```
----- P R O D U C T   M A R K E T   S H A R E   I N F O R M A T I O N  -----
```

SAMAR Period 10	Segment	Segment M.S. % U	Segment M.S. % $	TOTAL M.S. % U	TOTAL M.S. % $
SAMZ38	C	9.6	10.4	2.4	3.1
SAMZ56	B	15.4	15.2	1.9	3.3
SAMZ75	A	12.0	11.8	0.8	2.1
ATOZ17	D	18.3	14.2	10.2	4.5
ATOZ22	D	59.2	61.2	33.0	19.4
ATOZ39	C	17.9	18.4	4.5	5.4
ATOZ60	B	66.3	66.2	8.2	14.2
KENZ22	D	20.7	22.4	11.6	7.1
KENZ65	B	3.0	3.5	0.4	0.8
KENZ78	A	33.0	30.8	2.3	5.4
KENZ81	A	54.9	57.4	3.8	10.1
PITZ28	D	1.7	2.2	0.9	0.7
PITZ41	C	69.6	68.1	17.4	20.0
PITZ45	C	2.8	3.2	0.7	0.9
PITZ59	B	15.2	15.1	1.9	3.2

EXHIBIT 2
(continued)

```
----------------   P R O D U C T   P O S I T I O N I N G   ------------------

   SAMAR                                             Period : 10

user price ($)                                   Name    $/swot

  260 +                                        A:ATOZ17  1.94
  240 +                                        +:ATOZ22  2.00
  220 +                                        +:KENZ22  2.09
  200 +                           M            B:PITZ28  1.96
  180 +                        KL              C:SAMZ38  2.50
  160 +                 J                      D:ATOZ39  2.31
  140 +                                        E:PITZ41  2.10
  120 +              GHI                        F:PITZ45  2.22
  100 +        C  F                             G:SAMZ56  2.30
   80 +        DE                               H:PITZ59  2.19
   60 +      B                                  I:ATOZ60  2.17
   40 +    A +                                  J:KENZ65  2.32
   20 +                                         K:SAMZ75  2.51
    0 +-+-+-+-+-+-+-+-+-+-+-+-+-+-+-+-+-+-+-    L:KENZ78  2.28
      0   1   2   3   4   5   6   7   8   9     M:KENZ81  2.47
             swotage (*10 swots)
```

```
------------   C O M P E T I T I V E   I N F O R M A T I O N   --------------

 SAMAR
 Period  10        Segment       User price $       Marketing resources K$

   SAMZ38            C               95                   1000
   SAMZ56            B              129                   1100
   SAMZ75            A              188                    900

   ATOZ17            D               33                   1304
   ATOZ22            D               44                   3634
   ATOZ39            C               90                   1265
   ATOZ60            B              130                   3141
   KENZ22            D               46                   1379
   KENZ65            B              151                    155
   KENZ78            A              178                   1195
   KENZ81            A              200                   1981
   PITZ28            D               55                    138
   PITZ41            C               86                   3643
   PITZ45            C              100                    232
   PITZ59            B              129                    589
```

EXHIBIT 2
(concluded)

SAMAR	--------------------- M A R K E T		F O R E C A S T	---------------------		
	---------- Results period 10 ----------				Forecast	period 11
	Market volume K U	Market growth % U	Market value K $	Market growth % $	Market volume K U	Market growth % U
Segment A	183	-7.7	35061	-8.0	174	-5.0
Segment B	328	-1.9	42780	-2.6	322	-2.0
Segment C	667	0.1	58720	-0.2	667	0.0
Segment D	1485	0.5	63222	0.4	1485	0.0
TOTAL	2664	-0.5	199784	-2.0	2648	-0.6

EXHIBIT 3
Evolution of Net Contribution under the Status Quo Scenario for SAMAR

E X H I B I T   4

Evolution of the Zompert Market under the Status Quo Scenario for SAMAR

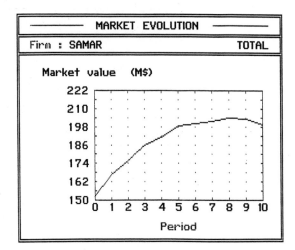

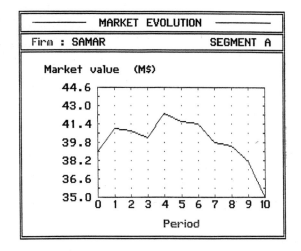

E X H I B I T   4
(continued)

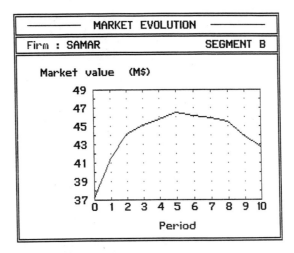

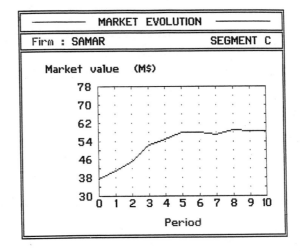

E X H I B I T   4
(concluded)

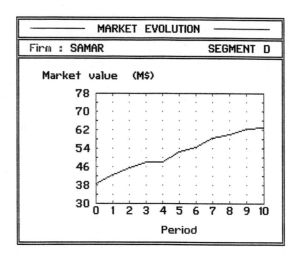

E X H I B I T   5
Instructions to the SAMAR Software

1. Switch on system and wait for ">" prompt.
2. Insert the SAMAR simulation disk in drive A, type SAMAR, and press the return key. (You can also select to load the SAMAR software on your hard disk.)
3. *Initialization.* Give a name to the simulated firm that you want to run (e.g., SAMAR). The name needs to be composed of at least three letters and should be different from ATO, KEN, or PIT. You can also specify some parameters for your computer configuration including the disk unit on which you want to save your data files. This is usually "B:" or the hard disk, but *do not* use the same diskette as the one on which the SAMAR software is located as there is not enough space available for a complete data file.
4. *Master Menu.* To select an option in the Master Menu, move the cursor to the appropriate line, and press the return key, or press the key corresponding to the desired option (e.g., "O" for "Operating Instructions").
5. *Display or print results.* To obtain the results in a given period. Print only when you want to keep a record of these results. When testing different strategies, just displaying the results and writing down a few of the key results is sufficient. Note that when displaying results the "Analysis mode" allows you to have a graph of past historical results.
6. *Next decisions.* To enter your decisions for the next period. Note that pressing "H" for "Historical" will give you information on decisions made in the past.
7. *Change decisions.* To change your decisions for the current period.
8. *Run simulation.* To run the simulation and produce the results for the next period, based on your decisions.
9. *Other useful hints:*
   a. Help messages. Whenever you have to provide an input to the SAMAR software, a help message will be displayed to guide you. You will see this message at the bottom of the screen.
   b. Caps lock. This key sets your keyboard in the capitals or uppercase mode and is usually called Caps Lock. If you have set your keyboard to operate in uppercase mode, the letters CAPS will appear on the bottom left of your screen to remind you of this.
   c. Num lock. On the right side of your keyboard you can see a group of keys, or numerical board, corresponding to the numbers 0 to 9 as well as arrow keys. You can usually set these keys in numerical mode by pressing a key called Num Lock. If you do so, the letters NUM will appear on the bottom right of your screen to remind you of this.
   d. Escape key. On your keyboard there is a key called the Escape key, usually indicated as ESC. Unless otherwise shown, pressing the ESC key will "retrace your steps" to the last menu which you accessed, and eventually back to the Master Menu.

Name Index

Subject Index